Beyond Secularism and Jihad?

A Triangular Inquiry into the Mosque, the Manger, and Modernity

Peter D. Beaulieu

UNIVERSITY PRESS OF AMERICA,® INC.
Lanham • Boulder • New York • Toronto • Plymouth, UK

In Memory of my Parents
and my wife, Kristi—

"…her lamp will never go out"
(Proverbs 31:18).

Contents

Preface

Four thousand years ago Abraham paused on a desert night and came to know that he would be the father of a great nation with descendents outnumbering the stars (Gen 12:2). For Arabs of the desert and now for all Muslims a legend persists, possibly true, that one of these stars crashed to earth. The Black Stone of the Ka'ba in Mecca, the site of annual pilgrimage by Muslims from around the world, is possibly an ancient meteorite and by one legend was placed there by Abraham himself. The Prophet Mohammed claimed to have recovered the original faith of Abraham and then led his people to stand apart from the idolatries of tribal Mecca.

Six hundred years earlier, and two thousand years ago, another star is said to have remained stationary in the sky over Palestine to guide star gazers from the east to a backwater village of the Roman Empire, in Judea, called Bethlehem. It is held that in this town there came to earth not an asteroid from the sky, but the very God of the universe and the human heart. Modern science demonstrates that a celestial conjunction actually occurred in that sky at that time and place, and that by the earth's seasonal path the phenomenon appeared move as a beacon pointing to the one called Christ.[1] The child "grew in wisdom and age and grace before God and men" (Lk 2:52), and it is because of this wisdom and grace that he was crucified by a race both graced and fallen. But there were witnesses to his words and deeds and who first came to be known in Antioch as Christians. Christians witness to the oneness and mercy of God, and that this is a Triune Oneness who by his mysterious design chose to reveal his own inner life into the inner hearts of pilgrim mankind, now strangers in a strange land.

The book of the Muslims is the *Qur'an*, the "recitations" of the final Prophet Mohammed, which are believed to be dictated from heaven and in Arabic, and since the ninth century to be of the very essence of God. The earlier Christians also have a book. The heart of this book is the gospel, the "good news" of the New Testament. However, the symmetrical comparison to be made between Islam and Christianity is not between these books, but between the *Qur'an* and the one to whom witness is given in the Bible. Some of what follows in the book in the reader's hands is explained by the asymmetry between the followers of Islam who adhere to "the word made Book" and the witnesses to Christ who proclaim the "Word made flesh" (Jn 1:14). Another part is about the onlookers of secular humanism who equally discount both sets of writings. Their fascination is the physical universe as another kind of book measured not in thousands of years but in events infinitely small at one end and, at the other, measured in billions of years. The Christian vision and the Islamic memory are collapsed by the anonymity of modern man whose first belief is of himself as the measure of all things.

Or, does "Paradise lies at the feet of mothers"? This little known pronouncement is attributed by the followers of Islam to their founder the Prophet Mohammed. And centuries before Mohammed was a twinkle in his father's eye, Mary who is held by many to be the Mother of God, stood at the feet of Christ crucified while He offered paradise to the "repentant thief," one of his last companions in this world. A possible healing path to the future—a future that goes *beyond both secular-ism and jihad*—might be based upon such a direct appreciation of a relational God and the transcendent dignity of the human person. While the cultural event called the West flows from the combined influence of Christianity and the Classical world, the recent tendency of narrow modernity is to omit any mention of such Christian ingredients—as in the exclusively secularist Charter of the European Union. The darker side of modernity would have us believe that maternity and the paradise are no more than quaint anachronisms in a much larger universe of accidents within a larger chaos, bent toward order by the laborious and sometimes heroic workings of mankind.

In one definition of modernity, John Paul II wrote that "if by modernity we mean a convergence of conditions that permit a human being to express better his or her own maturity, spiritual, moral, and cultural, then the Church saw itself as the 'soul' of modernity."[2] A more secular modernity, and especially a radically dehumanized modernity, can be more of a solvent than a construction worthy of man. With its excesses there comes a mathematical and digital universe and the erosion of real "things" which are knowable as such and which are always a step beyond complete human understanding and control. But consistent deference for the scientific method as the reliable path to understanding can so capture the imagination that a doctrinaire resistance is erected to the reality of many things that are otherwise knowable as real, such as motherhood or paradise. Modern beliefs against the realities of man and God—sometimes less a defect of intellect than of character—patronize the underpinnings of tradition and faith, holding that things that cannot be quantified are merely subjective opinion. "If it cannot be quantified, it cannot be managed" becomes the new religion.

The deeper heritage of the West proposes that things of faith and things of reason best defer to one another and that they expand and grow best in the light of each other. Pascal remarked that "the last act of the reason is to recognize its limitations." The low ceiling universe of rationalism, often held to be religion at a higher level, suspends those questions pushed to the edges. The start point is still a confidence in at least the coherence of things measured. As part of scientific inquiry, Einstein and a colleague affirmed that "without the belief that it is possible to grasp the reality with our theoretical construction, without the belief in the inner harmony of our world, there could be no science. This belief is and always will remain the fundamental motive for all scientific creation. Throughout all our efforts, in every dramatic struggle between old and new views, we recognize the eternal longing for understanding, the ever-firm belief in the harmony of our world, continually strengthened by the increasing obstacles to comprehension."[3]

What is the inner source of such confidence? Systematic skepticism that rejects skepticism toward itself is not science but ideology. Ideological disbelief, as a start point for inquiry, is the comfort zone of the radical secular-*ist* and of free thought intolerance of all things labeled as religious. Ersatz religion is as responsible for this reactionary attitude as radical secularism is for giving modern secular institutions a bad name. In Revolutionary France, Robespierre sought to destroy church steeples as too expressive of old things undemocratic and opposed to a new spiritual community of liberated people. Modern day Robespierres salute a symbolic skyline of business and cellular phone towers, but now find themselves asked to consider minarets at key locations in the West, sometimes converted from empty churches.

Because the dominant religion in a post-modern period of Christianity in decline might be some version of Islam rather than an ever ascendant modernity, mosques and minarets may some day outnumber the steeples of empty churches on the skyline of many European cities. But for the global Christian minority, the star of Bethlehem—and indeed the billions of other stars as well—will still point back to something so near and simple as a manger in the history of Palestine. The term mosque is a translation of "prostration" (*masjid*) and symbolizes "*submission* or resignation to the will of God." The manger symbolizes a more trusting *surrender* and a freedom that expands as humility increases. The manger invites trust in a transcendent God who is approachable because He has first approached us. It is only because God is transcendent—the key tenet of Islam—that the theoretically possible Incarnation must be a totally unique event as proclaimed by Christianity.

Between the two world wars of the twentieth century, a Protestant theologian penned words worthy of us today as we stand between the recent Cold War and a new and less bi-polar globalism:

> The Christian analysis of life leads to conclusions which will seem morbidly pessimistic to moderns, still steeped as they are in their evolutionary optimism. The conclusion most abhorrent to the modern mood is that the possibilities of evil grow with the possibilities of good, and that human history is therefore not so much a chronicle of the progressive victory of good over evil, of cosmos over chaos, as the story of an ever increasing cosmos creating ever increasing possibilities of chaos.[4]

The new globalism is intercultural and market-based, and defined politically by tensions and multiple balances of power at the regional level. With the Soviet Empire dismembered, the new and chaotic landscape especially pits the world of historic Islam against the post-Christian West. Like the Cold War threat between the West and the former Soviet Bloc, Islamic ideology also divides the world into a "zone of peace" and a "zone of war." The formula of co-existence is again proposed, together with specific ways of dealing with former Third World nations mostly of Africa, Asia and Latin America. The essential difference in today's new landscape is that the former communist bloc was atheistic toward both man and God, while the Islamic world is assertive in its monolithic view of God, and its corresponding and a still nascent view of the human person in contrast with values still found in the Western tradition.

The modern world is a three-way intersection among the adherents of not two but three major world belief systems: a Christian faith much divided; the at least equally fractious Islam, and the relativism of secular humanism whose model of the universe places each individual at the center of a private narrative. Secular humanism raises the question whether at any time in history multicultural ideology, identity politics, and self interest are a sufficient foundation for mutual respect. Can a completely secular civic culture lift itself by its own bootstraps? Today, measures of social mobilization, economic productivity, efficiency, networking, and even sensitivity posture as serious substitutes for the discarded universality of what is poorly labeled as natural law.

What does it mean to be fully human? Might the irreducible dignity of each person—the universality of the natural law—depend upon the actual subsistence of a transcendent God outside of ourselves? In late 2006 Pope Benedict XVI stood alongside Muslim leaders inside the central square of an Istanbul monument. He prayed alone for a moment in the freedom of silence.

The structure was Santa Sophia, the awe inspiring sixth century Christian church, later recast as a mosque when overrun in the fifteenth century, and then recast again as a secular museum early in the twentieth century. In the earliest years of Islam and like the current pope, when Omar the second successor to Mohammed claimed Jerusalem (687 A.D.), he remained outside the tomb of Jesus. Omar accepted surrender on the terms that the churches remain undamaged and the Christians be allowed to worship freely. Today the Mosque of Omar still marks the spot where Omar paused in prayer only a few steps from the Holy Sepulcher.[5]

This research is not part of any official dialogue that breaks this shared silence, such as the Catholic-Muslim forum between spokesmen of the Vatican and the Islamic world, or the several other regional and thematic dialogues co-sponsored by the United States Catholic Conference of Bishops (USCCB). Nor does this work pretend to add anything to the reconciliation of secular modernity, as belief system, with the world religions. Your author is not a specialist on any of the disciplines referenced, yet he takes some refuge in the remark made by H. G. Wells in the introduction to his much more wide ranging *Outline of History*. Of that sweeping work—and that author's lack of specialization in history—Wells explained that no historian had stepped forward "who was sufficiently superficial, shall we say sufficiently wide and sufficiently shallow to cover the vast range of the project." What is lost in disciplinary rigor can sometimes be made up in peripheral vision.

The present triangular inquiry asks the same kind of indulgence from general readers and more credentialed scholars, some of whom are gratefully cited in this work. The focus here is less on any of the many well-developed areas of academic specialization—especially scripture scholarship—than on bridges between them, and on occasional visits by the symphonic muses and rare flashes of originality. Ultimately, the focus is on such broadly human questions as whether God is, and if so whether and how He communicates, and how accurately man possibly listens and responds—or whether all such questions are subjective and arbitrary narratives. These questions call for a fundamental departure from the picture painted by Mr. Wells. Wells airbrushed the bulk of history with the presumption that the key to all history is scientific and technological advancement. He trumps our first two religious options of Christian faith and the religion of Islam with the premise (now discredited by history itself) of omnipotent technical progress.

In early 1969 the first astronaut to return from a trip around the moon remarked that "man can now do anything he wants to do technically." Later that year the first astronauts to set foot on the moon returned to earth with forty pounds of samples from the lunar surface. Islam reveres the Black Stone as possibly an asteroid collected on the earth's surface by Abraham; and Christianity points to the star of Bethlehem, and modernity gathers samples from our nearest neighbor in space.

Grouped together in our cover design is an inner chamber to the Great Mosque of Cordova, Bernini's colonnade that shapes St. Peter's Square in Rome and, suspended in space, the singular greenish-blue earthsphere as discovered by mankind who is now in lunar orbit. For seven centuries (until 1492) Cordova served as the Muslim capital of Moorish Spain. A century and a half after the final reconquest of Spain, Bernini envisioned his Baroque colonnade and piazza fronting on St. Peter's basilica in Rome. As construction neared completion it was decided that the arms of the colonnade should not entirely enclose the oval plaza, but instead should remain as open arms outstretched to invite and embrace the City on the Tiber and the horizon beyond. In our current century technology fully reveals the earthly horizon as a singular greenish blue sphere suspended against a darkened backdrop of one hundred quintillion infinitely distant suns, The inquiry of the following chapters examines the intersection—the triangular *encounter*—among all three worldviews: the Mosque, the Manger, and Modernity.

NOTES

1. The star was quite possibly the triple conjunction of Jupiter, Saturn and Aires in April and December 6 B.C. A rigorous argument is provided by a highly credible researcher (Michael Molnar, former manager of the Physics Instructional Laboratories at Rutgers University, *The Star of Bethlehem: The Legacy of the Magi*, Piscataway, New Jersey: Rutgers University Press, 1999).

2. "General Audience Homily of November 24, 1999," quoted in Tracey Rowland, *Ratzinger's Faith: The Theology of Pope Benedict XVI* (New York: Oxford University Press, 2008), 152. The Church's self understanding contrasts with a prediction offered by Alexis de Tocqueville in his survey of America (1835): "By whatever political laws men are governed in the ages of equality, it may be foreseen that faith in public opinion will become for them a species of religion, and the majority its ministering prophet" (Democracy in America, Vol. II, Bk. 1, Ch. II).

3. See Albert Einstein and Leopold Infeld, *The Evolution of Physics* (New York: Simon and Schuster, 1938), 313.

4. Reinhold Niebuhr, *An Interpretation of Christian Ethics* (New York: Harper and Row, 1935), 97f.

5. Michael La Civita, "The Orthodox Patriarchal Church of Jerusalem," *One* (New York: Catholic Near East Welfare Association, May 2011), 24.

Acknowledgments

I first wish to acknowledge debts that long precede actual preparation of this work. Two scholars at the University of Washington were especially helpful to my doctoral research (1972–5) which focused on political and economic change in post-colonial settings. Based largely on his field work in the late 1950s, one member of my dissertation committee, Daniel Saul Lev (1993–2006), is affectionately known even today by many in mostly Muslim Indonesia as "Bapak (Father) Dan." In the classroom Lev conveyed with unusual clarity the political issues of multicultural societies adapting to a world of "nation-states," the dominant political identities of modernity. A passionate campaigner in Indonesia for human rights, he was also a man of vigorous and open classroom inquiry. Harold Amoss, my committee chair, brought the added perspective of an anthropologist. With a career "interest in things Islamic," his academic and field specialization was pre-revolutionary Afghanistan. A wide range of coursework was also available to me through other professors in disciplines later consolidated into the Jackson School of International Studies at the University of Washington. I wish to note my exploratory studies under George Taylor, Jerry Bacharach, Imre Boba and Paul Brass, George Modelski, Simon Ottenberg, and Pierre L. van den Berghe, whose upper division and graduate-level course offerings, respectively, introduced me to the history of the Far East and of the Middle East, East European ethnic populations, the national politics of India and South Asia, as well as world politics, urban anthropology in West Africa, and in general the sociology of *communally segmented* societies.

At the time of my studies as a student, a large segment of social science research (political science) was documenting the case that collective integration in some form, e.g., socialism, is not inevitable, but is often contradicted by the complexity of the subject matter and by the churning of deeper and resistant themes. And beyond the methods and findings of the very diverse social sciences, I am indebted to other groups of thinkers known to me only through their writings and many of whom are identified in my citations and bibliography. Among these mentors I also include my father-in-law, the medical doctor Richard E. Orr. Over the nearly quarter century before his death, our widely varied conversations at his table in the clear air of central Idaho were for me and the extended family a consistent source of fascination and intellectual challenge. Mentors such as these are needed reminders of those deeply human questions that decline to be domesticated by facile cultural presuppositions such as positivism sometimes staked out within the social sciences.

The substantial contributions of social science research are complemented with the understanding that an exclusively secular anthropology of the human person deprives us of a broader account of human experience and possibilities. A finding of social science itself is that human history is not a natural science and usually or often does not repeat itself even under identical circumstances. Not all wars, or social achievements, are economics-driven or status-based. The cross-cutting questions behind historic and current events find a hearing in theology and philosophy and varied traditions. While this current book does not pretend to be a broad synthesis, it hopes to offer a weave of themes, parallelisms, and contact points. For your author and the reader, common themes between all of us are the questions of personal life and death, love, and of "good" and "evil" in the world. These are also the universal preoccupations of the world religions, especially Christianity and Islam.

The hope is that this inquiry into sometimes non-replicable events, and our interreligious and intercultural similarities and differences, will add a few points of clarity to an awaited three-way conversation, and foster personal fascination for the events addressed and ways of thinking about the future. I acknowledge and welcome in advance my future debt to those who might extend or redirect thoughts offered or omitted here, and especially any distortions of firmly held positions, religious or otherwise. A guide for all is the advice given by the fifth century St. Augustine: "In essentials, unity; in non-essentials, liberty; in all things, charity."

Introduction

In late 2006 Pope Benedict XVI visited face to face with ranking followers of Islam. This personal gesture is both pre-modern and a possible opening toward a deeply modern future. Other more political meetings are between heads of Western and secular nation-states and the leaders of Islamic mosque-states still fused with the religion of Islam. In Istanbul the head of Christianity met with important religious leaders in Turkey which is also the only Muslim state with a clearly secular constitution. Much earlier in our history (451 A.D.) it was another white haired pope, Leo the Great, who made such an encounter outside the gates of Imperial Rome. Pope Leo's actual conversation with Attila (406?-453) on a sandbar of the Mincio River is lost in the silence of the unrecorded past. The words spoken remain one of the great mysteries of history. Attila's army reversed its course and spared Rome from conquest and pillage. Today, and in the context of the new Third Millennium what is behind Pope Benedict's historic trip, and what was said?

At first glance, the a-political and multi-state Muslim community, or *ummah*, might seem to resemble a past entity called Christendom, which was based at least implicitly on natural law notions of the common good. But, the natural law applies to each and all persons irrespective of communal grouping, while the breadth of the ummah is both communally bounded and more abstract. The ummah is confined to the globe-spanning community and domain of Islam (*dar al-Islam*), outside of which are all others—the infidels (*dar al-harb*). A case is made by some Islamic scholars that *jihad* is not the Muslim way. It is argued that members of the ummah theoretically must first consider emigration—not jihad—whenever they find themselves in a third or "composite" middle case ("domain") if the prevailing institutions prevent them from practicing the Islamic way of life.[1] The modern world is such a middle case, so what then is the legitimate adjustment that might be made by mainstream Islam to the world of nation-states, Church-state separation and secularism?

And what adjustments might be needed in the West? To Western secular eyes, the institutional comparison between Western and Islamic societies compares the ummah to pre-secular and often totemic political forms found in the early history of the West. The Islamic state partly resembles pre-European caesaro-papism as it existed under Charlemagne or in the Byzantine Empire to the East, or less frequently a medieval papal theocracy. A defining difference is that with Islam the fusion of belief and political sovereignty theoretically situates the leadership fully within the ummah, rather than above it as in the stratified Western empires and monarchies. The global ummah is also theologically a world apart from the more recent Christian community which operates within secular society under a distinction (aka separation) between Church and state. Within the Christian community unity is not political and it is less abstract than for the ummah. In addition to the institutional churches and ecclesial communities, unity is found primarily in any group of more than one: "For where two or three are gathered together for my sake, there am I in the midst of them" (Mt 18:20). In religious comparison, the *Qur'an* claims no such indwelling by the Holy Spirit, but it also acknowledges God's presence everywhere ". . . He is with you wheresoever ye may be. And Allah sees well all that ye do" (Q57:4).

Entering the twenty-first century, how is there to be the needed and enduring conversation between the "modern" West and "pre-modern" Islam, so fundamentally at odds politically and theologically and at so many levels? It is at this juncture and at the cultural and interreligious levels—deeper than the political or economic—that the Church in the person of the pope intervenes as one religious and historic factor. Pope Benedict XVI restores to the table the reality that people do live by what they believe, and not simply by their interests. This perspective—both pre-modern and post-modern—is as much an opening to Islam as it is a challenge to modern Western ideology. Islam holds that all religions are subsumed under Islam, while Western ideology often holds that societies face no deeper challenge than to adjust their respective scriptures to social and economic imperatives in a way that defuses religious extremism and generally demotes religious content. Social science, and political and market actions, are critical to societal harmony, but have not fully displaced enduring theological insights into the nature of the human person. The reader is invited to remain open to the possibility that at least some political errors are ultimately theological in origin.

The following chapters identify and explore "contact points" between the world of Islam, Christianity, and the secular West. The overall structure focuses one chapter on each of the three corners of a triangular inquiry: the

Mosque, the Manger, and Modernity (respectively, key parts of Chapters 3, 4 and 5). Chapter 1 explores the meaning of personal and cultural "encounter" in the twenty-first century. It peeks below the so-called and large scale "clash of civilizations." Chapter 2 is a broad history with highlights of comparative theology and brief excursions into historical and literary parallels to Islam. Included is an examination of Mohammed the man, together with a treatment of whether Islam is in some sense a Christian "heresy" eligible for ecumenical rather than interreligious status with Christianity. This Muslim preference toward an ecumenical starting point is not supported. From Islamic sources, Chapter 3 explores the unitary Islamic State as a "communal theocracy." Our inquiry points to the natural law as a very tenuous, but possible "grammar" for a largely non-theological dialogue with the followers of Islam. Chapter 4 follows the evolution of the secular nation-state, the modern political idiom but not the end of history, and of the distinct Church in the West. Particular attention is given to the crisis-response of the Church in the recent First and Second Vatican Councils. In addition to a clarified self-understanding, the Church *proposes* guidance for decisions and actions for others who are directly responsible for the common good. Just War theory and jihad are compared.

Chapter 5 sets the modern "crisis of Islam" against the opposite crisis of the West—excessive attention to things of faith versus a nearly exclusive commitment to rationalism. It touches on the scientific or experimental method which continues to complement and strain in different ways those deeper inspirations found in the West and in elements of Islamic culture. Chapter 6 expands the coherence between faith and reason, a familiar theme in the new Islamic dialogue, to also consider human memory and will, two other human faculties at the root of Western and Christian thought and institutions.

The lasting legacy of Pope John Paul II casts its light upon major parts of this book. This legacy includes in part the need for a "new evangelization," a treatment of the economy and politics within his wider appreciation of ethical values, and the philosophy of interpersonal engagement ("personalism") attentive to many valid insights offered by modern philosophy.[2] This work also draws from widely selected works by many other different thinkers. *The Concept of State and Law in Islam* (Farooq Hassan, 1981) is one invaluable source by a prominent Muslim scholar and attorney.[3] Following the Iran Hostage Crisis of 1979, Hassan wrote his volume to fill a void specifically for Western readers and to compare the distinctive features of *Shari'a* to Western political science. At the certain risk of oversimplification Chapter 3 relies upon this Pakistani presentation of the Mosque-state. Islamic interactions in other parts of the world leave us with a broader mosaic of cultural and political partial adjustments toward modernity. Another valuable and very recently available Muslim work *is A Muslim View of Christianity: Essays on Dialogue by Mahmoud Ayoub.*[4]

Medieval Western polemic is well documented by Norman Daniel in *Islam and the West: The Making of an Image.*[5] A post-Medieval source still typical of this genre is Prideaux's diversely documented seventeenth-century *The Life of Mahomet*[6] which gives a remarkably detailed and probable account of Mohammed's life. Although this work is scarred by a high degree of critical anti-Islam bias carried forward from earlier Medieval commentators, it still can be mined for underlying factual detail.[7] The author (writing in 1696) casts Mohammed as a deliberate and flagrant imposter,[8] but even on this narrative defect two points are useful to remember. First, this work is based either directly or indirectly on a wide variety of early sources including Arabic, Hebrew, Chaldee (modern day Iraq), Greek, Latin, English and French. Citations include Abu l'Feda (born Isma'il, 1273–1331 A.D.) whose own writing is based on much earlier works and is the first source to serve as a basis for the oldest European accounts of Mohammed.[9]

Second, the clear distinction so commonplace today between deliberate imposter deception and an "ideology" such as class identity did not become part of Western social science until over a century after Prideaux's volume was written. The classic work is Karl Mannheim's *Ideology and Utopia* (1931). The task of cross-cultural interpretation, especially across fourteen centuries, requires stepping out of one's own world. How should modernity classify Islam, shaped in its earliest days by a nomadic culture inclined to gather wealth and ideas from converging caravan routes and inclined to find its successful leaders to be both warriors and prophets? In addition to Prideaux, we also draw from other writers including the more sympathetic and equally detailed, but less documented, Muslim biographer Maulana Muhammad Ali.[10]

Christian sources for our analysis include several of the documents of the Second Vatican Council.[11] This Council, the twenty-first of the history of the Catholic Church, was convened in 1962 and concluded in 1965. Like Islam, the Church is a major world religion with its beginnings in ancient times. In convening the most recent council, the Church sought to renew itself and only then to deeply encounter the modern world and the followers of other religions. As a theologian and witness to faith, and one who took part in the Vatican Council, Pope Benedict XVI stresses a vertical axis to any meaningful encounter. This vertical axis is the possibility of graced "supervention" from One other than ourselves. Benedict advocates a solid grounding in prayer, conscience, and reason as a first step toward any durable "alliance for civility" intent on jointly promoting human rights.[12] Even in Proverbs we are reminded of the difference between our grand designs and the Designer's path: "In his mind a man plans his course, but the Lord directs his steps" (Prov 16:9).

Real encounter entails more than the presumed forward pressure of social Darwinism and natural history in the making. Openness to the possibility of supervention suspects that rather than a set of trend lines, human history is more a sequence or array of potential tipping points, each more or less open to the working of grace, each more or less present to the Presence. All three of the monotheistic and historical religions—Judaism, Christianity, and Islam—are largely of one mind on the need and reality of a human encounter that does not exclude God. They "see existence in terms of the encounters between a personal God and human beings, and these encounters 'take the form of historical acts and events in the world.'"[13] Luigi Guissani, founder of an inspired lay Christian movement in the West, reminds us that "(R)eligion is in fact that which man does in his solitude, but it is also that in which the human person discovers his essential companionship . . . Such companionship is, then, *more original to us than our solitude*" (italics added).[14] This essential companionship is more original to us than our current global divisions aggravated by identity politics. Such friendship potentially rises to challenge this solitude and any self-idolatry, and is partly knowable by our shared capacity for reason. This original companionship is a short definition for the universal—and too easily discarded—natural law.

The emerging global struggle today between the West (and Christianity) and the world of Islam takes place on many levels. This confrontation gives us pause as possibly the greatest and most threatening novelty we face in the coming century, if not millennium. The former pope John Paul II worded Benedict's vision of fully human cooperation and the possibility of supervention in this way: ". . . in order that the demands of justice may be met, and attempts to achieve this goal may succeed, what is needed is the gift of grace, a gift which comes from God." Grace, in cooperation with human freedom, constitutes that mysterious presence of God in history which is Providence.

The year 2007 marked the Twenty-first International Meeting for Peace, attended by leaders of more than the Catholic and Muslim religions, but also of the Orthodox, Protestant, Jewish, Hindu, Buddhist, Shinto and Zoroastrian traditions. The group quoted the words of Benedict: "Never can evil and violence be justified by invoking the name of God," and in their statement they added that "a world without dialogue is a world without hope, where people are fated to fear each other."[15] Pope Benedict XVI extends the footsteps of St. Augustine who in the fifth century penned the *City of God*, even as imperial Rome drifted toward its own extinction. Might it be that history will show that dealing with a Europe in decline, the Church's end game in an increasingly Islamic and secularist world will be to secure through dialogue, both hopeful and realistic, a mutually respectful "reciprocity" toward what the pope sees as the Christian and "creative minorities?"

Within the Christian tradition, the creative minorities are communities of believers who very personally decide for Christ—for the unambiguous self-disclosure and presence of God—and who sustain one another and inevitably leaven a new world from within.[16] This is less a call to exclusivity than it is a call to renewed evangelization, a sharing of the unsullied gift of the "good news" with others. But first of all it is a claim by the Church to simply have the space to be what it is. Recalling the concession to Muslims to build mosques across Europe, in Turkey Pope Benedict petitioned the equivalent concession (reciprocity), or right, to found new seminaries in Turkey. Perhaps this assertion on behalf of Christians in Muslim lands is also intended to better ensure at least the continued institutional autonomy of the Church in the future Europe,[17] and a continued place for those human values that under the earlier St. Benedict were the taproot of European culture.

To a certain modern mentality in the West, Pope Benedict also warns against any facile "ideology of dialogue." But in his address to the United Nations (April 2008), he also spoke of "giving attention and encouragement to even the faintest sign of dialogue or desire for reconciliation." He assured diplomats that they "can count on the results of dialogue between religions, and can draw fruit from the willingness of believers to place their experiences at the service of the common good . . . . Their task," he adds, "is to propose a vision of faith not in terms of intolerance, discrimination and conflict, but in terms of complete respect for truth, coexistence, rights, and reconciliation."[18]

In the first year of the Second World War, the Anglo-Catholic T.S. Eliot produced his own urgent and brief analysis *The Idea of a Christian Society*.[19] On the current value crisis in the West, his still timely premise was that any society that falls into the cult of Neutrality is destined either to restore itself as a Christian society or to descend into paganism. In today's context this work is worth reconsidering. Today the moral ambivalence or crisis of the West is brought into sharp relief by a resurgent Islam. As a distinctly non-Western culture, Islam declines to make any basic distinction between either belief or society and the state. Islam proposes to fill the void Eliot identifies as neutrality. At the same time, the Western elite generally presume that a sociological or neutral understanding of the West and other societies provides a path for the future of both. In the West, Church and state have been sorted out and altered by many centuries of growth and revolutionary disruption. The prevailing multicultural ideology is that Islam might also make pragmatic adjustments if given the time and the correct political and economic ingredients. Questioning these worldviews—and the reason for a triangular encounter as developed in the following chapters—is the purpose of this book. A full chapter (again, chapter 4) is devoted to historical institutional change in the West, and a full chapter (Chapter 3) is devoted to the different content and personality of Islam. Rather than sociological churning, a distinctly classical and Christian understanding of the human person is proposed as the necessary ingredient for positive modernity in both the West and the world of Islam.

Almost anticipated by Eliot (above) is the recent refocusing in the Christian world beyond any past evangelization of nation-states and toward a deepening re-evangelization of society itself. This re-evangelization by the Catholic Church is based largely on the mystery and intrinsic dignity of the human person, and on the primacy of the common good over any ideology or sociology of falsely neutral or facile common ground. This re-evangelization proposes—does not impose—messages consolidated and developed at the Second Vatican Council (1963–65) and in later decades. It is on the basis of the inviolable dignity and eternal destiny of each human person that the Church joins in the call for global "immunity from coercion in civil society . . . on the part of individuals or social groups and any human power . . ."[20] and proposes its "social principles" protective of the human person and society, and our politics, economies and cultures.

Backlighting this exploratory effort are the five transcendentals that can serve to both frame and open the borders of our inquiry. As measures of the fully human and hints of the divine, the transcendentals are *love*, the *one*, the *true*, the *good* and the *beautiful*. The One is a very foundational premise of Islam as presented in Chapter 2 and 3. The natural law vision of the human person and the common good is treated in Chapters 3 and in greater depth in Chapter 4. The possible fit between faith and such reasoning is a recurring theme. The recent Muslim request to unpack the Commandment of Love as a possible "common word" among diverse religions also surfaces in Chapter 5 and in Chapter 6 is explored further.

Modernity is largely allergic to the One and the True largely because of rationalism and then the ideological warfare especially of the recent century. The exhaustion of history helps explain the spiritual malaise affecting previously Christian Europe today. Another transcendental—the Good—is sullied by a false understanding of human freedom as an escape from restrain rather than a liberation for the deepest good. But, finally, there is Beauty. For the reader and for the author, the direct sense of Beauty—in itself and as a fresh and open window to the other transcendentals—is possibly the most inviting surprise discovered in the weaving of this triangular inquiry into the Mosque, the Manger and Modernity.

Pointing to a restored and well grounded moral vision of the mystery of the human person, this inquiry proposes an alternative to the excesses of rationalism in the West and the engulfing theology of Islam. To hope that Western secularity can untangle the Gordian knot of the Islamic State is like expecting mathematics to disprove poetry. Conversely, the Islamic State should not assume that cultural osmosis can render irrelevant that need in politics and culture for a coherent relationship between things of faith and things of reason. The contribution of the current triangular inquiry is to notice predispositions like these, and to review more clearly our multiple similarities and multiple incongruities at all levels—social, cultural, and political, but also theological and scriptural. The many parallels and discontinuities offer portals for mutually respectful engagement and conversations in place of the many monologues that so often dominate our modernity.

These conversations might be less between faith, religions, and worldviews than between actual "persons" in pivotal situations. Just as the natural sciences face the non-replicable event of the "big bang," the social sciences come up against non-replicable human freedom and responsibility understood as more than statistical anomalies. The trend lines of personal and group histories are laced with tipping points—encounters—that become trend lines only in retrospect. This is the proposition explored in our triangular inquiry between three groups. These groups are, first, those of no faith whose confidence is grounded exclusively in human reason; second, those who believe in the unambiguous oneness of the God of Abraham; and third, those who reason that Christ is the non-replicable Incarnation of this God in human history.

The conflicted circumstances today involve a tension between resulting institutions, particularly the tension between Church-state separation in the Western nation-states and in the multi-state Islamic world the unitary Islamic State, and within all of society. Our triangular format of inquiry enables a dialogue that is not forced into the familiar two-dimensional tension between Islam and the West.

- First, scholars and others of a rigid secular-ist predisposition are invited to refrain from classifying religion as pre-modern and subjective in nature, and specifically from bulking Christianity and Islam together as "pre-modern" residues.
- Second, followers of Islam are invited to distinguish the Christian faith from non-Christian and even anti-Christian features of the West that they find morally offensive.
- Third, distinct from the civic realm, the Church continues its own introspection and engagement with the multicultural modern world, and as part of this process proposes general principles (Chapter 4) to be weighed by the Western nation-states and by other leaders responsible for the common good.

NOTES

1. Yahya Michot, *Muslims UnderNon-Muslim Rule: Ibn Taymiyya* (Oxford: Interface Publications, 2006).

2. The legacy of John Paul II was informally identified by papal biographer George Weigel at a gathering of Catholic Professionals in Seattle, Washington, on October 18, 2010. He introduced his new book *The End and the Beginning* (New York: Doubleday, 2010).

3. Farooq Hassan, *The Concept of State and Law in Islam* (Washington, DC: University Press of America, Inc, 1981). Hassan is author of dozens of books and hundreds of articles, and remains active in advancing human rights as a member of the World Family Alliance. Born in Pakistan and educated at Oxford, Columbia and Harvard, he holds doctoral degrees in constitutional law, international and comparative law, and international affairs. Hassan's work is partly a needed alternative to the less systematic and more inflammatory Imam Khomeini (translated and annotated by Hamid Algar), *Islam and Revolution: Writings and Declarations* (London: KPI, 1981). Khomeini justifies the hostage taking as a response to United States' alleged shielding of the deposed and dead Shah's financial assets.

4. Mahmoud Ayoub in Irfan A. Omar (ed.), *A Muslim View of Christianity* (New York: Orbis Maryknoll, 2007). The author of several books and dozens of articles, Ayoub teaches at Duncan Black Macdonald Center, Harford Seminary, Connecticut, and is a research fellow at the Middle East Center, University of Pennsylvania.

5. Norman Daniel, *The Making of an Image* (Oxford: Oneworld, 1993 [1960]).

6. Documented historical detail is from Humphrey Prideaux, *Life of Mahomet* (partial title), (London: Curll, Hooke, Fleetstreet, Mears and Clay without Temple-Bar, MDCCXVIII [and 1696]). Following the medieval tradition, Prideaux gratuitously maligns Mohammed's character, but for factual material draws from a wide range of non-medieval, annotated and now relatively inaccessible primary sources: Arabic, Hebrew and Chaldee, Greek, Latin, English and French.

7. Norman Daniel regards Prideaux as the last major contributor to still work within the medieval image of Islam, asserting that is work "outdoes almost any medieval writer in its virulence" (Norman Daniel, *Islam and the West: The Making of an Image* [Oxford: Oneworld, 1960, 1993], 309, 318).

8. The complete title of Prideaux's two-part book is *The True Nature of Imposture Fully Display'd in the LIFE OF MAHOMET with A Discourse annex'd for the Vindication of Christianity from this Charge*. The volume served as a defense of Christianity against continental Deism which at the time of the writing charged Christ as being an imposter.

9. Prideaux's work predates by two centuries the biographical source cited by the renowned Muslim writer Mahmoud Ayoub (see Bibliography). The principal authorities are listed as these three: Ibn Ishaq (767–8), the grandson of Yasar (died 633), a contemporary of Qadi Malik who was the first compiler of the tradition; Ibn Umar al-Waqidi (died 823) whose value is that he quotes from Ibn Ishaq in a pristine form prior to Ibn Hisham; and Ibn Sa'd (died 844) who was al-Waqidi's secretary. This

note is based partly on de Lacy O'Leary, *Arabia Before Muhammad* (New York: E.P. Dutton and Co., 1927), 210–16.

10. Maulana Muhammad Ali, *Muhammad the Prophet* (Lahore, Pakistan: Ripon, 1984 [Ahmadiyya Anjuman Isha'at Islam, 1924]).

11. All following citations from the council are from Walter Abbott (ed.), *The Documents of Vatican II* (New York: American Press, 1966).

12. "Believing in the Reason common to all Peoples," *L'Osservatore Romano*, Vatican City: May 13, 2009.

13. M.C. D'Arcy, *The Meaning and Matter of History: A Christian View* (New York: Meridian Books, 1959), 115. Internal citations are from "Toynbee's Vision of History," by Albert Hourani in the *Dublin Review*, No. 470, (1955).

14. Luigi Guissani, *The Religious Sense* (San Francisco: Ignatius Press, 1986), 75.

15. *Catholic World Report* (San Francisco: Ignatius Press, December 2007), 11.

16. In the United States, Benedict's term "creative minorities" is drawn from the historian Oswald Spengler and is not to be confused with professional careerists of today who self-identify themselves as the "creative class."

17. In his later writings, Jurgen Habermas, sometimes referred to as "the pope of secularism," now seems to call for a "two-way understanding of tolerance: the church-state relationship . . . (as) one based upon reciprocity." This wording is from commentator Virgil Nemoianu ("The Church and the Secular Establishment: A Philosophical Dialog between Joseph Ratzinger and Jurgen Habermas, *Logos*, 9:2 [St. Paul, Minnesota: University of St. Thomas, Spring 2006], 22). The secularist Habermas offers this seasoned reflection: "Christianity, and nothing else, is the ultimate foundation of liberty, conscience, human rights, and democracy, the benchmarks of Western civilization" (citation p.41, fn. 19).

18. New York Times News Service, November 24, 2008, written comments to Marcello Pera regarding his book *Why We Must Call Ourselves Christian.*

19. T. S. Eliot, *The Idea of a Christian Society* (New York: Harcourt, Brace and Co., 1940).

20. Second Vatican Council, *Declaration on Religious Freedom*, nn. 1, 2.

Chapter One

New York to Rome and Istanbul

Five years after the savage killing of over three thousand in the twin towers in New York—like Pearl Harbor "a day that will live in infamy"—a pope journeyed from Rome to the historic city of Istanbul. The distance is measured with at least two different yardsticks. It is measured either as the crossing of a geographic territory or as an allegory separating two very different religious and cultural worlds. Both yardsticks are true. Even prior to his historic visit to Istanbul in November of 2006, in his *Regensburg Lecture* of September 2006, the pope invited the followers of Islam to intercultural and interreligious dialogue. This level is not the province of Western political or economic leaders. He began by simply asking whether aspects of their understanding of God are sufficiently compatible with universal human *reason* as to reject radical Islam's totally new phenomenon of suicide terrorism.

The protest in much of the Islamic world still hovered in the November skies over Istanbul. Speaking to an academic audience, Pope Benedict had quoted views not his own but those of a Byzantine Emperor Manuel II Paleologus in the fourteenth century: "Show me just what Muhammad brought that was new, and there you will find things only evil and inhuman." While the indirect use of this citation to an academic audience is still questioned, the pope's later apology was not that of a chameleon politician. Rather than a retraction of a truth spoken, the apology applied to the misunderstanding it caused and the injury done by reactionary demonstrators.[1] The times call for this degree of clarity beyond the well-honed language of professional diplomacy as was the possible shortcoming of some of Pope Pius XII's nuanced statements against mid-century political trends in Europe.[2]

The *Regensburg Lecture* equally challenged Islam and Western materialism. The pope elicited constructive questions from an initial thirty-eight Muslim imams who also "applaud(ed) the pope's efforts to oppose the dominance

1

of positivism and materialism in human life." This was followed by a more developed statement to the Christian world from 138 Muslim leaders entitled "A Common Word Among Us and You."[3] Less reported in the Western press than Muslim hostility was the absence of response in the West to the call for an opening between Western ethics and the wider vista of faith. At Regensburg the pope remarked: "In the Western world, it is widely held that only positivistic reason and the forms of philosophy based on it are universally valid . . . . A reason which is deaf to the divine and which relegates religion into the realm of subcultures is incapable of entering into the dialogue of cultures."[4] This high ground of human culture, exemplified and taught by the pope, combines the very broad elements of faith with reason.

Such language might appear to be so general as to be vacuous. What is meant by the coherence or harmony between faith and reason? The rationalist dismisses faith as superfluous while the person of faith dismisses the doctrinaire empiricism as reductionism. Each in his own way believes that reason involves the willingness and ability to both investigate and to notice things other than what one is *not* looking for. The rationalist faults the age of belief for the religious wars, while the person of faith holds the age of ideology—a surrogate faith—responsible for narrowing the human mystery to what might be controlled, and inevitably for the carnage of modernity's recent centuries. Faith and reason together yield two books rather than one, the book of nature and the book of scripture. This violin of more than one string comes as much from the Church as from Galileo.

Steered by secular modernity, the Preamble to the charter for the European Union charts the future by acknowledging only rationality and classical thought as the solitary taproot for the cultural event called Europe. It shrinks from any explicit recognition of the finiteness of human thought before the infinite. This near schizophrenic orientation is the flip side of Muslim belief largely insulated from reason as an innate human capacity to discover truth. The dire consequences of Western rational self-sufficiency are scattered throughout history. Theoretically, German Chancellor Angela Merkel and the German *Basic Law* (1947), which is based on a vivid and accurate memory of the Holocaust and the entire Second World War, could help shape a more balanced charter for the Union. The *Basic Law* is a bulwark against any future ideological insanity as Germany, particularly, suffered under Nazism. As a reasoned document, the *Basic Law* also recognizes the religious basis for human rights as transcending, preceding, and limiting any willful actions of parliaments, powers and principalities.[5]

At this time for potential Western introspection, Turkey provides a possible "bridge opportunity" for Christianity and the West to also engage the re-emerging world of Islam. This encounter takes place on a political landscape

shaped by enormous recent events. The end of the First World War ushered
in the final demise of the Muslim Ottoman Empire, as well as the two other
multinational Empires of the West, Czarist Russia and the Austro-Hungarian
Empire. The successor landscape today, featuring the nation-state model, is
possibly accountable to principles higher than this new political idiom, but
nation-states are also vulnerable at every step to being co-opted by political
ideologies or ethnic charismatic leaders. With the recent collapse of state
sponsored communism—the Soviet Empire, an event equivalent to Gibbon's
gradual decline and fall of the Roman Empire, the Western nation-states
remain, nevertheless, challenged by a sweep of history larger than their own
short narratives.

The quite different model, the Islamic-state, rises up from a dormant history that predates even the Ottoman Empire. Almost six centuries after the
time of St. Paul, Mohammed was born into a world entirely different than our
own. Certainly one of the most profoundly charismatic figures of history, his
pre-modern mission was to replace Arab paganism with a restored version of
Jewish and Christian monotheism centered on the common origin, Abraham.
The distinction of Abraham is that he accepted the mysterious call to leave
behind the land of Ur and of his ancestors, and then—in a then deepening
relationship with his God—changed his identity and name from Abram
(possibly recalling a Sumerian deity) to Abraham, meaning "father of many
nations." In a later millennium the major geographic encounters between
the offshoot Islam and Christian West serve almost as ceramic molds in the
shaping of modern Europe as we know it. The three centers of early Western
civilization prior to 1000 A.D. were actually Muslim—the Byzantine Constantinople to the East, and the Muslim Caliphates of Cairo and of Cordova
in the contested region of Spain. The oldest university in the world and the
primary center of Islamic scholarship today is Al-Azhar in Cairo, founded
in 969 A.D. Between the continental invasions in the eighth and seventeenth
centuries many benefits flowed from Islam to the West. Commerce connected new peoples, and there was a heightened sense of national identity
stimulated by the Crusades. Contact with Classical Western thinkers came
largely through the diligence of Muslim scholars in what is now Spain.[6] In
the late eleventh century after King Alfonso VI of Castile recaptured Toledo
from the Islamic Moors (1085), the rediscovered works of Greek philosophy
and of Aristotle were embraced by Western translators and transmitted to the
University of Paris. A century later these writings were to contribute to the
Christian harmony between faith and reason as articulated in the thirteenth
century by the Dominican St. Thomas Aquinas (1225–1274). Centuries before Christ, Aristotle already had affirmed the fit between belief and reason:
"To believe is nothing other than to think with assent . . . Believers are also

thinkers; in believing, they think and in thinking they believe . . . If faith does not think, it is nothing."[7] Compatibility between supernatural faith and natural reason had been lightly outlined by the fifth century St. Augustine in his *City of God.* Centuries later developments in education and logic, including Aquinas' *Summa Theologica* (Summary of Theology), reinforced tendencies toward what was to become Western humanism.

From multiple sources Aquinas developed a Christian-Aristotelian dialogue. This work—initially condemned by the local bishop of Paris and then the bishop of Canterbury—significantly refuted the proposition attributed to some Muslim scholars (e.g., Averroes) that between philosophy and theology there can be equally valid but genuinely contradictory truth claims.[8] Aquinas did not simply assimilate Muslim scholarship, but hoped to convert the Muslims with a timeless principle of Christian thought. Error, he said, "is not so much a fault as an inconsistency, an unfaithfulness to one's own self."[9] At the intellectual level, Aquinas' integrative breakthrough—that things of faith and of reason are neither inherently contradictory nor reducible one to the other—is not weakened by the fact that Aquinas in his time was confined to Aristotle's science or cosmology.[10] In recent centuries Aristotle's science has been vastly superseded by centuries of independent scientific discovery.

Western scholars recognize that apart from some other rejected Muslim additions to Aristotle, many foundational concepts used by Thomas Aquinas were influenced especially by the Aristotelian Muslim Avicenna (980–1037).[11] Avicenna pioneered the important distinctions as between the very nature of specific things (their essence) and their existence, between human intelligence and a higher illumination, and philosophically (not scientifically) between matter and the principle of individuation—the question why in our human experience, instead of oneness, is there a multiplicity?[12] In Aquinas the approach of Aristotle is not simply borrowed, or even baptized; it is totally "transfigured." As Maritain explains, Aquinas gives us a metaphysics not of any *be-ing*, or the good or of the beautiful, but of the universal *act of existing*. This metaphysics has as its primary object the "primordial and all embracing intelligible reality—(and therefore has) the capacity to welcome, recognize, honor, set to rights all that is."[13] Prior to Islamic or Thomistic commentaries, the basic distinction between be-ing and existence is traced ultimately to biblical accounts (Gen 1:27, and Ex 3:14: "I am who I am").[14]

This theology of being and existence can do justice to all that is true in other theologies and philosophies "because it includes all of them and yet is "truer than any of them taken separately."[15] The core philosophical insight is to treat the existence of all things (the *is*-ness of all things) apart from their specific essence (their specific *what*-ness). It is in this sense that Thomism embraces the truth of all other philosophies that deal truly with anything at all. By discovering that such inclusiveness is a feature of the act of being—of philosophy—rather than of the One behind all of existence—of theology and divine revelation—the approach of Aquinas is untouched by the kind of trap and modern crisis that now besets the theology and inclusive worldview of Islamic thought and the Mosque-state.

Like the earlier and now encysted Hellenistic Greek culture that preceded it, early Muslim culture excelled famously in many fields: mathematics, geography, astronomy, and medicine. Arabic numerals with a recurrent use of zero, so critical to all of later Western science, were transmitted through the Muslim world from India, possibly in the early ninth century.[16] The West today is richly decorated with Islamic vocabulary, and place names, and scholars find that a range of Medieval writers were routinely influenced by Muslim works. This influence is particularly apparent in the rise of romance literature and chivalry up through the thirteenth century. Dante's *Paradiso* is probably directly patterned after passages in the *hadith* (the sayings of the Prophet) depicting Mohammed's layered visit to heaven, and by a Muslim writer active a full century before Dante during the final years of Moorish control of Iberia. In the world of architecture, the Gothic cathedral, so expressive of the coherence of faith and reason owes much to Islamic influences. Faith is symbolized in the transparency of the stained glass walls, and reason is exercised in the counterbalanced matrix of intersecting vaults, ribs and flying buttresses. The structural key to the Gothic is the pointed arch, an invention echoing the decorative pointed arches discovered by the Crusaders when they took Sicily from the Muslims (1061–90).[17] But unlike Islamic piety toward the encased black stone of the Ka'ba in Mecca, in Christianity the human members themselves are likened to "living stones . . . built into a spiritual house to be a holy priesthood to offer spiritual sacrifices acceptable to God through Jesus Christ" (1 Pe 2:5).

Analogous to Turkey today, Moorish Spain in the West was the bridge between Europe and Islam for the seven centuries leading up to 1492. As with the earlier Spain, the landscape of Turkey was actually Christian prior to the rise of Islam, as were Egypt, present-day Sudan, and much of Ethiopia. In 1923 the Turkish nation became the leading remnant of the much more extensive but ailing Ottoman Empire, the "Sick Man of Europe."[18] Mustaffa Kemal Ataturk (the mountain fighter turned national leader, and Father of the Turks), eliminated the territorial Sultanate in 1923 and the left over Caliphate in 1924. He banished from the new secular nation-state the Sultan's hereditary son and positioned himself as the unchallenged executive.[19] Under the 1923 Turkish constitution the religion of Islam decidedly is not listed as the state religion. After six centuries the Christian cathedral of Santa Sophia, seized at the conquest of Constantinople in 1453, was converted in 1935 by

Ataturk from a mosque to a secular museum open to all of the populace. The Christian mosaics, covered for centuries with plaster, now look down from their timeless abode onto passing visitors, including Pope Benedict XVI during his visit in late 2006.

Given its own peripheral geography with Europe, secular Turkey seeks membership in the European Union, much as many remnant states of the Soviet Empire have also done since 1991. If Turkey were to be admitted by Western nations into membership in the Union, it would be the most populace member.[20] At Istanbul the newly selected pope—as a religious observer—reversed his own earlier opposition to Turkish membership. Turkish membership, he considered, would not necessarily be evidence of a further Western slide into relativistic and leveled multicultural-*ism*.[21] Regarding the popes revised position: "This perhaps speaks not so much to his confidence in Islam as his lack of confidence in secular Europe: the depth of the crisis is so great that even a European encounter with Islamic monotheism becomes helpful."[22] Are we witnessing one of the great ironies of history, that as the Muslim world possibly struggles to conform the Islamic State more to the universal natural law, the West at the same time jettisons its own natural law foundation in favor of militant secularism superficially disguised as open door multicultural-*ism*?

Demonstrating part of the Western heritage—the distinction of Church from state—the pope invited his Muslim audience to notice that the actual decision on Turkish membership in the Union resides with the secular members and clearly not with the Church. His most immediate and ongoing goal with Turkish Muslim leaders is to work toward religious "co-existence" and religious freedom in Turkey. Such "reciprocity" would include the right to found Christian seminaries and new dioceses within the secular Turkish nation-state.[23]

Opposite to the Turkish experience, another quite different reaction to the modern world came at a different point in the Muslim world in the late 1970s. The religious leader Khomeini seized power in Iran to replace the secularizing Shah Pahlevi. He proclaimed a "constitutional state," but did not use this term in the Turkish sense that Iran might be run by a parliament. Rather, under the "constitution" the machinery of state was still accountable to the *Qur'an* and hadith.[24] Between the bookends of Turkey and Iran are a range of other Muslim adjustments to the West. One intriguing example is Nigeria, roughly half Muslim and half Christian.[25] In tribally divided Nigeria (mostly Hausa in the north, Yoruba in the West, and Christian Ibo in the east) inter-religious clashes in the Muslim north were recently addressed in the so-called Kaduna Compromise (1999). Under this agreement, the Shari'a criminal code was put in place only at the state level and not at the federal level, and further, it applies only to Muslims and is not always strictly imposed. Thus far, at the federal level the secular democratic constitution remains intact.[26] In Nigeria, as in other post-colonial regions, the state boundaries are often an arbitrary inheritance from the earlier administrations or the protectorates assigned after the First World War. Federated systems like Nigeria are the pragmatic reverse of historical Islamic practices to encase non-Muslim populations as second class enclaves (*dhimmis*) within Muslim society.

Besides Turkey and Nigeria, another "democratic" and relatively tolerant Islamic state is Indonesia. The largest state of Muslim population in the world, Indonesia also has a higher literacy rate than many. In 2007 the incoming Indonesian president took his oath of office with his hand on the *Qur'an*, but relations with minority non-Muslims are somewhat "normalized" due to day-to-day shoulder rubbing with these mostly Hindu and animist neighbors. Indonesia's new ambassador to the Holy See reaffirmed his government's "position of condemning terrorist violence, under whatever pretext it occurs, as a criminal offense, which by its contempt for human life and freedom, undermines the very foundations of society."[27] Other pragmatic tailoring between Islam and the West prominently include Egypt. This uneasy history includes the assassination of the Westernizing President Sadat in the early 1980s as well as civil and military steps in 2011 toward some form of democracy. Malaysia also theoretically offers freedom of religion, but a recent case is that of a woman convert to Christianity who was constrained from re-entering the country to join her Muslim husband. Early in 2010 controversy also arose over whether non-Muslims can use the term Allah as in Malay-language Bibles.

Overall, the larger and long-term picture emerging from the pope's engagement with Islam at Regensburg and Istanbul is the possibility of new but limited interreligious and intercultural dialogue. Following Regensburg, the pope specifically invited dialogue with Islamic imams, and in October 2006, at the end of Ramadan, the initial group of thirty-eight imams respondents increased more than three-fold and delivered their open letter to the pope and to the leaders of other Christian Churches and denominations ("A Common Word Between Us and You," above). In his response, Pope Benedict XVI reaffirmed the need for continued work together based on three factors: respect for the integrity of the human person, more "objective knowledge" of each other's religion, and the sharing of religious experience. The Pontifical Council on Interreligious Dialogue continues to be engaged, and the Muslim delegation also was reminded of the Pope's words from 2005: "I am profoundly convinced that we must not yield to the negative pressures in our midst, but must affirm the values of mutual respect, solidarity and peace. The life of every human being is sacred, both for Christians and for Muslims. There is plenty of scope for us to act together in the service of fundamental moral values."[28] The now ongoing Catholic-Muslim Forum issued a joint statement affirming the very general obligations of love, of working toward religious freedom and mutual education, and of the need in the world for shared witness to the reality of God.

Facing ethical challenges in the West, the pope's primary goal during his earlier November 2006 visit to Istanbul was to meet with the Greek Orthodox Patriarch Bartholomew I. The Patriarch co-signed a pledge to combat the "increase of secularization, relativism, even nihilism, especially in the Western world" and "to preserve Christian roots, traditions and values, to ensure respect for history, and thus to contribute to the European culture of the future . . . ." In September 2009 the Russian Orthodox Archbishop Hilarion remarked: "We live in a de-Christianized world, in a time that some define—mistakenly—as post Christian . . . Contemporary society, with its practical materialism and moral relativism, is a challenge to us all. The future of humanity depends on our response . . . More than ever before, we Christians must stand together."[29] Unification of the Latin and Orthodox Church's would establish an expansive spiritual geography extending from the otherwise secular European Union eastward to the Urals and across most of Siberia toward the Pacific. Hilarion's lines are strikingly similar to a petition heard many years earlier from the Muslim world at another interreligious gathering: "It is a prime duty of our two monotheistic faiths to establish real and abiding friendship, not only among their own adherents, but also between themselves and the followers of the other faith as well. We should collaborate as believers in the one God in defending the world against the menaces of atheism and materialism."[30]

As part of his intercultural message to new Islamic contacts in Istanbul, the pope noted in passing that the French constitution was used as a model for the secular constitution of Turkey.[31] Such reference to a Western constitution is a good opening, but it is also problematic. The proposed sectioning off or separation of Church and state can take many cultural forms, some of them abusive.[32] According to the pre-eminent Jewish scholar of Islam, Bernard Lewis, respect for the physical sciences was not meaningfully accepted within the Ottoman Empire until after the French Revolution—and the attempted establishment of an anti-religious French culture and secular state.[33] Science, he says, became acceptable because with the Revolution science was totally detached from the European context of Christian religion.[34] Lewis adds that later Muslim thinkers saw the danger to both Christianity and Islam of the atheist message even when it was attached to the worldly benefits of science.

The French Constitution of 1905—roughly concurrent with Ataturk's secular Turkish constitution—should be compared to the United States Constitution. The earlier American First Amendment assures personal freedom of religion. In the United States the federal government is forbidden to define the Church which "alone is competent to define herself." The often repeated wording "wall of separation" between government and religion is taken not from the Constitution, but simply from the private writings of Thomas Jefferson, as cited in the 1947 Supreme Court case *Everson v. Board of Education.* The actual wording of the First Amendment to the United States Constitution reads simply that (the government shall) ". . . make no law respecting an establishment of religion, or prohibiting the free exercise thereof." Today the public exercise of religion, as in the display of nativity scenes on public grounds, is routinely misinterpreted by the courts as a prohibited federal "establishment" of religion.[35]

The Jesuit John Courtney Murray's analysis of the different American and French political experiments is reflective of European cultural history. His words are worth quoting at length as background for our later treatment in Chapter 4. Influenced by the difference between the European and American experience, the focus of the Second Vatican Council (1963–5) moves from Church-state relations to a non-political concern for the moral and spiritual needs of the underlying society. Murray writes:

> This is one of the important respects in which separation of Church and state in the United States differs from the Continental separations. There is hardly a point of comparison between the First Amendment to the U.S. Constitution and, for instance, the first article of the French Law of Separation of 1905, in what regards context, history, theory, or further articulation in law. Without going into the matter, it might be said that the First Amendment simply declares the U.S. *government incompetent to legislate in religious matters*; in consequence, in American laws the Catholic Church is literally ignored, at the same time that, in American society, the Church is free to be what she is. On the contrary, in the French law, as has been said, 'The State pretends to ignore the Church; in reality it never took more cognizance of her.' The French government *assigned her an explicit juridical stature* articulated in forty-four articles, whose general effect was to reduce her to the explicit status of an *association cultuelle*, or a union of them, chartered by the State as corporations of private law, and most minutely regulated.[36]

The original recognition that government is "incompetent to legislate in religious matters" has no commonality with the judicial presumption today, and that of government (public) schools, that the state is entitled to establish and then enforce pre-emptive multiculturalism as a public ideology. Unlike the United States constitutional provision, Murray does find commonality between the French tradition of government intrusion and the Italian and

Spanish histories as well.[37] The French experience also resembles the late nineteenth century *Kulturkampf* ("struggle for civilization") in Otto von Bismark's new Germany, which sought to eliminate the Church or at least subordinate it as a department of state. Compared to both the historical French model of state dominance and the Islamic model—which regards the state as an administrative feature of the much broader Islamic cultural zone—the American model, as a constitutional republic, simply distances the state from religion altogether. Church and state fulfill distinct realms. This delineation is possible because of the special circumstance of a presumed religious population in America. A religious society, quite apart from the state, carries a civic morality directly rooted in natural law.[38] The American premise, now greatly tested, was that a prior and common morality can stand on its own.

In Chapter 3 the Islamic state is contrasted by Muslim writers with the separation model, and is explained by Muslim writers as an indispensable tutor and enforcer for righteous living. The difference between the American model and the European experience of Church-state relations is apparent in research by the scholar Bernard Lewis. He recounts an early report on how the French were seen by some Muslims at the time of the Napoleonic invasion of Egypt in 1798. This perspective is not entirely out of date today: "In the name of God, the merciful and the compassionate. O you who believe in the oneness of God, community of Muslims, know that the French nation (may God devastate their dwellings and abase their banners) are rebellious infidels and dissident evildoers. They do not believe in the oneness of the Lord of Heaven and Earth, nor in the mission of the intercessor on the Day of Judgment, but have abandoned all religions and denied the afterworld and its penalties. They do not believe in the Day of Resurrection and pretend that only the passage of time destroys us and that beyond this there is no resurrection and no reckoning, no examination and nor retribution, no question and no answer."[39]

Napoleon claimed that he was foretold in the *Qur'an* (much as Mohammed found himself foretold in the Bible) and in the interests of political expediency he even pretended an interest in converting. The Sheik of Alexandria had taken a liking to the Emperor, but to this cynical conversion he responded: "The French observe no religious worship . . . (And then) Why not, therefore, declare yourself Moslem at once, and remove the only obstacle betwixt you and the throne of the East."[40] Later kidnapping the pope to Paris and always seeing himself as another Charlemagne, Napoleon enjoyed referring to himself as either a Caliph[41] or a Caesar.[42] The more secular politics of our own day confronts us now with widespread spiritual malaise at all levels of society especially across much of Europe. A European Union survey in 2005 depicts this stark decline in religious belief. The centers of strongest belief in God are Turkey (Muslim), Malta, Cyprus and Romania, all still at over ninety percent believers. Portugal and Poland are also above seventy-five percent. The centers of lowest belief are Estonia, the Czech Republic and Sweden at between sixteen and twenty-three percent. Much of the former Yugoslavia is also below twenty-five percent.[43]

Pope Benedict's comments on this loss of faith and this even despising attitude toward its own religious past, with succinct and necessary clarity and even bluntness. He decries Western "self hatred that is nothing short of pathological."[44] By this assessment, Western decline and post-modern graffiti manifest cultural dementia and worse. And thinking globally and of the future he adds, "The Islam that is sure of itself has to a large extent a greater fascination for the Third World than a Christianity that is in a state of inner decay."[45] This decay can be traced only in part to the weariness of two world wars in one century and the tiresomeness of the many ideologies that have been imposed on national populations. The seventh century was a similar period of Byzantine Christian demoralization, and of additional government oppression and internal dissension. As in the seventh century, the temptation once again is toward intercultural syncretism. Subsequent chapters develop the theme of encounter at the personal and institutional levels. The sequence scans Islamic-Western history, then examines Islamic political institutions, the alternative evolution of the West and of the Church, and some aspects of scientific thought which secularism would bend to its purposes as willingly as Islam absorbs the state.

NOTES

1. As published the Lecture includes a footnote that reads in part: "I hope that the reader of my text can see immediately that this sentence does not express my personal view of the *Qur'an*, for which I have the respect due to the holy book of a great religion. In quoting the text of the Emperor Manuel II, I intended solely to draw out the essential relationship between faith and reason. On this point I am in agreement with Manuel II, but without endorsing his polemic."

2. Critics allege that as pope Pius XII failed to sufficiently confront Hitler. Beginning in the early 1960s, this campaign might well have been triggered by a 1960 Kremlin "super-secret plan for destroying the Vatican's moral authority" (retired KGB general Ion Mihai Pacepa, cited in *National Review Online* (Jan. 25, 2007) and quoted in *National Catholic Register*, Feb. 18, 2007). In 1963 Hochhuth's play, *The Deputy* (1963), repeated the Soviet slander. Pacepa reports that Hochhuth drew from an earlier play produced by Erwin Piscator, a fervent communist, based on tampered documents stolen from the Vatican archives. The pope's anonymous role in rescuing 860,000 Jews finds new documentation in the work of Gary Krupp (*Examining the Papacy of Pius XII* [2009], or Pave the Way Foundation at ptwf.org.)

In 1937 Pius XII already had spoken out against a broad "conspiracy of silence" in the press regarding horrors in Russia, Mexico and Spain (*Divine Redemptoris*, encyclical on communism). Factors counseling papal "silence," that is, Pius XII's non-specific condemnations of Fascist violence, included vulnerability of Catholic populations (as shown in Holland) and of Church relief and charitable operations including sanctuary networks. Dangers from a break in papal neutrality also could have heightened exploitation in Allied news coverage (a papal position cited in Jose Sanchez, *Pius XII and the Holocaust* [Washington, DC: Catholic University Press], 157–8). Historically and under similar circumstances the Vatican excommunication of Elizabeth I backfired, resulting in the severe persecution of Catholics in England.

3. The verse "common word (etc.)" comes from the *Qur'an*: "O People of the Scripture! Come to a common word as between us and you: that we worship none but God and that we shall ascribe no partner unto Him . . ." (Q 3:64).

4. Pope Benedict XVI, "The Regensburg Lecture," n. 58 as reprinted in James Schall, S.J., *The Regensburg Lecture* (South Bend, Indiana: St. Augustine's Press, 2007), Appendix I. In 2004 Cardinal Ratzinger (now Pope Benedict) briefly introduced the "intercultural dimension" of human existence as part of his dialogue with the secularist and positivist Jurgen Habermas (Jurgan Habermas and Joseph Ratzinger, *The Dialectics of Secularization* [San Francisco: Ignatius Press, 2006]). Habermas proposes liberal political rule justified by "nonreligious or postmetaphysical" *procedures* (22) while Ratzinger maintains human rights that are "incomprehensible without the *presupposition* that man *qua* man . . . is the subject of rights and that his being bears within itself values and norms that must be discovered—but not invented" (71). References to Islam (the third pole addressed in the current book) are tangential to the dialogue between secularism and natural law. Habermas reports that "In Teheran, a colleague once said to me that the comparative study of cultures and religious sociology surely suggested that European secularization was the odd one out among the various (postmodern) developments—and that it ought to be corrected" (38). Ratzinger finds that "Islam has defined its own catalogue of human rights, which differs from the Western catalogue" (61).

5. Of the twenty-seven member states of the European Union (EU), Germany is the only one opposed to a possible European Union Directive presented in 2008 by the European Commission and approved by the European Parliament in April 2009, which would invite legal action favoring homosexual rights as distinguished from human rights.

6. Christopher Dawson, *Medieval Essays* (Garden City, New York: Image Books, 1959), p. 107. Dawson finds in the cosmopolitan character of tenth century Mediterranean culture a cooperative and international movement among Muslim, Christian and Jewish scholars.

7. Cited by John Paul II in *Fides et Ratio* (On the Relationship between Faith and Reason), (September 14, 1998, no. 79).

8. In the General Introduction to St. Thomas Aquinas, *On the Truth of the Catholic Faith (Summa Contra Gentiles)*, Vol. I, (Garden City: Image Books, 1955), 15, 21. Falsely attributed to Averroes by contemporary Latin critics was the theory of "double truth." Under this theory philosophy provides the scientific formulation of truth

while theology then supplies an allegorical expression to the apparently contradicted Scripture, for the benefit of the less educated. Theology would become fully subordinate to philosophy. Averroes' subtle theory of allegory is contained in a translation by George Hourani, *On the Harmony of Religion and Philosophy* (London: Mssrs. Luzac and Col., 1967 [1961]).

9. Jean Guitton, *Great Heresies and Church Councils* (New York: Harper and Row, 1983), 107.

10. In addition, Arab versions of the ancients imported into the Medieval West were apparently alloyed. The translators destroyed the originals, while revising Aristotle toward theosophy by mixing astronomy with astrology, and similarly modifying medicine (Leopold Ranke, *History of the Popes*, Vol. 1 [London: George Bell and Sons, 1878], 47.

11. Many of the works of Aristotle were available in translations from the Greek either before or alongside the Arabic translations, e.g., the works of Boethius, Robert Grosseteste, William of Moerbeke (Copleston, op. cit., 233–5). Moerebeke finally accessed the Byzantine libraries some fifty years after the crusaders ravaged Constantinople in 1204.

12. Frederick Copleston, SJ, *A History of Philosophy: Medieval Philosophy* (Vol. 2: Part 1), Garden City, New York: Image Books, 1962, 220, deferring to a commentary by Roland-Gosselin. Syrian Christians in the fourth century were the first to translate Aristotle from Greek into their language and then in Baghdad into Arabic (c. 832). Also influential to Aquinas was the eleventh century Jewish Maimonides who harmonized Judaism with Aristotle, while still retaining the necessity of revelation (John Hardon, *Religions of the World*, Vol. 1 [Garden City, New York: Image Books, 1968], 266).

13. Jacques Maritain, *The Peasant of the Garonne* (New York: Holt, Rinehart and Winston, 1968), 133–4. Maritain and Etienne Gilson are the two most prominent Thomistic scholars of the twentieth century.

14. This point is lodged by John Paul II, "Biblical Account of Creation Analyzed" Sept. 12, 1979, *The Original Unity of Man and Woman* (Boston: Daughters of Saint Paul, 1981), 23–26.

15. Ibid, citing Etienne Gilson.

16. The quantity zero was introduced by the Arab mathematician Muhammad Ibn Musa al-Khwarizmi in 810 A.D., but he credited as his source the Indian Brahmagupta of the early seventh century (Ariana Fallaci, *The Rage and the Pride* (New York: Rizzoli, 2001), 47. Indian numerals are mentioned in 662 by a Syriac Christian bishop, and a translation into Arabic is dated 754–75, a generation before al-Khwarizmi (W.H. McNeill, *The Rise of the West* [New York: Mentor, 1963]479, fn. 25).

17. Earlier the pointed arch had been borrowed by the Muslims from Persia (c. 641), and came originally from Assyria and Mesopotamian aqueducts (722 B.C.). Sir Banister Fletcher, *A History of Architecture* (New York: Charles Scribner's Sons, 1961), 367.

18. In 1853 the Tsar of Russia remarked of the Ottoman Empire to the British Ambassador: "We have on our hands a sick man—a very sick man . . . He may die suddenly upon our hands . . . ."

19. The Sultan is a territorial position while the Caliph, as a successor to the Prophet, is universal and non-territorial. The Sultan of Turkey, who was also the Caliph, was aligned with the British when they occupied Istanbul in 1920. Since the revolution of 1908 he had served as a constitutional monarch with an advisory council and a parliament. Kemal, who was being supplied by Soviet Russia in what was partly a Western struggle for regional influence, denounced the Sultan and in turn was excommunicated. The Sultan called for the murder of Kemal, even declaring jihad against him and his nationalist fighters (all Muslims). See Jawaharlal Nehru, *Glimpses of History* (New York: John Day Co., 1942 [1934[), 696–704.

20. Full Union membership by a country of Islamic citizens may come later, or never. Even lukewarm interest by members of the Union is diminishing. The newly elected French President Nicolas Sarkozy (2007) is openly opposed while the current Chancellor Merkel of Germany envisions a possible tiered system of memberships.

21. "What eclecticism and cultural leveling have in common is the separation of culture from human nature. Thus cultures can no longer define themselves within a nature that transcends them and man ends up being reduced to a mere cultural statistic" (John Paul II, *Veritatis Splendor* [The Splendor of the Truth], August 1993, nn. 33, 46, 51, repeated in Pope Benedict XVI, *Caritas in Veritate* [Charity in Truth], June 2009, n. 26).

22. George Neumayr (ed.), *Catholic World Report*, January 2007.

23. In a world divided between Christian-ruled and Muslim states, seven centuries before our own time, Pope Clement V (1311) prohibited the holding of Muslim services in those Christian-ruled countries also inhabited by Muslims. Pilgrimages to Mohammed's shrine were prohibited, as well as the use of his name (Walter Ullman, *Medieval Papalism: The Political Theories of the Medieval Canonists* [London: Methuen Co. Ltd., 1949], 122).

24. John Laffin, *The Dagger of Islam* (New York: Bantam, 1981), 130. An original source is Imam Khomeini, translated and annotated by Hamid Algar, *Islam and Revolution: Writings and Declarations* (London: KMI, 1981), 53: "Islamic government is neither tyrannical nor absolute, but constitutional. It is not constitutional in the current sense of the word, i.e., based on the approval of laws in accordance with the opinion of the majority (sic). It is constitutional in the sense that the rulers are subject to . . . the Noble *Qur'an* and the Sunna of the Most Noble Messenger" (Mohammed). . . . Islamic government may therefore be defined as the rule of divine law over men."

25. Still useful in the study of non-class based "communal" politics in non-Western countries, e.g., religious groupings including Muslim, is a broad article based in part on Nigeria as a case study. Federated structures are only one of a wide spectrum of possible outcomes in communal political settings. See Robert Melson and Howard Wolpe, "Modernization and the Politics of Communalism: A Theoretical Perspective," *American Political Science Review*, LXIV:4, Dec. 1970, 1112–30. The source is revisited in Chapter 3.

26. One observer notes also that the federated democratic system "has also allowed the many divisions *within* both Islam and Christianity to rise to the surface to be debated locally." This, he says, "takes some pressure off the Muslim-Christian rift" (Darren Kew, "Why Nigeria Matters," *First Things* [New York: Institute on Religion and Public Life, Nov. 2007], 17–19).

27. Comments by Benedict XVI, cited in *National Catholic Register*, Nov. 25, 2007.

28. Text signed by Vatican Secretary of State Cardinal Tarcisio Bertone, addressed to His Highness Prince Ghazi bin Muhammad bin Talal (Amman, Jordan), November 19, 2007, carried in *L'Osseratore Romano*, December 5, 2007.

29. Cited in Edward Pentin, "Archbishop Hilarion's Speech at Sant' Egido (Sept. 17, 2009), *National Catholic Register*, July 31, 2009.

30. Statement of Moslem observers to the World Council of Churches, (Abdullar Igram, DeanHekim, M. Yousef Sharwarbi), 1954, private printing, cited in John Hardon, op. cit., Vol. II, 100.

31. Also adopted were the Swiss Civil Code, the Italian Penal Code and the German Commercial Code.

32. The 1905 French Law of Separation of Church and State repealed the Napoleonic Concordat of 1801. The earlier Law would have removed all state support for religions *and* would have claimed for the state all goods of the Church. It would have entrusting churches and chapels to elected "cultural associations." This radically secularist formula would have disrupted the *internal* life of the Church, and was intended by some as a first step to "detach the nation, families and individuals from the Church" (Henri Daniel-Rops, *History of the Church of Christ* [17 volumes]: *A Fight for God* [Garden City, New York: Image, 1967], 217).

33. Amicable diplomatic relations between Turkey and France began in the sixteenth century when Francis I found himself excluded from the Mediterranean by Austrian expansionism. A treaty signed in 1536 came in the form of an order from the Sultan (Hatti Sherif) and in this sense was the model for all subsequent treaties or "concessions" granted to European nations by a soon in decline Ottoman Empire until the eve of the First World War. The French were granted rights of extraterritoriality, trade and free exercise of religion. See Edwin Bliss, *Turkey and the Armenian Atrocities* (New York: M. J. Coghlan, 1896), 183–194.

34. Bernard Lewis, *The Emergence of Modern Turkey,* London: Oxford University Press, 1961. Also repeated in *What Went Wrong?* (New York: Harper Perennial, 2002), p. 104, where Lewis cites as his source a book by Jean Chesneau, 1887.

35. John Harmon McElroy, "Understanding the First Amendment's Religion Clauses," *The Intercollegiate Review*, 46:1 (Wilmington, DE: Intercollegiate Studies Institute, Spring 2011), 33–40. In a 1962 case, Engel v. Vitale, the United States Supreme Court ruled that the Federal Government could overrule state actions with regard to the public exercise of religion, a principle not contained in the First Amendment and misapplying the Fourteenth Amendment's Equal Protection Clause passed after the Civil War specifically to ensure citizen rights to freed slaves.

36. John Courtney Murray, S.J., *Government Repression of Heresy*, Proceedings of the Catholic Theological Society, no date (c. 1950), p. 58, fn. 35, italics added. Murray's classic work came ten years later: *We Hold These Truths: Catholic Reflections on the American Proposition* (New York: Sheed and Ward, 1960).

37. In 1967 and by a vote of 391 to 9, the Spanish Parliament removed restrictions against non-Catholic religions and granted full religious liberty to all denominations, closely following key wording in the Second Vatican Council Declaration on Religious Liberty.

38. McNamara is among those who go so far as to trace key wording and the five principles in the Declaration of Independence to a more original and more Christian source preceding not only the French Revolution (1789) but even the widely credited *Second Treatise on Government* by the Englishman John Locke. See Sylvester J. McNamara, *American Democracy and Catholic Doctrine* (Brooklyn: International Catholic Truth Society, n.d., c. 1920), 106–122, esp. 155. Mc Namara documents evidence that philosophy of *Declaration of Independence* (and the Virginia Declaration of Rights which he also wrote) derives in large part from the writings of the Jesuit Robert Cardinal Bellarmine. The greatest similarity between Jefferson and the original Bellarmine, who is generally viewed as monarchist (and who preached against the "divine right of kings") is in the content and exact wording of Jefferson's five principles in the preamble: sovereignty, equality, divine and natural law, the right to select magistrates, and the right to change the form of government.

McNamara draws from Filmer's *Patriarcha* (a compendium of Bellarmine's philosophy). Jefferson's copy of *Patriarcha* remains in the Library of Congress. The incomparable term "self-evident" (truths) was altered by the Benjamin Franklin from Jefferson's original "sacred and undeniable" (Paul Johnson, *A History of the American People* [New York: Harper Perennial, 1999], 155). Jefferson's original proposal corresponds to Bellarmine's "this power (to institute civil power) is in the divine law." Among the colonies and prior to the *Declaration of Independence*, Lord Baltimore's (Catholic) Maryland was unusual for its religious tolerance. But in 1692, after non-Catholics gained control of the legislature and then agitated in Parliament, King William voided this 1649 policy.

39. Bernard Lewis, *What Went Wrong?* 130–1.

40. Author of Waverley (Sir Walter Scott*), The Life of Napoleon Bonaparte: Emperor of the French*, (Exeter: J & B Williams, Vol. I, 1832), 298. During the Reign of Terror, less than three centuries after Santa Sophia in Constantinople was converted into a mosque, Notre Dame was converted into a "Temple of Reason," and the Paris church of St. Genvieve, the burial place of Voltaire and Rousseau, became a temple to French nationalism.

41. Walter Scott, 91.

42. In 1810 Napoleon reproached the clergy of Holland for pronouncing the bull of his excommunication by the pope: "The principle of the Christian Church, as these gentlemen (turning to the Protestant deputies) can teach you, is, as they have just professed, to render unto Caesar the things which are Caesar's . . . I bear the temporal sword, and know how to use it. I am a monarch of God's creation, and you reptiles of the earth dare not oppose me...."

43. Tom Hundley, "Does God have a Prayer in Europe?" *Chicago Tribune*, May 10, 2006. A 2008 American Religious Identification Survey conducted by the Program on Public Values at Trinity College (Hartford, Conn.) makes findings for the United States. The share of those professing no religion is fifteen percent, up from 1990.

44. Pope Benedict XVI, *Without Roots* (New York: Basic Books, 2006), 78.

45. Josef Cardinal Ratzinger (Pope Benedict XVI), *Turning Point for Europe* (San Francisco: Ignatius, 1991), 170.

Chapter Two

Islam and the Map

In 1799 Napoleon suffered the first great defeat of his career, in his attempt to erect an Empire on the Euphrates, on the ancient battlefield Plain of Esdraelon east of the coastal Mount Carmel in Palestine. Two centuries later and in the wake of a crumbled Ottoman Empire, in 1979, the West entered its newest phase in its relations with the Muslim world. Confounding some of modern social science and its ideology, history reversed direction as a traditional Muslim cleric deposed and replaced the secularizing Shah Pahlevi of Iran. Barely a decade later in 1991 came the collapse of the Soviet Union and the abrupt end of the Cold War. The global table was set for a encounter between the West and rising Islam in the Middle East. Pealing back the layers of history in reverse will unveil the Islamic worldview and in this way might give some insight into the longer-term picture for the future.

In August of 1914 the assassins of Archduke Ferdinand in Bosnia triggered a world poised to collapse into the trenches of the First World War. The Versailles Treaty (1919) marked the beginning of an accelerated phase of Western nation building. In Europe the Austro-Hungarian Empire was reduced to a fourth its original size. The new treaty completed the European revolutions of 1848 by fully dismantling the *multi-national* political *form* associated with monarchies and empires. The Russian Revolution of 1917 had already eliminated the Czar and a second widespread Russian empire. The third dynasty, the Ottoman Empire, already in decline for centuries, and a wartime ally of Germany, was also eliminated and replaced mostly by a patchwork of European protectorates. Wedged against southeastern Europe was an Islamic exception, the buffer Turkish nation-state, the final remnant a broad Turkish invasion from the east of nearly a millennium before (the Seljuk Turks, 1071).

The First World War completed the breakdown of most hereditary monarchies, which in the ideal at least denote a role for monarchs as multi-national mediators. (The exception, the world-spanning British Empire, dissolved following the Second World War.) Following the First World War, shell-shocked post war observers offered an early assessment of the new state of affairs: "The years covering the period of the Great War have taught, however, that knowledge of the arts and sciences, and great intellectual development and material prosperity do not necessarily produce humane principles or methods of warfare above those held by the savages since the beginning of recorded history."[1] Under yet another quirk of history, the separated autocratic regimes of Europe soon were replaced by totalitarian dictatorships. The old monarchic and aristocratic order in Europe gave way to the alternative populist and sometimes aberrant nation-states, soon to be captured by a new range of continental ideologies—Nazism in Germany, but also Communism in Russia and Italian Fascism.[2] In Germany it was the Catholic culture centered in southern Germany that held out longest against the parliamentary rise of Hitler and National Socialist party in 1933.[3]

At the beginning of the twenty-first century the emergence of regional zones of conflict, in place of the Western and Soviet power blocs, returns the world to a situation much like the end of the First World War. The Versailles Treaty supplies three perspectives for this new environment and especially the multinational world of Islam. First, Versailles ushered in an era of fully separate nation-states in Europe, and gave birth to such dismembered or artificial nation-states as the late Czechoslovakia and especially Poland (a buffer between the Germany and Russia). Second, the boundaries of new colonial mandates in the Middle East were overlaid more or less arbitrarily onto the diverse post-Ottoman Islamic populations.[4] Much of the ferment of the Islamic world today is the story of these disparate Islamic sects seeking an identity with respect to the West and toward each other. And third, in 1923–4, under Mustafa Kemal Ataturk, Muslim Turkey wrenched itself away from the surviving Islamic Caliphate and toward an unambiguously secular and Western style political constitution. This Turkish constitution, rather than Islam, served Turkish nationalism and provided a defensive path against further dismemberment by the European powers.[5]

Prior to Versailles, a nineteenth century traveler from a wealthy pedigree tracing back to the Crusades, retired deep into the Sahara. Charles de Foucauld (1858–1916) was a high living Foreign Legionnaire who later turned priest. He lived for fifteen years as a solitary monk and teacher partly among the nominally Muslim Touareg peoples. Like Mohammed he had been orphaned at eight. As a young man he converted to Christianity. This turning point happened in a Paris confessional rather than in a cave as was the case with Mohammed when he discovered monotheism. Among the Touaregs de Foucauld gained many converts, not by conquest but by the witness of his personal poverty and simplicity. Of missionary peoples, he said, "Neither does our role as Little Brothers include working for their adaptation to the Western materialistic, technological form of civilization, which, moreover, comes far from representing the only conceivable idea of a really human civilization."[6] His own conversion from a dissolute, comfortable and bored existence continued in Morocco where "through the faith of an entire people of Moslems, he had glimpsed something of the greatness of God."[7]

Almost exactly seven hundred years earlier, in 1219, we catch up with one of many other mendicant monks on Muslim territory. St. Francis shared the same pure motives as Charles. In a simple brown robe and alone in human terms, he confronted the Sultan Malek al-Kamil at Damietta on the Nile Delta, then under siege by an army of the Fifth Crusade.[8] While he failed to convert al-Kamil to the peace of Christ it was possibly here that he might have met a young woman named Hula. It is said that she prepared with him the now familiar words to the Prayer of St. Francis,[9] so cherished within the Christian world: "Lord, making me an instrument of your peace . . . ." And, because Francis received the handshake of al-Kamil and his permit of safe passage, the Franciscan Order was permitted to remain in Islamic territories even through the later centuries of the Ottoman Empire and into the present (e.g., in Herzgovina) while other religious orders were expelled.

LIFE OF MOHAMMED

It was still farther back, six centuries before St. Francis visited the Muslim outpost that the founder of Islam was born at Mecca, a crossroad of foreign civilizations on the northern and southern frontiers, and amidst a confusion of indigenous local idolatries and warring tribes. The mixed Arabian culture was salted with Christian theological disputes seeping in from the bordering Byzantine Empire. The first full biography of Mohammed was not produced until about one hundred twenty years after Mohammed's death, by Ibn Ishaq (704–773 A.D.).[10] The only version of this work now available was edited by Ibn Hisham (d. 835 or 840) a full two centuries after Muhammed. Mohammed was born in 571 A.D. Mohammed came from a clan within the noblest tribe of Arabia, the Qurayish. With his father dead when Mohammed was only two months old and his mother in his eighth year, he was cared for by his grandfather, but for only one year before he too died, and then by an uncle.[11] At age twenty-five Mohammed met a rich widow, Khadijha, probably fifteen years his senior. After working for three years at Damascus and elsewhere in her trade and caravan business they married (c. 595 A.D.).[12] Mecca was on the direct trade route between the matriarchal Saba in the south, the still active civilization of Yemen,[13] and the patriarchal and more warlike regions of Sinai and Palestine to the north.

In traditional societies social advancement could be achieved through commerce in support of the urban elite or through construction of a genealogy. In his marriage to Khadijha Mohammed enjoyed both upper-class family ties and commercial success. As an Arabian he was descended from the Ishmaelites,[14] and this biblical connection was to give legitimacy and profound emotional power to the religion he later founded.[15] Humphrey Prideaux, the seventeenth century historian and Christian polemicist, maintained that Mohammed's opportune marriage and then his religion of Islam served mostly as a useful path to personal advancement into the Meccan establishment.[16] Mohammed's well known mystical visions began in 610 A.D. when he was forty and at least fifteen years into his marriage. He had been meditating in cave on Mount Hira outside Mecca. Khadijha, possibly a Christian according to both Western and Muslim accounts, came to share his convictions. As a well-positioned advocate, his wife also continued to afford him access to a prominent and extended family of supporters.[17] Following a reported three years of private religious experiences, Mohammed preached for the first time in 613. He began with selected leaders of his home city, Mecca, who later became his nine disciples and generals.[18]

Muslim commentators hold that Mohammed most probably learned about religions of the day from fellow travelers during his earlier trade missions on the camel routes to and from Mecca. A common Western view about Mohammed's visions is that these lessons simply re-emerged in later trances, which could account for the recordings in the holy book, the *Qur'an* (Q 16:103, 25:4, 44:14).[19] In any case, Mohammed was scandalized by the warring tribes and increasing anarchy of Arabia and especially by their denial of providence and by their fragmented idolatry in Mecca. Some 360 deities ruled the city. Mohammed saw a need for reform and for "a moral law to replace tribal laws of kinship and blood feud."[20] Influenced by the Jews and Christians, many theists in Arabia had already rejected idolatry and were turning toward more ascetic religion, and Mohammed must have been partly influence by these Arabian monotheists as well (the *hanifs*).[21] Mohammed's first biographer (Ibn Ishaq) provides the only early story of his life. It records how an uncle criticized him for eating meat which had been sacrificed to idols. It concludes: "After that I never knowingly stoked one of their idols nor did I sacrifice to them until God honoured me with his apostleship."[22] The Christian sociologist, Christopher Dawson, remarks that the hadith cites in several places the puritanical spirituality of the Christian St. Gregentius, the apostle to the Himyarites in south Arabia.[23]

The self-image of Islam is that of restored fidelity to what was given to Abraham at the beginning:[24] "Mohammed did not pretend to deliver to them any new Religion, but to revive the old one, which God first gave to Adam; and when lost in the corruption of the Old World, restored it again by Revelation to Abraham, who taught it to his Son Is(h)mael their Forefather; and that he, when he first planted himself in Arabia, instructed Men in the same Religion which he had received from Abraham; but their Posterity afterwards corrupted it into Idolatry, and that God had now sent him to destroy this Idolatry, and again restore the Religion of Is(h)mael their Forefather."[25] But, as a reformer Mohammed is in a unique category. Other reformers will come: "God's teaching is and will always be continuous, but there has been and will be no Prophet after Mohammed"[26]—and "Mohammed is . . . the Apostle of Allah, and the Seal of the Prophets: and Allah has full knowledge of all things" (Q 33:40).

Long before the coming of Mohammed, the restoration of Judaism in exile under a God who keeps his promises (Covenant) is found in the Old Testament writings of Ezra-Nehemiah. These writings record the return of the remnant Jews from Babylon to Judea under the Persian emperor Cyrus (538 B.C.). The remnant is permitted to rebuild the Temple in Jerusalem (515 B.C.), but Judaism still awaited an eventual messiah who would fully restore the golden age of King David. In the seventh century after the coming of Christ, Mohammed discovers a quite different kind of restorer in himself as the final Prophet (Q 33:40). He selects from the Torah, and then diminishes and displaces to a merely prophetic role the coming of Christ in the New Testament (Q 41:6, 3:87). As a restoration and partly eclectic religion— rather than a new faith—Islam resembles in some ways the earlier syncretic or blended 'mystery religions of the late Roman Empire. Mani (c. 216–277), whose form of dualism at first attracted the young St. Augustine, revived Jesus, Buddha, Zoroaster and others. He believed himself to be the Holy Spirit and also saw himself as restoring an original truth. Like the later Mohammed, he was eclectic and "utterly repudiated the notion that his doctrine was in any way new."[27]

The greatest difference was that rather than regarding Christ as one of the prophets as does Mohammed, Mani saw Him as wholly supernatural. Manichaeism resembles the Monophysite heresy on this point, and in this important detail is opposite from the Nestorian heresy (351–451 A.D.) which influenced Mohammed. Nestorius[28] affirmed an indivisible Christ, but taught that he was a combination of two distinct persons, one divine and the other human—rather than a unique unity of two natures in one person. Since this Christ of two halves was not a unity, fully God and fully man, it held the Mary was mother to only the human Jesus.

Based on the works of Friar Richard, a Dominican monk who traveled to Baghdad in 1210 to research Islam first hand and from earlier writings, it appears that inclusion of Jewish and Christian elements into the eventual *Qur'an* was directly assisted by both a Jew and a Nestorian Christian. Abdia Ben Salon, later changed to the Arabic Abdollah Ebn Salem, was a Persian Jew and the first influence. The second influence was possibly an excommunicated Syrian and Nestorian monk known in various early writings as either Sergius by Western writers or Bahira by Eastern writers.[29] Held by some to be legendary, tracing at least as far back as the late seventh century St. John of Damascus, Bahira might be referenced in the *Qur'an* itself (Q 14:103).[30] When modern sources sometimes still mention Bahira, they are unconvinced about his authenticity partly because of conflicts in the conjectured timing and place of his appearance and meeting with Mohammed. The possibly legendary Bahira may have come from Syria rather than with later migrants returning from Christian Abyssinia. The migration date renders Bahira problematic because of Qur'anic verses recorded in Medina after 622. But in the Syria account, Bahira meets Mohammed earlier in either Jerusalem or "Bostra" and they return together to Mecca.[31] Islamic sources often propose that Bahira first met a very young Mohammed when he was only twelve, and as a monk announced even then his future role as a prophet.

Thus, a very direct Nestorian influence on the later *Qur'an* is historically plausible. The Nestorians were one of many late offshoots from early fourth century Arianism,[32] the finely grained teaching that denied the real divinity of Christ as the perfect image of God made flesh (e.g., 2 Cor 4:4, Col 1:15; Heb 1:3). Acceptance of the Incarnation/Resurrection is acceptance of an unexpected and infinite act of kindness without any hedging second thoughts by finite minds. This consent of mind and will is an act of humble faith, not of inadequate imagination. The bishop Arius is the author of unorthodox Arianism, and represents a range of many always inadequate human efforts to imagine the Incarnation. Like the Islam that followed, he taught that God ever remains finally incapable of communicating Himself. For Arius as under Islam, we have the unrelieved doctrine of inaccessible Unity. Instead of the gospel "Good News," we have a departure into absolutely less almost-good news. Nestorianism settles for a God who is One and who might be infinite love—but not quite. Applying Greek categories of thought to a God who always exceeds these or any thoughts, God is restricted from freely entering fully into His creation. He is not a "person" fully God and fully man, but more of a guarded mingling of the divine with the elements. The Muslim thinker is in step with the doubt whether God actually enters time and history or only manifests himself from an unsullied distance. To overcome this doubt the frail human mind might have to conclude that God himself is composed of elements and therefore is subject to change—no longer God. Under paganism—rejected by Islam—the different elements of nature often warred with each such that the human mind fashioned separate and multiple gods.

Theoretically Arius and the later Nestorius would lead the Christian to conclude that the one God is specifically not triune in His nature. God is solitary and not relational, not a God who loves as his essence and who is love (1 Jn 4:16). Christ is dismissed as a lesser and created being, rather than being co-eternal with the Father. As a spin-off of Arianism, the later Nestorianism reduced Christ to a dichotomy, with divinity residing inside of Christ, but not fully together with his human nature as a unified "person." The particular doctrine of Nestorianism—missing the mystery of two complete natures in the one unified person of Christ—asserted that Mary was only the mother of Jesus, but not of Christ: "God-bearing" (*Theotokos*). The reality of the Incarnation escapes and so too does humanity's promise of life in his resurrection. By the time of Mohammed, the widespread Nestorian missions already had reached into Arabia and Turkish Central Asia (a full century before Mohammed), and then in the eighth century to the Talos River halfway to China, and later reached into China itself.[33] Nestorians, possibly including the legendary or real Bahira, would have been familiar faces and voices on the trade routes to Mecca.

A different account of Christ's non-divine stature is offered by the prominent and modern day Islamic scholar Mahmoud Ayoub. He leaves no room for even a Nestorian influence as under Bahira. In attending to orthodox Christian doctrines, Ayoub concedes the Annunciation to Mary (Lk 1:35, Q21:90–1), but refers instead to a Syro-Arabic and unorthodox Christian tradition and to the work of the Jacobite bishop Theodore Abu Quarrah (d. 825). It is on the basis of linguistics that Ayoub argues for a Christ who is human, but not divine.[34] Following Ayoub's account, the Muslim understanding of Christ as only a prophet traces not to the original influence of an unorthodox Nestorian Christian monk, but instead to a later unorthodox reaction against Nestorianism, and then to the works of Islamic commentators working from secondary verses in the *Qur'an*.[35] Monophysitism, another reaction against Nestorianism, began under Eutyches (d. 454) who claimed that the humanity of Christ was absorbed into the single nature of His divinity, leaving Him with only this one divine nature. This school of thought came still two centuries before Mohammed and might have had a hearing in Arabia. Today Monophysitism, viewed under Islam as a corrupt form of Unitarianism, continues to maintain a presence in Syria, Iraq and Egypt.

From the mixing zone of Arabia, Mohammed rose to restore to Arabia a political unity and his own understanding of the religion of Abraham. He challenged the pagan gods in Mecca, the loose morals of the Arab tribes and their social inequalities, and the hold of pagan ancestors. Clearly a threat to all levels of Meccan society, Mohammed was met immediately with hostility, especially since his condemnation of the Ka'ba cult directly threatened the market for idols and the lucrative pilgrimage trade. He appropriated pagan reverence for the Black Stone housed within the Ka'ba—possibly an ancient meteor that is believed to have been placed by Abraham himself.[36] Mohammed's adoption of earlier practices, such as retaining the Ka'ba, as part of his new monotheism finds parallels even in the Christian religion. As but one example, from the same period, in 601 A.D. Pope Gregory instructed that pagan temples in Britain could be cleansed of their pagan idols and dedicated and used for Christian worship.[37] Christian days of celebration sometimes coincide with earlier pagan holidays. But ultimately, in the Christian tradition the bridge to the Father is not a physical rock, like either the Ka'ba or Golgotha, but instead the silhouette of the cross erected on top of Golgotha. Christians celebrate the mediation of the Son who without interruption is forever one with the Father: "the Lord above us," but also "the Lord with us and the Lord in us." We have "received a spirit of adoption, through which we cry, 'Abba, Father!'" (Rom 8:15).

During the early engagement with the pagans at Mecca, death took Mohammed's first wife Khadijha and then it took his uncle Abu-Talib, a second family protector. One of the earliest converts to Mohammed's religion, the rich merchant and nephew Abu-Bakr, was father to Mohammed's soon favorite new wife A'isha. (Immediately after Mohammed's death in 632 Abu-Bakr was to become Mohammed's first successor or caliph.) Within one year of Khadijha's passing, converts from Yathrib (Medina) appeared on the scene and offered their protection to this now isolated, self-proclaimed, and vulnerable prophet. Mohammed and seventy followers[38] fled north from Mecca to Medina, a distance of some two hundred seventy miles.[39] This is the "Hijrah," which marks the first year of the Muslim calendar (622 A.D.).

The Hijrah is a very major tipping or turning point of both Muslim and Western history. Established at Medina as a non-local mediator between disputing parties, Mohammed suppressed feuds among Arab tribes and especially disputes involving tribes who had converted to Judaism.[40] The dispossession of earlier Jewish immigrants into Arabia is perceived by Muslims as a restoration.[41] The parallel event in the Christian narrative is the crusades (the repeated attempts by Christendom to restore the Holy Land.) Mohammed formed the ummah confederation of a dozen tribes all under the authority of Allah. An imposed mono-idolatry might have served the same political function as the new monotheism. Members of the ummah accepted Mohammed as the final prophet and messenger of the one God, Allah. They no longer fought one another and professed belief in the Day of Judgment. The first *jihad* raiding parties against non-aligned tribes in Arabia began almost immediately in 624.[42] The first Qur'anic authorization for defensive warfare dates from this Medina period (Q 22:39–42). In the ten years before his death Mohammed had been involved in probably twenty military expeditions.

Mohammed complained how the clemency of Moses, the wisdom of Solomon, and the righteousness and miracles of Christ all have been insufficient to "enforce conviction," and asserted that "I, therefore, the last of the prophets, am sent with the sword. Let those who promulgate my faith enter into no argument nor discussion; but slay all who refuse obedience to the law. . . the sword is the key to heaven and hell." The casual biographer (source of the plausible foregoing quote), Washington Irving, stresses that the new warlike enterprises "betray the lurking resentment" held by Mohammed against his own tribesmen who had rejected him at Mecca.[43] His lieutenant Abdallah was not only permitted to openly attack a caravan to Mecca, but to do so during the holy month. "His disavowal of the violence committed by Abdallah, yet his bringing the *Koran* (note: Q 9:36) to his aid to enable him to profit by it with impunity, give still darker shades to this transaction; which altogether shows how immediately and widely he went wrong the moment he departed from the benevolent spirit of Christianity, which he at first endeavored to emulate."[44]

The *Qur'an* includes among its prophets the militaristic Alexander the Great.[45] In addition to the military theme, Alexander's curious placement in the *Qur'an* also affords a more promising contact point between Islamic theology and the role of human reason which found such a crucial and more fruitful opening in the West. Even in pursuit of Darius, Alexander complained in a letter to Aristotle that he (Alexander's tutor) should not have published certain metaphysical pieces which he wanted for himself. Alexander said that "he had much rather surpass the rest of men in the knowledge of sublime and excellent things, than in the greatness and extent of his power."[46] Under the influence of a more single-minded and purer Islam, many Muslim thinkers tend more to submerge any such autonomous "knowledge of the sublime" of the "prophets" under later Qur'anic theology and often militaristic parsing of jihad. Alexander saw a reasoned choice where Islam simply combined careers. Clearly, religious warfare remains a prominent feature of the earlier biblical history of the chosen people, fragments of which influenced Mohammed. Religious warfare is later and equally mixed history of the Christian West, even though it is not an explicit part of the actual Christian New Testament and faith. Based on the Old Testament Pentateuch, the *Qur'an* recalls Yahweh's instructions regarding the Canaanites: "You must lay them under ban. You must make no covenant with them nor show them any pity . . . (otherwise) the anger of Yahweh would blaze out against you and soon destroy you" (Deut 7:2–4).

Later at the time of Mohammed and further Islamic expansion under his immediate successors, the collapsed Roman Empire in the West left in place only the stability of the land. Byzantine culture survived for another thousand years in the East, until it was largely overrun by Islam in 1453. In the West, the particular religious element survived in the already established diocesan structure of the centralized (and, significantly, apostolic) Church. To avoid the onslaught of the Huns in the West, Constantine already had moved his center of Christianity to Constantinople in the East. Admitting to these and many other differences, in both cases—early Western Europe and Arabia—the earthly task at hand in both instances was to bring bordering tribes within the orbit of either a surviving order or a new confederation. This political objective drove events as much in the forested European peninsula as in the more fluid deserts of the Arabian Peninsula and then beyond. The fusion of loyalty with the martial arts and conquest is a dominant theme on both peninsulas. The comparison can even be read into Western feudalism. In Arabia the general picture is one of a unifying religion, nomadic jihad, and plunder. Merovingian Europe offers a similar but agrarian feudal structure in support of knights. The support of knights was costly and depended upon an "endowment" consisting of lands. Under this interpretation, these lands were confiscated from the Church by Charles Martel, the victor in the West against the Muslims (the Moors) in 732 A.D and the great grandfather of Charlemagne, specifically for this new social purpose.[47]

At its core the military goal during Mohammed's lifetime may have been more pan-Arabism than it was the religion of the *Qur'an*. Under this reading of history, the goal was the defensive and progressive incorporation of local resistance groups. It was only after Mohammed's death that jihad became a tool for dramatically more expansive economic and religious conquest. It was partly coincidental that this energy was against the followers of another religion—the Christians—who governed most of the territories surrounding Arabia.[48] Mohammed's immediate followers assembled into the *Qur'an* many parts of the Old and New Testament.[49] This gathering-in might recall the assembly of the Jewish scriptures, partly to salvage a national identity, immediately following the end of Hebrew exile in Babylon. But Mohammed the Prophet concluded that the Jews by their infidelity to the God of Abraham and Moses had corrupted the original revelation and that the covenant was irrevocably broken. Christianity was also found to be fatally flawed since the doctrine of Christ's divinity transformed the original Abrahamic revelation of the one God into polytheism and idolatry.[50] Christianity was generally on a par with the paganism of Mecca. At first Mohammed looked for Jewish and Christian help in his campaigns (of monotheism) against the pagans of Mecca. Knowing their deeper differences, the Jews and later the Christians declined. Islam regards the Judeo-Christian narrative as a box canyon of infidelity, to be reset by returning to origins in the religion of Abraham.

The *Qur'an* recalls the initially different encounters with Jews and Christians from the Medina period:

> Thou shalt find the Jews to be very great Enemies to the true Believers; and the Christians to have great Inclination and Amity towards them, for they have Priests and Religious, that are humble, who have Eyes full of Tears when they hear mention of the Doctrine which God hath inspired into thee, because of their knowledge of the Truth, and Say, Lord we believe in thy Law, write us in the number of them who profess thy Unity. Who shall hinder us from believing in God, and the Truth wherein we have been instructed. We desire with Passion, O Lord, to be in the number of the Just (Q 5:82).[51]

The term Unity refers to the pre-emptive Unitarianism of Islam, a continuation of the Jewish God and a truncated revelation compared with Trinitarian Christianity. Jewish and Christian rejection of a composite monotheism accounts for Mohammed's decision to reorient the direction of Muslim prayer away from Jerusalem, and toward Mecca as the new Holy City with its traditional shrine of the Ka'ba. Practical steps toward an amalgamated monotheism had included such concessions as the timing of Ramadan (in 623) to begin on the Jewish fast of Expiation, and then the extension for forty days to match the Christian Lenten season[52] first used by the Greek Churches in 337 A.D.

In 629 A.D., apparently on the pretense that two or three years of truce had been broken by others,[53] Mohammed finally crusaded directly against Mecca, the center of Arabian polytheism. The oneness of God was asserted and the assembly of Meccan idols destroyed. A peaceful surrender is often reported, but critics offer details, "On his entry into it (Mecca), having put to Death such as had been most violent against him, all the rest, without any further Opposition, submitted unto him, and embraced his Religion."[54] The twentieth century Muslim apologist Assfy describes the entry into Mecca as "uneventful," resulting in the death of two Muslims and then a slaughter of twenty opponents, after which the enemy panicked and fled.[55] Several accounts of clemency toward even personal enemies are recorded, one for the party who killed Mohammed's uncle and another for a former scribe who had mocked the faith by falsifying lines in the *Qur'an*.

Some sources report a later and costly counterattack by several nomad tribes,[56] but recent knowledge of Old Testament precedents could support the view that carnage was limited. The archeological record for the "invasion" of Canaan allows for two possibly complementary models of Israelite migration from Egypt and final settlement in Palestine. One is the traditional view of abrupt invasion and the other is more of a mixed pattern of infiltration including assimilation. Under the second and richer record, Old Testament intertribal genocide could have been preceded by an opportunity extending over decades for resident populations to emigrate with their defeated gods. Target populations were free to move to other lands not reserved by the god of whichever tribe was victorious on the new field of battle. Under this theory Old Testament genocide was more limited in scope than is generally believed. It was inflicted only on the last resistant and threatening holdouts, and on their youngest and orphaned children who otherwise would have been left to wander into eventual starvation.[57]

In addition to the pagan Ka'ba at Mecca, Mohammed retained other pagan practices including pilgrimage.[58] This was the most important of the many pragmatic compromises with earlier Arabian culture. And the earlier Arabians, it is said, "always held, that there was but one only God . . . (Allah Taal) . . . But being (as they held) so great and high as not to be approached to by Men while here on Earth, but through the Mediation of Advocates or Intercessors . . . was the reason that they set up Images, and built them Temples, and directed their Worship and Devotion unto them."[59] In this regard, Islam might be seen as a purified continuation of Arabian religious impulses which beneath the surface might have approached a kind of implicit monotheism. Hinduism and Greek paganism are often described in the same way, as fundamentally monotheistic but with myriad expressions often attached to various aspects of nature.

As an assertion of the unknown, unknowable, and monotheistic God against the idolatry of Mecca, Islam recalls to Christians St. Paul's encounter centuries earlier with the pagan Gentiles in Athens. There St. Paul preached the monotheistic but Trinitarian Godhead, known by the historical Incarnation in history and by faith, in place of the "Unknown God" he found enshrined side by side with the rich variety of pagan temples.[60] In Mecca and in his radical simplicity, Mohammed denied both the detested female deities of the Arabs, and St. Paul's Jesus Christ of the Trinitarian and one God. The Christian teaching is that Christ is radically unlike the mythic pagan figures who are *half* god and *half* man, but that He is rather *fully* God and *fully* Man, two natures in one "person"—the fullness of revelation in the fullness of time, the Son of God and always fully one with the Father.[61] With St. Paul, we are no longer slaves to the unknowable, but rather, as the Risen Christ invites us, "I no longer call you slaves, because a slave does not know what his master is doing. I have called you friends, because I have told you everything I have heard from the Father" (Jn 15:15). St. Paul preached the sunrise of the new life of Christ within (especially Eph 4:25–32, and Eph 5 and 6). As a bond among persons, the new life is both concrete and transcendent. Paul preached

Christ as the new life and as the self-revelation of the God of heaven and earth and of all creation material and spiritual: "To be in Christ means being a completely new creature. Everything of the old is gone, now everything is made anew" (2 Cor 5:17, also Rom 8:1–13). Rather than excelling in external acts, "Your inmost being must be renewed, and you must put on the *new man*" (Eph 4:23–4, italics added).

The earliest Muslim God seems to be a conceptual hybrid who coincides with both Judeo-Christian monotheism and with Arabian mythology. All of the tribal images in Mecca were offspring of Allah and his wife Al-hat, and their three daughters.[62] The new doctrine held that there is but one God, Allah the God of Abraham, and all pagan idols were banished. Viewed through the same lens, the Christian Trinity also was dismissed as idolatry—a trilogy of gods. Prideaux elaborates on Mohammed:

> Those who say God hath Sons or Daughters, or that there are any other Gods officiated with him, are impious, and ought to be abhorred. By denying him Sons and Associates, he reflected on the Christians for holding the Doctrine of the Trinity, and that Jesus Christ is the Son of God; the Belief of both which he doth in many places in his Alcoran vehemently forbid. By denying him Daughters, he condemned the Idolatrous Practice of the Arabians, who worshiped Allat, Menah, and Al Uzza, Female Deities, which they held to be the Daughters of God, whose idols and Temples he afterwards every where destroyed.[63]

By banishing the daughters of paganism, Islam also loses the truth content of imagination and with this the suspicion at least of the real fatherhood of God.

Compared to historical Christianity, Mohammed claimed a solitary role as "messenger" for the angel Gabriel,[64] while Christ announced a witness role for himself toward the Father, a role to be shared by the witnessing of his apostles: "As the Father has sent me, even so I send you" (Jn 20:21). In the *Qur'an* instead of a triune God who in the person of Christ delivers himself, we find an intermediary angel who delivers a message: "This day I have perfected your religion for you and completed My favor to you. I have chosen Islam to be your faith" (Q 5:3). As a founder and messenger of religion Mohammed is more parallel to the apostles and especially St. Paul than he is to Christ even considered as a "prophet."[65] Confronting the pagan idols of Mecca and Arabia (628 A.D.), Mohammed confirmed his message not with miracles but by a personal report of his own after-sundown trip to heaven (Q 17:1).

Mohammed died on June 8 in the year 632 of the Christian calendar (dating from the Hijrah, the year ten of the Muslim chronology). Some legends hold that he was poisoned, and one recurring account says that he had been deliberately poisoned three years before he finally succumbed. He spat out the tainted food, but the lingering effects eventually took his life. Of the culprit, a servant girl, the accounts of early writers are summarized: "The Maid (daughter of leader of Caibar, a defeated town of Jewish Arabs) being asked why she did this, answered, that she had a mind to make trial whether he were a Prophet, or no. For were he a Prophet, said she, he could certainly know that the Meat (a shoulder of mutton) was poisoned; and therefore would receive no harm from it; but if he were not a Prophet, she thought she should do the World good Service, in ridding it of so wicked a Tyrant."[66] By some accounts the maid was executed.

Near the point of Mohammed's death there was lost his possibly final message, a final book which due to dissension even then around his bedside he never dictated.[67] That Mohammed's closest followers were not to "contend in his presence" recalls by coincidence similar Qur'anic wording applied to God: "God will say: 'Do not dispute in My presence. I did forewarn you. My word cannot be changed, nor am I unjust to My servants" (Q 50:28). In contrast, St. Jerome recounts the non-contentious and very peaceful passing of Christ's close apostle, St. John. When asked for a last message, John repeated twice, "Little children, love one another," and then added "It is enough, for it is the Lord's command." He spoke not of himself, but of Christ,[68] as Christ had spoken not of himself, but of the Father. In the Bible we read this . . . "Whoever speaks on his own is bent on self-glorification" (Jn 7:18).

Another account of Mohammed's last words is this: "O Allah, Pardon my sins. Yes, I come," and "If I owe anything to anybody it may be claimed. If I have offended anybody he may have his revenge."[69] Discrediting the charge that the complex Mohammed was insincere and an imposter are other lines such as these: "My last command to you is, that ye remain united; that ye love, honor and uphold each other; that ye exhort each other to faith and constancy in belief, and to the performance of pious deeds; by thee alone men prosper; all else leads to destruction."[70] With his death came the second critical juncture—another tipping point in the history of Islam—the first having been his invitation and successful flight Medina from a hostile rejection at Mecca. Now and on their own, Mohammed's followers decided to continue the campaign begun under his astonishing charismatic leadership and military brilliance. As with his own decision in 622 to continue with new supporters and to use Medina as a new base, at Mohammed's death the renewed resolve of his followers was a clear decision not to walk away, but to sustain and expand the tribal confederation.

From the earliest days after the death of Mohammed the two largest sects within the resulting Islam trace to an ancestral contention over tribal succession. Within the new family of Islam, who should be the caliph or temporal and spiritual successor of the Prophet? These major sects are the majority Sunnis (eighty-five percent of Muslims today) and the less numerous Shi'ites (e.g., Iran and Saudi Arabia). Shi'ites hold to the clan tradition which would support a family line successor, his cousin and son-in-law Ali. Ali's wife was Mohammed's treasured and short-lived daughter Fatima. The majority Sunnis trace back to a different and consensus-based tribal tradition and selected and successfully placed Abu Bakr as the first caliph. A third splinter group is the puritanical Kharidjites or Seceders, whose doctrinal look-alikes are the modern day and "fundamentalist" Wahhabis.[71] Numerous additional sects also exist, and all sects hold each other accountable for the divisions within congregational Islam.

It might have been partly under external Byzantine influence that the early Ummayad chiefs, forerunners of the Shi'ites, adhered to the hereditary succession of leadership. As potential hereditary successors, Mohammed had six children, all under Khadijha but all of whom predeceased their father, except for Fatima who outlived him by only sixty days.[72] He had no recognized surviving sons, but through the line of Ali, his cousin and Fatima's husband, he was provided two grandsons. Mohammed might have had one surviving male offspring, the infant son Ibrahim borne of the Coptic slave Mariya. This boy either died a few months ahead of Mohammed[73] or else disappeared earlier into Egypt, possible at the doing of a jealous A'isha.[74] Following the death of Khadijha, A'isha (the daughter of Abu Bakr) became the Prophet's favorite and most prominent wife. A telling and compromising verse finds its way into the *Qur'an*, apparently to justify Mohammed when A'isha and another favored wife first discovered him with Mariya. The *Qur'an* begins to at least confine early Arabian polygamy by setting a limit of four wives, but there is added an exemption for Mohammed: "O Prophet, why dost thou forbid what God hath allowed thee, that thou may'st please thy wives? God hath granted *unto you* to lie with your Maid-servants" (Q 66:1, italics added).[75] Apparently permitted is sexual relations with women taken captive under jihad: "(Prohibited are) women already married, except those whom your right hands possess" (Q 4:24).

The first modern legal controls on polygamy in the Muslim world began in the Ottoman Law of 1917 shortly before secular Turkey emerged from the old empire. Today, except for Saudi Arabia, Muslim polygamy is not widely practiced. This is due mostly to changing social views and economic limitations for most families. In the different non-Western culture of late sixteenth century China the Jesuit missionary Matteo Ricci was highly praise for advocating Western monogamy, but he also found in Peking and Nanking an unchallenged world of multiple "wives and concubines and softened boys."[76] In the Western context a possible ecclesial parallel with polygamy was a managerial practice of celibate churchmen in past centuries. The frequent claim on multiple bishoprics or other incompatible offices was widespread.

This practice was finally limited by the Fifth Council of the Lateran (1512–1517) to only four such offices, and then by the Council of Trent (1545–63) to only one.[77] In the secularized West of today, other institutional parallels to the moral ambivalence behind polygamy might be political pressures to define same sex pairings as part of a new condominium definition of marriage and the family, or more established acceptance of arbitrary divorce and remarriage ("sequential bigamy"), or the predisposing technical severance of the unitive and procreative meanings of human sexuality.

Within Islam the minority Shi'ite sect does not recognize the first four non-hereditary successors to the Prophet. Because Sunni loyalty departs from an original tribal custom of family line, they are seen by the Shi'ites even today as usurpers. For the more consensual Sunnis the non-hereditary caliph is to be elected from among the historic Qurayish tribe, the broader tribe of the Prophet. The Sunnis served as auxiliaries of the Romans, and from the beginning were well positioned to set up the first Caliphate, in Syria (Damascus) in 661, barely a generation after Mohammed's death. The Sunni caliphs are not regarded as prophets, while the Shi'ite imams (a parallel term for caliph) enjoy this status.

An early crisis in Islam was the doctrine that the *Qur'an* was created in time, a Mu'tazilite and state imposed teaching under Abbasid caliphs between 833 and 848 A.D. and then rejected largely under the leadership of Ibn Hanbal.[78] Shi'ite imams are mediators who were "with God from the beginning as his first act of Creation."[79] At the interreligious level, the Shi'ite imams are remotely parallel to an Arian understanding of Christ who (for Arians) was created in time rather than eternal. The Shi'ites now wait for the return of the twelfth imam, the Mahdi, who is believed to have disappeared at the age of ten in 873 A.D. A possible echo of Hebrew prophecy, the Mahdi is held to be a future messiah.[80] The Shi'ites cannot accept that the twelfth and final imam perished for if there is no imam, they say, the "world could not endure for the twinkling of an eye."[81] One presumed Mahdi, revered by the Ahmadiyyas sect, holds that as a prophet, Jesus Christ departed to Kashmir after his resurrection, where he is believed to have lived on to the biblical age of one hundred and twenty. The messianic element of Imamism may have been introduced into Islam by Christian and Jewish converts. The later and most direct European counterpart for the imam cult might have been the expectation among many Medieval Christians that the dead Charlemagne one day would return.

Some Shi'ite sects have been less patient in waiting for the restoration of purified Islam and society and have favored messianic revolt. Wahhabism (from Abd al-Wahhab, d. 1792) erupted in the eighteenth century as one of numerous such reform movements internal to Islam. Wahhabism attached itself to the Sunni Saud family and today is centered in Saudia Arabia.[82] In the 1920s Wahhabism consolidated control of the peninsula and Holy Sites and then was propelled into prominence and the modern world indirectly by Western technology and oil diplomacy. Well funded and extremist Wahhabi education and indoctrination centers are widespread today especially in those secularist Western countries that refrain from supervising the content of "religious" education, especially Germany and the United States. In American public schools an atmosphere of secular humanism often replaces substantive moral teaching which is prohibited under dogmatic Church-state separation.

In the early days Christian conversion to Islam could be a relatively easy matter since there often was no need to directly deny faith in Christ. As with multiculturalism today it was only necessary to refrain from the claim that the Christian faith is uniquely true. The *Qur'an* dilutes differences by thinking less in terms of distinct monotheistic creeds than of cultural assimilation. As a theologically composite religion, Islam also seeks a *condominium* monotheism as a mandate from God. "It is He Who has sent His Apostle with Guidance and the Religion of Truth, to proclaim *it over all religion*, and enough is Allah for a Witness" (Q 48:28, italics added). The Islamic way of life is broadly a culture in that it consists of "concrete human attitudes, such as *islam* (total submission or obedience to God), *iman* (sincere faith in God) and *ihsan* (righteous living or the performance of good deeds)."[83] Islam discounts the intellectual clarity of distinct monotheistic creeds in favor of a way of life and inter-cultural mixing. The followers of Islam see Islam as a religious substrate, and tend to see infidels as the accidental result of having simply been born into other religious groups.[84]

While conversion into Islam is promoted, conversion from the Islamic way of life is severely prohibited. Historically, in the original tribal confederation the Qur'anic death penalty applied only to cases of treason as against the family of Islam, rather than to individual conversion. This kind of limitation is said to apply today. In the Western context, the condominium model of monotheism initially assumed and proposed by Mohammed almost recalls pagan Rome as well as Mecca. In Rome it was a simple matter to combine one's own cult with the cosmopolitan pagan cult and the emperor.[85] The intolerable eccentricity of Christians was a faith that was no longer based on cults or nationalities (or today, identity politics) of any kind. This act of faith—the core of a "new life"—is a response to the unique event of Christ, and in him the self-revealed Fatherhood of God. This Fatherhood as directly revealed with concrete clarity through the Incarnation who is one with the Father. Given this faith toward a Trinitarian unity, a shared condominium religion with Unitarian Islam is a contradiction.

The Islamic path of cultural assimilation and leaving unsaid important differences resembles some forms of Christian ecumenism even as found in the first years of the Reformation.[86] Multicultural equivalence of truly conflicting truth claims was rejected in the fourth century by St. Ambrose. Imperial powers tried to force Arian use of his Milan Cathedral and in this way to reduce Christianity to the status of one equivalent religion among many.[87] The premise of all such cases of syncretic religious consolidation is that all religions are essentially human *expressions* toward the transcendent or toward the "elemental spirits of the universe" (Col 2:8). The unique truth claim of Christianity is the affirmation of God's incarnate *self-disclosure* of Himself toward man (Eph 1:9)—a revelation to be received, rather than a human expression. The core creed of the Christian is that "Jesus is Lord (and that) God raised him from the dead" (Rm 10:9), while a core belief of Islam is that "There is no God but Allah, and Mohammed is his prophet." It is because there is no fatherhood of God that there appears a self-identified final messenger from a less relational God, a final prophet.

Bainton speculates that the initial and brushfire spread of Islam across the Christian frontier in Africa was aided by a particular split within the resident Christian community. He points to the fourth century Donatist heresy (311–411 A.D.). Donatism arose over the question whether to readmit into the Church repentant apostates who had yielded to Roman threats or torture. The Donatists admitted to no readmission and went so far as to erect a parallel Church hierarchy. With the intervention of the secular Julian the Apostate (361–363) the Donatists began to occupy a vast amount of Church property across North Africa. Theologically Donatism was but one of many claims of rigorous spiritual purity as compared to the rest of the Church. Donatists maintained that sacraments presided over by previously apostate bishops— initially Caecilian, elected to the See of Carthage—were invalid. Donatism was "the first clear instance in Church history of a coincidence of a split in the Church with a fissure in the social structure."[88] Still two centuries prior to Islam, Donatism set the cosmopolitan and Rome-oriented upper class against the local layers of the Church in Africa.

Bainton summarizes his thesis, "Other schisms and heresies died out; Donatism lasted until the Mohammedan invasions and may then have succumbed only because Islam offered a better way of resisting Rome."[89] Donatism had been disbanded in 405 A.D., driven underground and financially penalized after 412, but lingered until the coming of the Saracens (Saracen: "a man who holds the same religion as Mohammed") in the seventh century. A similar vulnerability is more frequently reported of the Byzantine world in the eastern Mediterranean. Islam offered an alternative to the divided and "Byzantine" politics of the East. Today the global challenge for Christians is more the reverse. The challenge is first to resist external Islamic expansion and intrusion against the West in general, but equal to this, it is the task of avoiding conflicts between the major sects *internal* to the Islamic world. Sectarian differences within Islam are at least as intractable as the interreligious or intercultural differences between Islam as a whole and the West.[90]

THE PASSION OF ISLAM: SOME VIEWS

The eminent Catholic sociologist Christopher Dawson accepts Mohammed as a "religious mystic" whose actual trances are recorded in the *Qur'an*.[91] Islamic writers paint an endearing picture of the Prophet as one who maintained the common touch, and who exemplified a highly moral life, for example, chastity and monogamy until the age of fifty-four, and a life of consistent generosity toward friends, family, and the poor. To his daughter Fatima he would say "respect your children," and to his followers he would say "paradise lies at the feet of mothers."[92] With a broad brush the Islamic apologist, Rashid Rida, has suggested from the *Qur'an* the ". . . possibility that God has sent prophets to the ancient Chinese and Indians to lead them to the level of felicity they had enjoyed," only later to be contaminated with polytheism.[93] Within the Christian tradition, and beyond what we know as its "normal means" of grace (the sacraments), the Church affirms that the Spirit "apportions to each one individually as he wills" (1 Cor 12:11). Pope John Paul II stressed the conviction that "every authentic prayer is prompted by the Holy Spirit, who is mysteriously present in every human heart."[94] Western rationalism presumes that all such experiences are mere intuition and never anything else and that in all cases subjective intuition is the root of a mislabeled "revelation."

Many early Christian critics understood Mohammed's experiences to be demonic, self-induced, or physiological in origin. Within the specifically Catholic self-understanding, for which the incarnate Christ is the final *public* revelation, a case still might be made for at least Mohammed's initial religious experience. As a mystic he might have received a *private* and gifted insight or "locution," or an enviable stage of contemplation, or even a private revelation[95] of the Oneness of the true God (Tauhid) and his mercy and compassion, and even a powerful intuition of our calling to live in his guiding truth (objectified in the West as "natural law"). This intuition colors and tends to override all daily experience and thoughts and even accurate self-understanding. Surah 53 is the only direct entry in the *Qur'an* claiming evidence of a vision and validating Mohammed's prophetic role. The rich details of this heavenly visit are assembled and reported in the hadith only many years after his death. Western critics have debated for centuries whether Moham-med was an imposter or a true prophet or something in between. Thinking in non-western categories, might it be that he simply and even innocently saw only the hand of Allah, everywhere without the distinctions that characterize (western) thought? No only does Islamic fatalism reject the interventions of autonomomous and physical laws of external nature, but similarly might the Prophet have overlooked the distinction between divine revelation and his own inner impressions, intuitions, decisions and expediencies throughout each day? As recorded in the *Qur'an* all of this comes directly from Al-lah. A reading of Ibn Ishaq's very anecdotal first biography seems to point to this possibility. Turning to its own inner life, the Church distinguishes and recognizes private revelations only very selectively, and even for these warns against subjective distortion or even the attachment of deceptive evil camouflaged as the good. Among indigenous peoples the greatest example is the sixteenth century appearance of Our Lady of Guadalupe to the Mexican peasant Juan Diego, which in only a few years brought an end to human sacri-fice and the conversion of some eight million. Mohammed's possible private revelation is "public" in the sense that he elaborates his initial experience by mingling with it some centuries-earlier public revelations drawn from the Old and New Testament. Private illuminations such as this are suspect and often erroneous and have left a well-documented trail of chaos in history. Aware of the risk of delusion, in Moorish Spain, the Christian mystic Theresa of Avila examples a life of painstaking searching for authenticity over a span of three decades. Confining his remarks to Western experience the historian Friedrich Heer remarks: "Modern artists, poets and geniuses think that they can transcend such painstaking self-discipline. The spiritual history of the last four hundred years has seen countless examples of men, from Rousseau to Nietzsche, in whom a moment of inspiration created havoc and disorder because they ignored the wisdom of Theresa."[96]

If Mohammed did receive privately a locution, a plausible claim, could such a genuine experience then be blurred by Mohammed with subjective imagery and self vindication with the Qurayish tribe in Mecca? Selecting one of the Hebrew fragments, Islamic monotheism theologically seems a lengthy footnote to a single Jewish verse in Exodus, spread across history: "You shall not worship any other God, for the Lord is 'the Jealous One;' a jealous God is he" (Ex 34:14). Of private spirituality within the family of Islam, the eleventh century al-Ghazali warns against Sufi enthusiasm. He writes that

> Their 'state' ascends from the vision of forms and likenesses to stages beyond the narrow range of words: so if anyone tries to express them, his words contain evident error against which he cannot guard himself. But speaking in general,

the matter comes ultimately to a closeness to God which one group almost conceives of as 'indwelling,' and another as 'union,' and another as 'reaching,' but
all that is wrong . . . The charisms of the 'saints' are in reality the first stages
passed through by the prophets. *Such was the initial state of the Apostle of God
. . .* when he went to Mount Hira, where he would be alone with his Lord and
perform acts of worship, so that the Arabs of the desert said: Muhammad indeed
passionately loves his Lord (italics added).[97]

In the Christian tradition this oneness of the Lord unfolds itself in time
through the incarnate Christ who is the public self-disclosure of the inner life
of the one God. The doctrine that the divine nature is relational and triune
is based on historical events witnessed through Scripture. In a manner that
images the Triune Oneness, Man himself is also known as relational in his
very nature. Likewise in true marriage there is "one flesh" rather than anything more divided or separately autonomous or multiple as in paganism or
polygamy. The oneness of Christ, too (as defined precisely at the Council of
Constantinople, 381 A.D.), is a true unity of a fully human nature with a fully
divine nature in a coherent "person" without contradiction or alloy. Among
the New Testament letters dealing with the oneness of God and the fallen actions of man is this: "You believe that God is one; you do well; the demons
too believe, and tremble" (Jas 2:19).

In Christian history documented private locutions, as might have been
enjoyed by Mohammed in 610 A.D., include those of Julian of Norwich (b.
1343). During a severe illness on May 8, 1373 and a short period of less than
a day she witnessed sixteen distinct locutions of Christ and the Trinity. This
Christo-centric experience sets her apart from the unknown medieval author
of the *Cloud of Unknowing* whose less Christo-centric mysticism resembles
in this respect the non-Trinitarian mysticism of Mohammed. He focuses directly God, but does not fully exclude God's interior life revealed in Christ.
In contrast with *The Cloud*, Julian, a religious recluse in Britain, received a
private and enwrapping revelation of the more clearly Trinitarian God.[98] She
explained that while God remains ever hidden from our view, it was He rather
than an angel who almost directly made this revelation to her. Researchers
explain from Julian's writing that while she "saw" personally the divine love
of God, this was still an indirect (though highly gifted) and contemplative vision or image.[99] Julian's written testimony establishes her as the first woman
to write or dictate a book in the English language.

A more recent written testimony of private locutions is the early twentieth century *Diary: Divine Mercy in My Soul* written by St. Maria Faustina
Kowalski, the first saint canonized in the third millennium. The writings were
produced only under obedience to her confessor and tell of our oneness with
a God who is truly one, and that "mankind will not have peace until it turns

with trust to God's mercy." It is because of the Trinitarian inner life of God that our path is one of trust rather than a more tentative submission.[100] The Christian God is so much one that He is what He does: "God is love" (1 Jn 4:16). Kowalski comments on private revelation or locutions. A God who is "compassionate and merciful" (the Qur'anic refrain) offers his mercy through the blood of the Cross. She writes of her private revelations from Christ:

> There are, in my life, times and moments of spiritual insight; that is, divine illu-
> minations, when the soul receives inward instruction about things it has not read
> in any book and has not been taught by any person. These are times of great inner
> knowledge which God himself imparts to the soul. These are great mysteries . .
> . I often receive light and the knowledge of the interior life of God and of God's
> intimate disposition, and this fills me with unutterable trust and a joy that I cannot
> contain within myself; I desire to dissolve completely in Him . . .[101]

As part of a possible locution, the present proposition is that at Mount Hira Mohammed entered into a compelling experience or intuition of self-awareness as a created being subject to the inner law that is imprinted on all of humanity from the beginning. In the Western and Christian tradition, this would be the universal natural law normally known by use of reason than by a local revelation confined to the Arabic language.

From the traditional Muslim perspective, Mahmoud Ayoub understands Christ in a moral sense (in our view along the lines of natural law). Christ is not the fulfillment of prophecy and the incarnation of God: "Christianity came with a call to morality and with a synthesis of the truth that people were looking for."[102] Ayoub then paints Mohammed as a counterpart to this socio-logical Christ, who six centuries later threw a similar and broader net into a confused pagan Arabia. Ayoub also concurs with others that Mohammed might have lived for a while with the already monotheistic hanifs (the "pious ones"), but holds that he could not join either the Jews or the Christians of the East because of the scandalous internal disputes he saw with each. Early Christological controversies are known now to have been largely cultural and linguistic, but it would be another century or two before the Church Council's clarified the articles of faith implicit in the Incarnation and Resur-rection events. Precision and clarity were perceived by a culturally different Arab mentality as a narrowing of the divine oneness into multiple gods and idolatry.

Islam emerges from either personal intuition or biblical roots as an offshoot with Arabian trappings, but not as a new and separate faith or religion. From Mount Hira, Islam claims to restore the religion of Abraham as found in the Torah or the Old Testament and only later codified on Sinai (and surpassed in the Sermon on the Mount). The *Qur'an* reads: "The Jews say that Christians have nothing on which to stand and the Christians say the Jews have nothing on which to stand, yet both of them read the scriptures" (Q 2:113).[103] From the Christian perspective, Christ is more than a moral leader and catalyst for synthesis of divergent schools of thought and spirituality.

If Mohammed did experience a locution, in the Christian sense, of the one-ness of God, might he then have added his own "successive words" to the received insight, all in answer to either one question or challenge or another? Even within the Catholic tradition the mystic St. John of the Cross writes of this kind of confused phenomenon—a real visitation followed by less gifted impressions or edits: "And when the understanding is illumined and taught in this way by the master, and comprehends these truths, it begins of its own accord to form the words which relate to the truths that are communicated to it from elsewhere. So that we may say that the voice is the voice of Jacob and the hands are the hands of Esau."[104] With openness to the workings of the Spirit in history, the biblical St. John also counsels us in all cases, "Be-loved, do not trust every spirit but test the spirits to see whether they belong to God, because many false prophets have appeared in the world" (1 Jn 4:1). Initially Mohammed inquired of relatives, at least, what they thought of his extraordinary visions. Later entries into the final *Qur'an* become more fanci-ful, particularly at the time of Medina and after.

To consider Mohammed not from a mystical but from a purely natural perspective, we can ask how deep were his emotional wounds acquired along the way, especially on the eve of Medina? First there was the early loss of both parents and then later the loss of his first wife and his protective uncle. Khadijha died during Mohammed's fiftieth year in 620 (or 621) shortly be-fore the flight to Medina.[105] His uncle and second protector Abu Talib died a year or two before, possibly in 619. Both losses came in about the tenth year of "the Call" to evangelize (Q 74:1–2), which by Muslims is referred to as Am al-Huzn or the Year of Grief. Following the death of Khadijha and his uncle, the first three of Mohammed's subsequent wives—A'isha, Sauda, and Hapsha—served to provide him with new protective patrons. He became the son-in-law to three of the most powerful men among his small band of followers.[106] Compounding his personal losses and rejection at Mecca, biog-raphers more often conclude that Medina was the reason that Mohammed's visionary enthusiasm was overtaken by a now more worldly, vindictive, and warlike final phase of life. At Medina Mohammed found himself finally treated as a prophet. He was respected as a chief and then possibly seduced by flattery as he became the leader of tribes ready to fight for him. His revela-tions became more opportunistic.[107]

This transition suggests the question: What was the exact nature of the original "visions" at Mount Hira? Were the multiple visions or locutions only

a delusion, and how strong was the possible need for self-validation?[108] On
the positive side of the historical record, there is much to support the sincerity of his belief. Prideaux is among even the severe critics who nevertheless
find no evidence that Mohammed was ever unfaithful to Khadijha, his first
wife of at least twenty years. His fidelity might have been because she was
possibly Christian and therefore monogamous, or because of her high social
status and clan connections, and that he dared not offend her with competing
wives. There are many accounts of Mohammed's tenderness. Muhammad Ali
recounts that long after Khadijha's death and "out of regard for (her) memory
. . . he would even send presents to her relations." Sir William Muir finds
that all authorities agree "in ascribing to the youth of Mohammed a modesty
of deportment and purity of manners rare among the people of Mecca."[109]
What then accounts for his radically altered personal disposition in 620 and
621? Not unheard of in Arabian culture, Mohammed is committed to a favorite later wife when she was possibly only ten years old or nine.[110] After
the tragic death of his first and older wife he seems to have relapsed more
into the Arab culture of the time, and in addition to concubines even had up
to eleven wives at one time and perhaps twenty-one altogether.[111] Islamic
apologists consistently divide Arab history into the "days of ignorance,"
the Arab culture before Mohammed about which little is known, and all the
years after the Prophet.[112] In Jewish history and in the time of the Hebrew
kings, Solomon—a symbol of vain luxury as well as wisdom—had as many
as seven hundred wives and one thousand concubines. The same is true for
Buddha who in early life was presented by his father with tens of thousands of
dancing girls to restrain his mysticism.[113] By comparison, the Old Testament
Gideon also had many wives, and these gave him seventy sons (Jdg 8:30). In
addition to his concubines, David also had several wives. And prior to David
and Solomon and in keeping with the Sumerian code of Hammurabi, Abraham himself had Ishmael by the Egyptian servant girl Hagar, and in addition
to the six male offspring by his second wife Katurah, he also had other "sons
of his concubines" (Gen 25:6). These were all in addition to his prophesied
son Isaac by his wife Sarah—the beginning of all the Jewish people.

The historian De Lacy O'Leary is another who is careful to place Mohammed's personal record in the context of the norm in Arabia at the time. In
the early Arab world polygamy (or more exactly polygyny: multiple wives)
was an improvement over an earlier practice.[114] Possibly echoing new social
theories of his time, O' Leary reports that in the days of ignorance the consort remained with her own tribe, and her offspring simply became part of
her clan. The transition from earlier group living is "a recent change in the
Prophet's time." This change is also broadly cited as evidence that Arabian
centers such as Mecca and Medina were not entirely isolated from the influ-

ence of the surrounding and more civilized empires.[115] Mohammed's many wives are not credited with providing him any heirs, although throughout each month he favored each of them on a rotating daily schedule. Several of Mohammed's marriages—with Saudah, Hassah, Zainab, Umm Salamah, Juwairiyah, Safiyyah, Mary the Copt, and Maimunah—were for compassionate or political reasons. These reasons include the depletion of male partners due to tribal warfare and his concerns for widows who were often not young, for the release of prisoners from the tribes of widows taken in marriage by the Prophet, and for the formation by marriage of a network of intertribal alliances.[116] The confederation of tribes through marriage is indicated in the *Qur'an* itself: "The Prophet has greater claim on the faithful than they have on each other. His wives are their mothers" (Q 33:6).

Based possibly on Muhammad Ali, the Christian writer "Bosworth Smith" attributes almost all of Mohammed's multiple wives to pity for those concerned, since they were neither beautiful nor wealthy. A'isha is the very youthful exception.[117] Because of the imbalance between males and females in the tribal years, the *Qur'an* allows for polygamy but also requires that multiple wives each be treated justly by their shared husband.[118] Yet, critics note that it is to Mohammed alone that the *Qur'an* curiously grants wide latitude in taking as wives his close relatives and also slave-girls "whom God has given you as booty . . . . This privilege is yours alone, being granted to no other believers" (Q32:50).[119] Guillaume finds in some translations of the *Qur'an* authorization for having wives *for pay*, and refers to early authorities of the *Qur'an* who assert that the wording "for a specified period" (that is, prostitution) has been deleted. The entire surah in question (Q 4:28, italics added) appears to have been shortened and much diluted in a recent translation.[120]

In addition to familiar Old Testament practices and others already noted, scholarly ethnography provides other examples of early marriage customs giving security in cultures of persistent male imbalance caused by warfare. In southeastern Europe male depletion due to tribal feuds among the Highland Ghegs of Albania resulted in increased rather than decreased respect for women. From whatever tribe, the women were so valued that they were secure from attack even when traveling alone on mountain trails. This particular accommodation was so absolute that even men traveling with women were safe. Thus, in tribal Albania, polygamy (again, polygyny) was common, but ethnologists also find that polygamy was limited to the Muslim populations. The practice was not found among the Christians where monogamy was the respected standard[121] as was possibly the case with Khadijha.

Mohammed's rejection of the Judeo-Christian revelation, while at the same time turning back to the religion of Abraham—is this ambiguity a kind of polygamy? What can be made of his combination of the cleansing faith of

Abraham with post-Meccan polygamy, plunder, and eclectic religion? Rejection of the Christian Trinity comes under the Qur'anic verse that God at least "does not have a consort" (Q6:101/102; Q 112:1–4). The nearly final entry in the *Qur'an* reads, "Say: God is One, the Eternal God. He begot none, nor was He begotten. None is equal to Him" (Q 112:1–4). In these entries the *Qur'an* seems to carry forward the memory of early pagan intermediate gods—half man and half god—begotten by the deities and their consorts, the coupling of gods with humans. In the *Qur'an*, is the Christian revelation of Christ—who is fully God and fully man—retained as a prophet but not recognized because the lingering lens of the pagan imagination is mingled with devout monotheism? Thoughtful Muslim scholars hold that the teachings of Islam are distinct from the life of its charismatic and revered founder the Prophet, but the *Qur'an*, compiled by others after his death, celebrates and confuses both. Near the time of his death, Mohammed's favorite wife asked if he at least might be entered into heaven through compassion alone, not needing the mercy of God. With admirable transparency, three times he solemnly replied: "Neither shall I enter paradise unless God cover me with his mercy."[122]

One secular writer links sexual perversion and aberrant forms of religious intensity: "It belongs to the province, not of the theologian but of the psychologist, especially interested in the study of depraved emotion and diseased imagination. Its foundation is that perverted sexuality which is so strangely connected, as a matter of psychological fact, with intensity of religious enthusiasm."[123] The late Erik von Kuehnelt-Leddhin would find this reading of history to be largely the fiction of self-justifying modernity. The Jewish tradition admonishes against sexual license (the sixth and ninth Commandments) while Christianity preaches a broadly "new life" which keeps, fulfills and transcends the Law and which through Christ is possible even in this world. Religion is not defined by the pagan mystery cults and their fertility cults and temple prostitutes, including the contemporary tabloid and Hollywood cults.

In Scripture sexual immorality is closely identified not with authentic religion, but with idolatry (Num 25:1–5, 1 Cor 10:8, Rev 2:14). Von Kuehnelt-Leddhin associates "sadistic bestiality," perversion and political stupidity not with religion but more clearly with the unreason of pagan and atheistic belief systems, particularly the events of 1789 and later convulsions in the anti-religious West. He lists in one dense page a complete litany of cruelties in the twentieth century alone, descendent in his mind from the ideological excesses set loose by the unrestrained rationalism of the French Revolution. Coupled with new technology (coupled: an appropriate term), these excesses lead to twentieth century victims numbering between one hundred and three hundred million,[124] compared for example to probably two or three thousand actual victims during the three hundred fifty years of the Spanish Inquisition (admittedly more in the witch trials in Germany and other regions). In summary, Von Kuehnelt-Leddhin associates sexual perversity, as in the treatment of victims in the Vendee of 1793 France, with "leftism" as he defines it—that is, in terms of the targeted family, and as always including symbolic or actual "murder of the father." This theory—the ascendancy of ideology over fatherhood and family—provides a parallel between secular ideological movements in the West and the superficially "religious" terrorism attached to Islam in our present day. The ambivalent and post-Medina messages of Islam with regard to jihad would lend further support to the proposition that chaos most follows corruption and a turning away from unambiguous religious and ascetic devotion. Such devotion values the created things of this world and each other more truly, rather than less so. The lay Catholic theologian Von Hildebrand explains that these goods are to be loved *for their own sake*, and not as any narrower means toward some other goal or even our own higher spiritual fulfillment.

> Many religious persons erroneously believe that in reference to created things no . . . "joyful immersion" . . . of one's self in the essence of an object, as it were, is commendable; they hold the narrow view that no created object has any "use" for our eternal aim except in a purely instrumental sense, as a subordinate means of our pursuit irrespective of its intrinsic value . . . *It is not from what we undertake with a view to our transformation, but from the things to which we devote ourselves for their own sake, that will issue the deepest formative effect upon our habitual being* (italics in original).[125]

In a review of rising nationalism and mass hatreds in the West, historian Friedrich Heer concludes that "This combination of creative activity (which draws on the resources of love) with deadly hatred is a specifically European trait, exposing man in all his grandeur and wretchedness."[126] The link is between autonomous creativity and hatred. Bernard Lewis finds instead that only when Western secularism took hold in the seventeenth century did the West overcome its own religious intolerance of unbelievers,[127] but this view does not fully account for the seven demons of modern ideology—including nationalism—that have rushed in to fill the vacuum in the human soul. Actual sexual perversion throughout history prompts Pope Benedict XVI to offer this biblical insight: "Corresponding to the image of a monotheistic God is a monogamous marriage. Marriage based on exclusive and definitive love becomes the icon of the relationship between God and his people and vice versa, God's way of loving becomes the measure of human love. This close connection between *eros* and marriage in the Bible has practically no equivalent in extra-biblical literature."[128]

Benedict proposes that rather than destroying eros, Christianity rescues it from the notion that it is a kind of "divine madness" by which man experiences supreme happiness. Regarding *eros* alone, he recounts:

> In religions, this attitude found expression in fertility cults, part of which was the 'sacred' prostitution which flourished in many temples . . . The Old Testament firmly opposed this form of religion, which represents a powerful temptation against monotheistic faith, combating it as a perversion of religiosity. But it in no way rejected eros as such; rather it declared war on a warped and destructive form of it, this counterfeit divinization of eros actually strips it of its dignity and dehumanizes it . . . It is part of love's growth toward higher levels and inward purification that it now seeks to become definitive, and it does so in a twofold sense: both in the sense of exclusivity (this particular person alone) and in the sense of being 'forever.'[129]

Exclusivity in a good marriage dissolves aggression and even unrecognized defensiveness. Applied to the Church, this kind of exclusivity enables a unity without boundaries, and might be contrasted with the additive and congregational, but always bounded, unity of Islam. The unity of the ummah is finally exclusive, and is generally defined by the boundary between two domains, dar al-Islam (the House of Islam) and dar al-harb (the House of War). In contrast with the apostles sent forth by Christ, beginning in Medina in 622 Mohammed's monotheism even in his scripture is compromised with polygamy—a relic of paganism—at the same time that Mohammed begins to distinguish himself as a warrior. These combined tendencies would seem to be always at risk of relapse into the ambient madness of tribal Arabia and its "days of ignorance." Mohammed does seek a kind of theological unification, hoping for an alliance with monotheistic Jews and Christians, in his military crusade against the idolatry of Mecca. The impasse—and the crisis of Islam today—might be due to these two different views of unity. One is nuptial and spiritually inclusive, while the other is amalgamating and defensively exclusive. Mohammed's middle ground morality is at once primitive and very much in step with modernity. The difference, again, is that the conflicting elements are written directly into and revered in the *Qur'an*, while Western courts of law today allegedly make it their cause either rewrite the (United States) *Constitution*, or else interpret it outside of the context of the natural law, i.e., as premised in the *Declaration of Independence*.

At roughly the same time as Mohammed's "defensive" military conquests in Arabia, Christian Europe was, nevertheless, equally violent. Within Christendom, the tribal leader and founder of the Merovingian dynasty, Clovis (466–511), is both like and unlike Mohammed, the tribal genius of Arabia a century later. Clovis embraced Trinitarian Christianity against the Arian and

Nestorian-like belief that Christ is not divine. But this very partial conversion did not prevent him politically from taking decisive steps to sideline or eliminate princely competitors to his family. And nearly three centuries later, at the "bloody verdict of Verdun" on his northern frontier, Charlemagne (crowned emperor in Rome in 800 A.D.) executed over four thousand assembled and disarmed Anglo-Saxon tribal chieftains, all at one time, for their continued pagan worship outside the pale. Like Clovis and Mohammed he grafted defeated tribes into his own expanding army, all of them under the same political/religious banner. In later years Charlemagne deeply regretted this action, although in this instance paganism involved human sacrifice and ritual cannibalism. Possible high-tech equivalents to first-millennium cultures still linger under our modern day "culture of death" (Pope John Paul II's counterpoint to a "culture of life".) These practices include organ extractions from executed prisoners in China and, in the West, late term abortions (especially), the cultivation of tissue growths or even commercial products derived from *embryonic* stem cells, and euthanasia of the elderly and those labeled "vegetative."

Charlemagne carried on a tradition of conversion or death. He also had five wives in succession (rather than up to four at a time as under Islam), and at least as many concubines, all resulting in eighteen children of which nine were legitimate. Charlemagne's youthful and favorite wife (Hildegard) gave him these nine children and his most happy family life before she died at age twenty-six (they married when she was only twelve).[130] Unlike the religion of Islam, Charlemagne's Church disapproved of his non-monogamous ways, but apparently tolerated these excesses which were part of the times. The difficulties of succession are powerfully illustrated by the equally charismatic Charlemagne and Mohammed. The alternative to personal succession, achieved and imposed by modernity, is the benefit and scourge of rationalization and the administrative state. Upon his death, Charlemagne's empire would have been divided among his three sons. But with the untimely deaths of Pepin and Charles, the realm remained intact and fell to his least capable son, Louis. The unstable empire was succeeded (or restored) in 962 by the Holy Roman Empire with the coronation of the German king Otto I. Following Mohammed's death, potential successors took part in a struggle allowing only one winner for a regime that was to expand dramatically outward in barely one century.

Mohammed openly recognized and conceded his inability to perform miracles like the Christ of Christianity. The *Qur'an* accepts the miracles worked through the words of Christ, but explains that these were accomplished not by a divine Christ, but by Christ as only a man and only with "God's permission" (Q 3:48–50, 5:110–112).[131] Islam asserts a dichotomy between Christ and God, while Christ used his miracles precisely to teach the unity of a present and living God: ". . . the Father is in me and I am in the Father" (Jn 11:38). Neither did Mohammed prophecy the future as did Christ as on the coming destruction of the Temple in Jerusalem (Mt 24:2, Lk 19:43–44) in 69 A.D. Instead, to advance and justify his convictions, Mohammed appealed at key points to three personal favors. First and foremost was a sequence of messages from the Angel Gabriel during the years 610 to 613. Second, Mohammed reported a uniquely privileged trip to heaven at least as a vision.[132] The *Qur'an* makes only one brief and cryptic entry: "Glory be to Him who made His servant go by night from the Sacred Temple to the farther Temple whose surroundings We have blessed, that We might show him some of Our Signs. He alone hears and observes all" (Q 17:1). The more detailed account of this key event is found only in the hadith completed only two centuries later. The third favor claimed by Mohammed came during the final period of martial conquest. Mohammed claimed a special ability to see angels at the ready in order to encourage and assist his army in combat. He also claimed to see angelic interventions that caused the enemy to perceive his own armies to be enlarged three-fold from what they were in reality.[133] In a crude parallel, the eleventh and twelfth century popes granted remission of sins to those who took part in Crusades to recover the overrun Christian territories of the Holy Land.

Mohammed's first personal favor, visitations by an angel, is addressed above. This cornerstone to Islam now calls for a closer look. Other than as a "locution," how else might Christians and Jews, indeed all non-Islamic believers in revealed religion, view the special favor of divine inspirations or possible "revelations"? Frederick Denny offers almost in passing a vocabulary explanation. Again, not knowing at first what to think of his experiences at Mount Hira, Mohammed consulted his possibly Christian wife and then sought the advice of her trusted and aged cousin, Waraqua ibn Naufal, an Arabian monotheist and hanif and Jewish convert to Christianity. Because of the very central role of Gabriel to Mohammed's message and to the *Qur'an*, the complete quote from Denny is provided here: "Waraqua knew something of the older scriptures and declared that what had come upon his cousin's (Khadijha's) husband was none other than what had previously descended upon Moses, the *namus*. This term seems to have been understood by the Arabs as meaning an angelic messenger, especially Gabriel, but it is a corruption of the Greek *nomos*, meaning 'law,' or Torah."[134] Is it possible that Waraque correctly interpreted the visitations as similar to the *law*, while from Waraque's words Mohammed might just as easily have heard an additional reference to angels? The later *Qur'an* is based largely on the Law, the Pentateuch of the Old Testament delivered to Mohammed, it is believed, by the angel Gabriel. Recall of countless stories gathered on the trade routes to Mecca could have equipped Mohammed to recount the law with the help of a vivid memory thought to be the work of an angel.

A common denominator between the origin of Islam and some cultic inspirations within Christianity is the possible interplay between subjective or perhaps mystical personal experiences, overreaching validation from other persons, and all of this mediated by imperfect human language. This hypothesis is professionally explored in connection with the full range of authentic and inauthentic Marian apparitions in the Catholic world, by Sandra L. Zimdars-Schwartz, an associate professor of Religious Studies at the University of Kansas. She finds that tangible definition to an initial experience is often given by others to the often vague subjective experience of the possible mystic. She finds that an added role can be played by earlier instances of personal suffering and rejection and the occasional tendency to "project into their post-experience environment the negative aspects of what they have experienced for example, paranoia leading to racism, anti-Semitism, hyper-nationalism."[135]

A possible parallel of this kind between Mohammed's visions as a turning point in Arabian history and a turning point in Western history *might* be Constantine's vision at the Milvian Bridge. The early Church historian Eusebius (263–339 A.D.) reports that a "most marvelous sign appeared to him from heaven," the cross "bearing the inscription Conquer by This." The already familiar symbol of Christ—the superimposed Greek letters X[*chi*] and P [*rho*])—is then painted on the shields of his men. Constantine defeats Maxentius and becomes undisputed ruler of Europe. Norwich traces the account of the "vision" to Lacantius, tutor to Constantine's son Crispus, who describes the experience as only a dream rather than a vision.[136] Constantine had been "in a state of grave religious uncertainty" and from 310 A.D. onwards, before the dream or vision, his coins already showed only one god, the Unconquered Sun (*Sol Invictus*). From a sociological perspective, religion is used as a rallying point and insignia for conventional conquest—Trinitarian monotheism by Constantine in 312 A.D., and Unitarian monotheism three hundred years later by Mohammed. Christianity, the religion of about one-tenth of the Roman Empire, was formally tolerated under Constantine and then declared the religion of state by Theodosius the Great in 380.[137]

As a predisposing condition for his own visions, Mohammed also might have suffered from the "falling sickness" or epilepsy.[138] The least serious reference to epilepsy or feigned prophecy was repeated by Roger Bacon, to the effect that Mohammed routinely engaged in days to weeks of debauchery, only to return to the palace to feign epilepsy or self-induced possession and prophecy.[139] Gibb and Kramers are among those who conclude that Mohammed's revelations were straightforward epileptic artifacts, echoes of ordinary lessons he had heard from other people around himself, for example on the trade routes to Mecca: ". . . the voice heard by him only uttered what he had from time to time heard from others and which now cropped up out of his subconscious."[140] Thus Gibb and Kramers are also among those secular researchers who see Mohammed not as a deceiver, but as a sincere believer in his missionary role as Messenger.[141] The possibility remains that Mohammed's experiences included at least one truly profound personal locution, from *outside* of himself, as to the oneness of God.[142] Similar instances occur in the early Church (Philip in Acts 8:26). This experience might have been simultaneous with—but not fully explained by—his possible epilepsy. If so, then Mohammed and St. Paul are a little alike in that each is a mystic of either lesser or greater degree, and each had a physical affliction of some sort. The Catholic convert Malcolm Muggeridge, during his modern day journey in the footsteps of St. Paul, suggests that the tireless St. Paul "must have been an insomniac! But anyway reading his letters one can see quite clearly that he had the sort of temperament that today would be called manic-depressive."[143] Paul complains of a "thorn in my flesh" and was particularly attuned to the fact that "God chose the weak of the world to shame the strong . . ." (1 Cor 1:27) and "For when I am weak, then I am strong" (2 Cor 12:10).

Overall, in the religion of Mohammed is certainly one of great passion across the centuries. Islam displays an intense theological enthusiasm and devotion to the transcendent oneness of a God who is forever larger than the human mind. This particular message is both true in what it affirms and extreme in what it omits. The easily compromising hallmark of theological reflection, the word "reason," does not even appear in the *Qur'an*.[144] In Asian theology generally there is less use of analysis and synthesis than in the West. A more direct relating of the individual to the Whole is done through religious symbols. The *Qur'an* itself is such a symbol. In comparison with symbolic religion: "The Church Fathers found the seeds of the Word, *not in the religions of the world*, but rather in philosophy, that is, in the process of critical reason directed against the (pagan) religions, in the history of progressive reason, and not in the history of religion."[145] Humanity breaks from clans and customary symbols as did Abraham, and with the coming of Christ we come to believe finally in the *Logos* as the self-revealing reason of Being itself, gratuitously made fully present.

One graphic portrait of the non-Western and early Arab mind, more than a stereotype, is provided by T.E. Lawrence in his *Seven Pillars of Wisdom*. A First World War organizer of the Arabian tribes against a common enemy, the Turks, Lawrence came to understand much of the Arab mind from the inside. Of Arabian culture he wrote: "The fringes of their deserts were strewn with broken faith . . . .The Arabs said there had been forty thousand prophets: we had record of at least some hundreds."[146] Of this multitude, Islam is the one that survived and spread by military conquest far beyond its desert incubator. In contrast with the Christian and Western attentiveness to the personal interior life, the Bedouin of the desert "Could not look for God within him; he was too sure that he was within God. He could not conceive anything which was or was not God, Who alone was great . . . ."[147]

Appreciation of this cultural predisposition, and even genius, fostered in part by the severity of the Arabian Desert is essential to our understanding of early Muslim (Arabian) resistance to more nuanced thought, and especially to Trinitarian monotheism. The simplicity of the desert resonates in Islam's bent to divide the world into two camps, those who are of the house of Islam and those who are not: dar al-Islam and dar al-harb. Lawrence continues:

> In the very outset, at the first meeting with them, was found a universal clearness or hardness of belief, almost mathematical in its limitations, and repellent in its unsympathetic form. Semites had no half-tones in their register of vision. They were a people of primary colours, or rather of black and white, who saw the world always in contour. They were a dogmatic people, despising doubt, our modern crown of thorns. They did not understand our metaphysical difficulties, our introspective questionings. They knew only truth and untruth, belief and unbelief, without our hesitating retinue of finer shades . . . (but then) They inhabited superlatives by choice. Sometimes inconsistencies seemed to possess them at once in joint sway; but they never compromised: they pursued the logic of several incompatible opinions to absurd ends, without perceiving the incongruity.[148]

An earlier Hebrew scholar paints a similar picture, but then gives a different interpretation more favorable to Mohammed. At the turn of the twentieth century, George Adam Smith wrote, "the creed of the desert nomad is simple and austere—for nature about him is monotonous, silent, and illiberal." He adds that the lush setting of Syria, in contrast, fostered a sense of indulgence, accompanied by any number of deities to which one might appeal. Looking upon the lavishness of Damascus, it is said that Mohammed "gazed, but turned away, and would not enter the city . . . 'Man' he said, 'can have but one Paradise, and mine is above.'"[149]

To the Western mind as it has flourished over time, the uniform sweep of Islamic belief across all aspects of life resembles the unity of the desert wind with its unrelieved dominance of the sand dunes as they continually reshape each other. The former Catholic nun, Karen Armstrong, explains that for Muslims, "salvation" does not consist in redemption, but rather "puts into practice God's desires for the human race . . . there is no dichotomy between the sacred and things of this world, the religious and the political, sexuality and worship . . . the aim was *tawhid* (making one), the integration of the whole of life in a unified community, which would give Muslims intimations of the Unity which is God."[150] It is this predisposition away from distinctions in the categories listed, this pre-emptive expansion of the unity of God to engulf all things created by Him that renders so difficult any deepening dialogue on real distinctions such as the differences and relations between Church and state. Also discounted is the dialectical and concrete unity (not abstract dichotomy) of the Old and New Testament stressed by St. Augustine, and appreciated by the later Pascal's analytical mind, "of image and truth, of sin and redemption, of nature and grace, of earth and Heaven."[151] With the predisposition toward unity based on clarity, the Christian waits "for the Savior, our Lord Jesus Christ, until he, who is life, appears, and we appear with him in glory."[152]

St. Gregory of Nyssa offers a clear picture of redemption as it begins even now in a distinct "world" that is found by God to be "very good" (Gen 1:31). Gregory combines two of the Lord's sayings: "Blessed are the pure of heart, for they shall see God . . .The kingdom of God is within you." He explains that "the man who cleanses his heart of every created thing and every evil desire will see the image of the divine nature in the beauty of his own soul."[153] With the coming of Christ, salvation involves a radical and personal conversion, not absorption, and a reuniting best understood as the unity of atonement, that is, at-*one*-ment. Conversion as a turning around looks deeply at obvious offenses, and more deeply at the clever bluntness of interior blindness. Interior conversion is a turning away from those ingrained resentments and self-justifications that are so easily confused with self-respect. The fully converted Christian distances neither from the true self nor from God or men, but from "the world": "To make the world your friend is to make God your enemy" (James 4:4).

The broad brush of the sociologist Christopher Dawson paints picture similar to that of Lawrence. He contrasts the opposite flaws of the West and of Islam:

> Behind every civilization there is a vision . . . The faith in Progress and in human perfectibility which inspired the thinkers of the eighteenth and nineteenth centuries in Europe, was essentially of this order, just as much as was that great vision of the vanity of human achievement which Mohammad saw in the cave of Mount Hira and which made civilization and all temporal concerns as meaningless as 'the beat of a gnat's wing,' in comparison with the splendour of Eternal Power, burning alone like the sun over the desert.[154]

Dawson continues: "Nor can we doubt that the material progress of modern Europe as opposed to the material stagnation of Islam is, at least to some extent, the result of the different psychological effects produced by these two different visions." Several aspects of early Arabia are carried forward in new form by the unitary vision of Islam. In addition to the psychology of the desert, there is the divisive tribal combat Mohammed determined to bring to an end. Is not jihad in its martial form partly the extension of tribal combat as originally found in the borrowed Pentateuch, but with broadened boundaries now projected centuries ahead into the present? Alongside Islamic exhortations toward chastity and even purity of the eyes (Q 14:30–34), the contradiction and concession to pagan polygamy also continues. Pagan pilgrimage (*hajj*), a valuable tradition, also continues as one of the five pillars of the new Islam. But under Islam parts of the Old Testament monotheism are actually grafted onto the stubborn patterns bequeathed by the expelled pagan gods of Mecca.

And yet, Islam is more than either absconded Judaism or an Arabian anachronism. The Christian Augustine and Aquinas asserted that human nature is the capacity for God (*capax Dei*). Human nature "has room for God because it has an innate capacity, even a need, to transcend itself . . . The urge that drives us to seek God is the same as the urge that drives us to smash things. The old psychologists were absolutely correct in the ambiguous role they ascribed to our power of anger. It is the power that smashes through limitations, leading us either to become visionaries or to become vandals."[155] The passion of Mohammed is that he is wedded to both masters; in Islam one does not distinguish and therefore does not choose between the path of piety and the path of conquest which is the other face of submission. As in all religions, the contradictory paths of heightened spirituality and of the fallen world are ever at risk of being laminated into one seamless movement. The allure of "having it both ways," of choosing the knowledge of both good and evil as a middle ground, is found from very near the beginning. It is only "in the cross (that) there is no mingling of good and evil, as in the tree of paradise . . . ."[156]

THE CROOKED LINES OF HISTORY

A superficial scan of historical meeting points between the West and Islam will serve as common background for reviewing the inner life of each culture in Chapters 3 and 4, respectively. It will also reinforce a theme hinted earlier that religion can be both a "cause" of violence in history and a restraint. Given the freedom of the human person, the core of the universal natural law, this resistance to being reduced to physical laws and effects is readily apparent in history as a human artifact and less as a case study by those who seek to overextend their appreciation for the laws of nature by imposing oracular interpretations dressed up as economic laws or sociological ideologies. Crooked lines of history made by human hands on the ground bring the world today both forward and to where it was immediately following the First World War.

Different Western scholars paint the crusades as either a pious religious enterprise or as a cruel military adventure fueled by hopes of plunder and aggrandizement. Likewise, early Islamic expansion lends itself to conflicting interpretations. For example, following the death of Mohammed: "The driving force of the Muslim conquests was religious; other motivations were subordinate and secondary." Citing Donner, the like-minded Warren Carroll continues: "It was Islam—the set of religious beliefs preached by Mohammed, with its social and political ramifications—that ultimately sparked the whole integration process and hence was the ultimate cause of the conquest's success."[157] Daniel-Rops (a Catholic like Carroll) suggests instead that with Mohammed's death the merchant class reasserted itself and seized jihad as a path to material gain and that it was only happenstance that placed those of another religion (Christians) in their path.[158] Karen Armstrong paints a similar picture: "the objective of Umar (second caliph after Ali) and his warriors was entirely pragmatic: they wanted plunder and a common activity that would preserve the unity of the ummah . . . . Later, when the Muslims had established their great empire, Islamic law would give a religious interpretation of this conquest . . . ."[159] Rarely acknowledged by modern social science is a motivation more basic than abstract "religion" or economics, the pre-modern loyalty to Mohammed and his unifying memory and example. Theologically, the contrast is between the counsel of St. Paul against personal loyalties to Apollos or Cephas and always toward a Christ who is divine and undivided (1 Cor 1:12–13), and the conflated blurring under Islam of such a distinction— "there is no God but Allah, *and* Mohammed is his prophet."

Barely one century after Mohammed's death in 632, Islam was extended over vast territories, gaining in this short period an area much larger than did all the Roman legions in eight centuries. Only the Mongol Empire of the thirteenth and fourteenth century claimed a larger domain stretching from Korea to Hungary and even invading the Islamic world. Norwich captures the first century of rapid conquests under the sword of Islam: "In 633, they burst out of Arabia. After three years they had taken Damascus; after five, Jerusalem; after six, all Syria; within a decade, Egypt and Armenia; within twenty years, the Persian Empire; within thirty Afghanistan and most of the Punjab . . . In 711, having occupied the entire coast of North Africa, they invaded Spain; and by 732, less than a century after the first eruption from their desert homeland, they had crossed the Pyrenees and driven north to the banks of the Loire—where they were checked at last."[160]

Dawson places the beginning of the so-called Middle Ages at the mid-seventh century, rather than at the more widely accepted fifth century. The threshold between eras was when the Roman Empire and "the whole civilized world seemed about to become Moslem."[161] Other more familiar accounts accent mostly internal reasons for the decline of the Roman Empire, and then the eventual ascent of Christianity. Edward Gibbon, the English literary historian, saw the triumph of Christianity over paganism as simply the replacement of many early superstitions by another. The primary cause is "the convincing evidence of the doctrine itself, and (to) the ruling providence of its great Author," and his famous five other secondary causes are: "exclusive zeal, the immediate expectation of another world, the claim of miracles, the practice of rigid virtue, and the constitution of the primitive church."[162] Gibbon advances a post-Enlightenment understanding of the Church as essentially a political competitor in society. He cites "The union and discipline of the *Christian republic*, which gradually formed an *independent and increasing state* in the heart of the Roman Empire."[163] Even the non-believer Leslie Stephen takes Gibbon to task for failing to understand the core explanations for the spread of Christianity within the Empire: "the true causes of the greatest of all spiritual movements lay in a religion altogether inscrutable by his methods of inquiry . . . Gibbon, indeed, is as incapable of understanding the spiritual significance of the phenomenon as of assigning a cause for it."[164] With Christianity the human person sees an eternal destiny and never again will fit neatly into any purely secular state or empire. Personal openness and human access to eternity must be considered in explaining the cultural event of Europe and the West.

Many historians explain Europe in terms of a larger map of the ninth century. Boundaries were set by outside pressures from an expansive Islam such that Charlemagne rose to fill the "island" between the territory of Islam to the south and the frontiers of barbarism to the north.[165] Later European consolidation in turn reinforced the widening division between Western Christianity and Byzantium far to the East, a division that was formalized by mutual excommunications in 1054. The seeds of this internal division of Christendom were planted centuries earlier in the fourth century when Constantine's empire was divided East and West partly by the pressure of migrating invaders from the northeast. The last formal remnant of the Roman Empire West fell when its last emperor in 476 was replaced by a more local king (Odoacer). The severed Byzantine East continued for another millennium. From these complex beginnings. The contested Pirenne Thesis attributes the particular path of Western growth largely to Islamic pressures after the seventh century:[166]

The very lands where civilization had been born were torn away; the Cult of the Prophet was substituted for the Christian Faith, Moslem law for Roman law, the

Arab tongue for the Greek and the Latin tongue. The Mediterranean had been a
Roman lake; it now became, for the most part, a Moslem lake. From this time on
it separated, instead of uniting, the East and the West of Europe . . . Without Islam, the Frankish empire would probably never have existed and Charlemagne,
without Mohammed, would be inconceivable.[167]

Running parallel to Western events, the history of Islam begins with the
early era of the caliphs (632 until 1258) spanning three periods. The universally accepted three early successors (632–661) are followed by the Umayyad
Caliphate (661–750), and then with the massacre of the princely blood line,
the Abbasid Empire (750–1258) of the finally dominant Sunnis sect. In the
first years of Abbasid rule (752) the capital was moved from Damascus to
Baghdad. The learned ones or *ulema,* rather than family descendents of the
Prophet, seized their place as the true heirs to the Prophet. The more settled
and urban Abbasid Caliphate combined the Arabic language and religion with
the learning from older and surrounding civilizations. They expanded and
altered Islam from an Arab confederation to a multicultural Islamic dynasty.

The most familiar aspect of Muslim history from the vantage point of the
West came later in the combined history of the crusades, retrospectively
divided into eight phases (1095–1291). By the time of the crusades the weakened Byzantium already had been defeated by the savage Seljuk Turks at the
Battle of Manzikert (1071). This "invasion was a scourge far heavier than that
of the Saracens. While the latter, when bent on permanent conquest, offered
the option of tribute as alternative to the 'Koran or the sword,' the Seljouks
were mere savages who slew for the pleasure of slaying."[168] Well over a million were slaughtered at Manzikert, as many as the number of Jews slain by
the Romans in the siege of Jerusalem in 70 A.D. Access by pilgrims to the
Holy Land was now all but blocked.

The Byzantines had struggled for centuries to regain territory lost to Islam,
with the greatest progress in the mid-tenth century when in 975 the overex-
tended armies still fell short of taking Jerusalem. By the late eleventh century
an endangered Constantinople pleaded with Rome for outside protection
and help in reopening pilgrimage routes to the Holy Sites. Factors enabling
this support were a general calming of Europe itself, a newly cleared route
through Magyar territory on the Danube, and new fleets capable of using
Venice as a jumping off point.[169] The crusades continued to reinforce European unity by allowing the powers to concentrate on a foreign threat.[170]

The next three centuries of crusades failed to retake the Holy Land. The
First Crusade (1095–1101) was the only one of all eight that was militarily
successful. It came as a response to the capture of Antioch by the Seljuk
Turks in 1085.[171] Pope Urban II's call to arms at Clermont appealed to many

motives and the assembled crowd erupted with almost Islamic simplicity, "God wills it! God wills it!"[172] By the time Jerusalem was besieged it had changed masters back from the feared Turkish invaders to the original and milder Saracens. In exchange for routine tribute, the Saracens had given hospitality and protection to Western pilgrims. On the verge of the assault and in hopes of peace they now offered gifts, but the European leaders now were propelled by sacred vows to rescue the city from all Muslim infidels. By widespread account Jerusalem was retaken with great brutality: ". . . amid scenes of hideous carnage, the soldiers of Christ battered their way into Jerusalem, slaughtering all the Muslims in the city and burning all the Jews alive in the main synagogue."[173] The stark choice given to Muslims infidels was to either convert where they stood or be executed.[174]

In Europe yet another round of Jewish persecution broke out. Persecution had smoldered from over two centuries earlier. The newest acts were less at the hands of the crusaders than the rag tag camp followers and their own charismatic leaders. Discriminatory legislation appeared only later under the Third and Fourth Lateran Councils (1179 and 1215). Throughout, individual bishops often housed and protected Jews from the fury. At Worms the bishop hid them in his castle and offered baptism to escape slaughter, a scene repeated centuries later during the Second World War when Pope Pius XII supplied baptismal certificates to countless Nazi-hunted Jews in Rome. But at Worms all eight hundred victims refused baptism and chose suicide. A thousand others perished together in Mainz, and additional cases are reported at Cologne, Regensburg and Prague. In May and June of 1096, some four to eight thousand Jews perished and at least one migrating mob is reported to have practiced cannibalism en route to the Holy Land.[175] During the same period Jews may have suffered as much under Islamic "tolerance" in Andalusia. "In Granada in 1066 rioting Muslim mobs assassinated the rabbi and visir Joseph Ibn Naghrela and destroyed the entire Jewish community. Thousands perished— more than those killed by mobs in the Rhineland at the beginning of the First Crusade."[176] The Rhineland massacres were condemned by the pope.

The *Second* Crusade (1145–8) set out to avenge the fall of Edessa. This campaign was generally a disaster although Jerusalem was retained. The *Third* Crusade (1188–92) responded to the startling fall in 1187 of Jerusalem to a newly unified Islam under Saladin (a Kurd).[177] Unity under Saladin's leadership was galvanized by early Christian victories in Palestine. Beginning in 1171 Saladin consolidated his position as the Muslim leader with conquests outside of Palestine: in Egypt, Syria, Mesopotamia, Assyria, Armenia and Arabia. The three strongest rulers in the West now came to provide a more coordinated Western effort: Frederick I of Germany, Philip August of France, and Richard I of England. Without consolidated leadership the first century of the crusades had been marked by internal dissension on both sides. Until the year 1200, "relations between Muslim and Christian . . . were sometimes better than the relations between Muslim and Muslim or Christian and Christian."[178]

Recalling how Jerusalem had been earlier put to the sword during the First Crusade, Saladin's remarkable restraint in the battle for Jerusalem is surprising:

> Saladin's magnanimity was already celebrated. Every Christian, he decreed, would be allowed to redeem himself by payment of a suitable ransom. Of the twenty thousand poor who had no means of raising the money, seven thousand would be freed on payment of a lump sum by the various Christian authorities . . . There was no murder, no bloodshed, no looting. Few Christians ultimately found their way into slavery.[179]

Saladin singled out and with his own hands killed and beheaded Reynald of Chatillon who had instigated the renewed hostilities. From Kerak in southern Jordan (1176–1178 AD), Reynald had dispatched routine pillaging parties into Muslim controlled territory and finally one of the intercepted caravans was made up of only Muslim pilgrims bound for Mecca. This raid signalled a threat against the holy places of Islam—a mirror image of the Christian motive for the crusades.[180] From Jerusalem Saladin moved on to recapture other centers in Palestine and Syria taken by the Christians nearly a century before. In 1191 Richard Duke of Burgundy beheaded nearly three thousand captives,[181] but in 1192 it was Saladin who imposed a truce to end the Third Crusade. Jerusalem remained a Muslim holding, but Christian pilgrims received permission once more to visit the Holy Sepulcher.

Pope Innocent III represents the high water mark of papal power in Europe and in 1202–4 and called for the *Fourth* Crusade so tragic to Christian unity. Fearing that all of Christian Asia Minor might be lost, he was also disgusted with much of the behavior of the troops in earlier campaigns. He remarked: "Christians in name only . . . these wretched Christians who betrayed one another, hated one another, and scandalized one another."[182] He even appealed to the Sultan of Aleppo to protect the Latin patriarch of Antioch from the Christian prince of Tripoli.[183] Lured off track by local Byzantine political intrigue and by the need to supplement Venetian finances for the expedition to the Holy Land, the Fourth Crusade was rerouted into the fateful sacking of ancient Constantinople. The pope excommunicated temporarily the entire expedition even as they left Venice for the Dalmatian coast, but also hoped for reunion between the Eastern and Western Churches and might have seen Constantinople as a good path to Jerusalem.[184] The Muslim conquest of this bastian in 1453 was less consuming than this self-inflicted sacking of the same Christian city in 1203 by crusaders: "By the sack of Constantinople,

Western civilization suffered a loss greater than the sack of Rome in the fifth century or the burning of the library of Alexandria in the seventh—perhaps the most catastrophic single loss in all history."[185] Countless religious relics were pillaged, most of these finding their way to France where they were later destroyed by post-Christian zealots of the French Revolution.[186] Early in the siege of Constantinople the initial damage to the city actually was not due to the crusaders. The fire was ignited during a brawl between Greeks and Latins already living in the city. The murder of the newly reinstated Emperor Alexius by his bodyguards and the usurper Murzuphlus then crystallized the resolve of the occupying Western army. The army was encouraged by clerical denunciation of the guilty and reassurance of the rightness of the Latin cause.[187] Distracted in this way and totally spent, the Fourth Crusade never reached the Holy Land.

In 1212 the spontaneous and incredibly naïve Children's Crusade victimized tens of thousands of the young of nearly all early ages, mostly French and some German, who either died en route or ended up in the prostitution rings of Christian Europe or as slaves in Muslim Baghdad and Alexandria.[188] Twenty-first century readers need not justify ourselves by demanding how the Medieval world could allow such things to happen. More systematic victimization is very much with us today with the casually reported international trafficking of women and children, nearly one million each year, partly to serve the now global markets of prostitution.[189] Another failed attempt to retake Jerusalem, the *Fifth* Crusade, set out in 1221 to reach the holy sites through Egypt. It was during this expedition that St. Francis journeyed unharmed to the tent of the Sultan to propose his conversion. In the *Sixth* Crusade (1228–9) and armed with multilingual skills including Arabic, the German emperor Frederick II finally secured Jerusalem through direct negotiations with the sultan. The sultan was already preoccupied with an internal struggle for control of Damascus.[190] Pious writers pin his success on the fact that the sultan was the same al-Kamil who during the Sixth Crusade had entertained St. Francis on the banks of the Nile, but during the previous two decades the Muslims had offered four times to surrender Jerusalem under treaty arrangements.[191] Due partly and ironically to his religious indifference,[192] Frederick found a pragmatic way to simply declare Jerusalem a city of three religions and then to divide the Holy Sites among the three allegiances.[193] Following this modest interlude the *Seventh* Crusade (1248–54) again was unsuccessful. The French monarch St. Louis IX was imprisoned and sent home and in the *Eighth* Crusade, also a disaster. He was finally killed in North Africa. Crusader occupation ended when Acre, the last of the crusader kingdoms, fell in 1291.

Centuries later and near the end of the First World War, General Allenby labeled his entry into Damascus as finally ending the crusades. But in 1981,

Mehmet Ali Agca readied for his attempted assassination of the pope with
these words: "I have decided to kill John Paul II, supreme commander of the
Crusades."[194] A contrasting personality, Louis IX was later elevated to sainthood and in Europe practiced the civilizing and religious Truce of God between
combatants. Dating from a Church council in France in 975, the Truce of God
restricted warfare with holidays assigned to several dates and seasons of the
year having Christian religious significance. In 1139 the Second Council of the
Lateran imposed the penalty of excommunication for breaking the truce. These
historic *religious* interventions to violence are echoed only rarely in modern
times. In the trenches of the First World War the guns fell silent on Christmas
Eve of 1914. Combatants found themselves singing Christmas carols and sharing camaraderie, first among themselves and then together across the cratered
No Man's Land that separated and joined members of the opposing armies.[195]
While the medieval Truce was to be applied only between Christian combatants, it appears surfaces in crusader history in the Holy Land. The opposing
armies often found interludes for gift exchanges and tournaments. Western
armies often cared for and returned Muslim children captured in battle, and of
the Muslims, Oliverisu Scholasticus, a member of a defeated Frankish army,
offers this striking report: "Who could doubt that such goodness, friendship and
charity came from God. Men whose parents, sons and daughters, brothers and
sisters had died in agony at our hands, whose lands we took, whom we drove
naked from their homes, revived us with their own food when we were dying of
hunger, and showered us with kindness even while we were in their power."[196]
St. Paul spoke especially to Christians of such moments: "Never repay injury
with injury . . . But if your enemy is hungry, feed him; if he is thirsty, give him
something to drink . . ." (Rom 12:17, 20).

The Christian Truce of God finds a counterpart in ancient Arabia. Following
the peaceful era of the Elephant, recorded later in the *Qur'an*,[197] Mohammed at
the age of twenty joined his uncle Abu Taleb in battle for the first time in the late
sixth century Impious War. But prior to this war and Mohammed's involvement,

> . . . it was an ancient Constitution through all Arabia, to hold four months of
> the Year sacred, in which all War was to cease . . . as soon as any of those
> Sacred Months began, they all immediately desisted, and taking off the heads
> from their Spears, and laying aside all other Weapons of War, had intercourse,
> and intermingled together, as if there had been perfect Peace and Friendship
> between them, without any fear of each other; so that if a Man should meet on
> those Months him that had slain his Father, or his Brother, he dusrt not meddle
> with him, how violent soever his Hatred or Revenge might prompt him to it.[198]

In all of these cases the universal natural law is trampled by warfare, but
never defeated entirely. The long memory of the Church expresses this truth

about man its social doctrine to the modern world: "Man receives from God his essential dignity and with it *the capacity to transcend every social order so as to move toward truth and goodness.*"[199]

In Europe, the international experience of the crusades and later has fed many new currents. Muslim reverence for the Arabic language preceded the cult of language spread by Greek emigrants especially following the fall of Constantinople in 1453. Aided and abetted by moveable type and gunpowder, Europe began to discover itself in the different European languages as principles of local unity.[200] In the East, Arabic and Islam remain fused, and in the West the new evolution was toward language-based nation-states first with their state religions and then ever more secular and removed from traditional religion. Western reactions to the crusader centuries include the pacifism of the heretical and Manichean Cathars and sometimes the new religious order founded by St. Francis. Baptists and Quakers are later and very moderate offshoots of such early pacifism.[201] The non-violent path to freedom in India in the 1940s was due as much to new global visibility as it was to the leadership of Gandhi. Public surveillance and outrage toward repressive British reactions were as vital to the decolonization of India as were parliamentary institutions transplanted from colonial Great Britain. Most recently, global visibility played a key role in the unraveling of the Soviet Empire and, in the Arab world made possible the 2011 removal of President Mubarak from power in Egypt. In Chapter 4 we will consider the imponderable calculations demanded by "just war theory" as contrasted with the ideological nature of Islamic jihad.

Well before the crusades and extending from the tenth and into the sixteenth century, the reach of Muslim merchants and teachers vastly extended the political control of Islam. Then from outside both the West and the Muslim world, and coinciding with the last crusade, a Mongol grandson of Genghis Khan came from the east to sack Baghdad in 1258. The search for booty and conquest by his own tribal confederation matches the similar history of Islam at its beginning six centuries earlier. With the Mongols, the non-territorial Caliphate (632–1258) was replaced with territorial military commanders (sultans in the West and khans in the East). To narrowly educated Westerners, the fall of Baghdad might barely appear as a spot on a discarded calendar, But within the memory of Islam at least hundreds of thousands of residents were slaughtered. The city was put almost totally to the sword. It was a full two centuries before the city recovered. In yet another wave of invasion the Ottoman Turks lay siege to the nearly encircled eastern outpost of Christendom at Constantinople. This external threat to Europe came on the heels of the Plague (1348–50) and coincided with the end the draining and internal Hundred Years War (1337–1453) which fostered a greater sense of national identity within much of Europe.[202]

After over a millennium of impregnable security the Eastern Empire fell
with Constantinople when its walls were finally breached (May 29, 1453).
Between one hundred and three hundred thousand Muslims moved against a
much smaller force of only seven thousand defenders. Norwich captures this
moment:

> By now, too, the omens had begun. On 22 May there was a lunar eclipse; a
> day or two later, as the holiest icon of the Virgin was being carried through the
> streets in one last appeal for her intercession, it slipped from its platform. A few
> hundred yards further on, a violent thunderstorm caused the whole procession
> to be abandoned. The next morning the city was shrouded in fog, unheard-of at
> the end of May; the same night the dome of Santa Sophia was suffused with an
> unearthly red glow that crept slowly up from the base to the summit and then
> went out. The past phenomenon was also seen by the Turks in Galata; Mehmet
> himself was greatly disturbed, and was reassured only after his astrologers had
> interpreted it as a sign that the building would soon be illuminated by the True
> Faith. For the Byzantines, the meaning was clear: the Spirit of God itself had
> deserted their city.[203]

On the final day the prayerful flock huddled in the cathedral of Santa Sophia:
"Matins were already in progress when the berserk conquerors were heard
approaching. Immediately the great bronze doors were closed; but the Turks
soon smashed their way in. The poorer and less attractive of the congregation
were massacred on the spot; the remainder was led off to the Turkish camps to
await their fate."[204] After the fall of Constantinople the victorious Mohammed
II found it necessary to repopulate the city and guaranteed liberty of conscience
to any returning Greeks. He restored the city and even the patriarch who still
was useful politically as an opponent to the tenuous Bull of Reunion (1439)
between Rome and the Greek bishops.[205] In the decades following the siege
of Constantinople, eastern Islam expanded more completely into the Balkans,
Greece, and up the Danube. The Orthodox Eastern Church disintegrated over
the centuries into well over a dozen autonomous national churches, especially
including the prominent Greek Orthodox Church. (It was the current Greek patriarch whom Pope Benedict XVI visited during his historic journey to Istanbul
in late 2006.) In 1516 and 1517 Islam solidified control in the south over Egypt
and Syria. By 1526 Suleiman the Magnificent had restrained a rising Persian
dynasty[206] and then advanced into Europe even as Europe struggled with the
opening days of the Reformation. In this year alone (1526) Suleiman captured
one hundred thousand men, women and children to be delivered to the slave
markets of Istanbul. The next year some three million more were sent to Damascus, Cairo and Algiers. The numbers in future years were constrained only
by the economic law of diminishing returns. In 1529, finally beaten and turned

back in Austria, the receding Muslim army left its mark by rounding up and impaling thirty thousand unsuspecting peasants.[207]

During this broad period of European troubles, both internal and external, Muslim encirclement of continental Europe was temporarily stalled at the navy Battle of Lepanto in 1571 in the Gulf of Corinth, another event that has been called the last battle of the crusades. The battle of Vienna late in the next century (1683) actually marks the farthest extension of the eastern Islamic invasion. In the West, the first Muslim invasion of Europe had been stopped at Tours in central France nearly a millennium earlier, during the eighth century (732). Without the decisive intervention at Vienna of twenty-five thousand cavalry under the Polish King, John Sobieski, further inroads into the Europe we know today would have been assured.[208] The final defeat of the Sultan in the east came in 1697, blocking his final attempt to establish an outpost north of the Danube, the original frontier of ancient Rome. Near the town of Zena some thirty thousand troops of the Ottoman army fell to the Austrians, on September 11, a date possibly immortalized in 2001 by the terrorist attack on the World Trade Center in New York.

Internal to Europe, the Diet of Augsburg in 1555 brought some order to Reformation period, with its pragmatic principle *cuius regio, eius religio*— the ruler of a region determines its religion. Greater resolution came only after the exhaustion of the Thirty Years War (1618–1648). And the Peace of Westphalia further entrenched the Augsburg formula by recognizing Calvinist alongside of Lutheran and Catholic princes, and resulted in France's undisputed dominance in Europe. The Thirty Years War marked the tipping point from a European Christendom toward political modernity and toward more overt balances of power among now secular states. The papacy hesitated, still clinging to an earlier world, officially declaring the Peace of Westphalia as "null and void, and of no effect or authority for past, present, or future."[209]

Dynastic structures still prevailed and loss of the Habsburg line in Spain triggered the War of Spanish Succession (1701–14). The French Revolution of 1789 gave way to a new Caesar in Napoleon. National resistance movements to his imperial ambitions mark the end of the ancient German Holy Roman Empire (962 to 1806). The Pandora's Box of nationalism was partly contained by Prince Metternich's principle of legitimacy and his refined balance-of-power politics set in place at the Congress of Vienna in 1815. With Russian involvement, the successful Greek revolt of 1830 against the Ottomans signaled a series of mid-century national revolutions and then the ascendancy of Prussian Germany over France in 1871. Metternich's Concert of Europe generally maintained international stability for nearly a century until in 1914 the intricate web of secret alliances totally unraveled into the trenches of the First World War.[210]

For centuries the Western monarchies and then nation-states had bumped against Islam to the east. In the early sixteenth century the Portuguese discovered sea routes around Africa and interference by Muslim competitors in the Mediterranean. By 1828 the Ottomans had executed eleven patriarchs of Constantinople as well as nearly one hundred bishops, and several thousand priests, deacons, and monks. In southeastern Europe the sultans had conscripted possibly one million Christian boys, either captured or surrendered under a quota system to supply a highly trained and non-indigenous Janissary military elite of unquestioned loyalty.[211] Recent centuries brought to the Ottoman Empire a relative decline in armaments and sea power, and then in 1798 military defeat at Battle of the Nile by Napoleon.

Impressed by Western institutions, the Ottomans finally turned cautiously toward political modernity under the Tanzimat Reforms and the new Ottoman Constitution of 1876. The actual effects of these reforms remained mostly on paper until 1908 and the eve of the First World War. Reasons for the general decline of Islamic culture from its golden age under Sulieman the Magnificent (1520–66) are multiple. Legal thought was stunted in the thirteenth century under the new khans and sultans following the Mongol invasion. Draining battles between the Ottomans and Safavid nationalism in Persia (1534–1619) also weakened and tipped Islam toward decline. The Ottomans stopped translating Western philosophy after the fifteenth century, and then limited themselves to only what was directly useful such as history and military topics.[212] A persistent cultural liability was the aversion to making meaningful intellectual and institutional distinctions as between theology and philosophy, between philosophy and the experimental mind of science, and between mosque and state. Islam is very much a culture of amalgamation within the oneness of Allah, and a composite religion including even Greek, Chinese and Hindu influences. Early Islam eventually became parasitic on encysted Christian communities from which it borrowed so much. The atrophy of these confined communities may help account for the decline of the larger but dependent Muslim world itself.[213] The influx into Europe of silver and gold from the New World devalued Ottoman exports of grain and textiles. The Empire generally lacked military sea power in a fast emerging maritime world and in the seventeenth and eighteenth centuries became increasingly subject to pressure from not only neighboring Russia but also the maritime powers of France and Britain.

The severe dislocation in the Islamic world today recalls historical parallels. The Hebrew people experience such emptiness following their exile and release from Babylon (587–538 B.C.), and defined themselves in terms of their own recovered scriptures which were compiled into the Old Testament. Muslim rigorists such as the Wahhabis will always attribute loss of Islam's golden age to a failure in strict Islamic purity before their own Shari'a law. This message was a large part Khomeini's 1979 revolution in Iran (ancient Persia). Very crude parallels might be drawn with the series of Hebrew prophets who periodically recalled battered Israel back to the Torah and away from any mingling with Canaanite idolatry. Christian parallels include the fourth century Donatists in St. Augustine's North Africa who held that they alone were pure enough to be called Christian.

Alternative to insular purity as the key to successful civilizations is the view that diverse interactions ensure ascendancy. Of the far flung Islamic empire and its lost Golden Age, the sociologist Christopher Dawson writes: "Unfortunately Moslem Spain, in spite of its high civilization, was based on insecure social foundations, and the very age which produced so brilliant a flowering of intellectual culture was also the age of its political decline and fall. The Moslem State in Spain no less than in Egypt and Mesopotamia was an artificial creation which had no organic relation to the life of the people and rested its power on mercenary troops and on the class of slaves and freed-man from which most of its servants and officials were drawn . . ."[214] Dawson found this "premature blighting" to be "typical of the fate of this (Islamic) Mediterranean world as a whole. Everywhere, we find the same wealth of material and intellectual culture and the same lack of social vitality or free political activity."[215]

By the late twentieth century a newly reshuffled political landscape features a resurgent Third World Islam. Secularists see Islam as filling the global vacuum left by the dismantling of the Soviet Union in 1991 and the end of the Cold War. The Christian is inclined toward a less political explanation based on the permanent tension between man and a fallen world—whether in the form of Gulag repression, a resurgent Islam, or the universal solvent of modern secular humanism. But, politically, the post-colonial Western influence has helped transform several monarchies in the Islamic Middle East into republics. Besides Turkey in 1923, there are Syria and Lebanon (1943), Egypt (1953), and Sudan, Tunisia and Iraq (the late 1950s). Other monarchies remain in Morocco, the moderate Jordan and the exceptionally traditional Kingdom of Saudi Arabia. The conventionally optimistic assessments of Islamic modernization from the final years of the twentieth century are now mixed with profound apprehension and speculative hope.

Eighty percent of Muslims are not found in the Arab oil oligarchies of the Middle East. A merely class-based or economic approach to global intercultural engagements serves mostly to maintain appearances for Western elites and their imitators. Entering the new millennium, speculation also abounds as to the very future of Europe itself. Apart for the threat of radical Islam, what are the intended or unintended effects of moderate and job-seeking Islamic immigrants? Most writers suggest that a de facto demographic invasion of Europe is underway. More alarmist than many, the late Richard John Neuhaus (d. 2008) wrote this: "Through terrorism and the mass immigration of Muslims in Europe, the jihadists are pressing for the reversal of the military outcome of 1683" (Vienna). To which he reported this alarming response from one well-known Muslim spokesman, Tariq Ramadan, the controversial research Fellow at Oxford: "We are here, we are coming, don't even think of stopping us. Europe is ours at least as much as it is yours. Get used to it."[216]

Less abrupt Muslim responsdents is simply to notice that because Muslims are already citizens of Western nation-states these states are by definition multicultural. Under this concession of first principles, the implied next move is cultural blending where distinctly different things are no longer distinguished. This step proposed by Islam is to adjust the political institutions to fit what is proposed as already a *fait accompli*, to ratify an invertebrate and syncretic consensus. Civic and institutional tensions insert themselves into the demographic and cultural stagnation of Europe. Global in scale, these tensions combine with "an ever larger proportion of the earth's people living in . . . Africa, Asia and Latin America," where the political texts of Karl Marx and Chairman Mao will be replaced by religious scriptures, sometimes equally and even more apocalyptic. Pondering the role of religion in a convoluted modern world, the Protestant scholar Philip Jenkins remarks, "We may be entering the great age of Vatican diplomacy."[217]

Good luck and patience are the minimum required to navigate the current turning point for Islam, better than was done with the Ottoman Empire on the eve of the First World War. In 1839, before the empire succumbed to a history not fully its own, the Sultan Abd-ul-Medjid proposed a document described as "one of the most remarkable documents of history." In *Hatti Sherif of Gulhane* he outlined ways of "guaranteeing and insuring to our subjects *perfect security of life, honor, and fortune" (life, mind, property)*. While couched in terms of "subjects" rather than citizens, and still attributing the Ottoman decline to "disregard for the sacred code of laws and the regulations flowing therefrom,"[218] even the modern reader is struck by a modest harmony between these words and Western constitutional language based on natural law rather than Shari'a. This opening failed because of Sultan Abd-ul-Medjid's successors, the "inertness" of the English Embassy in Constantinople, and especially the derailing effects of incursions by the Czar into the Bosporus. Ottoman entanglements in European politics had begun very early under in the sixteenth century and the politics of Francis I, and played into the dismemberment of the "sick man of Europe." Dismemberment enabled creation of modern Turkey, but this success was partly a protest against long-discussed partition of Anatolia by the European powers.

In 1832 Lord Stratford, Britain's resident supporter of Abd-ul-Medjid's failed initiative to bridge the Middle East into a cleaner future, sent a dispatch to England that read in part: "That chance (shoring up the Empire) is a very precarious one at best, and should it unfortunately not be realized, the dismemberment which would ensue could hardly fail of disturbing the peace of Europe through a long series of years."[219] The First World War removed the veil from crippling divisions within the Arab world at the same time that both the region and the West entered into a new twentieth century of increasingly shallow-rooted political and economic experiments. The twenty-first century ushers in a sharpening encounter between the defensive aggressiveness of Islam's archaic origins and the brittle ideologies and economic nostrums of a highly secularized West. To reconstruct at least a triangular discussion involving these two cultural residues and Christianity is the mission of Chapter 3, 4 and 5. Introductory reflections on the fit between religion and the chaotic and costly playfulness of human history are attempted in the following section.

RELIGION IN HISTORY/ETERNITY IN TIME

Cultures other than the Islamic world offer parallels to the encounters between Christian culture and the Middle East. Two cases involve nineteenth century personalities whose intense but marginally Christian views might compare with Mohammed. A third case is misuse of modern science by the religion of secular humanism.

As the prominent local religion and civic code of China, Confucianism eventually became the subject of a Rites Controversy that also divided Catholic missionary groups. Decided finally by the pope in 1715, the Controversy affected all of China and then India. Yielding to the possibly insular advice of a commission of nine Italian cardinals unfamiliar with the East, Pope Clement XI found local customs to be incompatible with missionary Christianity. Of the two competing views, the Jesuits proposed that reverence for ancestors was a civic code and did not entail worship of ancestors. The prevailing faction was the Dominican and Franciscan missionaries who held that Confucianism was a religion.[220] Pope Clement permitted to Christian converts only those customs "that can in no way be interpreted as heathen in nature."[221] Because of the Rites Controversy the Chinese Emperor Kangxi in 1721 dropped further interest in Christianity even as a moral support for society like Confucianism. As in Mohammed's Arabia and in the West the later Galileo incident, the spread of the Gospel was undermined at least partly by jealousies among religious orders within the Church. More than a century of earlier cross-cultural discourse begun under Matteo Ricci (1552–1610) fell by the wayside.

After three centuries China was in long-term decline and ripe for the anti-Christian and anti-human ideology of Karl Marx (1818–1883).[222] But for the Rites Controversy, China might be either more Christian today or more likely and as was feared, the Christian element might have been folded into an amalgam religion—in this respect similar to Islam. Entering the twenty-first century, four of the five or six remaining communist countries in the world are in the Far East and within the historic Chinese orbit. In addition to China this list includes Cambodia, North Korea and Vietnam. The others are Cuba and the newly infected Venezuela. A twentieth century Chinese Communist executioner of Christians paused to remark to a Christian pastor: "I've seen many of you die. The Christians die differently. What is their secret?"[223]

Today, the Church struggles to assert the autonomy of the missionary Church from all government structures, and in China to promote unity between the government controlled Chinese Patriotic Church and the underground and persecuted Church still in full visible communion with the universal Church.[224] The Christian population in China is growing and is possibly one hundred thirty million, fully one-tenth of the total population—the same ratio as when Constantine recognized Christianity in the Roman Empire (313 A.D.). The vast majority of Chinese Christians are either Protestant or a mixture of Christianity with Taoist and Buddhist ingredients,[225] much as Islam is a collage of Old Testament and early Arabian features. A very recent trend is the re-introduction of ancient Confucianism (Confucius died in 479 B.C.) with its civic code of obedience. Confucianism is called upon to fill the "ideological chaos" of a nominally Communist regime now in hot pursuit of global economic profit. The potential outcome is seen as neither democracy nor dictatorship, but a creed of "socialism with Chinese characteristics."[226]

The Church's message to modern China is that the Catholic Church is a faith of "inculturation"—the grafting of Christianity into all that is good and compatible with the natural law in indigenous cultures and ways of life. The result can be a symphony of all cultures supportive of the fully human person. The Second Vatican Council explains that "The Church, sent to all peoples of every time and place, is not bound exclusively and indissolubly to any race or nation, nor to any particular way of life or any customary pattern of living, ancient or recent."[227] One participant in the council, Cardinal Danielou, cites Andre Gide to propose that such universality actually celebrates the genuinely particular: "There is nobody more English than Shakespeare and no one more universal; none more Italian than Dante and no one more universal; none more French than Racine and no one more universal."[228] The dream of Matteo Ricci for a Chinese Catholicism remains to be realized. And the world awaits a future where the best of human flourishing is more than an interlude between ages of oppression in the ancient world and more ages of possibly unenlightened neo-paganism in the future.

In the nineteenth century responses to the West in China and in the Arab world were generally the same. In both cases the path was to adopt Western science separate from the morally ambivalent Western humanism. Leading intellectual figures were Feng Kuei-fen in China and al-Afghani in the Muslim world. At the sociological level, Mohammed finds a personal counterpart in a similarly situated nineteenth century figure in China. Mohammed's contest with the Qurayish leadership in Mecca compares to Hung Hsui-ch'uan's competition for the respected status enjoyed by government officials across China and especially in the capital Beijing. In the turbulent 1850s personal success and esteem in China continued to be measured by scholarly achievement within the traditional scholar-gentry class (*shen-shih*). Rather than successful trade as in Mecca, it was a series of examinations built around the Confucian texts[229] that offered the path to prestige, security, and personal acceptance.

Hung Hsui-ch'uan suffered a nervous breakdown under the strain of these tests. With this affliction he begins to resemble Mohammed with his possible epileptic tendencies. In recovery Hung reported a vision revealing that he was a younger brother of Jesus Christ, much as Mohammed reported a visit to heaven to validate his claimed role as the final messenger of a jealous and monotheistic God. Instead of Mohammed's later jihad from Medina against a resistant Mecca, Hung ignited in central China the Taiping Rebellion (1851–1864). This outbreak was one of the largest insurrections in Chinese history and sought to topple the wobbly and ethnically separate overlords of Manchu China in Beijing (*T'ai-p'ing t'ien-kuo*: the Heavenly Kingdom of Peace). Hung's quest for reform—significantly assisted by his distorted view of Christianity—brought death to between twelve million and twenty million souls who perished either directly from combat or from widespread devastation and starvation.[230]

Like Mohammed, Hung co-mingled a religious message and fervor with economic and social disarray and political upheaval, in this case against the Manchu dynasty. Hung's movement was both a peasant-based political campaign and a religious war. Hung confuses himself with the Holy Spirit, and might even have drawn from parts of Islam.[231] Western writers see the Taiping government as theocratic: "(Hung) was both the spiritual and political head of the movement, and his proclamations derived their binding power on his followers in so far as they were considered to have come directly from God."[232] Numerically he exceeded both Charlemagne and Mohammed many times over in his mixing of violence with sexual excess. He kept as many as sixty concubines (and his allied father kept three hundred in addition to sixty-eight wives).[233] Parallel to the role of the Nestorian Christian Bahira with Mohammed, Hung absorbed fragments of Protestant Christianity directly from the prominent missionary Issachar J. Roberts, and the writings of others.[234] Rejection of past Chinese ancestor worship gives a further parallel to Mohammed's rejection of pagan idolatry. This feature of Confucianism predates other elements of the tradition that Hung chose to retain, like Mohammed, to ensure credibility with well placed followers. But unlike Mohammed who shunned any concept of God as Father, Hung took this term literally and anthropomorphically when he identified himself as the younger brother of Jesus Christ.

Decline of the central Manchu government increased its dependence on regional warlords to suppress the Taipings. The nineteenth century Western powers found it opportune to continue to deal with the weakened central government of China. In striking contrast with the isolation and failure of the Taipings in nineteenth century China, Islamic expansion succeeded to an extraordinary degree in the seventh and eighth century Middle East. Enlisted from the outside an ever widening circle of reconciled tribal groupings moved against those ever more distant cities and regions still individually opposed to the growing movement. Tribal independence was forfeited for the benefits of membership in the family of Islam, the ummah. Where imperial Rome's strategy for controlling its European periphery was divide and rule, the strategy of jihad was combine and advance. In China the absence of outside help placed the Taiping movement at the mercy of its own internal dissensions and shortcomings. Unlike Islam in Arabia and beyond—the Taiping Rebellion in China "became (only) another relic in the history of Chinese rebellions."[235]

Pseudo-religion and specifically pseudo-Christian alloys have an erratic effect on most cases of social transition away from the past. But with regard to the course of Islam, Muhammad Ali summarizes his namesake's achievements in glowing terms:

> It is remarkable that before the appearance of the Holy Prophet, three different movements were set afoot, all aiming at the reformation of Arabia (Judaism, Christianity, and the unitarian Hanif). Keeping at work for centuries with all the advantages that worldly power can afford, all these movements vanish in smoke. But then arises an individual who achieves, single-handed and in a state of utter helplessness, what they had failed to achieve. In the course of a few years, he brings about a transformation unparalleled in the history of the world.[236]

The second of our cases of historical culture contact with the West offers a much closer comparison with the details of Mohammed's religion. Historical Mormonism in the Western United States is unrelated to seventh century Islam,[237] but in many particulars Mormonism is comparable as a *type* that may be historically inevitable to the human imagination in the absence of Christian orthodoxy upholding the incarnation as fully and uniquely human and divine. Islam attributes a restored text—the *Qur'an*—to messages received by Mohammed directly from the Angel Gabriel beginning in 610 A.D. The founding prophet of Mormonism is believed to have been visited by the Angel Moroni beginning in 1823. The prophet Joseph Smith carries an exactly transcribed and untouchable text delivered on hidden tablets of gold. Islam's untouchable Arabic script (Q 13:37, 42:5, 46:13) is duplicated for Mohammed from an identical text in heaven. Both religions (and many others) have a supplemental set of writings, respectively the Book of Mormon and the Muslim hadith. Both religious leaders experienced initial persecution, the mystic Joseph Smith in Missouri and Illinois and Mohammed at Mecca. Both migrated to a selected new base of operations, Joseph Smith west to Salt Lake and Mohammed north to Medina. Islam is preached first to the tribes of Arabia, while Mormonism initially saw its mission among the indigenous tribes of North America. Mormons have believed that the American Indians are migrant descendents from the Israelite patriarch Lehi arriving via Arabia to the New World in 590. B.C. (coincidentally twenty years before Mohammed's birth), but do not reject possibly Asiatic origins. Under Islam the Prophet's lineage is from Ishmael who was to be the ancestor of "a great nation" (Gen 21:18).[238]

As with the *Qur'an*, where Christ is recast as a prophet pointing toward the coming of Mohammed (Q 61:5), the Book of Mormon also places words into the mouth of Christ. Under Mormonism we find Christ conferring unending life on three figures chosen to direct the new church in America. Islam grew by a system of conquest and plunder while the more peaceful Mormonism also expands its base, but differently through convinced and aggressive proselytism combined with permanent tithing.[239] Mormonism, like Islam, claims to be a restoration rather than a new religion, and claims an option for ongoing revelation.[240] Mormonism would restore a corrupted Christianity while Islam would restore the earlier and corrupted faith of Abraham from the very beginning of the Judeo-Christian narrative. Mormon apologists refer to a universal apostasy by a Church extinguished under Diocletian and ravaged by later strife among Protestants.[241] Islam is scandalized by early Byzantine Christian theological disputes of about the same period.

A defining difference between Islam and Mormonism is apparent in the writings of Elder Roberts who concludes with a *non-sequitor* that is poles apart from Islam: "Thus, after centuries of controversy the simple truth of the scriptures which teach that man was created in the likeness of God—*hence God must be the same in form as man*—was reaffirmed."[242] Islam shuns anthropomorphism.

Modern day and breezy theology makes a similar logical error as Mormonism on this point when it implies that because "God is love," it must be that love (only) is God. Islam and Mormonism differ in other subtle but very important respects. While Islam and Mormonism each tends to see itself as the perimeter religion that brackets all others,[243] the Mormon religion is theologically the opposite book end from Islam. Mormonism holds that Jesus himself is limited by "eternal law" which is "independent and co-eternal with God, *just as matter is.*"[244] Independent and eternal matter is a doctrine rejected by Christianity, and introduces a degree of pantheism that is accepted only by some Sufi mystics and overwhelmingly rejected by the rest of Islam (see Chapter 3).

A Mormon philosopher explains that "God does not have absolute power . . . but rather the power to maximally utilize natural laws to bring about his purposes."[245] When Christ heals the leper by touching him and saying "I do *will* it, be cured" (Mk 1:41, italics added)—the Christian is converted to Christ, not to the laws of nature. The Muslim attributes the miracle to a One who is other than Christ and other than any (autonomous) laws of nature. The Mormon awaits yet unknown laws of nature to explain all things. Under Islam, even the twelfth century Aristotelian Averroes conceded that at least the *Qur'an* was a miracle willed by God apart from the laws of cause and effect, although scholars do differ in the meaning of his statement.[246] Regardless of his actual meaning, Averroes' effort toward allegorical interpretation of the Book and away from divine intervention was later rejected in the history of Islam. On this point—the denial of the unbounded freedom and creative love of God—Mormonism is more allied with the secular thought of today than with the followers of Islam. Modern scientific pantheism—e.g., Stephen Hawking's quest to fully know "the mind of God" mathematically—also holds that God acts only through natural laws fully discoverable by our scientific method of replicable experimentation.

Considered together, the Muslim and Mormon religions appear to be very similar, but at a deeper level they are very *opposite* when viewed as alternative deconstructions of the Incarnation. Islam asserts a consistent transcendentalism mingled with earthly preoccupations, while Mormonism contains the spiritual and the divine within an exaggerated naturalism. Where Mohammed banished from Mecca the three sister offspring deities (related to Venus, to the rains, and to the sun), all of these three deities possibly of Syrian origin (Q 53:19–20), Mormonism teaches that "man has not only a Father in heaven, but a Mother also"—and that it is we who are the offspring.[247]

On a subtle point, unlike the Nestorian roots of Islam, Mormonism also holds that while Christ was not God, He in time did become fully divine, though still in a limited way.[248] Mormonism retains the Christian sense of God as Father, but holds that he was not always so. He also "came to his present exalted position by degrees of progress . . . there has been and there now exists an endless line of Gods, stretching back into the eternities, that had no beginning and will have no end."[249] Islam turns fully away from even the appearance of such multiple deities. And Mormonism, instead of tracing its legitimacy through the Old Testament lineage of Ishmael to Abraham as under Islam, believes instead that one of Christ's original twelve apostles never died. Instead, he held a ministry that is reflected now in the "prophets, seers, and revelators" of the Mormon community.[250] In Islam, the Shi'ite sect awaits the return of the twelfth Mahdi from the ninth century, who also did not die. Very much unlike Islam and also unlike orthodox Christianity, Mormonism proclaims that the New Jerusalem is terrestrial, and "will be built upon the American continent; that Christ will reign personally upon the earth; and that the earth will be renewed and receive is paradisiacal glory."[251]

The Muslim critique of Christianity, and that the Trinity constitutes polytheism and idolatry, would seem to actually apply better to the apparent polytheism of early Mormonism. Jesus Christ and the Holy Spirit are held by early Mormons to be "separate and distinct personages and subordinate gods"[252] to God the Father. Roberts explains that this triad "does not strike out of existence the many other Gods and Lords that live and have dominion in other universes and worlds . . . ."[253] Despite its own deities (plural), Mormonism claims to be monotheistic in the sense that while it acknowledges these additional gods, it does not worship them. Islam generally makes no claim to being a new revelation, while the self-understanding of Mormonism involves both a restoration and an ongoing revelation.[254]

For all of its theological confusion as viewed through orthodox Christian eyes, Mormonism still serves well today as a remarkable example and even persecuted defender of sound family values. This commitment to family is the feature for which Mormonism is increasingly subject to media attack in the West by radical secularists. In comparison, Islam is not nested and vulnerable within secular society and instead is a comprehensive "way of life" that redefines the family, society, and the state in a way that finds no counterparts in Western political theory (see Hassan in Chapter 3). Muslim polygamy is a compromise with the obscure Arabian culture already in place from the "days of ignorance" prior to Mohammed. The Mormon cult officially renounced polygamy altogether in 1890 in order to qualify for formal entry as a state into the broader United States (1896). Its founder, Joseph Smith, had had fifty or more wives, and earlier had been criticized in the press (the *Nauvoo Expositor*, 1844) for attempting for create a church-state (like the Islamic-state). To take on the form of modern nation-states, territorial areas of the Islamic ummah have made no such concessions beyond those allowed in the *Qur'an* and hadith. While no longer common, polygamy remains doctrinally accepted and a latent option even among Islamic immigrants into Western countries. This feature of Islam may yet become a point of growing intercultural friction, more so than is something so seemingly benign as the Muslim dress code.

Unlike Islam, for the past several decades Mormonism as a whole sees itself as moving away from citadel isolation and more toward mainstream Christianity. Getting at the core of Christianity—the nature of Christ—Islam dates the Christian fall from monotheism mostly in the fourth century and the Council of Nicaea (325) and the explicit doctrine of the Trinity. Mormonism sees Church corruption coming earlier at the end of the first century. In comparison to both Islam and Mormonism, the various Protestants sects remain Trinitarian, but assign a generous range of possible dates for the apostasy, reaching from the first decades to the moral scandals of the Middle Ages or to the materialist and rationalist excesses of the Renaissance popes.[255] With regard to human fallibility and worse, the Catholic Church distinguishes between actions of unworthy individuals, often great in number, and the Church itself as informed by the merciful indwelling of the Holy Spirit given at Pentecost.[256] Judging from history, there will always be those in all arenas who are corrupt or who more cleverly lead double lives.[257] Secular humanism would discredit religions other than itself in favor of a more radical new belief system—its own resistant belief in unbelief. Even at the expense of legitimate science, some scientists cannot imagine any distinction between their own calling and that of theologians. Our third narrative, in addition to the examples of China and Mormonism (above), accepts science but then proposes a leap of imagination and then a leap from imagination.

Our scientific and often spatial imagination scoffs at the seductive and mere idea of "eternity." Where did this unimaginable idea come from? For the believer, religious faith is precisely the willingness to believe what we cannot imagine. Revelation discloses both the presence of God and the capacious nature of the human person for God. "Christ the Lord, Christ, the final Adam, by the revelation of the mystery of the Father and His love, *fully reveals man to man himself* and makes his supreme calling clear."[258] By this Trinitarian doctrine we are freed from any anthropomorphic deity and are shown instead our shared Christocentric humanity. The Christian understanding of Christ is that, "He took the nature of a servant . . . *enlarging our humanity without diminishing his divinity.*"[259] How might we imagine all of this, and then leave inadequate imagination behind?

St. Patrick illustrated to the inhabitants of a north Atlantic island the threeness-in-one through the very imperfect analogy of a three-leaved clover. Other cultures have resorted to Euclidean geometry and the triangle. In the more sophisticated and equally inadequate thought of today, we might appeal to non-Euclidean fractal geometry for a mental image that at least begins to communicate to the modern mind. In fractal geometry, unlike Euclidian geometry, the shapes are irregular *and* remarkably exhibit the "*same* degree of irregularity at *all* scales."[260] Fractal geometry displays less a sense of symmetry, completeness and control. It gives us more of a restored sense of being on the edge of something that is at once both familiar and yet ever larger. A good example is a satellite photograph of a sandy coastline. This coastline image is *indistinguishable* from the edge of a single grain of sand as seen through a microscope.[261] Indeed, science now tells us that the entire universe is not self sufficient and eternal, but an unfolding of an original "singularity" smaller in size than a single proton, at the front edge of space-time, and pointing beyond itself to the unfolded and nearly endless cosmos as we know it through such modern means as the Hubble telescope.

Even if this natural cosmos bewilders the deliberate patterning assumed by a scientifically unsophisticated Aristotle, such a finding has no bearing on another purposive human universe in which we also find ourselves. Using fractals as an analogy, however insufficient, we might come to know in more than a physical sense, that rather than being isolated, every person is more originally part of a truth ever larger than himself or herself. Fractals might serve as the mathematical expression of the Medieval and perennial thought of Thomas Aquinas, his *analogy* between finite thought and infinite Reality. Fractals, like analogy, locate us at the edge rather than at the center, as if peering into ever new discoveries through either the Hubble telescope or simply an open window.[262]

In the reading of Scripture—no less a revelation than is all of the universe— the literal sense of interpretation points to a surplus of meaning and to interpretations that are more than literal, not less, and more deeply spiritual. The spiritual sense is something categorically different than the scientific quest to expand our knowledge of physical reality by constantly expanding boundaries and making new connections.[263] The spiritual sense points at once to an inborn morality here below, to allegorical insight, and even to a future life of eternal unfolding "face to face" with "God" (anagogical). Confounding our spatial imaginations, fractal geometry shows us that the detail is in the Gestalt and the Gestalt is in the detail. "The stone the builders rejected has become the cornerstone" (Ps 118:22). The poetry of the *Qur'an* recalls in this way the word of God to the Israelites: "Whoever saved a human being shall be regarded as having saved all mankind" (Q 5:32). In the Christian Scripture, we listen and God speaks, finally in the Word becoming flesh (Jn 1:14). This is because God is love and because with every breath we abide in Him (1 Jn 4:16).

A fractal enthusiast would feel no more diminished by the hundred billion galaxies or the hundred billion stars in each galaxy, more or less, than he would feel expanded by the same number (a hundred billion) of tiny neurons within his own relatively immense brain. With these measures, the Christian finds within himself a framework of moral imagination, and surprisingly again, he is elevated as the statistical "center" of this expanded and deepened universe. A primitive but overreaching science demanded in the Middle Ages how many angels can stand on the head of a pin. Science has spent the next few centuries discovering that within an original "singularity" much smaller than a single proton all of the countless galaxies once easily fit without risk of falling off.[264] And, according to Albert Einstein's Theory of Relativity, each and every planet and star and dust particle is a coordinate system rendering all planets, stars and dust particles—even our earth—equally the center of "the universe." Recalling Galileo, to say that *either* "the earth rests" or that "the sun rests" is a convention attached with equal validity to one or the other event in a consistent physics of coordinate systems.

Totally freed of our spatial imaginations, we are free to reconsider another reality as well. Is the unique genetic union involving the genome already the whole child unborn, a person with potential, rather than only a potential person eligible for extermination? Likewise, rather than an accident in essence, the cosmos conceals a universe open to more than statistics and mathematical reconstruction. Might the universe as a whole conceal an ever larger and divine romance revealed by the divinity? The English writer G.K. Chesterton remarked to his agnostic readership, "The size of the scientific universe gave one no novelty, no relief. The cosmos went on for ever, but not in its wildest constellation could there be anything really interesting; anything, for instance, such as forgiveness or free will."[265]

Even from the scientific perspective, the detail that most caught the eye of the lunar astronauts was not their own footprints on the moon, but—looking back—the blue-green wonder of our unique home rising "earthrise over the lunar landscape." Is there an inkling here that not only does human nature still have a place in the grand scheme of things, but that possibly the mystery of the human person *is* this "scheme," a grounded creation capable of "knowing" always more and having a "face to face" destiny with the Source? Nine years after publication of his *Origin of Species*, Charles Darwin—apparently only partly in step with his modern day imitators—rejected the notion of a colleague (Professor Asa Gray) that "variation has been led along certain beneficial lines." But then taking a side step, Darwin in the same breath also retained the humility of what we have noticed here as fractal incompleteness. Of the full range of human inquiries, he at that time still acknowledged that "*On the other hand,* an omnipotent and omniscient Creator ordains everything and foresees everything. Thus we are brought face to face with a difficulty as insoluble as is that of free will and predestination."[266] (As an exaggeration of both human fallen-ness and the gratuitousness of divine grace, this doctrine merited Darwin's judgment as a "damnable doctrine.")[267]

Today Darwin's resilient fractal insight—his "on the other hand"—points to a divide between two modern day scientific camps. First are those who posit an infinite number of universes as a way of overwhelming the statistical improbability of intelligent life evolving randomly within a single universe such as ours. Second are those who raise the ontological argument: how to account for the *existence* of any evolutionary process? Is existence due to a mechanism, or does the mechanism—as we reduce it—ingest within itself a freedom and pure act of love that we call creation? Always finite, the human mind finally avoids reducing either the scientific method of what and how, or the ontological argument (why anything rather than nothing?), to a mere detail or subset of the other.

Even in science, whether in leaps or increments, we build from what we know. And part of what we know is always remembering what we do not know. Rather than an error, Newton's law of inertia is a subset of the deeper and "special" theory of relativity, and this theory in turn fits within the still broader and "general" theory of relativity. But the reverse paradigm is not true: the deeper level of understanding cannot be conformed to the lower—relativity is not a subset of Newtonian physics. Within the scientific method of advancing theory and measurement there remains the imagination and the memory, and yet something more. By comparison religious and political revolutions too often impose apostasy in order to erase memory and often those who might have helped us to remember, moving ever in circles away from concrete reality and toward the closure of an imaginary millennium[268] or a final restoration of primordial beginnings.

Scientific models help explain *what* things are,[269] but not with any finality the mystery *that* they are. For those who see the ontological question—why is there anything?—the analogy of fractal openness might calm any stirrings against a living God of all that is. Fractal perception is a corrective to the ingrained mechanical universe of Descartes. There is "room" above, below, and within for a God who throughout all of human history, and uniquely in the Incarnation, is with us—a Trinitarian God who is "over all and through all and in all" (Eph 4:6). Against the accidental void of the agnostic, such a God presents Himself as the singular "person" of Christ. Catholics particularly are attentive to the ever renewing words of Christ at the last supper. He becomes present, really and not only symbolically, in each consecrated host of the Eucharist, because He now indwells the Church as a whole. He indwells the Church because he is sacramentally present. In the consecrated host is to be found in person the One, and the True, the Beautiful and the Good. The Son of the Father—also our True Self—is present to our individual selves without ever leaving the heavenly Father. This is not our humiliation before the truth, but the humility of the Truth *setting aside* its splendor for our benefit. In that splendid term of Simon Weil, God is not powerless, but rather "power free." The thing about the crucified Christ, remarks Weil, is not that he was innocent, but than within his innocence he did not retaliate.

In the recent century, the obscure Cistercian monk Dom Boylon in Ireland gives us a Trinitarian picture more advanced than St. Patrick's clover leaf, again untroubled by our regnant Cartesian and mechanistic rather than fractal mathematics: "The pattern of the whole is found in each of its parts, and in fact the parts are only incorporated into the whole by being made conformable to the whole—who is Christ. For Christ is all in all. The whole Christ—head and members—resembles Christ the head, for each Christian is another Christ."[270] It is not that God multiplies himself, but that *what exists* is one creation and this one creation is transparent, and at its heart uncreated and undimensioned. In the canticle of Mary we have this remarkable and perennial expression: "My soul doth magnify the Lord" (Lk 1:46).[271]

With an insight equal to that of Andre Gide, and to others who find that the universal dwells in the particular, Pope Benedict XVI links the receptivity of faith toward the truth to the capacity of reason (*logos*) to know the truth. He finds that "logos means an option for a personal, creative meaning . . . it is at the same time an option for *the primacy of the particular as against the universal*. The highest is not the most universal but, precisely, the particular, and the Christian faith is thus above all also the option for man as the irreducible, infinity-oriented being."[272] At the theological level, and nine centuries before fractal mathematics (and yet anticipating the self-similarity of fractals) St. Bernard of Clairvaux, the preacher of the Second Crusade, gave us this: "In those respects in which the soul is unlike God it is also unlike itself."

ISLAM: A CHRISTIAN "HERESY"?

Mohammed made no claim that Islam is a new religion. Islam sees itself as a restoration of the monotheism of Abraham which has been either corrupted by Jews or mingled by Trinitarian Christians with idolatry.[273] The Trinity, the Incarnation and the Resurrection as the central teachings of Christianity are all dismissed by Islam, and by various heretical movements within the Christian West. These denials are among eighty-eighty heresies of the first four centuries identified by St. Augustine. In his elaborate treatise on the Trinity, St. Augustine remarks: "Yet, when the question is asked (of the Trinity), What three (?), human language labors altogether under great poverty of speech. The answer, however, is given, three 'persons,' *not that it might be (completely) spoken, but that it might not be left (wholly) unspoken.*"[274] As in the articles of the Nicene Creed regarding the Trinity, finite reason does its best to encircle the event of Christ which it can never fully define. "Since our weak minds cannot comprehend the Father or the Son, we have been given the Holy Spirit as our intermediary and advocate, to shed light on that hard doctrine of our faith, the incarnation of God."[275] The Church uses the term *circumincession* for the inner life of the one God—the constant movement and mutual indwelling. The formal definition is "the indwelling of the three distinct Persons of the Blessed Trinity, *the Father being whole and entire in the Son and in the Holy Spirit, and each one in the other as well as in the Father.*"[276]

The early twentieth century Catholic writer, Hilaire Belloc, reopens the ancient question whether Islam itself is not a different religion, but a Christian heresy. It would be the only heresy to emerge outside the geography of Christendom.[277] Politically, even on the eve of the Second World War, Belloc saw beyond current events of mere power and ideology in Europe to warn against a still deeper struggle between the West and the dormant world of Islam. In 1938 he wrote:

> I say the suggestion that Islam may re-arise sounds fantastic—but this is only because men are always powerfully affected by the immediate past—one might say that they are blinded by it. Cultures spring from religions; ultimately the vital force which maintains any culture is its philosophy, its attitude towards the universe; the decay of a religion involves the decay of the culture corresponding to it—we see that most clearly in the breakdown of Christianity today. The bad work begun at the Reformation is bearing its final fruit in the dissolution of our ancestral doctrines—the very structure of our society is dissolving.[278]

Belloc joins others by defining heresy in partly positive terms as "The dislocation of some complete and self-supporting scheme by the introduction of a novel denial of some essential part therein."[279] Yet, by its denial or reductionism the heresy becomes a counterfeit for the real. And the real is Christ who is both the path and the goal: "the way, the truth and the life" (Jn 14:6). To carve away at this abyss of truth is to remove man entirely, even in this life, from the Risen One who fulfills the transcendentals of human flourishing—love, the one, the true, the good and the beautiful. Like Christianity, Islam is monotheistic, but the path of "submission" begins by dismissing the Trinity, the Incarnation, and the Resurrection as late Christian accretions to a more original Islam which is prior in history and in time, but not prior in the chronology of self-disclosing *being*. To what extent is Islam a Christian heresy or instead an independent and syncretic movement that simply happens to borrow into the *Qur'an* incidental Christian elements?[280] The Trinity "began" with the eternal Christ, not with its human definition at the Council of Nicea (325 A.D.). Already in the third century St. Irenaeus compared earlier Gnostic heresies to the core Rule of Faith of early Christianity.[281] The Rule is the original Trinitarian baptismal formula which serves as an advance look at the later and more comprehensive Nicene Creed centered on the historical presence of God—the Incarnation which is Christ—and his resurrection.[282]

Besides Belloc, other early Church Fathers also saw Islam as a heresy. The leading example is the eighth century John of Damascene who, like his father, served in Damascus as Treasurer of the Caliphate before becoming a monk. Likewise, in his *Divine Comedy* the thirteenth century poet Dante (1265–1321) portrays Mohammed as a heretic[283] and possibly refers to Islam as a Christian schism (a "dragon" or Satan).[284] Dante expresses the Medieval Christian understanding. Among Muslims the proposition that Islam is a Christian heresy is highly resented, although they do seek a role in dialogue more under the ecumenical label (that is, within an unbounded Christian dialogue) than clearly and more correctly as interreligious. Abdullah Yusuf Ali proposes that Islam supplanted the fragmented Eastern Church in the eighth century and that the Western Church "has since worked on definitely new lines, and its offshoots among the Protestant Churches have, consciously or unconsciously, been influenced by the broad principles of Islam."[285] The radical activist of the mid-twentieth century, Sayyad Qutb,[286] calls upon Muslims not to trust either the Jewish or Christian communities, but according to a modern apologist apparently centered his disdain only on those corrupt non-Muslims (described in Q 5:82–85) who claimed that Muslims were really Christians, "those who said we are Christians."[287]

Many modern Christian writers find "heresy" too harsh and culture-bound a term. These observers are more open to the notion that human traditions pointing back to "men of old" can carry an authentic intuition of the divine, even if not in the precise sense as self-disclosures from God.[288] The German Catholic philosopher Josef Pieper explains that the "men of old" could not have suspected God's later Incarnation, but still did think that it was possible that God would be the "'liberator of man'—which amounts to believing *fide implicita* in Christ" (with implicit faith). There could by what Pieper terms an "affinity of content" between the "holy tradition" of Plato, for example, and the Christian Annunciation.[289] St. Augustine proposed that Plato's ideas were inspired in part by Plato's possible familiarity with the scriptural "I am who AM" (Ex 3:14).

Another such connection in history would be between the birth of Christ in Bethlehem and the arrival of somehow expectant wise men from the east, who significantly were Gentiles and not Jews.[290] Holding aside its recent date, might the original elements of Islamic thought resemble a tradition from "men of old"? Islam comes chronologically later than Christ (unlike Plato, Buddha, Confucius, Lao Tzu and other men of old) and even rejects Him. But in its geographic and cultural isolation, as a monotheistic religion might it still be in a logical and spiritual sense prior to Christ possibly with "implicit faith" in Pieper's pre-Christian meaning of the term? In his commentaries on Scripture, the Presbyterian scholar William Barclay observes: "Never has there been any time in any nation when the Spirit of Christ was not moving men to seek God and guiding them to find him. Sometimes they have been blind and deaf, sometimes they have misinterpreted that guidance, sometimes they have grasped but fragments of it, but always that revealing Spirit has been there to guide the searching mind."[291] Might this overview also apply to a religion that borrows much of its insight from both elements of the Judeo-Christian tradition even as it prunes so much more from both, claiming as it does to replace Judaism and rejecting the whole Christ?

As a mystic Mohammed might have experienced a genuine private revelation or locution on the supreme oneness of God, but short of the Lord's self-disclosed inner and Trinitarian nature. After the first mystical experience, there came a long period before the next, months and perhaps even more than a year. This is *fatrat al-wahy*, or the cessation of revelation.[292] In the instance of Islam, the Jewish and Christian elements eventually become heavily alloyed with fragments common to all paganism and colored by tribal Arabian culture and Mohammed's own personal biography. The trappings of Arabian paganism include polygamy, additional slave mistresses, summary divorce attainable at will, annualized tribute or outright plunder, a lingering place for the *jinn* or demons, and transfer of Islamic leadership legitimacy based on the competing tribal customs. The traditional understanding of tribal chivalry (*muruwwa*) or "honor and revenge" is carried forward, although the *Qur'an* restricts the aggrieved from wide-sweeping vengeance and blood revenge: "Not for thee (but for Allah), is the decision: whether He turn in mercy to them, or punish them, for they are indeed wrongdoers" (Q 3:128). Jean Guitton summarizes this temporizing root of what is now the crisis of Islam: "Islam has not wanted to choose between Heaven and Earth. It proposed instead a blending of heaven and earth, sex and mysticism, war and proselytism, conquest and apostolate. In more general terms, Islam proposed a blending of the spiritual and the temporal worlds which neither in Islam nor among the pagans have ever been divided."[293] As in all cultures, the worldly alloy is the cleverness to accept the will of God as an endorsement of our own will. This tendency, in all of us, is the root evil of choosing to know both good and evil (Gen 2:16–17). Universal human willfulness is worse than a contaminant and an alloy. In the powerful term applied by C.S. Lewis (in *The Great Divorce*) such willfulness "vetoes" the will of God.

Even the record of Old Testament is often a mystery in this regard. To the will of God, Abraham offers his own son for sacrifice (Gen. 22:2), in a test of loyalty that is also a misguided practice of the early Semite culture he is called to leave behind. The patriarchs and others are polygamous (e.g., Gen 30:1–19, Dt 17:17 and 21:15–17) and are permitted concubines as prisoners or slaves (Dt 21:10–14, Est 21:7–11). Divorce is allowed because of the hardness of their hearts (Deut. 24:1–4). Some medieval Christian philosophers, e.g., Occam, simply concluded that while the natural law is permanent, as to its actual application God still can impose his overriding will. The later Aquinas tied natural law to both God's will and his intellect.[294] In the depth of our revealed fallen state we are inclined to attribute even to God the things that rise up within ourselves and that we do. It is at this point, that the Christian revelation speaks most clearly. The triune God accepted *for our sake* even this attribution of a weakness that is ours as the suffering of Christ who is the image of the Father.

Mohammed's mixed record is well-captured in the balanced picture painted of King David. Daniel-Rops writes of David:

> his humanity is no less remarkable than his greatness. We admire him as a hero, and we cannot refrain from loving him. Certainly his character is not perfect, and although he has some of the characteristics of a saint—his boundless love for the One God, his trust in providence, his faith—we cannot overlook the fact that he is the product of a barbarous age, in which neither violence nor treachery were judged by the standards of our own laws and literature, if not our behaviour.[295]

Mohammed's very small band at Medina, in danger of likely extinction, is absorbed by the ethic and passion of tribal self-assertion—at first defensive, but pointing to an ever broader definition of interiorly righteous and then exteriorly self-righteous jihad. The crucial compromise with earlier "days of ignorance" might have come less with the final messages of Mohammed than with a separate decision by his immediate successors who consolidated and edited the polyglot *Qur'an*. It was their decision to preserve a tenuous tribal alliance and to then extend this unity beyond Arabia through ever expanded conquest.[296]

In this Arabic culture, biblical historians might see the echo of Pharaoh in the life of the Exodus Jews. It was to the plundered gifts of Egyptian gold (and the old life) that the Jews in flight became too attached, finally to fashion the golden calf at foot of Mount Sinai. Of Mohammed's non-material borrowings from his environment, an unsympathetic Swiss historian, Jacob Burckhardt (1818–1897) proposes: "From his youth on, Mohammed, with the aid of at least ten people, looks over the faiths of the Jews, Christians, and Parsis, and steals from them any scraps that he can use, shaping these elements according to his imagination. Thus everyone found in Mohammed's sermons some echo of his accustomed faith."[297] Today one or two modern Islamic scholars even propose a much broader eclecticism. They propose that the people of all major religions—Confucian and Hindu, etc.—should be regarded as "people of the book."

Or again, rather than a Christian heresy, or a more worldly alloy still seeking God, is Islam more like a Jewish sect along the lines of the half-converted Judaizers of apostolic times? The Islamic stress on submission to a mostly distant God of the Law is more in harmony with the esthetics of early Judaism than it is a heretical distortion of the new life of Christianity.[298] But unlike a Jewish-like sect, Islam is a denial of the resilient reality of the Jewish Covenant[299] which is never rescinded by God, and the Jewish hope in a messiah. Especially in his oath to David, Yahweh's covenant is unconditional (Ps 2:7, 2 Sam 7). The self-understanding of Christianity is that the Church carries forward the promise made to David that his "house . . . shall be blessed forever" (2 Sam 29). With Christ as messiah, it is God who sustains and then fulfills the unbroken Covenant. The fulfillment is both continuity and, more, a bringing of Israel (and each of us) to the point where in faith we might not reject the incomprehensible nuisance of God appearing at a discrete point in human history. The fulfillment "means not only rationality and freedom . . . but also, from the very beginning, the capacity of having a personal relationship with God, as 'I' and 'you' . . . and therefore the capacity of having a covenant."[300] Islam replaces both hope in the covenanted Messiah and Christ the fulfillment, with a book as the "confirmation" and "fuller explanation" (and usurper) of earlier revelations (Q 10:37). The *Qur'an* is the "word made book" as delivered through the final Prophet. The remnant and reshaped hope of a messiah carries over only in the Shi'ite sect as it waits for an earthly return of the Mahdi.[301]

To help advance his particular view that Islam is a Christian heresy, Belloc groups Islam with four other mostly later heresies in the West. The first heresy is early fourth century Arianism—the idea to kill the Church by demoting its founder from the level of divinity to something else if only a shade less.[302] Very much like the later Islam, Arius insisted on the totally transcendent oneness of God: "God is incommunicable, otherwise we should have to admit that He is composed of elements, susceptible to divisions and changes."[303] The offshoot heresy of Nestorianism influenced Mohammed, but Belloc casts Islam itself as a direct heresy in its own right: "The attributes of God he (Mohammed) also took over in the main from Catholic doctrine: the personal nature, the all-goodness, the timelessness, the providence of God, his creative power at the origin of all things, and His sustenance of all things by His power alone. . . . Mohammed preached with insistence that prime Catholic doctrine, on the human side—the immortality of the soul and its responsibility for actions in this life, coupled with the consequent doctrine of punishment and reward after death."[304]

Of the remaining three European heresies treated in Belloc's presentation the first is Medieval Albigensianism or Catharism which in Europe came between the times of the fifth and sixth crusades. Albigensianism was centered in Spain and southern France. As a Manichaean sect it preached radical enlightenment and spiritual purity, and accounted for evil and the physical world by attributing both to a second god. Theologically it held that the Church, because it preached an incarnate God, was of satanic origin. It rejected any continuity between the Old and New Testaments. Ideologically it was strangely modern in that it had no prohibitions against suicide, contraception, the now routine and unspeakable crime of abortion or euthanasia. Another of Belloc's heresies was the Protestant Reformation which he defined as an effort to establish a counter-church.[305] The triggering scandal for Luther was the buying and selling of "indulgences," a practice that began as an incentive for taking part in the Crusades against Islam. The final heresy is our Modern Age which typically imposes—as an article of faith—the proposition that only experimental knowledge can tell us anything about reality.

A family of heresies that Belloc does not identify, and that also has a shaping influence on later Islam, is Gnosticism.[306] Early Gnostic thought preceded Christianity and then shortly after the writings of the evangelists emerged in the Gnostic gospels. Gnosticism typically claims revelation of secretive knowledge and delivery of this knowledge through a single and favored individual. Gnosticism displays a radical dualism in the form of light over darkness and often preaches—and probably begins as—a break between belief and morality. Gnosticism disdains the created world. Islam often disconnects belief from morality, but it does not go so far as to preach a Demiurge or second and lesser god as the source of physical reality.

Gnostic Moslems think of the world more as a necessary emanation from God than as a free creation, and place a "way of life" above the natural law, but it is expansive modernity that more often resembles and reinvents ancient Gnosticism. For some, science replants religion on a plane within itself to fill any psychological gaps left behind by the scientific method. This tendency toward monism—the blurring of the material and the spiritual—includes the promise of building a heaven on earth, if only we will set aside for a moment the troublesome moral squint of natural law and yield to inborn pride in any of its legion of forms. "All these things I shall give to you, if only you will prostrate yourself . . ." (Mt 4:9). Unlike secularist modernity, Islam accepts the resurrection, but with modernity it denies redemption.

A distinct and possibly Gnostic-like sense of special and sufficient *guidance* is also given in the *Qur'an* (for example, Q 2:38), to confirm "the guiding light of all those who achieved the highest enlightenment on spiritual matters."[307] Or again, "Nothing can prevent men from having faith and seeking forgiveness of their Lord, now that guidance has been revealed to them . . ." (Q 18:55, also Q 10:35, 45, and Q 47:16, etc.). Is this the guidance a presumed revelation, or is it the implicit wisdom of natural law and Josef Pieper's "men of old" (above)? Enlightenment in either the Gnostic or philosophical sense alerts the conscience but continues to miss the human need for redemption. Muslim scholars sometimes recruit Christian Gnosticism as useful in their own apologetics. They point to the non-canonical and allegedly Gnostic-era Gospel of Barnabas as verifying the Islamic proposition that Christ is less than divine.[308] With its general aversion for dichotomies or distinctions, as between the Redeemer and the Fall, or between theology and philosophy, to what degree is it still possible that the "guidance" given to Adam and reported in the *Qur'an* (Q 2:38) is less a dilution of Christian revelation than simply a vague understanding of what has been articulated in the West as the universal natural law? At first this seems most unlikely under some Qur'anic verses: "Say, 'we believe in God and that which has been revealed to us; in what was revealed to Abraham, Ishmael, Isaac, Jacob, and the tribes; to Moses and Jesus and the other prophets of the Lord. We make no distinction among any of them, and to Him we submit' . . . If they accept your faith, they shall be rightly guided; if they reject it, they shall surely be in schism" (Q 2:136–7).

But under what new Islamic leadership might the ambivalent concept of guidance be better understood as the natural moral virtues? In the Christian world the moral virtues—justice, prudence, temperance, courage—were first developed by non-Christian classical thinkers and only later adopted and spiritually deepened by Christianity. If pressed on this point of a universal natural law knowable by (and including) human reason, Muslims would almost certainly assign all truth to direct revelation. Islam discounts any implication that an autonomous God leaves an accessible and enduring imprint on any of His works other than the *Qur'an* and Shari'a law.

In contrast with the formative role of the Islamic State—within Christianity it is the morally formed human person who engages culture, the economy and politics even including the state. Christianity understands guidance, conscience, and the Law as including reason and then something more: *expectation.* Even of the Gentiles who (also) lacked the additional and fulfilling revelation, St. Paul said: *"They show the work of the Law written in their hearts"* (Rom 2:14–15). Pope Benedict writes that when Paul identifies the Gentiles as "a law unto themselves" (ibid.) he refers to:

The same experience that Israel itself had already had in contact with the 'God-fearers.' In the Gentile world, Israel had encountered something that was confirmed anew in the experience of the messengers of Jesus Christ: *their preaching responded to an expectation*. It encountered a basic *prior knowledge* of the essential elements of the will of God that had taken written form in the commandments, and this knowledge is found in all cultures. This primal knowledge develops all the more purely where it is not distorted by the arrogance of 'civilization.'[309]

The powerful insight here is the combination of prior knowledge and expectation, the natural law and the vista of hope.

Bedeviling the modern world is its own total substitution of activism—either individualist or collectivist—for prior knowledge and expectation. The *Qur'an* reasserts itself as a creation of the intersecting edges of Byzantine civilization and Arabia. It asserts a restored message formerly lost to Jewish corruption and deceit (e.g., Q 5:13) and Christian forgetfulness and polytheism (e.g., Q 5:14). Islam is expectation in reverse. In the *Qur'an* we find memory of parts of the Old and New Testament, but also a forgetting of the real history of God's patient and unfolding presence and final self-revelation to an expectant people as narrated in the full scriptures. The self-understanding of Islam on these points is that it stands outside of time, and is free of human engagement. In the Judeo-Christian tradition even human time is a gift of growing relationship, first in "the garden," then successively in family, clan, tribe and a chosen people, and finally in a faith that beckons even the Gentiles. Consider the glance between Christ on the cross and the repentant thief—his last companion in this world. Their eyes meet and suddenly, "This very day you will be with me in paradise (Lk 23:43)." History is long, but eternity takes only a moment.

For both the Jew and the Christian, history is the patience of God exercised within his own creation. In the order of reality, rather than only the order of sequential time, the *new life* of the Christian fulfills and infinitely surpasses the sacrificial Old Testament and the universal natural law it contains (the Decalogue).[310] This crowning new life of the commandments and beatitudes finally is written directly in minds and hearts as part of a fulfilled new covenant (Heb 8:7–13). Christ teaches that he came to fulfill the law (Mt 5:18): "It was not you who chose me, it was I who chose you to go forth and bear fruit" (Jn 15:16). John places revelation in order when he writes, "We, for our part, love *because he first loved us*" (1 Jn 4:19, italics added). The new life is not an abstract bond as is the Muslim ummah; it is a belonging personally to the Risen One. This new life admits to "no parallelism between grace and sin, nor even a kind of symmetry or dialectical relationship. The influence of evil will never be able to conquer the force of grace and the radiance of good . . . ."[311] The new life is described in an early Letter to Diognetus:

(And yet) there is something extraordinary about their lives. They live in their own countries as though they were only passing through. They play their full role as citizens, but labor under all the disabilities of aliens. Any country can be their homeland, but for them their homeland, wherever it may be, is a foreign country. Like others, they marry and have children, but they do not expose them. They live in the flesh, but they are not governed by the flesh. They pass their days upon earth, but they are citizens of heaven. Obedient to the laws, they yet live on a level that transcends the law.

The contemporary Muslim writer, Mahmoud Ayoub, admirably summarizes this contact point, this sign of contradiction between Christianity and Islam. He explains that the Muslim is to "let God be God," and that Humanity is fulfilled by his prophet and friends. Then he adds: "Christianity has insisted, and with equally uncompromising seriousness, on 'letting God be man" in order for "man to be divine.' The gap between an extreme Islamic view and an extreme Christian position on this point is admittedly vast."[312] Ayoub understands the extravagance of the Christian claim more clearly than do many and perhaps most Christians, but is his formulation of this extreme view accurately stated? It is not simplistically that God becomes man but that the Son, who is the glory of a Trinitarian unity, becomes man and points us to his Father. Ayoub proposes to resolve the difficulty by reducing it to "one of theological terminology rather than intent," and then by restating as a presumed substrate truth the untouched Muslim view. Ayoub simply collapses Trinitarian Christianity into Muslim Unitarianism.

Islam is "submission" (a term derived from the word *salaam* which also means peace) to a sovereign and (presumed) un-communicating God. Ayoub imagines a global homogenization of other religions into the always more original Islam: Judaism is stripped of hope through the covenant and Christianity is asked to deny Christ as the fulfillment of revelation in the fullness of time. The Christian response to Ayoub remains that *because* God is God, let the "new man" come to be through the indwelling of the Holy Spirit.

One of the very few parallels in the New Testament to Islamic *submission* to an ever distant God is found in St. Paul. But as an injunction the selected verse is to be interpreted in the context of the preceding and following two verses. Taken together, we read: "Defer to one another out of reverence for Christ. (And only then) Wives should be *submissive* to their husbands as if to the Lord . . . (and then) Husbands, love your wives, as Christ loved the church. He gave himself up for her . . . ." (Ephesians 5:20–25). Marriage is submission only within the encircling, shared, and transforming deferral to one another. As such, marriage is also an icon for Christ's relationship to his Church and even to the inner life of a triune God. In this mutual transparency and presence, the Christian proposes—does not impose—a fulfillment: "And we have come to know, and have believed, the love that God has in our behalf. God is love, and he who abides in love abides in God, and God in him" (1 Jn 4:16).[313]

Contrary to Muslim fears, the Christian does not claim divinity, but instead accepts the divine invitation to *participate* in God's divinity as He first participates in our humanity. That the Incarnation is possibly a concrete reality transforming history and transfiguring ourselves, rather than a merely conceptual "position," remains for both Islam and modernity not only unsuspected but unwelcome. "In the beginning was the Word, and the Word was with God; and the Word was God . . . And the Word was made flesh, and dwelt among us. And we saw his glory—glory as of the only begotten of the Father—full of grace and of truth" (Jn 1:14).[314] In comparison and under Islam the earlier insularity found in the once chosen people of Judaism is simply replicated in tribal Arabia and then expanded in the accreted global ummah. The resulting boundary line between insiders and outsiders of the conglomerate mega-tribe remains unquestioned and has become only clearer over the centuries. In 622 when Mohammed was rejected by Christians as well as Jews in Medina, he no longer attempted to amalgamate a sort of condominium monotheism from what he initially saw as Jewish, Christian, and Muslim branches.

There remain the similarities and the differences. Today as we enter the third millennium, John Paul II offers a comparative overview of Islam and the two other world monotheisms:

> Whoever knows the Old and New Testaments, and then reads the Koran, clearly sees the process *by which it completely reduces Divine Revelation*. It is impossible not to note the movement away from what God said about Himself, first in the Old Testament through the Prophets, and then finally in the New Testament through His Son. In Islam all the richness of God's self-revelation, which constitutes the heritage of the Old and New Testaments, has definitely been set aside . . . . Some of the most beautiful names in the human language are given to the God of the Koran, but He is ultimately a God outside of the world, a God *who in only Majesty, never Emmanuel*, God-with-us. *Islam is not a religion of redemption*. There is no room for the Cross and the Resurrection. Jesus is mentioned, but only as a prophet who prepares for the last prophet, Mohammed. There is also mention of Mary, His Virgin Mother, but the tragedy of redemption is completely absent. For this reason not only the theology but also the anthropology of Islam is very distant from Christianity.[315]

Pope John Paul II did genuinely admire the piety of the *followers* of Islam. His previous remarks continue as follows: "(Nevertheless), the religiosity of Muslims deserves respect. It is impossible not to admire, for example, their fidelity to prayer. The image of believers in Allah who, without caring about time or place, fall to their knees and immerse themselves in prayer remains a model for all *those who invoke* God, in particular for those Christians who, having deserted their magnificent cathedrals, pray only a little or not at all."[316]

Compared to Christianity, it is not that Islam as a religion offers "no half-tones in their register of vision" (T.E. Lawrence, above), but that it is all monotone almost as if sun bleached. Islam offers resurrection but no redemption, a transcendent God but one whose transcendence is finitely bounded from real entry into this world—distant and above but not close and within. Allah is merciful but not mercy itself, and while he knows our suffering he does not suffer with us. Rather than a heretical defection from Christian monotheism, Islam is more of a distant and distorted echo. From the Old Testament the *Qur'an* retains references to Moses and to his Commandments, but even these are not actually listed. An early twentieth century perception was that Muslim nations and their members exceed even some Western actors in violation of the Decalogue and natural law:

> Sin is merely a transgression of statute. Falsehood, deception, robbery, murder have no moral quality whatever. There are entirely legitimate when used for the furtherance of the Moslem and even for the furtherance of individual advantage . . . the great mass of the Moslem community is utterly ignorant of what evangelical Christians understand by the sense of sin. Mistakes are to be atoned for by punishment, penance or remission of penalty; forgiveness in the Christian sense of the term is almost absolutely unknown.[317]

Abdullah Yusuf Ali remarks that sin is more a victimization by "the tree of Evil" than a self-inflicted betrayal of our selves and of our God who indwells at our center. In his commentary on the *Qur'an* Ali blurs the nature of sin when he presumes that earlier and rejected biblical texts confuse sin with human sexuality.[318] The more complete Christian insight begins with the two situations or states of the human person. One is the state of original sin and the deeper state is that original innocence which is the original covenant with God so soon "broken in man's heart."[319] Under this full doctrine of original sin the human person is more than what he seems—*not less*—and to some degree is most whole and free when he is a "resident alien" (St. Augustine's term) in a fallen world. The sin original to ourselves from the beginning, finally, is not only our undeniable and chosen distance from the freedom and infinite love which is God, but also from ourselves as the intended capacity to receive Him. The Christian notices that all of the capital sins gain entry through the most understandable sin of possessive lust. All infidelities are detected as versions of lust. St. Augustine says of women: "Those things are Yours, O God. They are good, because You created them. None of our evil is in them. The evil is ours if we love them at the expense of Yourself—these things that reflect your design."[320] He goes on to explain that the faces of lust are legion: the lust for revenge is anger, and then there are the lusts of avarice, obstinacy, vanity and—what "comes to light in every civil war"—the lust for domination.[321]

Abdullah Yusif Ali endorses in substance the meaning if not the full doctrine of original sin—pride—when he writes that "The great root of Evil and Unbelief is Self-glory or Arrogance . . ." (reference to Q: 38:74–76).[322] The denial of humility, or our ongoing participation in the effects of original sin, seems trivial to the imagination, nothing more than a reflex of self-sufficiency in place of trust. Under Islam, humanity seems bedeviled more by a cycle of forgetting good actions and then of remembering once again, but this reading of the full human condition is inaccurate and hints more toward the mystery cults. It is in the mystery cults—

neither Christian nor even Muslim—where the emotions "fade to a memory of no consequence. They are not capable of generating the spiritual transformation which is the stuff of conversion . . . ."[323] Islam has no place for baptism, and yet does call for remembrance and transformation in an ongoing conversion. Clarifying the Muslim teaching, Abdullah Yusuf Ali writes that "The Arabic word for 'Repentance' (*tauba*) means 'turning,' and the intensive word (*tawwab*) for God's forgiveness ('Oft-Returning'or 'Ever-Returning') is from the same root. For repentance, three things are necessary: the sinner must acknowledge his wrong; he must give it up; and he must resolve to eschew it for the future."[324]

For the Christian, it is only in the light of the total self-donation of Christ that we regain the *lost trust* which is restored within, because coming from above. The particular act of baptism, not to be repeated, is the normal path that finally touches the inner flaw and that unconditionally affirms each person in particular as truly destined for eternal life. Reception of this new life and trust brings continual conversion and the added vision of our fully human stature—as intended from the "beginning"—for eventual face-to-face presence toward the Presence. Church theologians propose that Adam represents "the truth that man and his sinful choices, *not* God or creation as he intended it, is the basis of the universal condition of 'unsalvation' in the world."[325] Christ serves as backlighting for the human condition, finally illuminating our understanding of the human past as well as our hope for the future.

The clear understanding of the mystery of evil is indicated, but still never exhausted, in the New Testament. Beyond (Muslim) "submission," the Christian knows that he is already claimed by a complete Giver. The author of Hebrews compares the Levitical motif of annual sin offerings, valuable to a point as fostering remorse, to the absolute self-offering of Christ who is not simply a messenger, but the "Good News" in person (the Gospel). Of the first sin offerings the New Testament writer explains, "In those sacrifices there is only a yearly remembrance of sins" (Heb 10:3). Then we read of the ultimate offering of Christ to the Father: "Behold, I come to do your will . . . By this 'will' we have been consecrated through the offering of the body of Jesus *Christ once and for all*" (Heb 10:9–10, italics added). Christians recognize in Christ the fulfillment of the promise made to Abraham and of the Law later delivered to Moses (Gal 3:17–18).

Is Islam less a heresy than it is a relapse into the Levitical world? Was Mohammed essentially misled by dissensions between Christians and Jews, and among Byzantine Christians themselves regarding the continuity of the Covenant and ultimately the undiluted mystery of the Incarnation? The entire saga of Islam might even be viewed as a footnote to St. Augustine's lamentation two centuries before the birth of Mohammed: "(a)ll who want to live piously in Christ Jesus . . . realize how many would-be converts are driven into perplexed hesitancy because of heretical dissention."[326] The *Qur'an* comments: "None disputed it (the Scripture) save those to whom it was given, and that was through envy of one another, after veritable signs had been vouchsafed them…" (Q 2:113). Muslim commentators interpret the Arian and Monophysite controversies of the Byzantine world as signaling the collapse of Christianity and permanent loss of its ability to influence pagan corruption. The early Caliph Ali speaks of the Taghlib (Christian) tribe in these words: "All they have borrowed from that Church is the practice of a wine-bibbing."[327] In his sermons, in early fifth century North Africa, St. Augustine repeatedly scolded the Donatist sect for this and other excesses and scandals. A Muslim commentator summarizes: "In short, Christianity—last of the revealed religions of the world—was practically defunct. It had lost all driving force towards moral reform."[328]

The worldview offered by Islam proposed that the biblical verses on the coming of the Holy Spirit upon the Apostles are metaphorical and refer to the later coming of the Holy Spirit through the final Prophet Mohammed. Because the one God is not understood as Father and triune, Mohammed—or his later compilers and editors—individualize even the Holy Spirit as the gift in history of Mohammed.[329] For the Christian, when Christ sends his Holy Spirit at Pentecost he is fully available to all those throughout history who are drawn into the community of witnesses, his Church. In their decision to include Gentiles within the fold, the apostles do not make this landmark decision alone: "It has seemed good to the Holy Spirit and to us" (Acts 15:28). Likewise, in the Christian doctrine of the Ascension—and unlike Mohammed's restoration of the faith of Abraham or his own singular journey to heaven— *all* are restored directly and lifted up to the One revealed in Christ, as Father.

Under Islam, the Trinity of God as Father, Son and Holy Spirit, is almost replaced by a parallel Triad of the One and unknowable, the *Qur'an*, and a highly revered Mohammed. One Muslim commentator writes: "The first link of the Israelite chain of prophets, Moses, was the embodiment of power and glory and the last, Jesus, that of humility and meekness, *but the Holy Prophet gave expression to both of these phases in his own person*. Thus every spiritual luminary sent forth but one ray, a beam of light in one particular direction, but the Prophet Mohammed was the center from which went forth rays of light in every direction . . . ."[330] Underscoring the finality of Mohammed the Prophet, the commentator refers directly to the *Qur'an*: "Muhammed is the father of no man among you. He is the Apostle of God and the Seal of the Prophets. Surely God has knowledge of all things" (Q 33:40).[331] To guard against the proliferation of further prophets, there are no physical descendents. To many Christian eyes, Muslim reverence for Mohammed eclipses and replaces devotion to the Mystical Body of Christ and the Church's sacramental life given by the indwelling Holy Spirit. With Western acquiescence, history would be reset to give us a final prophet in place of a totally new and everlasting covenant. Early Christian infighting over expressions of the Christian creed of the Incarnation scandalized Mohammed, but these steps toward doctrinal clarity reflect a deep necessity for reasoned accuracy on the unfathomable mystery of God and Man as revealed in Christ.

Belloc asks whether Islam as a possible Christian "heresy." More precisely, to what degree is Islam at its core Nestorianism in a turban? On this exact point Mohammed himself was not baptized and therefore cannot be a "heretic." No scholar has ever suggested that Bahira both proselytized this bright Arab boy or young man *and* baptized him.[332] Mohammed's religion is a rich tapestry of treasured Christian threads, sometimes distorted to fit a subjective pattern of personal inspiration from whatever source and Arab folk literature. In addition to the tribal elements carried into Islam, the *Qur'an* is held by some scholars to be an oral tradition itself rather than a fixed book. Theologically, it is a "self-aware" process open to divine "writing" and "rewriting."[333] Mohammed tested his early visions against his immediate his possibly Christian wife (Khadijha) and her Christian cousin (Waraqua, above). Within Christianity and the Church, movements of the Spirit are no longer to be tested with clan, but against the indwelling Spirit himself, given through the self-revelation of God in Christ as known through His Gospel witnesses. John writes: "Beloved, do not trust every spirit but test the spirits to see whether they belong to God, because many false prophets have gone out into the world. This is how you can know the Spirit of God: every spirit that acknowledges Jesus Christ come in the flesh belongs to God, and every spirit that does not acknowledge Jesus does not belong to God" (1Jn 4:1,2).

Mohammed's understanding of Christ probably was most influenced by Nestorian Christianity through Bahira, the possibly excommunicated Nestorian monk, and by other anonymous Christians met on the trade routes to Mecca. Of Bahira, legend holds that "(when they first met) . . . he remained a holy man, and taught Mohammed to believe in one God and to love Jesus Christ and His Mother."[334] But if Bahira was later driven from his monastic community, is it at least possible that he found Mohammed personally useful as a rising prophet in the desert?[335] Or if Bahira first met Mohammed when he was still a youth, might Bahira have relished the opportunity to proselytize the intelligent nephew of the guardian of the Ka'ba in order to introduce Christianity into Mecca? Would this cast of events classify Islam as a heresy planted in Arabia by a Nestorian? Mohammed's teachings were assembled and later edited by his followers into the *Qur'an*. The *Qur'an* points back to Abraham and misses the divinity of Christ. Christ is reformulated: "And of Jesus son of Mary, who said to the Israelites: 'I am sent forth to you from God to confirm the Torah already revealed, and to give news of an apostle that will come after me whose name is Ahmad' (another name for Mohammed meaning "The Praised One") (Q 61:6).[336]

Speaking on his own authority, the Christ of the Bible had this to say about himself and the God of Abraham: "If I glorify myself, my glory is nothing. It is my Father who glorifies me, of whom you say that he is your God" and "Abraham your father rejoiced that he was to see my day. He saw it and was glad" (Jn 8:54, and 8:56). Christ is the "I AM" revealed to Moses (Ex 3:14). While the eternal Christ is revered in the *Qur'an*, he is a Nestorian Christ created in time, "Jesus is like Adam in the sight of God. He created him from dust and then said to him: 'Be, and he was'" (Q 3:59). This verse of the *Qur'an* (Q 61) actually contrasts with a verse of the same number in the Old Testament Isaiah. In the temple Christ announced his mission by reading from Isaiah: "The Spirit of the Lord is upon me because he has anointed me; to bring good news to the poor he has sent me, to proclaim to the captives release, and sight to the blind; to set at liberty the oppressed, to proclaim the acceptable year of the Lord, and the day of recompense" (Isa 61:1–2; Lk 4:18–19). And, "*Today this scripture passage is fulfilled in your hearing*" (Lk 4:21, italics added).

The Christ of the *Qur'an* is Nestorian. When the Franciscan William of Rubruck was sent in 1253 by Saint Louis to visit the Great Khan in Asia, he found many Nestorians along the way and in the high courts.[337] The seventh century Islamic phenomenon easily might be understood as a prior and equally large field under Nestorian influence. If Islam itself were to qualify as a Christian "heresy," then either it was founded by Bahira as inquired above—an implausible and fanciful conjecture—or the definition of heresy must be gerrymandered beyond the definition given by Belloc. In similar cases, the early heresies of Gnosticism, Montanism, and Manichaeaism (and others) did not begin as distortions of selected Christian truths—Belloc's definition of heresy. Instead these theories are *imported* into Christianity from without, either from Judaism or heathendom.[338] In the very different case of Islam the definition of heresy would have to be distorted to embrace any non-Christian movements whenever they accrete or re-label deformed Christian elements as their own. Belloc's definition of heresy as an error of deletion would be expanded to include the opposite errors of fusion.

As an Orthodox monk, Bahira would have been familiar with the spirituality of the early *Philokalia*, an ancient collection of Orthodox writings. Contributions to this work began in fourth century and continued into the fifteenth. Parts would have been available to Orthodox monasteries beginning in Byzantine times and would have constrained Bahira from teaching many of the excesses eventually lumped into Islam. The term philokalia is defined as the exclusive "love of the beautiful, the exalted, the excellent, understood as the transcendent source of life and the revelation of Truth." Islam is a religion that relishes beauty, even claiming that the Arabic poetics of the *Qur'an* are part of what demonstrates its divine origin. Orthodox priority is also placed on the spirituality of inner stillness and of stable meanings. The concept of jihad—defined originally by Islam as inner struggle—is unstable and even in the early years evolved under historical opportunism to include external conquest. Such degeneration of meaning is generally warned against especially in the several later volumes of *Philokalia*.[339]

There does remain the novel possibility that Western Protestantism expresses a deeper negation than is commonly understood as "heresy" in the Western tradition. This negation might also apply to Islam, and is the rejection of the Church's self-understanding as a profoundly sacramental partaking in the body of Christ, prior in time and substance to the translation of oral tradition into writing (the basis of later Protestant *sola Scriptura* theology). Christ as the Word (*Logos*) invites us in words to be corporately one with his divine Person just as He is one with the Father. Beyond the scope of this study is whether Protestantism in the West finds a direct counterpart with Islam on this point of sacramental membership. Islam, earlier in history than Protestantism, would be essentially an early protest less against the doctrine than the fact of the mystical body of Christ, even as it was a protest against the pagan cults of Arabia rather than any of their writings, per se. Instead of asking whether Islam is a Christian heresy, one could then ask whether some of the Reformation heresy addressed by Belloc is genetically akin to the phenomenon of Islam.

Arabia supplied Mohammed with a mixing zone of surrounding civilizations and local tribal culture. Islam is much more of an alloyed accretion onto a jealous monotheism than it is a heretical splinter away from Byzantine Christianity. Because Mohammed is not a Christian heretic and Islam is not a heresy, modern day dialogue between Christianity and Islam cannot be ecumenical as hopeful Islamic scholars sometimes propose. And as in Mohammed's time, Christianity is not eligible for inclusion between the brackets of an absorbent Islamic religion and culture. Instead, the relationship is inter-religious and intercultural; it yields to neither a Christian ecumenical format, nor to Islamic amalgamation. And because Islam does not easily distinguish between Mosque and State, the relationship between the West and Islam is an institutional and political riddle as well.

Chapter 3 begins with a partial examination of Shari'a law as an array of biography and folk culture and of Judeo-Christian borrowings, all authorized by Mohammed's private illumination for delivery to an Arabic-speaking region. The chapter concludes with an inquiry into the fused Islamic State. Chapter 4 matches this inquiry with a parallel inquiry into the distinct institutions of Church and State in the West and the historical and interactive developments of each. The lens for viewing these complex, and even overwhelming themes is the nature and history of the Catholic Church, and especially relevant outcomes of the two nineteenth and twentieth century Vatican Councils. The Protestant and liberal historian Lord Thomas Macauley (1800–59) is a remarkable and fitting transition:

> There is not and there never was on this earth, a work of human policy so well deserving of examination as the Roman Catholic Church . . . She saw the commencement of all the governments and of all the ecclesiastical establishments that now exist in the world; and we feel no assurance that she is not destined to see the end of them all. She was great and respected before the Saxon had set foot on Britain, before the Frank had passed the Rhine, when Grecian eloquence still flourished in Antioch, when idols were still worshipped in the temple of Mecca. And she may still exist in undiminished vigour when some traveler from New Zealand shall, in the midst of a vast solitude, take his stand on a broken arch of London Bridge to sketch the ruins of St. Paul's (review of Leopold von Ranke's *Political History of the Popes*, in 1840).

NOTES

1. George Wharton and Alan Burgoyne, in James Miller and H.S. Canfield, *The People's War Book*, Part II (Cleveland: R.C. Barnum, 1920), 13.

2. Writing prior to the Soviet collapse in 1991, one school of historians sympathized with the lost order: "National self-determination . . . opened the way for the later, more vicious ones (ideologies) by destroying the Habsburg Monarchy and its tolerant, humane traditions...Those nationalities 'liberated from the yoke of Hapsburg oppression' now suffer from a denial of personal liberty unimaginable in the

old Monarchy" (Bruce Pauley, *The Habsburg Legacy 1867–1939* [Malibar, Florida: Robert E. Kreiger, 1972], 169).

The Christian monarch was often a responsible person and ideally a mediator among factions and between the people and the experts. Contrary to Jacob Burckhardt's popular maxim, absolute power does *not* necessarily corrupt absolutely: "The fact that a monarch is responsible 'to God alone,' rather than to an assembly or a popular majority, is rather shocking to an agnostic mind . . ." (Erik von Kuehnelt-Leddhin, *Liberty or Equality*, [Caldwell, Idaho: Caxton Printers, 1952], 158).

3. Voting records for 1932 reveal that resistance to Hitler centered in southern and Catholic Germany. The Concordat between Germany and the Vatican was signed in 1933. Ignored, it led to Pius XI's anti-Nazi encyclical *Mit brenneder Sorge* (With Deep Anxiety, 1937).

At Versailles in 1918 Pan-Germanism was commented upon by an ideological President Wilson: "But this would mean the establishment of a great central Roman Catholic nation which would be under the control of the papacy, and would be particularly objectionable to Italy" (*Letters of Franklin K. Lane*, ed., A.W. Lane and L.H. Hal (Boston: Houghton, Mifflin, 1922, 297, cited in Erik von Kuehnelt-Leddihn, *Liberty or Equality*, op. cit., 244 and 355). German religious identity and the divergent regional voting outcomes for 1932 are shown on detailed maps, Figures 2, 3 and 4 inserted between pp. 224–5.

4. The two areas free from colonial control were the new and secular Turkey and Wahhabi Saudi Arabia.

5. Alan Palmer, *The Decline and Fall of the Ottoman Empire* (New York: Barnes and Noble, 1992), 262. Western powers noted specifically that a caliphate "could never be simply a spiritual leader, like a post-1870 pope . . . ." The needs of non-Turkish Armenians and Kurds within the new Turkish state of 1923 were not explicitly addressed in the constitution. Today, as part of possible restoration of relations between Turkey and Armenia, the two countries are considering formation of a commission to research the deaths of up to one million Armenians at the end of the First World War. The earlier period, or earlier stage, of savage Kurd and Ottoman persecution of Armenian Christians under Abdul Hamid (1894–5) is documented by eyewitness accounts in Edwin Bliss, *Turkey and the Armenian Atrocities* (New York: M.J. Coghlan, 1896).

6. In Rene Voillaume, *Seeds of the Desert* (Notre Dame, Indiana: Fides Publishers, Inc., 1964), 134.

7. Ibid., 15.

8. In the *Paradiso*, Canto XI, Dante says that St. Francis sought martyrdom and that failing this he left; and implies that the Sultan might not have been attracted to Lady Poverty. In the mid thirteenth century, fearful of the Mogul invasions, other Franciscans made their way to Mongolia in unsuccessful efforts to convert the Khan, and with the remote possibility of even joining in an alliance against Islam. One of these (John of Pian de Carpine, 1180?-1252) had been a companion of St. Francis (See Daniel Boorstin, *The Discoverers* [New York: Random House, 1983], 128–133.).

9. No published source: A discussion in 1995 with the Very Rev Stephen Barham, an archimandrite of the Melkite Greek Catholic Order.

10. The English translation of Ibn Ishaq's biography became available in 1955: Alfred Guillaume, *The Life of Muhammad: A Translation of Ibn Ishaq's Sirat Rasul Allah* (Oxford: Oxford University Press, 1955 (1967).

11. Many of the following biographical details are from Humphrey Prideaux, *Life of Mahomet* (London: Curll, Hooke, Fleetstreet, Mears and Clay without Temple-Bar, 1718 [and 1696]). A more friendly and uplifting account is given by Tariq Ramadan, *In the Footsteps of the Prophet: Lessons from the Life of Muhammad* (New York: Oxford University Press, 2007).

12. An alternative account holds that Khadijha fell in love with Mohammed from afar, and that they married without delay. She was wealthy and removed his financial inability to support a wife (Zaid H. Assfy, *Islam and Christianity* (York, England: William Sessions, Ltd., 1977), 65.

13. Yemen had been already in long decline and was overrun by the Persians the year before Mohammed's birth.

14. The lineage toward a great nation of twelve tribes is found in Gen 17:20 and 25: 12–17. Gen 17:19 also applies: "God replied: "Nevertheless, your wife Sarah is to bear you a son, and you shall call him Isaac. I will maintain my covenant with him . . . ." In a different setting, and with dependence on imagination alone, the genealogies of all the early kings of all the English kingdoms were traced by a priest in the late eighth century to the god Woden and excluded all sons born out of wedlock or to concubines. In the epic *Beowulf*, the mother of Grendel is traced to the outcast Cain in the Old Testament (Peter Brown, *The Rise of Western Christendom* [Hoboken, N. J.: Wiley-Blackwell, 2003], 306,314).

15. On the American continent the Sioux prophet Sitting Bull, who is mistakenly regarded more as a warrior, looked back in a similar way to tribal origins. The former clergyman W.H.H. Murray recounted these words as part of his eulogy at the time of the prophet's death: "You tell me of the Alenaznis. They are our forefathers and the forefathers of all red men. They were the men of the Dawn. They came from the East. They were born in the morning of the world. The traditions of my people are full of the Alenaznis. They rocked the cradles of our race" Fletcher Johnson, *Life of Sitting Bull and History of the Indian War* [Edgewood Publishing, 1891], 194–203).

16. Mohammed's possibly considerable inheritance had been deflected to his uncles when Mohammed's grandfather outlived his father. We also read in the *Qur'an*: "Give orphans the property which belongs to them" (Q 4:3), and "Let not the rich guardian touch the property of his orphan ward (Q: 4:7), and of an uncle, "May the hands of Abu-Lahab perish! . . . Nothing shall his wealth and gains avail him . . . ." (Q 111:1). Note the possible parallel to the Psalms "Lord . . . you turn your ear to protect the rights of the orphan . . ." (Ps 10:18).

17. Prideaux, 6.

18. Less than a century earlier, and scandalized by the corruption of Rome, the young St. Benedict spent a similar three years meditating in a cave outside of the city, before becoming the founder of Western monasticism.

19. Gibb and Kramer, p. 275. By convention, citations of the *Qur'an* are identified by Q followed by the chapter or *surrah*, and then the verse or *ayat*.

20. Dawson, 131.

21. N.J. Dawood, *The Koran* (New York: Penguin, 1956), 2.

22. The full citation is in Alfred Giullaume, *Islam* (New York: Penguin Books, 1982), 26.

23. Dawson, 131. For a fifty-year interlude the Himyarites were actually a Christian kingdom.

24. Even as a restoration, the *Qur'an* is also portrayed as a revelation, e.g., "It is We Who Have sent down the *Qur'an* To thee by stages" (Q 76:23), and "...We have revealed it by stages" (Q 17:106).

25. Prideaux, 11. By comparison, under Christianity and as a fulfillment of the Old Covenant, there is a deeper kind of *restoration*: "Salvation entails the restoration of the image of God by Christ who is the perfect image of the Father" ("Communion and Stewardship: Human Persons Created in the Image of God," International Theological Commission, July 23, 2004, n. 47).

26. Abdullah Yusuf Ali, *The Holy Qur'an: Text, Translation and Commentary*, Lahore, Pakistan: S.H. Muhammad Ashraf, 1983 (1938), 1119n3731.

27. W.H. McNeill, *The Rise of the West* (New York: University of Chicago Press, 1953), 442–3. Some commentators often present Islam less as a restoration than as a final culmination of flawed Jewish and Christian portrayals of the divine.

28. Nestorius (d. 451) was a Syrian Christian, Patriarch of Constantinople in 428, and exiled to Egypt in 431. His purpose was to avoid the subtle and opposite heresy that the divine Christ lacked a human mind (Apollinarianism, 360–381 A.D.).

29. Prideaux, 25–6, citing Friar Richardi (who in 1210 studied in Baghdad), and two other early sources: Cantacuzenus, emperor of Constantinople who resigned his Empire to son-in-law John Laleologus in 1355, and Bartholemaeus Edessenus, monk of Edessa (date unknown). The *Qur'an* barely notes the saying that "a mortal taught him" (Q 16:103). Some Muslim scholars believe that Bahira first noticed a twelve-year old Mohammed in Syria while he was still working for his uncle. Prideaux contends the meeting came only at a later date when Mohammed was beginning to define his monotheism. According to Prideaux's sources, Muslims hold that Bahira saw in the young Mohammed the same "Prophetic Light" that had shown first on Adam and then on Abraham and Isaac and following generations of prophets, but that the light placed on Ishmael was suppressed until the coming of Mohammed.

30. "We know indeed that they say, 'It is a man that teaches him.' The tongue of him they wickedly point to is notably foreign, while this is Arabic, pure and clear" (Q 16:103).

31. Prideaux, 26, compared to the more skeptical Mahmoud Ayoub in Irfan A. Omar (ed.)r, *A Muslim View of Christianity* (Maryknoll, New York: Orbis, 2007), 204.

32. Of Arianism, the nineteenth century Cardinal Newman writes: "The Church of Rome is not idolatrous, unless Arianism is orthodoxy" (Philip Boyce [ed.], *The Virgin Mary in the Life and Writings of John Henry Newman* [Grand Rapids, Michigan: William Eerdmans Publishing Co., 1999], 193).

33. In 1605 when the Jesuit missionary Matteo Ricci reached Peking, there remained living evidence that Nestorian recruits in the Khan's Empire at the time of Marco Polo might have been garrisoned in the city (possibly referred to by Polo as

Cambaluc). Such reports of a Nestorian presence were also made by Franciscans in the thirteenth century, including John of Plano Carpini, one of St. Francis' first companions. See Vincent Cronin, *The Wise Man from the West* (Garden City, NY: Image, 1957), 205–9. Where Nestorian Christian elements were retained in Arabia and the *Qur'an*, by Ricci's time (writes Cronin) the few followers in China had been persecuted by the Muslims and converted to either Islam or Buddhism.

34. Ayoub in Omar (ed.), 120–1.

35. In historical fact, the referenced Jacobite Church is named after Jacobus Baradai, sixth century Bishop of Edessa and member of the broader Monophysite sect, long before the ninth century events cited by Ayoub.

36. The stone may serve the human need to connect ourselves to a distantly transcendent god or at least to the cosmos. During the Enlightenment meteorites were discarded from French museums because of the scientific contempt for "lay people" witnesses to impact events. The bishop of Zagreb countered this bias in 1751 when he credited eyewitness accounts and collected a recent meteorite. The results were published in 1794 by the German physicist, E.F. Chladni marking the beginning of the modern science of meteorites (Stanley Jaki, *Miracles and Physics* [Front Royal, VA: Christendom Press, 1989], 94).

37. Bede the Venerable, *History of the English Church and People*, Leo Sherley-Price and R.E. Latham (trans.), (New York: Penguin, 1986), 1, 30, 92.

38. By coincidence seventy is also the traditional number of the Jewish Sanhedrin, and the number of Hebrew scholars who in the first century A.D. translated the Hebrew Bible into Greek, the *Septuagint*, and at one point was the number of Christ's disciples. Muslim apologists notice that just as there are twelve imams, so too did (the earlier) Christ select twelve apostles (the number of the biblical tribes of Israel). The founder of the second century Manichaeism also mimicked Christianity with twelve teachers and seventy-two bishops.

39. By coincidence, following the Ascension the persecuted Christians fled from Jerusalem, north fifty miles and across the Jordan to Pella in Peraea. The catastrophic Roman siege of Jerusalem followed almost immediately in 70 A.D.

40. By comparison, we see that Christ's kingdom was not of this world. When asked to solve an inheritance dispute, he declined: "Friend, who appointed me as your judge and arbitrator" (Luke 12:13–15).

41. Abdullah Yusuf Ali, 1522n.5379.

42. From this initial period we read of the Battle of the Ditch south of Mecca. Prideaux recounts how a certain King and Arab (Du Nawas) converted to Judaism and constructed the ditch as a furnace into which were thrown those Christians who refused to renounce their religion and convert to Judaism. Following his overthrow by the warrior uncle of the Ethiopian King Aryat, and under new Ethiopian rule, a famous church was built. This church attracted converts from the pagan Temple of Mecca which then fell into neglect. The Arabs desecrated the church following a failed attack on Mecca by elephant riders. Prideaux observes that the *Qur'an* (Q 105, titled "the Elephant") records this encounter and effort to protect the Temple of Mecca, although the attack took place in the year of Mohammed's birth and therefore too early for his personal experience (*The Life of Mahomet*, 46–8).

43. Washington Irving's undocumented quotations from the *Qur'an* partly include Q 61:1–14 (*Mahomet and his Successors* [New York: George P. Putnam, 1850], 153–4).

44. Ibid., 155–8.

45. In the *Qur'an* Alexander is Dhul-Qarnayn (Q 18:82–98). N.J. Dawood, *The Koran* (New York: Penguin, 2003), 212, fn. 1. St. Augustine writes that Alexander wrote a letter to his mother that Leo, an Egyptian high priest, revealed to him that all of the (polytheistic) gods, were mere mortals (*The City of God*, Part I, Bk. 8, Ch. 5). Were compilers of the *Qur'an* influenced by this Christian writing?

46. Cited from extant letters, by Charles Rollin, "History of Alexander," *Ancient History* (Cincinnati: George Conclin, Pub., 1844), 528.

47. Lynn White, *Medieval Technology and Social Change* (New York: Oxford University Press, 1962), 2–14, and: "The chivalric class never repudiated the original condition of its existence: that it was endowed to fight, and that anyone who could not or would not meet his military obligations forfeited his endowment" (31).

48. Henri Daniel-Rops, *The Church in the Dark Ages* (Garden City, New York: Image, 1962), 36.

49. One is reminded how on their return from Exile in Babylon (531 A.D.) the remnant Israel rebuilt itself around those parts of the Torah brought back by Ezra to Jerusalem.

50. "The only true faith in God's sight is Islam. Those to whom the Scriptures were given disagreed among themselves, through insolence, only after knowledge had been vouchsafed them" (Q 3:19). The foundational placement of the term "knowledge" might also suggest a Gnostic component to Islam and to the ulema interpreters (learned ones).

51. Prideaux stresses the docility of Eastern Christians in Mohammed's time, 43.

52. Prideaux, 57–8. Christians will also recall other later substitutions: the Dome of the Rock (site of Mohammed's legendary night journey to heaven, Q 17:1) directly above the Christian Church of the Holy Sepulcher in Jerusalem and, from 1453 until its conversion into a museum in the 1920s, the use of the Christian church of Santa Sophia as a mosque.

53. Ibid., 71.

54. Ibid., 72. Mohammed appears to follow the pattern in the Old Testament where holy war is moderated over time to require that terms of peace to be offered before laying siege (Deut 20:10–14). Centuries earlier, in 66 A.D., the presumption that God's ways are our ways led Jewish Zealots to take up the sword against the Roman Empire. The result in this unfavorable case, unlike that the Meccan conquest, was the devastation of Jerusalem and the Diaspora of the Jews for the next two millennia.

55. Zaid H. Assfy, *Islam and Christianity* (York, England: William Sessions, Ltd., 1977), 88.

56. Prideaux, 73. Mohammed restored wives and children to the defeated tribes, and then their belongings after they embraced Islam.

57. http://www.christian-thinktank.com/qamorite.html.

58. Examples of Christian assimilation are the very familiar basilica church design which may be an adaptation of the Roman hall of justice (with the grand entry-way

moved from the side to one end) or even pagan temples; and the term "Easter" which comes from an Anglo-Saxon word derived from the pagan goddess of the dawn. Some Christian holiday dates were selected to coincide with pagan festivals to aid the transition from pagan practices to the Christian faith. The cult of Saturnus (the Sower) recalled the Golden Age of Italy and celebrated the seedtime and harvest in a seven-day festival extending from December 17 to 24. As the event and mutual gift exchange became more corrupt 'Christianity stepped in and diverted its purpose by the adoption of the same season as Christmas'" (R. J. Campbell, *The Story of Christmas* (New York: The Macmillan Co., 1941), 61–62).

59. Prideaux, citing Pocock (1604–91), an Oxford scholar who in 1650 published a valuable collection from Arab writers. This view is compatible with the current Muslim apologist, Farooq Hassan (*The Concept of the State and Law in Islam*, 21).

60. St. Paul in Athens: "As I walked around looking at your shrines, I even discovered an altar inscribed, 'To a God Unknown.' Now, what you are thus worshiping in ignorance I intend to make known to you" (Acts 17:23). The difference between a pagan "monotheism" arrived at by deletion (the Egyptian Akhenaton), and the Jewish monotheism of a *transcendent* God, is stressed in Stanley Jaki's commentary on Psalm 104 (*Praying the Psalms: A Commentary*, Grand Rapids, Michigan: William B. Eerdmans, 2001, 182–185). The transitional case (not a hybrid), where the Roman myth of the Sun (*sola Invictus*) is maintained alongside a genuinely Christian monotheism in the time of Constantine, is addressed in Michael R. Molnar, *The Star of Bethlehem* (New Jersey, Rutgers University Press, 2001), 104–9.

61. Aquinas warns that the Trinity cannot be proved by natural reason alone, and that "to bring as a proof of the faith reasons that are not necessary is to expose that faith to the scorn of the infidels; they will think that it is upon these reasons that we base ourselves, and it is on account of them that we believe" (*Summa Theologiae*, cited by Jean-Pierre Torrell [Robert Royal, trans.], *Saint Thomas Aquinas*, Vol. 1 [Washington, D.C.: Catholic University of America Press, 1996], 109).

62. Edwin Bliss, op. cit., 52.

63. Prideaux, 10.

64. The Medieval critic, San Pedro Pascual held that Mohammed's claims was to have received a progressive insights over a period of twenty-three years, but that this experience was only later attributed to revelation from God, and (based on Islamic authorities) this attribution was later suggested by Umar. Pedro de Alfonso held that biblical entries were added to the *Qur'an* by the compiler Uthman the third caliph, fifteen years after Mohammed's death, with the forced assistance of Christians and Jews. See Norman Daniel, *Islam and the West* (Oxford: Oneworld, 1903 [1960], 51–2, 55.

65. Initially Paul approached Damascus to scatter the Christians. But unlike Mohammed, who returned to Mecca to destroy the pagans, Paul encounters Christ and then continues to Damascus as a man of the new life. Later he writes, "I became a minister of this church through the commission God gave me to preach among you his word in its fullness, that mystery hidden from ages and generations past but now revealed to his holy ones" (Col 1:25–26).

66. Prideaux, 71. This story is traced to Abul Feda (b. 1273) from the family of Jobida (of which was Saladin the famous Sultan of Egypt); Al Kedai (d. 1062); Al

Janabbi (*History*, 1588); the *Disputatio Christiani* (in Arabic by a Christian officer in the Court of a Saracen king, translated for Peter of Cluny in 1130); Richardi Confutatio (Dominican researcher who visited Mecca, c. 1210); Pocock (Oxford Professor of Arabic and Hebrew), *Specimen History of Arabia* (1650).

67. Prideaux, 76. Citing several sources including the ancient Al Bochari (809–869 A.D.), one of the original compilers of the hadith, Prideaux offers this account: "He called for a Pen, Ink, and Paper, telling them that he would dictate a Book to them, which should keep them from erring after his Death. But Omar would not admit this, saying the Alcoran sufficeth, and that the Prophet, through the greatness of his Malady, knew not what he said. But others who were present, were of another Mind, and expressed a great desire that the Book might be wrote, which their Prophet spoke to them of; whereon a Contention arose between them, some being of Omar's mind, and some of the contrary; at which Mohammed taking offence, bid them all be gone, telling them, That it did not become them thus to contend in his Presence. So the Book was not wrote; the loss of which was afterwards lamented by some of his Followers, as a great Calamity to their Cause."

68. William Barclay, *The Gospel of John*, Vol. 1 (Philadelphia: Westminster Press, 1975), 18.

69. http://users.belgacom.net/gc674645/grave/lastword.htm, and Maulana Muhammad Ali, *Muhammad the Prophet* (Lahore, Pakistan: Ripon, 1984 [Ahmadiyya Anjuman Isha'at Islam, 1924], 276.

70. Washington Irving, 321. Irving's biography is based on sources researched during his sojourn in Spain, mostly a translation from the Arabian historian Abulfeda, shelved in the Jesuit Library of the Convent of St. Isidro in Madrid (*Mahomet and His Successors*, Vol. I [New York: George P. Putnam, 1850].

71. Dawson, 135.

72. Ibid., 87. W.H. McNeill holds that hereditary claims to succession grew in importance only later "when familiarity with Persian and Byzantine ideas of hereditary rulership had penetrated the Moslem community" (*The Rise of the West* [New York: Mentor, 1963], 465, fn. 9).

73. Gibb and Kramers, in *Shorter Encyclopedia of Islam* (Cornell, University Press, 1953), 402.

74. Muhammad Ali also reports that the Copt gave birth to a son named Ibrahim. He confirms that Mohammed lost all of his children in his own lifetime, except Fatimah who died six months after the Prophet. Ibrahim is also referred to as coming from a wife other than Khadijah and whom he married in Madina. This son died after eighteen months (Maulana Muhammad Ali, *Muhammad the Prophet* (Lahore, Pakistan: Ripon, 1984 [Ahmadiyya Anjuman Isha'at Islam, 1924], 55,307).

75. Prideaux, 86. One need not accept Prideaux's diatribe against Mohammed in order to reflect on Mohammed's control over his two favorite and simultaneous wives, Aisha and Haphsa (reported in the *Qur'an*). They had threatened to reproach him before their fathers for his activities with the fifteen year old Mariya of the Jacobite sect.

76. Vincent Cronin, *The Wise Man From the West* (Garden City, New York: Image, 1957), 181.

77. Philip Hughes, *The Church in Crisis: A History of the General Councils* (Garden City, New York: Hanover House, 1961), 296, 314. One purpose of Trent was foster political peace to enable a united effort against the Turks.

78. Yahya Michot, *Muslims Under Non-Muslim Rule: Ibn Taymiyya* (London: Interface Press, 2006), 15, fn. 1.

79. Ayoub in Omar (ed.), 137.

80. Dawson, 143–4.

81. Ayoub in Omar (ed.), ibid. The Christian cannot help but notice the parallel to Bible verses linking time and eternity, that "with the Lord one day is like a thousand years and a thousand years like one day" (2 Pe 3:8), and that at the resurrection we will be changed "in an instant, in the blink of an eye" (1 Cor 15:52).

82. The German Treaty of Peace (in Sec. VII) reads: "Germany is to restore within six months the Koran of the caliph Othman, formerly at Medina, to the king of the Hedjas, and the skull of the sultan Okwawa, formerly in German East Africa to his Britannic majesty's government." Othman was the third caliph after Mohammed; at the War's end Hedjas became Saudi Arabia.

83. Ayoub in Omar (ed.), 189.

84. The Muslim articles of faith define a very large tent: the unity of God, life after death, and divine decree (often seen by the West as fatalism); together with belief in Allah's angels, prophets, and revealed books (www.dremali.com). While Islam is incorrectly characterized as promoting only violence, the shortcoming is more accurately the ambivalence of its prohibitions against violence.

85. On Rome, see Philip Hughes, *A Popular History of the Catholic Church* (New York: MacMillan, 1947), 31.

86. In the sixteenth century, Melanchthon understated several parts of the emerging Lutheran doctrinal crisis by omitting them in his *Augsburg Confession* (1530) which in this attempted middle path more nearly resembled Catholic teachings clarified later at the Council of Trent (John Dolan, *History of the Reformation* [New York: Mentor-Omega, 1967], 255–64).

87. In 496 the emperor and his mother demanded use the Christian cathedral for state-supported Arian ceremonies, this for the sake of social cohesion in a time of political disintegration. The record of his courageous resistance marks a defining moment for the distinct role of Church as apart from state in Western Christendom and then the modern world.

88. More familiar in the West is the sixteenth Reformation which, in part, served to divide northern and southern Europe along cultural lines as well as theological lines.

89. Roland Bainton, *Early Christianity* (Malabar, Florida: Krieger Publishing, 1960), 66. A counter-Church of nearly three hundred Donatist bishops existed alongside the legitimate hierarchy, most often in the same dioceses.

90. As a typical year, government discrimination against Christians occurred in twenty-three countries in 2009, twelve of these in Islamic countries (excluding secular Turkey). There were sixteen cases of government discrimination against Muslims, and eleven of these were by Muslim majorities against Muslim minorities (*International Religious Freedom Report for 2009* [U.S. Department of State[, also

cited in *Catalyst,* 36:10 [New York: Catholic League of Religious and Civil Rights, Nov. 2009], 120).

91. Dawson, 131.

92. Maulana Muhammad Ali, *Muhammad the Prophet* (Lahore, Pakistan: Ripon Press, 1984 [1924]), 268–286.

93. Citation in Ayoub in Omar (ed.), 219.

94. John Paul II, *Redemptoris Missio* (The Mission of the Redeemer), December 7, 1990, n. 29. St. John Chrysostom notes (Homily xxiv on Acts) that in the Acts of the Apostles, the singular example of the Spirit entering where He will is with Cornelius and his family. The manifestation did not await the later sacrament of Baptism (Acts 19:5,6).

95. Western scholastic thinkers distinguish between *scientia* (discursive knowledge) and *sapientia* (wisdom), or contemplative and mystical knowledge which transcends even meditation, and which is received as a gift. Within the Church tradition, private revelations can be approved if they refer back to the one public revelation of Christ and therefore contain nothing contrary to faith or morals.

96. Friedrich Heer, *The Intellectual History of Europe* (New York: The World Publishing Co., 1953), 276.

97. Al-Munqidh min al-Dalal, translated by R.J. McCarthy, *Al-Ghazali's Path to Sufism: His Deliverance from Error* (Louisville: Fons Vitae, 1999 [1131A.D.]), 57–8.

98. Brant Pelphrey, *The Theology and Mysticism of Julian of Norwich* (Salzburg: The University of Salzburg, 1982), 63. In his thorough study of Julian, Pelphrey stresses briefly the difference between *The Cloud* and the theology of Julian.

99. Ibid., 121.

100. The Second Vatican Council uses the earlier term "submission," but within the context of intellect and will: "'The obedience of faith' (Rom 16:26; cf 1:5; 2 Cor 10:5–6) must be given to God who reveals, and obedience by which man entrusts his whole self freely to God, offering 'the full submission of intellect and will to God who reveals,' and freely assenting to the truth revealed by Him (*Dei Verbum*, n. 5, citing the earlier Council of Trent).

101. Maria Faustina Kowalski, *Diary of Divine Mercy in my Soul* (Stockbridge, Mass.: Marians of the Immaculate Conception, 2002), 410 (n. 1102).

102. Ayoub in Omar (ed.), 10.

103. Ibid. By the time of Mohammed's birth, the institutional Church already had manifested its unity in five of its now twenty-one general councils.

104. *Ascent of Mt Carmel,* xxix, 196, cited in P. Marie-Eugene, OCD, *I am a Daughter of the Church: A Practical Synthesis of Carmelite Spirituality,* Vol. II (Allen, Texas: Christian Classics, 1997 [1955]), 247–8. With locutions, the message received is inevitably filtered through and possibly modified by personal and subjective imagery and intellectual errors and circumstances.

105. Ayoub in Omar, 80.

106. Ibid., 30.

107. The Medina turning point is stressed in Washington Irving, op. cit., 336–7. The Islamic encounter with modernity would benefit from a systematic to understand the *Qur'an* in some more principled order than the life sequence of Mohammed (a

proposal of Mohammad Iqbal [1877–1938] and the contemporary Islamic scholar Fazlur Rehman). If the *Qur'an* lends itself to a non-biographical order, then the watershed change at Medina could be highly explanatory as proposed in our text, and in this way could provide a clearer nexus with Western self-understanding as well.

108. In her study of Joseph Smith and Mormonism, Fawn Brodie refers in part to Dr. Phyllis Greenacre who proposes that imposters "struggle between two dominant identities" and that the false identity cannot be sustained without an external audience: "It is the demand for an audience in which the (false) self is reflected that causes impostures often to become of social significance" ("The Impostor," Psychoanalytic Quarterly, 27:359–82 [1958], cited in Fawn Brodie, *No One Knows My History* [New York: Henry Knopf, 1995], 418–19). Greenacre's analysis might also explain much of contemporary political and judicial activism.

109. Muhammad Ali, 283–4.

110. Ali makes an intricate case that A'isha was ten when married and fifteen when the marriage was consummated (ibid., 304).

111. Ali reports that most of these were relatively unattractive widows (not virgins), usually from warfare, while Prideaux suggests that Mohammed later exempted himself from sexual morals enjoined on others (e.g., he cites Q 33:50–51), but some apologists say this permission is then revoked by Q 33:52. Critics claim evidence of slave sex, concubines and pedophilia.

112. Six centuries before Mohammed, St. Paul referred to the days before the coming of Christ as the "times of ignorance" (Acts 17:30).

113. Before concluding that ultimate reality is "emptiness," Siddhartha (Buddha) was married to one woman (Bimba, or Gopa) and had a son. When at the earlier age of sixteen his father awarded him three palaces and forty thousand dancing girls to restrain him from renouncing the world and its endless reincarnations.

114. De Lacy O'Leary, *Arabia Before Muhammad* (New York: E.P. Dutton and Co., 1927), 214. At the turn of the twentieth century the discovery of customs of organized sexual license led to theories of the gradual evolution of the family from ages of promiscuity. Dawson (relying on Malinowski) finds instead that even early societies tribal law and morality served to repress instinctive behavior, largely as a protection against the destructive results of incest (Christopher Dawson, *The Dynamics of World History* [New York: Mentor Omega, 1962], 158–67).

115. De Lacy O'Leary, 191. A more critical view faults Islam for its lack of moral content in its appeals to fanaticism and its spread by force of arms, and for "promising to its followers a paradise of sensuality" (Kearney, "The Religion of Tomorrow," *in The Catholic Philosophy of Life* [the Shanghai Catholic Radio League], Shanghai: T'ou-se-wei Press, 1939, 16).

In a different setting, the mingling of pagan and of Christian ways is evident in the Spanish conquistadores in the sixteenth century. Some twenty newly baptized women were distributed by Cortez to his captains, and later when the husband of one returned to Spain he claimed her for himself (from a record written in 1568, cited in Joseph Mc Sorley, *An Outline History of the Church by Centuries* [St. Louis: Herder Book Co., 1945], 557 n.).

116. Muhammad Ali, 304–7.

117. Ibid, 308–14.

118. Verses in the *Qur'an*, often muted by patriarchal custom, grant inheritance rights to women (Q 4:10–13). Similar legal rights only appeared in the West in the nineteenth century (John Esposito, *Islam: The Straight Path* [New York: Oxford University Press, 1998], p. 95–100).

119. The Islamic themes of booty and Holy War (etc.) are either anticipated or rooted in the Jewish Bible (the Pentateuch), e.g., Num 31:25–54, and Deut 20:10–18. Marriage to a slave girl is permitted in Deut 21:10–14.

120. Alfred Guillaume, *Islam* (New York: Penguin Books, 1982), 103–4, and N.J. Dawood, *The Koran* (New York: Penguin Books, 2003), 64, which reads simply: "Believers, do not consume your wealth among yourselves in vanity, but rather trade with it by mutual consent." Guillaume's complete version reads: "You are permitted in addition to seek out wives with your wealth in modest conduct but not in fornication; give them their pay for the enjoyment you have had of them for a specified period as a duty." The wording appears in Shi'ite books, but the wording and practice are rejected by Sunnis.

121. Lucy Garnett, *The Women of Turkey and Their Folklore* (London: David Nett Strand, 1891). Mentioned in passing by F. Engels is the recent South-Slavic Zadruga extended family involved the descendents of one father and multiple wives, all under the authority of a Family Council consisting of all adult members, women and men. Engels proposes an evolutionary and economic explanation of the finally monogamous family, apart from human spirituality and the additional Judeo-Christian tradition (*The Origin of the Family, Private Property, and the State* [Moscow: Foreign Languages Publishing House, 1891], 94).

122. Washington Irving, op. cit., 340.

123. A.S. Turberville, *Medieval Heresies and the Inquisition* (London: Archon Books, 1964), 231. He writes the Flagelates were so extreme as to be excommunicated from the Church. Farther back, radical Anabaptists in Westphalia were led by an ex-priest and Lutheran, Bernard Rottman who had four wives, and by John of Leyden, who had sixteen (Joseph Mc Sorley, *An Outline History of the Church by Centuries* [St. Louis, Missouri: Herder Book Co., 1945], 614).

124. Erik von Kuenhelt-Leddhin, *Leftism: From de Sade and Marx to Hitler and Marcuse*, New Rochelle, New York: Arlington House, 1974, 418–19, and passim.

125. Dietrich von Hildbrand, *Transformation in Christ* (Garden City, New York: Image, 1963), 188, 192.

126. Freidrich Heer, *The Intellectual History of Europe*.

127. Bernard Lewis and Buntzie Ellis Churchill, *Islam: The Religion and the People* (Wharton School Publishing, 2008), 146.

128. Benedict XVI, *Deus est Caritas* (God is Love), 2006, n. 11. One modern day Islamic information source defends polygamy within Islam by asserting as if it is common knowledge, and incorrectly, that Christianity also approves polygamy: http://www.usc.edu/dept/MSA/notislam/misconceptions.html. The duplicitous position of the possibly referenced 1988 Lambeth Conference, Resolution #26, did not speak for Christianity when it said: "This Conference upholds monogamy as God's plan, and as the ideal relationship of love between husband and wife; nevertheless

recommends that a polygamist who responds to the Gospel and wishes to join the Anglican Church may be baptized and confirmed with his believing wives and children"...under listed conditions.

In the early period of biblical Judaism polygamy is common but was later abandoned. Not representative of Christianity, Luther is reported to have supported bigamy over divorce for Henry VIII and for Philip of Hesse, referring to the Old Testament and the patriarchs. At the time of Luther, many Catholic theologians held the same position (John Dolan, 266).

129. *Deus Caritas Est* (God is Love), nn. 4,6.

130. Richard Winston, *Charlemagne: From the Hammer to the Cross* (New York: Vintage, 1954), 57.

131. The most complete text on Christ as other than divine is Q 4:169–70 (sometimes Q 171–2). Detecting arm's length belief even among those who walked with him, Christ remarked: "If it is by the finger of God that I cast out demons then the kingdom of God has come upon you" (Lk 11:20, Mt 12:28).

132. Prideaux, p. 31. "For the People calling on him for Miracles to prove his Mission, and he being able to work none, to salve the Matter, he invents this Story of his Journey to Heaven; which must be acknowledged to have Miracle enough in it, by all those who have Faith to believe it." The ascension might have occurred at Jerusalem, or might not, and might have involved travel by means of a ladder or alternatively by a winged donkey.

133. Ibid.

134. Frederick Denny, *An Introduction to Islam* (New York: Macmillan, 1994), 64.

135. Sandra L. Zimdars-Schwartz, *Encountering Mary*, Princeton (New Jersey: Princeton University Press, 1991), 270. In a separate and ambitious work dealing with self-image and political outcomes, Alan Bullock examines the psychological influences behind Hitler and Stalin (*Hitler and Stalin: Parallel Lives* [New York: Vintage Books, 1993], 3–17). In the life of Hitler, early family tensions and a sequence of rejections (dismissal from a Vienna art school) contributed to his fantasies and Wagnerian self-image, his strong resentment for German victimization at Versailles, and his racial ideology. Stalin's only systematic education was ten years in a particular monastic setting where a dogmatic, suspicious and watchful environment earned his lifelong disdain. Based carefully on Freud, Erik Erickson (on adolescent development) and Erich Fromm (on narcissism), Bullock finds that when Stalin discovered Marxist ideology this reinforced his already acquired personal dispositions. Bullock concludes that the particular monastic model of his upbringing served partly as a template for Lenin's Soviet police state. This interpretation overlooks the fact that under the Czar, Stalin spent four years as a prisoner in a Siberian camp near Turukhansk from 1913–1917. This point is alluded to in cynical camp folklore from the Gulag period (reported in Mihajlo Mihajlov, *Moscow Summer* [New York: Farrar, Straus and Giboux, 1965], 76–85).

136. John Julius Norwich, *A Short History of Byzantium* (abridged single volume) [New York: Vintage, 1999], 6–7. Norwich bases his skepticism on the additional fact that Eusebius fails to mention the event at all until his later *Life of Constantine*, source of our quote in the text (not the more relevant *Ecclesiastical History*, c.325).

He writes that no other reference is given even from Constantine himself, although he did claim to have had a prior vision, years before in 312 pointing him toward monotheism. Daniel-Rops is not skeptical and points to the inscription on the triumphal arch erected in 313, which reads "by an inspiration of the deity."

137. The first to accept Christianity as the religion of state was the Kingdom of Armenia in 301. In its constitution of 1889 Japan tolerated Christianity alongside Buddhism and Shintoism, although this missionary religion was embraced by less than a quarter of one percent of the population.

138. Prideaux documents nearly a dozen much earlier historians who report that Mohammed was "subject to the Falling Sickness" (*Life of Mahomet*, 12), citing Rodericus Toletanus (twelfth century archbishop of Toledo, Spain) and Ricardi (eleventh century Dominican Friar who in 1210 studied in Baghdad). Byzantine authors are cited by Gibb and Kramers, 393 (Theophanes' *Chronographia*, edited by de Boor). Citing a Muslim source, Karen Armstrong reports that Mohammed believed the convulsions which were accompanied by profuse sweat on cool days and by voices were the result rather than the cause of the revelation: "Never once did I receive a revelation, without thinking that my soul had been torn away from me" (*Islam: A Short History* [New York: Modern Library, 2002], 5). Norman Daniel regards the possibility of epilepsy as legendary (op. cit, 266).

139. Citations in Norman Daniel, op. cit., 51.

140. Gibb and Kramers, in *Short Encyclopedia of Islam* (Ithaca: Cornell University Press, 1953), 402.

141. The less generous charge that Mohammed was "an imposter" is usually traced to Medieval diatribes against his inability to perform miracles and toward his exaggerated sexual excesses. See Bosworth, Donzel, Heinrichs, Pellat, editors, *Encyclopedia of Islam*, Volume VII (New York: E.J. Brill, 1993), 380.

142. The italics here distance this comment from Karen Armstrong who in this instance and generally tend blur the critical distinction between inspiration, heightened consciousness and discovery as fully explanatory, and the still different meaning of revelation as of divine origin and initiative (*Muhammad: A Biography of the Prophet* [San Francisco: Harper Collins, 1993], 84–6.

143. Malcolm Muggeridge and Alec Vidler, *Paul: Envoy Extraordinary* (New York: Harper and Row, 1972), 73.

144. Raymond Charles, cited in Jean Herbert, *An Introduction to Asia* (New York: Oxford University Press, 1968), 155. In the West we possibly find in Descartes a vivid parallel and contrast to the calling of Mohammed. Descartes' entire deductive method of reason (with faith bracketed) is foundational to later Western rationalism and traces back to three dreams he had on November 10, 1619. In these dreams Descartes found his calling was to demonstrate the truth by the use of reason alone.

145. See Pope Benedict XVI, *On the Way to Jesus Christ* (San Francisco: Ignatius, 2005), 72, italics added. Barclay comments that while Paul first presented Christ to the Gentiles, in the Greek city of Ephesus John also worked among Gentiles. To reach them, he used the rich concept of "the word." To the Greeks the Word is Logos, or Reason (including the ability of the human mind to discover truth). For Jewish readers the term "word of God" was used in vernacular or Aramaic translations of the

Hebrew Old Testament (the *Targums* from the first century before Christ) to convey the notion of God's transcendence and to avoid anthropomorphic expressions. See William Barclay, *The Gospel of John*, Vol. I (Phil.; Westminster Press, 1975), 27–32.

146. T.E. Lawrence, *Seven Pillars of Wisdom* (New York: Anchor Books, 1991), 39. The Islamic scholar Mahmoud Ayoub gives a higher number of 124,000, adding that only twenty-one are named in *the Qur'an*.

147. Ibid.

148. Ibid., 38–43.

149. George Adam Smith, *The Historical Geography of the Holy Land* (London: Hodder and Stoughton, 1900), 88. The quotation may be from the hadith.

150. Karen Armstrong, *Islam: A Short History* (New York: Modern Library, 2002), 15, 24. The International Theological Commission retains a deeper definition of salvation as "…nothing less than a transformation and fulfillment of the personal life of the human being, created in the image of God and now newly directed to a real participation in the life of the divine persons, through the grace of the incarnation and the indwelling of the Holy Spirit" ("Communion and Stewardship: Human Persons Created in the Image of God," July 23, 2004, n. 47).

151. See "Pascal" in Hans Urs von Balthasar, *The Glory of the Lord: A Theological Aesthetics,* Vol. III: Lay Styles (San Francisco: Ignatius, 1986), 172–238, 228.

152. Second Vatican Council, *Sacrosanctum Concilium (Constitution on the Sacred Liturgy)*, n. 8.

153. From a homily of St. Gregory of Nyssa, *Liturgy of the Hours,* Vol. III, (New York: Catholic Book Publishing Co., 1975), 412–14.

154. Christopher Dawson, 50. That religious vision is the source of high culture is generally still accepted.

155. Fr. Simon Tugwell, O.P., *The Beatitudes: Soundings in Christian Traditions* (Springfield, Il.: Templegate Publishers, 1980), cited in *Magnificat* (Yonkers, New York: Magnificat, Feb. 2010), 390.

156. St. Theodore the Studite, in *The Liturgy of Hours*, Vol. II (New York: Catholic Book Publishing, 1976), 677.

157. Warren Carroll, *The Building of Christendom*, Vol. 2 (Front Royal, Virginia: Christendom Press, 1987), 237, citing Donner, *Early Islamic Conquests*, 269.

158. Henri Daniel-Rops, *The Church in the Dark Ages*, Vol. II (Garden City: Image, 1962), 36.

159. Karen Armstrong, 29–30. The alternative view is that Armstrong is reading present ideologies into past events. The *ideologically* driven carnage of the twentieth century demonstrates the ideological fallacy that the only or greatest global threat today is intolerance among the fanatical fringes of the world religions.

160. Norwich, 94–5.

161. Dawson, *The Making of Europe*, 136.

162. Edward Gibbon, *Christians and the Fall of Rome (*New York: Penguin Books, 2004), 2, 70; extract from *The Decline and Fall of the Roman Empire*, Vol. I, first published 1776.

163. Ibid., 3. The insight of a state-within-a-state finds a parallel today. This comparison is between the undermining of Roman strength by the military recruitment of

tribal invader descendants (e.g., Attila), and the recent discrediting of the priesthood (and the Church) by those entrants who see their abnormal behavior as unrestricted by the vow of celibacy as normally understood.

164. Leslie Stephen, *History of English Thought in the 18th Century* (3rd ed.), Vol. I, 449, cited in Christopher Dawson, 326.

165. In the ninth century the *Qur'an* was pronounced part of the divine essence. Near this time Charlemagne was well imbued with the more reasoned Catholic understanding of scriptural interpretation. He exhorted his abbots to the humble study of letters to better understand "the mysteries of the Holy Scriptures. For as these contain images, tropes, and similar figures, it is impossible to doubt that the reader will arrive far more readily at the spiritual sense according as he is the better instructed in learning" (from "Charlemagne's 'Capitulary of 787'," in Richard Gamble, *The Great Tradition* [Wilmington, DE: Intercollegiate Studies Institute, 2007], 244–5).

166. Critics point to a long history of declining commerce in the Mediterranean, and the small share carried out between the Orient and the West. White grounds the emergence of northern Europe on an agricultural revolution and technologies supporting increased productivity: the heavy plow, crop rotation, the modern harness (Lynn White, Jr., op. cit., 77.

167. Henri Pirenne, *Medieval Cities* (New York: Doubleday and Co., Inc, 1925), 16, 18. Others attribute the decline of the Frankish presence on the Mediterranean Sea to Byzantine sea power, or a greater emphasis on internal unification. Recent archeological evidence tend to refute the Pirenne Thesis and to support the thesis that Carolingian Europe and Islam both simply filled in the vacuum left by the Roman collapse, but that Charlemagne underwrote internal stability wit h silver secured from the Muslim world through overland trade (Richard Hodges and David Whitehouse, *Mohammed, Charlemagne and the Origin of Europe* [Ithaca, New York: Cornell University Press, 1983]).

168. Sir Charles Oman, *A History of the Art of War in the Middle Ages (378–1278)*, Vol. I (Mechanicsburg, Penn.: Stackpole Books, 1991 [1924],) 222.

169. Ibid., 232.

170. Roland Bainton, *The Medieval Church* (Malabar, Florida: Krieger Publishing, 1962), 38.

171. 171. To be noted is the parallel between this strategy to maintain unity and the strategy of early Islam to expand its realm by uniting the previously warring tribes of Arabia against such new and external enemies as the Byzantines and Persians.

172. In the West, the year 1085 also marks the Christian recovery of Toledo in Moorish Spain.

173. Thomas P. Neill (ed.), "Urban II Calls for a Crusade," in *The Building of the Human City* (Garden City, New York: Doubleday Christendom Books, 1960), 100–104. Pope Urban II included economic motives: "Let none of your possessions detain you, no solicitude for your family affairs, since this land which you inhabit, shut in on all sides by the sea and surrounded by mountain peaks, is too narrow for your large population, nor does it abound in wealth; and it furnishes scarcely food enough for it cultivators."

174. Norwich, 260; and Norman Cohn, *Pursuit of the Millennium* (New York: Oxford University Press, 1970), 68.

175. Norman Cohn, 61–8.

176. Cohn., 69.

177. Dario Fernandez-Morera, "The Myth of the Andalusian Paradise," *Intercollegiate Review*, Fall 2006, 23–31, citing *Rambam: Selected Letters of Maimonides, Letter to Yemen, Discourse on Martyrdom*, Abraham Yaakov Finkel (trans.), Scranton: Yeshivah Beth Moshe, 1994. Bernard Lewis (himself a Jew) writes: "The golden age of equal rights (in Spain) was a myth, and belief in it was a result, more than a cause, of Jewish sympathy for Islam. The myth was invented by Jews in nineteenth-century Europe as a reproach to Christians" ("The Pro-Islamic Jews," in *Islam in History* [Chicago: Open Court, 1993], 148). Christian resistance to Muslim occupation of Spain is surveyed through a hereditary lineage of twenty-four generations (711–1451) in Warren Carroll, *Isabel of Spain: The Catholic Queen* (Front Royal, Virginia: Christendom Press, 1991), 4–14. In the thirteenth, fourteenth and fifteenth centuries the Jews were expelled respectively from England, France and Spain, a fate that contrasts with the often moderate encapsulation of minority populations (dhimmis) within the history of the Muslim world.

178. Saladin had risen from the level of slave (in Egypt), as did two or three popes in the early years of the Church.

179. John Teall, in Lewis Spitz and Richard Lyman (eds.), *Major Crises in Western Civilization*, Vol. 1 (New York: Harcourt, Brace and World, 1965), 116.

180. Norwich, 296.

While slavery is consistent with Islam, Mohammed lessened the burden he found in pagan Arabia. He saw manumission as and act of piety and originally "murder or maiming of slaves was to be punished by retaliation" (D,S, Margoliouth, *Mohammed and the Rise of Islam* [London: 1905] 461–2). In a later sermon Mohammed exhorted: "And your Slaves! See that ye feed them with such food as ye eat yourselves; and clothe them with the stuff ye wear. And if they commit a fault which ye are not inclined to forgive, then sell them, for they are the servants of the Lord, and are not to be tormented" (cited in Muir, *The Life of Mahomet* [New Delhi: 1992], 473). The foregoing citations are found in Andrew G. Bostom (ed.), *The Legacy of Jihad: Islamic Holy War and the Fate of Non-Muslims* [New York: Promethius Books, 2005], 530. The Foreword is by Ibn Warraq (pseudonym) who applauds "this comprehensive anthology that gainsays the myth of Islamic tolerance in an irrefutable way" (21).

181. Ayoub in Omar, (ed.), 305.

182. Ibid.

183. Joseph Clayton, *Pope Innocent III and His Times* (New York: Bruce Publishing, 1941), 103. In early Reformation Europe, interreligious alliances pitted Presbyterian Scotland and Catholic France against Anglican England, and later in the late 1630s and the Thirty Years War Cardinal Richelieu aligned France with Lutheran Sweden to contain the Catholic Habsburg Empire.

184. Villehardouin (1152–1218), comments on the "The Conquest of Constantinople" in Lewis Spitz and Richard Lyman (eds.), *Major Crises in Western Civilization*, op cit., 131. Villehardouin actually wrote more generally that the

issue was one of resisting dissidents who would have the army disbanded, and that the pope "knew well that without such forces the service of God could not be accomplished" (Joinville and Villehardouin, *Chronicles of the Crusades* [New York: Penguin, 1963], 51).

185. Norwich, 306. The destruction of Alexandria might have been at the hands of earlier Roman invaders or possibly the later Emperor Theodosius. Of the Saracen invasion, it is also written that the libraries of Alexandria were used to heat the water in the 4,000 baths in the city. The fuel was sufficient for a full six months (Daniel Haskel, *Chronological View of the World*, New York: J. H. Colton, 1846, 91). The Saracen Omar I is quoted (by Emerson in *Representative Men*) as having said, "Burn the libraries, for their value is in this one book" (the *Qur'an*).

186. Geoffrey Hindley, *The Crusaders* (New York: Carroll and Graf, 1983), 154.

187. The clerics assured the Crusaders "that the war is just and lawful, and if you fight to conquer this land with the right intention of bringing it under the authority of Rome, all those of you who die after making confession shall benefit from the indulgence granted by the Pope" (Joinville and Villehardouin, 79, 85).

188. Three centuries later, as a child, the lifelong Christian contemplative and mystic Teresa of Avila (author of *The Interior Castle*) embarked with her brother Rodrigo toward the Moors in the hope of being martyred: "I want to see God and to see Him we must die."

189. Today an unwilling 800,000 children and adults are subject to international human trafficking each year, and millions more fall victim within their national boundaries (*The Trafficking In Persons Report*, U.S. Department of State, June 2007, www.state.gov/g/tip).

190. It is possibly through Frederick II that Arabic numerals and Algebra made their way into Europe. Christians can consider that the tension between Latin and Greek Churches, culminating in the Schism of 1054, is due in partly to the language barrier separating Latin and Greek Christians.

191. Hindley, 177–8.

192. Ibid., 192. Frederick had a Muslim bodyguard and friends, and in earlier years he had declared that history had produced three "imposters," these being Moses, Christ and Mohammed.

193. Frederick rejected the Medieval view of limited kingship with his theory of absolute state power and royal supremacy in all things temporal and spiritual. While Frederick was in Rome bartering to have himself declared heir to the papal throne, the new pope Innocent IV escaped by sea and the following year (1245) had Frederick deposed at the Council of Lyons.

194. Attributed by Amin Maalouf, in *The Crusades Through Arab Eyes* (New York: Schocken Books, 1984), 266.

195. R.J. Campbell, op. cit., 158–68.

196. Friedrich Heer, *The Medieval World* (New York: Mentor Books, 1963), 144. Reports of humanitarian treatment are numerous, but exceptional. The same is true in the 21st century. The 2010 Christmas season carried reports of thirty-eight Christians killed in Nigeria (and two thousand more earlier in the year), the Christmas Day

bombing of a Catholic chapel in the Philippines, and eleven bomb attacks on Christians in Iraq, and also in Iraq the arrest of dozens of Muslim converts to Christianity, and the memory of two million Sudanese Christians killed over the past twenty years.

197. "The Elephant" is Q 105.

198. Prideaux, 48–9.

199. John Paul II, *Centesimus Annus* (One Hundred Years), n. 38, italics added.

200. The fall of Constantinople coincides with Gutenberg's invention of movable type and the printing press. The creation of language-based nation-states (and fragmentation into national religions) in the West marks a different politics of language than has occurred in the Islamic world.

201. Ibid.

202. The interplay between the Crusades and European history includes the marital tensions in Antioch between second crusader King Louis and his wife Eleanor. The battle lines of the Hundred Years War reflect regional allegiances that followed from Eleanor's divorce from Louis and her quick marriage to Henry II, taking with her much of southwestern France (Hindley, 80–81).

203. Norwich, 377–8. Apparent consensus between Latins and Greeks on the underlying *filioque* debate—the distinction between and relationship of equality and oneness (the "procession") among the Father, the Son, and the Holy Spirit—had been achieved at the Council of Florence in 1439.

204. Ibid., 380–1.

205. Christopher Koch (translated from the French by J.G. Cogswell), *History of the Revolutions in Europe to the Congress of Vienna*, Vol. 1 (Middletown, Connecticut: Edwin Hunt, 1835), 206.

206. The Safavids in Persia (modern day Iran) were a new center of Shi'ite power, troublesome to the Sunni Ottoman Turks, a relationship which in the history of Islam is most often compared to the Reformation within Christendom.

207. Ariano Fallaci, *The Force of Reason* (New York: Rizolli, 2006), 46–7.

208. Koch, Vol. II, p. 47.

209. *Zelus domus Dei* (Bull of Nov. 20, 1648), cited in "Janus," The Pope and The Council (Boston: RobertsBrothers, 1870), 25.

210. Outside of the West, the 1889 Japanese constitution was patterned after the new German (Prussian) constitution, and the Chinese civil code of the 1930s was based on the Swiss code, which also was closely related to the German code. The main principles of the German code derived from the Code of Napoleon.

211. George Cardinal Pell, "Islam and Us," *First Things* (New York: Institute on Religion and Public Life June/July 2006), 34. The Janissaries were abruptly brought to an end in 1826 when murdered in the barracks by the Ottoman sultan Mahmud II.

212. Bernard Lewis, *What Went Wrong?* (New York: Harper Perennial, 2002), 139–40. Medieval translations had included medicine, astronomy, chemistry, physics, mathematics and philosophy.

213. The relationship between multinational groupings, cultural achievements, and political power is a theme proposed by Robert Kann in connection with the Habsburg Empire (1526–1918). See *A History of the Habsburg Empire* (Berkeley: University of

California Press, 1977), 521–564. Based mostly on the Habsburg multinational setting, Kann suggests that when the threat of political dominance subsides, distinct cultural interaction and achievement thrives.

214. Christopher Dawson, *Medieval Essays* (Garden City: Image, 1959), 115. See "Continuity and Development in Christopher Dawson's Thought," John Mulloy, in Christopher Dawson, *Dynamics of World History* (New York: Mentor Omega, 1962), 403–457.

215. Ibid., 117.

216. *Time Magazine*, Nov. 27, 2006.

217. *The Next Christendom: The Coming of Global Christianity* (New York: Oxford University Press, 2002), 85, 159–61 and passim. The reader is invited to revisit the opening paragraph to our Introduction.

218. Edwin Bliss, *Turkey and the Armenian Atrocities* (New York: M.J. Coghlan, 1896), Ch. XIII (225–37). The text includes the *Hatti Sherif of Gulhane* in its entirety.

219. Ibid.

220. Maria Ambrosia and Mary Willis, *The "Secret" Archives of the Vatican* (New York: Little Brown/Barnes and Noble, 1996), 261–2. In 1939 American Indian converts were allowed by the Vatican to continue ancestor veneration as a form of filial respect rather than religious worship.

221. John Fairbank, Edwin Reischauer and Albert Craig, *East Asia: The Modern Transformation* (Boston: Houghton Mifflin Co., 1965), 58. A minority of the Jesuits (the "Figurists") proposed that the Chinese classical texts recalled figuratively the Hebrew tradition rooted in Noah, a legitimization tracing even farther back than Islam's connection to Ishmael and Abraham.

222. Failing to gain Western sympathy, the nationalist Sun Yat-sen turned to Russia in 1924 for support. He accepted the Communist Borodin as an advisor and communist members into his Kuomintang party. After a party split and the Second World War, China came under total Communist control in 1949.

223. http://users.belgacom.net/gc67645/grace/lastword.htm. Eyewitness accounts and first hand testimony of religious persecution in China following the Communist takeover in 1948 are given in Jean Monsterleet, *Martyrs in China* (Chicago: Henry Regnery, 1956), with a foreword by John C.W. Wu.

224. "Letter of the Holy Father, Pope Benedict XVI, to the Bishops, Priests, Consecrated Persons and Lay Faithful of the Catholic Church in the People's Republic of China," May 27, 2007.

225. Francesco Sisci, "China's Catholic Moment," *First Things* (New York: Institute on Religion and Public Life, June/July 2009), 27–30.

226. Andrew Higgins, "Chinese Dust off ideas of Confucius," *Washington Post*, May 16, 2010. Beyond the scope of this book is the possible similarity between the unitary Islamic State with a religion of submission and a Chinese state imbued with a pre-Christian civic religion or philosophy of obedience.

227. Second Vatican Council, *The Church in the Modern World* (Gaudium et Spes), n. 58.

228. Jean Cardinal Danielou, *Prayer as a Political Problem* (New York: Sheed and Ward, 1967), 115.

229. Confucianism is more of a civic code than a revealed religion. Still the Boxer Rebellion (1899) affords a rough parallel to the impact of the West on the world of Islam. As a backward looking reaction to modernity, the Rebellion was later followed by growing acceptance in China of Western technology disassociated from empiricist philosophy, and then by revolution. In the separate case of Japan, the Meiji Restoration (1868) marked the decisive beginning of modernization. The hereditary (and distinctly pre-Fascist) Emperor, whose unique participation in divinity was irrevocable, is more analogous with Islam and its divinized *Qur'an*. At the end of the Second World War Japan was allowed to retain the Emperor but only as a demythologized figurehead.

230. At the same time as the Rebellion (1860), French and British troops marched on Peking and decimated the Imperial Summer Palace, burning its books and treasures in bonfires that lasted for days, a reminder of the Saracen destruction of the Western library at Alexandria in the seventh century.

231. Citations in Vincent Y. C. Shin, *The Taiping Ideology: Its Sources, Interpretations and Influences* (Seattle: University of Washington Press, 1967), 406–7, e.g., "…born from a brain teeming with confused and often erroneous ideas of the teachings of Christianity, not unlearned in the writings of Confucius, and *perhaps imbued with some portions of the faith of Mahomet*" (italics added). Based on Taiping writings, qualified twentieth century specialists reject the notion that Hung was simply politically motivated and an impostor. They identify a progressive mental derangement, a messiah complex and possibly a "aschizophrenic-paranoic element in his illness" (Shih, 448–9). In the different case of Mohammed, some commentators regard biblical references to the coming of the Holy Spirit as referring to Mohammed. This view is proposed in Maulana Muhammad Ali, *Muhammad the Prophet* (Lahore, Pakistan: Ripon, 1984 [Ahmadiyya Anjuman Isha'at Islam, 1924]), 43–5.

232. Citation from George Taylor, in Vincent Y.C. Shih, 435.

233. Ssu-yu Jeng and Jeremy Ingalls, *The Political History of China, 1840–1928* (New York: Van Nostrand, 1956), 54, 80–81. A very complex movement, the Taiping Rebellion is also credited with instituting monogamy and freeing women from foot binding, and other reforms (e.g., Shih, 446).

234. Roberts was later prohibited by Hung from evangelizing the troops, a possible parallel to Mohammed's discontinued use of Bahira. Bahira might have been executed when he was of no further use and perhaps "knew too much" (Prideaux, 27). The citation regarding Bahira reads: "And therefore not long after this Monk for some great Crime being excommunicated, and espell'd his Monastery, fled to Mecca to him; and being there entertain'd in his House, became his Assistant in the framing of that Imposture, which he afterwards vented, and continued with him ever after . . . till at length the Impostor having no further occasion of him, to secure the Secret, put him to death." An original source is Richardi, reported in the extensively annotated bibliography as a Franciscan Friar who in the Year 1210 went to Baghdad, "to study the Mohammedan Religion out of their own Books . . ." (198). (*Richardi, Confutatio Legis Saracenica*). Other sources are named as Theophanes, Zonaras, annotated as two Byzantine historians. An alternative theory to Mohammed's killing of Bahira is that he was murdered by those jealous of his influence.

235. Vincent Y.C. Shih, xix. John Bagot Glubb, who lived with the Bedouins for fifteen years between the world wars, details six reasons why early Islam was so successful in expanding its perimeter and carving out a role as more than a footnote in Arabian history. In summary, these reasons were Mohammed's political charisma, the shallowness of the targeted pagan devotion among the Arabs, the fusion of Islam with traditional tribal loyalties, the unifying outlet offered by Islam for traditional tribal bravery and plunder against the new and external targets of Byzantium and Persia, followed by the inertial of cumulative success in battle and the allied belief that Allah rewards his followers even in this life,and finally the suitability of an uncomplicated Islam and its revelation in the Arabic language to uncomplicated and straightforward Arab minds (*The Life and Times of Muhammad* [London: Hodder and Stoughton, 1979], 381–383).

236. Muhammad Ali, *Muhammad the Prophet,* 32.

237. Joseph Smith did make at least one comparison between himself and his understanding of Mohammed. At an agitated moment in Missouri he said he would "trample down our enemies and make it one gore of blood from the Rocky Mountains to the Atlantic Ocean . . . I will be to this generation a second Mohammed, whose motto in treating for peace was 'the Alcoran or the Sword.' So shall it eventually be with us—'Joseph Smith or the Sword!'" (Fawn M. Brodie, *No Man Knows My History* [New York: Alfred Knopf, 1995], 420). A more recent and heavily documented critique of Mormon teaching possibly traces the Book of Mormon (1830) to an earlier and unpublished biblical fiction written the Rev. Solomon Spalding (Wayne Cowdrey, Howard Davis and Arthur Vanick, *Who Really Wrote the Book of Mormon: The Spalding Engima* [St. Louis: Concordia, 2005]).

238. In a roughly analogous way within Christendom, the historic Protestant communities trace their origins less clearly to Peter who with the apostles was commissioned by Christ, than to Luther, Calvin, or St. Augustine of Canterbury (Anglican).

239. The long-term insolvency of the Social Security System in the United States derives partly from the Mormon system that succeeds on a smaller scale. Social Security is undermined today by the changed demographics of this larger national system. The bounded pool of younger and contributing members is no longer larger than the supported older population.

240. In 1978 the admission of formerly excluded Blacks as full members was based on a new revelation. Mission work in Africa was a factor. Some interpretations of Islam hold that the *Qur'an* is "self-aware" as part of an ongoing process of divine revelation (Daniel Madigan, *The Qur'an' Self-Image: Writing and Authority in Islam's Scripture* [Princeton, 2001]).

241. Elder B. H. Roberts, *New Witness for Christ* (Salt Lake City: George B. Cannon and Sons, 1875). For detailed Mormon rendition of the "apostasy" see James E. Talmadge, *The Great Apostasy* (Salt Lake City, Utah: The Deseret News, 1909). In its own self-understanding, the Church asserts that rather than succumbing to the apostasy of some of its members, the living Church as an institution indwelled by the Holy Spirit always lives on.

242. Ibid., 173, italics added.

243. The self-understanding of Islam is as a community of religions. In the case of Mormonism Brigham Young remarked: "Our religion is simply the truth. It is all said in this one expression—it embraces all truth, wherever found in all the works of God and man" (in George Seldes, *The Great Quotations* [New York: Pocket Books, 1970], 830). Hinduism sees itself in the same way. Hoping to avert a communal partition of Pakistan from India, Ghandi claimed to be "a Muslim, a Hindu, a Buddhist, a Jew, a Parsee." In contrast, Christianity is a centering faith in a unique Incarnation, and is addressed to all persons rather than to other religions. "The Word was made flesh, and dwelt among us" (Jn 1:14).

244. Citation from the *Encyclopedia on Mormonism* (Brigham Young University), in Bruce Porter and Gerald McDermott, "Is Mormonism Christian?" *First Things*, New York: Institute on Religion and Public Policy, October 20, 2008, 35–41 (italics added). The citation is from the panelist McDermott.

245. Ibid. The cited Mormon philosopher is David Paulsen.

246. "For those religious sayings in the precious book which are expressed to everyone have three properties that indicate their miraculous character...etc." (Averroes[George Hourani, trans.], *On the Harmony of Religion and Philosophy* [London: Mssrs. Luzac and Col., 1967, 1961], Ch. 3, 70).

247. Roberts, op. cit., 461.

248. A divide between the Mormon construct and Islam, and one that would be readily detected by Muslim scholars, is that Mormonism subordinates even the power of God to laws of nature. Mormon philosopher David Paulsen writes, "God does not have absolute power . . . but rather the power to maximally utilize natural laws to bring about His purposes" (cited by Gerald McDermott, "Is Mormonism Christian," *New Things*, New York: Institute on Religion and Public Life, October 2008, 41).

249. Roberts, 466. The Christian will notice the similarity to Aristotle who taught an eternal universe, and perhaps the poetry of Carl Sagan who offered a merger of science with Hindu mysticism and endless recurrence into the future and endless recession into the past.

250. Isaiah Bennett, *Inside Mormonism* (San Diego: Catholic Answers, 1999), 246. Because he is a lapsed Mormon, Bennett is probably dismissed by Mormon thinkers as a secondary source.

251. Ibid., Appendix III, the Articles of Faith, 503–4.

252. Ibid. (quoted phrase and elaboration), 253–66. Mormons do not regard themselves as polytheists; while they do recognize more than one deity, they worship only the one God the Father.

253. Roberts, 473. To the scientific proposition toward multiple universes, the Christian might respond as follows. The one God might well sketch on a near infinite number of canvases to arrive at the infinitely improbable canvas of our universe. And it is in his creative self-disclosure that as an artist, rather than a random numbers generator, He chooses to enter into His own work as the Incarnation, through whom all honor and glory is given to the Father.

254. The elementary difference between progressive revelation and *development* of doctrine within a revealed "deposit of faith" in the Catholic Church (noted in Chapter

Four) is sometimes lost on rationalist biblical scholars (e.g., Stephen L. Harris, *Understanding the Bible* [Boston: McGraw Hill, 2003], 611). A case in point is the progressive revelation to the Mormon president in 1978 that the ban should be lifted against blacks entering the priesthood, an action that enabled Mormon proselytizing in Brazil and Africa (Newell Bringhurst, author of two books on Mormonism, in the *Washington Post*, "In Nigeria, the new Face of global Mormonism," carried in the Seattle Times, Nov. 26, 2007).

255. In the second century, Montanism divorced Christianity from the alleged corruptions of the Jewish heritage by rejecting any continuity with the Old Testament. In the tenth and eleventh centuries Catharism, imported from Bulgaria, so radically rejected human imperfection that it denied both the natural world and the sacramental life, rejecting even marriage and the begetting of children. Suicide by starvation, echoed in modern day euthanasia, was approved.

256. "During its pilgrimage on earth, this People, though still in its members liable to sin, is growing in Christ . . ." (*Unitas Redinegratio* [Ecumenism], n. 3, italics added).

257. Under the scrutiny of the Church's formal teaching authority (the magisterium) any blending of worldliness with the call to holiness remains outside of the Scripture and Tradition, and is opposed by the official teaching about morality and Christ as the True Self, within whom "we live, and move and have our being" (Acts 17:28). See Chapter 4.

258. Second Vatican Council, *Gaudium et Spes* (The Church in the Modern World), n. 22, italics added.

259. Letter of St. Leo the Great, *Liturgy of the Hours*, Vol. II, 1746. St. Bernard remarked in a sermon: "The lesser he became through his human nature the greater was his goodness; the more he lowered himself for me, the dearer he is to me" (ibid, Vol. I, 448).

260. Benoit Mandelbrot (coined the term "fractal"), in Nina Hall (ed.), *Exploring Chaos: A Guide to the New Science of Disorder* (New York: W.W. Norton and Co., 19910, 122–35 (italics added).

261. With the eyes of the heart, this was already known to the prophets: "Behold, the nations count as a drop of the bucket, as dust on the scales; the coastlands weigh no more than powder" (Isa 40:15).

262. "Try me . . . shall I not open for you the floodgates of heaven, to pour down blessings upon you without measure"? (Mal 3:10).

263. For a delightful exposition on the progressive interplay of science and imagination, see Jacob Bronowski, *The Origins of Knowledge and Imagination* (New Haven: Yale University Press, 1978).

264. Infinitely smaller than the cosmos, and yet infinitely larger than the singularity is a single drop of blood. Witnesses to the twentieth century mystic and stigmatist Teresa Neumann report that as she reclined the flow blood from her inexplicable wounds defied gravity, e.g., "The force of gravity would undoubtedly have induced it to flow towards the ankle. The drop did not do this, but flowed almost vertically upwards towards the toes. This was the direction in which Our Lord's blood had flowed almost 2,000 year before on the cross" (Baron von Aretin, in *Berliner Heften*, April

1946 on the events of July 8, 1927, cited in Charles M. Carty, *The Two Stigmatists: Padre Pio and Teresa Neumann* [St. Paul, Mn.: Radio Replies Press Society, 1956], 133).

265. G.K. Chesterton, *Orthodoxy* (Garden City, New York: Image, 1959), 62.

266. *Variation of Animals and Plants under Domestication*, Vol. II (New York: D. Appleton and Co., 1883 [1868]), 428. At a higher level, Benedict XVI comments: "To him who as spirit upholds and encompasses the universe, a spirit, a man's heart with its ability to love, is greater than all the milky ways in the universe" (*Introduction to Christianity*, San Francisco: Ignatius, 2004 [1968], 146).

267. Within Christianity, the original Lutheran doctrine asserted a total corruption of the human person who then is lifted up by totally gratuitous grace. The Calvinist doctrine of predestination (with its parallel in Islam) is both opposite and equal in content. The consistent Catholic doctrine is that while fallen man has a tendency toward evil (concupiscence), this weakness does not corrupt absolutely. Human free will remains intact to respond to the gift of divine grace. The tie between faith and works is addressed by Lutherans and Catholics together in *the Joint Declaration on the Doctrine of Justification* (Grand Rapids, Michigan: William B. Eerdmans, 2001). The Declaration reads in part: "By grace alone, in faith in Christ's saving work and not because of any merit on our part, we are adopted by God and receive the Holy Spirit, who renews our hearts while equipping and calling us to good works" (n. 15).

268. A principle theme of Erik von Kuehnelt-Leddihn, citing Mortimer Adler (*Leftism Revisited : From De Sade and Marx to Hitler and Pol Pot* [Washington D.C.: Regnery Gateway, 1990], passim. and 26, with fn. 41 on p. 349). Also, "If the Spirit of God lives in us, then what every believer has within himself is greater than what he admires in the skies" (Pope Leo the Great, Sermon in *The Liturgy of the Hours*, Vol. III, 192).

269. It might even be that a diversity of models (e.g., various string theories) will remain irreconcilable, each version of physical reality applicable to specific physical situations (see Stephen Hawking and Leonard Mlodinaw, *The Grand Design* [New York: Bantam Books, 2010]).

270. Dom Boylon (d. 1963), "The Journey to Eternal Life," in Peter Cameron (ed.), *Magnificat*,10:3, Yonkers, New York: Magnificat, May 2008, 98–9. Pope Benedict XVI points to Holderlin's preface to the Hyperion: "Not to be encompassed by the greatest, but to let oneself be encompassed by the smallest—that is divine" (*Introduction to Christianity*, 146).

271. In the sixteenth century the Christian mystic Teresa of Avila reported how once she saw in prayer "with perfect clarity, how all things are seen in God and how within Himself He contains them all. . . . In all Three Persons there is not more than one will and one power and one dominion, so that none of Them can do anything without Another; so, however many creatures there may be, there is only One Creator" (Marie-Eugene, O.C.D., *I am a Daughter of the Church*, Vol. II [Allen Texas: Christian Classics, 1997], 259, 263).

272. Josef Cardinal Ratzinger (Pope Benedict XVI), *Introduction to Christianity*, 158, italics added.

273. "It is not claimed that Islam tells us anything which has never been heard before, but rather that Islam is the confirmation and continuation of the same fundamental

teaching which has been the guiding light of all those who have achieved the highest enlightenment on spiritual matters" (Hassan, 225).

274. On the Trinity, in Philip Schaff (ed*.), Nicene and Post-Nicene Fathers of the Christian Church* (Grand Rapids, Michigan: Wm. B. Eerdmans Publishing Co., 1998 [1887]) Book V, Ch. 9, italics added.

275. Treatise on the Trinity by St. Hilary, *Liturgy of the Hours*, Vol. II, 997–999. Giussani defines the "incarnation:" when the "enigmatic presence . . . became a phenomenon, a regular *fact* that could act upon and be registered in the trajectory of history" (*At the Origin of the Christian Claim*, [Ithaca: McGill-Queen's University Press, 1998], 29, italics added).

276. Robert Broderick, *The Catholic Encyclopedia* (New York: Thomas Nelson Inc., 1976), 118. St. Hilary, bishop, writes of the Trinity: "One power, (which) brings all things into being, one Son, through whom all things come to be, and one gift of perfect hope" (in *Liturgy of the Hours*, Vol. II, 998).

277. Based on Genesis, another Catholic writer, Henri Daniel-Rops, holds that "the descendents of Ishmael, the Arabs of the desert, know that they, too, have received the promise, and that the will of God himself has made them a great nation" (*Israel and the Ancient World* [Garden City, New York: Image, 1964], 37, italics added).

278. Belloc, 76 (italics added).

279. Ibid., Short of actual denial, a principle of Western theology is that to affirm one truth is not to deny another.

280. Muslim apologists propose that Mohammed had few contacts with foreigners and that he made only one trip beyond his homeland, that he was illiterate and could not personally study other scriptures, and that the Bible was not translated into Arabic until many centuries after his death.

281. The Gnostics sought salvation through a secretive and elitist appeal to esoteric knowledge, and discounted human free will and other elements. Gnostics accepted Luke, but not the other synoptic writers (Matthew and Mark) since they reference the crucifixion and resurrection. The Gnostics then added other gospels which by their dated content appear to be too late to have been suppressed as an original but minority testimony (Philip Jenkins, *The Hidden Gospels* [New York: Oxford University Press, 2001], 54–81).

282. Hilaire Belloc, *Against the Heretics*, e.g., Book 1, Ch. 10. Gnosticism is very much with us today. Eric Voegelin develops the thesis that the ideology of Modernity—the full replacement of truth by world imminent action—is the result of splicing Gnostic enlightenment with the need for certainty within history (*The New Science of Politics* [Chicago: University of Chicago Press, 1952]).

283. Dante, *Inferno*, XXVIII: 22–33. Citing Nardi and Asin Palacios, Frederick Copleston holds that Mohammed is placed in hell by Dante simply because he was not a philosopher. Muslim philosophers, to whom Dante owed a great deal, are more highly placed (*The History of Philosophy: Medieval*, Vol. 2 [Garden City, New York: Image, 1962], 225).

284. Dante, *Purgatory*, XXXII: 130–5 (Mark Musa, *The Portable Dante* (New York: Penguin, 1995), 380.

285. Abdullah Yusuf Ali, ibid., Appendix V, 413.

286. Qutb was an Egyptian Muslim radical who after an extended stay in the United States saw the world as beset by *jahilliyya*, or the "days of ignorance" as they existed prior to Mohammed, and as seductive and capable of destroying Islam. He concluded that there was no middle ground between Islam and Satan (*The 9/11 Commission Report*, 2004, 51). Qutb was executed by Egyptian President Nassar in 1966.

287. Ayoub in Omar (ed.), 205.

288. As formally and precisely defined by the Catholic Church: "Inspiration is a supernatural impulse by which the Holy Spirit has inspired and directed the sacred authors, and assisted them in their writing, so that they should preserve accurately, and with to report faithfully, and express with an infallible verity all that God directs them to write, and that only" (Pope Leo XIII, *Providentissimus Deus* [Providence of God], italics added; citation from Henri Daniel-Rops, *Israel and the Ancient World*, Garden City, New York: Image Books, 1964, p. 326). The Second Vatican Council reiterates the boundary of inerrancy for "that truth which God wanted put into the sacred writings for the sake of our salvation." Inerrancy cannot be called upon to validate a literalist interpretation of cosmology or geologic history (*Dei Verbum* [Revelation], n. 11).

289. Josef Pieper, *For the Love of Wisdom: Essays on the Nature of Philosophy* (San Francisco: Ignatius, 2006), 205. This view finds a place at the Second Vatican Council: "Nor does Divine Providence deny the aids necessary for salvation to those who, without blame on their part, have not yet reached an explicit belief in God, but strive to lead a good life, under the influence of God's grace" (*Lumen Gentium*, nn. 2–16).

290. Some propose that the wise men were descendents of the ten lost tribes of Israel dispersed by the ethnic cleansing of the invading Assyrians. Monotheism finds its way into Zoroastrianism near the time of Cyrus the Great, in the sixth century B.C.

291. William Barclay, *The Letters of James and Peter* (Philadelphia: Westminster Press, 1976) 181.

292. Muhammad Ali, 64.

293. Jean Guitton, *Great Heresies and Church Councils* (New York: Harper and Row, 1983), 116. Citing Goldziher, Nicholson greatly credits the differences between theoretical Islam and the receiving Arabian culture: "It was not the destruction of their idols that they opposed so much as the spirit of devotion which it was sought to implant in them: the determination of their whole lives by the thought of God and of His pre-ordaining and retributive omnipotence, the prayers and fasts, the renouncement of coveted pleasures, and the sacrifice of money and property which was demanded in God's name" (from Ignaz Goldziher, *Muhammedanische Studien* [Halle, 1888–9], 1–39)…The Bedouin who accepted Islam had to unlearn the greater part of his unwritten moral code. As a pious Moslem he must return good for evil, forgive his enemy, and find balm for his wounded feelings in the assurance of being admitted into Paradise (Q 3:128). Again, the social organization of the heathen Arabs was based on the tribe, whereas that of Islam rested on the equality and fraternity of all believers. The religious bond cancelled all distinctions of rank and pedigree; it did away, theoretically, with clannish feuds, contests for honor, pride of race—things that lay at the root of Arabian chivalry….(Rather than heartfelt coversion)…what chiefly inspired them, apart from love of booty, was the conviction, born of success, that

Allah was fighting on their side" (Reynold A. Nicholson, *A Literary History of the Arabs* [New York: Charles Scribner's Sons, 1907]178–9).

294. Heinrich Rommen, *Natural Law* (Indianapolis: Liberty Fund, 1998), 58.

295. Henri Daniel-Rops, *Israel and the Ancient World* (Garden City, New York: Image, 1964), 195.

296. In a Western setting, the cult of the Ghost Dance and invincibility in battle arose among the plains Indians partly because the peaceful message of a messiah was unacceptable. Commenting on a local prophet, Chief Porcupine (a Cheyenne Sioux) "...said that the Indians who had gone to hear this new Christ with him had gone hoping to hear him preach some incendiary doctrine, and that they were disappointed at hearing that the new creed required them simply to work and behave themselves; that, being known by their people to have visited this new Messiah, they concluded on their return home not to relate strictly what this man had told them, but to put into his mouth doctrines more agreeable to the Indians" (Fletcher Johnson, op. cit., 270).

297. Harry Zohn, (trans.), *Judgments on History and Historians* (Boston: Beacon Press, 1958), 47.

298. James of the New Testament, however, does translate: "'God resists the proud but bestows his favor on the lowly.' Therefore *submit* to God . . ." (James 4:7, italics added).

299. The *Qur'an* does speak of "Allah's Covenant" with Father Abraham, e.g., Q 2:27.

300. John Paul II, *The Holy Spirit in the Life of the Church and the World* (Dominum et Vivificantem), (Boston: Pauline Books and Media, 1986), n. 34.

301. Biblical scholarship offers the Documentary Hypothesis which holds that Genesis is comprised of four distinct sources. It is almost as if Islam tapped into the very early Elohist oral tradition of a distant God, apart from its historical combination with the later Jawhist tradition of a more anthropomorphic and accessible God. Both traditions contribute to a balanced Old Testament. The Arabic Allah is linguistically related to the Hebrew Elohim. In the same vein, the *Qur'an* reflects the late Greek *Targums*, translations of the Aramaic dating from the century before Christ, and which also preserved a more distant Godhead.

302. Arianism was the cause of the Council of Nicaea in 325. Muslim scholars assert that Christianity was unitarian (like Islam) up until this Council. The Christian doctrinal issue was resolved finally in the seeming detail of a dotted "i"–*homo-ousios* versus *homoiousios* (Christ as uncreated or "of the same essence or substance" as the Father versus created in time or of only a "similar substance."). If the weight assigned to single words or even a letter within a word arouses the dismay of the modern mind, we might reflect on the critical difference between military "first strike," or "preemptive" strike, or on the pre-requisite "shape of the table" for peace negotiations.

303. Cited without source in Henri Daniel-Rops, *The Church of Apostles and Martyrs*, Vol. II (Garden City, New York: Image, 1962), 199.

304. Belloc, 43.

305. In at least one interesting detail the Protestant movement in Europe is interactive with Islam on the frontier of European Christendom. In the 1520s the Turkish invasion into Hapsburg territories led to a proposal to maintain temporarily the reli-

gious status quo in German territory, with Catholic Masses to be tolerated until a later date. In 1529 the Second Diet of Speyer protested and rejected this imperial demand for even-handed toleration, giving rise to Jacob Strum's coined term "Protestantism." The specific protest was against toleration (John Dolan, 256).

306. Nicholson makes the case that Sufi Islam absorbed features of not only Christianity and Gnosticism, but also earlier Buddhism and Neo-Platonism in what later became Islamic domain Reynold A. Nicholson, *The Mystics of Islam* (New York: Penguin, 1989 [1914]).

307. Quoted phrase from Hassan, 225.

308. Ayoub refers to an early twentieth century translation which maintains that rather than being crucified, Christ was carried to heaven by angels and his place on the cross was taken by Judas who was made to look and sound like Christ (in Omar [ed.], 173). Not unlike the Islamic interpretation, some modern-day scholars also oppose the unique divinity of Christ with the alternative divinity of all through self-enlightenment, e.g., Elaine Pagels. Critical to this view is the actual date of parts of the *Gospel of Thomas*. Philip Jenkins finds evidence that this early writing is edited with later Gnostic insertions, possibly 150 years after Christ (*The Hidden Gospels* [New York: Oxford University Press, 2001], 70–72). In *The Gnostic Gospels* Pagels purports that the doctrine of monotheism and the Church hierarchy served to consolidate power against the diversity of the Gnostics. Paul Mankowski shows that Pagel's documentation is not only "conflated" as she admits, but a non-scholarly invention that suppresses context, omits wording, and shifts phrases "to pervert the meaning of the original" (cwnews.com and "The Pagels Imposture," *Catholic World Report* [San Francisco: Ignatius, May 2006], 38–9.

309. Joseph Cardinal Ratzinger (Pope Benedict XVI), *Values in a Time of Upheaval* (San Francisco: Ignatius Press, 2006), 93. Our attention was drawn to Ratzinger's words by Gil Bailie, "Raising the Ante: Recovering an Alpha and Omega Christology," *Communio*, Washington, D.C.: Communio, Inc., Spring 2008, pp. 83–106. See also Psalms: "My God, I delight in your law in the depth of my heart" (Ps 40:9).

310. Even the God of the Old Testament fails to satisfy the Western stereotype of a vengeful and fickle sovereign in need of subservient submission. Jonah is sent even to the spiritual and moral sinkhole of Nineveh with the consistent message of repentance and compassion (Jon 1–3).

311. International Theological Commission, *Memory and Reconciliation: The Church and the Faults of the Past*, December 1999, n. 3.4.

312. Ayoub in Omar (ed.), 177. In a separate but interesting parallel, early cosmology assumed that the laws governing the heavens were different than the laws governing things of earth. Newton's revolutionary discovery of universal gravitation altered this imagined split-level worldview.

313. Guillaume has the historical Sufi figure Hallaj also teaching that "God is love" (Alfred Guillaume, *Islam* [New York: Penguin Books, 1956], 146).

314. Rather than a merely human idea, Revelation is the *self-disclosure* to us of the *living* God: "In His goodness and wisdom, God chose to reveal Himself and to make known to us the hidden purpose of His will (cf. Eph. 1:9) by which through Christ, *the word made flesh*, man has access to the Father in the Holy Spirit and comes to

share in the divine nature" (*Dei Verbum*, Second Vatican Council, n. 2, italics added; cf. Eph. 2:18, 2 Pt 1:4).

315. John Paul II, *Crossing the Threshold of Hope* (New York, Alfred Knopf, 1994), 92–3.

316. Ibid. John Paul II quotes the Council: "Even if over the course of centuries Christians and Muslims have had more than a few dissensions and quarrels, this sacred Council now urges all to forget the past and to work toward mutual understanding as well as toward the preservation and promotion of social justice, moral welfare, peace, and freedom for the benefit of all mankind" (*Nostra Aetate*, 3).

317. Edwin Bliss, op. cit., 61.

318. Ali writes that "it was carnal-minded men who invented the doctrine of original sin," adding later that within Islam the word "guidance" means "Guide us to and in the straight way" (Abdullah Yusuf Ali, 25, 88, and 15 [notes 50, 249, 22]).

319. John Paul II, *The Original Innocence of Man and Woman* (Boston: Daughters of St. Paul, 1981), 36.

320. Attributed by Peter Brown, *Augustine of Hippo* (Berkeley: University of California Press, 1969), 326 (from the *City of God*, inaccurate citation).

321. *The City of God*, Book XIV, 15.

322. Ali, op. cit., 25 (note 50), 1217 (note 4148).

323. Citation from Gustave Bardy in Don Luigi Giussani, *Why the Church?* (San Francisco: Ignatius, 2001), 190–1.

324. Abdullah Yusuf Ali, Q 2:37, n. 55.

325. Robert Egan, S.J., *New Direction in the Doctrine of Original Sin* (doctoral dissertation), Fordham University, 1973, 196 (italics added).

326. St. Augustine, *The City of God*, Book XVIII, Ch. 51.

327. Citing the Dominican monk Ricardi (c. 1210) and the French Ricaut (n.d.), Prideaux attributes the prohibition of wine (Q: 5:90) to the good judgment of Mohammed responding to a tendency to overindulge combined with the effects of the hot climate (*Life of Mahomet*, 63–4). The precipitating event was a marriage feast that degenerated into male embracing and then fighting and bloody dismemberments. Alternatively, sacrificial blood came to be regarded by Arabs (and Hebrews) as too sacred to be consumed, and finally was absolutely prohibited by Mohammed (William Robertson Smith, *Lectures on the Religions of the Semites* [London: A. and C. Black, Ltd., 1927, 1989], 234–5).

328. Muhammad Ali, 14.

329. Where the successor third caliph Uthman is said to have destroyed all conflicting texts, the parallel in Chinese history is that of the first emperor of the Ch'in dynasty. In 211 B.C. he is said to have burned nearly all of the books in the empire because of their different interpretations of the Chinese past, and to have buried 460 scholars alive in a mass grave (Bill Porter, *Road to Heaven: Encounters with Chinese Hermits* [San Francisco: Mercury House, 1993], 178).

330. Ibid., 295, italics added.

331. Ibid., 45. Ali also cites this ayat: "This day I have perfected your religion for you and completed My favour to you. I have chosen Islam to be your faith" (Q5:3).

332. Ablution is prescribed in the *Qur'an* and seems to carry forward ritual purification from the Pentateuch. In both cases washing with water (or with sand) prefigures the one-time baptism for the forgiveness of sins of the New Testament, "for Allah doth blot out sins and forgive again and again" (Q 4:43).

333. Daniel Madigan, op. cit.

334. Norman Daniel summarizing a much early writer, 110.

335. Norman Daniel dismisses as legend the concept that the Arabs were corrupted by Sergius, but includes a version written by the medieval William of Auvergne: (Sergius or Bahira) appeared to be of such piety and holiness that Muhammad wished to make him his teacher; and sometimes he called him 'Gabriel the Archangel'—hiding what he dared not reveal, that the lunacies which he delivered to those whom he deceived he had learned from a man" (105).

336. Note the similarity to the Old Testament prefiguring of Christ, e.g., "A prophet like me will the Lord, your God, raise up for you...to him you shall listen" (Deut 18:18). Some Church Fathers, and others, claim that after the coming of Christ and his rejection, the Messianic prophecies were altered in the Talmud. In some cases the prophecies are seen as referring to David or Solomon, or even to the Jewish Nation itself. The *Qur'an* also implicitly has Moses foretelling Muhammad (Q 46:10).

337. Friedrich Heer, *The Medieval World*, 153.

338. G.A. Williamson (ed.) in Eusebius, *The History of the Church* (New York: Penguin, 1965), 23–4.

339. On the spirituality of philokalia, see G.E.H. Palmer, Philip Sherrard, and Kallistos Ware (trans.), *The Philokalia*, Vol. I (Boston: Faber and Faber, 1983 [1979]. The parenthetical definition is from the introduction (13). A telling contrast between the *Philokalia*, compiled from centuries of monastic tradition and centered on the Jesus Prayer, and the *Qur'an*, compiled in less than two decades from the writings of a celebrated intertribal and mystical leader, is that the former is inseparably "bound up with (the) sacramental and liturgical life" (15) of a Church tradition. To separate philokalia and its path to stillness (*hesychai*) from its ecclesiology would be an "abuse" and "to act with a presumption that may well have consequences of a disastrous kind, mental and physical" (15). The radical wing of Islam asserts that all forms of jihad in the world depend on the greater (inner) jihad, and that "if we succeed in the greater jihad, then all our other strivings will count as jihad, and if not, they will be satanic" (Imam Khomeini, *Islam and Revolution: Writings and Declarations* [London: KPI, 1981], 385). Exploited by unreasoned interpretation and the accretions of history, the subjective sense of inner jihad gives license to suicide bombings as among "all our other strivings." Prior to his Medina period, Mohammed himself might not have recognized this aspect of Islam today.

Chapter Three

The Mosque:
Shari'a and the World

The overall Muslim worldview is well expressed in this way: "(The modern European mind is) . . . so accustomed to regard religion and metaphysics and the various natural sciences as independent and autonomous fields of knowledge that it is difficult for us to comprehend a system in which physics and metaphysics, cosmology and epistemology were all combined in a single unity."[1] To the traditional Western mind, Islam tends to homogenize into false unities such distinct realities as faith and reason, church (mosque) and state, world and heaven, inspiration and folk literature, revelation and natural law, and peace and war (jihad). The less traditional Western worldview of today errs in another direction. This is less the propensity to conflate than to subsume all modes of thought under one method, namely the experimental method of the natural sciences. To understand the commingled crises of Islam and of the West is also to examine divergent presuppositions. Chapter 3 begins with the Islamic "way of life" based on the *Qur'an*. Chapter 4 focuses the Western distinction between Church and State and then on the Christian "new life" and morally based principles proposed by the Church (not imposed) to achieve the common good, partly through the state. Chapter 5 deals broadly with Modernity, the third leg of the triangular encounter suggested in the subtitle to this book.

THE *QUR'AN* AND THE NEW TESTAMENT

The *Qur'an* and the New Testament are not comparable, since the first points to a religion of the book, while the latter is witness statements about and from Christ as the Word made flesh. This section explores this difference, but also provides a back-and-forth review of some of the contents of each writing. The theological divide between Islam and Christianity is that Islam is attentive, exclusively, on the transcendence of Allah, while Christians proclaim a transcendent God who by his own free choice has revealed his inner life (the Trinity) in the incarnate Christ. Interpretation of scriptures is dissimilar, since the *Qur'an* is believed to be dictated, while the Christian witness is inspired, but not dictated.[2] These themes serve as background for the section to follow which explores the unitary Islamic State.

During the first twenty years after the death of the Prophet his followers compiled and edited his verbal messages into the written *Qur'an* or "recitations." This point-in-time "revelation" to a single prophet contrasts with the Old Testament as a covenanted encounter through the centuries between the Israelites as a people and Yahweh. The *Qur'an* also differs from the New Testament testimony of the first Christians, a testimony supplied by *witnesses* to the oneness of Jesus with the Father, and to His death and resurrection within human history (Mk 16:9, 28:9; Lk 24:13, 34, 36, 50; Jn 21:1, 20:24). Christ is witnessed by men other than himself, by his words and his works (Jn 5:36), and by the Father: "This is my beloved Son, with whom I am well pleased" (Mt 3:17; see also Mk 1:11, Lk 3:22, Jn 1:32–4). This witnessing is repeated later on Mount Tabor, and more is added "listen to Him" (Mt 17:5). In contrast the *Qur'an* refers directly to Mohammed as a messenger: "We sent down the (*Qur'an*) in Truth, and in Truth has it descended: and We sent Thee but to give Glad Tidings and to warn (sinners)" (Q 17:105).

Theologically, Islam and Christianity are not symmetrical nor fully comparable. The comparison with Christianity is that *the Qur'an as a scripture is made parallel to Christ—rather than to the Christian Bible.* William Cantwell Smith distills this core asymmetry: "What corresponds in the Christian scheme to the *Qur'an* is not the Bible but the person of Christ—it is Christ who is for Christians the revelation of God. And what corresponds to the Bible (the record of revelation) is the Islamic Tradition (hadith)."[3] Muslim scholars consistently compare the *Qur'an* directly to Christ, the memory and hope of Christians: "the Word became book, rather than the Word became flesh."[4] Again, the two religions are not symmetrical on the place each assigns to scripture. Under Islam the *Qur'an* is the *uncreated word of God*—an exact copy of the original text in heaven (Q 85:22).[5]

The task for interreligious dialogue is not so simple as to avoid profiling one religion with selective quotations from the scriptures of the other. For Christians the living biblical tradition of the combined Old and New Testaments traces from the faith of Abraham, through Isaac and forward to fulfillment in Christ, the self-disclosure of a God who is so self-giving that in the fullness of time he saturates his own creation personally with himself. The

coming of Christ is the understood meaning of Nathan's prophecy to David
that the Lord would "make his kingdom secure . . . (and that it) shall endure
forever before me" (1 Sam 7:12,16). "I will not withdraw my favor from him"
says the Lord (1 Sam 7:15).

The *Qur'an* of Islam asserts a break in this history, Rather than to Isaac,
it connects tribal Arabia directly back to Ishmael (Q 19:54), son of the slave
girl Hagar, as an alternative to the unbroken path beginning with Abraham
and tracing through his wife Sarah and their son Isaac (Q 2:136, 19:54).[6] Of
the witnesses in the Bible narrative: "They were dismayed at his teaching, for
he taught them as one who had authority, and not as the scribes" (Mk 1:22).
And St. Paul writes: "For they are not all Israelites who are sprung from Israel; nor because they are descendants of Abraham, are they all his children;
but through Isaac shall thy posterity bear thy name" (Rom 9:6–7).[7] In the Old
Testament account God said of Abraham's first two sons, "I will make of him
(Ishmael) a great nation. But my covenant I will maintain with Isaac, whom
Sarah shall bear to you . . ." (Gen 17:20–21).

The significance of Abraham to Jews, Christians and Muslims is partly
this: when called from "the land of your kinfolk," he turned toward the
promise. He turned away from family and clan, and their cultic rituals so
depended upon to domesticate the cosmos. He turned away from all that
was known—and even all that is knowable by the exercise of human imagination and reason (Gen 12:1–4). Abraham left behind the astrologers and
moon worshipers atop the citadel of Ur. But from their different beginnings,
Islam and the Judeo-Christian tradition are on already different paths. Like
Judaism and Christianity, Islam reveres the power of God, and his beauty:
"He is Allah, the Creator, the Maker, the Fashioner. His are the most beautiful names. Whatever is in the heavens and the earth declares His glory;
and he is Mighty and Wise" (Q 59:24). But Mohammed casts Christianity
as a fragment of terminal Judaism. He selects for himself themes from the
Pentateuch (The first five books of the Old Testament beginning with Genesis) in the writing of the *Qur'an*. Genesis is read by Islam as a promise not
only of lineage, but also of its own rise in the seventh century as a distinct
religion of restoration.

In the New Testament of the Christians the last prophet is John the Baptist
who had this to say about the difference between clan lineage and the actual
descendents of Abraham, "Do not presume to say to yourselves, 'We have
Abraham as our father.' For I tell you, God can raise up children to Abraham
from these stones" (Mt 3:9). Christ is finally asked, "Art thou greater than
our father Abraham, who is dead? And the prophets who are dead. Whom
dost thou make thyself?" And Jesus answered: "If I glorify myself, my glory
is nothing. It is my Father who glorifies me, of whom you say that he is your

God. And you do not know him, but I know him . . . and I keep his word. Abraham your father rejoiced that he was to see my day. He saw it and was glad. The Jews therefore said to him, 'Thou art not yet fifty years old, and hast thou seen Abraham?' Jesus said to them, "Amen, amen, I say to you, before Abraham came to be, I am" (Jn 8:53–58).

Within the original Christian tradition it is the Church as the Body of Christ—more than any Scripture—that is the living imprint of the eternal:

> You surely cannot be ignorant of the fact that the living Church is the body of Christ; for Scripture says: God made man male and female . . . Now the male signifies Christ, and the female signifies the Church, which, according to both the Old and the New Testament, is no recent creation, but has *existed from the beginning.* At first the Church was purely spiritual. . . . (but now) the body of the Church is *a copy of the Spirit*, and no one who defaces the copy can have any part in what the copy represents.[8]

Unlike the followers of Islam, the witnesses to Christ point to the Word rather than the beauty of their words. The witnesses to Christ point to the resurrection, to the nuptial beauty of the Church's martyrs, and to the most unlikely flourishing of the early Church under Roman persecution. The proof of the incarnate Christ is itself incarnate. The irony is that this proof is demonstrated under afflictions drawn out by non-believers—whether by the Roman state, or by the years following the rise of militant Islam in 620, or by the years following 1789 in the West.

Muslim scholars explain that Islam is distinguished as a complete "way of life." Islam is not falsely divided as was early Christendom into separate domains for mosque and for state. Such a division in the West, Muslim scholars propose, traces back to the historical accident of Christians persecution in the pagan Roman Empire. Culturally, Islam advanced victorious and undivided from its beginning, undistorted by any merely historical divide between the ruled and the rulers. As a theological system, the *Qur'an* still reveres Christ but as only a prophet, a limited stature that Christ himself explicitly dismissed in a discourse with his apostles (Mt 16:15). At this point, the *Qur'an* constructs a consistency between itself and the Bible by inserting words into the mouth of an only prophetic Christ: "And of Jesus son of Mary, who said to the Israelites: 'I am sent forth to you from God to confirm the Torah already revealed, and to give news of an apostle that will come after me whose name is Ahmad' (another name for Mohammed meaning "The Praised One") (Q 61:5–6).[9] But on the Road to Emmaus, six centuries before Mohammed and his editors, we hear this: "Beginning, then, with Moses and all the prophets, he interpreted for them every passage of Scripture which referred to him . . . ." (Lk 24:13–35).[10]

Islam harkens back Abraham and through him to "guidance" given early
to the fallen Adam (Q 2:37, 38). St. Paul also preaches that God has "manifested" himself to all through his creation, such that there is no excuse even
for those who do not know Christ for not giving glory and thanks from the
beginning (Rom 1:18–21). "For since the creation of the world his invisible
attributes are clearly seen—his everlasting power also and his divinity—being understood through the things that are made" (Rom 1:20). In Christian
history, the heretical fifth century priest Pelagius proposed further that without divine grace natural human perfectibility was sufficient for salvation.
Responding directly to Pelagius, St. Augustine points again to St. Paul: "I
will not make void the grace of God: for if righteousness comes by the law,
then Christ is dead in vain" (Gal 2:21).[11] Under Islam Christ is but one of the
several prophets all preceding Mohammed as the final restorer of lost guidance given to all. The *Qur'an* accepts Christ's miracles, but holds that these
divine actions were done only with the outside permission and power of an
ever distant God (Q 3:48–50). The Christ found in Scripture, however, claims
beyond any earlier guidance the authority to act: "If I do not perform my Father's works, put no faith in me. But if I do perform them, even though you
put no faith in me, put faith in the works so as *to realize what it means that
the Father is in me and I am in him*" (Jn 10:37–8, italics added).

In sum, the central compromise or dichotomy of Islam is its partial attentiveness to the otherness of God and, therefore, the apparent rejection of
His most intimate presence as discovered in Christ. The fullness of Christ as
"savior" in word and deed gains no entrance in Islam. In place of the Fall
and the Redeemer, Islam holds that God immediately extended to Man only
a more attenuated mercy: "But his Lord chose him (Adam). He turned to him
and gave him guidance" (Q 20:122). The Christian St. Irenaeus says much the
same: "From the beginning, God had implanted in the heart of man the precepts of the natural law. Then he was content to remind him of them. This was
the Decalogue."[12] But with Islam there is no further need for salvation history
and personal redemption as participation in the life of God. By comparison,
there is a more harmonic remembering and forgetting, of repentance and of
sin. Beyond this cycle so familiar to all mankind, the human need for redemption at least reminds all of us that our will is not necessarily God's will.
The redemptive cross is a sign of contradiction. Non-redemptive ideology
reappears in modern secularism which also erases original sin and original
innocence from the language of ideas. The Christian insight, expressed with
the permanence of a doctrine, is that the instinctive pride of self and pride of
life is a self-inflicted desertion from a revealed and ever larger life in the "garden" presence of God. Our understanding of the "original" stature of man is
actually elevated by the fact that by humiliating each other we also humiliate

our Source. As both the perpetrator and the victim we place ourselves in need of an original salvation from outside of ourselves. Modern psychiatry frees us from the notion that the emotionally disturbed are demoniacs, but modernity should also sense that even modern psychology is not alchemy.

For the Muslim there still remains a Day of Judgment and of possible mercy from above, assisted possibly by the prayers of Mohammed. But muted in the Islamic understanding of justice is a more feminine mystical theology found in the richer Christian tradition. This feminine element, well demonstrated by Julian of Norwich (b. 1373), understands God's relationship to us less in juridical and masculine terms and more in the terms of a mother's care for her children. Rather than a cycle of forgetting and remembering, this tradition points to growth and healing and finds ways of loving the Lord and Redeemer while still in the world that is also loved.[13] In the words of Christ himself: "(Jerusalem) how many times I yearned to gather your children together as a hen gathers her brood under her wings, but you were unwilling" (Lk 13:34).

Islam and Christianity focus on the encounter of humanity with the divine. Both point to a final judgment concluding and transcending the flux of history and time. But with the *Qur'an* the encounter with God is periodically restored in a wave pattern of forgetting and remembering. This paradigm is possibly influenced by a cyclical understanding of history still lingering from a rejected pagan world. Even Christ's reference to the coming of the Holy Spirit, the Paraclete and the Comforter (Jn 14:15–17, 14:26, and 16:12, 13, 17), is understood by Muslim scholars as referring to the coming of the final Prophet Mohammed.[14] Where the *Qur'an* is to be contrasted with Christ rather than the Bible, Mohammed's successors also substitute him for the Holy Spirit. Because of the gap that confines God to remaining a distant God and man to remain a man outside redemption, the self-giving descent of the divine is reduced to a conceptual position alternative to the apologetics of Islam. Where the incarnate Christ says "I and the Father are One" (Jn 10:30) and "Whoever has seen me has seen the Father" (Jn 14:7), the Prophet Mohammed instructs his followers, "I am but a man like you" (Q 41:6). Islam sees Christianity as polytheistic, while Christians see in Islam a God of finite transcendence, near but apart. The gap is compensated by Mohammed and his possible prayers; where Christians know God to be closer to us than we are to ourselves, Islam proclaims "The Prophet is closer to the Believers than their own selves" (Q 33:6).

The transcendence of Allah seems so encompassing as to even trump human reason. On this point Muslim apologists have second thoughts: "Modern Muslims have laid much stress on reason as the final arbiter of truth, again in accordance with the Qur'anic emphasis on the necessity of understanding and reason . . . (and further) revelation must accord with reason...(and) . . . the probability of the truth of any idea must in the end be determined by reason."[15] The Christian faith responds to a complete salvation and lifting from above, which it finds to be coherent with reason, i.e., not unreasonable: "What we shall later be has not yet come to light, we know that when it comes to light *we shall be like him, for we shall see him as he is*" (1 Jn 3:2, italics added).[16] For Christians the gulf between God and man is not fully bridged by reason, but is finally crossed from the other side by a God who would share his inner life with us, beginning even now in this world. This is the "new life" of the Gospel especially as proclaimed by St. Paul.

A prominent Jewish self-understanding differs from both of these positions. While messianic as is Christianity, the Jewish view is of a messiah who comes at the end of time and who is more of a sage than a redeemer. Islam places "guidance" in Adam at the beginning of history and in the faith of Abraham as retrieved from the ravages of history by Mohammed. Within Judaism, Rabbi Neusner proposes that its three current branches—Conservative, Reformed and Orthodox—all give evidence a new and common search for ways to move forward with increased segregation from others in the world. For well over fifteen hundred years survival was achieved within a Christian culture. But today's post-Christian culture of nations and classes now calls for another major adjustment by Judaism. This contemporary searching, he argues, remains as before in that it is based on the original "dual-Torah" of the written word combined with the more flexible oral traditions (which were not written until the third to the seventh centuries, e.g., the Mishnah).[17]

Unlike Judaism and Islam, Christianity is not insular—St. Paul went to the Gentiles and opened the faith to the world of Greek thought (reason). The specifically Catholic self-understanding, unlike the Protestant sects, centers on a living and sacramental Tradition, rather than on the Bible as the foundation (*sola Scriptura*). The Church proposes both Scripture and Tradition. Islam is insular like Judaism, but centers on the word made book (*Qur'an*) combined with the later hadith (sayings of the Prophet). Within the Catholic tradition, St. Thomas Aquinas provides a resilient Christian treatment on intricate but central points such as the fit between things of faith and things of reason. Authentic things of faith are coherent with reason, but not reducible to reasoned probabilities. Developing the concept of *analogy*, he proposes a distinct and open faith together with distinct and open reason. Faith and reason are coherent. Already a millennium before Aquinas, St. Irenaeus (135–200 A.D.?) saw how with finite minds we still detect God, through analogy: "The Father is beyond our sight and comprehension, but he is known by his Word, who tells us of him who surpasses all telling."[18] Today, the modern philosophy of phenomenology deals with how we perceive what is in fact a "world" around us and especially other persons or other "selves." We find ourselves in a place, and then place ourselves in the place of others—not in the sense of being identical, but in the sense of understanding and empathy, and finally the compassion of "suffering with." We know others by empathy—and analogy. Thomas noticed in detail that this is also how we know God. His thinking is extended in modern research on human empathy by Edith Stein, the early twentieth century Jewish intellectual who converted to Catholic Christianity and then was martyred at Auschwitz in 1942 (and canonized in 1998).[19]

Analogy is a bridge between the known and the unknowable. Analogy holds that things can be *similar in some respects while still dissimilar in others*, as between human goodness and the ever greater, dissimilar, and infinite goodness of God. God who *is* the good is imaged in us, but also remains ever more infinitely beyond us. Beyond Aquinas' own faithfulness and reasoning and his own human authorship of "analogy," there remains the ever more gifted abyss: "For from the greatness and the beauty of created things their original author, by analogy, is seen" (Wis 13:5, written a century before the coming of Christ). Pope Benedict XVI meditates that we approach God through analogy and participation precisely because we are not God. Analogy is grounded in God and therefore is also always young and open rather than closed. "To conceive God as the Act of being pure and subsisting by itself, cause and end of all other beings, is by the same token to give oneself a theology that can do justice to whatever is true in other theologies, just as metaphysics of *esse* has what is needed to do justice to whatever is true in other philosophies."[20] *By analogy we know that man is like God, but that as this likeness is advanced, the unlikeness advances infinitely more.* In this solution Aquinas was preceded by and builds upon the early fifth century St. Augustine's maxim: "I believe in order to understand," and St. Anselm who preached a "faith seeking understanding." Abu-Bakr, the first caliph following the passing of Mohammed (632), remarked: "Not to be able to comprehend understanding is already to understand!"

The purpose of understanding is to love the truth (*philo Sophia*: love of wisdom, not grasping for) and in this way not to simply conquer the truth. Reason cannot prove the faith, but as the nineteenth century John Henry Cardinal Newman explains, reason can disarm any obstacles to the faith that reason itself raises. The seed of faith remains forever a gift from a Giver; it is not a construct of the human intuition. The direct relevance of analogy to the modern person, too, and our own quest for truth, cannot be overstated. Modernity still confronts an analogue universe—a cosmos of real things and their relations—even if this encounter through symbolic and explanatory mathematics. In its openness to science, analogy never forgets the mystery of the questioner, the question of who I am and why, alongside the equal mystery of others including God. The

Christian seeks to become a fully human person, that is, in his heart and will to become one with a God who makes himself known, and in his intellect to both know the cosmos, and to be "like Him, for we shall see Him as He is" (1 Jn 3:2).

Islam, centuries before Aquinas, struggled less successfully to reconcile its abstractness with earthly human reason. In this effort, and yet to protect the unity of God, the ninth century Mu'tazila school proposed that the multiple divine attributes of God listed in the *Qur'an* could be interpreted allegorically. His adherents also maintained that man has free will and the power to choose his acts.[21] Mu'tazilites looked for ways to soften such inconsistencies in the *Qur'an* as the teaching that man is responsible for his actions, but that all things are decreed and in effect that man can be condemned eternally for doing what he is commanded by Allah to do. But the historian Friedrich Heer comments that even the later twelfth century Muslim philosophy "was never more than a struggle between conservative and liberal tendencies among the mu'tazila, who were by definition removed from the world."[22]

In the tenth century, al-Ashari already had attempted a compromise whereby the attributes of God simply are not at all like human qualities. He also asserted a world of continuous divine intervention absent any laws of nature, which meant that he too also denied any place for human free will.[23] Dawson writes that the later Mu'tazila "movement actually owed its origin to the influence of Christian theology rather than to Greek science . . . ."[24] The Greek thinkers such as Aristotle and then the later Muslim Averroes held that the universe is moved by absolute determinism, that human liberty is an illusion, and that there is no immortality of the soul since intelligence is not personal but impersonal and is held in common by the whole human race.[25] Overall, the attempted Mu'tazila opening to human reason was a broad one and not simply the work of a single sect. Adherents were from both major camps, the Sunni and Shi'ite.

Yet the Mu'tazilites were suppressed, and for at least three reasons. Mu'tazila was deemed dualist in asserting two sources of autonomy and action (God and Man) rather than one. Second, it was blasphemy to hold that God *must* do what is good for man and that his unsearchable will is less than total and arbitrary. And third, it undermined the purity of superior revelation by asserting categories of good and evil in the universe independent of the *Qur'an*.[26] Rationalistic philosophy in Islam finds its greatest figure in the Sufi al-Farabi (d. 950), who saw religion more as a branch of political science. He felt that under Islam the possibility remained for the rational society proposed by the Greek thinkers, for example, Plato and Aristotle, who later provided the vocabulary of ideas that so enriched the work of Christian thinkers in the Middle Ages.[27] Within the world of Islam, a direct remnant of the early

Mu'tazila still survives into our century, but this school is confined geographically to part of Yemen at the southern edge of Mohammad's Arabia.

The *Qur'an* retains at least a memory of free will: "Some chose the world; others chose the world to come" (Q 3:152). In this line is a striking parallel to St. Augustine's treatise on the centrality of free will as it struggles between two loves. For Augustine this struggle is the key to ongoing and unfolding human history as elaborated throughout his *City of God*: "One city is that of men who live according to the flesh. The other is of men who live according to the spirit."[28] The West finally surpasses Augustine by acting in "hope to construct a third city, which would be temporal like the earthly city, yet just in a temporal way, that is striving toward a temporal justice obtainable by appropriate means. Such an idea seems never to have occurred to St. Augustine; at least he never spoke of it."[29] Nor has such an idea occurred to Islam which asserts a mandate for the Islamic State to impose the timeless and abstract *Qur'an*. Risking selective quotation, the *Qur'an* holds that "(T)he life of this world is but a sport and a diversion" (Q 6:32, and 4:36).

The careful differentiation in the West of faith and reason, each with its own validity and neither contradicting the other, is not achieved in Islamic culture. In the history of Islam we find an alternating and more ambivalent tilting back and forth between dominant belief and interrupted rationalism.[30] The prominent modern day Muslim scholar, Mahmoud Ayoub, does hold that Muslims in general assert "that what cannot be comprehended by human reason cannot be believed by the heart either." Is there no difference, possibly, between Christian understanding gained through analogy and what is meant here by "comprehend"?

The "basic philosophical foundation of Shari'a—the *Qur'an* with the collected sayings of the Prophet—is regarded *as a guideline for all times, in secular and religious matters . . . .*" (italics added)[31] very much as the Torah was and still is the "eternal Israel."[32] This historical outcome may be partly the result of a simplifying military action, the Seljuk Turk invasion and their installation of a new order of territorial commanders (sultans, and khans in the East). This interruption is one of several major military interventions after Mohammad that help account for the disruption of more creative thought within Islam. The second major military event was the taking of Constantinople in 1453.[33] But even during the life of Mohammed the Battle of Badr in 624, only two years after his flight to Medina, conferred on Islam its vindication as the favored religion. Early confirmation came in the sweeping victories of the seventh and early eighth centuries. Likewise, in early biblical times the tribal ethic held that the rightness of one's god was demonstrated by the successful taking of land occupied by those serving another god. The Old Testament story is largely one of repeated infidelities and then the return to a

God who punishes, but who through all of this does not break his promises. Ultimately the promise is Himself:

> For the Christian, the interplay of faith and reason is most evident in the doctrine that a Trinitarian God is revealed by a definitive encounter with Christ in human history. The doctrine of the Trinity did not arise out of speculation about God, out of an attempt by philosophical thinking to figure out what the fount of all being was like; it developed out of the effort to digest historical experiences . . . In the formative period of the New Testament comes a completely unexpected event in which God shows himself from a hitherto unknown side: in Jesus Christ one meets a man who at the same time knows and professes himself to be the Son of God. One finds God in the shape of the ambassador who is completely God, not some kind of intermediary being, yet with us says to God 'Father.'[34]

In this singular instance, human reason pauses at the absolutely total and alarming self-donation, and resurrection, of Christ at a particular time and place within history. Christ refers to a distinct Father and then the equally distinct coming of the Holy Spirit to indwell his people who become his "Church" (Acts 2:1–13).[35] From the beginning, the conclusions of the Council of Jerusalem were couched in these terms: "It is the decision of the Holy Spirit, and ours too . . ." (Acts 15:28). When the bishop Arius (Chapter 2) subtly rejected the unambiguous divinity of the person of Christ—presuming to restrict what is to be believed in the heart to what fits in the finite mind—the Church responded. In the early fourth century the Council Fathers at Nicaea (325 A.D.) and at Constantinople (a synod in 381 A.D., later confirmed by a general council at Chalcedon in 451) discerned the already existing Trinitarian and incarnational belief of Christians. This belief is based on testimony dating from an encounter in history with the eternal Christ. At Nicaea the driving fact was not neo-Platonic ideas, but rather the alarming and perplexing fact, words, and deeds of Christ in human history.[36]

As a protection against human despair in the face of an unknowable and ultimate reality, writes one historian of Christianity:

> Trinitarian Christianity presents itself, *not* as a dogma, but as the rejection of dogma, *not* as the assertion but rather as the denial of anthropomorphism and myth, and it calls for a final and conclusive expulsion of these elements from the description of ultimate reality as the preliminary to a starkly realistic account of the nature of man (italics added).[37]

Far from being an imposed and exhaustive doctrine, the doctrine of the Trinity and the Incarnation preserves a received truth from both rationalism and absorption into the Eastern mystery religions. While not a Christian heresy in the normal sense, the Unitarianism of Mohammed still resembles one or two of the dozens substitute "heresies" for the orthodoxy of the Trinity and Incarnation. In its offshoot Nestorian expression Arianism is either an ancestor or a close cousin to Islam.

But even within the seemingly stark theology of Islam itself, there are happy parallels to Christian piety. The personal mysticism of Sufism survives today as a legitimate and tolerated personal experience, so long as it sees itself as partaking in the reflection of God and not directly in the divine.[38] Equivalent wording in Christianity might be that the mystic "participates" in, rather than is, the life of God. According to Guillaume the text in the *Qu'ran* that appeals most to the Sufis is this: "A People whom He loved and who love Him" (Q 5:59). Among Christians, the similar expression of St. John is key: "God is love" (1 Jn 4:16). Of one prominent Sufi, Hallaj, it is written: "He taught that man was God incarnate, and he looked to Jesus rather than to Muhammad as the supreme example of glorified humanity."[39] Hallaj's message is described more completely: "God is love, and in his love he created man after his own image so that man might find that image within himself and attain union with the divine nature."[40] Within Islam, this appears to be a remarkably Christian perspective. Hallaj even uses the term *hulul* which translates as "indwelling." Guillaume finds in other Sufi writings favorable references to the Christian doctrine of the incarnation. But then at the extreme, Hallaj is quoted as claiming of himself, "I am the truth." It is for this blasphemy—what Christians might see as confusion between private inspiration toward the ground of our being and actual revelation received from God—that Hallaj himself was crucified by fellow Muslims, mimicking how Christ was falsely accused and then crucified in Jerusalem. Hallaj might also have said these additional words so familiar to Christians, "Father, forgive them for they know not what they do,"[41]—but he is not credited by witnesses with miracles and he did not rise from the dead.

The hadith holds that everyone is born in the simplicity (original disposition) of Islam: "There is not a child that he or she is born upon this *fitrah*, this original state of the knowledge of God. And his parents make him a Jew, a Christian, or a Zoroastrian . . . and if they are Muslims, Muslim."[42] Likewise from the *Qur'an* directly: "There was a time when mankind was but one community. Then they disagreed among themselves: and but for a Word from your Lord, long since decreed, their differences would have been firmly resolved" (Q 10:19). In his own religious search, the famous Al-Ghazali (1058–1111), an eleventh century Muslim philosopher (Friedrich Heer calls him the Pascal of Islam), turned finally to personal mysticism. Influenced partly by classical thought and Jewish and Christian ideas, his autobiography—*Deliverance from Error*[43] —is compared to the late fourth century *Confessions* of St. Augustine.[44] Both writers stress the interior life and the path from repentance, to renunciation, and illumination which is revealed by God to man.

Al-Ghazali criticized some Sufi mystics because they believed matter to be eternal, or believed that God knew nothing of particular beings (only universals), and because they denied the unity of man by confining human immortality to the soul while excluding the body. He held that theology and philosophy (faith and reason) could not be in conflict. In words that sound like they came out of the Christian and scientific West, he asked: "Have they not considered the dominion of the heaven and the earth, and what *things God has created*."[45] St. Augustine attends to such things, and then opens the door even further to a Christian anthropology of man: "And yet (men) leave themselves unnoticed; they do not marvel at themselves." Of himself, St. Augustine wrote "I entered into my inmost being . . . (the truth) was above my mind, *because he made me*, and I was beneath it, because I was made by it. He who knows the truth, knows the light, and he who knows it knows eternity."[46]

The Christian St. Thomas Aquinas was an intellectual beneficiary of St. Augustine as well as Muslim scholars and the Jewish Maimonides. After a prolific career of reconciling the always distinct faith and reason, partly through the doctrine of analogy, on December 6, 1273, Aquinas saw more completely into the light of ultimate reality. As with Mohammed, he too had visions beginning at the age of forty. From these intense mystical experiences comes his famous statement about any future writing: "I cannot; such things have been revealed to me that all that I have written seems so much straw." He put down his pen, wrote nothing more, and died the following year at the age of forty-nine.[47] Is it possible that a small part of what was visible to Aquinas, and to Augustine and al-Ghazali as well, was a God who not only creates and sustains, but who overwhelms all things into being, but without so much as quenching a smoldering reed (Isa 42:3) or consuming a burning bush (Ex 3:2)? Were they pricked by the crowning nature and mystery of the human person made in His image? The fourth century St. Gregory of Nyssa explains that the pure of heart see God in the sense that "the man who cleanses his heart of every created thing and every evil desire will see the image of the divine nature in the beauty of his own soul."[48]

In Genesis, "increase and multiply" (Gen 1:28) follows the verse "Let us make man to our image and likeness..." (Gen 1:26). Might this revelation mean that the whole person is both relational and fecund ("male and female" together) *and* continuously called to "increase" in both numbers and relational *being*? To "multiply" becomes a call toward deepening through interpersonal communion, and is poorly mimicked in the inclusiveness of plunder, or any openness toward a harem culture and analogous cultural amalgamation. Muslim scholars insist that apparent contradictions in the *Qur'an*, especially regarding jihad, must always be read in the context of the entire

Qur'an. This guidance is too easily dismissed as simply another example of "having it both ways," not only as a way of life but in the scripture itself. The Catholic interpretation of Bible, too, is always subject to a comprehensive reading of the entire Scripture, especially as both the Old Testament and the New Testament center on the singular reality of the Incarnation. This reading is done in a manner open to a personal and communal guidance indwelled by the Holy Spirit.[49] "Christianity is the religion of the 'Word' of God, a word which is 'not a written and mute word, but the Word which is incarnate and living.'"[50] John Paul II and the Pontifical Biblical Commission explain that Christian scriptural interpretation seeks to harmonize our understanding of the fulfillment of revelation through time (diachronic) with our understanding of cultural settings at any point in time (synchronic), for example, those insights to be gained by believers through the historical-critical method of interpretation.[51]

Under the Catholic Tradition first proposed by the monk John Cassian (360–435), long before being fleshed out by the thirteenth century Aquinas in his *Summa Theologiai* (1,1,10, ad.1), there are four *senses* for interpreting the written Scripture, especially the Old Testament. The first sense, and foundational to the others, is the literal and potentially "fundamentalist" reading of what the words and the human writers of Scripture actually say.[52] Scripture itself places the disciples in the role of witnesses.[53] The eyewitness source of the Gospels, as apart from either the initial literal sense or any later historical distortion, is convincingly rescued in recent research. Drawing especially from the early Bishop Papias, Bauckham ties events witnessed by John in his Gospel to what was heard directly by St. Polycarp (d. 155) from the aged John while he was still alive, and then passed on to St. Irenaeus. Of the unity in Scripture and Tradition (like this), particularly as seen through this eye witness testimony, Bauckham remarks: "It is only the excessive individualism of the modern Western ideology that tempts us to the view that testimony should regularly and generally incur our suspicion, while our own personal perceptions, memories, and inferences should not."[54]

Within the literal reading of scripture there is also the more-than-literal (not less) and *spiritual* sense. For the Catholic there is in the literal sense always a surplus of meaning, like drinking from a spring that is never exhausted. Through the literal sense we have an additional spiritual sense that comes in three forms. The *moral* sense has to do with human action. The *allegorical* sense has to do with actual meanings deeper than the literal (allegory: "another sense"). And finally the *anagogical* sense has to do with the next world.[55] The Catholic self-understanding is that the Church is not built atop scripture, but that the living tradition of the Church—consistent with verses in its Scripture—is the lens by which even Scripture is to be ever more deeply understood without novel addition or deletion. St. Paul writes to the Thessalonians: "Hold fast to the *traditions* you received from us, *either* by our word *or* by letter" (2 Thes 2:15, italics added). By comparison, where the Church admits to additional private revelations Islam sometimes sees itself more as an oral tradition than a religion of the (written) book. The *Qur'an* is part of an ongoing and self-aware divine "writing" and "rewriting."[56] In this view, the *Qur'an* is self-authorized to interpret itself, and this may explain why Muslims also regard the *Qur'an* as the instrument for correctly interpreting the Bible as well. Defensive critics of Islam might counter this presumption with an opposite charge . . . without at least an implicit natural law element, the Arabic language in the divine *Qur'an* has the potential to function like a pagan oracle always capable of multiple meanings. The script and undifferentiated vocabulary simply substitutes for carved images which are forbidden by the *Qur'an* and Islamic religion.

In the Bible it is largely by the allegorical sense of Scripture that we are taught of the Fall. This is not because Old Testament peoples are primitive, but because in important ways they are like us. To reduce "knowledge" of all truth to the intellectual pride of an outside observer is the Fall. The only remaining path left into such a fallen soul is by hint and suggestion, the route of allegory. Even pagan idolatry is much more than a primitive invention on the evolutionary path to modernity. Whether in ancient Rome of the Arabian "days of darkness," idolatry is the "eyes that *cannot* see" (Ps 135:16). This is the context for what we discover later in Mark: "Having eyes, see ye not? And having ears hear ye not? And *do ye not remember*?" (Mk 8:18) and then "blessed are your eyes, for they see: and your ears, for they hear." (Matthew 13:16). Christ's curing of physical blindness, so alarming to all generations, is only a sign for His direct removal of that tricky point of twilight blindness so near the center of our heart. The inability to believe, or the decision to not see with the eyes of spiritual clarity or faith, is itself evidence of the fall. We settle for "fig leaves" of our own making (Gen 3:7), or in today's idiom, we settle for personal and busy micromanagement of mundane issues.

The Bible is open to wise interpretation; it is "inspired," not dictated. By comparison, the *Qur'an* is held by Muslims to be exactly "dictated" and to be read in only one literal sense, and most authentically only in the Arabic language of dictation. Regarding the anagogical sense of scripture, Muslims join Christians in our belief in a final judgment higher than history. They also join in our belief in a life beyond our current experience, that is, an afterlife.[57] Very significantly, Christianity and Islam share the wellspring of expectation and hope for eternal life. The *Qur'an* reads: "This Book is not to be doubted . . . it is a guide for the righteous . . . who believe in what has been revealed to you (Muhammad) and what was revealed before you, and *have absolute faith in the life to come*" (Q 2:1–2, italics added).

The only part of the Christian Scripture that might be literally regarded as "dictated" is the account of Moses and the tablets of the Decalogue: He came down the mountain "with the two tablets of the commandments in his hands, tablets that were written on both sides, front and back; tablets that were made by God, having inscriptions on them that were *engraved by God himself*" (Ex 33:15–16, italics added). The surprising revelation *within* this revelation might be that the Law is written on both sides. The law is written on the stony heart, but even if we erase this truth from our conscience, the truth of God still remains with him although no longer visible to our darkened selves. The fulfillment of this eternal Law revealed to Moses is the person of Christ who is prefigured by the front and back of the tablet—who is near to us as fully man but who is also fully our infinite God. Pope Benedict calls upon the allegorical sense of Scripture to interpret the parable of the Good Samaritan. This figure who helped the outcast Levite on the road between Jericho and Jerusalem represents more than simply good human behavior (Lk 10:25–37). The motive is not unredeemed humanism, but a shared participation in divine love. Speaking to the spiritual senses, Benedict shows us "God, *though so remote from us*, has made himself our neighbor in Jesus Christ."[58] In this one sentence, we find the complete biblical response of Trinitarian Christianity to the remotely Unitarian God in all its manifestations including Islam.

The twenty-seven books of the Christian New Testament were compiled by members of the Church and mostly in Greek (only the original Matthew was in Hebrew), all in the several decades almost immediately following the death of Christ.[59] The letters of Paul came first, possibly beginning in 51 A.D., and Revelation and the letters of the school of John came last in 85 to 100 A.D. The authorized version of the *Qur'an* was completed in an even shorter period under Uthman, the successor of Omar the second Caliph, between 644 and 656 A.D. Versions incongruous with the accepted and edited text are said to have been burned. Also, the first version was possibly completed in a difficult script (Kufic) which would account for some variability in later readings.[60] The edited composition of the *Qu'ran* is about equal in length to the New Testament and consists of one hundred fourteen *surahs* (chapters) arranged from the longest to the shortest, not chronologically as are the Old Testament, generally each of the three synoptic Gospel narratives (synoptic: to be seen side by side) in the New Testament, and St. Luke's Acts of the Apostles. Within the *Qur'an* the surahs divide into some six-thousand two hundred *ayats* which are equivalent to single verses of the Bible.[61]

The complete systematic development of the Shari'a consists of both the *Qur'an*, and the later hadith or additional sayings of Mohammed. Collection of the hadith consumed the first two centuries after the death of the Prophet. Abu Darr offers this summary of the moral rules (grounded in the universal natural law?) embedded in the hadith:

> My friend (the Prophet) has given me a sevenfold admonition—Help the poor and be near to them; look at those who are beneath thee and not at those who are above thee; never ask anything of anybody; be faithful to thy parents even if they offend thee; tell nothing but the truth even if it is bitter; do not let thyself be turned aside from the way of God by the blame of those who blame; repeat often: 'There is no power or force but through God for this comes from the treasure that is hidden under the Divine Throne'[62]

With its two sources, the *Qur'an* and the hadith, the Shari'a is organizationally parallel to the Hebrew Bible and the Talmud, or in the Catholic Church to the Tradition and Bible on the one hand, and canon law (first fully codified in 1234 A.D.). Unlike Shari'a, the internal canon law is distinct from the Church's social principles proposed for society and the secular powers outside the Church (Chapter 5).

The first Arabic printing of the *Qur'an* came near the time of the Gutenberg Bible (1455) in the West, and was accomplished in Venice in 1485 and 1499.[63] The first printing press did not arrive in the Islamic world until 1727 in Istanbul, and it was only in 1874 that the Ottoman government gave permission to print the *Qur'an* even in Arabic. The Egyptian government first officially published the *Qur'an* in 1925. In 1931, as part of his Westernizing revolution in Turkey, Ataturk outlawed Arabic script and the *Qur'an* was only then translated into the vernacular Turkish.[64] A detailed survey of Bible publications shows a rich history of partial or total translations, even many centuries before Luther's 1521 translation at the Castle of Wartburg from Erasmus' Greek and a Hebrew Bible. By the second century translations of scripture already had been made in the vernacular—from the Greek to Latin for those Western Christians who did not understand the original Greek. The most common was the Old Latin, or *Itala*. Of the complete translations, a Gothic version is dated in the fourth century still near the same time that St. Jerome in the East translated the Vulgate from Greek to Latin. A sampling of either partial or complete and mostly early translations are in Gaelic, Anglo-Saxon, Italian (1500), Cyrilic (ninth century and which first required Sts. Cyril and Methodius to invent a Slavic written script), German (980) Armenian (fourth and thirteenth century), Icelandic (1297), French (807 under Charlemagne, others in the fifteenth and early sixteenth centuries), Russian (New Testament, tenth century), Flemish (1210), Polish and Bohemian (six editions beginning in 1478), Italian (1471), Spanish (1478 and 1515), and Slavonick (early sixteenth century). Between the invention of printing and

Luther's extolled German version, early complete German editions after 1462 were numerous, with five editions at Mentz, fifteen at Augsburg, and others at Wittenburg, Nuremburg and Strasburg. The vast majority of other translations or copies no longer exist due either to religious wars, invasions and the pillaging of the Reformation,[65] all adding to a cumulative loss of monasteries, libraries and manuscripts. Over the centuries these self-inflicted European losses must rank alongside the historic devastations of Constantinople by the crusaders and the Library at Alexandria to the Saracens.

From the Islamic perspective, the modern day Muslim Hassan opines of the Bible that "because of time and lack of authentic recording, the original words were lost and replaced by the words of different men, admittedly saints and disciples, but still not the words used by God."[66] Muslims believe that the Bible was not written until a century after Christ—that there is a break between this writing and the earlier message of God. But Christian witness is to Christ as the incarnate message of the Father, not a book, and attests that the Gospels about and from Christ were written within living memory (80–95 A.D. at the latest, and possibly 50–100 A.D.).[67] These writings are augmented by the letters of St. Paul whose testimony is the earliest in the New Testament (roughly 50 to 70 A.D.). He concisely contrasts belief in Christ to all other religions (including much later Islam): "if Christ has not risen, vain then is our preaching, vain too is your faith" (1 Cor 15:14). The distinctive self-understanding of the Catholic Church is that it is not primarily a Bible-based assembly, but instead is rooted in Tradition beginning at Pentecost as testified in oral tradition and recorded by Luke in the Acts of the Apostles (Acts 2:1–13).

In the Christian tradition the Bible is "inspired" ("to be breathed upon") not "dictated" (like the *Qur'an*). For the Christian the allegedly lacking "word(s) used by God" is Christ himself as the Word made flesh. It is the incarnate Christ, not a lesser message either written or oral, who is encountered and who is to be followed. Christ's invitation in word and deed to his disciples is "Follow me" (Mk 2:14). Christ is more than the human founder or restorer of a religion who neglected to personally transcribe any messages. Instead of a reporting a private visit to heaven, Christ is heaven uniquely transfigured at one point here on earth, as witnessed by persons other than himself (Peter, James, John and even the prophets of old, Moses and Elijah): ". . . his face shone like the sun and his clothes became white as light" (Mt 17:2).

The Prophet Mohammed made no claim to found a new religion. Instead he set about ending paganism in Arabia by confirming fragments of previous scriptures as correctly understood only by himself (Q 10:37–8). The *Qur'an* purports to restore the original religion of Abraham, partly by borrowing from the scriptures of Judaism and Christianity. It contains portions recognizable from the Pentateuch and from the Gospel. Where the Bible is translated into numerous languages, the *Qur'an* is the Arabic version of the Hebrew and the Syriac. The *Qur'an* holds that its "revelations are exactly the same as what was said to the earlier prophets and that, if they were to be recited in a foreign tongue, the people would not understand."[68] The Arabic *Qur'an* claims to restore what has already been received, but is not a mere translation or innovation. In particulars the *Qur'an* accuses Judaism of tampering with the Old Testament (Q 2:76–9) and does not accept the prophetical works (Isaiah, Ezekial, Daniel). The Gospel stories of the New Testament are recounted more as messages related to Christ than as witness testimony about and from Christ—both His words and deeds. Of the Gospels it accepts only Christ's "sermons, maxims, and precepts," while regarding the rest as pious attachments from either later history or from opinion or legend.[69]

Islam holds that the *Qur'an* is not only the accurate accounting, but that it is in itself of the *essence of God*. Human beings can translate only the "ideas" in the *Qu'ran*, but not the divine *Qur'an* itself which remains in the presumed language of Arabic dictation as coming directly from God and through Gabriel.[70] The *Qur'an* discards the biblical record of an unfolding Judeo-Christian revelation culminating in Christ the Incarnation, who said, "Think not that I have come to abolish the Law and the Prophets; I have come not to abolish them but to fulfill them" (Matt 5:17). The Christian seeks not merely a Plan or even a "way of life," but personal incorporation into Christ the incarnate truth, the "new life" even beginning in this life. He finds an altogether new life in the Spirit as sons and daughters of a God who is Father (Rom 8:1–13, 14–30; 31–39). St. Paul states it this way: "Whatever you eat, then, or drink, and whatever else you do, do it all for the glory of God" (1 Cor 10:31). For the early Church, and the Church today, the applicable term is *communio* in Latin, or *koinonia* in Greek, meaning a new way of being and acting, a way to the new life, each with others and with God.[71]

In Arabia the *Qur'an* is entrusted to Mohammed. The resurrected and Eucharistic Christ, the actual fulfillment of revelation, is manifested in his Church where members entrust themselves to Him. Ironically, the Muslim self-interpretation as a way of life constructs an anthropomorphic God. Allah performs in too human a way. Rather than maintaining His covenant relationship with his once chosen people of Israel, He follows their lead and also breaks it. A resentful God turns away from Israel because of their infidelity and the golden calf, a replica of one of the greatest pagan idol of the Egypt they so recently left behind. Rather than a faithful God, Allah decides to reset his self-revelation through a chronologically more final prophet, Mohammed. The conclusive Christian revelation is that God as Father transcends our fallen state. God's anger is unlike Man's. He does not erase his promise; his fidelity is not a human-like and wavering cycle of remembering and forget-

ting. Unlike man, He says: "My heart is overwhelmed, my pity is stirred, I will not give vent to my blazing anger, I will not destroy Ephraim again, *for I am God and not man*" (Hosea 11:8, 9, italics added).

Also in the Old Testament Psalms the Lord reassures that, "I will never be false to David, His dynasty will continue forever . . ." (Ps 89:36–7). The greatest prophet of the Old Testament other than John the Baptist explains: "Can a mother forget her infant, be without tenderness for the child of her womb? Even should she forget, I will never forget you" (Isa 49:15). With the voice of Jeremiah, Jahweh beckons: 'Return, rebel Israel, says the Lord, I will not remain angry with you; for I am merciful, says the Lord, I will not continue my wrath forever" (Jer 3:12)'."[72] In Jeremiah we are assured that after the days of the golden calf the Lord does *not* abandon his people. Where Mohammed looks back from the golden calf to Abraham, the Church finds in Jeremiah (a prophet recognized by Mohammed) the promise of a new covenant yet to come: "I will make a new covenant with the house of Israel and the house of Judah. It will not be like the covenant I made with their fathers the day I took them by the hand to lead them forth from the land of Egypt; for they broke my covenant, and I had to show myself their master, says the Lord. . . I will place my law within them, and write it upon their hearts; I will be their God and they will be my people" ("the Gospel before the Gospel": Jer 31:31–4). New Testament revelation unveils us as more than we might ever suspect according to human perception: "We are the sons of God, and it has not yet been disclosed what we shall be; but we know that when he appears we shall be like him, because we shall see him as he is" (1 Jn 3:2).

The single point of discontinuity is also a thread continuity, between the Old Testament and the New. St. Makarios reflects on the Gospel (Mt 21:33–34) to say that when Israel did break the covenant in the rejection of Christ, that his "prophecy, priesthood and service were taken from them and were entrusted to the Gentiles who believed."[73] An early apologist of Islam (Rida) reflects on the universal Christianity of St. Paul and notices the apparent disruption. This break is seen as an opening for the later arrival of Mohammed as yet another prophet of the Old Testament sequence and this time the final prophet. Apparently unaware of the complete Matthew (5:17, above), Rida asked: "How is it possible for Paul to annul the Law of Moses and Jesus and yet not possible for God to send another Prophet with a law more perfect and nearer to reason than both . . ."[74] Rida also wrote: "Christianity was originally a heavenly religion of divine unity, but Christians later turned it into the worship of human beings such as Jesus and his mother"(sic).[75] When the *Qur'an* refers to the Trinity, this "triad" (a familiar pagan construct) is construed as Allah together with the separate Jesus, and with Mary—rather than in the unity of the Holy Spirit—as the third "person." Some Muslim scholars prefer

to trace the origin of this triad view to a splinter Christian sect in early Abyssinia (Ethiopia).[76] Of the Christians, the *Qur'an* reads: "Unbelievers are those who declare: 'God is the Messiah, the son of Mary'" (Q 5:16). But the Torah or Old Testament reads: "the virgin shall be with child, and bear a son, and shall name him Immanuel" (Isa 7:14), God is with us. On such points Islam "completely reduces Divine Revelation."[77]

In an assuming tone, Abu Zahrah demands under the *Qur'an* that other monotheists should live up to the Bible: "It is the Gospel by which the *Qur'an* challenges Jews and Christians to abide" (Q 5:47). This comment affords a particularly incisive contact point for interreligious dialogue. Part of the Gospel "new life" of love is the humility to judge no one (Lk 6:37–38). It is our own actions that we are to measure against the Gospel teachings of Christ and the echo of this Law already in our hearts.[78] A common and genuine appeal to the two great commandments would be a more non-exclusive call that does not confuse righteousness with self-righteousness. This is the Gospel to which Christians abide: "Why do you notice the splinter in your brother's eye, but do not notice the wooden beam in your own eye" (Mt 7:3). And despite the recurring violence of Christians, no less than others throughout history, Henry Perreyve presents to us the beautiful consistency of the Gospel: "Nowhere in the Gospel will you find a warrant for the doing of violence to even one single soul, for the disregarding of the honour or of the rights of the least of your fellowmen, nothing to authorize that haughty and assuming tone of voice, those proud and bitter words, or that overbearing and contemptuous manner, by which certain ministers of the Gospel too often think to impress their hearers."[79]

St. Gregory of Nyssa (330–395) defined Christianity as "an imitation of the divine nature." He goes on "So Moses, in philosophizing about man, where he says that God made man, states that 'He created him in the image of God,' and the word 'Christianity,' therefore, brings man back to his original good fortune."[80] An early Jerusalem Catechesis reads: "Let no one imagine that baptism consists only in the forgiveness of sins and in the grace of adoption. Our baptism is not like the baptism of John, which conferred only the forgiveness of sins. We know perfectly well that baptism, besides washing away our sins and bringing us the gift of the Holy Spirit, is a symbol of the sufferings of Christ."[81]

Coming centuries after the time of Christ, recorders of the *Qur'an* selectively appropriate Christian commentary on the Bible for their own purposes. "After the conception of eternity and the uncreated-ness of the word of God had become known to Muslim theologians through the polemics of Christian theologians, it was applied by them to the copy in heaven and then finally by the strictly orthodox school to the Arabic copies of the *Kur'an* and expressed

epigrammatically in the sentence 'what lies between the two covers is the word of God'."[82] The central message in the Bible—the eternal generation of the Son and his incarnation in time, within the oneness of the Trinity— is rejected by Islam under a pre-conceived and naturalistic notion that all "generation" is sexual. Prior to Islam a common theme of widespread pagan mythology shows us mythical gods often consorting with humans to create hybrid deities. Is it partly out of this heritage that the rhetorical and dismissive question of Allah is posed in the *Qur'an*, "How can He have a son as He has no consort?" (Q 6:101/ 102)?[83] In addition to the *Qur'an*, the companion hadith contains a similar assertion from God himself speaking of Christians: "The children of Adam have uttered lies about me . . . Their insult is their saying that I have an offspring. Far glorified am I above having a consort or offspring."[84]

In critiquing a similar confusion found even in the Western writings of Albert Schweitzer, who dismissed Christ as but one of many apocalyptic figures of the day, Cardinal Ratzinger (now Pope Benedict XVI) pointed out that the divine Sonship is not biological. The Sonship is ontological—of the order of being, not the order process—and is based on the "I Am" of John's Gospel[85] (e.g., Jn 8:22–24). Islam would have the *Qur'an* understood in terms of its opening lines in the first *ayat* (verse): "Praise be to God, Lord of the Universe, the Compassionate, the Merciful, Sovereign of the Day of Judgment. You alone we worship, and to You alone we turn for help. Guide us to the straight path . . ." (Q1:1–6). For Christians, it is the person of Christ, not any book, which is the straight path and a graced path as well, "the Way, and the Truth and the Life" (Jn 14:6). Muslims reject the divinity of Christ and cast him as a messenger, one among many. "We know Jesus brought a Bible as previous Messengers revealed Divine Laws. But where is the Gospel? We do not have any such manuscript, neither Christian nor Muslim. Perhaps someone buried or concealed it; or it was destroyed and broken in war or unsettled times."[86]

Until recently, and as was the case with Medieval Christian interpreters of the *Qur'an*, Muslim interpreters of the Bible spent little time with the Bible itself or with Christian interpretations. A growing number of Muslims now look directly to biblical scholarship by reputable Christian writers. The result is a typically hybrid presentation. The Muslim Abu Zahrah takes note of the nineteenth century biblical theory of "Source Q" (*Quelle* from the German "Source").[87] Many and perhaps most Christian biblical scholars today still hold that the hypothetical Source Q (50–70 A.D.?) is an original compilation of the sayings of Christ, and that this source underlies the later Gospels of Matthew and Luke, both of which also depend in part upon Mark.[88] Other credible theories are that the gospels are simply interdependent, or that the three synoptic Gospels all had access to a living memory of short sayings, stories, writings and finally collections of writings originally produced to aid local oral proclamation and catechesis to very different audiences, first in Palestine and then in the pagan world.[89] Building on the Muslim theory that the four Gospels (and others non-canonical) are all later corruptions of an earlier true Gospel of Jesus more akin to Islam, Abu Zahrah suggests that the elusive Source Q was possibly this writing. He holds that Source Q was deliberately destroyed by Christians because of a resemblance to the later *Qur'an*. Muslims also appeal to one or two of the non-canonical Gnostics gospels such as *Barnabas*, which (they hold) was "perhaps written by a Christian convert to Islam."[90]

The Muslim-friendly absence of central Christian doctrines such as the Trinity from the hypothetical Source Q quotations or from yet another non-canonical Gospel, that of *Thomas*, is easily explained by the non-Catholic scholar Philip Jenkins. Jenkins writes, "(T)he notion that the essential doctrines of a religion can or should be plainly laid out for everyone in scriptural form, as opposed to liturgy or oral teaching, is a distinctively modern and Protestant view."[91] This is also an Islamic view. The Catholic view in particular is that the source behind any hypothetical Source Q is the living Christ, sacramentally present and constituting his Church Eucharistically. Beginning at the public descent of the Holy Spirit at Pentecost, the Church comes into being to receive and accept the ongoing role to guard, unpack, and advance the truth of God and of the whole man *as revealed in the Incarnation*, and as then proclaimed orally in Tradition and in the written Scripture. Pentecost is not a golden age to be recovered from the past, but rather continues as the ever present indwelling *today* of the Spirit who has acted throughout history, beginning with the prophets. It is this living memory—or much more the memory of living truly—which accounts for the already existing Church during the first four centuries. It was four centuries before the canon of New Testament scripture was sifted and compiled by the same Church in the Muratorian Canon of 170 A.D. and then later at the Council of Carthage in 397, to be reconfirmed in 419[92] and finally more definitively proclaimed at the Council of Trent in the sixteenth century.

The historical *fact* of revelation is retained intact throughout, but is to be distinguished from its faithful interpretation and deepened meaning gained under the guidance of the same indwelling Holy Spirit:[93] "I am with you all days, even unto the consummation of the world" (Mk 28:20); and "the Paraclete, the Holy Spirit who the Father will send in my name, will instruct you in everything, and *remind you* of all that I told you" (Jn 14:26, italics added).[94] Rather than a final prophet, there is in history the less remote and actual fulfillment of revelation. It is the Church in its living Tradition—not the *Qur'an* (Q 10:37)[95]—that is responsible for handing on and interpreting its own Scriptural witness to the mystery of Christ, "the same yesterday, today and forever" (Heb 13:8), and the center of history.

Jewish thinkers scattered from the Temple by the Diaspora in 70 A.D., now point to their own deepening insights into the mind of God. Prophecy is not yet fulfilled. Mohammed, the final Prophet, short-circuits the Jewish expectation as much as he reshapes the Christian revelation. His greatest claim, before being driven from Mecca, was his night visit to heaven. As a possible allegory, Mohammed's visit is only vaguely alluded to in one verse in the *Qur'an* (Q 17:1). The visit is given elaborate detail in the separate and later hadith. In the earlier New Testament, St. Paul's religious experience of actually having been "snatched up to the third heaven" (2 Cor 12:2) was so extraordinary that he was incapable of expressing it at all (2 Cor 12:1–5).[96] From the lack of scriptural account, we might also conclude that after being dead four days the resurrected Lazarus (Jn 11:42–3), too, was far beyond words.[97] The apocalyptic visions recorded in St. John's Book of Revelation are not lacking in detail, but a key passage in Scripture still applies: "Eye has not seen, ear has not heard, nor has it so much as dawned on man what God has prepared for those who love him" (1 Cor 2:9 and Is 64:3). But heaven approaches earth. At Christ's baptism in the Jordan, it is eternity that is made near and enters our experience. The heavens were "torn open and the Spirit, like a dove, came from the heavens, 'You are my beloved Son; with you I am well pleased'" (Mk 1:10).

A light and useful way to explore this interpretive challenge to interreligious scriptural dialogue might involve a scripture-like allegory in Western poetry. In literary poetry the early Renaissance Dante Alighieri (1265–1321) tried to imagine "what God has prepared" in heaven. Jeffrey Burton Russell writes, "The *Paradiso* . . . is the most sublime portrait of heaven from the Book of Revelation to the present."[98] Dante's work specifically ties in with our earlier treatment of the four senses of scriptural interpretation, *and* is even shaped in part by Mohammed's self-reported visit to a seven storied heaven. Guillaume refers to a discovery in Madrid of a love poem by Ibn Arabi (1165–1240), a predecessor of Dante who exercised a strong Muslim influence on the Florentine poet.[99] Arabi wrote his own love song first, and this writing was based in turn on Mohammed's ascent to Paradise as reported in the hadith.[100]

Of Mohammed's trip and whether it is legendary, Guillaume finds two early writers who give an account of another trip by Mohammed unrelated to any heavenly visit. He suggests that a night pilgrimage to "the farther mosque" was to a place neither in Jerusalem nor in heaven, but to a place called al-Jirana some fifteen kilometers from Mecca. This trip offers "a perfectly natural explanation of this verse in the *Qur'an*, which expresses Muhammad's feelings of gratitude to God for having helped him perform the pilgrimage at night at a time when the polytheists had not been excluded from its rites and when he would have compromised his position had he gone openly in the day."[101]

While the *Qur'an* remains largely within a Semitic orbit, the Medieval/Renaissance *Paradiso* and the complete *Divine Comedy* fits within the orbits of both pagan Antiquity and Christianity. Dante uses numerous biblical references and is monotheistic and Trinitarian,[102] but in this epic work his specific references to the incarnation and redemptive suffering are relatively brief and understated. Dante is a bridge both from Antiquity to the modern world and from the nearer Age of Faith to modernity. He is first guided through hell (*Inferno*) and purgatory (*Purgatorio*) by Virgil who represents reason (a dimension absent from Mohammed's account in the hadith), and then by his beloved Beatrice. But in the end he can be pointed to the final stages of heaven (*Paradiso*) only by a redeemed Christian, St. Bernard. Possibly in a minority, Balthasar writes of Dante's overall message: "The image of God is not really Trinitarian but an extraordinarily intensified, Christian version of the Eros of Antiquity. And it is quite clear that the relationship of Dante to Beatrice, of Gabriel and Mary, of earthly and heavenly love, of Eros and Agape within an Eros that is regarded as embracing all, is the last word of the poet."[103]

By comparison Mohammed often promises a more terrestrial heaven to be found not in a beloved and sainted one (Beatrice), but in the almond eyes of seventy-two maidens.[104] From the *Qur'an*, the saved "shall sit with bashful, dark-eyed virgins" (Q 37:48 and 55:52–78). Or again, "Dark eyed houris (maidens) We shall wed them . . . (and) there shall wait on them young boys of their own, as fair as virgin pearls" (Q 52:20–25). Islamic commentators insist that such lines are allegorical, that there is no question of sex in heaven, and indicate the non-carnal feminine virtues, particularly the intense luster of the eyes as compared to dullness and lack of expression.[105] The *Qur'an* and the *Paradiso* are both pre-Cartesian. There is a place in both for spiritual reality and angels. Neither is burdened by the rationalistic premise that man is essentially an isolated observer of a foreign and only physical universe that can be comprehended and dominated in terms of physical measurement and mathematical constructions.

This literary harmony between the *Qur'an* and *Paradiso* frees us in the West from a substantive competition between the words of the *Qur'an* and the person of Christ as the Word made flesh (not a book). While the two writings, the *Qur'an* and *Paradisio*, do not serve as a parallelism between Islam and Christianity, Dante's work suggests the genre of poetic imagination as a common frame of reference between two heavenly writings. An obstacle to scriptural dialogue is that "form criticism" used on the Bible is generally forbidden on the *Qur'an*. Where the Bible is inspired and accessible, the deified *Qur'an* is dictated and untouchable. Although dictated in the human Arabic language it is believed to be unmediated by human hands such that different forms or genres, e.g., poetry, cannot be called upon to understand its possible meaning as folk literature. Folk literature usually begins in *oral* tradition and unfolds over time by the community as a whole. The *Qur'an* originated from one individual, but was assembled over a short period of decades from the many segments possibly written during his lifetime.

Might form criticism apply to the *Qur'an* at a higher level? Might form criticism apply in an external and *inter*-scriptural way to the entire text, rather than internally to various parts of the *Qur'an*?[106] This is to say that as a whole the *Qur'an* incorporates and modifies earlier revelation found in the altogether separate Jewish and Christian scriptures. Rather than parts of the *Qur'an*, the entire writing is eclectic and redactive as a literary form. Further, the version passed on by the compiler, Uthman the third caliph, is lifted out from all other incongruous versions which he also collected and then reportedly burned. The entire *Qur'an* discounts the unbroken covenant of Yahweh with Israel (the Jewish Bible), redefines Christ (the New Testament) as only a forerunner for Mohammed, and subordinates both to the recitations of this final Prophet.[107] To the Christian understanding, the *Qur'an* is like the Gnostic gospels to which is added biographical and editorial poetry. Like the *Qur'an*, Dante's *Comedy* and its *Paradiso* are a form of inspired poetry, and can be examined alongside the *Qur'an* as a whole. As the *Qur'an* borrows parts of other scriptures, the *Paradiso* probably draws from those parts of the hadith that recount Mohmammed's mystical visit to heaven.

A treatment of Dante's work suggests a level of inspiration—less than a public revelation—that might apply Mohammed's private recitations collected into to the *Qur'an*. Dante's description of his work follows Christian Tradition in holding that *Paradiso* is to be understood in four senses.[108] With Dante, Russell holds that human language can be only literal or allegorical, while it is God alone who can speak the remaining two spiritual senses, the moral and anagogical words of "ultimate reality." Muslims would locate every Arabic word of the *Qur'an* in these two divine categories. Russell introduces a most intriguing writing generally held to be from Dante himself. The "Letter to Can Grande della Scala" touches on what Dante intended by writing *Paradiso*. As an introduction to the poem, the letter "indicated Dante's belief that the *Paradiso*, like the Bible, uttered all four senses, expressing reality as God knows it."[109] Dante is said to have had a profound vision of his beloved and unattainable Beatrice, in 1296, when he was studying theology and philosophy. Russell tells us that commentators "read the *Divine Comedy* not *as* Scripture, but in some way *like* Scripture, applying the four senses of interpretation." Russell says that Dante,

> Knew that the Christian community recognizes only the Bible as guaranteed revelation. But this means only that no other work is in fact revealed. Christian tradition also allowed that some works, though falling short of revelation, could be inspired by God. Dante may have viewed the *Paradiso* as less than revealed but more than merely inspired . . . . *The Divine Comedy* is about language, not only Dante's language about heaven, but God's own language. In the *Comedy* one cannot separate the medium from the message.[110]

For Muslims, the *Qur'an* is likewise the divine medium and the divine message. What are we to think of the close parallel between the "inspired" *Paradiso* and Mohammed's visit to heaven noted in only one verse of the *Qur'an,* and then detailed in the hadith? The followers of Islam assert the divine origin of the *Qur'an* precisely because it is most beautiful, while coming from the mouth of one who claimed to be only a messenger and who many still claim could neither read nor write (Q 29:48–49).[111] To the respectful observer from the West, might this stature mean, as with the *Paradiso*, that the *Qur'an* is in some sense "less than revealed but more than merely inspired?" (In Chapter 2 we discovered the possibility of a locution or a private revelation incorporating exiting public revelations, e.g., the Pentateuch.) The difference between Dante's literary work and St. Paul's testimony in the Bible could apply equally to what is recalled in the hadith of Mohammed's experience:

> Dante's model was the experience of St. Paul; he goes to heaven even before his death as Paul did, and, as Paul did, returns. But unlike Paul, who said that he was not permitted to relate what he experienced in his vision, Dante tells us what he saw. And where Paul was ambiguous about his state of existence during his ascent—'whether in the body or out of the body I do not know' (2 Cor 12:2)— Dante's pilgrim journey is in the body. By choosing Paul as model, Dante chose a precursor who 'went' as well as 'saw.' Debates as to whether Dante was a poet or visionary are pointless. He was both: a master of language and the recorder of real spiritual experience.[112]

Of the Muslim scriptures, it is only since the ninth century that the *Qur'an* has been held officially to be more than a revered book. Popular piety, demonstrated in street riots in Baghdad, prevailed over the more moderate views of the caliphs. Rather than originating in time as a creature of God, the book becomes "*an integral part of the divine essence.*"[113] with all parts equally dictated and equally beyond human interpretation.[114] During the early Abbasid period popular piety in the streets of Baghdad helped overrule the

The Mosque: Shari'a and the World 151

earlier caliphs and under the Abbasids (Caliph Wathiq in 847 A.D.) tipped the scales for all time toward this unquestionable starting point or doctrine that the *Qur'an* was not created in time. Suppression of the Mu'tazilites was first attempted through the power of the ruler, but ended in the simple supremacy of the *Qur'an* and the hadith. The prevailing Ash'arite school was one of four theological schools of the Sunni sect and whose legalistic "mode of thought . . . (was) distinct from Shi'ism."[115]

Was cultural consolidation with the world beyond Arabia more possible under the Sunni consensus process of *Ijma,* combined with a now invulnerable *Qur'an*? An analogous transition in much earlier Jewish history is the first Hebrew monarchy under David. The Jewish tribes united under a king against the common external threat of the coastal Philistines. Instead of a David-like monarch, the more divided Islamic sects agreed on a deified text that also elevated the stature of the Prophet Mohammed. Transcendence of the Muslim sects by ijma or popular consensus is consistent with a fundamental point presented by Avicenna in the twelfth century. This scholar held that it was not only the question of Mohammed's successors, but especially the misuse of allegorical interpretation of the *Qur'an* by the Mu'tazilites, and their controversy with the Ash'arites, that actually heightened (rather than simply responded to) sect hostility in Islam.[116]

A modern day equivalent to ninth century Muslim unanimity on the divine nature of the *Qur'an* might a pre-emptive agreement sometimes used in Western parliaments. Given the choice between filibuster and closure, they choose simply to close debate through "cloture." At the political level of intertribal strife, deification of the *Qur'an* is a pre-modern exercise of modern cloture (for a third option, see Newman in Chapter 4). In our post-modern world, instances of gridlocked views on moral first premises those in charge of the podium declare them "irreconcilable" as a ploy to move on. The public forum dating back to the Greek agora is increasingly restricted under modernity to only secondary questions.[117] Marx was a pioneer of modernity when dealing with the mystery of the human person as not totally self-created. Of this premise, he announced, "The question of contingency is forbidden to socialist man."[118] Forbidden to the followers of Islam is any discourse that might consider the inner nature of the one God as Trinitarian. And forbidden to modern man is the challenge to "walk and chew gum at the same time," that is, to accept "evolutionary" conclusions while not at the same time accepting "ontological" distinctions between the order of becoming and the order of *being.*

The patchwork rationalism of Western political correctness and the rationalism of Islam as a collage of practices and beliefs—rather than being a "clash of civilizations"—possibly reinforce one another. Western rationalism holds all moralities to be equally subjective, and equally valid or irrelevant, while the Islam holds that any human autonomy to decide values, distinct from the autonomy of God, is invalid. In the years ahead, the possible outcome in the West is politically correct (Shari'a-like) prosecution of the constitutional freedoms of speech and thought as phobias and "hate crimes." It is politically correct to ferret out cases of exploitation and grooming of the young in a Church whose clergy was in effect infiltrated under lax admission policies,[119] but it is intolerant to notice the trend in other institutions or steps in the broader society to groom an entire generation through media conditioning and aligned text books. The natural law approach would be one of consistent and uncompromised respect for each person and the common good, and therefore would not stoop to state enforced public mainstreaming of one disordered life style or another. In a parallel situation, United Nations resolutions are proposed to discourage at the international (and national) level critical commentary on any Islamic tenets. The secularist West would bracket to the side residual polygamy while Islam would presumably disregard other moral aberrations in the West. The greatest naivete of multicultural modern ideology is to presume that it can colonize a re-energized Islam without being assimilated into the larger cosmopolitan amalgamation it has been throughout most of its history. In place of our Christian roots—now passed over in silence, for example, in the charter of the secularist European Union—post-modern multiculturalism might yield to Islamic fideism as the resident spiritual voice in the secularist and even Christophobic West. Value neutrality cannot easily domesticate Islamic conviction. At best, across the board dialogue is narrowed by a mutually imposed silence (agressive tolerance) on what in better times are the enduring questions of the human condition and the very nature of the human person,

Up to a point the Church is sympathetic with the historically later Muslim tenet that nothing is exempt from the divine. The Second Vatican Council (1963–5) teaches that "even in secular affairs there is no human activity which can be withdrawn from God's dominion."[120] But in addition, based on two millennia of Christian thought and western experience (as compared to Muslim rejection of their own Mutazilites of the ninth century, see Chapter 2) the now marginalized Church also affirms the human person and the universal natural law, and therefore the coherence between genuine faith and inquiring reason. Politically, the Church proposes the urgent distinction and harmony, both, between our rights and our personal duties as members of the Church and as members of a well grounded secular society. Morally, it proposes principles of intrinsic human dignity realized in community, alternative to any post-modern "tyranny of relativism" (Chapter 4). And in the life of the Church itself, as recorded in the Acts of the Apostles, a deeper unity comes not from consensus below, but from the single divine fire from above, at Pentecost. ". . . They were filled with the Holy Spirit and began to *speak in different tongues*, as the Spirit enabled them to proclaim . . . (every nation under heaven staying in Jerusalem) gathered in a large crowd, but they were confused because *each one heard them speaking in his own language*" (Acts 2:4–6, italics added). The diverse publics were unified as enabled directly by the Spirit, and all understood in his own language. The unity was not found in a book yet unwritten or possibly dictated as in Arabic.

Islam borrows heavily from the inspired Jewish and Christian scriptures. The *Qur'an* goes so far as to identify *itself* as the interpretive instrument in place of either Catholic Tradition outlined above, including the writings of the early Church Fathers, or the much later *sola Scriptura* claims of the six-teenth century Protestant communions (Q 10:37).[121] Where Protestant com-munions protest the institutional Catholic Church as an invention not found in the Gospels (although it is in the first decades of oral Tradition that Christian-ity finds the Bible), Muslims reject both Catholic and Protestant Christianity because they believe it was at least a century after the birth of Christ that the Gospels were written. The presumed inaccuracies are corruptions of the mis-remembered message, the principles of the *Qur'an* which has existed from the very beginning and was later restored by Mohammed.

One small but significant cooperative step among Muslim, Jewish and Christian leaders was initiated in the years prior to the 2006 papal addresses at Regensburg and Istanbul. This earlier step was the formation of the *Foun-dation for Interreligious and Intercultural Research and Dialogue* in 1999 by the joint action of the then Cardinal Ratzinger (now Pope Benedict XVI), Jor-danian Prince El Hassan bin Talal, Orthodox leaders, the then-chief rabbi of France, and others. The first project, now complete, was to publish together the Hebrew Bible, the New Testament and the *Qur'an*, each in its original language. If it is still true that Muslims generally defer to the *Qur'an* and its Muslim commentators for their information on the Bible, then this joint project may be a step toward more objective understanding of one another. The Foundation seeks to encourage a tri-lateral dialogue for common reflec-tion. In diplomatic language, common reflection will be done by "scrutinizing the mystery of God in the light of our religious traditions and our respective wisdom, to discern those values capable of enlightening all men and women no matter what their culture or religion."[122]

Other than comparing the scriptures or at least presuppositions of those who profess monotheistic religion, another promising and more relaxed path is to compare the respective *commentaries* on the different scriptures. Might commentaries on the oneness of God, as proclaimed by all monotheistic religions, still find harmony in possibly surprising ways? Different than the

Thomist synthesis of faith and reason is the work of a successor theologian, the Franciscan Duns Scotus (1265?–1308). Without actually contradicting the broad coherence discovered by Aquinas, Scotus proposed that there can be intuitive knowledge of things apart from sense perception as Aquinas maintained, *and* that intellectual certainty does not depend upon illumination, an earlier position of St. Augustine. Scotus is one of a family of commentators showing us that between God and Man there is both a radical continuity and a radical discontinuity, and that both of these are incomprehensible to finite minds. Where modernity falls into the first camp (rationalism), Islam falls into the second ("Let God be God"). The Church rejects neither posture and possibly insists on both. The Church does theology on its knees.

By placing priority on the *will* over the *intellect,* Scotus was actually influenced by the Muslim thinker Avicenna. Carried too far, the emphasis on the will yields a God who once again is unknowable and arbitrary. Under William of Occam in the West the outcome is the "nominalist" worldview. Nominalism loses touch with the reality of universals—such as "man" or "natural law" or "reason." The Occamist mindset is illustrated by the mirror crises of Islam and modernity. The first crisis is "religious" fatalism and the second is dominance of the quantitative method. Morality itself becomes only a field of applied mathematics. Islamic rationalism disallows a distinction between mosque and political life or the state under the natural law, and Western rationalism embraces the state while further isolating political life from the universal natural law.

But in the Western intellectual tradition might there be a valid nominalism as simply a love of the particular? Beginning with the "very good" of creation that delighted God himself (Gen 1:31) and the five overarching and immeasurably real transcendentals—love, the good, but also the one, the beautiful, and the true—might the more intuitive Scotus also offer a path for interreligious dialogue with Islam? Islam sees all things as instances of unique acts of creation. The Scotus path would not be in the realm of creeds, but in the realm of a different transcental, that of beauty.[123] Initially Scotus—beatified by Pope John Paul II in 1993—might help speak to both the oneness of God, an idea so fixed in Islam, and to the beauty of the gratuitous, incarnational and singular form of this oneness—the message of Christian witnessing. Within Christendom, Galileo accepted Scripture as inspired and inerrant, and found fault rather with "its commentators, who wished to cling to its pure literalness."[124] In the broader instance of Islam, Muslims regard every line of the *Qur'an* as dictated (literal) rather than inspired. Still, comparisons between the respective commentators, rather than the two books, seems to hold promise among those of good will. (The possible contribution of Duns Scotus to dialogue with Islam is reopened in Chapter 6.)

SUBMISSION AND FREEDOM IN THE WORLD

On the death of John Paul II, Sayyid Syeed, secretary general of the Islamic Society of North America, expressed "profound grief." He recalled the pope's words in 1999, that "Muslims, like Jews and Christians, see the figure of Abraham as a model of unconditional submission to the decrees of God."[125] The telecast from Rome and spontaneous expression offered by John Neuhaus was simply that we must "hear the Gospel, and go with it." Unconditional submission—but in Christianity we find or are found by something more. Because of our freedom the better word might be "surrender." The term surrender better reflects an analogical and even nuptial relationship between the Divinity and his followers (his Church), a relationship which for Christians is also an icon of the inner life of the triune God. One of the very few places in the Bible where the more unilateral doctrine of Shari'a-like submission seems to occur is subordinated to the transforming Christian nuptial imagery as a more ultimate reality. "Wives should be submissive to their husbands as if to the Lord (Eph 5:22, italics added), *but* this guidance comes within the context of the lines preceding and following: "Defer to one another out of reverence for Christ" (Eph 5:21), (and) "Husbands, love your wives, as Christ loved the Church" (Eph 5:25), surely meaning exclusively and reciprocally.

The *Qur'an* would have the husband treat his potentially multiple wives equally under the umbrella of guardianship. But the Bible proclaims that in their complementary ways spouses from the beginning are *equal to one another* as a unity of persons in one flesh. "God created man in his image . . . male and female he created them" (Gen 1:27). Monogamous marriage is an interpersonal icon of the unity found in the Triune oneness of God. Pagan multiplicity, mimicked in polygamy, violates this covenant. The first historian of the Church, Eusebius (263–339 A.D.), relates that even before the fourth century the heretic Cerinthus and the Nicolaitans attempted to import directly into Christianity the "notorious licentiousness of western Asia Minor." They taught that Christ's kingdom would be on earth and open to "unlimited indulgence in gluttony and lechery at banquets, drinking bouts, and wedding feasts . . . ."[126]

For the devout Christian salvation is quite different, beyond this or any imagination: "Dearly beloved, we are God's children now; what we shall become later has not yet come to light" (1 Jn 3:2). To the current promiscuity in all its forms in the West, the current Pope Benedict exposes and warns of the old whisperings: "Do not cling to this distant God, who has nothing to offer you. Do not cling to the covenant, which is so alien to you and which imposes so many restrictions on you. Plunge into the current of life, into its delirium and its ecstasy, and thus you will be able to partake of the reality of life and of its immortality."[127] Benedict explains that the biblical serpent—a symbol drawn from pagan fertility cults—does not deny God, but simply asks for "information," which then lures us from trust and into self-assertion and finally self-preoccupied mistrust. The likeness between harlotry and modern Western ideologies is in seeking possession of the political and natural world. Male dominance in the West resonates especially with the earlier thinking of the seventeenth century Francis Bacon. Bacon advanced the legitimate inductive scientific method underlying Western advances. But he also spoke of inducing nature—as a sort of harem—to betray her secrets so that they could be used to advance technical control even against nature. In 1945 the nuclear bomb test site at Alamagordo, New Mexico, was anointed with the name "Trinity" . . . finally causing at least some to wonder at the cultural reasoning behind this selection. Not in a direct reference, one figure who came out of the spiritual darkness of the Cold War era wrote this:

What little I know of the stars I have passed on to my son over the years . . . we often stop to watch through the apple trees the great sky triangle tipped by the evening stars: Veg in Lyra, Altair in Aquila and Deneb, burning in the constellation of the Swan . . . I want him to have a standard as simple as stepping into the dark and raising his eyes whereby to measure what he is and what he is not against the order of reality. I want him to see for himself upon the scale of the universes that God, the soul, faith, are not simple matters, and that no easy or ingenuous view of them is possible. I want him to remember that God Who is a God of Love is also the God of a world that includes the atom bomb and virus, the minds that contrived and use or those that suffer them, and that the problem of good and evil is not more simple than the immensity of worlds. I want him to understand that evil is not something that can be condescended to, waved aside or smiled away, for it is not merely an uninvited guest, but lies *coiled in foro interno* at home with good within ourselves. Evil can only be fought . . . I want him to know that it is his soul, and his soul alone, that makes it possible for him to bear, without dying of his own mortality, the faint light of Hercules' fifty thousand suns.[128]

Abraham raised his eyes to the stars. So too did the wise men of the east who found the Lord of the universe below this canopy. On the mystery of the human soul and its burden of evil coiled within, and not yet complicated by the multiplier of technology, the fifth century St. Augustine saw the fallen intellect always tending toward its own imaginings and then acting not on what it is and is not "against the order of reality," but on these fantasies. The Marxist fantasy tramples reality as it jousts against alienating economic superstructures, and millions of people—each one precious to God—are sacrificed at the altar of history. The end justifies the means. Stalin comments that "to kill one person is murder, but a million is statistics." Augustine gave a name to this kind of cerebral distancing and then deception so influential in both Islamic and modern history. What we call ideology, he calls it *fantastica fornicatio*—"the prostitution of the mind to its own fancies."[129] Looking back at the Gulag, Solzhenitsyn finds that it is ideology that "gives evildoing justification and gives the evildoer the necessary steadfastness and determination . . . Thanks to ideology, the twentieth century was fated to experience evildoing on a scale calculated in the millions."[130]

The Franciscan St. Bonaventure (1221–1274) sees the highest category as goodness rather than even truth. "For St. Thomas the supreme goal towards which our desire is oriented is to see God . . . for St. Bonaventure, on the other hand, man's ultimate destiny is to love God—the encounter and union of his love and ours."[131] And for Bonaventure, faith ever remains an *imprint* given from the inexhaustibility of God. Bonaventure might hint that even the natural law as an imprint is an anticipation of our fulfillment in Christ, the True Self. The initial discovery of the natural law is in the Classics, but even this is not its real origin. The faith of Bonaventure is the initial difference between seeing and not seeing, and in extreme cases is a protection against "intellectual harlotry."[132] Martin Luther who began as a monk in the order of St. Augustine remarked that except for practical questions reason is the enemy of God, "the source of the sources of all evils . . . reason by itself is a whore" in the sense that with a carrot and a stick you can lead it anywhere.[133] The scholar Thomas Molnar reminds us that concrete reality must not be substituted with imagined and arbitrary *starting points* for political bartering based only on circumstances of the moment.[134] Rationalization with no opening beyond itself is a playground for willfulness.

Aquinas exercises the notion that reason is part of seeing. Absent reason as a dimension of the natural law, the sense of wonder and then of justice disappears. Worse than forgetfulness, ungrounded willfulness leads us to participate in genuine evil. Even the reality of the Holocaust is dismissed as if it is but another false memory of revisionist history. And today, more accessible and efficient than Auschwitz and Treblinka, neighborhood abortion clinics are "poisoning the lives of millions of defenseless human beings, as if in a form of 'chemical warfare'."[135] Mothers are amputated from their own maternity, just as Descartes isolated man, the subjective observer, stands apart from the external and objective universe. This fact-value dichotomy in Western thought is not part of Islamic history. This dichotomy submerges man's spiritual estrangement beneath a calculating mentality such that our very existence is only a problem to be solved, possibly by subtraction. Today, young women are steered to imagine abortion "rights" as an equalizing rite of passage into unquestioned modernity.

Such modernity is ancient, finding parallels in the pre-modern Roman Empire. To know all of the answers of life the demented early fourth century Emperor Maxentius resorted finally to witchcraft: "full of magical notions, he sometimes ripped up pregnant women, sometimes scrutinized the entrails of new-born babies . . . ."[136] Again today, not far behind the *objectifying* cult of abortion is euthanasia, first voluntary and eventually more calculated under a rationing mentality, and involuntary. The medical industry even now traffics in aborted fetal products in the form of child vaccines that are now required for entry into government (public) schools, and cosmetics that recall Nazi Germany's fashionable lampshades made from human skin as reported by Nuremburg convict, Albert Speer (*Inside the Third Reich*, 1970). In the United States today embryonic stem cells are harvested from human fetuses under the pretense of medical benefits sometime in the future, even when patient-derived adult stem cells already show a wide range of medical benefits, and without bazaar side effects. Embryonic cell lines are inventive and eligible for patent protection, while adult stem cells are not. Veterinary ethics can be applied equally at both ends of the human life cycle under the economics of abortion and euthanasia.

The European historian Friedrich Heer's assessment of doctrinaire and Revolutionary France seems to apply: "they waged war on the mothers, everything feminine or changing, especially the Church and the people, both of which they saw as feminine. Descartes and Pascal sought to subject female matter to male mathematics."[137] Mohammed destroyed the assembly of pagan deities in seventh century Mecca and among these were the three sister deities (Chapter 2).[138] These were related to Venus, to the rains, and to the sun, all possibly of Syrian origin (Q 53:19–20). The father of these three female deities (Q 16:59, 52:29) was possibly retained by the process of elimination to become a solitary and monotheistic deity congruent with Allah (Q 2:61, 6:09, 29:65, and 31:31). Mohammed rejected the directly generated female deities and all others, but by breaking up this pagan family, the truth content veiled behind the myth—the fatherhood of God and the sacredness of human maternity—also were removed. The deletion of the fatherhood quality from a key pagan deity might have been as significant an action as was Mohammed's more notorious removal from Mecca of all of the pagan idols.

Today, Muslim scholars have found a way to respond directly to a Father who is both beyond us and yet so close as to take upon Himself our self-crucifixion by sin. They conclude that the Christ in history was not actually killed. Instead, he was replaced by a willing stand-in, and was still physically alive when a figure was "lifted up." He did not ascend after death (Q 41:56). There is no physical resurrection and glorification of Christ as testified by John: "And just as Moses lifted up the serpent in the desert, so must the Son of Man be lifted up, so that everyone who believes in him may have eternal life" (Jn 3:14). This rejection of the Trinity and of redemption through Christ and the cross is not at all original to Mohammed. The earlier Platonist writer Celsus held that John's Gospel falsely deified a prophet Christ and that the earlier synoptic Gospels—Matthew, Mark, and Luke—stopped short of this step.

The modern Muslim scholar Abu Zahrah calls on Christians to carry the Protestant Reformation far beyond itself. Christians should return all the way to the alleged Unitarianism he suggests existed prior to the formal rejection of Arianism at the Council of Nicaea (325 A.D.) and "which is Islam in its essence."[139] And yet, before Nicaea and before any of the Gospels were committed to writing, St. Paul in the earliest Christian writings already reminds us, "if Christ has not risen, vain then is our preaching, vain too is your faith" (1 Cor 15:14). Also and again centuries before Nicaea, St. Paul proclaims Christ within the context of a Trinitarian God: "The grace of the Lord Jesus Christ, and the love of God, and the fellowship of the Holy Spirit be with you all" (2 Cor 13:13). The author of the Second letter of Peter (c. 70 A.D.) mentions the Father (1:17), the Son (1:17) and the Holy Spirit (1:21).[140]

At Nicaea the last remnants of paganism and Judaism are discarded with faith, resolve, and intellectual clarity. The Council of Nicaea was convened not to invent the Lord's divine nature, but more precisely to determine whether or not the bishop Arius stood in contradiction to what was already believed from the beginning about the Incarnation.[141] Outside of the Scriptures, the earliest written evidence as to what was already believed survives in the *Didache* ("The Teaching of the Twelve Apostles"). Not accepted as an inspired writing, this document is valuable as the earliest writing of the Christian community outside the Scriptures (65–80 A.D., and the early second century). The Didache records the Trinitarian baptismal formula: "pour water three times on the head, in the name of the Father, and of the Son, and of the Holy Spirit" (Ch. 7.3). And the canonical Gospel narration gives this: "(I)f you really knew me, you would know my Father also. From this point on you know him; you have seen him' (Jn 14:7–8). And, "Do you not believe that I am in the Father and the Father is in me?" (Jn 14:10), and yet again, "Believe me that I am in the Father and the Father is in me, or else, believe because of the works that I do" (Jn 14:11).

At the Transfiguration it the Father speaks, "Behold my beloved Son, listen to him" (Mt 17:5, Mk 9:7). The three disciples who were with Christ at Gethsemane and earlier at the Transfiguration are so affected that at the very front of each of their first writings they already proclaim the new birth that is given to us (Jn 1:13, James 1:18, 1 Peter 1:3). Peter, singled out by Christ, has in his letters: "It was not by way of cleverly concocted myths that we taught you about the coming in power of our Lord Jesus Christ for we were eye witnesses of his sovereign majesty. He received glory and praise from God the Father when that unique declaration came to him out of the majestic splendor: 'This is my beloved Son, on whom my favor rests.'" (2 Pe 1:16–18).

On such points the contemporary Muslim scholar Mahmoud Ayoub calls for "true dialogue (as) conversation among persons and not a confrontation between ideas."[142] To the Christian, whether Catholic or Protestant, the significant fact of Christianity is not an idea or a certain logic, but a devoted encounter and conversation with the actual person of Christ. The whole point, the asymmetry between Christianity and Islam (and Modernity), is that Christ is not an idea. To assume that encounters between basically different religions are essentially a clash of *ideas* might be, in itself, an excess of imported Western rationalism (Kantianism).[143] Happily, within the doctrinal differences and worldviews and lives of members of Christ and the followers of Islam, there is a still deep similarity capable of dialogue. Adherents of both surely agree at some level that monotheism, whether Trinitarian (Christian) or Unitarian (Islam), is more than an idea.

Secular commentators often dismiss religions other than their own beliefs as temporary emanations from agrarian cultures as they transition to urban and modern life. To scholars of this latter secularist view, religion is explained in terms of multigenerational demographics, migrations, and now a further stage of globalization.[144] Defenders of the deeper and even historical basis of traditional religion know of the Trinity by reflecting on actual events remembered and narrated in the Gospels.[145] In the Gospels we also read that it was the words of Christ himself, in the beginning, that introduced us face to face with the mystery of the Trinity, "Go, therefore, and make disciples of all nations, baptizing them in the name of the Father, and of the Son, and of the Holy Spirit" (Mt 28:19).

With her strong sense of the individual, the writer Simon Weil (1909–1943) saw her vocation as being, yes, a Christian but one who remains outside of the institutional Church. She rejected her mental image of the Mystical Body as too collectivist. And then, ironically, she proposed in her own words the very same Pauline understanding of the Church: "Our true dignity is not to be parts of a body, even though it be a mystical one, even though it be that of Christ. It consists in this, that in the state of perfection, which is the vocation of each one of us, we no longer live in ourselves, but Christ lives in us, so that through our perfection Christ in his integrity and in his indivisible unity, becomes in a sense each of us."[146] Paul's testimony to the "mystical body" witnesses to the same reality:

> I live, no longer I, but Christ lives in me" (Gal 2:20). Under the Old Testament, the term used for the Jewish covenant is *berith*, a term which maintains a (Muslim-like?) distance between the oneness of the Creator and his creatures.

> But of the New Covenant, the term used is actually *chaburah*, meaning more
> than a covenant in the old sense of contractual subordination (and possibly fate-
> ful submission). Implied is a *relationship of communion* between God and Man
> 'in and through the person of Jesus Christ.'[147]

As all of the monotheistic religions know, "Man cannot in fact transcend
himself, *but* God can enter into him."[148] Rather than a new "scripture," the
New Covenant is the new life as foretold in the Old Testament scripture, and
as now proclaimed through the unbroken succession of apostolic witnesses.[149]

As "*hearers* of the word" who are to live this new life, all Christians are
sent into the world as lambs among wolves. Before any of the gospels are
written, St. Paul leads by preaching to the Gentiles. The messenger Mohammed is parallel—but not equivalent—to St. Paul and to the other apostles
who were also sent into the world by Christ.[150] St. Paul preached a living
person who after His resurrection demanded of St. Paul, "Saul, Saul, why do
you persecute *me*" (Acts 9:4)? St. Paul, like many of Mohammed's followers
down through history, persecuted the witnessing Church in the name of the
Law in some form.[151] Paul was converted on the Road to Damascus by an
encounter—not by an idea. He was converted to live and preach the complete
crucifixion and resurrection as total redemption and as later narrated in the
Gospels. "And if Christ has not been raised, then empty is our preaching;
empty, too, is your faith" (1 Cor 15:14).[152]

This new messenger of Christ, St. Paul, is dismissed by Jews[153] and again
centuries later by the followers of Islam. For Paul faith in Christ replaces the
waiting of the Jews under the law—the new life replaces any lesser way of
life. Christ ransomed us "that the blessing of Abraham might be extended to
the Gentiles . . . that we might receive the promise of the Spirit through faith"
(Gal 3:14). In the Pauline and related writings we find unambiguous clarity:
"In times past, God spoke in fragmentary and varied ways to our fathers
through the prophets; in this, the final age, he has spoken to us through his
Son, whom he has made heir of all things and through whom he first created
the universe" (Heb 1:1)?

Like Judaism and Christianity, Islam defends a wide "context of humanity's relationship with God." Of God's presence it is explained: "the
miracle of Jesus, like the miracle of the *Qur'an*, is not a once-only event
but an everlasting source of blessing, guidance and salvation."[154] Islam
asserts that "there is no compulsion in religion" (Q2:256). The *Qur'an*
also reads: "The truth is from your Lord. So whosoever wishes shall
believe, and whosoever wishes shall disbelieve" (Q 18:29). Ironically,
similar wording appears in the writings of Mao-tse Tung (1955) so long
as the good of his atheistic Chinese state is not in question.[155] On the point
of non-compulsion in religion the *Catechism of the Catholic Church*

(1994, n. 160) reads: "Man's response to God by faith must be free, and . . . therefore nobody is to be forced to embrace the faith against his will. The act of faith is of its very nature a free act." Under the Christian scripture faith produces hope, and both faith and hope are enriched by reason: "Always be ready to give an explanation to anyone who asks you for a reason for your hope, but do it with gentleness and reverence . . ." (1 Pe 3:15). In his *Refutation of All Heresies,* Saint Hippolytus clearly separates Christian evangelization from conquest: "God wished to win men back from disobedience, not by using force to reduce him to slavery but by addressing to his free will a call to liberty."[156] While abuses under the Inquisitions (plural) are often exaggerated but cannot be denied, the practice cannot be supported easily by citations of Christian scriptures. The parable in Luke, "compel them to come in"(Lk 14:23) is likely meant merely as "persuasion" according to a clerical critic and a supporter of St. Augustine's limited approval for Imperial policies against the Donatists.[157]

Under the *Qur'an,* "The right way is indeed clearly distinct from error" (Q 2:256, ff.)?[158] And: "Whoso obeyeth the messenger obeyeth Allah, and who so turnesth away: We have not sent you (O Muhammad) as a warder over them" (Q 4:80, similarly 10:109, 41:48, 50:45). The *Qur'an* also reads: "grant a delay to the unbelievers: give respite to them gently (for a while)" (Q86:17). Might the Islamic understanding of free religious choice come under a caution offered by St. Augustine? Augustine held that true freedom "cannot be reduced to a sense of choice: it is freedom to act fully . . . For a sense of choice is a symptom of the disintegration of will: the final union of knowledge and feeling would involve a man in the object of his choice in such a way that any other alternative would be inconceivable."[159]

Again involving the concept of compulsion, the biblical parable of the wedding feast has the master giving instruction to go out to the highways and to "compel" the previously uninvited to come in (Lk 14:23).[160] In this instance the political theorist Hugo Grotius writes that the term "compel," as used here and in other parts of the New Testament, means nothing more than an "earnest request." Pope John Paul II said this about compulsion *and* freedom: "Human freedom and God's law meet and are called to intersect, in the sense of man's free obedience to God and of God's completely gratuitous benevolence toward man. Hence obedience to God is not, as some would believe, a heteronomy, as if the moral life were subject to the will of something all-powerful, absolute, extraneous to man and intolerant of his freedom. If in fact a heteronomy of morality were to mean a denial of man's *self-determination* or the imposition of norms unrelated to his good, this would be in contradiction to the revelation of the covenant and of the redemptive incarnation."[161]

NATURAL LAW AND SHARI'A

Political life under Shari'a Law—the *Qur'an* and hadith—contrasts with political life in the West with its heritage of universal natural law embedded within the human person. The natural law is written directly on the human heart of all men and women, whether Christians or not. This is true even though belief in the natural law, knowable by both reason and revelation, is no longer widely accepted. Even from the Christian perspective, St. Paul instructs us, "When the Gentiles who have no law do by nature what the Law prescribes, these having no law are a law unto themselves. They show the work of the Law written in their hearts" (Rom 2:14–15).[162] And "Love does no evil to the neighbor, hence, love is the fulfillment of the Law" ((Rom 13:10). Paul continues: "Clearly you *are* a letter of Christ which I have delivered, a letter written not with ink but *by the Spirit of the living God,* not on tablets of stone but on tablets of flesh in the heart" (I Cor 3:2–3, italics added). The Old Testament anticipates this proclamation: "For the command which I enjoin on you today is not too mysterious and remote for you. It is not up in the sky, that you should say, 'Who will go up in the sky to get it for us and tell us of it, that we may carry it out?. . . No, it is something very near to you, already in your mouths and in your hearts; you have only to carry it out" (Deut 30:11–14).

Heinrich Rommen defines natural law in terms of two central and self-evident principles. These are *"What is just is to be done, and injustice is to be avoided,"* and what he terms the age-old venerable rule, *"Give to everyone his own."*[163] Good and evil are original categories of reality, not simply symbols of experience. In his comparison of secular Western political science and the Islamic State, the Muslim scholar Farooq Hassan mistakes this natural law with superficial post-Enlightenment writings such as the works of empiricist Jeremy Bentham. Bentham's "greatest good for the greatest number" imposes an arithmetic that often violates the natural law, as does the compulsory freedom under Rousseau's General Will which forces dissidents to be free (to conform), and the Leviathan state of Thomas Hobbes. These are departures from the natural law to which Hassan holds up the *Qur'an* as containing the deeper Law, possibly similar to the natural law. Reinforcing Hassan's point at the political level, a Member of the Muslim Mission in Baltimore helped defeat pro-homosexual legislation in Baltimore in 1980 on the grounds that it would "open the door for legal perversion."[164]

The Psalms imply throughout, a natural law, e.g., "Long have I known from your decrees that you have established them (your commands) forever" (Ps 119:152). In the *Qur'an* might the references to "guidance" (e.g., Q 10:35: "It is Allah who gives guidance to Truth . . .") begin to actually refer to reasoned natural law as capable of standing distinct from revelatory divine law? The unraveling of this line of inquiry is in the fact that the *Qur'an* and the broader Shari'a add cultural contradictions from multiple sources. These contradictions include brutal Old Testament and Arabian penalties for violating whatever fragments of natural law might be present. The self understanding of some Muslim writers is that Islam is at once a revelation and the universal religion of nature: "Previous religions strove to unite individuals into communities—in itself a great service—but Islam, *the Religion of Nature*, came to amalgamate these petty nationalities into one vast Brotherhood" (italics added).[165] Again, between divine law and natural law, and between these and the laws of nature, there is no functional distinction.

The Muslim view might be that because the natural law as guidance is rooted ultimately in the unsearchable God, our only access is through his dictation in Arabic, the *Qur'an*. Unlike Hassan, the Christian Heinrich Rommen holds that while natural law is permanent, "the idea of a natural law can emerge only when men come to perceive that not all law is unalterable and unchanging divine law."[166] The difference is that positive law is based on the reasonably discernible morality of universal natural law. Just as the laws of nature become open to scientific investigation when Christianity replaces pagan nature worship, so too do the universal moral laws become clear when differentiation of human laws allows them to take on more of a life of their own. In the West the Medieval conflict between the German empire and the Catholic papacy actually advanced the distinction that made possible natural law theory and constitutionalism.[167] Nevertheless, the historical conflict is not the origin of natural law which is as old as philosophy. The Decalogue precedes late Medieval constitutionalism, the Christian New Testament, and certainly the *Qur'an* of the seventh century.

Abdullah Yusuf Ali finds that the moral law as portrayed in the *Qur'an* (Q 17:23–39) partly reflects the Decalogue, but then goes beyond it by noticing motives and giving attention to the weak and helpless. The love of God involves love and help to one another.[168] The most promising contact point between the West and Islam on the theme of natural law is found in one line of the *Qur'an* that parallels the (above) natural law principles of the West and of Christianity. The *Qur'an* reads: "The true believers, both men and women, are friends to one another. They *enjoin what is just and forbid what is evil . . .*" (Q 9:71, italics added). The divergence with the West is in the meaning of what is "just." From the start is justice "correct belief in the face of external opposition . . . (and opposing injustice) . . . "within the community?"[169] Or is justice found in principles of universal natural law discernible by human reason and applicable to all of humanity, not simply "the community" (the ummah)? For Christians Christ fulfills and confirms the natural law found in nature and in Scripture. Under Islam the *Qur'an* comes last and claims to explain the natural law and the Scriptures in terms of itself (Q 10:37).

Thomas Aquinas and other Medieval Christian writers sought harmony between the New Testament and the natural law writings of such early Classical thinkers as Socrates (470–399 B.C.), Aristotle (384–322 B.C.), the Stoics (e.g., Zeno, 335–263 B.C.) and the Roman Cicero (106–43 B.C.). The path of coherence between faith (divine law) and reason (natural law) need not have narrowed itself later to the rationalist pretense of the Enlightenment project. This pretense includes the naïve doctrine that in a fallen world, unnatural tendencies can simply be educated out of us with worldly knowledge absent the healing touch of the divine—that beyond better managed practical outcomes there is no Good and Evil.

Added to the above citations from the *Qur'an,* the natural law is arguably reflected in other beautiful entries in the hadith:

> O People! Listen to my words as I may not be another year with you in this place. Be humane and just among yourselves. The life and property of each are sacred and inviolable to the other. Render faithfully everyone his due, as you will appear before the Lord and He will demand an account of your actions. Treat woman well; they are your helpmates and do nothing by yourselves. You have taken them from God on trust. O people! Listen to my words and fix them in your memory. I have revealed to you everything; I have left to you a law which you should preserve and be firmly attached to, a law clear and positive, the Book of God and the Examples (hadith).[170]

Abdullah Yusuf Ali proposes that the real Covenant of Israel "is about the moral law, which is set out in the *Qur'an*: And remember We took a Covenant from the Children of Israel (to this effect): Worship none but Allah; Treat with kindness Your parents and kindred, And orphans and those in need; speak fair to the people; Be steadfast in prayer; And practice regular charity" (Q 2:83).[171]

George Weigel, a Senior Fellow at the Ethics and Public Policy Center and prominent defender of the natural law, suggests that "the development of an Islamic 'social doctrine' capable of sustaining tolerance, civility, and pluralism engages the most serious questions of Islamic self-understanding and reminds us that great social and political questions are, more often than not, ultimately theological in character."[172] Favorable citations notwithstanding, is there something about even the Islamic writings that precludes natural law as a possible Rosetta Stone or shared grammar between the West and the world of Islam? Freedom of religion is a key ingredient of natural law. Jordan is the most interreligious of the Muslim states, and at least here the constitution assures freedom of religion. Christians are free to build churches and to take part in the nation's government. Islamic scholars continue to identify shared Christian and Muslim principles and to host interreligious conferences. The Pontifical Council for Interreligious Dialogue encourages this engagement. At the first colloquium in a series, the Amman-based Royal Aal al-Bayt Institute for Islamic Thought and the Council jointly developed very general and concise language on democracy and the rule of law, the role of religions in civil society, the role of civil societies in "creating space for and encouraging dialogue," the dignity of persons and the right of religious freedom, and the need to reject violence in favor of "peaceful coexistence on the basis of full citizenship."[173]

A deepening multicultural inquiry between the world of Islam and the West might come in two parts. First, at the theological level is the understanding that in Islam the *Qur'an* is equivalent to Christ, not the Bible. The second contact point is whether the *Qur'an* is more parallel to the distinct development of natural law in the West. Are openings to the universal natural law embedded in the uniformly deified *Qur'an*? If so, the dual challenge is (a) for Muslims to reconsider whether the natural law—accessible to reason apart from faith—is discernible within the collage-like and communally limited *Qur'an*; and (b) for the West to reconsider whether its progressive dismissal of the natural law in favor of unrestrained positivism is a prudent precondition for global, intercultural, and interreligious engagement in the twenty-first century.

The *Qur'an* imposes a vaguely bounded set of occasionally contradictory religious and moral *positive dictates* delivered from God. Beyond this, different Muslim groups prefer sometimes different collections of practices in the hadith, the sayings of the Prophet. By comparison, under the Christian tradition the first three Commandments refer man to God, but the fourth commandment—to honor father and mother—elevates the natural law. It leads into the remaining six injunctions which are prohibitive or negative. For Muslims, the Shari'a tells *what to do*; for Christians the universal natural law first tells us who we are in the freedom of God, and then the outer boundary of *what not to do*. The last six commandments define only what must be avoided because love of God is positive and extends to esteem and respect for one another. To violate these commandments is sin. Paired with the commandments are the beatitudes (Lk 6:20–22)—calls for mercy—which fully release us to act as we might in charity (but lack of perfection in these matters need not imply moral disorder). Combined, the commandments and the beatitudes give the guidance of an absolute and reasonable morality with an open-ended invitation to charity.

The Bible does not construct a social geography as does Islam and its strongly "felt" ummah. The ummah is based on a simple act of will to be a member of Islam,[174] and leaves in its eclipse the apparently inevitable division between the House of Islam (dar al-Islam) and all others or the House of war (dar al-harb). Some scholars dispute the actual teaching rendered by the key historical figure associated with this binary worldview,[175] but are still faced with specific entries in the *Qur'an* itself. The root difference between the West and Islam is that in Christianity as a faith, and as a response to our common human destiny, we are called to a *non-exclusive* brotherhood toward all persons.[176] Isolationist movements like Catharism that confine the term Christian to the self-identified pure and elect are rejected as heretical. Societies fit for human flourishing are not an imprint from timeless theology, but are grown imperfectly through the moral virtues. During the age of expansion and colonization of the New World recognition of the dignity of indigenous peoples in the New World came partly in early instructions from Pope Eugene IV (1435) and then Paul III (1534–1549). In contrast the non-ecclesiastical nineteenth century *Dred Scott* Supreme Court decision classified an escaped black man as property to be reclaimed, and the 1973 decision (*Roe v. Wade*) disenfranchised an entire class of the unborn as less than persons.

As an historical artifact, the ummah is a reminder that in all early Semitic religions "the god was the god of the nation or of the tribe, and he knew and cared for the individual only as a member of the community."[177] In the very different Western context, membership is twofold, either by baptism or most usually by birth into a political community. In the religious realm, baptism is the normal entry point into a lifetime of ongoing conversion, and is conferred in person on each new member from each new generation. It is sacramental, not hereditary. But the communal dimension of sacramental baptism is also evident from the beginning, as when Peter or Paul baptized the entire household (Acts 10: 47–8, 18:8). In the political realm the principle of "subsidiarity" (unlike the ummah) recognizes multiple voluntary social groupings either "below" the national level or independent from the nation-state or any form of government. Unlike Shari'a, the natural law is a law of human freedom and responsibility and presumes personal moral virtues, especially the virtues of justice and prudence. The moral virtues involve exercise of the will on a daily basis, and are not displaced by one willful act to join the ummah. Prudential judgment, as exercised in political matters, is the capacity not only to assess the appropriateness of action, but for the acting person himself, cooperating with grace and with others, to form himself by this engagement.

Compared to the Shari'a and even to the enactment of "positive law," the natural law "*remains as it were latent. But it makes itself felt whenever the positive law, in itself or in the eyes of a large number of people, appears to be in conflict with the natural law*" (italics added).[178] From the more religious perspective, in addition to the four moral virtues drawn from Classical times, namely justice and prudence, temperance and courage, there are seven other virtues by which Christians personally measure themselves. Each one of these opposes one of the seven "capital sins." The virtues are generosity (growth away from avarice), humility (compared to pride), chastity (rather than lust), meekness (in place of anger), temperance (replacing gluttony), brotherly love (quieting envy), and diligence (overcoming sloth or acedia). St. John offers broad guidance on authentic freedom acting in the world but not of the world: "Do not love the world. If anyone loves the world, the love of the Father is not in him; because all that is in the world is the lust of the flesh, and the lust of the eyes, and the pride of life; which is not from the Father, but from the world" (1 Jn 2: 15–16).

The *Qur'an* reads: "Who but a foolish man would renounce the faith of Abraham? We chose him in the world, and in the world to come he shall abide among the righteous. When the Lord said to him: 'Submit,' he answered: 'I have submitted to the Lord of the Universe'" (Q 129–130). What is termed the "crisis of Islam"[179] and the crisis of Shari'a Law is the difficulty in seeing natural law as a meeting of two distinct but not opposed freedoms. These freedoms are not mutually exclusive or in a zero-sum relationship—the uncreated freedom of a creative God and our own created freedom toward God and one another, as receptive persons because made in His image. Century after century Islam has paused and nearly stopped at the question, how can the autonomy of God be preserved if the human person also has autonomy? The crisis of Islam is that Shari'a Law makes no distinction between faith, religion, a way of life, and civil law.

To gain membership into the Islamic ummah all that is required is to accept the *Qur'an* and "the five pillars."[180] In common with earlier Jewish law three of the pillars are the observance of prayer,[181] fasting, and almsgiving. For Muslims, prayer is ritual prayer five times each day; almsgiving is partly specified in the *Qur'an*; and fasting is done for a full month (between sunrise and sun down) each year during Ramadan. To these three pillars is added a fourth, to make a pilgrimage to Mecca during one's lifetime. And the fifth pillar which is also uniquely Islamic, is to profess Allah and to accept Mohammed as his messenger: "*There is no God but Allah, and Mohammed is His Prophet.*"[182] This injunction is very similar to the morning and evening prayer of the earlier Jewish community: "Hear, O Israel! Jahweh our God is the one God." Mohammed claimed to have found the words of the fifth pillar listed on the gates of each of the seven heavens his visited on his legendary visit to Heaven, and finally in the seventh heaven at the right side of the throne of God: "*La ellah ellallah Mohammed resul ollah.*"[183] For the Christian it is the resurrected Christ who is our advocate at the right hand of the Father, not Mohammed who throughout the *Qur'an* parcels out his prayers to the deserving.[184]

In addition to the pillars, Muslim law includes a moral code drawn partly from the Ten Commandments, or as conjectured by Hassan (above) the embedded natural law generally to do good and to avoid evil. But unlike the responsible freedom of the universal natural law as developed and understood in the West, the *Qur'an* and hadith first confine the message to members of the ummah (Q 48:29), and then specify in positive detail what these moral actions are—including radical departures from Judeo-Christian morality. Residual polygamy and stoning are two examples.[185] In the past the Muslim code has not applied equally to all persons—equality of persons is only for those within the House of Islam (dar al-Islam).[186] And at the personal level in the real world—and perhaps only partly supported by Shari'a—the code also sharply reduces women to submission relative to men. Genital mutilation of young girls is diminished but still widely practiced,[187] and in Pakistan especially conviction rates in cases of rape and domestic violence are low.[188] Other basic features of Shari'a address domestic welfare and economics within the ummah. One of these features is the *zakat*, an annual tax on *all* property (land, jewelry) of Muslims. Until the Ottoman period the zakat served as a source for alms in place of any tax on annual income which under Shari'a is prohibited. The zakat often has been collected by the government (a concession opposed by Shi'ites) at no overhead cost to be used for the needy within the community of Islam, but also often to support the imams.

The hadith prohibits the taking of interest on loans, and instead modern bank deposits yield profits as is also the case with stock ownership in the West. In this way economic common sense is served while still observing the religious prohibition against usury.[189] The Muslim law is economically democratic on paper in that it discourages the formation of cartels. The Organization of Petroleum Exporting Countries (OPEC) and the domestic oligarchies in Arab states are the most conspicuous and unexamined exceptions. In Pakistan, also in the early 1970s, Ali Bhutto came to power on the platform that Islam contained a socialistic outlook. In a range of national instances including criminal codes, immigration, and civil service, administrative rules are given latitude provided they do not directly conflict with the higher laws of Shari'a.[190] Islamic law also provides for private property, unions and fair treatment of employees, and for free enterprise. Influenced by early twentieth century Western nationalism and socialism, Shari'a also features the liberal right of the state to acquire the means of production of social welfare.[191] Iran is a leading example of a resulting split-level economy consisting of entrenched state-owned businesses and patronage structures alongside a separate niche-level economy of very small scale street venders.[192]

In broad overview, because of the natural law embedded in the human heart, the human person is oriented first of all toward responsible freedom, and truth, justice and solidarity.[193] These principles define the human person as a person, and apply universally, even to those outside the Western experience and even to supposed infidels. Natural law supplies the uncorrupted man with negative boundaries on what not to do, leaving him free to pursue together the personal and common good, and is open to such positive biblical actions as are encouraged by the beatitudes. "The true believers, both men and women, are friends to one another. *They enjoin what is just and forbid what is evil . . .*" (Q 9:71, italics added). Muslim scholars (e.g., Hassan) point to other hints of natural law in the *Qur'an* and hadith: "Allah be worshipped and evil be shunned" (Q 16:36), and "God's creation cannot be changed" (Q 30:30).

While these lines are *in* Muslim law, they might not really *of* Muslim law. The Gordian Knot for Muslims of good will is to see this distinction. In the West the reasoned discovery of natural law came in Classical thought and before Christ (in the order of time, not the order of reality). The self-understanding of Islam is in crisis today is the difficulty in unwinding its history in the backwards direction. In Christian thought the natural law is part of divine law and was discovered chronologically before the coming of Christ and is knowable without revelation. Grace perfects nature . . . does not erase nature. Within Islam does the natural law persist, but engulfed within a dictated "revelation?" The natural law coincides with the Ten Commandments delivered to Moses on Mount Sinai to a forgetful people. The *Qur'an* recounts parts of these entries in a more poetic format (Q 2:83–85). Significantly, the commentator Abdullah Yusuf Ali remarks that "the real Covenant is about the moral law, which is set out (here). The moral law is universal . . ."[194] The difficulty with regard to universal morals is the fatalistic presupposition that those not favored with specifically Islamic belief remain beyond the pale of universality and are doomed to punishment (Q 39:20).

At this point an entry cited above from the hadith invites reasoned inquiry: "There is not a child that he or she is born upon this fitrah, this original state of the knowledge of God. And his parents make him a Jew, a Christian, or a Zoroastrian . . . and if they are Muslims, Muslim."[195] The congruence on some points between philosophy and theology is noted by al-Ghazali: "It is not farfetched that ideas should coincide, just as a horse's hoof may fall on the print left by another . . ."[196] Fitrah has been intensely discussed within and without Islam. Proposed here is a potentially fruitful joint inquiry on the possible double meaning of fitrah as a "hoof print" for both the natural law and divine law. Various translations of fitrah compatible with this proposal are "natural disposition, constitution, temperament, e.g., what is in a man at his creation, a sound nature, natural religion (and) the germ of Islam."[197] The interreligious nexus is whether fitrah refers more to natural law as stable meanings anchored in the nature of man or whether it authorizes continuous revelation more akin Western process theology. The self-understanding of Islam is that the *Qur'an* is the ongoing divine "writing" and "rewriting" of revelation.[198] Process theology offers the same flexibility, but in the alternative sense (historicism) that the content of faith depends upon the evolution of culture. Multicultural approaches to religion obscure such varied premises. Catholic propositions regarding historicist theology admit to development of doctrine, but not that doctrine is indeterminate or always an approximation subject to paradigm shifts, as occur in the empirical sciences.[199]

St. Paul refreshes: "When the Gentiles who have no law (meaning Christ) do by nature what the Law prescribes, these having no law are a law unto themselves. They show the work of the Law written in their hearts" (Rom 2:14–15). Can Muslims of good will distinguish between this law *already written in each heart* of themselves and of others, and its echo (congruence) in texts that many have never read? Should we not hope that the universal natural law, the Decalogue—*bracketed* for a moment from its Christian fulfillment—adds to the needed "grammar" of discourse between the West, the witnesses to Christ, and most of the followers of Islam? To entertain this intricate possibility may be to grasp at straws, but it is not necessarily naive or blatantly secularist. With the hindsight of another century or two (and possibly beyond the immediate threat of jihad), we might see afresh that the Spirit moves where he will.

THE ISLAMIC STATE

What is the relationship between the domain of Islam and the particular case of the territorial Islamic State or Mosque-state? The Qur'anic verse: "There is no compulsion in religion" (Q 2:256) predates the rise of the fused Mosque-state. In the Christian world, where Church and State are separate, a similar concept appears in the writings of the Second Vatican Council (1963–5): "(the truth) does not impose itself except by the strength of the truth itself."[200] The defining difference is the immunity enjoyed by members in civil society from external coercion by the state.[201] The council asserts the personal right to freedom of religion (see below). With Shari'a a distinct realm for autonomous civil society does not clearly exist.

Much is misunderstood in the West about the foreign Islamic concept of the state. To help bridge this gap, in 1981 and immediately following the 1979 Iran Hostage Crisis, the Pakistani jurist and scholar Farooq Hassan wrote a comprehensive and lucid profile of the Islamic State: *The Concept of the State and Law in Islam*.[202] Although details differ in important ways between his homeland Pakistan and politics in the rest of the Islamic world, this is an invaluable source. Hassan explains that the bifurcation between Church and state in the West results from historical circumstance. From the beginning, the Jewish and Christian communities were under the leadership of priests and existed apart from either the Pharaoh or the pagan Roman Emperor. Under Islam, however, there is no such historical and accidental distinction between the ruled and ruler. From the beginning victorious Muslims were ruled by Muslims.[203] As a result of Islam's special history, the separation of Mosque and state would be an unwarranted "dichotomy" based on an imported peculiarity of Western experience.

A different reading of Western history would notice the pivotal event for both Judaism and Islam in the destruction of the Temple in 70 A.D. This tragedy marks the beginning of rabbinic Judaism absent the Temple. Like Judaism from this point forward, Islam also displays a reduced role of atonement as found in earlier Judaism and in the continuing faith life of Christianity. Judaism and the later Islam are defined by prayer, fasting and almsgiving. Islam rounds out its five pillars with the pilgrimage to Mecca (as a kind of temple), and reverence for Mohammed as the final prophet of Allah. Modern Judaism and Islam are both shaped by a pivotal act of Roman militarism. Both Judaism and Islam tend to dilute a theology of atonement between creature and Creator with one of reverence combined with cultural identity. Modern secular humanism is intent on relocating historically rooted cultural identities within a broad multiculturalism domesticated by the proceduralism of day-to-day civility.

The connection between Roman institutions and today's Church-state distinction differs in yet another respect from Hassan's interpretation. Before destruction of the Temple, the Jews in the Hellenic part of the Roman Empire actually enjoyed protection from interference by those members who might disrupt the quiet practice of their religion. As a potential instigator, Christ was brought before Roman justice, and the later Paul was also brought before a Roman court. The edicts of Claudius reaffirmed the privilege of toleration dating from the triumviral period and the later Augustus. Claudius' wording is that "It is proper that the Jews through the world under Roman rule should keep their native customs without let or hindrance."[204]

The separation of Church and state in the Christian West is much more than an artifact of Roman persecution. To claim otherwise is to reverse cause and effect. The Church began in persecution because the intrinsic dignity it proclaimed for each human person, as now revealed by Christ, is *irreducible and transcends the Roman state and any state*: "my kingdom does not belong to this world" (Jn 13:36). Scriptural scholar Dougherty expresses it this way: "Behind the struggle between the Christian Church and the Roman Empire were aligned the heavenly and the infernal powers . . . a rehearsal for that final great conflict between them when God's victory will mark the end of this world and the beginning of *the other world*. The Apocalypse is a Christian philosophy of history."[205] Under Islam, the reason the mosque and state remain fully absorbed within each other is that Islam too often shuns distinctions.

Hassan stresses that Islam takes a unified and comprehensive view of life. The Islamic State is not comparable to the modern Western state.[206] The Islamic State is even seen as part of a culture and the cornerstone to reclaiming something of past glories for the world of Islam.[207] Hassan finds that there is a lack of moral content in the way of life of secular nation-states. Such an assessment pertains less directly to *political* institutions as such than to Western *society* with its many institutions outside the state, including religious institutions. But Hassan's general insight (1981) is not lost on religious leaders in the West. In a recent interview Pope Benedict XVI offered his assessment of the Muslim worldview as it pertains to life in the West. Benedict summarizes what he finds in the Muslim self-understanding:

> We (Muslims) are somebody too; we know who we are; our religion is holding its ground; you don't have one any longer. This is actually the feeling today of the Muslim world: The Western countries are no longer capable of preaching a message of morality but have only know-how to offer the world. The Christian religion has abdicated; it really no longer exists as a religion; the Christians no longer have a morality or a faith; all that's left are a few remains of some modern ideas of enlightenment; we (Muslims) have the religion that stands the test.[208]

A rising Islam also fills the political vacuum left by the collapse of the Soviet Union and the confrontation of the Cold War. Political analysis of the new landscape is superficial because the new terrain rests on deeper and almost geologic formations. To be recognized in the twenty-first century is a world consisting possibly of three cultural-religious zones. These are the spiritual vacuum in China as is evidenced by the inability of the regime to successfully suppress religion as a human need, the spiritual vacuum in the West as seen in the unprecedented superficiality of political and cultural discourse, and thirdly, the renewed presence of the Islamic State and its pre-modern communal culture and clear beliefs (even if five-times-daily prayer is neglected by the majority of Muslims on the street).

The religious core of the Islamic State resembles to some degree the Western kingdoms of medieval times and the confessional states of the later sixteenth and seventeenth centuries. Throughout its history any theoretically purer and congregational kind of Islamic society has given way to forms of centralization. Modernization in the West is both a departure and a sharpening of these models. Scientific thought, industrial and military society, and replacement of traditional identities with individualism are all part of the modern chemistry. But as an organizing principle, religious creed has been replaced by ideology and trade routes. The Italian statesman Fanfani looked back on this transition: "the State became more favourably disposed towards capitalism; it had no longer a creed to defend, but only interests, and in this sphere it was not hard to reach an understanding."[209] The current Pope Benedict XVI follows a similar track and is also partly in step with Hassan's critique of the West: "Then, the conviction that the economy must be autonomous, that it must be shielded from 'influences' of a moral character, has led man to abuse the economic process in a thoroughly destructive way."[210] But unlike Hassan's solution of the unitary Islamic State, Benedict observes that within society there are distinct layers, ultimately protective of the human person. He distinguishes between the market, the state, and civil society.[211]

In the Muslim world the Islamic State—unlike much of the West—still has a vigorous self image and belief to defend and spread. Out of step with the Western experience toward modernization, the multi-state ummah is an extraordinary and unique example of what Western social science broadly classifies as a traditional identity or "communal" group. Communal groups exist prior to and apart from (Western) individualism and modern or rationalized social groupings, such as economic or vocational classes. Communal groups are typically presumed to be easily organized by the politics of new and overarching secular states, each with its geographic boundaries of sovereignty.

Common features of communal groups are recited in the literature as, first, a common culture and identity with a *strongly felt* solidarity; second, an included set of networking that works throughout *the entire life* of the individual members; and third, a way of including *within itself* the full range of (Western) differences in terms of economic status and power.[212] At the local scale, the communal group tries to absorb modernity, rather than the other way around. Communalism understands people primarily as members of "pre-modern" groups, ethnic, linguistic or religious and so on.

Academic political theory, especially until the rise of Ayatollah Khomeini in Iran in 1979, has held that communal groups eventually assimilate into a class-based and rationalized social structure. Such structures involve self-evident "stages of development" and in modern history are usually constructed as secular nation-states.[213] The evidence suggests, however, that at least in the foreseeable future, rather than a transformer, modernity itself is just as easily encapsulated within the more resistant or even new communal groupings and especially religious groupings. Communal groups are not necessarily the raw material of applied social science.

Resilient communal identities are symbiotic with state machinery as an enabling framework and idiom for repositioning themselves in the new environment. For the global ummah of communal Islam, as in the West, all politics is still local. The fused Islamic State is a particular outcome, possibly in response to early Byzantine pressures. Secular Turkey and the several Muslim republics of the Middle East are others more recent. In its religious content, the diverse and multi-state Islamic community, the ummah, spans the globe from West Africa to Indonesia. Different than the dismantled sacramental Christian commonwealth, and in contrast with the successor Western nation-states, the Islamic State is "not temporal in the modern sense of the term, since the modern state is not guided by religion, and it usually lacks moral conscience and a moral basis for administration and application of its laws."[214]

The anomalous modern event in the world of Islam is the Turkish nation-state, specifically the attachment of the Turkish and Muslim people to what is on paper a fully secular state apparatus. The Turkish solution is a poised balance under the watchful eye of a secular military. The exceptional event among nation-states in the West, far beyond the separation of Church from state, is the apparent co-option of nation-state institutions by interests actually hostile to religion. Public expression of religion is increasingly suppressed, either Lenin's "private matter" in former communist states or more commonly as simply a subjective experience to be displaced by media culture and the market place of monetized appetites—the consumer culture.

The institutional architecture responsive to communal and multicultural populations is not limited to the unitary Islamic State or the civility of the secular nation-state. Before Versailles the Western multinational empires retained monarchic or extended family approach. Another approach is federalism[215] which can apply to all kinds of communal groups other than the religious, such as ethnic, language and dialect, or racial. India is a secular (three-fourths Hindu) nation-state but geographically a confederation of two dozen language-states. Unlike supervisory colonialism, pure *federalism* provides semi-autonomous territorial governments when these groups conveniently divide geographically on the map. For other mixed populations, another federated approach is to successfully foster *consensus among the elites*, as in the predominantly Muslim Federation of Malaysia with its multicultural coalition of Hindu, Chinese and Malay political parties into the ruling Alliance Party. Historically in the Islamic world the leaders of Christian subgroups (or dhimmis) were accountable to the sultan or khan, but the group members were not confined to any particular geographic territory in his domain. This is one of many examples of *encapsulation*.

Other institutional models shaped by communal groupings would include strong man rule or *coercion* (the recent Iraqi regime of Saddam Hussein), *economic interdependence* or "globalization" on a small scale, and *communal representation* in parliaments, possibly with rotation of key positions among the major religious groups. In Lebanon especially, national survival depends upon this kind of religious cooperation. "Lebanon is not just a nation, but a message" (Pope John Paul II). Others models are the *neutrality of leadership* with regard to its own ethnic or communal background (mid-twentieth century Tanzania, and the monarchic principle as sometimes practiced in early Europe), and more forceful *ideological manipulation* which was a large part of Ataturk's creation of modern Turkey. Abusive cases include forced *expatriation* of minorities as in the expulsion of non-converting Jews from Spain (1480 and 1531). The opposite and rare case would be the creation or restoration of a secure (and likely disputed) homeland as in the settling of the New World or the creation of the state of Israel.[216] Recent and unhappy examples of expatriation include the mutual relocation of Greek and Turkish religious populations following the First World War, and the expulsion and severe tribulations of nearly three million Sudenten Germans from Czechoslovakia in the two years following the Second World War.[217]

Yet another solution is *assimilation* or the "melting pot" which to a possibly declining degree is the exceptional American enterprise. On a small scale, the Singapore city-state achieves "inimitable" multiracial and multilingual harmony as a one-party "administrative state" committed to evenly distributed economic growth, four official languages with the external English as the dominant one, and a commonly understood internal concern for secure nation-building in the larger and volatile southeast Asian region.[218] The model of the recent British Empire was unique in concept and scale, that of a *commonwealth* of independent nations under the headship of a figurehead monarchy.[219] *Military coup* has been the most common default solution to political complexity in the post-colonial world. Where it exists, universal conscription is a legacy of the Napoleon, and as a nation-wide institution the military is a tool for social stability or enforced social change for good or ill. In the 1970s after the removal of colonial powers around the world, probably two-thirds of states were under military control. Today, especially with the collapse of the Soviet empire, the ratio is reduced to probably one-third.

By far the most prominent and widespread communal identity is the Islamic ummah. The ummah, or dar al-Islam tests geographic categorization in a very large way. The ummah is a domain—not a mapped territory—encompassing all places where the Muslim is secure in his person, religion and property. Hassan begins his analysis of the territorial Islamic State, as a particular case, with four elements held in common with the modern nation-state.[220] Modernity's centralized nation-state, says Hassan, in all cases consists of a territory, a population (understood here to include a shared culture and history[221]), an organization, and sovereignty. Some of the parallel and distinctive characteristics of the Islamic State are that sovereignty resides in God, that all basic laws already exist in the Shari'a but that there still remains a limited legislative function, that all laws fall directly under moral review because sin and crime are almost indistinguishable, that there is no separation between Mosque and State, that the economic system is midway between Capitalism and Communism, and that the purpose of the State "is to foster ties among the international community of Islam."[222]

Unlike the ummah as a collage of diverse peoples within an abstract (non-historical) Muslim identity, the Western understanding of much more recent "national" histories and identities entails a fifth concept in addition to Hassan's four. National citizenship is a synthesis of nationalism, or more reasonably patriotism, and personal freedom and responsibilities. And from this feature of citizenship comes possibly a sixth feature. To be fostered by the modern state and a range of other community structures is service to the common good, as part of the universal natural law reaching beyond any particular state. The uncorrupted Western nation-state would be more than an administrative unit, and even entails a foundational choice by the governed of their governmental organization or political system.

Within Hassan's four-part definition, the key divide between the West and the world of Islam is the meaning of "sovereignty." In the West and as a natural right sovereignty resides not in the state, but in the body politic itself and ultimately in the free and responsible human persons of which the state is an instrument.[223] Despite its troubled history, this aspect of modernity is largely a Christian heritage. Under Islam it is only God who is sovereign (not additionally the people in some nuanced sense), while the state exists to ensure and even supervise Hassan's goals of fraternity, equality, liberty and justice. Hassan explains that "the essence and aims of the Islamic law (are) the protection and promotion of human rights . . . All of the positive and negative injunctions frequently used from Quranic sources revolve around some aspect of the human rights philosophy. Since man (not States as in Western political theories) is the center of the universe, laws are made with a clear mandate behind them for his welfare. Therefore, *inter alia*, the source of human rights protection laws is the highest in Islam."[224]

Hassan proposal—startling to Western ears—is that it is only with the abolition of monarchy and feudalism after the French Revolution, that such Islamic ideals as equality, liberty and justice gain a reception in Europe.[225] This ethnocentric image of dar al-harb history would seem to be marginally softened by a sense of universal justice. "The notion of justice in the Shari'a," he writes, "binds a Muslim not only to God, but also to his fellow men including non-Muslims."[226] The Christian message is non-exclusive from the beginning. St. Paul writes: "So then, while we have the opportunity, let us do good to all, but especially to those who belong to the family of the faith" (Gal 6:10). The contradiction between Western history and Hassan's claims for Islam reinforces the thesis introduced and implied above that some parts of Islam might be better understood in the West as an assertion of the universal natural law (not divine revelation), but an assertion unfortunately fossilized inside of a divinely dictated Islamic folk literature and worldview. In only partial response, Western political theory does not place the state over man, and the West, despite its own shortcomings, is not convinced that all Islamic laws by definition advance personal and social welfare, or that justice (based on inalienable human rights) is done uniformly with Muslims and non-Muslims. Further, much of the history of the West, even before the rise of Islam, turns on the actual tension between liberty and equality. Hassan begins to show that in the Islamic State, the Western safeguard in the separation of governmental powers exists to some degree, although the zone of application is limited.[227]

Critiquing the West from the Islamic vantage point, Wael B. Hallaq makes the case that the simplifying power of nation-state sovereignty—and female subordination in the household—is a result of the broadly influential French Civil Code. In his view it is the French Civil Code and modernity and nation-state ideology—rather than features of Islam—that are responsible now for the disconnected nuclear family and for the patriarchal dominance that results. He holds that it is these Western intrusions that best account for the absence in post-colonial Islamic laws of earlier extended family roles and the pre-modern web of safety-nets and supports for the wife relative to her husband.[228] Western thinkers will find this assertion one-sided, yet it is a formal teaching of the Church (termed "subsidiarity") that the socialist state poses a real threat to a wide range of natural and intermediate groups and associations supportive and respectful of the human person, especially including the family (Chapter 4).

Hassan holds, at a different level, that membership in the universal Muslim family, the ummah, is so abstract and is such an "absolute standard of evaluation" that it is simply invulnerable to such "accidental, historical, and social influences that surround the individual."[229] In this respect, the ummah is parallel, but not equivalent to the early Christian community. Dawson describes the Christian community as a "fellowship of believers, which abolishes all distinctions of race and tribe and social rank."[230] As a religion rather than as a collection of states, the ummah is essentially different than the Church especially as the Christian community first began. At the descent of the Holy Spirit at Pentecost the words of Peter and the apostles were received not abstractly, but concretely and personally and by many very different fellow travelers: "How is it that each of us hears them in his native tongue?" (Acts

2:8). Those present and astonished included visitors from Cappadocia (part of modern day Turkey) and even from Arabia, six centuries before the coming of Mohammed. The counterpoint in the *Qur'an* seems to concede a permanent human disunity, untouched by either Pentecost or an inborn natural law, and attributes this tribal premise to God. It reads, "Had your Lord so wished he would have made all of humanity one ummah" (Q 11:118). Islam acts in place of God to edit Babel out of the human picture, but then declines to explain the factionalism within the ummah. For Christians the coming of Christ illuminates and redeems us from the primordial flaw within us all, termed original sin.

Under the universal natural law, all of humanity actually is one family. Some of the earliest and culture-bound expressions of natural law resemble the divinely political sovereignty still claimed today by Islam. We have this from St. Paul: "Let everyone be subject to the higher authorities for there exists no authority except from God, and those who exist have been appointed by God. Therefore he who resists the authority resists the ordinance of God; and they that resist bring on themselves condemnation" (Rom 13:1–2). In its reaffirmations of the Christian faith, especially against what later became the Communism State, Pope Leo XIII pointed explicitly to the real and deeper accountability contained within the political principle of sovereignty: "Whatever be the nature of the government, rulers must ever bear in mind that God is the paramount ruler of the world, and must set Him before themselves as their exemplar and law in the administration of the State."[231]

Today territorial and political sovereignties exist largely as administrative conveniences for the strongly felt Muslim community or ummah, however much divided by sectarian loyalties: "The quintessence of the Quranic Principles is that they, being of divine origin, are equally applicable to the whole of mankind, irrespective of a person's status, position, color, race, sex, language, or nationality.[232] If a thing is declared legal, it is legal for all in any shape or form . . . We can, therefore, conclude that owing to the restricted right of legislation, nobody is regarded as a 'legislator' (in the modern sense of the word) in an Islamic State. *The authority of authorities in such a State can only be regarded as that of executors of law, basically made by God"* (italics added).[233]

Western law distinguishes between what is "declared legal" and those universal principles of natural law that are not identical with discretionary positive law but are to be consistently respected. In asserting a total sovereignty of God devoid of nuance as it does, Islam is preceded by and largely replicates an early phase in the unfolding history of Judaism. David in the Old Testament said this: "Yours O Lord, are grandeur and power, majesty, splendor, and glory. For all in heaven and on earth is yours; yours, O Lord, is the *sovereignty*; you are exalted as head over all" (1 Chron 29:11, italics added). In the days before David and Saul, as carried forward in this verse, there was no king stationed between God and his people; there were only "judges"—charismatic leaders in the early days of competition for the land of Canaan. Undistorted by any later political structures, the original "congregational" Islam might best be thought of as modeled after the period of "judges" who are parallel to imams and who directly enabled the populations to live in obedience to the Lord.

The Western observer can readily agree that the Islamic State is decidedly unlike the modern state in the West: "Since its chief function (the Islamic State*) is to protect Islam and to promote its cause both within and without*, and to administer both religious and temporal affairs in accordance with the *Qur'an* and the Sunna, this State may be regarded as religious as well as temporal. It should, however, be made clear that the State religion of the Islamic State must be Islam for whose protection and maintenance it is called into existence and continues to exist."[234]

Medieval canonists in the West struggled in a similar way with the origin of law. In the thirteenth century papalists held that only the pope received his power directly from God while the emperor received his indirectly through the pope. At the zenith of this thinking, Pope Innocent III referred to papal and secular power in language similar to Hassan's. Both the pope and the emperor were God's "instruments" and "artificers," the one dealing with human law and the other the divine.[235] He addressed a letter to the independent towns of central Italy. While even then the Church and towns were not fused as are the Mosque and state, his letter included language at least remotely similar to Hassan's. He wrote: "you should always endeavor to act in a way which would add to the honour and growth of the Roman Church so as to deserve and strengthen the pledge of her favour and friendship."[236] Nearly a millennium after Innocent III, the fused Islamic State continues to exist to protect Islam and the Muslim community, the ummah. Since the thirteenth century the separate nations in the West have displaced the Medieval Mystical Body of Christ as the context for politics. And without ranking the spiritual condition of different cultures, a strong tradition in Western thought laments the decline over centuries of the spiritual condition of the West. Writing less than a decade before Hassan, Eric Voegelin documents "the revolutionary crisis of our age." He writes that the current crisis "is distinguished from earlier revolutions by the fact that the spiritual substance of Western society has diminished to the vanishing point, and that the vacuum does not show any signs of refilling from new sources."[237]

In the recent Western context the United States *Declaration of Independence* reads "we hold these truths to be self evident. . ." This is a secular proclamation respectful of religion but pointing to natural law. And the Church's social teachings, largely a critique of ideological Europe in the twentieth century, insists on: "necessary limits to the state's intervention and on its instrumental character inasmuch as the individual, the family and society are *prior to the state* and inasmuch as the state exists in order to protect their rights and not stifle them."[238] Not at all in conflict with knowable truth, the Western state is re-centered not as the "executor" of divine law, but as the guardian of the distinct natural law and as the protector of the *human person and the shared common good*: "The promotion of the appropriate conditions of life in both the economic and the cultural sphere is, then, the purpose of the state."[239]

Unlike the Islamic worldview, the Christian view is that divine and human autonomies are neither identical nor mutually exclusive. The "autonomy" of shared self-government by citizens is both legitimate and good. And further, the particular form of government and the designation of leaders as by elections derive from authentic and responsible human freedom.[240] Unlike Islam which sees the political order as *delegated* under the *Qur'an*, in the specifically Catholic political philosophy the political order is a consequence of a personal human dignity known by both reason and revelation. In 1901 the author of the Church's first social encyclicals dealing with the Church in the modern world, wrote: "for the laws of nature and of the Gospel, which by right are superior to all human contingences, *are necessarily independent of all particular forms of civil government*, while, at the same time, they are in harmony with all that is not repugnant to morality and justice."[241]

Such a synthesis of necessary "independence" and "harmony" is almost inconceivable to the Shari'a and the Islamic State. Yet, for the Christian as well as for the Muslim, the state is not above our understanding(s) of morality. Under Islamic and Catholic political theories, an "immoral" law is not a law. In the Christian world ideology is to be judged by informed personal and public conscience, not the reverse. To the religious mind and heart the radical secularist imposes a worldview lacking both religion and consistent moral justice. With regard to permissive laws for abortion, the ultimate child abuse, John Paul II reminds us of ". . . the grave and clear obligation to oppose them by conscientious objection."[242] It was generally Muslim states, not Western states, that joined the pope at the 1994 Cairo Conference to successfully oppose a proposed United Nations redefinition of abortion as a human right. Pope John Paul II uses the very strong terms "conspiracy" and "betrayal" in his accusation that states have negated "the long historical process leading to the discovery of human rights."[243] This critique also applies to the recent decision by the United States (2009) to fund abortions internationally, and to make foreign aid conditional on acceptance of this policy for countries often desperate for help.

Institutionally the Islamic State differs fundamentally from the Western and from Catholic political thought. Yet, Islam is not to be classified under Western terminology as a theocracy. The leaders are not at the top of an institutional pyramid as was John Calvin at Geneva or Henry VIII in England. Hassan writes that "In the Shari'a, God is God and man is man," and even the Prophet is mentioned as but a man (Q 18:110).[244] The caliph or successor of Mohammed is a mere "representative of the people."[245] (In the vast majority of Islamic states that are Sunni, the historic caliph is equivalent to the Shi'ite imams as the defender of Shari'a.) The caliph is characterized as a trustee with wide geographic authority. His role pertains to a collective right of all who identify themselves as Muslims under the absolute sovereignty of God. This role theoretically is not reducible to the service of any particular clan or class. Muslim writers explain that Islam is a *"congregational theocracy."* Further, the universality of Shari'a law (like natural law in the West) is equally binding not only on all Muslims but on all mankind,[246] an understanding that on many points is threatening to members and especially to infidels outside of dar al-Islam. Under Islam as a conglomerate or congregational theocracy, "The Caliph and citizens are responsible to each other and to God."[247] Religious and temporal functions are not separated, and penalties for violation are both certain and often primitive. The Islamic State exists to protect and maintain Islamic religion and culture. While it is like an ideological state "(The Islamic State) differs fundamentally from all of them (modern States) and stands in a class by itself."[248]

As an institution outside the Western state, the Catholic Church is to be contrasted with the Islamic State in its religious dimension. While the self-understanding of mosque-state Islam is as a congregational theocracy, the self understanding of the Church—distinct from the Western state—is as a *"hierarchical communion."*[249] In its original meaning, "hierarchy" means "sacred ruler" or "sacred origin" (from the Greek), and need not be confused with patterns of careerism and domination. Institutionally, the Church government consists of a hierarchy of territorially responsible bishops tracing back to the apostles commissioned by Christ, who is more than a prophet. They stand in union with the pope as the bishop of Rome who traces directly back to the historical St. Peter[250] whose bones repose in the excavations beneath the main altar of the basilica in Rome bearing his name. This hierarchical communion combines with a laity who equally share "the universal call to holiness" and "the priesthood of the faithful," but whose special role is to witness to Christ in the world.[251] These relationships exist within a communion that is both a mystery and an institution.

The hierarchical communion is neither a simplistic pyramidal model of papalism nor a dispersed model of episcopacy.[252] Internal to the Church today

the fitting image for "hierarchical communion" is more of an "ellipse" uniting the episcopacy tracing back to the apostles, but with the papal primacy
uniquely tracing back to St. Peter. From the beginning these come always
together, never one isolated from the other.[253] The hierarchical communion
is not an "executor" of divine law in the world. In the worldly realm it is the
role of Church members, generally not the Church as such, to become directly
engaged in secular affairs. This role and special vocation of the laity in the
world is not a delegated one. Rather, "Through their baptism and confirmation, all are commissioned to that apostolate *by the Lord himself*."[254] The inevitably vigorous debate on political matters calling for discernment on how
to apply moral principles to "contingent" situations is not a sign of disunity.
It is a sign of a deeper respect and unity under the natural law which includes
a right to participation and engagement.

From the Islamic perspective, Hassan finds deficiency in the Western
democracies—as distinct from the Church which he does not address. He
faults the democracies for protecting human rights by *restricting* government
authority more than by positive action. Under Shari'a the Islamic State itself
is believed to be a positive force for human advancement, both secular and
religious. There is no formal hierarchy and therefore there is no laity, and
there is no citizenship clearly distinct from the Islamic ummah. Hassan writes
sweepingly and glowingly of Shari'a Law: "(Under Shari'a) it may be seen
that the solutions for man's problems are already available and have been for
a long time. It shows and proves that the Shari'a is not only supreme and in
accordance with the needs of man, but it also contains principles which are
for universal application in the future as well. This basic philosophical foundation of Shari'a as a guideline for all times, in secular and religious matters,
is the essence of Islamic polity, its concept of law and State."[255]

In the theory of the Islamic State there is no fully independent civil society, and alongside the state no deeper culture of associations to directly
advance the common good. The state is the "executor of divine law,"[256] not a
more limited legislator of positive law accountable to a recessive natural law
imprinted by God in the citizens themselves.[257] For Muslims, sovereignty is
singular and belongs to God. But according to thinkers like Hassan, in politics
this sovereignty still admits some scope for interpretation according to the
"rules of derivation."[258] This is especially true for entirely new situations not
anticipated in the *Qur'an* or the hadith. Thus, there is some room for flexibility and for characteristic pragmatism around the edges of Shari'a and the
Islamic State.

The three major elements of Shari'a in the Islamic State are the *Qur'an*,
the hadith, and to a lesser extent a third feature of limited flexibility called
Ijtihad.[259] Again, the *Qur'an* is a divinely revealed message delivered to

Mohammed as Allah's Prophet. It is believed to be the restored religion of Abraham and, as a sacred and precisely dictated book, the definitive essence of God. In addition to this is the hadith or Sunna which is a diversely collected record of the prophet's deeds and sayings. This is the tradition of the Prophet which, unlike the *Qur'an,* may admit to some added scope for free will. The hadith is based in part on Mohammed's reported journey to heaven where, in addition to the writings of the *Qur'an,* he is said to have been instructed by God himself. The *Qur'an* and hadith together constitute the Nass, or the eternal law, the basic principle for legislation in Islam for addressing all issues. Finally, the rulings or *fatwas* of individuals can deal even arbitrarily with a wide range of what in the West would include civil matters addressed by positive law.[260]

The hadith was arrived at by the first caliphs and scholars through consensus judgment. This consensus is Ijtihad, the "systematic development by different schools of Muslim jurisprudence to examine and codify the content of . . . Islam." Ijtihad is precisely defined by Hassan as "the derivation of rules through explicit reasoning from the basic defined guidance."[261] To the Western observer, reason remains bounded and eclipsed by the *Qur'an.* Ijtihad today is a less widely accepted tool than is *Qiyas* which is the use of analogy looking toward past cases and precedents, as the basis for new opinions and the correct derivation of new rules of law. Ijtihad is self exertion to form an opinion, again providing that the "rules of derivation" are followed. On the theological and less political plane there is no mediating structure like the *magisterium* or teaching authority of the Church to assure accountability from any localized consensus and more especially to insulate the message from worldly compromises.[262]

Hassan and others, e.g., the late Benazir Bhutto, depart from many orthodox views in holding that historic Ijtihad of the first two centuries of Islam remains today an available approach which under the pressures of modernity should be used more widely. Most other commentators hold that the door was closed on any further Ijtihad in the tenth (or possibly the twelfth) century with completion of the hadith. Hassan stands apart from those "who cling to eighth century solutions" and whom he identifies as "the ill educated Mullah class whose education and understanding are both superficial and limited."[263]

The minority Shi'ite community continues to use Ijtihad under the governance of its mujtahids or ayatollahs. Less than fifteen percent of Muslims are Shi'ite, although this sect was in power throughout the Islamic world in the eleventh and twelfth centuries, prior to the Seljug Turk invasion. The verdicts of mujtahids under Ijtihad are not timeless and can be changed in later generations, and in this respect are similar to civil law in the West which is open to new legislative and judicial reversals. Explaining the possibilities offered by Ijtihad to deal with the opportunities and stresses of modernity, Hassan writes "Whosoever cultivates these capabilities must come forward for this task (Mujtahid). The non-Mujtahid must follow his Mujtahid and work for the betterment of his political, social, economic, and spiritual life according to the verdicts of Mujtahid."[264]

The current form of group Ijtihad (Ijma) is the consensus among mujtahids[265] which by some accounts may be of any size ranging from the entire former Ottoman Empire to a small circle of devotees. Two Western scholars, Gibb and Kramer, are among those who maintain that Ijma is not achieved unless it is Muslim-wide. In practice, local Ijma can become so strong as to exclude all other Muslims who do not agree, and as in the case of Osama bin Laden, can render even these fellow Muslims as "outside Islam" and even subject to death. In place of Shi'ite mujtahids, the Sunnis *ulema* or "learned ones" are more of an informal class somewhat parallel to Christian theologians. The ulema also retain the authority to criticize political leaders, but nevertheless are subservient to the Islamic State.[266] Historically, the ulema displace the suppressed Mu'tazila reformers of earlier centuries. Now, as then and as in the West, the political issue at least as much about personal power as it is about philosophy or theology.

Hassan goes on to characterize Islamic State legislatures as "consultative assemblies" in that they are advisory to the executive who remains ultimately responsible for Shari'a. Hassan explains the limited functions of Islamic legislatures.[267] First, the legislature of the Islamic State cannot contravene directives of God, but it can codify these directives. Second it can deal with directives that under Shari'a have more than one interpretation. Third, the legislature can address areas where there are no explicit provisions in the Shari'a. And fourth, it can deal with areas where there is no guidance, under the principle that whatever has not been disallowed is allowed. The parallel in the West, with significant differences, is the relationship between routine legislation and the underlying (secular) constitution.

The basic point is that in Islam the law and religion remain united or (to the Western mind) confounded. Differing from the emperor-worshipping late Roman Empire, religious authority under Islam is highly decentralized, layered and fractious. From the outside, the congregation consists of the transnational ummah as taught and monitored by either Sunni uleman or Shi'ite imams, varied and competing sects stemming initially from alternative views on the Prophet's successors, four major schools of theology (*fiqh*[268]), the additional and spontaneous consensus groups (Ijtihad and Ijma) and fatwas issued according to the will of one imam or another. This frayed fabric is overlaid with random and poorly assimilated political boundaries and political trappings inherited from the West, and in many areas falls within a culture of pre-Islamic violence and family vendettas. The objective Western observer might notice parallels to the dynastic wars of Europe's past and the interest-driven incoherence of modern politics, society and economics.

Hassan compares the early advances of Muslim law to events in Christian culture and prominently the much later *Magna Carta* (1215).[269] These parallels again suggest the benefit of comparing Islamic religious values with what is distinguished in Western and Christian views as natural law (not divine revelation). Centuries before the Magna Carta it was the Christian vision of the human person that released him from being simply an isolated individual fully contained within any terrestrial order, specifically the *polis* or ancient city of the Roman and pagan state—or even as a member as defined by any communal group. Describing the classical or ancient city, Foustel de Coulanges summarizes:

> (the city) had been founded upon a religion, and constituted like a church . . . the citizen was subordinate in everything, and without any reserve, to the city; he belonged to it body and soul. The religion which had produced the state, and the state which supported the religion, sustained each other, and made but one; these two powers, associated and confounded, formed a power almost superhuman, to which the soul and the body were equally enslaved.[270]

Under Islam the state is claimed by religion to the same monolithic effect as we find in ancient Rome—with the radical difference that Islam is theoretically a flat culture free of social hierarchy (an emperor). In the case of Christianity and Rome:

> Religion, law, and government were confounded, and had been but a single thing under three different aspects . . . (but under Christianity) It is the first time that God and the state are so clearly distinguished. For Caesar at that period was still the *pontifex maximus*, the chief and principle organ of the Roman religion; he was the guardian and the interpreter of beliefs . . . But now Christ breaks the alliance which paganism and the empire wished to renew. He proclaims that religion is no longer the state, and that to obey Caesar is no longer the same thing as to obey God . . . Law was independent; it could draw its rules from nature, from the human conscience, from the powerful idea of the just that is in men's minds.[271]

The new Christian vision of the transcendent human person, together with the universal natural law as above positive law, is precisely the reason why the Christians were a hunted people. They would not burn incense before the emperor's shrine. Suppressed status under the ancient city finds an echo today in the lost or absent freedom to express ones religion in public—most especially for non-Muslims living in Islamic states. As in Islam, the earlier history of Eastern Christendom featured a fixed Byzantine fusion of empire and church, more so than in the West. Unlike the Latin West, Byzantium lasted a thousand years after the final Roman Emperor in 476 A.D. This Byzantine state certainly is not incomprehensible to Islam and may have imprinted the Muslim world with its political form today—the Islamic State. In its earliest days in the seventh century, Muslim expansion was based partly on the promise of freedom from Byzantine dominance, and on the replacement of intricate control systems with a simple and less demanding collection of annual tribute to Islam. But the Byzantine political form is contagious.

Separate growth pains in the West include the Roman period of religious persecution already mentioned, but also the practical subordination of ecclesial powers by princely powers. More commonly there was a symbiosis between Church and state. The eventual crisis traces back to the spoils system exercised by Charles Martel, great grandfather of Charlemagne. The first large scale investing of bishoprics and properties by the secular power was by Martel, for those who helped him repulse the first Moslem invasion of Europe at Tours in 732.[272] For centuries later the tension between Church and state worked in both directions. Pope Gregory VII (1073–85) claimed an ecclesial authority to depose emperors, offsetting the long standing princely and feudal practice of appointing bishops who were frequently drawn from among important landholders.[273] This new order was the end of the Investiture Controversy[274] and begins the period of greater autonomy for both the Church and the state. Had Gregory's struggle with German emperors within Europe been less distracting, he might have followed through with assistance to the Byzantines as soon as they were routed by the Turks at the Battle of Manzikert (1071).

The Investiture Contest and generally the separation or even the distinction between the two realms of religion and secular responsibilities have no parallel in Muslim thought or the Muslim world. However, the rise of the papal bureaucracy in Rome, the curia, was due in part by the Investiture Controversy, and the Islamic State is likewise partly a byproduct of external political pressures. In the West the hardly contested truce over investiture was formalized in the Concordat of Worms in 1122.[275] This mutual accommodation brought thirty years of peace between pope and emperor (1122–53), but in the long run was replaced by such episodes as French lay dominance and again royal control of the Church. For nearly a century following papal deposition of the German Emperor, the popes found themselves under the thumb of French monarchs and relocated to the papal residence to French Avignon (known as the Babylonian Captivity, 1309–1377). In the German empire at the same time, clerical presumption of supremacy in secular affairs led to a papal excommunication of the emperor.

A nationwide interdict (suppression of the sacraments) was disregarded by the population and contributed to the resentments behind the Reformation in the sixteenth century. Continued monarchic tendencies of the papacy in the new secular realm played into the emerging local and linguistic nation-states and the linked new Reformation ideology, all to produce national churches in the Protestant regions of northern Europe.[276] The Renaissance poet Dante was deeply scandalized by irregular arrangements between princes of the world and princes of the Church in southern Europe—"fornication of the Bride of Christ." In addition to Mohammed, in his *Divine Comedy* he places most of the early Renaissance popes in Hell. By soft-pedaling parts of the Luther's doctrine, Melancthon's version of Lutheranism (the Augsburg Confession, 1530) adhered closely to traditional theology and even went so far as to "condemn every heresy which has sprung up contrary to this article, such as the (list) . . . Mohammedans . . . ."[277] In the twentieth century, Edith Stein provides an analysis of medieval legal practices. Stein began as an atheist ethnic Jew, was converted to Catholicism, and then as a Catholic Jew was among those exterminated in Auschwitz (1942) in post-Christian Germany. Her insights into Medieval law apply to Shari'a in the modern world: "According to that concept, law that has been in effect since time immemorial is unalterable; and it's permissible to make new law only if it derives from the old law and shows itself to be a consequence of the old law, or if you can show that the new law abolishes habitual injustice and restores the older law."[278] Stein's overall thesis on the Western state, also applicable to both the Islamic State, is that the legitimate state is only the implementer of deeper law, not its arbitrary source.[279]

For Westerners who are justifiably offended at the Islamic practice of issuing personal and repressive fatwas that violate the natural law or common decency, for example death threats, we might consider remotely parallel inroads in our own culture. Through modern technology, self-appointed Hollywood elites and their media and educational sycophants gain entry into every neighborhood and classroom. An increasingly captive audience serves as a market for the relativistic moral tone and permissive fatwas of unrelieved secular humanism. For all of its professed secularism and modernity, popular entertainment is in this way an anachronism, a popular idolatry. Celebrities do not directly immolate or cannibalized their own children, as did even the early Israelites (Jer 32:35, Lam 2:20, Bar 2:3, Ps 106:36–8), but they and their camp followers are willing enough to marginalize and ridicule the viewing family. Meanwhile, the modern social sciences quantify and update current trends. For the cynic this is primarily to justify additional infusions of fiat currency to support more peer-reviewed and admired research and to possibly offset the damage.

In the Islamic world, a hybrid institution with Western political values is the Turkish secular constitution. The ongoing commitment to a secular state with a Muslim Turkish culture is partly why Benedict XVI regards the land of the Turks as a possible bridge between the West and the world of Islam. While Turkey is ninety-nine percent a Muslim population, the state constitution is unambiguously secular. As revised in 1928, *Article 2* reads: "The Turkish Republic is a national, democratic, secular and social State governed by the rule of law, based on human rights and the fundamental tenets set forth in the preamble." This wording replaces that of 1924: "The religion of the Turkish state is Islam." *Article 4* of the constitution reads: "Sovereignty is vested in the Turkish Nation without reservation or condition."[280] Political sovereignty resides in the *nation*, not God. Turkey aspires to be a nation-state, not an Islamic State. Hassan sees within the new Turkey no alteration of the religion or the Islamic way of life, other than that the call to prayer is in Turkish rather than Arabic. "What transpired in Turkey was not that Islam itself had been changed or that an attempt was made to change Islam; rather, the Turkish people were told that there was another approach in looking at affairs of state . . . it can be maintained that there did not take place any real measure which aimed at de-secularizing (sic for secularizing) the 'content' of Islam, but instead Islam was reduced to the place of any other religion in Turkey."[281] In place of any Islamic government under the direct surveillance of imams, the secular government is held in place largely by the military.

A significant change to Islam under Ataturk, however, is that polygamy was abolished. But in general, in Turkey the universality of Shari'a Law—or the Muslim way of life—is politically encapsulated with respect to its international setting. (The opposite Islamic view, equally valid, is that the state has been encapsulated as an idiom for continuing the Muslim way of life in a new global setting.) Under favorable conditions, a pragmatic Islam is basically capable of attaching itself to new ways without being radically changed by them. However, as a geographic bridge between the Muslim Middle East and Europe, secular Turkey soon may have to deal more directly with the resulting contradictions. Governing Turkey's possible entry into the European Union still may be the so-called Copenhagen criteria which establish the conditions for membership. This early Turkish "Roadmap to Europe" consisted of fifty-two separate subheadings. Still on paper, the initial 2000–2004 period called for a phased and total rewrite of the Turkish legal system. For 2001, the criteria would have rescinded the death penalty (subhead 20) which is prohibited by all European Union member states.[282]

Besides Turkey, many other Islamic states also experiment to a lesser degree with pragmatic parliamentary advances toward modernity. Culturally, polygamy is no longer widely practiced in Muslim countries. As in Turkey, the practice is illegal in Tunisia (since 1956) and is punished. Even in Shi'ite Iraq financial equity for each prospective wife must first be demonstrated to a judge.[283] In Egypt child marriage is accepted under Shari'a as from the beginning, but now is seen as repugnant. Shari'a remains intact but chooses not to interfere in cases that come before civil courts. In early 2007 bills were introduced in Pakistan to simplify the prosecution of rape cases and to outlaw forced marriages.[284] The post-colonial Algerian constitution typically allows freedom of religion, however, a parliamentary decree in 2006 tightly restricts how religions other than Islam actually can be practiced. As is commonly the case, proselytizing by other religions still is regarded as potentially weakening the belief of Muslims, and is prohibited. In the most moderate kingdom of Jordan, Islam is the state religion but other religions are clearly permitted. In Pakistan heightened Islamization is the trend under tightened blasphemy laws.[285]

Based on the *Qur'an* (Q 13:12) even the early reformist writer Muhammad Iqbal (1876–1938) found a way to see man as more of a co-worker with God. Traditionally this view is "perilously near heresy." Iqbal wrote, "God will not change the condition of man until they change what is in themselves."[286] On this fundamental point, the Islamic State and the constitutional state in the West cannot be directly compared. The Islamic State assumes the "positive" role of executing a moral society, while Western political institutions are more inclined to be "negative" in the sense that they presume the existence of an underlying and third factor, a moral society, and then provide the institutional architecture—a system of checks and balances—to both institute political power and minimize its abuses. Because the two models of government are not symmetrical even on this point, Islamic critics (for example, Hassan) conclude too broadly that Western government, like the unitary Islamic State, is responsible for providing a moral grounding.

Discounted in Islamic thought is the positive appeal to a distinct and articulated natural law. In the United States the *Declaration of Independence* is founded on inalienable rights, and the Preamble to the United States *Constitution*, seeks to "establish Justice, insure domestic Tranquility, provide for the common defense, promote the general Welfare, and secure the Blessings of Liberty . . ." The Islamic State is more akin to a voluntarily chosen monastic setting, a vocation for a very few rather than a general population. Undivided obedience of will is given to one's monastic superior as to God, as the path to personal perfection and a holocaust of service to God, but even with the vow of obedience instructions in violation of the natural law are not binding.[287] Utopian Marxism, the great enemy of Islam, in a sense is also a misapplication of the monastic ideal. It expects the general population to fall under the monastic vow of personal poverty and communal ownership.

In the Muslim world, the Prophet's example is the married state; there is no ideal of celibacy in Islam as there is in much of the Christian world. Monasticism and life in the world are less differentiated. From an interreligious and intercultural perspective, the task facing Islam is less political than it is to first free future generations from a pseudo-monastic kind obedience to the unitary Islamic State. In Chapter 4 we turn to the openness of natural law, as transmitted partly by the early monastic Church, as this law is found to indwell the human person rather than any single institutional form such as Church or State (or the Islamic State).

NOTES

1. Stanley Yaki, holder of doctorates in theology and physics, defines *scientism* "as the obstinate attitude that wants every area of human experience and reflection to be interpreted by the quantitative, experimental method of physical science" ("Demythologization of Science," in *The Absolute Beneath the Relative*, vol. 3[Lanham, Md.: University Press of America, 1988], 211).

2. The *Qur'an* is written in Arabic and the Jewish Bible is confined to the Hebrew. The Jewish Bible excludes books written in Greek and later incorporated in St. Jerome's translation of the Old Testament from Greek to Latin. The Greek version used by Jerome, the Septuagint, was accepted by "Jews of the Dispersion" and was available to Christ and later Christians and Gentiles. In the Reformation Luther used the Hebrew translation, and this accounts for his omission of several books of the Old Testament found in the Catholic Bible.

3. William Cantwell Smith, *Islam in the Modern World* (New York: Mentor, 1957), 26.

4. Reference to John 1:14.

5. In the earlier history of Judaism, the Jewish sanctuary was a copy of the pattern shown to Moses on the mountain (Heb 8:5). As literature, some compare the *Qur'an* text to the Psalms in that both nurture poetic truth and not confined to terrestrial history. Dawood's translation of the *Qur'an* calls specific attention to the similarity between surah 55 and the biblical Psalm 136 from which it may have been borrowed (N.J. Dawood [trans.], *The Koran* [London: Penguin Books, 2003], 376). Other Christian investigators suggest that the Qur'anic description of heaven was borrowed from the New Jerusalem and particularly the biblical book of Apocalypse.

6. In early Greek and Roman culture the family hearth was transcended in the institution of the *gens*, an extended family united by common ancestry and a more broadly shared religion (Foustel de Coulanges, *The Ancient City* [Garden City, New York: Doubleday, n.d., original 1873]). Unconventional family patterns also were common in ancient society. (In early Greek and Roman society slaves ceremonially entered their patron families and by adoption shared permanently their religion [114–115]. In more distant cases, to perpetuate the family line in early Athens adultery was forbidden, but

incest was permitted, while marriage with a woman from another city was not [97].)
The gens stood in contrast with the "populus romanus," or the broader roman populace.
In the modern world does the Ishmaelite root serve as a kind of family hearth for the
Arab peoples and all members of global but insular Islam, i.e., the ummah?

7. "We are not sons of a slave, but of a free woman" (Gal 4:31, clearly a reference to Ishmael and Isaac). In Genesis (22:2) Abraham is told that he has but one
son, Isaac.

8. From a homily written in the second century, in *The Liturgy of the Hours*,
Vol. IV (New York: Catholic Book Publishing Co., 1975), 521–522 (italics added).
Somewhat like Islam, the Protestant understanding of the church as spiritual but not
institutional resembles the Old Testament religious gathering.

9. Note the similarity to the Old Testament prefiguring of Christ, e.g., "A prophet
like me will the Lord, your God, raise up for you . . . to him you shall listen" (Deut
18:18). Some Church Fathers, and others, claim that after the coming of Christ and
his rejection, the Messianic prophecies were altered in the Talmud. In some cases the
prophecies are seen as referring to David or Solomon, or even to the Jewish Nation
itself. The *Qur'an* also implicitly has Moses foretelling Muhammad (Q 46:10).

10. "The law was but a shadow of the good things to come, not a living likeness
to them" (Heb 10:1). Hassan tells us that seventy-eight verses (ayats) in a variety
of chapters (surahs) refer to Christ: Q 2 -10, 19, 21, 33, 39, 42, 43, 57, 61, 72, and
112 (Farooq Hassan, *The Concept of the State and Law in Islam* [Washington D.C.:
University of America Press, 1981], 243). In the eleventh century the Jewish scholar
Maimonides, already having chosen exile over forced apostasy into Islam, rejected
Muslim claims that the Old Testament pointed to Mohammed rather than to a Jewish
Messiah. He found such interpretations "totally opposed to common sense" ("Letter
to the Jews in Yemen" [1172], referenced in M. Friedlander, *The Guide to the Per-
plexed* [New York: Dover Publications, Inc., 1956 (1881, 1904)], xx.).

11. "A Work on the Proceedings of Pelagius" (417), Ch. 20, and "On Nature and
Grace," Ch. 69, both in Philip Schaff, *The Nicene and Post-Nicene Fathers of the
Christian Church,* Vol. 5: "St. Augustine—Anti-Pelagian Writings" (Grand Rapids,
Michigan: William B. Eerdmans, 1956). The case is made that by the grace of God,
Pelagius actually means simply nature, as in knowledge of the law.

12. Cited in Joseph Cardinal Ratzinger, *On the Way to Jesus Christ* (translated
by Michael J. Miller), (San Francisco: Ignatius, 2005), 162. A possible parallel exists between Islam and original Lutheran theology which saw the human person as
a permanent duality of good and evil. The Catholic teaching that man at the core is
good, but marred by an original sin resulting in evil *inclinations* (concupiscence). By
the sacramental life of grace we can be and are restored fully, not ambivalently. The
Council of Trent declared that the baptized are themselves "...made innocent, without
stain, pure, no longer hateful, but beloved sons of God, heirs, indeed, of God and joint
heirs with Christ (see Rom 8:17) so that absolutely nothing delays their entrance into
heaven...." (Canon 5).

13. See Brant Pelphrey, *The Theology and Mysticism of Julian of Norwich* (Salzburg: University of Salzburg, 1982), passim. and 84–87. Christian scholars might also
find in Julian of Norwich an overlooked key to understanding the perplexing differ-

ence between John's Gospel, which stresses the glory of Christ, and the three synoptic and less mystical Gospel narratives. Julian's *Revelations* represents twenty-five years of reflection on her extraordinary day of private visions bonding the crucifixion to the transfiguration. Likewise, John completed his gospel reflections decades after the earlier gospels. Significantly, he was the only disciple to have personally been present at both the transfiguration and the crucifixion. The depth of the incarnate Christ's self-donating glory—as witnessed objectively and in the flesh only by John—seems a more reasonable explanation of John's Gospel than is the prevalent rationalist notion that his work is a gratuitous overlay of subjective theological distortion.

14. Maulana Muhammad Ali, *Muhammad the Prophet* (Lahore, Pakistan: Ripon, 1984 [Ahmadiyya Anjuman Isha'at Islam, 1924]), 43–5. The Greek term "Paraclete" (Holy Spirit) is substituted by Muslim commentators with the presumably correct "Periclyte,"the Greek form of Ahmad or Mohammed (Abdullah Yusuf Ali, *The Holy Qur'an: Text, Translation and Commentary* [Lahore: Sh. Muhammad Ashraf, 1983 [1938], Q 7:157, fn. 1127), 388).

15. Ibid., 218–19. It is on a very fine line that Muslims and Christians might debate the reality, or not, of the Incarnation. Ayoub notes for the reader that Qur'anic references to reason include Q 2:164, 5:153, and 8:22 (Mahmoud Ayoub in Omar, *A Muslim View of Christianity* [New York: Orbis, 2007]).

16. "Life within God is not eternally the same, is a sense which would imply a kind of everlasting boredom. Rather, God's Trinitarian life is a 'liveliness' characterized by the always new and by 'surprise': in the words of Speyr, Trinitarian life is a 'communion of surprise' (in the sense of an infinite ever-flowing fulfillment . . . .)" (David L. Schindler, *Heart of the World, Center of the Church* [Grand Rapids, MI: William B. Eerdmans, 1996] 226).

17. Jacob Neusner, *Death and Birth of Judaism* (New York: Basic Books, 1987), passim., 348, 352.

18. "Against Heresies," cited in *The Liturgy of the Hours*, Vol. III (New York: Catholic Book Publishing, 1975), 63.

19. Stein, Edith (Waltraus Stein, trans.), *On the Problem of Empathy*, Washington D.C.: ICS Publications, 1989. Stein's definition of empathy is not to be confused with a post-modern redefinition that aligns empathy with special interest politics and jurisprudence, i.e., empathy euphemistically as "a keen understanding of how the law affects the daily lives of American people."

20. Etienne Gilson, quoted in Jacques Maritain, *The Peasant of the Garonne* (New York: Holt, Rinehart and Winston, 1968), 134.

21. Esposito, John, *Islam: The Straight Path* (New York: Oxford University Press, 1998), 71. The obvious parallel (not an equivalency) with Christianity is in Arianism and later Nestorianism, both of which held that Christ was not quite divine. Under Christian theology the incarnation of God is the unified person of Christ, and not a split personality. And likewise, under Catholic biblical scholarship, the Bible is protected from reductionism. It is interpreted both by what it literally says and by the surplus value of the three spiritual senses (e.g., the allegorical).

22. Friedrich Heer, *The Intellectual History of Europe* (New York: World Publishing Co., 1953), 98.

23. Karen Armstrong, *Islam: A Short History* (New York: Modern Library, 2002), 64.

24. Christopher Dawson, *The Making of Europe* (New York: Meridian Books, 1956), 142.

25. Torrell reports that Averroes is misrepresented by early translators in that he did not hold that there is only one intellectual soul for all men (*Thomas Aquinas*, Vol. I, [Washington, D.C.: Catholic University of America Press, 1996], 192–3). If Torrell is correct, an accurate portrayal of Averroes could be important in advancing modern day Christian-Islamic dialogue.

26. Alfred Guillaume, *Islam* (New York: Penguin Books, 1956), 129–33.

27. Karen Anderson, *Islam: A Short History* (New York: Modern Library, 2002), 72–3.

28. St. Augustine, *The City of God* (Garden City, New York: Image, 1958), Book XIV, Ch. 1.

29. St. Augustine, *The City of God*, the Foreword by Etienne Gilson, 32.

30. Therese-Anne Druart writes of al-Farabi: "In the *Book of Religion* al-Farabi states that true religion imitates philosophy and that the part of a virtuous religion which deals with actions receives its universals from practical philosophy" rather than, say, moral theology (in Bazan, Andujar and Sborocchi (eds.), Volume I, "Al-Farabi on the Practical and Speculative Aspects of Ethics," *Moral and Political Philosophies in the Middle Ages* [New York/Ottowa/Toronto: Legas, 1995], 478, 482).

31. Hassan, 122 (italics added). For Hassan's credentials, see the footnote citation in the Introduction.

32. From Rabbi Neusner, cited in Pope Benedict XVI, *Jesus of Nazareth* (New York: Doubleday, 2007), 108.

33. The fall of Constantinople in 1453 motivated Nicholas de Cusa, an early voice for Church reform in the West, to advocate a less insular attitude that could in some way restore the ecumenical mission of the Church to unify all things in Christ. He sought the universal themes in all religions, but still without undermining Christ, the Trinity and the Church (John Dolan, *History of the Reformation* [New York: Mentor Omega, 1965], 167–183).

34. Joseph Cardinal Ratzinger (Pope Benedict XVI), *Introduction to Christianity* (San Francisco: Ignatius, 2004 and 1968), 163.

35. Not understanding the nature and role of the Church, the respected Muslim apologist, Rashid Rida (d. 1935), argued that there were no authorities of transmission for either the Old Testament or the New Testament (Ayoub in Omar, ed., 218).

36. Confirmation of key events from non-Christian historians includes the writings of Tacitus (55–117 A.D.) and the Jewish Josephus (37–100 A.D.).

37. Charles Norris Cochrane, *Christianity and Classical Culture* (New York: Oxford University Press, 1974), 432. Charles Freeman fails to consider this point in his freelance writing, A.D. 381 (New York: Overlook Press, 2008). Freeman sees the Trinitarian doctrine as a sort of straight jacket for the supernatural, imposed by the emperor Theodosius, rather than as a protection against rationalism and reductionism in all of their historical and modern variants.

38. Patrick Lang, "Islam: Monotheistic but not Monolithic," *One* (Catholic Near East Welfare Association, Jan. 2007). In a parallel situation and condemned in the

West as a heresy, "ontologism" claimed that the human intellect can in this life have unmediated knowledge of God (Joseph McSorley, *An Outline History of the Church by Centuries* [St. Louis, Missouri: B. Herder Book Co., 1945], 832).

39. Guillaume, 145.

40. Ibid., 145–6.

41. Ibid. Armstrong reports that some scholars translate the key phrase as "I *see* the truth" and reports that Hallaj was executed specifically for "claiming that it was possible to make a valid *hajj* (pilgrimage to Mecca) in spirit, while staying at home (op. cit., 75). Rabinnical Judaism also claims as one of its saints, Aquiba who was martyred, his body pierced with spikes as he repeated "Hear, O Israel! Jahweh our God is the one God" (Henri Daniel-Rops, *Israel and the Ancient World* [Garden City, New York: Image, 1964], 369).

42. From the hadith as reported by Bukhari (Sahih, I 34), and cited in Hassan, 97, and worded more completely here by Ayoub in Omar (ed.), 13.

43. Available under Al-Munqidh min al-Dalal, translated by R.J. McCarthy, *Al-Ghazali's Path to Sufism: His Deliverance from Error* (Louisville: Fons Vitae, 1999).

44. Guillaume, 148.

45. Albert Hourani, *A History of the Arab Peoples* (Cambridge, Mass.: Harvard University Press, 1991, 174, italics added.

46. *Confessions*, Bk. 7, Ch. 10:16, italics added.

47. Did the Dominican scholastic Aquinas experience the mysticism of his contemporary the Franciscan St. Bonaventure(?): "If you should ask how these things (mystical communion with God) come about, question grace, not instruction; desire, not intellect; the cry of prayer, not pursuit of study; the spouse, not the teacher; God, not man; darkness, not clarity; not light, but the wholly flaming fire which will bear you aloft to God with fullest unction and burning affection" (St. Bonaventure (George Boas, trans.), *The Mind's Road to God* [New York: Liberal Arts Press/The Bobbs-Merrill Co., Inc., 1953], 45 (n. 6)).

48. *Liturgy of the Hours*, Vol. II, op. cit;, 412–413.

49. The Church "is not above the Word of God, but serves it, teaching only what has been handed on; by divine commission, with the help of the Holy Spirit, the Church listens to the text with love, watches over it in holiness and explains it faithfully" (Second Vatican Council, *Dei Verbum* [the Word of God], n. 10). By comparison, the Islamic understanding of jihad radically expands during the life of Mohammed, and partly through compiled and much later reminiscences in the hadith from the Prophet Mohammed (see Maulana Fazlul Karim, *Al-Hadith: An English Translation and Commentary of Mishkat-ul-Masabih*, Vol. II [New Delhi: Islamic Book Service, 1999], 334–364).

50. *Catechism of the Catholic Church*, Librera Editrice Vaticana, 1994, n. 108.

51. Pontifical Biblical Commission, *The Interpretation of the Bible in the Church* (with Address by John Paul II, n. 14, and referring to *Dei Verbum*, 4), 1993, 54. Pope Benedict XVI urges Christian Scripture scholars to reconsider as a presumed *starting point* their presumptive historical method of reading Scripture. He writes: "if instead we take (this) conviction of faith as our starting point for reading the texts with the help of historical methodology and its intrinsic openness to something greater, they are

opened up and they reveal a way and a figure that are worthy of belief" (Joseph Ratzinger (Pope Benedict XVI), *Jesus of Nazareth* [New York: Doubleday, 2007], xxiii).

52. The creation of the world on Sunday, October 23, 4004 B.C., is a calculation of the literalist Anglican Archbishop Usher, in his Annals of the Old and New Testament.

53. See for example Mt 10:18 and 24:14, Mk 13:10, Lk 1:1–4 and 21:12–14, Jn 15:27, and Acts 1:21–22.

54. Richard Bauckham, *Jesus and the Eyewitnesses: The Gospels as Eyewitness Testimony* (Grand Rapids, MI: William B. Eerdnams, 2006), 478.

55. Ibid., nn. 115–117. a very crude parallel in Islamic thought is the *suppressed* work of the twelfth century Averroes who for the *Qur'an* distinguished three methods of interpretation shaped as much by audience as content: the *demonstrative* (apparent) interpretation for elite and qualified readers also schooled in philosophy, dialectical interpretation or accurate *allegory* to safeguard against disbelief among less learned followers of Islam, and thirdly, *rhetorical* presentation for the class incapable of any interpretation (Averroes [George Hourani, trans.*], On the Harmony of Religion and Philosophy,* 1179–1180 A.D. (London: Messrs, Luzac and Co., 1967 [1961], Ch. 3).

56. Daniel Madigan, *The Qur'an's Self-Image: Writing and Authority in Islam's Scriptures* (Princeton, N.J.: Princeton University Press, 2001). The Christian proclamation is that by action of the Holy Spirit the Word is written into the hearts of the People of God, and further (for Catholics) that they participate directly in the "rewriting" of their lives by being incorporated sacramentally into the complete Word made flesh. "You will not change me into yourself, as you change food into your flesh, but you will be changed into me" (St. Augustine, *Confessions,* Bk. 7, Ch. 10). Under Islam, the written revelation is in the *Qur'an* seemingly prior to the heart. Islam's hadith reports that "whenever anything was revealed to (Mohammed), He used to "call to those who write" and to say 'Place these verses in the chapter in which there is mention of such and such (verse)'" (Maulana Fazul Karim, *Al-Hadith,* Vol. III, 705).

57. The Muslim naturalistic paradise, different than the Christian, is described in the *Qur'an* (e.g., Q 3:16, 37:45–8, 55:48–78).

58. Pope Benedict XVI, *Jesus of Nazareth* (New York: Doubleday, 2007), 200 (italics added).

59. Ibid., xxii. Pope Benedict XVI writes: "As early as twenty or so years after Jesus' death, the great Christ-hymn of the Letter to the Philippians (cf. 2:6–11) offers us a fully developed Christology stating that Jesus was equal to God, but emptied himself, became man, and humbled himself to die on the cross, and that to him now belongs the worship of all creation, the adoration that God, through the Prophet Isaiah, said was due to him alone (cf. Is 45:23*)."*

60. N.J. Dawood, *The Koran* (New York: Penguin Books, 1956), 3. A brief account of the assembly and later discovery and destruction of divergent texts is translated in Bernard Lewis (ed. and trans.), *Islam: From the Prophet to the Capture of Constantinople* (New York: Oxford University Press, 1987), 1.2.

61. The numbering system for the *Qur'an* is the same as for chapters and verses in the Bible, e.g., 10:23; when shown as 10:23/24 the final digits appear for those cases that differ under Cairo edition of the *Qur'an*.

62. Jean Herbert, *An Introduction to Asia* (New York: Oxford University Press, 1965), 62–3.

63. Hassan, 267. Erpenius translated an Arabic New Testament in 1342 (Leicester Buckingham, *The Bible in the Middle Ages* [London: Thomas Cautley Newby, 1853], 44. Earlier translations include Latin (Cluny, 1143 and published in 1543), German (Nuremburg, 1616), French (Paris, 1647), Russian (St. Petersburg, 1776), and more in French (1783, 1840), English (from the French, in 1647, and from the Latin, in 1734), (Abdullah Yusuf Ali, op. cit., xiv).

64. Daniel Boorstin, *The Discoverers* (New York: Random House, 1983), 545–7. Within Christendom, and much earlier, Cyril and Methodius invented the Slavic (Cyrillic) script for evangelizing the Slavs who did not yet have a written language (c. 800 to 900). Long before the Gutenberg Bible made mass publication possible, hand translations of the Bible into local Middle Eastern languages was fairly common: Armenian, Syriac, Coptic, Arabic, and Ethiopic (Henry Graham, *Where We Got the Bible* [St. Louis: Herder Book Co, 1952 and 1911] 15). The first Latin translation of the *Qur'an* was made in 1143 (Cluny) and published in 1543, and then translated into Italian, German and Dutch. Other later translations were in German (1616, 1773 and 1828), French (1647, 1783 and 1840), and Russian in 1776. The first *Muslim* translation into a European language was into English in 1905 (Abdullah Yusuf Ali, op. cit., xiv, xv).

65. Buckingham, passim, 44–65, and 155–162. In the modern languages and before the first Protestant version was issued from the press, six hundred twenty-six complete or partial editions of the Bible were published by the Church, and of these one hundred ninety-eight were in the language of the laity (64–5).

66. Hassan, 26. The Bible warns against false prophets: Mt 7:15, Mk 13:22, 2 Pe 2:1.

67. Harris is among those who treat all of the Gospel writers as "anonymous," but dates them in the first century as follows: Matthew (80–85), Mark (66–70), Luke (85–90), John (90–95). The less skeptical Navarre Bible defends earlier dates: Matthew (Aramaic 50–55 and Greek 68–70), Mark (60/64–70), Luke (62/67–70), and John (98–100). See Stephen Harris (California State University), *Understanding the Bible* (New York: McGraw Hill, 2003), 404; and the *Navarre Bible* (St. Mark volume), (Dublin, Ireland: Four Courts Press, 1988), 28.

68. Daniel Madigan, op. cit., 136.

69. Rashid Rida, cited by Ayoub in Omar (ed.), 217–18.

70. Jacques Jomier, *The Bible and the Qur'an* (San Francisco: Ignatius, 2002), 5.

71. Don Luigi Giussani, *Why the Church?* (San Francisco: Ignatius Press, 2001), 95.

72. Citation from *Israel and the Ancient World* (Garden City, New York: Image, 1964), 238–9. In Psalms we find this: "By my holiness I swore once for all: I will never be false to David. His dynasty will continue forever, his throne, like the sun before me. Like the moon it will stand eternal, forever firm like the sky" (Ps 89:36–38). The Islamic self-understanding is that "If ye turn back (from the Path), He will *substitute in your stead* another people; then they would not be like you" (Q 67:38, italics added).

73. G. E. H. Palmer, Philip Sherrard, and Kallistos Ware, *The Philokalia*, Vol. 3 (Boston: Faber and Faber, 1995 [1984]), 316.

74. Rashid Rida cited by Ayoub in Omar (ed.), 218.

75. Ibid.

76. Jomier, op. cit., citing L. Beven Jones, *The People of the Mosque*, 1932.

77. John Paul II, *Crossing the Threshold of Hope* (New York, Alfred Knopf, 1994), 92–3.

78. In his address "Christian-Muslim Relations in the 21st Century," Cardinal Francis Arinze from Nigeria speaks of the daily Christian self examination of conscience, and asks "my Muslim friends whether in Islam there is a similar practice." (Center for Muslim-Christian Understanding, Georgetown University, Washington D.C., June 5, 1997, www.sedos.org/english/arinze.htm).

79. Quoted in Guibert, *On Kindness*, n.d., 20.

80. "On What it Means to Call Oneself Christian," in John A. Hardon, S.J., *The Treasury of Catholic Wisdom* (San Francisco: Ignatius, 1995 and 1987), 63.

81. *Liturgy of the Hours*, Vol. II, 597. With St. Gregory, by a new creation, St. Paul means "the indwelling of the Holy Spirit in a heart that is pure and blameless, free of all malice, wickedness or shamefulness" (Vol. IV, 337–9).

82. Gibb and Kramer, 285.

83. Under paganism the multiplicity of gods was generated in part by liaisons between Zeus and mortals. This pagan mythology of half-humans resembles Muhammad's terse dismissal of Christ's divinity. In contrast, Christian witness develops a coherence between revelation and reason: "We thereby affirm that the two natures being brought together in a true union are different, but the result of the two is one Christ and one Son; for the difference of these natures is not taken away by this union, but rather the divinity and the humanity, by their ineffable and inexpressible union, make perfect for us the one Lord Jesus Christ" (Letter from Cyril of Alexandria to Nestorius, approved during the fourth general council, the Council of Calcedon, in 451 A.D., cited in the weekly General Audience of Benedict XVI on October 3, 2007, reported in the *National Catholic Register*, October 14, 2007).

84. Reference to Ibn Kathir cited by Ayoub in Omar (ed.), *A Muslim View of Christianity* (Maryknoll: Orbis, 2007), 126.

85. Josef Cardinal Ratzinger, *Introduction to Christianity*, 276. Giussani recounts how Schweitzer himself, an intelligent and profoundly dedicated humanitarian in Africa, questioned Charles De Foucauld (see Chapter Two) on how he received the level of love and devotion Schweitzer so dearly wanted. The difference was that while Charles did less, he lived more directly with his people as he shared his "certainty of hope" in the ever-present Christ (citation from Gilbert Cesbron [1952] in *Is it Possible to Live the Way?*, Vol. 2: Hope, [Ithaca: McGill Queen's University Press, 2008], 149–50]).

86. Zaid H. Assfy, *Islam and Christianity* (York, England: William Sessions, Ltd., 1977), 57.

87. Ayoub in Omar (ed.), 222–29. Source Q is not to be confused with our convention for citing verses in the *Qur'an*, e.g. (Q 2:113).

88. The "two source" theory of the scripture (Source Q and Mark) finds an alternative scheme in the "two Gospel" thesis (Mathew and Mark). The minority but credible

view is supported by Alfred Wickenhauser who wrote at the University of Freiburg. Agreeing that Mark was the oldest Gospel composed in Greek and that canonical Matthew and Luke depend upon Mark, Wickenhauser also proposed that the author of the earlier source Q is the Apostle Matthew (consistent with the sequence reported by the early historian Eusebius, 263–339 A.D., in his *History of the Church*). Source Q was a hypothetical source of Christ's sayings in Aramaic and is generally regarded as an independent source for Matthew and Luke (*New Testament Introduction*, referenced in John Dougherty, *Searching the Scriptures* [Garden City, New York: Image, 1963], 118–9.).

Whitehead develops a different case for Two Gospels (Matthew and Luke, with Mark as simply as an abridgement), in contrast with the Two Sources (Source Q and then the Gospels). See Kenneth Whitehead, "Biblical Scholarship in Positive Vein," *Catholic World Report*, Ignatius, 1998, 54–7. St. Iranaeus held that "Matthew published a written gospel for the Hebrews in their own tongue, while Peter and Paul were preaching the Gospel in Rome and founding the church there" (that is, prior to 67 A.D.). Eusebius (263–339), *History of the Church*, V:8.

89. Xavier Leon-Dufour, translated and edited by John McHugh, *The Gospels and the Jesus of History* (Garden City, New York: Image Books, 1970), 174–5, 200–206. The author concludes that "none of the three Synoptics can be taken as a yardstick by which to judge the historical value of the other two, or of St. John" (205).

90. Ayoub in Omar (ed.), 222–229.

91. Philip Jenkins, *The Hidden Gospels* (New York: Oxford University Press, 2001), 78. In his treatise On the Mysteries, the late fourth century St. Ambrose writes of the sacraments: "If we had thought fit to teach these things to those not yet initiated through baptism, we should be considered traitors rather than teachers" (*The Liturgy of the Hours*, Vol. III, 482–3).

92. Henry G. Graham, 28–39.

93. John Paul II, *The Interpretation of the Bible in the Church*, Address of John Paul II and Document of the Pontifical Biblical Commission (Boston: Pauline Books and Media, 1993) nn. 3–4.

94. For an illustration of how this simple intuition actually works in everyday language, the reader is invited to skip back to the opening paragraph of Chapter 1.

95. Q 10:37: ". . . It (the *Qur'an*) confirms what was revealed before it and *fully explains* the Scriptures" (italics added).

96. "It is a mistake to assume that anything incapable of being stated in words does not exist. Stating is, by the same token, comprehending. But small indeed is the part of man which I have learned, so far, to comprehend" (Antoine de Saint-Exupery, *The Wisdom of the Sands* [Chicago: University of Chicago Press, 1979], 107).

97. By comparison, in the hadith Mohammed's journey to heaven offers extended detail. Within the tradition of Christian mysticism, (primarily Tersesa of Avila and John of the Cross) "ridiculous detail" characterizes pathological disturbances. (P. Marie-Eugene OCD, *I am a Daughter of the Church*, Vol. II [Allen, Texas: Christian Classics, 1997], 289).

98. Jeffrey Burton Russell, *A History of Heaven: The Singing Silence* (Princeton, New Jersey: Princeton University Press, 1997), 151.

99. Guillaume, 150. The truth of Arabi's possible influence on Dante's most sublime work serves a vital need for readers of the *Qur'an*. The relevant verse in the *Qur'an* reads: "This Koran could not have been devised by any but God. It is beyond doubt from the Lord of the Universe. If they say 'He invented it himself,' say: '*Bring me one chapter like it*. Call on whom you may besides God to help you, if what you say be true'" (Q 10:37–8, italics added).

100. Ibid. Western scholars also point to the Classical influences and to the Bible (the most cited source in the *Comedy*). The Old Testament book 2 Enoch describes ten heavenly levels leading to God. In Dante, the seven levels of purgatory correspond to the seven deadly sins, and the seven levels of heaven correspond to the seven planetary spheres of Aristotle and Ptolemy (coincidental with the seven heavens reported in Mohammed's account). Victor Watts connects Beatrice's speech at the end of *Paradiso I* to the influence of Boethius' (480–524): *The Consolation of Philosophy* (New York: Penguin, 1999 [1969]), xxix. Boethius straddles the Classical and Medieval eras as Dante straddles the Medieval and the Renaissance.

101. Guillaume, 110.

102. Dante's *Paradiso* expresses the Father, Son and Holy Spirit: "O Light Eternal fixed in Self alone, known only to Yourself, and knowing Self, You love and glow, knowing and being known" (XXX, 124–126); and at least esthetically the Cross: "I see that cross as it flames forth with Christ, yet cannot find the words to describe it" (XIV: 104–5).

103. Hans Urs von Balthasar, *The Glory of the Lord: A Theological Aesthetics*, Vol. III: Lay Styles (San Francisco: Ignatius, 1986), 101. Verses in the Comedy do include a trintarian reference ("O Triune Light which sparkles in one star...") and to Christ's sacrifice ("So now, appearing to me in the form of a white rose was Heaven's sacred host, those whom with His own blood Christ made his bride...") (*Paradiso*, XXXI, 1 and 29).

104. The term "heaven" derives from a Greek word meaning *expansiveness.* Might it be that the early nomads of the Arabian Desert found little consolation in a heaven conceived in the Greek way as expansiveness? Access to heaven is not denied to women: "Whoso doeth right, whether male or female, and is a believer, all such will enter the Garden" (Q 40:40; 16:97). In the New Testament the number seventy-two refers to the Gentiles, all of the assumed tribes on earth outside the twelve tribes of Israel.

105. Abdullah Usuf Ali, op. cit., (Q 54:64). 1352, fn. 4729.

106. Other than form criticism, the scientific examination of the Bible—the "historical-critical" method—is a blunter instrument for dissecting the *Qur'an*. The Muslim scripture was compiled from only one source (Mohammed) rather than many, and in a period of less than two decades rather than the nearly one thousand years of the Old Testament.

107. The editorial approach to scripture ("redaction criticism" in biblical studies) is particularly useful in understanding the conflicting meanings of jihad. The *Qur'an* is organized from the longest chapter first to the shortest, not chronologically. Chronologically he transition of jihad from an internal struggle to a military exhortation might fit the *sequence* of Mohammed's life and recitations beginning the cave at Hira (610 A.D.) and ending a few years after the attack on Mecca (628).

108. Again, these senses are the overt or literal, and within the literal the three spiritual senses: the allegorical, the moral, and the anagogical or eternal. See also the *Catechism of the Catholic Church*, 1992 (1994, 1996), nn.115–119.

109. Russell, 153–4.

110. Ibid.

111. Legends vary regarding Mohammed's early training. Norman Daniel refers to Moorish sources to the effect that he was "instructed in the natural sciences, the Catholic Religion and the Jewish Perfidy, under the guidance of a Jewish astrologer and magician who had also been his father's mentor" (*Islam and the West* [Oxford: Oneworld, 1993 and 1960], 108).

112. Russell, 156.

113. W.H. McNeill, *The Rise of the West* (New York: Mentor, 1963), 477, fn. 20 (citing Gardet and Anawati, *Introduction a la Theologie Musulmane*, 47–60). In 833 A.D. the Caliph Ma'mun imposed the Mutazilite doctrine that the *Qur'an* was a created good, and a leading opponent was scourged by this successor the Caliph Mu'tasim. As a consequence, "The palace was in danger of being wrecked by an angry mob which had assembled outside to hear the result of the trial." The Mutazilite dogma was abandoned by the Caliph Wathiq and in 847 declared heretical by Mutawakkil. "From that time to this the victorious party have sternly suppressed every rationalistic movement in Islam" (Reynold Nicholson, A Literary History of the Arabs [New York: Charles Scribner's Sons, 1907], 368–9). Within the Catholic tradition an exclusively literal approach to of scripture is avoided: "(The Bible is) . . . the words of God, expressed in the words of men" (*Dei Verbum*, n. 13). Barclay notes that in late Roman times, Caesar worship (like divinization of the *Qur'an*?), was "not imposed on the people from above. It arose from the people: it might even be said that it arose in spite of efforts by the early emperors to stop it, or at least curb it... Caesar worship began as a spontaneous outburst of gratitude to Rome" (for impartial Roman justice). See William Barclay, *The Revelation of John*, Vol. 1 (Philadelphia: Westminster Press, 1976), 16.

114. The Christian teaching expressed at Nicaea (325 A.D.) is that Christ is of the "substance of God" (*homoiousis*). The specifically Catholic teaching is that under the guidance of the Holy Spirit our reasoned understanding of this Incarnation event—our encounter with Christ—is reflected in an ever deepening "development of doctrine" consistent with the "deposit of faith."

115. Albert Hourani, *A History of the Arab Peoples* (Cambridge, Mass.: Harvard University Press, 1991), 36–37. "In Baghdad during the Abbasid period, Shafi'ism and Hanafism had given their names to urban factions which fought with one another" (158). By comparison, in post-Reformation Europe the accommodation was for the ruler of the territory to determine the religion of his realm.

116. *Averroes*, George Hourani (trans.), op. cit., Ch. 3, nn. 15–20 (p. 68). In his lengthy Introduction, Hourani confirms that in the absence of an ordained priesthood "orthodoxy has been defined in terms of acceptance by the Islamic community, whose consensus (Ijma) cannot be erroneous . . ." (29).

117. This is the widely accepted and politically correct thesis of John Rawls in *Political Liberalism* (New York: Columbia University Press, 1993). A criticism of the President's Commission on Bioethics appointed in 2009 is that it confines itself

to the technical application of new medical technologies, not the morality of such technologies.

118. *Writings of the Young Marx on Philosophy and Society* (New York: Anchor Books, 1971), 65–6; cited in Frederick Wilhelmsen, "Art and Religion," *Citizen of Rome* (La Salle, IL: Sherwood Sugden, 1980), 107.

119. Over eighty percent of sexual abuse victims were boys and ninety-five percent of abusers were not pedophiles. Critics of the final report (see below) agree with the first report that rather than pedophilia "the crisis was characterized by homosexual behavior." During the morally ambivalent 1960s and 70s the mix of seminary candidates might have been influenced by moral corruption in many seminaries, and then the handling of cases was marred by inadequate professional psychological advice and the pragmatism of many bishops. (See the "Report on the Crisis in the Catholic Church in the United States," 2004 (Finding A-3) and the followup "Causes and Context" report, 2011). The Church distinguishes between sexual orientation and immoral actions, and values the work of all of its priests who remain sexually inactive (celibate).

120. Second Vatican Council, *Lumen Gentium* (The Church in the Modern World [1965]), n. 36.

121. Pope Benedict XVI proposes that Melanchthon renders the *word* as the criterion for evaluating the *office* (authority) of the Church. Melanchthon's omission of office in Augsburg Confession (1530) reverses the Catholic self-understanding as author and interpreter of the Scriptures. The Protestant principle is vulnerable to the Islamic scripture (a millennium earlier) asserting that it—the *Qur'an*—is the criterion for understanding Christian scripture. (On the Protestant principle, see Benedict XVI, *God's Word: Scripture, Tradition and Office*, 44–45).

122. Pope Benedict XVI, *National Catholic Register*, Feb. 11, 2007.

123. On this transcendental approach, initially through beauty rather than truth (creed) or goodness (morality), see Hans Urs von Balthasar, *The Glory of the Lord: A Theological Aesthetics*, Vol. I: *Seeing the Form* (San Francisco: Ignatius Press, 1982).

124. Friedrich Heer, *The Intellectual History of Europe* (New York: The World Publishing Co., 1953), 305.

125. "Islamic Society of North American," *Origins*, Washington, D.C.: Catholic News Service, April 14, 2005, 693 (italics added).

126. Eusebius, *The History of the Church*, 3:28 (New York: Penguin, 1965), 138, with explanatory footnote by G. W. Williamson. On the biblical meaning of marriage see *Original Unity of Man and Woman: Catechesis on the Book of Genesis*, Boston: Daughters of St. Paul, 1981; included in *The Theology of the Body* (Boston: Pauline Books and Media, 1997).

127. Joseph Cardinal Ratzinger (Pope Benedict XVI), *In the Beginning: A Catholic Understanding of the Story of Creation and the Fall* (Grand Rapids, Michigan: Eerdmans Publishing, 1995), 65.

128. Whittaker Chambers, *Witness* (New York: Random House, 1952), 797–8.

129. Cochrane, 418.

130. Aleksandr Solzhenitsyn, *The Gulag Archipelego* (New York: Harper and Row, 1973), Part I, Ch. 4 (174).

131. Pope Benedict XVI, "Bonaventure and Thomas Aquinas" (General Audience of March 17, 2010), *National Catholic Register*, April 11, 2010, 6.

132. Hans Urs von Balthasar, *The Glory of the Lord: A Theological Aesthetics*, Vol. II (San Francisco: Ignatius, 1998), 266–282.

133. Unpublished comments by Erik von Keuhnelt-Leddihn to the G.K. Chesterton Society, Seattle, Washington, November 8, 1998; and documented quotes in Friedrich Heer, *The Intellectual History of Europe*, 223.

134. Thomas Molnar, *The Counter-Revolutionaries* (New York: Funk and Wagnalls, 1969).

135. John Paul II, *Centesimus Annus* (the Hundredth Year), n. 39.

136. Eusebius, *The History of the Church*, 8:14 (New York: Penguin, 1965), 346.

137. Heer, 336.

138. DeLacy O'Leary, *Arabia Before Muhammad* (New York: Dutton and Co., 1927), 194, 197–8.

139. Cited by Ayoub in Omar (ed.), 222–9. While identical in content, Western and later Unitarianism springs first from the time of the Reformation and Socinus, in 1570 (Socinianism).

140. Immediately before Nicaea we find in the writings of St. Athanasius, an influential participant at the Council, clear evidence of an already established Trinitarian belief. See *St. Athanasius on the Incarnation*, translated and edited by a Religious of C.S.M.V. [Crestwood, New York: St. Vladimir's Orthodox Theological Seminary, 1982], nn. 16,17).

141. In Cardinal Newman's words: "it must be borne in mind that the great Council of Nicaea was summoned, not to decide for the first time what was to be held concerning our Lord's divine nature, but...to determine the fact whether Arius did or did not contradict the Church's teaching, and, if he did, by what sufficient tessera (testing token) he and his party could be excluded from the communion of the faithful" (cited in Philip Hughes, *The Church in Crisis: A History of the General Councils, 325–1870* [New York: Hanover House, 1960], 17).

142. Ibid., 222, 226, 229.

143. One early eighteenth century writer comments on facts and words: "We alone believe in the Word while our dear enemies stubbornly persist in believing in Scripture." Edmund Burke's counterpart in France, Joseph de Maistre, makes this declaration with regard to Catholics and Protestants, in *On God and Society* (Chicago: Henry Regnery and Co., 1959 [1809]), 32.

144. Jean Cardinal Danielou finds atheism, not religion, to be the momentary product of the transition between the god-seeking paganism of rural civilization and industrial civilization. "The Christians of tomorrow," he writes, "will have to face a new type of paganism, a religion which is seeking to find itself, rather than an atheism which cannot long survive the boredom it engenders" (*Prayer as a Political Problem* [New York: Sheed and Ward, 1967], 100).

145. The divinity of Christ, as distinct from his full humanity, is stressed especially in Mark in the forgiveness of sins (2:10–12), expulsion of demons (1:28, 3:11), reading of hearts (2:8; 12:15), the Transfiguration (9:7) and the confession of the centurion (15:39).

146. Cited in Henry Leroy Finch, *Simone Weil and the Intellect of Grace* (New York: Continuum Publishing Co., 2001), 124, italics added.

147. Joseph Cardinal Ratzinger (Pope Benedict XVI), *Pilgrim Fellowship of Faith* (San Francisco: Ignatius Press, 2005) 74. Elaborating a "science of religion" W. Robertson Smith elaborates a distinction in ancient sacrifice, between tribute and "communion" with the deities. In these cases of hospitality with the deity, as if sharing the offering with another clan member, the communion remains mere ritual. It is not a communion between God and man. "A ritual system must always remain materialistic, even if its materialism is disguised under the cloak of mysticism" (W. Robertson Smith, *The Religion of the Semites* [London: A. and C. Black, Ltd., 1927 (1889)], 240, 396, 439).

148. Ibid., 118.

149. Joseph Cardinal Ratzinger, *God's Word: Scripture, Tradition, Office*, 22–30.

150. The term "apostle" is translated "to be sent" as by another.

151. Form Criticism of biblical texts holds correctly that the collective "we" was a prevalent linguistic form for any members of pre-modern communal groups. Additional clues to the doctrine of the mystical body of Christ, lie in the total experience of Paul and others, including his blindness and the divine instructions received through the messenger Ananias in Damascus (Acts 9:15–17).

152. Biblical testimony to the physical resurrection of Christ is found in Mt 28:9–10 and 16–20, Jn 20:11–18 and 20:19–23 and 24–29, Mk 16:9 and 14–18, and Lk 24:13–35 and 36–49.

153. To what degree did the later Talmud, in addition to parts of the Old and New Testament, decisively shape the contents of the hadith written in the two centuries after the death of the Prophet? Parts of the Talmud were apparently completed in the seventh century, and reflect the (disbelieving) Jewish reaction to the Christian religion: "At precisely the time when Christianity rose from modest beginnings to its first triumphs, the Talmud would become the defining document of those who refused to accept the new covenant." On the Talmud, see Peter Schafer, *Talmudic Jesus* (Princeton University Press), reviewed and quoted by Benjamin Balint in *First Things* (New York: Institute on Religion and Public Life, June 2007), 41–4.

154. Ibid., 115. A developed Trinitarian theology and the apologetics of Islam are not mutually exclusive on the point of continuous action by the Spirit in history. In Catholicism especially the sacraments are the "normal," but not the exclusive, path of grace: "(T)he spirit blows where it will" (Jn 3:8). The Second Vatican Council adds: "Those can attain to everlasting salvation who. . . sincerely seek God, and, moved by grace, strive by their deeds to do His will as it is known to them through the dictates of conscience . . .(even those who) have not yet arrived at an explicit knowledge of God" (*Lumen Gentium*, n. 16) . . . the Holy Spirit in a manner known only to God offers to every man the possibility of being associated with this paschal mystery" (*Gaudium et Spes*, n. 22).

155. Opposite to Islam, the atheistic state, can also speak still to religious tolerance. "On the principle of freedom of religious belief, all religions are tolerated in the Chinese liberated areas. Protestantism, Catholicism, Mohammedanism, Buddhism and all other religions will be protected by the people's government so long as the

believers abide by the laws of the government. Everybody is free to believe or not to believe in a religion; neither compulsion nor discrimination is allowed" (Mao Tse-Tung, *On Coalition Government* [Peking: Foreign Language Press, 1955], 109).

156. From St. Hippolytus, Treatise, *Liturgy of the Hours*, Vol. I, 459.

157. Reference is made to other scriptural passages denoting persuasion rather than compulsion: Gen 19:3, Matt 14:22, Lk 24:29, and Gal 1:24). Hugh Pope, *St. Augustine of Hippo: Essays* (Garden City, N.Y.: Image, 1961), 309.

158. For example, "Say: People of the Book, let us come to an agreement: that we will worship none but God...why do you argue about Abraham when both the Torah and the Gospel were not revealed till after him. Have you no sense?" (Q 3:62–5). The hospitality of the Second Vatican Council offers a contrast: "Catechumens who, moved by the Holy Spirit, seek with explicit intention to be incorporated into the Church are by that very intention joined to her" (*Lumen Gentium* [Light of the World], n. 14).

159. Augustine in the words of Peter Brown, *Augustine of Hippo* (Berkeley: University of California Press, 1967), 374.

160. Hugo Grotius, *The Rights of War and Peace: Including the Law of nature and of Nations* (Washington: Walter Dunne, 1901), 254.

161. John Paul II, *Veritatis Splendor* (The Splendor of Truth), August 6, 1993 (italics added).

162. See also Psalm 37:30–31: "The mouth of the just man tells wisdom and his tongue utters what is right, *the law of his God is in his heart* . . . ." Stated negatively: "The fool said in his heart: There is no God" (Ps 52:1). It is a misreading of Paul to hold that those ignorant of the laws of Christ were simply exempt, rather than that they could still live with merit the imprinted Natural Law.

163. Heinrich A. Rommen, *The Natural Law: A Study in Legal and Social History and Philosophy* (Indianapolis: Liberty Fund, 1998), 195. In Scripture, St Paul also teaches these precise points, e.g., Rom 12:10 and 13:7.

164. See Enrique Rueda, *The Homosexual Network* (Old Greenwich, Connecticut: Devin Adair Co., 1982), 262–4. The Muslim interpretation of Lot in the Old Testament is much like the Natural Law interpretation of traditional Christianity (Q 7:80–84, Q 9:77–83, Q 26:160–175, and Q 27: 54–58).

165. Maulana Muhammad Ali, op. cit., 293.

166. Rommen, op. cit., 4.

167. Dankwart Rustow, in Gabriel Almond and James Coleman (eds.), *The Politics of Developing Areas* (Princeton, N.J.: Princeton University Press, 1960), 380.

168. Op. cit., Q 17:39, p. 705, fn. 2224. Natural Law critics of Islam point to the practice of *al-Taqiyya*, an apparent license to lie to infidels at least in self defense. Al-Taqiyya seems to be widely invoked against those who are perceived as threats simply because they (infidels) decline to affirm Islam. Al-Taqiyya is based on the *Qur'an*: "Let not the Believers take for friends or helpers unbelievers rather than believers: if any do that, in nothing will there be help from Allah: except by way of precaution, that ye may guard yourselves from them . . . ." (Q 3:28). Compare this to the absence of guile in St. Peter: "Always be ready to give an explanation to anyone who asks you for a reason for your hope . . . ." (1 Pe 3:15). In exceptional

cases, whether it is permissible to "lie" is addressed by Cardinal Newman. He cites the positions that "it is allowable in certain cases to say what we know to be false, as, e.g. to escape from a great danger," or "when it is *impossible* to observe a certain other precept (other than truthful words), more important, without telling a lie" (italics added). A current example would be equivocation when concealing Jewish refugees in World War II Germany. The distinction is made between a material lie and a formal lie (sin). Worthy of probing interreligous discussion is a comparison between the range of positions extracted by Newman from Christian theology and the possibly similar provision for self-protection in the *Qur'an* (Q 3:28, above). See John Henry Cardinal Newman, *Apologia Pro Vita Sua* (Garden City, New York: Image, 1956), Appendix, especially 401–426.

169. Imam Khomeini, Translated and annotated by Hamid Algar, *Islam and Revolution: Writings and Declarations* (London: KPI, 1981), 109.

170. Hassan, 116. Note the similarity of the last line to Deuteronomy: "Give heed, O Israel, to the commands of the Lord, and inscribe them in you heart as in a book" Deut 4:1).

171. Abdullah Yusuf Ali, op cit., 39 and note 87.

172. George Weigel, *The Cube and the Cathedral* (New York: Basic Books, 2005), 141–2. Amir Hussain of Loyal Marymount University comments that Thomas Jefferson taught himself Arabic in order to study Islamic Law (Symposium, on "Faith and Reason in Christianity and Islam," University of Washington, Oct. 2008). The question presents itself on the timing of this avocation and Jefferson's (later?) well-known editing of a deist (and Muslim-compatible) version of the Bible, with all references to Christ's miracles and divinity deleted.

173. "Catholics and Muslims Dialogue," *National Catholic Register*, Circle Media, Inc., May 31, 2009.

174. Farooq Hassan explains that while cohesion in the West is based less on symbols and more on a heritage of shared action within history, Islamic membership in the *ummah* is radically different. It is based on a simple and *"common act of will* that identifies (them as) Muslims" (*The Concept of State and Law in Islam*, 89).

175. Yahya Michot documents a convincing case that the fourteenth century Ibn Taymiyya counseled flight, rather than jihad, for Muslims living in mixed domains between dar al-Islam and dar al-harb where the Muslim way of life was in jeopardy. See *Muslims under Non-Muslim Rule: Ibn Taymiyya* (London: Interface Press, 2006). From the philosopher's writings, he postulates a third "composite" case between dar al-Islam and dar al-harb and where Muslims would be capable of a civic culture.

176. Apart from the state, the Church fosters "that brotherhood of all men which corresponds to this destiny of theirs. Inspired by no earthly ambition, the Church seeks but a solitary goal: to carry forward the work of Christ Himself under the lead of the befriending Spirit" (*Gaudium et Spes*, [the Church in the Modern World], 3).

177. William Robertson Smith, *Lectures on the Religion of the Semites: The Fundamental Institutions* (London: A and C. Black, Ltd., 1927).

178. Ibid., 232.

179. A term possibly coined by Bernard Lewis, *The Crisis of Islam* (New York: Modern Library, 2003).

180. In the Christian world, the comparable case might be the notion that the church is a spiritual body alone, without common creed or an institutional structure.

181. One of the prayers, recited five times a day, is this: "O Lord you are Peace, from You comes Peace, and to You returns Peace, make us, O Lord, live in Peace and allow us to enter the house of Peace. O Lord of Glory and Grace, thine is the Bliss and Elevation" (Hassan, 239).

182. That Mohammed is the last of the prophets is asserted *not* by him, but by his successors shortly after his death during the wars of apostasy from his new ummah confederation. It is a teaching that we do not find in the *Qur'an* (Karen Armstrong, *Islam: A Short History* [New York: Modern Library, 2002], 26).

183. Humphrey Prideaux, *Life of Mahomet* (London: Curll, Hooke, Fleetstreet, Mears and Clay without Temple-Bar, MDCXVIII [and 1696]), 36.

184. See John "It is God the only Son, *ever at the Father's side*, who has revealed him" (Jn 1:18, italics added), and "...we have an Advocate with the Father, Jesus Christ the righteous one: (1 Jn 2:1). And "(Christ) took his seat forever at the right hand of God" (Heb 10:12, see also Rom 8:34).

185. Both Esposito and De Lacy O'Leary (*Arabia Before Muhammad* [New York: E.P. Dutton and Co., 1927]), explain that this permission actually serves as a compromise and restraint on the early Arabian practice of often having many more wives.

186. Within early Muslim society equality after conversion did not eliminate a four-level social structure. After the Arab Muslims came the converts of other non-Arab races, and these were followed by the secondary citizens of encysted communities adhering to other religions such as Jews or Christians, and then finally the slave class.

187. Periodically the press reports events nearly incomprehensible to Christians, such as the stoning of a thirteen year old rape victim (Aisha Ibrahim Duhulow) in the presence of one thousand spectators, in Mogadishu, Somalia, on the pretense that she had committed adultery with the three men she accused (Oct. 27, broadly reported on Nov. 2, 2008).

188. For an alleged lack of evidence, the Pakistan Supreme Court (not a completely independent judiciary as in the West) upheld an appellate court reversal of five earlier convictions in an internationally monitored case of gang rape. The sixth member received a reduced sentence to life imprisonment (*Los Angeles Times*, Islamabad, April 22, 2011).

189. Hassan, 171.

190. Thomas Lippman, *Understanding Islam* (revised) (New York: Mentor, 1990), 86–94.

191. Ibid., 174–7.

192. Borzou Daraghi, "Infighting rules Iran's power elite," *Los Angeles Times*, January 1, 2008. This contrast shows up periodically in Western news coverage. In early 2008 and on behalf of the Guardian Council, the Ayatolah Ali Khamenei overruled President Ahmadinejad to require the state-owned cartel to supply limited natural gas to remote villages outside the urban areas (Nazali Fathi, *New York Times*, January 22, 2008).

193. *Compendium of the Social Doctrine of the Church* (Pontifical Council for Justice and Peace, 2005), passim.

194. Abdullah Yusuf Ali, op. cit., 39, fn. 87 and 88. Margoliouth affirms that Islam is consistent on the biblical first commandment ("Thou shalt have none other gods but Me"), but the meaning of the remaining commandments is obscure and only scattered throughout the *Qur'an* (Remnants of a code are suggested in Q 6:152, 17:24, 25:65, 31:12 and 16:92). At least in the formative years of the *Qur'an* the second commandment is the simple "kindness to parents" (Q 31:14), but later is reduced for those parents who are Unbelievers (Q 29:7). Following the first historical vindication of Islam at the successful Battle of Badr, Moslems are told that there is perpertual enmity with Unbelievers, whatever their relationship (Q 9 and Q 50). Oaths are to be kept (Q 16:93), but if it is later judged opportune, perjury can be avoided by paying compensation (Q 5:91 and Q 56). See D. S. Margoliouth, *The Early Development of Mohammedanism* (The Hibbert Lectures of 1913), (New York: Charles Scribners' Sons, 1914), 47–8.

195. From the hadith as reported by Bukhari (Sahih, I 34), and cited in Hassan, 97, and worded more completely as here by Ayoub in Omar (ed.), 13.

196. Al-Munqidh min al-Dalal, op. cit., 39.

197. Al-Munqidh min al-Dalal, op. cit., 87–8, translator's footnote 34.

198. Daniel Madigan, op. cit.

199. Following the Second Vatican Council, Pope Paul VI addressed whether concepts expressing the faith are culture-bound (historicism), in *Mysterium Ecclesia* (The Mystery of the Church), 1973. From .n. 3: "One thing is the deposit of faith, which consists of the truths contained in sacred doctrine, another thing is the manner of presentation, always however with the same meaning and signification."

200. Second Vatican Council, *Dignitatis humanae* (Declaration on Religious Freedom), n.1.

201. The First Vatican Council (1869–70) had demanded the freedom of the Church apart from the claims of nationalist movements. The Second Vatican Council (1963–5) formally extends this earlier position by asserting for individuals immunity from coercion in religion, by any group, class, nation or state.

202. In the 1979 Hostage Crisis several dozens American citizens in Iran were seized and held for over a year as part of the revolution that toppled the secularizing Shah and elevated the mullah Khoumeini to power.

203. Hassan, 26.

204. A.N. Sherwin-White, *Roman Society and Roman Law in the New Testament* (Oxford: Clarendon Press, 1963), 102.

205. John Dougherty, *Searching the Scriptures* (Garden City, New York: Image, 1963), 139, italics added.

206. The illuminating comparison and contrast might be between the Islamic State and rather than the Western state, monastic institutions in the West. As the guide for group monasticism in the West, the *Rule of St. Benedict* (early sixth century) established a rule of law, somewhat as the Shari'a replaces tribal allegiances and their pagan gods with a single law. Both societies—Western monasteries and the Muslim ummah—are ostensibly oriented toward God within "a unified and comprehensive view of life," although the first is voluntary and celibate while the latter (Islam) is binding on all, even future generations, and is polygamous. In the West the state is held apart from monastic life, while under Islam the state is absorbed.

207. Coming out of Jewish culture, even at the Ascension, the disciples still hoped that Christ's purpose was to "restore the kingdom of Israel" (Acts 1:6).

208. Joseph Cardinal Ratzinger (Pope Benedict XVI), *Salt of the Earth* (San Francisco: Ignatius Press, 1997), 246.

209. Amintore Fanfani, *Catholicism, Capitalism and Protestantism* (New York: Sheed and Ward, 1935).

210. *Caristas in Veritate* (Charity in Love), 2009, n. 34.

211. Ibid., n. 38, and John Paul II, *Centesimus Annus* (The Hundred Years) 1991, n. 35.

212. Definition based on Robert Melson and Howard Wolpe, "Modernization and the Politics of Communalism: A Theoretical Perspective," *American Political Science Review*, LXIV:4 (Dec. 1970), 1112. Within the social sciences, prominent advocates of uniform processes of modernity included Talcott Parsons, Marion Levy, F.X. Sutton, Fred Riggs, Max Millikan, Donald Blackmer, Amatai Etzioni, David Apter, Robert Kearney, Jounaq Jahan, and Roger Scott. After the mid-twentieth century attention was drawn increasingly to discontinuous and communal tendencies in social and political processes. Leading exponents were C.S. Whitaker, Samuel Huntington, Karl Deutsch, Reinhard Bendix, S.N. Eisenstadt, Joseph La Polambara, Lucian Pye, Dankwart Rustow (not Walt W.), Clifford Geertz, Lloyd and Susanne Rudolph, Joel Migdahl, J.P. Nettle with Roland Robertson, and Joseph Gusfield.

213. The office of ayatollah as a religious leader emerged only in the nineteenth century. The office of caliph was head of both mosque and state as a single entity, a "practitioner of the arts of politics and sometimes war" (Bernard Lewis, *What Went Wrong?"* (New York: Harmer Perennial, 2003), 114.

214. Ibid., 46. A cultural divide amplifies the workings of the two different theologies. In the West the nation is temporal and has a history, a culture, a language and a past and a future. This opening to ethnic identity in the world received a large boost from Johann Herder (1744–1803) who contributed to German Romanticism and has indirectly influenced nationalist movements globally.

215. The following typology is drawn mostly from Melson and Wolpe, but is treated in a vast social science literature that includes at least thousands of case studies. The emergence of traditional Islam confounds the basic premises of much Western social science which largely is shaped by the class-based experiences of Western nation-states.

216. Conflicted views are the more common interpretation of "resident" Palestinians displaced after 1948, and the contrasting interpretation of Jews denied earlier access (after 1920) to the British Protectorate, in contrast with Arab immigrants. Joan Peters documents the latter view (*From Time Immemorial: The Origins of the Arab-Jewish Conflict Over Palestine* [New York: Harper and Row, Publishers, 1984]).

217. Kurt Glaser, *Czecho-Slovakia: A Critical History* (Caldwell, Idaho: The Caxton Printers, 1961), 124–132. Excluding this and other expatriations in the Soviet and Chinese orbit, the number of expatriations in the decade following the Second World War equaled the entire traffic of free migrants—45 million—across the Atlantic Ocean in the century between Napoleon and the First World War (tabulation in the *Encyclopedia Britannica*, 1970, 422).

218. Chan Hong Chee, "Political Developments: 1965–79," in Ernst C. T. Chew and Edwin Lee (eds.), A *History of Singapore* (Singapore: Oxford University Press, 1991), 158–79. After separation from Malaysia, the only nation to offer military advice in support of a security force was Israel, also a nation of about four million population in a much less accommodating region. See also the memoirs of Lee Kuan Yew, *From Third World to First: The Singapore Story: 1965–2000* (Singapore: Singapore Press Holdings, 2000).

219. Had the commonwealth model been in place in time, the American Revolution might well have been averted. Franklin's unsuccessful Albany Plan (1754) essentially proposed such as relationship between the colonies and Britain (Alfred Kelly and Winfred Harbison, *The American Constitution: Its Origins and Development* [New York: W.W. Norton, 1963], 61–2, 83).

220. Hassan, 34, 35.

221. On this important element, see also John Paul II, *Memory and Identity: Conversations at the Dawn of a Millennium* (New York: Rizzoli, 2005), 85. Arab identity is rooted in the biblical Ishmael while many other Muslims trace to the Persian Empire or the Golden Age of Islam. Even the anomaly of the Turkish nation reaches far back before our world of nation-states. These social anchors introduce a time scale that the West often fails to appreciate.

222. Hassan., 40–50.

223. Jacques Maritain, *Man and the State* (Chicago: Phoenix Books, 1951). Maritain played a key role in the 1947 preparation of the Universal Declaration of Human Rights.

224. Hassan, 115.

225. Ibid. 35.

226. Ibid., 120. He finds support in Q 4:58, 65,105,135; 7:29; 16:90, and 57:25. While some of these verses presume an arbitration role for Islam, none is explicit about justice and populations outside of Islam. (One reads in part, "Seek out the enemy relentlessly," Q4:105).

227. Ibid., 48.

228. Wael B. Hallaq, *An Introduction to Islamic Law* (New York: Cambridge, 2009), 121–4.

229. Hassan, 85.

230. Christopher Dawson, *The Making of Europe* (New York: Meridian Books, 1956), 132.

231. Pope Leo XIII, *Immortale Dei* (The Christian Constitution of States, 1885), n. 4. Obedience is commended in Scripture for the religious community e.g., Lk 10:16, Heb 13:17, 1 Pet 5:5, Col 3:18, and for all human institutions, e.g, 1 Pet 2:13–15.

232. Recalling St. Paul, "(T)here is in Christ and in the Church no inequality on the basis of race or nationality, social condition or sex, because 'there is neither Jew nor Greek; there is neither slave nor freeman; there is neither male nor female. For you are all 'one' in Christ Jesus(Gal 3:28)," comment and citation from the Second Vatican Council, *Lumen Gentium* [Light of the World], 32).

233. Hassan, 40. Rather than the executors of divine law, revolutionary Marxism positions itself as the executor of historical necessity in the absence of God. The no-

tion of executor also finds a parallel in Charlemagne's letter to Leo XIII. The emperor is "the representative of God who has to protect and govern all the members of God" (from Christopher Dawson, *Medieval Essays* [Garden City, New York: Image Books, 1959], 72).

234. Hassan, 46 (italics added). Compare this cornerstone idea to that of St. Augustine: "A State is an assemblage of reasonable beings bound together by a common *agreement concerning the objects of their love.*" (See Norman H. Baynes, *The Political Ideas of St. Augustine: De Civitate Dei*, [The Historical Association, 1968].)

235. Walter Ullmann, *Medieval Papalism: The Political Theories of the Medieval Canonists* (London: Methuen and Co. Ltd., 1949), 141–2.

236. Letter of November 3, 1198, in Anne Fremantle, *The Papal Encyclicals in Their Historical Context* (New York: Mentor-Omega, 1963), 70.

237. Eric Voegelin (John Hallowell, ed.), *From Enlightenment to Revolution* (Durhan, North Carolina: Duke University Press, 1975), 233.

238. John Paul II, *Centesimus Annus* (the Hundred Years), 1991, n. 11 (italics added), referring to the Church's first formal social encyclical, by Pope Leo XIII in 1891.

239. A very succinct definition of the common good is provided in this quotation by Dino Bigongiari, *The Political Ideas of St. Thomas Aquinas* (New York: Hafner Publishing Co., 1953), x.

240. Even in the mid seventeenth century, Cardinal Bellarmine held (in his *Treatise on Law*): "That particular forms of government, are by the law of nations, and not by divine law, since it depends upon the consent of the multitude to place over themselves a king, consuls, or other magistrates, as is clear; and, for a legitimate reason, they can change royalty into aristocracy, or into democracy, of vice versa, as it was done in Rome" (from a 1680 translation by Sir Robert Filmer, cited in S. McNamara, *American Democracy and Catholic Doctrine* [Brooklyn, New York: International Catholic Truth Society, n.d., c. 1920], 88). McNamara proposes that John Locke, in his refutation of the divine right of kings (*Two Treatises on Government*, 1689), drew directly or indirectly from the earlier Bellarmine (89–90).

241. *Graves de Communi* (On Christian Democracy), 1901, n. 7. In 1890 Pope Leo XIII had instructed the French hierarchy not to oppose the new republican *form* of government, even though later government policies of persecution were to come as no surprise, e.g., 13,000 parochial schools were closed by 1904.

242. John Paul II, *The Gospel of Life* (New York: Time Books, 1995), n. 73. And while upholding the primacy of conscience, Benedict XVI challenges the notion that "an erring conscience saves man by protecting him from the terrifying demands made by truth" (*Values in a Time of Upheaval* [New York: Crossroad Publishing Co., 2005], 79).

243. John Paul II, *Evangelium vitae*, (The Gospel of Life), nn. 12, 18, commentary by Hittinger in John Witte Jr. and Frank Alexander (eds.), *The Teachings of Modern Roman Catholicism: on Law, Politics, and Human Nature* (New York: Columbia University, 2007), 21.

244. Q 18:110: "Say, I am only mortal like you."

245. Hassan, 103.

246. In the Catholic Church, the distinction among members is not that of rulers and ruled, but a difference in roles. All are called to the same holiness. The place of bishops in the Church is reflected in Scripture from the earliest days of the Christian community: Phil 1:1; 1 Tim 3:1–7, 3:8–13, 5:17–18, 5:22; Titus 1:5–9; Acts 14:23, 20:17–38; and 1 Pet 5:1–5.

247. Some parallel can be found in early Lutheranism. Partly as a rejection of the Peasant Revolt, the ordained clergy of the Catholic Church were replaced by lay control in the form of the rising German state. Prideaux added to the countering Protestant bias against the Church. He claimed that Mohammed and the Bishop of Rome as "universal pastor" emerged at the same time, and proposed that each then advanced his respective empires, one in the East and the other in the West (ibid., 9–10).

248. Abdullah Yusuf Ali, op. cit., 414.

249. Second Vatican Council, *Constitution on the Church in the Modern World*, "Prefatory Explanatory Note," n. 2. The best informed commentary on the daily workings of the Council is Ralph Wiltgen, SVD, *The Rhine Flows into the Tiber* (Rockford, Ill.: Tan Books, 1978), 232. "With access to all official correspondence, documents and working papers received by the Council Fathers from the Council's Secretariat," Wiltgen published during the Council a news service in six languages, circulated to three thousand subscribers in one hundred eight countries.

250. Today the five patriarchs of Antioch and all of the East are all successors of Peter, but none is also the bishop of Rome.

251. Second Vatican Council, op. cit. The hierarchical priesthood differs from the priesthood of the faithful "in essence and not only in degree," but "each of them in its own special way is a participation in the one priesthood of Christ" (n. 10).

252. Of the First Vatican Council, Pope Benedict XVI writes, "The Vatican Council represents a condemnation of papalism just as much as of episcopalism. Actually, it characterizes *both* doctrines as heresies, and in the place of one-dimensional solutions on the basis of late theological ideas of those of power politics, it sets the dialectic of the reality already given, stemming from Christ, a dialectic and a reality that confirm their obedience to the truth in their very renunciation of a uniform formula satisfying to the intellect" (Joseph Cardinal Ratzinger, *God's Word* [San Francisco: Ignatius Press, 2008], 20). Intriguing possibilities for the future in relation to the Orthodox Churches are examined by Russell Shaw in *Papal Primacy in the Third Millennium* (Huntington, Ind.: Our Sunday Visitor, 2000). See also Thomas Kocik, *Apostolic Succession in an Ecumenical Context* (New York: Alba House, 1996), and the more recent *Dominus Iesus* (The Lord Jesus), Congregation for the Doctrine of the Faith, August 6, 2000.

253. Joseph Cardinal Ratzinger (Pope Benedict XVI), *God's Word: Scripture, Tradition and Office* (San Francisco: Ignatius Press, 2008), 15–22. The feature "together" is an ecclesial quality rather than an administrative design.

254. Second Vatican Council, *Lumen Gentium* (Constitution on the Church in the Modern World), n. 33 (italics added). Lay organizations that identify themselves as "Catholic" remain accountable to the criteria of fidelity, prudence and goodness.

255. Hassan, 122.

256. Ibid., 40.

257. In the West we can detect certain Shari'a-like trends toward radically secularist legislation from the bench, as in the 1973 *Rowe v Wade* abortion ruling in the United States, and notorious personal rights abuses and even truth abuses imposed more recently by the Human Rights Commissions in Canada.

258. Hassan, 126. The Islamic state is at least remotely comparable to the "divine right of kings" announced in 1598 by the Presbyterian King James I (and by Elizabeth before him): ". . . countable to that great God, who placed him as *his lieutenant* over them, upon the perill of his soule to procure the weale of both soules and bodies, as farre as in him lieth, of all them that are committed to his charge..." (italics added; in Thomas P. Neill, The *Building of the Human City* [Garden City, New York: Doubleday Christendom Books, 1960], 168–72).

259. In comparison to "rules of derivation," Christian moral discernment applies principles of *non-cooperation with wrongdoing,* e.g., the formal cooperation of an accomplice, or the sometimes acceptable material cooperation based on such factors as intent, remoteness, or avoidance of greater harm.

260. One critical example in early 2007 in Iraq was a fatwa preventing members of parliament from voting on the distribution of national oil revenues among ethnic regions. Distribution of oil revenues was a benchmark toward United States military disengagement. In early 2008 it was decided that the forbidden allocation could be handled not by formula, but as part of the adopted national budget.

261. Hassan, 125–6. Albert Hourani identifies five norms: those things which obligatory on either the community or on every single member, then in succession those that are recommended, morally neutral, reprehensible or forbidden (*A History of the Arab Peoples*, op. cit., 159).

262. The principle of Ijtihad is structurally akin to a key aspect of Protestant communions as contrasted with the Catholic Church which is a "hierarchical communion." Protestantism is rooted in a horizontal or congregational hypothesis based on shared individual interpretation of Scripture. The wording of John Huss—"The church of Christ is the community of the elect"—is pivotal to Martin Luther ("Luther at the Diet of Worms," the Speech of Dr. Martin Luther before the Emperor Charles," Carroll, Emgree et al (ed.), The *Development of Civilization: A Documentary History of Politics, Society, and Thought*, Vol. 1 [Chicago: Scott Foresman and Co., 1961], in 424–431).

263. Hassan, 78.

264. Ibid.

265. Hassan, 38.

266. Gibb and Kramer, 158.

267. Hassan, 75–6, 82.

268. Under the Sunni majority, four schools (*fiqh*) of Islamic Law can be found in different parts of the Western Muslim world. The Hanafi is widespread and is found throughout the lands of the former Ottoman Empire. The Maliki is confined to Western North Africa. The Shafi'I is in the Middle East, and the Hanbali is centered in Saudi Arabia and Qatar. All four are regarded as orthodox. These schools were already in place by end of the ninth century.

269. The Magna Carta arose in a complicated context. It is a listing of rights violated by King John, based on the earlier Charter of Rights granted by Henry I.

The principle author was Stephen Langton, a Catholic archbishop. The intricacy of Church-State disentanglement involved papal financial expectation from England to help prevent the Hohenstaufen dynasty from taking Sicily, threats of interdict and invasion, and the fact that King John had made England a papal fief, and that Langton's pope then opposed the Magna Carta as having been extracted under duress by the barons whom he excommunicated, and under oath which the pope regarded as invalid without his sanction. A revised version was produced in 1225.

270. Foustel de Coulanges, *The Ancient City* (Garden City, New York: Doubleday, n.d. [1864]), 219–220. The subordination of clan deities to the city finds a parallel in non-urban Arabia. Sanctuary grazing land lying between the waters of several tribes was open to all as common pasture-ground "where enemies could meet and feed their flocks in security under the peace of the god" (William Robert Smith, *Lectures on the Religion of the Semites* [London: A. and C. Black, Ltd., 1927 (1889)], 145).

271. Ibid., 389–395.

272. Ibid.

273. The notable exception to lay control of bishop appointments in the West was the network of almost 1,200 monasteries of the Cluniac Reform in the eleventh century. In this case the abbots were under direct papal jurisdiction and their election was exempt from local bishoprics and pressure from the civil powers (Benedict XVI, General Audience of Nov. 11, 2009 on "Humanism and the Future of Europe," *L'Osservatore Romano* [Vatican City: Wednesday, Nov. 18, 2009], 16).

274. See Gerd Tellenback *Church, State and Christian Society at the Time of the Investiture Contest* (New York, Harper Torchbook, 1959). In 1075 Pope Gregory VII confronted the German monarch Henry IV to end Lay Investiture of bishops. Formal relief came with the formal Concordat of Worms (1122) and the First Lateran Council (1123). It was a victory for the pope to distinguish between imperial investing of bishops with the scepter (temporal authority) and conferring of the ring and crozier (spiritual authority) by the Church. The German emperor also was to refrain from interfering in papal elections (Joseph Mc Sorley, *An Outline History of the Church by Centuries* [St. Louis: B. Herder Book Co., 1945], 340).

275. On the Italian peninsula, the secular state was advanced by the Ghibellines who based their political theory on the recently discovered Code and Institutes of Justinian. The Code provided an independent and fully developed legal system apart from the Canon Law used by the Vatican until this time without any mature competition.

276. Some historians stress a direct connection between our modern political freedom and self-governing merchant guilds that *predate* the Reformation. While the guilds were often monopolistic, they also cut across all economic classes. Mussolini's "corporations" of the 1930's are not to be compared since these were under the direct control of the Fascist state.

277. Included in citations in John Dolan, 256. Interestingly, the second-century syncretic religion of Manichaeism, like Lutheranism, retained only two of the Church's sacraments, Baptism and the Eucharist.

278. Edith Stein, (translated by Marianne Sawicki), *An Investigation Concerning the State* (Washington D.C.: Institute of Carmelite Studies Publications, 2006

[1925]), 83. As an ethnic Jew, Stein was among those Catholic Jews rounded up to be murdered in Auschwitz following the German bishops' protest of Nazi atrocities in Belgium.

279. Ibid., passim, and summarized in the Editor's Introduction: "States, she argues, can be neither explained nor justified by citing random historical causes or by projecting fanciful teleologies. Their true being is to implement law, *whose source subsists quite independently*" (italics added).

280. These features are not altered by Constitutional amendments of 1980, or by the Penal Code which in Section 301 prohibits statements against, not Islam, but Turkish-ness. A particular comparison with the West is the Portuguese Constitution (1933) which declares a separation of Church and state, but also affirms that "the Catholic religion may be freely practiced, in public or private, *as the religion of the Portuguese nation*" (Article 45).

281. Hassan, 150–1.

282. Bruce Maddy-Weitzman (ed.) *Middle East Contemporary Survey–2000*, Vol. XXIV (Tel Aviv University, 2002.

283. Thomas Lippman, *Understanding Islam*, op. cit., 103.

284. Associated Press, Feb.-28–2007.

285. The most controversial provision was adopted in 1986: "Whoever by words, either spoken or written, or by visible representation, or by any imputation, innuendo, or insinuation, directly or indirectly, defiles the sacred name of the Holy Prophet Muhammad (peace be upon him) shall be punished wit h death, or imprisoned for life, and shall also be liable to fine" (cited with a chronology of rising anti-Christian violence by Jeff Ziegler, "Under the Cross," in *Catholic World Report* [San Francisco: Ignatius, May 2011]).

286. Guillaume, 162, 172.

287. On monastic obedience, see Fr. Gabriel of St. Mary Magdelan, O.C.D. (*Divine Intimacy: Meditations on the Interior Life* [Rockford, ILL: Tan Books, 1996 [1964]), 359–374. Meditations are: Free Sacrifice of Liberty, Supernatural Obedience, Blind Obedience, and Difficulties in Obedience.

Chapter Four

The Manger:
The Human Person in the World

The principle of an inborn and universal natural law still supports the now uncertain political order in the West. The shared dignity of concrete human persons differs from the abstract unity of the Islamic community or ummah. However, hints toward the universal natural law can be found in the eclectic *Qur'an* (Chapter 3). The natural law is in the West, but it is *not of* the West. (It is more accurate to say that the West is of the discovered natural law.) While the intellectual basis of natural law comes with the classical thinkers, the theological basis comes from the east with Christianity and St. Paul: "When the Gentiles who have no law do by nature what the Law prescribes . . . they show the work of the Law written in their hearts" (Rom 2:14–15). It was this combination that created the cultural event called Europe or the West. The task of replanting these origins into the twenty-first century is one theme of Chapter 4. A major focus is the related and recent actions of the universal Church and its proposed principles in support of the dignity of the human person and a shared "common good" protective of responsible human freedom.

The difference between a culture based on the universal natural law and the culture of the Islamic State is reflected in the difference between parliamentary law and Shari'a, between civil society and the ummah, between impartial court decisions and fatwas, and between full citizenship and second class status for encapsulated religious populations or dhimmis.[1] If the West is to engage Islam on these institutional terms, the West must reconsider its own progressive drift away from both natural law and its distinct and historical Christian roots. Personal rights and freedoms, the dignity of the human person and concepts of the common good are all the fruits of classical thought, especially as illumined by the Christian revelation. The spread of cities and the printed word, new economics and the organization of labor and a middle class, the methods and findings of the natural sciences—these help shape historical and institutional outcomes in the West, but do not fully explain.

Today, the secularist worldview deprives the West of the universal natural law as a possible common grammar for coherent dialogue with the *followers* of Islam. If at its heart early Islam was in some obscure way a deification of inborn natural law (as also codified in the Decalogue), then clearer Western consent to the natural law might complete a common bridge or contact point for dialogue with the followers of Islam. Modernity and post-modernity too easily reject the universal natural law, imagining it to be a later biblical constraint against the liberty of Rousseau's mythical "noble savage," rather than an imprint of a deeper and fully human freedom to do the good and to avoid evil. Not something that we know because we construct it, the natural law is a *discovery* of what is already within ourselves—what we already know. Peter Lawler suggests that "Even the written law of the Bible, according to St. Augustine, had its origin in men's refusal to acknowledge and act *according to what they really know*."[2]

The universal natural law informs and is elevated by the Old Testament (and might also be borrowed into the later *Qur'an*): "This command which I enjoin on you today is not too mysterious and remote for you. No, it is something very near to you, already in your mouths and in your hearts; you have only to carry it out" (Deut 30:11, 14). The Thomistic philosopher Jacques Maritain, contributed to the United Nations Declaration of Human Rights (1948) which begins "all human beings are born free and equal indignity and rights" (Article 1). Maritain suggests that the natural law is "known through inclination or through co-naturality, not through conceptual knowledge and by way of reasoning . . . (he continues) what is consonant with the essential inclinations of human nature is grasped by the intellect as good; what is dissonant, as bad . . ."[3]

Unlike the detailed blue print injunctions of Shari'a, the natural law is often recessive. It creates a space for responsible freedom. It does not always tell us what to do or how to do it, but instead it tells us more what *not* to do. Natural law most often intervenes when the good is eclipsed or cancelled by the presumptive inventiveness of man.

> (The natural law) does not, for instance, tell us which of the many possible forms of laws about property is right in the abstract . . . But it judges each and every existing system of property in terms of justice . . . This quality of the unvarying natural law, which elevates it above the changing historical positive law, which makes it both the ideal for lawmakers and the critical norm for existing laws, renders it possible for the natural law to govern the acquisition and exercise of political power itself.[4]

The Western concept of justice differs from that under Islam where justice is conformance with the Shari'a in both its prohibitions and obligations.

In the West the natural law was a finding of reason reinforced by, but distinct from, things of belief and faith. And rather than a code imposed by executors for the benefit of the community, as with Islam, the natural law inheres in all of us from within, apart from belief or absence of belief. Natural law is not a fanatical imposition of irrational believers, nor is it to be rejected by Muslims as Christian evangelization. Under Islam, "justice" is easily equated with the *Qur'an* and the hadith. The universality of natural law (possibly) is subsumed into the communal ummah, and as a separate matter Western religious creeds are dismissed as artificial overlays to this belief. The most prominent creed of Islam (*Fiqh Akbar II*, c. 1000 A.D.) holds in one of its twenty-nine articles that man is created without belief or unbelief. Suspended at the beginning, man is simply given commandments which some choose not to believe.[5]

Matters of prudential judgment under (Western) natural law and positive law seem under Shari'a law to be amalgamated into a single package of revealed folk literature. Islam, as it faces a crisis of meaning in the modern world, finds itself unable to cooperate within a distinct realm of reasoned and universal natural law—in the same way that Islam has found itself immobilized historically with regard to science and autonomous laws of nature again distinct from the autonomous oneness of Allah. All autonomies—human positive law and scientific laws of nature—remain contained within and preempted by the autonomy of God, and the *Qur'an.*

"SEPARATION" OF CHURCH AND STATE

Dual access to the natural law, through reason and revelation, points toward a reasonable and faithful distinction between Church and state to the benefit of both. Finding and protecting this distinction is the secret of the West and its story. In the fourth century the emperor Constantine bluntly instructed bishop Cyril of Alexandria on the extent of his own imperial (and Shari'a-like) authority: "You should realize that Church and state are completely one, and, at our command and with the Providence of our God and Savior, we will become even more firmly united . . . and we will by no means tolerate any attempt of yours to cause disorder in the city or the Church."[6] From both sides Christendom struggled both to resist and to recognize conceptually, at least, the autonomy of each domain as well as the overall unity of the human person.

The famous formula of "two swords," one of God and the other of Caesar, was announced by Pope Galasius in the fifth century (492–496 A.D.), partly to free the Western Church from the kind of support and subservience given to the Eastern Church by the emperor. The Christ of the Gospel already makes the historic distinction of divided allegiances between life in the empire and the life of faith. When questioned directly by his disciples, He instructed them: "Render unto Caesar that which is Caesar's, and unto God that which is God's" (Matt 22:21), and "My kingdom does not belong to this world" (Jn 18:36). Yet, this guidance remains more of an invitation than a simplistic resolutions to the tensions experienced by Christians who remain in this world and now are also citizens of the City of God. On another occasion the same Christ teaches us that to render unto Caesar his image on a coin is not to diminish the higher service invited of all who are made in a different image—the image of God: No one can serve two masters. He will either hate one and love the other, or be devoted to one and despise the other. You cannot serve God and mammon (Mt 6:24).

Throughout western history, the practical relationship between the two swords has provided rich fodder for emperors, popes and especially skilled canonists ever since. For some, the pope's authority both derived directly from God and touches both the sacred and the temporal realms, but he was prudent not to exercise the latter. Christ told Peter: "Put up thy sword into the sheath" (Jn 18:11). For others the temporal power either derived directly from the citizens or else the emperor held no power until his coronation by the Church. The Christian commonwealth, like the Islamic state today, could not conceive of an autonomous state. The papal canonist held that "Since we form one body in Christ, it would be monstrous, if we had two heads."[7]

Christian freedom shatters not only the *polis* of the ancient world, but also the tribal allegiances of sixth century Clovis in barbarian Europe to the north, and equally the tribalism of seventh century Arabia—and today the ummah, and even Western nation-states when they annex themselves to extreme identity politics. In the political vacuum that followed the loss of a Western emperor and Roman political order, the prominence of bishops in secular affairs came largely as an historical aberration. The diocesan boundaries closely matched the Roman provinces. By default, bishops mediated civil affairs in much the same way that Mohammed, following his flight from Mecca, resolved disputes among the ungoverned tribes of Medina. It was only after centuries of usurpation in both West and East that Pope Callistus II in the twelfth successfully established the rightful autonomy of the Church. The Concordat of Worms of 1122 ended the practice of lay investiture, the selection of bishops by princes of state.[8] Overreaching, Pope Boniface VIII (1294–1303) issued the Bull (a major decree)*Unam Sanctam* (1302) in which he crowned centuries of papal sparring with powers of state by succinctly claiming not only the supremacy of the pope spiritual matters, but also papal supremacy over the emperor.[9] The emperor was answerable to the pope in things temporal. Dante's *Monarchy* (1309–1313) is partly directed at this pope and rebuts his theory. With other earlier writers Dante held that "the authority of the Empire is not derived from the authority of the Supreme Pontiff," and that the monarch's authority comes directly from God and not through the Church as an intermediary.[10]

While the use of religion for political purposes and vice versa are woven throughout much of Western history, under Islam religion is consistently dominant unless Islam today is primarily an ideology of clan or state control in the guise of religion. Shaped partly by Byzantine and early Turkish influences, the merging of mosque into the state comes from the religious side. Overreaching by either the state or religion is always about the truth of the *human person*. A Christian writer temporarily imprisoned under the Nazi regime explains:

> (Thus) all the real problems of political theory are influenced by the *presupposed theory of the nature of man*: the problem of freedom and political authority, of the end of the state, of the justification of political power, of the relation between Church and state, of the limitation of the state's supreme power and sovereignty, of the fundamental rights of man, and even of the superiority of monarchy, democracy, or aristocracy (italics added).[11]

This political theorist, Heinrich Rommen, is among those Catholic thinkers who render natural law unambiguously compatible with constitutional democracies. His classic work (*The State in Catholic Thought,* 1945) serves as a counterpart to the later Muslim work by Farooq Hassan on the Islamic State (Chapter 3). Catholic historians other than Rommen also stress that "liberality, humaneness, tolerance, the things that were constantly spoken about, existed under enlightened royal absolutism. Not many years lay between the abolition of capital punishment by Catherine the Great in Russia and Grand duke Leopold in Tuscany, and the invention of the guillotine."[12] Hassan was probably misled by relatively late Western writings when he confused original natural law theory with Hegel's evolutionary state as a manifestation of the spirit, and with the morally arbitrary positive law of Jeremy Bentham.[13] These late inventions are not what classical or biblical writers detected when they independently pointed to deeper and therefore much earlier roots for what has been termed the natural law. As under the later Islam, God is the ultimate source: "I will place my laws in their minds and I will write them upon their hearts . . ." (Heb 8:9–10).[14]

Speaking well before the current Western encounter with Islam, but with a message Islam might champion, many European intellectuals stress that the writing on the human heart also implied a Writer. One such voice in the mid-twentieth century wrote, "We (also) see the bankruptcy of *logical* ethics without a religious basis . . . Indeed there is no 'compelling argument' not to slit anybody's throat except the Commandments given on Mount Sinai."[15] Dostoyevsky saw the same truth: "If there is no God, everything is permitted." The nineteenth century English social critic and historian Thomas Carlyle as a young man shed all formal religion and later was the one who famously defined man as a "tool making animal." This limited definition was later seized by Karl Marx and converted by Lenin and Stalin into a weapon of mass destruction. But Carlyle also discovered that he was left "without God in the world, (to which he then added) nevertheless in my heart He was present, and His heaven-written Law still stood legible and sacred there."[16] Might man, the whole man, be an eternity-destined being called to be attentive within and in his actions to the kingdom of God?

It is from the Christian tradition and the natural law, confirmed in the trial and error of a long history, that the Catholic Church proposes a morality, a specific corpus of social principles, for human life and action in the world. The human person *is* an anomaly and a special holiday within the natural cosmos. His dignity is proclaimed above any social order or even national identity in one line from John Paul II: "Man receives from God his essential dignity and with it *the capacity to transcend every social order* so as to move toward truth and goodness" (italics added).[17] Principles based on this theme are proposed by the Church merit the special interest of the followers of Islam because they do not come directly from a foreign religious creed, nor from the Classical world, nor from secularized ideologies of Western nation-states or any state.

From the Muslim side of a possible dialogue, Hassan explains that the Islamic State embodies an already complete *way of life*, and then he identifies some similarities and intractable differences with Western civil law. The Islamic novelty as a way of life is that there is no distinction between principles and what in the West is has emerged as legislated or positive law.

> On the basis of the monotheistic nature of Islam, the Islamic notions of law, justice, and society are very similar. Whereas, for example, in Common law these three terms have different meanings and history, they may be used interchangeably in Islam . . . In Western legal systems it is justice according to law; in Islam, *legal justice is the same as abstract justice* . . . The man-made systems are operative only under a rule of enforcement by a body imposing them. The Shari'a system *being divine is operative forever;* it remains fixed and perennial.[18]

The one-to-one identification of positive law with abstract justice corresponds to the medieval stage of political thought in the West. Edith Stein's insight on the medieval world (Chapter 2) is instructive and extended here: "To my way of thinking, this medieval view is based on the idea of pure law. The idea of pure law is not yet separated from the idea of morality, and apart from the latter is interpreted falsely (by being tied to time). It's absurd to suppose that the fact of having been made long ago should require unalterability (though possibly for some other reason having no temporal point of origin)."[19]

In the Western and Christian view, the center of the common good is not so much a Western equivalent to Hassan's abstract justice as it is the concrete and responsible human person who act in concert and in time. Man (male and female) is a person of genuine engagement who acts less abstractly and through the four moral virtues of justice, temperance, courage, and prudential judgment. He works toward a communion of persons in anticipation of a greater communion always hereafter.[20] The irreducible fact of the human person is to be infringed by neither the Church nor the state. We are to obey legitimate authority (Rom 13:1–7),[21] but finally "God rather than men" (Acts 5:29). Wholeness with a higher life is to be lived fully even here and now. All of us, even slave and free (Gal 3:26–29), are one in Christ, and are made for happiness rooted in a self-respect that is best expressed as respect for others. We are personally worthy of esteem received from others in society and equally privileged to give it. Evil cannot be done even with the misguided intention that a practical good might come of it (Rom 3:8). Because of the nature of man as the "capacity for God" even a temporary suspension of God's law is the suspension of the eternal Christ on two planks of wood.

In probably its central message, the Second Vatican Council witnesses that by revealing God to man, the reality Christ also reveals "man to man himself."[22] In this affirmation, the Church frees itself from any defensive elements in the finally successful reforms of the Council of Trent five centuries earlier. Following Trent, Pope Pius IV had intended to publish the acts of that council, but upon his untimely death others decided to avoid inevitable arguments by pulling a veil over the proceedings. As a result the partisan and weakly informed London history by Paolo Sarpi "became the authority all over Europe." This English version was contested in alternative histories (1656, 1686), but not credibly until the Vatican archives were opened in 1857. The countless un-catalogued council records were opened for unrestricted research by the Oratorian priest Augustin Theiner during the two years of the First Vatican Council (published in 1873).[23]

At the fully reported Second Vatican Council (1962–65) the intrinsic right and vocation of the laity to form principled but unscripted associations for the common good is clearly seen as part of the natural law and the Christian new life. Added the natural law rights, this right is "a true and proper right that is not derived from any kind of 'concession' by authority, but flows directly from the sacrament of baptism to participate in the Church's communion and mission."[24] The lay mission of Church members to engage and act in the public square is not delegated by the clerical site of the Church. The initial right and obligation to govern well is a human right and obligation grounded in the nature of the human person, and extending to the formation of a body politic itself, under whatever form reasonably serves the common good in a given setting. Governmental forms thrown up by history have included democratic nation-states, but also multinational states, monarchies and aristocracies, and military dictatorships. For centuries in the West the dynastic family model amply proved itself both functional and susceptible to human imperfection and corruption. Measuring life here on earth against our eternal calling, the Church makes no claim to a direct worldly mission that belongs to civil authority. Referring always to the Gospel, and to the bitter lessons of experience, the Church clearly affirms that: "This (our eternal destiny), and this alone, is the principle which inspires the Church's social doctrine."[25]

The institutional preconditions for personal liberty, as they happened to unfold in the West, do not exist in the pure Islamic State. Nevertheless, Hassan detects a verse in the *Qur'an* which might be expanded upon by Muslims as a plausible natural law contact point between the Church, the West and Islam. He claims that "the law of Islam is framed on *human nature*." (italics added).[26] Unfortunately conflating a distinct natural law and the bulk of Islamic belief, the *Qur'an* reads: "Therefore, stand firm in your devotion to the true Faith, the upright Faith which God created for mankind to embrace. *God's creation cannot be changed.* This is surely the right faith, although most men may not know it'" (Q 30:30, italics added). How might acceptance of the universal natural law be parsed from this verse, and others in the *Qur'an* alluding to "guidance" given to Adam? For example, "Then He (the Lord) had mercy on him (Adam); He relented towards him and rightly guided him . . . When My guidance is revealed to you, he that follows it shall neither err nor grieve . . ." (Q 20:122–4). In the *Qur'an* the term fitrah (not fitnah) is defined by Sufis as guidance or a predisposition from within and from above, more than as an instinct. Fitrah leads to a truthful life for those who have a longing soul: "those who have faith and do righteous deeds."[27] To be explored as a contact point is the degree to which this is in both secular and Christian terms the natural law, to what degree it might be Gnostic pantheism.

Within the West, a common presupposition is that a superior modernity was released only when the religious orientation was broken. The assertion is that "(It was) the failure of Europeans to agree upon the truths of religion, within and across state boundaries, that opened the door to secularism and modern science."[28] Modernity is partly a product of the Alpine wedge driven between Protestant and Catholic Christian cultures in the Reformation. If this simplification is true and useful, it does not really offer Muslims a path to modernity in the more polyglot world of Islam. There is no convenient geographic divide today between Muslim religious sects. Historically, the best comparison between Islam and the watershed sixteenth century Reformation was the division in the same century between Shi'ite Persia (Iran) and the Ottoman sultanate to the West. This intra-religious wedge was not productive of a new culture and contributed to the long decline from the Ottoman golden age.

In contrast with the Islamic State today and the sovereign status of Shari'a, the Church in the Second Vatican Council speaks clearly of the autonomy of life on earth: "If by the autonomy of earthly affairs we mean that created things and societies themselves enjoy their own laws and values, which must be gradually deciphered, put to use, and regulated by men, then it is entirely right to demand that autonomy. Such is not merely required by modern man, but it harmonizes also with the will of the Creator. For by the very circumstances of their having been *created all things are endowed with their own stability, truth, goodness, proper laws, and order*" (italics added).[29] It follows that the Church's proposed social principles serve a discoverable common good and then are geared toward discernment of ends that are just, and decisions and actions toward these ends. The grounding principles are *not* another ideology, nor a Christian political theory. Instead, the principles are fully human, not political:

> Catholic political philosophy asserts that in *human nature* is the origin of the state. Here it must be stated that 'human nature' should be understood in its full philosophical meaning. Human nature does not mean the empirical, psychological nature as the politician or the advertising businessman sees it. The state originates in the bodily and spiritual nature of man. Nature or essence is also the end of man's activity and striving. Therefore the political status is necessary for the *fulfillment* of man's end, that state is an intentional disposition of human nature . . . the state is *not* a supernatural, immediately divine establishment. Yet, as originating in human nature, divinely established, the state is part and subject of the order of the Creator.[30]

Authorities of the Islamic State regard themselves as the "executors of the law basically made by God."[31] In the West, consistent with the truth discovered within, it is more the people who are the first executors and protagonists of their own true fulfillment as free *and* responsible beings. This is often to be done through associations other than the state. Islamic executors of divine law through the state are reminiscent of Charlemagne who was contemporary with early Islam:

> (T)he religion of Charles (Charlemagne) was like that of Islam, a religion of the sword, and his private life, in spite of his sincere piety, resembled that of a

Moslem ruler. Yet for all of that, he claimed direct authority over the Church and intervened even in matters of dogma. In the first letter to Leo III, he was 'the representative of God who has to protect and govern all the members of god,' he is 'Lord and Father, King and Priest, the Leader and Guide for all Christians.'[32]

Very much *un*like Shari'a law and the Mosque-state, in the West today the internal canon law of the Church is fully separated from civil law. This "separation" has been won with great difficulty to both Church and state over a period of two millennia.[33] Near our own time, beginning in the fifteenth century, new movements of nationalism were partly recognized through concordats between the Church and the emerging nation-states. Later centuries brought the French Revolution and nationalist reactions to Napoleonic conquest. The Industrial Revolution and the reactionary flight into Romanticism both contributed further to the formation of modern and always imperfect nation-states in the West.[34] This evolution of the Western nation-state is not homogeneous and does not offer a clear goal for Islam. Even the early outcomes varied widely "(The nation-state) was illustrated in different ways by Prussia, absolutist and narrowly Lutheran; by France, claiming theological support for the divine right of kings; and by England, building up parliamentary government on a basis of administrative indifference to the common people and of intolerance towards the Catholic religion."[35] The Church strives to separate itself from an earlier pattern of alliance with monarchies or more generally any particular form of government.[36] Such alliances were opportunistic artifacts cultivated mostly by the Jesuits during the Counter Reformation to offset Protestantism inroads with the lower social classes.

The modern Catholic view on Church and State relations has been concisely stated in recent correspondence with the Chinese people. In his historic letter to the Church in China (2007), Pope Benedict writes:

> The Catholic Church which is in China does not have a mission to change the structure or administration of the State; rather her mission is to proclaim Christ to men and women as the Saviour of the world, basing herself—in carrying out her proper apostolate—on the power of God. As I recalled in my *Encyclical Deus Caritas Est* (God is Love, 2006) . . . *The Church cannot and must not take upon herself the political battle to bring about the most just society possible. She cannot and must not replace the State. Yet at the same time she cannot and must not remain on the sidelines in the fight for justice.* She has to play her part through rational argument and she has to reawaken the spiritual energy without which justice, which always demands sacrifice, cannot prevail and prosper. A just society must be the achievement of politics, not of the Church . . . (italics added).[37]

The remainder of this chapter gives background and then begins to explore a possible body of fully Christian and yet interreligious and intercultural principles proposed (not imposed) by the Church. These principles apply to the modern world as well as the world of Islam which does not clearly recognize the temporal domain as a vocation for the laity. In the Islamic State there is no distinct laity because theoretically there is no distinct clergy.

INWARD AND OUTWARD ENGAGEMENT: THE TWO VATICAN COUNCILS

The Church's vision for distinct roles for Church and state is advanced by the combined work of the First and Second Vatican Councils (1869–70 and 1963–5). The comparison with Islam is the distinction between Church and state, a distinction with a well-grounded message about the human person and at the same time open to the world. This distinction is learned and rescued from a long and complex history. The world of Islam does not enjoy the costly luxury of centuries to find its own path. The two recent Church councils *together* constitute a phased encounter—both internal and external—between the Church and the modern world. Attention first shifts from the pretense of worldly power for the *papacy* to a clarified papal *primacy* within the Church. In late nineteenth century Europe, the *First Vatican Council* was convened at a crisis point partly pitting the autonomy of the Church against the advance of secular nation-states. This evolution especially includes the Gallican and Church-dominating state imposed earlier by Napoleon and then the last phases of Italian national unification. Was the Vatican to be reduced within Italy to a department of state and a municipal sector within its capital city of Rome?

In 1869 the Council first considered a conciliar document (*De Ecclesia Christi* [The Church of Christ]) touching on Church and state as two distinct societies. It affirmed the independence of the Church from the nation-states and especially from localizing tendencies of the states toward national churches and sometimes the destruction of the Church altogether.[38] In its Dogmatic Constitution, *Dei Filius*, the Council worked on the theological stumbling block found also in Islamic thought, namely the relationship between the autonomy of a distant God and the responsible freedom—the seemingly competing autonomy—of man. Writes the Council in the opening chapter: "By his *providence* God protects and governs all things which he has made . . . For 'all are open and laid bare to his eyes (cf. Heb 4:13), all those things which are yet to come into existence through the *free actions* of creatures" (italics added).[39]

The political and localizing tendencies challenging the Council had been symbiotic for centuries with the opposite trend of Church centralization. By the time of Henry VIII in England, nationalist tendencies across Protestant Europe finally provided a counter-identity to the Catholic Church and in Germany Martin Luther raised up the nation-state as a secular and religious power in place of the Church. The Ottoman's saw advantage in supporting Lutherans and Queen Elizabeth in England at least as "useful distraction of the Catholic powers."[40] The many variations of nationalism in Reformation Europe included not only the Lutheran model and the Calvinist theocracy in Geneva, but also the earlier fifteenth century Spanish church-state of the Moors. By 1682 the Gallican Articles in France worked to subordinate the Church to the state, by then the premiere monarchy in all of Europe. In 1813 Napoleon took Pope Pius VI prisoner and kidnapped him to France where he extracted a concession of subservience to the French Empire (the Concordat of Fontanbleau, 1813). Only after Napoleon was decisively defeated at Leipzig in 1814 was the pope reinstated in Rome.

At the Congress of Vienna (1815) the victorious powers of Europe restored the earlier monarchies as well as the Papal States. The Protestant historian Leopold von Ranke finds in the papal restoration one of those historical reversals that so often confound simple historical narrative. Papal supporters served the ideal of secular legitimacy and were mostly from the non-Catholic Alliance of Russia, Prussia and England, alongside Catholic Austria. Decades later, following the First Vatican Council in 1870,[41] Prussian German launched a short-lived attempt to domesticate its share of the universal Church as an administrative department of state (the *Kulturkampf*: cultural struggle). Added to these early modern political currents, the First Vatican Council also felt the lengthening shadow of materialism in its various forms. Marx's and Engle's publication of the *Communist Manifesto* (1848) proposed an international secular religion under its own altogether universal, materialistic, and communist ideology. The Council took an important step in overcoming the pitfalls of monarchic alliances, but it also was faced with heightened tensions between religion and science at the center of which were long-held resentments over the Galileo incident. With the success of the Italian army came broader access to the Vatican Archives (noted above) and at least partial publication of the Galileo manuscripts. These papers were only a small part of the massive collection pirated off to Paris by Napoleon in 1810–11 (and most was returned in 1817). In the environment of the late nineteenth century prudence now lay on the side of expedient access to the records rather than continued secrecy (example: Galileo was imprisoned for twenty-two days, not years, and was not badly treated).[42]

Doctrinally, the First Vatican Council considered whether it was "opportune" to clearly affirm and delimit—by defining—the permanent nature of Church authority. This authority is received from Christ and relates to the salvation of man as a spiritual and moral being in the world and yet destined for eternity. The Council surgically defined the role of the papal office within the broader "infallibility" of gathered witnesses—a Church—permanently indwelled by the Holy Spirit. Strong reservations of any such definition hinged on whether any definition was even useful. Would such a formal doctrine be perceived as the last left-over scrap from a fading and defeated world autocracy? Would it become a final barrier to reunion with the schismatic Orthodox Churches and rapprochement with Protestant bodies? Would it degenerate into license toward unrepentant conservatism, or alternatively, a license to invent truth and to even manipulate the new secular politics?[43]

A short time after Trent (1545–63), for example, Pope Paul IV still formally claimed (not infallibly) that the pope "has full authority and power over nations and kingdoms; he judges all and can in this world be judged by none."[44] Significantly, the precise title of the doctrine defined in 1870 is not broadly "the pope's infallibility," but narrowly "the infallibility of the pope's dogmatic pronouncements"[45] as these in one way or another proclaim the reality of the Incarnation. This infallibility is not a positive license toward novelty, as we find increasingly in secular applications of positive law (for example, politically correct redefinition of the "family"), nor is papal infallibility ever to be bulked together with Shari'a law as might be proposed by secular alarmists. The doctrine of infallibility and Shari'a are more opposite than similar. The effect of the definition is "not to enfeeble the freedom or vigour of human thought in religious speculation, but to resist and control its extravagance."[46] By the time of the council clarity on the internal accountability and nature of the Church—of the papacy in collegiality with the bishops—had already received an early boost even under the Gregorian reforms of the twelfth century, long before the paired Vatican councils dealt explicitly with these themes. From the beginning, the primacy of the papacy was distinct but inseparable from the episcopacy or the office of bishops.[47] The recognized important of bishops is seen later in their heightened role in the Council of Trent and their lead responsibility for carrying out its initiatives and long-awaited reforms.

With the theologian and philosopher Thomas Aquinas the Church holds that even prior to any divine revelation, the human intellect itself is "infallible" in a real sense. The intellect is the capacity to know the truth about being, however incompletely. With natural knowledge, false judgments are caused by incomplete information or human frailty. Under the natural law written directly on human hearts, and prior to moral decisions, the human person infallibly knows, however obscurely, the first objective norm of morality. The knowledge and practice of good and evil—of pretending to have it both ways—is either a betrayal or a deception, but it is not knowledge. The

First Vatican Council defended the proposition that even when every known human weakness and corruption is found within the Church, the Church distinct from any of its members remains intact, accountable, and secure in Christ as its head.

Compared to this model and ever new reality, Islam is archaic by confusing the Holy Spirit, sent by the incarnate Christ, with its own only human founder. Within Islam, al-Ghazali defended the mainstream against the Ta'limite sect by asserting "the need for an authoritative teacher who must also be infallible. But our infallible teacher is Muhammad—God's blessing and peace be upon him!" And then, "Today I have perfected for you your religion and have accorded you my full favor" (Q 5:3 or 5).[48] Near the time of the First Vatican Council, a prominent Anglican convert to Catholicism, John Henry Cardinal Newman, produced the *Essay on the Development of Christian Doctrine*.[49] Described as "the one man in Europe whose mind struggled with the predicament of the Catholic faith in a modern world of 'scientific history,'"[50] and now regarded as "the Father of Vatican II" (1962–5), Newman explains that a doctrinal understanding of revelation can be deepened while remaining essentially the same as from the beginning. Given the choice of either cloture or filibuster, he turns to an investigation that is both faithful and reasoned. His vision is based partly on the *Commonitorium* of the early fifth century St. Vincent of Lerins. To greatly generalize Newman's presentation, he proposed that authentic growth within revealed Truth must be always in clear continuity with—not abrogate—what has come before and yet may render explicit what previously was implicit.[51] While a gift can be unpacked, the gift remains the same. In a letter (1860) to William Wilberforce, a son of the earlier reformer of the slave trade in the British Parliament, Newman explained the core "deposit of faith" (2 Tim 1:14) this way: "Certainly a Catholic is required, simply to believe, what our Lord delivered to the Apostles to propound and promulgate—and again to believe that the Church has the gift of determining what those things are . . ."[52]

The role of the Church, neither conservative and progressive, is to proclaim with enduring clarity the "deposit of faith." Without this unbroken thread of continuity, the forever original revelation *received* from the Other, whether passed on in writing or orally—becomes an oracle subject to novel or pluripotent alteration. Even the faith could become a work of ventriloquism or a mono-idolatry. In his introduction to the *Catechism* completed in 1992–97, following the Second Vatican Council, pope "John Paul, Bishop and Servant of the Servants of God" summarizes the guiding mission: "Guarding the deposit of faith is the mission which the Lord entrusted to his Church, and which she fulfills in every age."[53] Natural science works in much the same way beginning with its external reference as the data of the physical universe,[54] rather than the historical and mystical datum of the witnessed Incarnation (Jn 14:16–17, Acts 2:1–13).

The Church's witnessing authority (e.g., Acts 20:28) on the reality of Christ—its magisterium—has greatest weight for things divinely revealed and "necessary for salvation," and which are definitively proposed. Other matters also benefit, such as things connected logically as is the natural law, or others that are often repeated by the Church.[55] That the Church is a visible institution is found in both Tradition and Scripture,[56] but it is also a mystery. More than an institution, it is the mystical body of Christ, with Christ rather than the pope as its head. This mystery is powerfully revealed to Paul on the Road to Damascus: "Saul, Saul, why do you persecute *me*" (Acts 9:3–6, italics added). The personal nature to us of this relationship is also witnessed by St. Paul: "I have been crucified with Christ, and the life I live now is not my own; Christ is living in me" (Gal 2:19–20); and even for us in the Beatitudes: "I was hungry, and you gave me food" (Mt 25:35).

The delineated teaching authority of the Church is a scandal to both the world of Islam and to secular thought. The magisterium contrasts with Islam by distinguishing between historical accretion and circumstances and the reliable core truth of the Incarnation as the received "deposit of faith." Islam admits instead to continous revelation within history. This ongoing revelation not only adds to, but may also cancel previous revelations. Authorization is contained in the *Qur'an* itself: "Whenever We suppress a verse or cause it to be forgotten, We bring one which is better or similar. Do you not know that God is Almighty?" (Q 2:106). Typically unresolved between commentators and critics is the critical question whether the early and peaceful definitions of jihad from the Meccan period are cancelled or only supplemented by later warlike connotations beginning in the Medina period (after 622 A.D.).

Islam is often interpreted in the West as a natural religion, but its own self-image also differs from this caricature, and it differs from the Christian fidelity to Christ as the ultimate public revelation of the divine in history. The self-image of the *Qur'an* is presented by scholars as less a book than a "self-aware" oral tradition that is part of an ongoing divine "writing" and "rewriting."[57] Where Christianity distinguishes between prophecy and fulfillment, and between public and private revelations, Islam makes no such distinctions. Within the Western experience, natural scientists might appreciate another distinction in that the greatly mishandled Galileo incident (1563–1641) has no connection to the Church's precisely bounded "infallible" and formal teaching mission regarding the salvation of man. A blunder and worse, resulting in "tragic mutual incomprehension" (John Paul II, 1992), the Galileo case involves more of an obtuse disciplinary error and even backroom intrigue rather than any formal pronouncement of "irreformable" teachings.

The Bible deals with faith and the salvation of man and is not a treatise on natural science. This view is well articulated by Galileo himself who drew support in part from St. Augustine: "The inspired writers knew what the truth was about the heavens, but the Spirit of God that spoke through them did not choose to teach it to men, as it was no use for salvation." Of this more original view Giorgio Santillana writes that "(T)he views concerning the interpretation of Scripture contained in Galileo's theological letters have become the official doctrine of the Church since Leo XIII's encyclical *Providentissimus Deus* (The Providence of God) of 1893."[58] In the seventeenth century, members of the Galileo commission refused to comprehend and probably manipulated[59] the proceedings at what was an early stage of the new scientific age.[60] The first religious figures to personally denounce the much earlier Copernicus (1473–1543) were the Protestants Luther and Calvin. Official reaction from Rome came more than seventy years later (when his book was placed on the *Index*, 1616). Free exploration of the book of creation, different than the book of Scripture, then was suppressed in Italy—the center of the Catholic world—and unwittingly handed to the Protestant nations. The deep cultural wound still festers today, "No further attempt was made to combine the world of matter and the world of faith."[61] In the eleventh century the Sufi al-Ghazali defined the relationship between science and things of faith "Great indeed is the crime against religion committed by the denial of (these) mathematical sciences. For the revealed Law nowhere undertakes to deny or affirm these sciences, and the latter nowhere address themselves to religious matters."[62]

Rarely mentioned and more amusing than the Galileo affair, was Pope Alexander's delineation of the global north-to-south Line of Demarcation in 1492. All discoveries by explorers to the west of the Azores were to belong to Spain and those to the east to Portugal. As in the Galileo case, no formal claim of infallibility was attached the geographical assumption that the split was fair.[63] Today, issue can be taken with a quite different and equally non-scientific "line of demarcation." The new edicts come from the secular power and by acclamation do claim a kind of secular and political infallibility in matters of life and death. Of the practice of "partial birth" abortions jurists debate the precise line at which a birthing child becomes a "human being," apparently taken to be the moment of complete contact with the air we breathe. Modern embryology and physiology . . . the very pre-modern Solomon, unschooled in modern sophistries, was quite able to decide without splitting the baby which of two claimants was the mother and real protector of a disputed child (1 Ki 3:16–28). And the combination of technological sophistication and marketing imperatives did not yet exist to use of fetal tissue in vaccines and in sweetener tests for some beverages.

In another discourse of our own day, the Church is not implicated in the debate between literal creation*ists* and evolution*ists*. The Church simply maintains, first, that *existence* at all levels is a gift in relation to a Creator who is more than a cause, but "the cause of causes."[64] The cause of causes is the self-sufficient (*sub-sisting*) act of being itself. According to modern physics the motion of any *ex-isting* body can be described by simple laws only when measured relative to all other existing matter in the universe. The moment of "creation" (of whatever duration) is an *act,* even an ecstasy. The inviolable soul that ponders such matters comes immediately from the creating God literally as another *given*.[65] Pope Benedict XVI makes this observation: "Whereas the Middle Ages had attempted a 'derivation of all science from theology' (Bonaventure), we can speak here about a derivation of all reality from 'evolution,' which believes that it can also account for knowledge, ethics, and religion in terms of the general scheme of evolution."[66] The human person—including every reader of these lines—is always more than an accident within a larger accident.

In the political scene of the nineteenth century, Napoleon had at least minimal regard for religion, "not as the mystery of the Incarnation, but as the secret to social order."[67] But with Napoleon—as possibly with Islam—the religion is one of rationalism and rationalization which in all cases distances us from the gifted presence of a God who is love. Not His existence—Deists accepted this—or even His sovereignty (the essence of Islam), but His unbounded and even sacrificial presence. As in Islam, Napoleon had a place for predestination; both conquests turned to this expression of fatalism as a way of mobilizing the troops to battle. In 1806 when Pope Pius VII rejected opportunities to capitulate to Napoleon and was taken captive, Napoleon wrote, "Your Holiness is Sovereign in Rome, but I am Roman Emperor."

Nearly a century after Napoleon, the First Vatican Council left his ghost and all the radical secularists behind, as well as the ultra-conservative "New Ultramontanes." The New Ultramontanes, mostly in France, looked back to the false certainties of pre-1789 prince-bishops and mergers of Church and crown.[68] In the final months prior to the Council, the specter of papal monarchism was set forth for the English speaking and especially the American audience in historic detail by Catholic Germans. Bulked together with the "Liberals," the writers were at once loyal, critical, and well-informed on history. They feared ratification of past papal pretensions and imagined that Pope Pius IX's wide-ranging grievance list—the "Syllabus of Errors" (1864)—might be generalized from specific cases and labeled infallible, and finally that despite all of history that the occupant of the papal chair might be declared free of personal faults. As an aside, the condemned final and sweeping proposition in the "Syllabus" asserted that "The Roman Pontiff can, and ought to, reconcile and come to terms with progress, liberalism, and modern civilization" (n. 80). If permanently endorsed this ideology would have committed the Church to one prevailing governmental form over all others and in all unforeseen circumstances.

Rather than this political agenda, the council agenda was an effort to offset the opposite ecclesiology of sixteenth century Luther, who held the (Islam-like) view that the popular *nation* and church are one[69] and that the nation-state is sovereign in all things. While in a minority, one modern central European historian makes an explicit comparison between early Protestant—not Catholic intuitions and Islamic culture:

> There is something decidedly Islamic is original Protestantism, with its idea of an all-controlling hidden God and His infallible Prophet, its secularization of marriage, its Puritanism and messianism. Even today some of the survivals of original (i.e., pre-liberal) Protestantism in remote parts of Scandinavia, Holland, Scotland and the United States have, at least culturally, more affinity with the Wahhabis than with Catholics from which they stem. It must be borne in mind that not so much the authoritarian organization but the liberal theology of Catholicism was the target of the reformers.[70]

Especially when compared to these and many other crosscurrents, the moderate tenor of debate at the First Vatican Council was widely praised by those who actually took part.[71] But these internal deliberations were overwhelmed by external political and military events. On the day after the final vote on the precise definition of the papal role in infallibility (July 18, 1870), war was declared between France and Germany (Prussia), the last two major European regions to constitute themselves as nation-states (1871). Italy was declared a kingdom a decade earlier in 1861, but the papal state had remained apart as a protectorate of France. The council's attention to internal collegiality between the pope and the bishops was not adjourned, but was disrupted by politics and gunpowder and then suspended indefinitely.[72] For the next two generations the pope turned down a state pension and the implied status as a state employee, and relied instead on the worldwide annual Peter's Pence collection. (This collection began as a funding source for the construction of St. Peter's Cathedral in Rome. When conveyance of these funds from Germany was blocked by the state, a more aggressive local sale of indulgences resulted, helping to shape the explosive ecclesial grievances of one Martin Luther.) For sixty years the besieged pope and his successors remained under self confinement as a "prisoner of the Vatican" (1870–1929). The concordat signed in 1929 between Pope Pius XI and the Fascist dictator Benito Mussolini mutually recognized the nation-state of Italy and the sovereign Vatican city-state.[73] It was only after this interregnum and two world wars that the complete internal definition of collegiality among the bishops was achieved, and that the Church re-engaged as a witness and moral voice in the modern world (the Second Vatican Council, 1962–1965).[74]

The signal contribution of the First Vatican Council to the future is two-fold. First is the clear demarcation of direct and limited matters of faith and morals, and second is the imposed and self-imposed exclusion of the Church from concrete solutions to intricate political and economic questions of the day. The pruned definition of infallibility draws from the use of both faith and reason. The entire definition is framed within a primary distinction between things of faith and morals, apart from other things of prudential judgment belonging to the governmental process. This pruning of historical accretions and errors contrasts with the parallel tipping point in the world of Islam. Apparently by a consensus process (ijma) in ninth century Baghdad, Arabia decided that the *Qur'an* as a whole was of the essence of God. The demands of sectarian and intertribal harmony mingled with the disruptions of the Mu'tazilite movement to position the *Qur'an* an undisputed rallying banner or icon of unity among factions as well as belief toward Allah.

In Europe and following the Council, the papacy no longer controlled the Papal States—territory in central Italy dating back a full millennium as a gift from Charlemagne. This loss added to the new and legitimate moral prestige of the Church. As a sovereign state, the Church now has only one hundred and ten acres and no territorial ambitions or special interests on the new land-scape of sovereign nation-states.[75] At the previous Council (Trent, 1545–63) the influence of the Catholic political sovereigns—France, Austria, and Spain (Protestant Germany having excluded itself)—was felt throughout the pro-ceedings, and the Council outcomes depended upon their concurrence. The Protestant historian Leopold Ranke finds this earlier alliance of the Church with the monarchies "in some degree analogous with the tendency of Protes-tantism to combine the episcopal and sovereign rights . . . (He adds that Pius IV at the Reformation Era Council of Trent) was the first pontiff by whom that tendency of the hierarchy to oppose itself to the temporal sovereigns, was deliberately and purposely abandoned."[76]

Following the First Vatican Council, cozy symbiosis with monarchies yielded to a different future. Today, the Church *proposes* principles and recommendations to those directly responsible for the common good. In the early twentieth century Pope Benedict XV regarded both the First World War and even its eventual terms of peace to be immoral. On August 15, 1917 he proposed "concrete and practical propositions" for peace, but these were ignored largely over the contentious issue of restitution of seized territories. Ludendorff feared that public support in Germany for the pope's peace with-out a victory surely would be followed in his country by public resentment and even revolution.[77] In early 1918 the pope's proposals did influence parts of the Fourteen Points of Peace promoted by President Wilson at Versailles.[78]

After a Second World War and well into the Cold War, the Church in the *Second Vatican Council* (1963–5) looked for new ways to better encounter and give hope to the modern world.[79] While celebrating the Feast of the Holy Family, shortly after the Council was convened, the new Pope Paul VI discovered at Nazareth a silence that relieves us of that "cacophony of strident protests and conflicting claims so characteristic of these turbulent times." A new tone already had been set for the Council by the convening Pope John XXIII. In 1961 his *Mater et Magistra* (Mother and Teacher) defended human rights and responsibilities in a modern and global world. *Pacem en Terris* (Peace on Earth, 1963) provided a needed context for approaching the struggle between the West and the Communist world. Teaching that human rights are "universal, inviolable, and inalienable," his document is credited for helping to create a new environment within which the 1963 Nuclear Test Ban Treaty could be concluded. Unlike all earlier Church documents, *Pacem en Terris* and others developed by the Second Vatican Council avoid anathemas and are addressed broadly to "all men of goodwill."

Beyond urgent secular affairs, the Council also sought to improve relations with other parts of Christendom and with other religions including Islam. Already decades prior to the Second Vatican Council, Pope Pius X had considered the adaptability of the Church as the bearer of a consistent message about revelation and natural law. He wrote, "Without ever endangering the integrity or the immutability of faith and morals and always preserving her sacred rights, she bends and accommodates herself easily in all contingent and accidental things, to the vicissitudes of times and to the exigencies of society."[80] Living the Christian revelation "today," a central theme of the Council, is termed in Latin "*aggiornamento*" and the prerequisite deepening of the Church's self-understanding, partly achieved in the First Vatican Council, is "*ressourcement*," (a French term meaning retrieval and renewal of what the Church is, especially as found in the early Church Fathers). The Council understanding of "updating" is in reality a "today-ing" in Christ who is the same Christ yesterday, today and forever (Heb 13:8).[81]

The Muslim approach to interreligious dialogue is different. It finds both its start point and end point in a first "principle of religious pluralism, which is crucial to any meaningful dialogue."[82] Under this imprint of a big tent, divine revelation and the human religious response are indistinguishable. All religions, especially if they are "of the book," are potentially equivalent as varied expressions of original Islam which regards itself as above all other religions. Islam and secularism appear very much alike in this premise. The alternative premise, termed by the Church the "deposit of faith" and which is accessible to conceptual clarity, is that revelation is clearly and distinctly something actually received from beyond ourselves. Mutual respect among various faithful is not to be confused with a conceptually obscure pluralism of beliefs.

Highlights of the Second Vatican Council touch directly and indirectly on the specific encounter between the Church and the followers of Islam. A key document is the dogmatic constitution *Dei Verbum* (Divine Revelation). Christianity is compatible with Islam in overlapping, beliefs and to the extent that Islam does not claim to be a new public revelation: "The Christian dispensation, therefore, as the new and definitive covenant, will never pass away, *and we now await no further new public revelation* before the glorious manifestation of the Lord Jesus Christ (cf 1 Tim 6:14, Tit. 2:13)" (italics added).[83] The certainty that we await no further public revelation comes with Christ as the fulfillment of Scripture, and with the assistance of the Holy Spirit indwelling in the Church from Pentecost forward (see Jn 14:16–17, 15:26, 16:7). The Christian believes that Christ is the very presence of God really with us (Emmanuel). Without leaving us He has also returned to the Father whom He never left. This presence—centered as the Incarnation—is the mystery of the eternal Trinity as it freely enters into and redeems created time and human history.

The difference between Christianity and Islam is not between the Bible and the *Qur'an*, but between Christ the Word made Flesh and the *Qur'an*. The Council teaches that "Jesus perfected revelation by fulfilling it through His whole work of making Himself present and manifesting Himself: through His words and deeds . . . (and His) death and glorious resurrection . . ."[84] From the Islamic perspective, the prominent scholar Mahmoud Ayoub today expresses the hope that interreligious understanding "will accommodate Islam not as a heresy of true Christianity but as an authentic expression of the divine and immutable truth."[85] One way that this hope might advance within the Christian worldview would be if Islam could be validated as partly a *private* revelation or locution (Chapter 2), but not a new public revelation from a God exercising damage control. On this count Islam itself claims to be a restoration of the religion of Abraham rather than anything new, but still the Trinity and knowledge of the divinity of Christ cannot be redacted from history as done my Muslim scholars.

Besides *Dei Verbum*, general engagement by the Church or its members in the world is chartered in a second of four dogmatic constitutions, *Gaudium et Spes* (The Church in the Modern World).[86] Misleading because selectively quoted, the opening line was not a one-dimensional call to false optimism. The complete opening phrase is "The joys and the hopes, *the griefs and the anxieties* of the men of this age . . . and . . . of the followers of Christ."[87]

Deeper than human optimism (the first half of the phrase) the Catholic Church sees the revelation of man's own essential dignity as contained not in human effort alone, but fully in the Incarnation: "Christ the Lord, Christ, the final Adam, by the revelation of the mystery of the Father and His love, *fully reveals man to man himself* and makes his supreme calling clear" (italics added).[88] Partly based upon this two-fold revelation the Council remarks:

> The political community and the Church are autonomous and independent of each other in their own fields. Nevertheless, both are devoted to the personal vocation of man, though under different titles . . . The Church, for its part, being founded in love of the Redeemer, contributes toward the spread of justice and charity among nations and within the border of nations themselves. By preaching the truths of the Gospel and clarifying sectors of human activity through its teaching and the witness of its members, the Church respects and encourages political freedom and responsibility of the citizen.[89]

St. Basil, a fourth century bishop of Asia Minor in modern-day Turkey, contemplates the total self-emptying of the incarnate Christ the Redeemer, his total participation in our "griefs and anxieties." He writes, "You must realize how great you are by reflecting on the price that was paid for you; look at the price that was paid for your ransom *and acknowledge your dignity*" (italics added).[90] The Council finds "a certain likeness between the union of the divine Persons" and our union in truth and charity. "This likeness reveals that man, who is the only creature on earth which God will for itself, cannot fully find himself except through a sincere gift of himself."[91] Also less clear in Islam is the redeeming insight that it is man as a person both male and female who is elevated above all the rest of creation. He/she is created and fully loved *for his own sake*—in the very "image of God."[92] Unsuspected without revelation, we are in fact temples of the Holy Spirit (1 Cor 3:16). The *Qur'an* never speaks of God as Father and His children, only of Lord and servants with whom he is most compassionate. But, from the totally gifted and better understood image-ness revealed in Christ comes profound personal dignity and freedom—a freedom *for* the truth found dwelling even within ourselves.

This freedom for the truth is fulfilled in relationship with others, and involves a most significant and distinct citizen role in the political domain. The political endeavor is for some a Christian vocation rather than the domain of "executors" of divine law in the Islamic State. Overcome finally in *Gaudium et Spes*, in the words of the theologian von Balthasar, is an earlier dividing line between the tradition of great theologians culminating in Aquinas, and the later "narrowing-down of Christian theology merely to the training of pastors or to academic specialization of the schools . . ." (Demanded afresh is a new) "understanding of revelation in the context of the history of the world and the actual present."[93] In the sixteenth century immediately after the Council of Trent, St. Francis de Sales remarked that religious devotion must and should be tailored to one's vocation and in very modern terms and that to dismiss this point could be "ridiculous, unorganized, and insupportable."[94]

Two other council documents that directly address non-Christian religions merit attention here. *Lumen Gentium* (The Dogmatic Constitution on the Church) speaks specifically of Islam:

> (But) the plan of salvation also includes those who acknowledge the Creator. In the first place among these there are the Moslems, who, professing to hold the faith of Abraham, along with us adore the one and merciful God, who on the last day will judge mankind. Nor is God Himself far distant from those who in shadows and images seek the unknown God, for it is He who gives to all men life and breath and every other gift (cf. Acts 17:25–28), and who as Savior wills that all men be saved (cf. 1 Tim. 2:4)[95]

A key scriptural phrase from St. Paul, much in harmony with verses appearing in the later *Qur'an*, regards the inscrutable decrees of God: "Oh, the depth of the riches of the wisdom and the knowledge of God! How incomprehensible are his judgments and how unsearchable his ways! For Who has known the mind of the Lord, or who has been his counselor?" (Rom 11:33–4). But, again, even more inscrutable than the unknowability of a distant God, and a consequence of this immeasurable personality, is the infinite degree of his totally free self-donation and his actual coming in Christ. God is with us (Emmanuel).

Finally, the *Declaration on the Relationship of the Church to Non-Christian Religions* "gives primary consideration . . . to what human beings have in common and to what promotes fellowship among them." Accompanying notes clarify that attention to commonalities "does not deny or neglect differences."[96] The Council is ever attentive to the mysterious workings of the Spirit, and therefore, the opportunity for dialogue among all of those of good will:

> The Catholic Church rejects nothing which is true and holy in these religions. She looks with sincere respect upon those ways of conduct and of life, those rules and teachings which, though differing in many particulars from what she holds and sets forth, nevertheless often reflect a ray of that Truth which enlightens all men. Indeed, she proclaims and must ever proclaim Christ, 'the way, the truth, and the life' (John 14:6), in whom men find the fullness of religious life, and in whom God has reconciled all things to Himself (cf. 2 Cor 5:18–19).[97]

In specific reference to similarities with Islam, the Council makes this extended observation:

Upon the Moslems, too, the Church looks with esteem. They adore one God, living and enduring, merciful and all powerful, Maker of heaven and earth and Speaker to men. They strive to submit wholeheartedly even to His inscrutable decrees, just as did Abraham, with whom the Islamic faith is pleased to associate itself. Though they do not acknowledge Jesus as God, they revere Him as prophet. They also honor Mary, His virgin mother; at times they call on her, too, with devotion. In addition they await the Day of Judgment when God will give each man his due after raising him up. Consequently, they prize the moral life, and give worship to God especially through prayer, almsgiving, and fasting.[98]

The relationship between the state and personal religious freedom is the topic of the Council Fathers *Declaration on Religious Freedom* (1965). This was the last and most controversial document promulgated by the Second Vatican Council. The First Vatican Council (and later Pope Leo XIII) had demanded the freedom of the Church from nationalist movements such as the consolidation of Italy in 1871 which left the pope a "prisoner of the Vatican." Where the first council asserted freedom for the Church as an institution, the second claims for individual persons freedom from governmental coercion or restraint with regard to their religion. We come full circle from a civil order that separates itself from religious entanglements, to the Church defending citizens of the new states from populist or elitist tyrannies masquerading as states having legitimacy under natural law or divine law.

While the "reference to totalitarian regimes of Communist inspiration is unmistakable,"[99] the *Declaration* in its generality does not direct or limit its remarks to communist states, which in the Cold War environment it could and perhaps should have done. Many Church Fathers called for greater clarity and even courage on this point. Instead, the Council (possibly staff infiltrated by Soviet operatives) spoke more obliquely of the civil order. On the later collapse of the Soviet Union in 1991, John Paul II proclaimed: "Thus, the root of modern totalitarianism is to be found in the denial of the transcendent dignity of the human person, who as the visible image of the invisible God, is therefore by his very nature the subject of rights which no one may violate—*no individual group, class, nation or state*" (italics added).[100] Today, nearly half a century after the Council, this part of the Church teaching applies equally to many possible futures. These futures include such examples as extreme individualism under the new *post-modern* political landscape, the new and unanticipated stirring of Islam acting through its states (or as powerless in controlling embedded terrorist networks), and the more hypothetical alternatives of a "new world order" or a global Caliphate.

Islam shares with the Council and Christianity a total rejection of atheism as found in Communist totalitarianism. But might it be that the Holy Spirit was at work in this broad and now prescient wording of the Council? The

Council speaks generically of personal and institutional freedom from coercion "either in the whole of mankind or in a particular country or in a specific community."[101] Under Islamic Law (Shari'a) the domain of unbelief (*dar al-kufr*) is opposed by the domain of belief (dar al-Islam), and if the former domain obstructs Islamic life it is identified as dar al-harb (the house of war). The contribution of the Second Vatican Council is to advance beyond the relations of Church and state (partly comparable to domain) and to specify the rights of the *person* to exercise his religion in any domain or in any state. The point of incoherence with Islam is that the Islamic State claims this right for its own members as based on the *Qur'an* rather than any distinct and universally accessible natural law.

Nearly three decades after the Council, in his assessment of the post-Cold War landscape, Pope John Paul II added these timely words:

> Nor does the Church close its eyes to the danger of fanaticism or fundamentalism among those who, in the name of an ideology which purports to be scientific or *religious*, claim the right to impose on others their own concept of what is true and good. Christian truth is not of this kind. Since it is not an ideology, the Christian faith does not presume to imprison changing socio-political realities in a rigid schema, and it recognizes that human life is realized in history in conditions that are diverse and imperfect. Furthermore, in constantly reaffirming the transcendent dignity of the person, the Church's method is always that of respect for freedom."[102] It is the Church's duty to teach "those principles of the moral order which *have their origin in human nature itself*"(italics added).[103]

Under historical Islam one often converted to Islam or else submitted. In the latter case the subject was usually allowed to retain one's religion while also paying annual tribute. The West conceives of a state respectful of the person and the informed personal conscience as such, regardless of religion or other group identity. Muslim membership in the ummah domain differs from Western citizenship in the territorial state. The self-understanding of Muslims is that membership is "achieved or at least initiated, by an act of will or by a commitment by an individual or society to place itself within the Muslim community (with the realization) that it is irrevocable and binding on future generations as well."[104] This imposition is only superficially like the inheritance of citizenship under Western social contract theory. Two differences are that in the Western civil case the individual is always free to change one's citizenship, and second, that religious membership is a completely separate matter usually of individual baptism into a Church or other religious community. The reality of personal conscience is also handled in the *Declaration*. In the Western context primacy of conscience applies to all "citizens" and even to atheists. The concept of "citizen's" consciences is more problematic under Shari'a and the Mosque-state where citizenship is secondary to group membership in the global ummah.

Under the influence of the American John Courtney Murray, S.J., the Council's *Declaration* pointed specifically to the American Constitution as one possible model for a future respectful of personal religious freedom apart from government pressures.[105] Any future role of the earlier European model of the confessional state[106] is not directly addressed, either favorably or unfavorably.[107] In this silence new confessional states do not appear to be ruled out as an option in an always indeterminate future. But even limited cases of this kind of outcome seem unlikely. Instead the foreseeable future offers a mix of post-Christian secular states possibly dismissive of both religion and natural law, a range of Islamic states where the future of Christian populations and of the Church is very uncertain, and an overlapping (non-territorial) domain where Muslims may or may not feel secure in the persons, property and religion. Church-Mosque relations must be worked out at more than one all-inclusive level. The Church-state question involves international security first of all, but also the minimal goal of "reciprocity" between religions, and attention to personal rights and responsibilities on cultural and intercultural questions such as the definition of "family" to be protected in civil law.

The recent Council helps replace this lengthy episode in Western history with a new focus for the future: the relationship between the church and society—not the Church-state question, but the *Church-society* question.[108] Murray's critics and even Murray himself saw the coming danger that the endorsed American political model—with a moral society sustaining a secularly defined state—might not endure. Future engagement between the nearly post-Christian West and Islam might be less over church-state relations within states than it is over society-society relations spanning across Western states and the ummah or collage of Islamic states. Distinguishable from the New Evangelization of post-Christian and other populations is a necessary openness to the distinct and universal natural law so foundational to the West possibly latent in the *Qur'an.*

As a communal society, Islam is more a way of life attached to nation-state paraphernalia than it is a state in the unambiguous Western constitutional sense. Secularized societies in the West seek to affirm personal human rights as foundational to political life within state boundaries, increasingly separate and even disdainful of religion or even universal natural law, while Islamic societies often equate social membership with the non-territorial ummah and a required submission to Shari'a Law and the *Qur'an*, which may contain a very few latent references to the natural law. Of this latency in the *Qur'an*, the clear meaning of the universal natural law is that the dignity of the human person, and his rights and responsibilities, are constitutive of each of the *followers* of

Islam themselves (and everyone else), whether or not they can be teased out of the *Qur'an*.

Today and following Murray's proposals, some commentators the Second Vatican Council read "the signs of the times" as trending toward a politics—*and* a society—based less on religious belief than on the non-sectarian natural law written on every human heart. Morality is held to be universal while specific religions are not. Under Shari'a it is Islam as a belief system that remains universal, while (other) religions are not. If morality is distinct from faith and religion, morally based laws cannot be assailed as if they were an imposition of any one religion on society as a whole. But if the *Qur'an* is the singular source of morality, even prior to the constitution of the human person as a person, then all other religions and the morality of a distinct natural law are foreclosed.

In the West, with its possible divorce between public morality and religion, the civic culture tolerates politicization of even moral issues, and an apparent "tyranny of relativism." From his first hand involvement, Bernard Nathanson, a one-time abortion czar in New York in the 1960s and who was personally responsible for the termination of sixty thousand unborn children, reports that from the very beginning the "anti-Catholic warp was a central strategy, a keystone of the abortion movement."[109] In another personal testimony, a former abortionist relates that after she had her own abortion, and to calm her personal sense of guilt, she reasoned that if she could induce others toward abortion and guilt, then perhaps she could rationalize away her own inner struggle. Even as she continued to selectively read the Bible, she set up clinics in the Houston area with the express agenda: to recruit young girls thirteen to seventeen years of age through classroom presentations to risk the promiscuous culture of "readiness," and then to deliberately supply them with low dose contraceptives, so that her network of clinics could count on three to five abortions each for teens in this market segment. With the personal economic goal "to be a millionaire," she later admitted responsibility for 35,000 abortions. Eventually she was apprehended performing and charging for abortions on girls who were not even pregnant[110]

At this Western tipping point toward cultural and moral decline, even freedom of religion is subject to verbal sleight of hand. The content-challenged term "freedom of worship" begins to replace the less marginalizing right to exercise religion publicly—"freedom of religion." By coincidence . . . the Muslim *Declaration of Human Rights* (1981) acknowledges (private) "freedom of worship" but not freedom of religion (publicly expressed) as assured in the *United Nations Declaration of Human Rights*, 1948). Secularist leaders in the West now privatize religion and by this internal logic also align unwittingly with Islamic understandings. The recurring code language "freedom of worship" renders religion little more than a private taste to be privately exercised, and risks being a half-way house to Islam which regards all other religions as imperfect expressions of itself.[111] In another modern and elastic transformation, freedom of conscience too easily becomes freedom *from* (informed) conscience. For Catholics, the term "freedom of conscience," in the subjective or possibly libertarian sense rather than in the sense of matched obligations and well grounded rights, is found *nowhere* in the thinking or writing of the Second Vatican Council.[112] In its statements, the Council speaks instead of religious liberty and defines this as "immunity" from coercion by the state in religious practices.

The modern and subjectivist monologue or "tyranny of relativism" would have us accept a new belief that the objective morality of *intrinsic* good and evil (the universal natural law) does not exist. Objective morality, like politics, is reduced to a branch of mathematics applied to extrinsic costs and benefits that can be deleted or reset as readily as any computer game imagery.[113] Pope Benedict terms this reduction of intrinsically evil actions to their external and problematic implications as a mere "calculus of consequences." In his 1993 post mortem for the flawed side of "Progress," Solzhenitsyn, survivor of years in the Gulag, offered a similar mathematics: "We have lost the clarity of spirit which was ours when the concepts of Good and Evil had yet to become a subject of ridicule, shoved aside by the principle of fifty-fifty."[114]

The Council continued to consistently teach that "In the depths of his conscience, man detects a law which he does not impose upon himself, but which holds him to obedience . . . For man has in his heart a law written by God. To obey it is *the very dignity of man*; according to it he will be judged."[115] Decades ago the Catholic novelist, Bernanos, unveiled one face of the widespread subjectivist assertion of moral relativism: "The modern world will shortly no longer possess sufficient spiritual reserves to commit genuine evil. Already . . . we can witness a lethal slackening of men's conscience that is attacking not only their moral life, but also their very heart and mind, altering and decomposing even their imagination . . . The menacing crisis is one of infantilism."[116] Foreseen by Bernanos, the brand of modernity carrying forward from the social revolutions of the 1960s is not complicated, but simple. It is not progress, but politically active infantilism in search of validation from the media-sensitive state.

The Council dealt mostly with the internal life of the Church which (like Islam) is a world religion. While the comparison cannot be overdrawn—between the Christian revelation and the religion of Islam—still there may be transferable lessons from one to the other. *Lumen Gentium* (The Dogmatic Constitution on the Church) helps us with a concise institutional comparison. The institutional form of Islam as a *"congregational theocracy"* (Chapter

3). In contrast, the Church in the two Vatican Councils proclaims a self-understanding that is separate from the state, and that in its own realm is both institutional and mystical. The form of the distinct Catholic Church is that of "*hierarchical communion* . . . not as a vague feeling . . . (but) an organic reality."[117] The Church continues the mission of the apostles *outside* of the state, unlike the strongly felt *ummah* which is a conflated hybrid of a global religion and almost world-spanning collage of government. In the hierarchical communion the "order of bishops is the successor to the college of the apostles (as taught by the First Vatican Council) in teaching authority and pastoral rule . . . (and the) subject of supreme and full power . . . (when they act) together *with its head, and never without the head*" (ialics added).[118] The bishops trace to the apostles and the pope traces uniquely to the bishop of Rome, St. Peter. Absent the apostolic succession, the mainline Protestant denominations (Lutheranism, Calvinism) are "congregational," and sometimes have been theocracies as in Calvin's early control of the Swiss republic. Without the unique source of apostolic succession, former Catholic alliances with the crown were similar in shape with Shi'ite mosque-states of today where imams are held to be direct descendents from the prophet Mohammed and have the ear of the throne or the gavel.

But unlike the succession of leadership from the Prophet, the new and key word here is "apostle." As successors to the apostles—apostle means to be sent—the bishops are personally sent *by Christ* as his witnesses acting through the Church which is His body. The first among the apostles is St. Peter. Christ based the gathering of his witnesses (Gr. *ecclesia*: Church) on Peter's profession of faith (Mt. 16: 18).[119] This is an extraordinary event and truth claim. Peter professes his faith in Christ who in each instant of our experience personally and in history is forever One with the Father. The finally total transparency of the infinite God confronts the stubborn opaqueness of the finite human mind and heart. The apostle or bishop is sent not by a prophet, but by the One who is the beginning and the end, the Alpha and the Omega, the one thing absolutely "new under the sun" (Eccl. 1:9).

The Church, with all of its personal shortcomings, is an institutional and mystical response in human history to the eternal and Trinitarian Other, who for our sake became man and *rose from the dead*. In Pope Benedict XVI's image, the collegiality of bishops is an ellipse with two focal points, the primacy and the episcopacy, rather than being a mimic of either a political monarchy or a democratic national assembly.[120] Even the several national Catholic conferences of bishops do not qualify a sort of presumptive church parliament. They exist rather to support "the inalienable responsibility of each bishop in relation to the universal Church and to his particular Church."[121] This form of Church is not comparable to Islam as a "congregational theocracy" with its factionalism and with its potential for religious-political consensus groups of Ijtihad or Ijma.

In the West the Church and State have found ways to mutually respect and separate from each other. Because the Church is connected hierarchically to its origin, as well as in mutual communion, its members as an institution remain open to the touch or supervention of the Holy Spirit initiated publicly at Pentecost. It is only by this indwelling Spirit that the Church's grace-giving sacraments become possible for each member always in communion with others.[122] Within the broad Christian world, the Church and the Protestant ecclesial communities are centered in their respective ways—either individually or also through his Church—on the *person* of Jesus Christ, not as an idea or a book or a proposition, but as a *response to an encounter*. The Faith becomes faithfulness: "Christ Jesus our hope . . ." (1 Tim 1:1).[123] We are called to respond to this love and dignity partly by how we work toward human dignity and the common good.

HUMAN DIGNITY AND THE COMMON GOOD

In late 1939 and the final months before the Second World War, the poet and cultural critic T.S. Eliot remarked to a lecture audience: "We are always faced both with the question 'what must be destroyed?' and with the question 'what must be preserved?' and neither Liberalism nor Conservatism, which are not philosophies and may be merely habits, is enough to guide us."[124] Is it possible that a coherent philosophy true to the dignity of the human person can be distilled from the shelves of a world religion that for two millennia has watched and struggled with the politics of the human soul in the world? What fully human principles might we find that include but are not delineated or limited by reactionary politics or movements toward ambivalent "democratization"?

At the Second Vatican Council, the twenty-first such council, the Church included its vision of the revealed human "person" and his inseparable relations with one another. Today one Western observer of his own culture writes of the Council that "the Catholic emphasis came to be on the natural dignity of the whole human person—in opposition to the modern view that our *dignity* resides only in our *autonomy*" (italics added).[125] The Church's social teaching affirms the dignity of the integral person and all persons and then supports principles for political life, economic life, and social and cultural life. For its part, Islam abhors any sense of autonomy that might be independent of the autonomy of God. The political outcome is not the unity of the human person, but the reach of the unitary Islamic State.

The Council proposes the reality and the universality of the natural law which while often obscured is detectible throughout history. The Jesuit missionary Pierre-Jean De Smet found it near the Rocky Mountains in American territory in 1840. A Flat-Head Indian chief, estimated to be eighty years of age, came forward and asked for baptism. De Smet encouraged contrition for any past "offenses he might have committed against his Maker." This chief, described as comparable in bearing to any Western aristocrat, gave this reply: "No doubt, I have done many things that have offended the Great Spirit— but it was unknowingly; I never in my life did anything which I knew to be evil; from my childhood it has been my constant endeavor to avoid sin, and I never did a second time any action, when I was told that it was wrong."[126] This simplicity reveals the accuracy of a theology that holds fallen man to be still intrinsically good. In distinctly Catholic theology the gift of sacramental grace is not added to nature, but instead perfects and transcends our nature which already is good in the eyes of the Father, but now both damaged and yet open to growth. Considering the whole man, the beginning is not only a *neutral* starting block pointing toward historical evolution. In harmony with the testimony of De Smet's chief is the more systematic social thinking of Mohandas Gandhi. A Hindu, he warned against seven deadly sins of the modern world: "politics without principle, wealth without work, commerce without morality, pleasure without conscience, education without character, science without humanity, and worship without sacrifice."[127]

The Church's social principles insert an explicit step of moral *discernment* in front of and above modernity's unexamined moral dynamism of action. Not a detailed template, the principles offer the spiritual and practical clues *on how we find and constitute ourselves* in all that we do, acting always in relationship.[128] An earlier lay intellectual, the Hungarian-born Thomas Molnar, approached the same reality in these words: "Theocentric man is also an action man, the difference between him and an activist is that he acts for God and that this permeates his work with prudence, patience, and charity. His action is concrete, directed to the here-and-now, and does not sacrifice generations for a hypothetical shiny future, does not sacrifice this concrete man here for the hypothetical masses of tomorrow. Only concrete action for real human beings resembles God's action in eternity."[129] Unlike Shari'a, Christian engagement in the world looks closely at those received rights that are inviolable and those other rights which in practice are subject to the moral virtues and conscientious discernment of concrete circumstances.

The Church's social teachings have been both proclaimed and drawn out in direct response to the challenges thrown at us by our pilgrimage through troubled history, especially the ideological conflicts of the nineteenth and twentieth centuries. In broadest outline, we are given the commandments as a *floor* beneath which we violate morality, but these Commandments point us to the Beatitudes as the *path* to perfection—not of any abstract society or political unit—but of the concrete human person.[130] "The Church is at once the sign and the safeguard of the transcendent dimension of the human person."[131] "Personal dignity is the most precious good which a human being possesses. As a result, the value of one person transcends all the material world."[132] Each of us enjoys innate self-possession, self-determination and inviolable rights, *none of which is created or conferred by the state, and none of which can be annulled by the state.* This is why in the West, in answer to Hassan (Chapter 3), it is no incidental matter that the state and society are constrained in a "negative" way from infringing on the human person.

For its part, the institutional Church "by reason of her role and competence, is not identified with any political community nor is she tied to any political system." Pope Benedict adds:

> Concrete juridical and social forms and political arrangements are no longer treated as a sacred law that is fixed *ad literam* for all times and so for all peoples. The decisive thing is the underlying communion of will with God given by Jesus. It frees men and nations to discover what aspects of political and social order accord with this communion of will and so to work out their own juridical arrangements . . . *The concrete political and social order is released from the directly sacred realm, from theocratic legislation, and is transferred to the freedom of man,* whom Jesus has established in God's will and taught thereby to see the right and the good (italics added).[133]

From the Second Vatican Council, *the Constitution on the Church in the Modern World* calmly affirms that "The Church guards the heritage of God's Word and draws *from it religious and moral principals, without always having at hand the solution to particular problems*" (italics added).[134] While moral absolutes exist, the Church cannot be cornered into the false role of defending static classical thought against more dynamic historical realities. The Council clearly separates itself from statecraft: "The Church has no models to present; models that are real and truly effective can only arise within the framework of different historical situations, through the efforts of all those who responsibly confront *concrete problems* in all their social, economic, political and cultural aspects, as these interact with one another."[135] These definitions provide much more distinct and complementary roles for revelation and for human responsibility and ingenuity than does the Muslim Shari'a. The Shari'a holds that "The man-made systems are operative only under a rule of enforcement by a body imposing them (and that) the Shari'a system being divine is operative forever (and) remains fixed and perennial," (and) generally that "legal justice is the same as abstract justice," (and) that man-made law is governed by "rules of derivation."[136] "Law, whether secular, non-secular, constitutional, public or private, must be *based on and derived from* the word or mandate of God as evidenced in the *Qur'an*, or from the traditions of the Prophet."[137]

A goal of Pope John Paul II was to place the Christian faith in the void left by the collapse of state-sponsored atheistic materialism. Since 1891 the Church has resorted regularly to social encyclicals to apply the Gospel message to the circumstances of modern history.[138] First addressed by the pope to the Church, more recently these letters are offered to all mankind. Following *Centesimus Annus* (One Hundred Years, 1991), a synthesis was folded into the more comprehensive *Catechism of the Catholic Church* (1992), an indirect product of the Second Vatican Council.[139] A more detailed *Compendium of the Social Doctrine of the Church* (2004) followed. In his *Caritas in Veritate (*Charity in Truth, 2009), Pope Benedict XVI combines earlier broad messages on human solidarity with moral statements affirming respect for each person in all stages of life.

Working outward from the irreducible dignity of each person and toward the common good, the compendium is both layered and transparent.

The Intrinsic Dignity of the Human Person[140]

The mystery and fact of the concrete person on the street, one at a time and over any group—whether a social class in the West or any non-Western communal category (Chapter 3)—*is the Church's core social principle.* As the start point for human rights and responsibilities, the intrinsic dignity of the concrete human person differs on a subtle point from human rights under Islam, which are believed to be "conferred" by Islam as an ideal code. Christians and Muslims agree that the dignity of the transcendent person is a received dignity,[141] and not a dignity to be either achieved or oppressed by tyranny or positive law. But beyond this affirmation, the West also distinguishes between the divine law and applications of the natural law. The person is more than a passive imprint of either a transcendent moral code alone or of any seeming imperatives of any particular time and place in history. Edith Stein remarks that "(we) can think of Caesar in a village instead of in Rome and can think of him transferred into the twentieth century. His historically settled individuality would then go through some changes, but just as surely he would remain Caesar."[142] And beyond philosophy, by transcendent it is meant that each person—as a person—takes part in some mysterious and concrete way in the reality of Christ who is "the same, yesterday and today, yes, and forever" (Heb 13:8).

More than any abstract principle, this transcendent dignity of the concrete person serves as the ground for all of the remaining principles. Actions directly attacking the human person are intrinsically evil. These are prohibited in the sense that there can be no common ground between the common good and direct assaults on that good however much individualized. We are bound to "consider every neighbor without exception as another self."[143] By what pretense do we presume to annihilate "other selves" including the unborn, by a prior forgetfulness, the self-deceit of first refusing to *see* them? The mystery of iniquity is not in the politics, but first of all in the lost willingness to see the real under the pretense of doing a larger good. History teaches us that horror comes when the reality of the concrete human person is nudged out of mind and when "the habit of abstract thinking" by those in power is accompanied by their loss of "the faculty to imagine that which they know."[144] This habit of thinking explains the Holocaust and the Gulag. It also explains a legal debate over what is self-evident, that the human embryo is in scientific fact a complete human being.[145]

At its core, the natural law written directly on the uncompromised human heart recoils from and forbids abortion, euthanasia, same-sex "marriage," and in our technocratic age human cloning[146] and the destruction of human embryos attendant to embryonic forms of stem cell research."[147] In vitro fertilization (IVF) unfolds into a new industry of special order baby manufacturing based on the colonization and harvesting of those women willing to be used in this manner. The Second Vatican Council proposes as an explicit teaching of the self-evident:

> (Furthermore), whatever is opposed to life itself, such as any type of murder, genocide, abortion, euthanasia,[148] or willful self-destruction, whatever violates the integrity of the human person, such as mutilation, torments inflicted on body and mind, attempts to coerce the will itself; whatever insults human dignity, such as subhuman living conditions, arbitrary imprisonment, deportation, slavery, prostitution, the selling of women and children; as well as disgraceful working conditions, where men are treated as mere tools for profit, rather than as free and responsible persons; all these things and others of their like are infamies indeed. They poison human society, but they do more harm to those who practice them than those who suffer from the injury. Moreover, they are a supreme dishonor to the Creator.[149]

Inseparable from the dignity of the person is a second principle, the shared *common good*. The common good "embraces the sum of those conditions of social life by which individuals, families, and groups *can achieve their own fulfillment* in a relatively thorough and ready way" (italics added).[150] The Christian life engages "contingent" matters which most often do not involve choices between good and evil, but between competing goods or between greater and lesser evils. In such cases "(citizens) should hold in high esteem professional skill, family and civic spirit, and the virtues relating to social behavior, namely, honesty, justice, sincerity, kindness, and courage, without which there can be no true Christian life."[151] Always affirming for all a personal human dignity, it is evil in the political arena to package affirmative programs with intrinsically evil actions on the pretense that on average good is being done. This is Bentham's "greatest good for the greatest number," mistaken by Hassan (Chapter 3) to be an expression of the natural law. In the extreme case, "Indeed, the failure to protect and defend life in its most vulnerable stages renders suspect any claims to the 'rightness' of positions in other matters affecting the poorest and least powerful of the human community."[152]

Family[153]

The family is the place where love and respect for others are mutually reinforced precisely because equality does not mean sameness. Affection and authority actually come together ultimately as a source and "sanctuary of life."[154] Contrary to much Western ideology, it is the family that is sacred, not the state. Writing fifteen years before the Council, the existential philosopher Gabriel Marcel observed: "What it is to belong to a family, and to be attached to it, is something which it seems to me that neither biology nor sociology is capable of probing right to the core; and on the other hand, speaking rather generally, one might say that the family relationship is not one which up to the present has sufficiently engaged the attention of metaphysics."[155] Under paganism when each family revered its own imagined god of the hearth, we were closer to the truth of the family than we are today where the family is seen too often as an arbitrary statistical bundle. Children and their parents are targeted as nationwide market segments for retailers of commercial products and government patronage.

Even the definition of the human family is in jeopardy of being gerrymandered to fit the criterion of equity in government benefits, or to base decisions of justice on superficial attention to "how such decisions affect people" (aka government constituencies). In the ongoing culture wars and under the banner of civil rights, the definition has been redrawn in half dozen of the United States and possibly the District of Columbia, and in the Netherlands, Belgium, Canada, Spain, Portugal, Spain, Norway, Sweden and South Africa. In the United States we enjoy a Fathers' Day and a Mothers' Day, and in the name of "equality"—a recent presidential proclamation of not one day, but thirty days (Gay Pride Month).

Scriptural guidance is sometimes denied, but clearly holds that sexual activity between those with the same gender identity is mutual degradation.[156] To be labeled and silenced by the state as a "phobia" is resistance to the politicized redefinition of basic concepts, including the meaning of foundational institutions that pre-exist the state, such as the family.[157] Just as Islamic rationalism redefines the meaning of jihad to embrace both interior struggle and martial aggression, Western rationalism would obscure the meaning of family. By peddling legal footnotes, the legal profession overlooks a broad cultural meltdown that can no longer distinguish between freedom of political speech and the most aggressive forms of pornography. Also dissolved is the distinction between latent inclinations or orientations and willful human actions (obesity is an "epidemic," and terrorism and treachery are mere "tragedies" like the acts of nature). Where Lenin conceived the family as an artifact of arbitrary economic relationships, others today would reduce the family to a linguistic artifact. Mark Twain exposed such subterfuge when he quipped that, "The difference between the almost right word and the right word is really a large matter—it's the difference between the lightning bug and the lightning." And Russian folk literature offers a like proverb that will outlive the dark side of modernity: "One word of truth outweighs the whole world."[158]

In the United States family deterioration is at the root of other more conventional evils. In the 1960s it was the breakup of black families—disrupted by generations of slavery, discrimination and then a culture of welfare politics—that was identified in *The Moynihan Report* as the major cause of poverty among blacks. The illegitimacy rate of forty percent in that decade is matched today by the Caucasian majority, but itself has climbed now to seventy percent. The universally corrosive effect and agenda of American television sit-coms (situation comedies) should be obvious even to those so addicted. Where Islam rejects the fatherhood of God, Western society discounts family fatherhood, often at tragic psychological costs to sons and daughters. In the watershed 1960s Marshall McLuhan foresaw the downside of the electronic era and the dark side of globalization. Families of any race or history are isolated from earlier community supports. The victims become commodities to be trafficked on an international scale.[159] Even Western culture regresses to an earlier barbaric level and begins to resemble the Arabian "days of ignorance" prior to the coming of Mohammed. In the *Qur'an* Mohammed prohibits the not uncommon practice of burying alive unwanted female babies[160]—a practice distinguished only by technology from clinical late-term abortions.

In his "Letter to Families" inaugurating 1994 as the Year of the Family, Pope John Paul II reminded us that "the family, as a community of persons, is (thus) the first human society . . . in a certain sense (a) sovereign society" and that "every act of begetting finds its primordial model in the fatherhood of God."[161] Looking across religions, the Christian world should appreciate that the Islamic scholar Hassan has served as ambassador to the United Nations for the World Family Alliance.[162] And when Pope Benedict met with Saudi Arabia's King Abdullah in late 2007, not as a head of state but to advance interreligious and intercultural dialogue among Christians, Muslims, and Jews, his purpose was "the promotion of peace, justice and spiritual and moral values, especially in support of the family."[163] In Cameroon in 2009 he repeated the message: "the difficulties arising from the impact of modernity and secularization on traditional society inspire you to defend vigorously the essential values of the African family . . ."[164]

As part of the immigration trend into Europe there comes a latent challenge to the Western understanding of the family as monogamous. In the twenty-first century, Europe especially will be faced with expectations for two incompatible sets of laws affecting the foundation of society—one indigenous set of separated civil and religious laws, and the other the imported Shari'a which is both civil and religious and which condones polygamy.[165] Contrary to Western misperceptions, polygamy is not widely practiced in most Muslim countries, and in at least Turkey and Tunisia is illegal, but unfortunately it is authorized scripturally and is not a more accidental and unofficial cultural accretion.

Solidarity as Mutual Responsibility, Friendship and Social Charity[166]

Superficially the most similar of the Church's social principles with the Shari'a way of life is the principle of *solidarity*. Similar in appearance, solidarity might be compared to the global Muslim community *or ummah*. Both protect against excessive individualism. But unlike the abstract ummah and the Islamic State, solidarity is a personal and shared sense of responsibility that can be neither absorbed nor delegated by the state. Further, even when it is particular it is non-exclusive. As a concrete definition of solidarity, John Paul II valued national identities such as Polish culture, but in the same breath challenged them to remain open to "non-exclusive solidarity." Non-exclusive solidarity is social and profoundly cultural, rooted as it is in deeply shared memories, but it is ultimately the memory of a shared human dignity. The Muslim and multi-state ummah is exclusive in that it sharply excludes non-Muslims, dating back to the Abbasid Dynasty (750–1258) which transformed Islam from an Arab confederation to a highly diverse mega-tribe. In the West, Hugo Grotius's foundational work on international law (*The Law of Nature and of Nations*, 1625) was written within a broadening Christian culture.

Under Islam, "The righteous man is he who . . . though he loves it dearly, gives away his wealth to kinfolk, to orphans, to the destitute, to the traveler in need and to beggars . . ." (Q 2:177). The limitation is that the ummah and even the possibly less restricted concept of *dhimmah* (or honor) are stalled as an abstract and "felt" kinship. This kinship within a supreme and exclusive loyalty is more felt than reasoned, and finally is a limited universe of dar al-Islam categorically exclusive of infidels (dar al-harb). However, while the Islamic State exists first and foremost to advance Islam, "a pious non-Muslim is considered higher than a non-pious Muslim."[167] The Catholic social principles are grounded not in what is felt or articulated in the history of Western development, but ultimately, in a reasoned *moral theology* applicable to each human person and every human setting. This grounding in moral theology is the possible opening to those cultures where secular Westernization has demonstrably less to offer.

It was Pope John Paul II who stressed that the Council's social teaching is not a Western ideology or political agenda, but "belongs to the field . . . of theology and particularly moral theology."[168] Moral theology stands between and above both Western positivism and any theories of ongoing revelation, Western or Islamic. The preaching of St. Paul to the Gentiles predates and summons the rise of the Western cultural event. Islam exists finally to protect the ummah, even at the expense of the individual, while Christian solidarity is rooted in the worth of every human person as he finds himself engaged in ever broader and global settings. In the parable of the Good Samaritan (Lk 10:25–37) we are challenged to be "neighbors" to all others and to be our "neighbor's keeper." In the modern and compact world we are to accept even global neighbors as friends however distant geographically. Such moral solidarity is enabled by modern communications and literature,[169] but still receives only varied degrees of legal recognition from one modern state to another. In Europe one who fails to help another in serious need is subject to civil and criminal penalties (under Romano-German law). The individualistic cultural slant in the United States has produced no such law. Instead, those who might cause harm when they help another in need have to be protected from litigation by "Good Samaritan" legislation.[170]

Faithful Citizenship

The principle of faithful citizenship recognizes a right to participate with others in political society. This is the only social principle that directly refers to (or depends upon) the existence of the state;[171] under Islam all principles of Shari'a are subject to authorities of the Islamic State as the executors of the God's law. The nineteenth century historian Lord Acton observed that rendering unto Caesar the things that are Caesar's "gave to the civil power, under the protection of conscience, a sacredness it had never enjoyed, and bounds it had never acknowledged." The principle of *faithful* citizenship alludes first to Christian "citizenship in heaven" and then at the same time affirms the duties of co-operation in democratic self-government. At a time of an imperial state St. Peter counseled loyalty to the emperor (1 Pe 2:13–15), but as a measure of citizenship today such submission would be an anachronism. The natural law runs deeper than authoritarianism. The Islamic state is challenged by the principle of faithful citizenship to distinguish between submission to the sovereignty of Allah and the role of citizens sharing in the common good. In the modern idiom this means elections untainted by corruption of factional identity politics. The West is challenged in more particular ways to assure "conscience clauses" for individuals and institutions working in the medical field where ethical relativism is a growing threat.

With their vocational expertise in the world, the well-informed lay Catholic role of faithful citizenship includes informed participation in possible *recommendations* made by the Church hierarchy on usually complex economic or political questions in specific need of moral critique.[172] But the Second Vatican Council also warns against politicizing the Church: "No one is allowed to appropriate the Church's authority for his opinion." A former Treasury Secretary of the United States, a lay Catholic, critiqued an early and probable lay staff *draft* of the national "Catholic Social Teaching and the U.S. Economy" (prepared in 1983 by for bishops conference in the United States). In his professional view, the draft was too much molded by the planks of a particular national political party. After the remaining eighteen months of discernment and editing, the bishops approved the more collaboratively developed final recommendation (*Economic Justice for All, 1986*).

Subsidiarity

The principle of subsidiarity was most urgently articulated during the rise of state Fascism in twentieth century Europe.[173] Subsidiarity reserves group and personal action to the closer levels of government whenever possible, and to private associations and communities and even communal groups apart from the state when these remain consistent with natural law. Today subsidiarity protects the right to personal participation "together with others" (especially including the family) in a range of natural associations such as a morally guided market economy. Other familiar examples are non-government or private schools and those many non-governmental organizations (NGOs) that, again, are not in violation of natural law.[174] People are fulfilled alone and together as protagonists in their own futures. This participatory aspect of human nature holds true even if we acknowledge that as a practical matter bounded "local" societies and communities, including personhood and families as foundational, are often highly networked and even global. The paired principles of social solidarity and subsidiarity are both to be preserved and fostered. Neither is to be sacrificed to the other as with divisive individualism and identity politics, or the alternative centralization of economic and political structures. Instead, in a community that is both spiritualized and historical— that is, incarnational—solidarity and subsidiarity reinforce, reaffirm, deepen and continuously test one another as they reaffirm the core principle of the concrete human person who is in history, but not simply of history.

The Islamic State has no relation to the Roman law which historically has shaped the fabric of subsidiary in Western institutions. Under Shari'a there are no corporate legal "persons" or entities such as the city or colleges as institutions.[175] Further, the Islamic State is held by Muslims to be an abstract rather than a historical entity. It possesses a direct, dominant and affirmative or "positive" mandate toward human betterment. This feature has been aggravated by the influence of Western socialist and nationalist ideology. To all of this, a corrective principle is subsidiarity.

And yet, resembling the Islamic State in form if not content is the transition of Western political institutions toward government by activist courts. Aggressive court rulings often challenge the personal right of association. Apparent in parts of the West is a culture of judicially driven social outcomes and court-enforced entitlements, and even the possible subordination of national constitutional law to transnational institutions. This culture begins to resemble the Islamic State and the transnational ummah or amalgam of Islamic society as a whole. An example of similarity in content as well as form would be an overly defined and enforced ideology of "tolerance." The expanded umbrella of tolerance allies fringe agenda activists and the Islamic international agenda to prohibit analysis of Islam or even modernity (like this book) as "hate crimes." The fatwa-like 2011 Presidential Executive Order refusing to defend the Congressional Defense of Marriage Act (DOMA, 1996) best illustrates this fusion at the top, particularly in the added ambivalence of continuing to enforce the Act while also anathematizing it unconstitutional. Such political finesse recalls T.E. Lawrence's (Chapter 2) observation that a signal trait of early Arab (and Islamic) culture was the ability to harbor conflicting positions without even noticing the contradictions.

Other than political subsidiarity, there is also economic subsidiarity which today implies some form of market economy. What Pope John Paul II termed "the subjectivity of society" calls for such an arena for shared freedom and responsibility. The form of the market economy should assure that an environment of moral responsibility is not swept aside by predatory profiteering, or even such abstract and purely instrumental criteria as efficiency and productivity. Historically, the rise of the centralized industrial states in Europe was feared early by the traditional Alexis de Tocqueville even a few years before the radical Karl Marx.[176] Other problematic tendencies include the absence of economic opportunities for the young and for families, a situation that is particularly pronounced today in the autocratic regimes of the Middle East. This region has become a seedbed for anti-Western resentment and despair even as the "revolutions" of 2011 especially in Tunisia and Egypt point to a new phase favoring either personal economic expectations or Islamic political culture. The migration pattern of those looking for work remains toward the more productive and democratic West, although the economic magnet has fallen into crisis for deep cultural reasons. Speaking in Spain in 2011 Cardinal Canizares proposed that "It is not possible to overcome the crisis . . . without a new and deeper moral conscience that is universal and valid for all, in which the truth about man, his dignity and the vocation he has because of the fact he is man is put first."

Rights and Responsibilities

The dignity of each human person carries with it his or her inalienable personal rights based on our responsibilities to ourselves and to others. The nineteenth century Cardinal Newman saw clearly that, "We have rights *because* we have responsibilities."[177] The human person constitutes himself by engaging not with abstractions like "humanity," but with *particular* others in conscientious action. We are personally fulfilled in each other.[178] John Paul II remarked that, "Error consists in an understanding of human freedom which detaches it from obedience to the truth and consequently from the duty to respect the rights of others."[179] The radical element of Islam renders obedience not to a divinely conferred truth *about man* and his rights and responsibilities,[180] but to an abstract and potentially arbitrary image of a distant and therefore less understood and less invoked God. For the radical Muslim, a fringe group of the total ummah, murder and suicide bombing become the will of God. Not well anchored in natural law and a functional distinction and linkage between faith with reason, the semi-modern Islamic State easily becomes a mere tools of power. The particular Muslim dilemma becomes one of suppressing Islamic extremism such as the Islamic Brotherhood, while at the same time using Islam as an identifying feature of the Islamic State.

Preference for the Poor and Vulnerable[181]

Christian society is not built on the overthrow of oppressive situations by violent means. Instead when Christians are inspired and constrained to do God's work they are to do it in God's way. We are to work with steady courage and not violence, against the malignant "structures of sin" flagged by the Second Vatican Council. The human predicament is one of genuine injustice, not simply flawed evolution or incomplete therapeutic government largesse. Among the structures of sin are economic injustices: "To destroy such structures and replace them with more authentic forms of living in community is a task which demands *courage and patience*" (italics added).[182] The presumption of the Liberation Theology of the 1970s and 80s was that we can set aside moral standards can be set aside, if only for a time, until legitimate grievances are first set right. It is precisely this sidelining of morality—taking a break from our humanity and the fatherhood of God in order to achieve possibly moral ends by immoral means—that is restrained by the Church's social principles. The end does not justify the means. Because each of us is a wholeness, made for true happiness, and worthy of giving and receiving unambiguous respect, we may not do evil even by democratic means that good might come of it (Rom 3:8). Justice is to be evenhanded: "Neither shall you allege the example of the many as an excuse for doing wrong, nor shall you . . . side with the many in perverting justice. You shall not favor a poor man in a lawsuit" (Ex 23:2, 3). The poor do have a right to preferential *attention* because when abused they are least able to protect the justice of their cause.

Radical liberation theology would be not only an evil in itself, but would immediately sink the *independent* Church into the level of ideological partisanship. Factional infighting within the Church always compromises its distinct and non-political core mission to "preach the word . . . in season and out of season" (1 Tim 4:2). This said, national and transnational solidarity with the oppressed, the poor and the vulnerable—those least able to help themselves—ever remains a universal Christian and human vocation. An unambiguous case is the need for more equitable access to global markets by lesser developed nations that are highly dependent upon an economy of agricultural production. These nations compete even within their own state boundaries with product dumping by state-subsidized agribusiness located in developed economies. The "loving preference for the poor" and vulnerable (previously miscast as a slanted *"preferential option* for the poor"[183]) again is based on moral theology. It is not a compromise or "third way" between capitalism and socialism. The great scandal of the future could be the triaging of rural populations by a managed world economy that subordinates the human right for food to the fluctuations of the commodities market. Projected climate fluctuations are expected to permanently disrupt regional crop productivity.[184]

The Church's social doctrine tilts toward market approaches as the *means* to personal self-fulfillment and the economic common good, but with attention given first to needed ethical preconditions. Asked if the fall of communism means that "capitalism" should be universally applied, Pope John Paul II proclaimed justice with a market face:

> The answer is obviously complex. If by 'capitalism' is meant an economic system which recognizes the fundamental and positive role of business, the market, private property and the resulting responsibility for the means of production, as well as free human creativity in the economic sector, then the answer is certainly in the affirmative, even though it would perhaps be more appropriate to speak of a 'business economy,' 'market economy' or simply 'free economy.' But if by 'capitalism' is meant a system in which freedom in the economic sector is not circumscribed within a *strong juridical framework* which places it at the service of *human freedom in its totality,* and which sees it as a particular aspect of that freedom, the *core of which is ethical and religious,* then the reply is certainly negative (italics added).[185]

A competent and ethically based market economy would not have created the recent global economic crises unloosed in Southeast Asia in 1997 and again globally in 2008. Ironically, a modern market economy would also protect against "usury" as this debunked and fragmented abuse actually reappears today at a global scale in such forms calculated currency devaluation.[186] A moral market economy would not include Darwinian cannibalism of predatory lending, commodities speculation, unrestrained public and private debt leading to confiscatory inflation, and simply unsound borrowing practices.

Theoretically, "the Islamic economic system might fall midway between the ideologies of capitalism and communism" in the way (it is said) that it encourages production based on private property, private enterprise, and family inheritance. Hassan calculates that if these incentives are ineffective in practice, the annual zakat (the historic tax on all Muslim property, generally two and a half percent per year) would have liquidated idle assets for the day-to-day benefit of the poor.[187] More than an economic system, the market economy in the West is at least potentially the means by which we as persons work together for ourselves and for each other. At the macro scale, the historic Ottoman decline might have been due in part to a combination of confiscatory taxation on total value alongside Western innovation and trade with taxes limited to annual transactions. Looking to the future, more important than the traditional economic building blocks of land or even capital, "today the decisive factor is increasingly man himself, that is, his knowledge, especially his scientific knowledge, his capacity for interrelated and compact organization, as well as his ability to *perceive the needs of others and to satisfy them*" (italics added).[188]

With the Church's singular mission of evangelization ever in mind, Pope John Paul II finally defines the concern for "the poor" broadly: "This option is not limited to material poverty, since it is well known that there are many other forms of poverty, especially in modern society—not only economic, but cultural and spiritual poverty as well."[189] To not be told the truth, to be denied the elementary freedom of religion, or to be profoundly humiliated or manipulated even if wealthy—to endure any of this is to be truly poor. The priest Werenfried von Straaten worked tirelessly to feed Central European refugees of the Second World War and continued in the field for decades. He was a respected critic of Vatican compromises with the Soviet Union in the 1970s and 80s and returned often to this layered formula: "There can be no peace without justice, and there is no justice without truth."

Dignity of Work and the Rights of Workers[190]

Islamic scripture agrees on what John Paul II expressed as "the primacy of persons over things." Globally, each person is "a part-owner of the great workbench at which he is working with everyone else."[191] Islamic ideology claims to be opposed to cartels and probably any kind of dichotomy as between labor and capital. Islam has a fierce hatred for Communism as demonstrated by its decade of resistance to the Soviet invasion of Afghanistan in the December 1979. In Christian terms work is not only a path to justice, but in itself is self-expression and self-fulfillment achieved by working with others. The human person can rightfully say that he is not simply part of the work or a "skill set," but that his work is donated as part of himself.

Within Islamic Sufism is a rising political power base on the generally rrural central plateau of secular Turkey. Here Sufism is practiced by export industrialists and capitalists who form a connection between this Islamic culture and the market opportunities of a global economy. This hybrid entrepreneurial-religious class appears to be reevaluating the statist and secularist thrust of the Turkish national constitution as well as the performance in recent decades of the ruling Justice and Development Party. This breakthrough gives rise to the informal term "Calvinist Islam" (also "Anatolian Tigers"), the notion that religious belief and economic liberalism are as compatible in Islamic Turkey as they have been in the West.[192] Intercultural research could compare Sufi economic development and the transitional cultures of late Medieval and later Protestant Europe.[193] Entrepreneurial Turkish access to global markets could foster an additional element of solidarity and subsidiarity, both compatible with the Church's social principles. On the other side of the ledger, the Turkish export sector is most closely tied to its immediate Islamic neighbors (the communal *ummah*). This economic sector grew twenty-fold in the decade between 1991 and 2008.

Care for God's Creation[194]

Personal self-fulfillment requires a right to private property ownership, but its use cannot be inconsistent with the "universal destination of goods."[195] When the Church lists care for creation apart from solidarity this is not a lapse into any political ideology of environmental socialism at the sacrifice of subsidiarity. Critics of formal government proposals dealing with "global warming" cite sections in support of global government, transfer of wealth, and centralized enforcement powers.[196] For ecological issues, the moral theology of subsidiarity challenges the modern world to find genuine structures of participation that extend to "(a) dialogue which involves past and future generations,"[197] but that does not pretend to confer moral status and equivalency to animals however much they are to be valued.[198] A fully human dialogue finds in the fabric of nature and the universe a beauty analogous to Scripture and to the sacraments. Nature, too, ultimately reflects the proportioning hand and presence of God. St. Francis conversed with the animals and stars and he is the patron saint of ecology.

Under the Genesis account, man is given "dominion" over the world . . . rather than over each other. This dominion is one of solidarity and stewardship rather than exploitation (Gen 1:26). In his *Liechentstein Address* (1993), Solzhenitsyn reaffirmed earlier remarks made toward technological society and the need for "self-limitation." He questioned the doctrine of productivity with the view that "in an economic race, we are poisoning ourselves." Two years earlier in a wide ranging address, Pope John Paul II also called for "important changes in established lifestyles, in order to limit the waste of environmental and human resources, thus enabling every individual and all the peoples of the earth to have a sufficient share of those resources."[199] In one of his hundreds of letters, St. Augustine sixteen centuries earlier connected growing passions and a finite world: "(the passions, he said) are more easily mortified finally in those who love God, than satisfied, even for a time, in those who love the world."[200] How are we to navigate intelligently, morally and realistically on a globe disrupted by strategic resource competition and depletion? Oil supplies at familiar prices are not infinite and yet are pressed upon by the conventional path of industrialization now offered to the aspiring new economies of China and India.

At least parts of mankind are demonstrably at risk of a self-inflicted "tragedy of the commons."[201] What is the possible alliance for shared action among the three monotheistic world religions? Like the Catholic social principle of solidarity, Islam proclaims at least for the ummah the reality of the common good and of property as a shared good. In this dimension Islam is open to possibly global ecological perspectives: "And eat not up your property among yourselves in vanity, nor seek by it to gain the hearing of the judges that ye may knowingly devour a portion of the property of others wrongfully" (Q 2:188). Christian and Jewish themes weave together a basic message for the benefit of both present and future generations, "(The Lord made the earth) not creating it to be a waste, but designing it to be lived in" (Isa 45:18).[202] In these verses we have an injunction for coming decades toward temperance, one of the four moral virtues.

In *Mater et Magistra* (Mother and Teacher, 1961) Pope John XXIII refined earlier confidences by noticing almost quaintly that nature has only *"almost* inexhaustible productive capacity" (italics added).[203] It was with an eye on rising per capita resource consumption, that Pope John Paul II more recently counseled "above all a change in lifestyle (and) models of production and consumption . . . (and) structures of power . . ."[204] Today the personal ecological footprint involves a layered web of often distant resource uses—land, water, air, and food chains. The level, distribution, and characteristics of the human populations are part of a vastly complex and randomly vulnerable set of relationships between human life and all other life and the sustaining ecology. Beijing, for example, a city of tens of millions, is dependent upon a rapidly declining reservoir of groundwater beneath. And in the United States, hormone laced sewage discharges from the upstream Mississippi River (due to contraceptive disposal) are possibly inflicting male sterility through even highly treated intakes and water supplies located downstream.

Beyond the balance of nature for current and future generations, we are reminded that "too little effort is made to safeguard the moral conditions for an authentic 'human ecology.'"[205] Pope John XXIII saw the connection between the globally-situated person and the inviolability of families. He already anticipated Pope Paul VI's (*Humanae Vitae*[206]) and the later Pope John Paul II (*Theology of the Body*) in their affirmations of integral human sexuality and family parenthood that is both unitive and open to procreation, neither severed from the other. Globalization "must serve solidarity and the common good . . . the human being must always be an end and not a means, a subject and not an object, nor a commodity of trade."[207] And earlier, in 1961 and still in advance of the Second Vatican Council, John XXIII wrote this of resource management, "But *whatever be the situation,* we clearly affirm these problems should be posed and resolved in such a way that man does not have recourse to methods and means *contrary to his dignity* . . ." (italics added).[208]

On human dignity, Zbigniew Brzezinski, author and former National Security Advisory under President Carter in the late 1990s, arrives at a specific prescription for America. He writes: "Only by identifying itself with the idea of universal human dignity—with its basic requirement of respect for culturally diverse political, social, and religious emanations—can America overcome the risk that the global political awakening will turn against it."[209] Brzezinski challenges America to engage "the global political awakening" in a way that involves freedom and democracy, "but also and "above all, (with) respect for the world's cultural and religious mosaic."[210] This apparent congruence between intricate secular strategizing and the Church's basic social principles is encouraging, but still inexact and subtly off the mark on a central point. The Catholic social principles see religious truth not as "emanations" from universal human dignity, rather human dignity is a consequence of man's relationship to God—religious truth. The start point validating a "mosaic" of cultures must be clearly the nature of the concrete human person, and the universality of natural law.

In summary, the Church's social principles are applications of the moral virtues—justice and prudential judgment, temperance and courage. It is courage, finally, rather than any intellectual exercise that enables us to see that each concrete human *person* is not a thing; that the *family* is not an arbitrary legal fiction either Qur'anic or Western; that *solidarity* means human relationships are real but not exclusive; that *subsidiarity* means the state and even the Islamic State is not the sum total of human community; that *human work* and the human worker are not commodities; that the *poor* of all kinds are not refuse; and that *creation* is a wonder which before it is found useful is given in the service of all.

The above social principles are proposed to those responsible for the common good. in addition, a unique *identity* attaches to the Church as a charitable apart from any state and state operations:

> The Church can never be exempted from practicing charity as an organized activity of believers, and on the other hand, there will never be a situation where the charity of each individual Christian is unnecessary, because in addition to justice man needs, and will always need, love . . . One does not make the world more human by refusing to act humanely here and now. We contribute to a better world only by personally doing good now, with full commitment and wherever we have the opportunity, *independently of partisan strategies and programs* (italics added).[211]

A cup of water or a kind word given personally in His name is a fractal of eternity.

THE JUST WAR: IDEOLOGY OR DISCERNMENT?

After Napoleon's bid for European empire and then the Congress of Vienna (1815), Prince Metternich's conservative balance of the restored nation-state powers controlled Europe. Despite internal social revolutions, especially those of 1848, this model held its place for a century before the entire subcontinent fell into the trenches of the First World War. Of Metternich's edifice and all politics the scholar and former Secretary of State Henry Kissinger writes: "(it) was the redefinition of the classic theological version of humility, 'Thy will be done,' with *reason taking the place of God*. It represented an effort to deal with the most fundamental problem of politics, *which is not the control of wickedness but the limitation of righteousness* . . . that order once shattered can be restored only by the experience of chaos" (italics added).[212] As a tool to control both wickedness and false righteousness, what is a "just war"? In entering the First World War President Wilson appealed to moral force over force of arms, confident in his campaign to make the world safe for democracy. The Emperor Franz Josef of Austria-Hungary had avenged the assassination of his heir apparent by mobilizing Austria-Hungary to pacify Serbia. Poised for this local action was the interwoven continental political landscape of Germany and Europe as a whole. Tinkering in backyard Serbia triggered the conflagration of total war. As with Frans Josef, in the twenty-first century the Western theory of the "just war" calls for an almost superhuman "calculus of *unintended* consequences" stemming from *either* action or inaction.

How do the Church's social principles, those apparent platitudes introduced above, actually serve as a moral compass at a compact global scale? Drawing the curtain on the Cold War was the collapse of the Soviet Union. This surprising event is sometimes compared to the fall of the Roman Empire which took centuries. Western tools of politics, economics, diplomacy or competitive military investment were all involved, but a crusade of prayer and self-identity in Poland also contributed.[213] The crusade in Poland is broken down by George Weigel into four steps serving as a possible model or at least inspiration for events elsewhere. First was a commitment to the *truth* of the dignity of each person called to rise above the Soviet "web of mendacity." Second, there was a willingness to take personal *responsibility*. Third, there was sincere *solidarity* with others, and fourth, in this instance the people followed a shrewd strategy not of pacifism but *non-violence*. The path of non-violence specifically deflected violent Soviet suppression as occurred in Hungary in 1956 and in Czechoslovakia in 1968.

The victory was due to "a doctrine and an ethic . . . that is why it worked . . . because the revolution, and the heroes who embodied it, broke through the hard shell of our power realism, our empiricism, and even our cynicism, to remind us that there is a *difference between good and evil*; that these categories are not irrelevant to politics (even to international politics); and that the human spirit can, indeed, overcome, from time to time" (italics added).[214] The moral virtue of courage, and the biblical injunction "Be not afraid" puts an always modern face on the moral virtue of courage.

The world of Islam asserts that the collapse of its mortal enemy, the Soviet Union, was brought about by their own Islamic jihad in Afghanistan.[215] Bernard Lewis observes that an incongruous Muslim role in the fall of communism is "not implausible."[216] The Islamic perspective on the significance of other historical battles at least admits to possible dialogue. From the Muslim perspective, the long-term military and geopolitical importance placed by many Western scholars on the Battle of Tours (732 A.D.) in Western Europe and on the Battle of Lepanto (1571) in the eastern Mediterranean may be much overstated. Further, both Islam and the West have theories on what qualifies as a "just war." With the separation of Church and State in the West such final decisions fall on those directly responsible for the common good, and are based on moral criteria (below). The Church is not this power, but is a source of moral influence. In Islam there is no distinction between Mosque and State, and the just war of jihad is theoretically limited to resisting aggression, but aggression is vaguely defined (see below). The religious leaders retain a trustee role over government and over the decisions of war and peace. Their role is not as presidents or monarchs within government, but as ever present monitors to safeguard against government violations of Shari'a.[217] In the West, the Christian Don Luigi Giussani remarks that faithfulness is a struggle, "not the opposite of peace . . . (and later) Peace is a war, but it is with ourselves."[218] Within Islam, the term jihad seems a contradiction, referring as it does to both this inner struggle and to external warfare. All jihad warfare to protect the practice of the religion of Islam against aggression whether real or only perceived is a just war. In the West, atheist Marxist ideology similarly holds that any war is justified by definition if one belongs to the correct and proletarian economic class.

Islam practices latent but *permanent* jihad as a "defensive" campaign against perceived threats from the infidel (dar al-harb). The general self-understanding of Muslims is that jihad is justified against others only if they launch or threaten actual attacks or if they forcefully prevent the preaching of Islam.[219] The Muslim scholar Michot documents the "composite" domain neither Muslim (dar al-Islam) nor aggressively infidel (dar al-harb), where the Islamic way of life is simply precluded. He points to a fourteenth century province in what is now southeastern Turkey and which was overrun by the Mongols. The correct path of Islam, misrepresented today by radicals, was not to resort to violent jihad but simply to peacefully emigrate to where Islam could be practiced.[220] Muslim jurists of the Makiki School likewise counseled Muslim emigration from areas overrun later by Christians, as in North Africa, Spain and Sicily.[221] From the side of the Christian nations, this was also the view of Pope Innocent IV, also in response to the Mongol invasion that came at the end of the simpler crusades territories lost Islam. As pope he held himself responsible for the salvation of all, but by this time he also felt constrained to act legally. For Innocent, aggressive intervention into regions no longer Christian was justified only if the infidels unjustly advanced "perverted" religions or repulsed Christian missionaries.[222]

In practice late Medieval Christian canonists still generally maintained that conquest was necessary for Christian penetration into non-Christian lands.[223] Hostiensis, the most influential canonist of the thirteenth century, held that because of their beliefs infidels had no rights.[224] Nevertheless, the nexus between religion and warfare is different in the foundational Christian and Islamic scriptures. To Western eyes, Islam seems to be more of a surviving martial ethic drawn from early Arabian tribal culture, combined with a borrowed Old Testament way of life. There is no central place for balancing the moral virtues of fortitude and courage with justice and temperance. Nor is there room for the Sermon on the Mount. Under reconstructed Old Testament history "Jericho" is invaded by the Hebrews who killed "men and women, young and old, even the oxen and sheep and donkeys, massacring them all" (Josh. 6:21). But even in this narrative the early Israelites gave as justification their hatred for the Canaanite practice there of child sacrifice (Deut. 12:31).[225] The modern historian Freidrich Heer concedes that, "The classical Muslim idea of a permanent holy war is analogous to the medieval Christian notion of the just war. Hostiensis maintained that any crusade is a just war."[226] But within this similarity, the difference is that a crusade was "neither scripturally ordained nor was it conceived as a permanent state of political, psychological, and military belligerence."[227] In Christianity warfare has been part of the culture, but it is not an integral part of the faith in the Savior Jesus Christ (the "deposit of faith," above). The more alloyed *Qur'an*, the core of Islamic faith, seems at best to be ambivalent in restraining righteousness and self-righteous aggression. Hassan disagrees, however, and likens jihad to the war of Saul and David against Goliath and the Philistines. He also cites examples from the hadith and the *Qur'an* (Q 2:256, 49:9, 109:6) that enjoin restraint in battle.[228]

Under New Testament morality of the "new life,," the traditional and formal Western and Christian just war theory consists *of relatively clear criteria for judging specific cases against the common good,* based on particular circumstances and merits.[229] It is the common good that is protected, not Church law which is conceptually parallel to Shari'a (but not equivalent). At the theological level the Catholic theologian Hans Urs von Balthasar draws upon the Old Testament Isaiah to suggest a possible opening for interreligious dialogue on holy wars. During the ancient period, "the holy war was an undertaking of God together with his people," and reflected an understanding of Jahweh as totally free and "unpredictable"—as He is under Islam (and) "to such an extent 'that the idea of faith, for example, the assured trust in Yahweh's action, had its true origin in the holy war.'"[230] But, he adds that in Isaiah this faith transforms into a waiting on the "miraculous working of God alone" simultaneous with the "trustful *keeping still* on the part of the people." The core message within the wording of the Old Testament, then, is less toward conquest on earth than toward attentiveness (toward God).

In the overall *Qur'an*, consistent attentiveness more of an ingredient to an ambiguous composite of moral and cultural guidance. When jihad becomes less an inner struggle and, in Mohammed's later years and thereafter more of an external and active warfare, it is then easily exploited by modern day radical terrorism. The elastic meaning of jihad and the consequences of simple and tragic misunderstandings find a possible parallel with cultural misperceptions between the West and Asia in the final days of the Second World War in the Pacific. In April 1945 Japan approached Russia to act as a go-between in possible peace negotiations. When the Western leaders insisted in the Potsdam Declaration on "unconditional surrender," Japan responded with "*mokusatsu*" which can mean anything from "withhold comment" to "unworthy of public notice." "Japanese opponents of peace pushed the harsher meaning in the press, and the Allies interpreted it (the response) as an outright rejection." Momentum continued toward use of atomic bombs on Hiroshima and Nagasaki in August 1945.[231]

Westerners in the twenty-first century are forced to take careful note of Islam's self-perception and its perception of the outside world: "The more sectarian and divided a people become, the greater the necessity of the message of Islam which preaches between warring factions as the religion of peace and unity."[232] Universal human reason toward peace and unity becomes a pretense for Islam as the unilateral custodian of righteousness. The *Qur'an* includes a wide range of messages on jihad, many of them contradictory. Probably the most quoted is this apparently peaceful verse when taken in isolation: "unto you your religion, and unto me my religion" (Q 109:6). Numerous endorsements of violence also appear, in some instances defensive and not as transgressors, but elsewhere clearly more aggressive. "Believers, make war on the infidels who dwell around you" (Q9:123), and "Make War on them until idolatry shall cease and Allah's religion shall reign supreme" (Q 8:34, see also Q 2:187/191, 9:5, 47:4). The violent verses are theoretically moderated or even abrogated by offsetting verses (Q 2:256, 60:8–9). Muhammad Ali cites the following as efforts to establish the Muslim understanding of religious freedom: "And fight with them until there is no persecution and *religion is only* for Allah" (Q 2:193); and "until all religions are for Allah" (Q 8:39, both italics added)[233] To the Westerner, this verse reads like many pagan-like oracles typically including contradictory meanings and therefore likely to be vindicated. Does Islam fight to suppress persecution, or does enforcement of Islam constitute persecution?

The modern Mahmoud Ayoub holds that the Qur'anic verses fostering disunity "referred to specific political problems between the Prophet and the Jews of Madinah" (Medina) or neighboring Christians," and should not be used to negate "more numerous and more emphatic" verses that are positive in content.[234] Modern Islamic apologists note that reinterpretation of Shari'a toward peace came in later centuries when conditions warranted suspension (at least) of jihad, particularly in the ninth century when territorial expansion was replaced by "the revival of intellectual and philosophical Islam."[235] Critics, on the other hand, ask whether the later and militant verses in the *Qur'an* really do abrogate the earlier and more peaceful entries.[236]

In either case, it is probably from the later period of Mohammed's life that we have this entry: "And slay them wherever you find them (or, gain mastery over them), and drive them out from where they have driven you out. The calamity (suffered by the believers) is more severe than the murder (of unbelievers); but do not fight them by the Sacred Mosque before they fight you there. If they fight you, slay them. Such is the reward of the unbelievers" (Q 2:186/190; and Q 2: 187/191).[237] To some Muslim factions the ambiguous and escalating meaning of jihad is amplified by the presumed overlord stature of Islam: "And if two parties of the believers quarrel, make peace between them; but if one of them acts wrongfully towards the other, fight that which acts wrongfully, until it returns to the command of Allah; then if it returns, make peace between them with justice and act equitably; surely Allah loves those who act equitably" (Q 49:9). Quarrels serve as entry points for false *righteousness* and possibly the aggressive imposition of Islam. In the secular and ideological West, state power is often similarly invoked by totalitarian authorities as a pretense to suppress disorder. Celebrating the shrewd and peaceful success of the Solidarity (political) movement in Poland and speaking in the context of the West, John Paul II said this, "violence always needs to justify itself through deceit, and *to appear, however falsely, to be defending a right or responding to a threat posed by others*" (italics added).[238]

Jihad, according to Hassan, "boils down to one of two things: defense against attack, and routing *fitnah* (the persecution inspired by religious prejudices and which eliminates freedom of thought and belief), or, in other words, *protection of the mission of Islam*" (italics added).[239] The Western reader will pause at the conflated and unilateral treatment of "freedom of thought and belief" and "protection of the mission of Islam." Hassan proposes that Muslims are only allowed to undertake a "just" war, and even that doctrines on just and unjust wars developed by classical thinkers and Hugh Grotius were borrowed from Islam.[240] Still, the presumptive mission of Islam sidesteps the prudential step and decision criteria (below) which in each case help discern the Western and Christian just war. Historically, the aggressive or pre-emptive interpretation of holy war, or at least the glorification of principled death, is not unique to Islam nor is early Christianity exempt: "The ancient Germans believed that whoever died in combat was received into Valhalla no matter what the morality of his life had been; this is bellicosity carried to a paroxysm of brutality and ferocity . . . We find a similar belief among the ancient Japanese and Mohammedans, etc. Christianity transfigures this: whoever dies in that battle of faith which is martyrdom is received among the saints, that death being a kind of new baptism which purifies him of every guilt."[241]

A close look now at Christian just war theory gives us St. Augustine's four moral *criteria* for case-specific evaluation. First, the purpose is not aggressive, but to *repulse* a clear aggressor whose damage is "lasting, grave and certain." Second, all *other means* toward a solution "have been shown to be impractical or ineffective." Third, there must be "*serious prospects of success*." And fourth, "the use of arms must not produce evils and disorders graver than the evil to be eliminated."[242] Where Islam seeks to restore the harmony it equates with the religion of Abraham, the Western theory of a just war seeks to restore the *common good* by repulsing stark evil while not adding disproportionately to it. Compared to these four moral criteria, the *Qur'an* counsels defensive religious war only in self defense and, in a general way, also counsels limits: "Fight in the Cause of Allah, those who fight you, But do not transgress limits, for Allah loveth not transgressors" (Q 2:190). Commentators interpret this guidance as meaning a vigorous defense, "but only to restore peace and freedom for the worship of God."[243]

Augustine's four conditions still can be highly problematic in specific cases. On the second criterion—the exhaustion of all other alternatives—non-doctrinaire pacifists still will likely stress the range of even very tenuous actions that might be taken to avoid being pushed by events into a corner with only a military option. On the third criterion—weighing the likely outcome—Pope John Paul II offers a sobering and inspiring insight on patriotism and national identity. At the front end of the Second World War an isolated Poland accepted the solitary burden of going to war against Hitler "despite the clear inferiority of her military and technological forces. At that moment the Polish authorities judged that this was the only way to defend the future of Europe and the European spirit."[244] The chance of success was nil, but the good to be defended was very broad and deep.[245]

Likewise, the later and tragic Warsaw Uprising was highly risky from the start,[246] but by our criteria was it therefore immoral? And on the Western front, was Churchill immoral in his many speeches before the House of Commons (1940) when he said, for example, "The whole fury and might of the enemy must very soon be turned on us . . . We would rather see London laid in ruins and ashes than that it should be tamely and abjectly enslaved." Again, the outcome was totally unknown, not calculated with the precision of a double-entry accountant to produce "fewer" (physical?) evils than were immediately threatened by the assailant. In yet another example within the West, during the early 1980s the option of new technology and investment was heralded by many as a breakthrough in the post-1945 Cold War. Mobile battlefield level missiles were to be deployed to offset the Soviet Union and Warsaw Pact's massive superiority in conventional armaments and new ground based missiles, but could be seen as either defensive or offensive. Other factors were risks of collateral damage and always the danger of escalation into nuclear Armageddon.[247] Research into the only actual use of nuclear weapons during warfare—the bombing of Hiroshima and Nagasaki—opens a case study on the complexities that can shape such escalations.[248] One line of reasoning in the debate of the 1980s turned ultimately not on battlefield inventories, but on whether a more basic regime change in the Soviet Union was the key to real peace.[249] The economic cost of a new cycle of Western arms investment was calculated to swamp the failing Soviet economy and to peacefully force a negotiated and verifiable nuclear test ban treaty sought by both hawks and doves in the United States Congress.[250]

The role of informed and tough statesmanship in securing the treaty demonstrates the need to engage hard core power, interests, and alliances armed with both solid principles *and* a sound grip on significant details. In a fallen world we are to be neither too clever nor too naïve, free to maneuver but not manipulate.[251] Classical just war theory does not address the fine distinction posed by the hair-trigger tensions of today, between a morally problematic pre-emptive strike against a threatening enemy and a more justified first strike against an immanent threat. In these as in all matters, individual Christians are called to be both "wise as serpents and innocent as doves" (Mt 10:16), with the cunning and the innocence inseparable complements to each other.[252] For its part, the Church as an institution generally restrains itself in such ambivalent and intricate matters beyond its direct mission to evangelize and its competence. Instead, it contributes its important but non-authoritative policy recommendations from the perspective of moral theology, while also affirming finally that the "evaluation of (these) conditions for moral legitimacy belongs to the prudential judgment of those who have responsibility for the common good."[253] In 1965 and speaking for the Church as a whole, the Second Vatican Council stated that the Church has "admiration" for those who individually forego violence—without harm to others, but also asserted the right and duty for defense, and accepted "deterrence" if this was a step toward nuclear disarmament, and therefore in the end stopped short of demanding a "freeze" in ownership of weapon arsenals.[254]

As Philip Jenkins speculates, in today's world an invited mediation role for the Church, possibly involving a religious figure like Pope Benedict XVI, always remains a possibility. But even mediation will be much more difficult than a century ago. The former Pope Benedict XV was rebuffed as a possible mediator on the eve of the First World War. This conflict was still among empires and nation-states rather than between these and the novelty of a global, non-territorial, non-state terrorist network nested in Islamic territories. Past applications of just war theory offer little guidance today against sub-national and autonomous tribal groupings and a widespread and hydra-headed terrorist network. Nation-states must also consider the reduced response time allowed by weapons of mass destruction as well much greater precision of defensive weapon systems previously considered to be indiscriminate in their damage potential (Armageddon).

A new pacifist bias in the West would not refine, but would undermine the coherence of just war theory in its current condition. The *justice of the cause to be served* cannot be factored out of the calculus. A leading advocate of this basic point writes, "That, and nothing other than that, is the 'starting point' for just war thinking," and reiterates as a motive the presence in the world of genuine evil, not simply interests and goals.[255] The Western starting point for a just war—the justice of the cause—applies to "the powerful currents of nihilism at work in the Taliban, al-Qaeda, and other contemporary terrorist organizations and networks."[256] The advent of terrorist suicide bombing is apparently a product of the twentieth century and according to scholar Bernard Lewis has no earlier precedents in Islamic history.[257] Underscoring the merit of purposive resistance to genuine evil, the jihadist network clearly knows that killing of innocents is immoral, but they are experiencing a horrified "desire to escape reality or transform it along the lines of a second reality more congenial to the *pheumopathological* terrorist imagination." The italicized term applies to a spiritual sickness rather than any psychological disorder or more rational thought process at least calculated to achieve justice, if by whatever means. They *know* what they are doing; "They are not psychopaths who cannot distinguish good and evil or innocence and guilt."[258] The writer finds that the West has not been exempt from similar manifestations of spiritual sickness at several times and even in the recent past.[259] In dealing with the radical fringe of Islam, any appeal to a common morality (our references to universal natural law) or even to what is often an irregular path toward modernity totally misses the point of totally willful evil. And it is the disrupted families of the present generation—so often with missing fathers—that assure the aberrations of the next.

Pope Benedict points to a widespread *deadening of conscience* in the West and more broadly:

> (First) I have been absolutely certain that there is something wrong with the theory of the justifying force of the subjective conscience . . . Hitler may have had none (guilt feelings); nor may Himmler or Stalin. Mafia bosses may have none, but it is more likely that they have merely suppressed their awareness of the skeletons in their closets. And the aborted guilt feelings . . . Everyone needs guilt feelings.[260] (And second) The loss of the ability to see one's guilt, the falling silent of conscience in so many areas, is a more dangerous illness of the soul than guilt that is recognized as guilt (see Psalm 19:12)[261] . . . To identify conscience with a superficial state of conviction is to equate it with a certainty that merely seems rational, a certainty woven from self-righteousness, conformism, and intellectual laziness. Conscience is degraded to a mechanism that produces excuses for one's conduct, although in reality conscience is meant to make the subject transparent to the divine, thereby revealing man's authentic dignity and greatness.[262]

When Hannah Arendt interviewed Adolf Eichmann, the captured overseer of Hitler's "final solution" to the Jews, she found him to be "quite ordinary, commonplace, and something neither demonic nor monstrous."[263] She concludes that his participation in the demonic was due less to choice than to a habit of thoughtlessness, which she understands as our way of "protecting (ourselves) from reality." We avoid moral dilemmas through a habit of forgetfulness. The coming of Christ illumines this previous "unsalvation" of the world. A primary point of contact between Christianity and Islam is the nexus between the Muslim dilution of sin within the habitual tendency toward "forgetting," in contrast with the Christian notion of knowing and deliberated choice? Islam is chronologically post-Christian, but its understanding of original innocence and sin remains shaded with Arabia's pre-Christian "days of ignorance."

In any event, and in an imperfect world, the purification of conscience away from the choice of evil (or the prior expedient thoughtlessness) carries its own risks. Vanguard movements by "the elect" include Leninist ideology and, in the 1950s and 60s, Sayyid Qutb's radical jihad against laxness in the Muslim world. His many writings had a formative influence Osama Bin Laden,[264] and included a critique of the West, shaped in part by his two years spent in the United States (1949–50). His visit evidenced a "superficial acquaintance with Western history and thought (and his) enormous loathing of Western society."[265] Here he found fault with materialism, racism, economics and so on, and (compared to Islamic culture) even the "animal-like" mixing of the sexes. On the last point, he must have been influenced in part by the

later discredited *Kinsey Report* (1948, 1953). The Report, purportedly a sta-
tistically valid survey of sexual practices in the West, promoted mainstream
casualness and pornography under the cover of scientific respectability.[266]
Followers of Islam are scandalized by the flaunting of moral decadence in the
West, much as Westerners disdain the toleration of polygamy and the sharp
inequality and suppression of women under Islam including the sexual mutilation of young girls. In 2011 when the icon of violence against corruption
in the West, Bin Laden, was tracked down and killed in Pakistan, a supply of
pornographic material was found in his compound shared with others for five
years. Cutting across societies east and west, the pharmaceutical neutering of
women under the pretense of individual freedom (and then the prophylactic
destruction of their unexpected and unborn children), has become part of the
common moral failure of conscience.[267]

   Universal human failings are what St. Paul meant in his discourse with the
Romans: "Do not conform yourselves to this age, but be transformed by the
renewal of your mind, that you may discern the will of God, what is good and
pleasing and perfect" (Rom 12:2). Shortly after the end of the Second World
War, the Catholic convert layman philosopher Jacque Maritain played a key
role in the original United Nations Declaration on Human Rights. Nearly two
decades later at the end of the Second Vatican Council he was honored by Pope
Paul VI. Maritain attributes to our common human nature a family of "spontaneous perceptions" toward "the existence of God, the sanctity of truth, the
value and necessity of good will, the dignity of the person (and) the spirituality
and immortality of the soul."[268] Now nearly fifty years after this remark and the
social uprisings of the 1960s, Pope Benedict XVI calls for "new forms of engagement."[269] His general proposal for *"integral human development" of each
person and all persons*—a concept pioneered by Maritain—would re-center
engagement toward a solidarity that includes the most elementary "right to life
of every people and every individual" and the "right to religious freedom."

   Given the global asymmetries between Western institutions and the unitary Islamic State, the pope also proposes that: "The State does not need to
have identical characteristics everywhere: the support aimed at strengthening
weak constitutional systems can easily be accompanied by the development
of other political players, of a cultural, social, territorial or religious nature,
alongside the State."[270] In the case of individuals and families and their associations, such institutions of the universal natural law exist not within the
state, but *prior to* the state. Do we find tentative parallels between this relationship and a similar situation within the world of Islam? Wael B. Hallaq
identifies the overlaid Western state as "the most overpowering project of
modernity." He finds that the permanence of the Western state model is the
"most fundamental dilemma for Muslims around the world: If Islamic law

governed society and state for over twelve centuries, and if the rule of law had a significance beyond and above the modern state's concept of such rule, then how is that sacred law accommodated by the irretrievable fact of the state, in effect the maker of all laws?"[271] The point for dialogue again appears to be the connection between universal natural law accessible by human reason because imprinted directly in human hearts, and corresponding but very latent wording of the more polyglot *Qur'an* and hadith.

The social principles of the Catholic Church are proposed as a possible opening toward a path through this "fundamental dilemma" specific to the Islamic State. More than a checklist, the principles and particular cases offer leavening insights into the concrete human person as the free and responsible intersection of nature and grace. Natural law principles predate and if necessary will surely survive the long polar night settling over many secular and positivistic Western nation-states no less than the Islamic states. With its long memory and a "future full of hope" (Jer 29:11) the Church as a world religion has encountered the benefits and the pitfalls of modernity, particularly through the combined Vatican Councils.

Muslim investigations into the Shari'a hint toward dialogue based to some degree on the accreted natural law absorbed into the *Qur'an,* the injunction to do good and to avoid evil: "Believers . . . enjoin what is just, and forbid what is evil" (Q 9:71). Needed is a fully open dialogue that in its most preliminary stage was suppressed with early Mu'tazilites in favor of closed membership in the mega-tribe "congregational theocracy": "Muhammad is God's apostle. Those who follow him are ruthless to the unbelievers but merciful to one another" (Q 48:29). Suppressing the inner space for the universal natural law and for the discernments of reason, the injunction to "avoid evil" has been parsed throughout much of history as a recurring call to arms in the mold of Old Testament narratives. But today, thoughtful Muslim scholars distill five principles hinting more toward natural law, from at least their comprehensive review of the Shari'a. These principles, supported by the second largest school of Sunni theology (the Maturidi), are *protection of life, mind, religion, property and offspring.*[272] These principles are identical with resuscitate the "basic goods" first abstracted from the *Qur'an* and Sunnah by Al-Ghazali nearly a millennium ago: "*religion, life, reason, lineage and property.*" In 1839 the Sultan Abd-ul-Medjid (Chapter 2) proposed ways of "guaranteeing and insuring to our subjects perfect *security of life, honor, and fortune" (life, mind, property).*[273]

The Church's social principles are not abstracted as are the above principles of Islam distilled from the *Qur'an* and the hadith. Instead, they are based on a sound anthropology of man as a moral theology of human reason, and the dignity of each concrete human person without exception. These principles fill a vacancy in the political thinking of Augustine no less than the parallel void of today in Shari'a. Augustine contrasted two mystical "cities" in his treatment of "the city of truth, of the good, of order, of peace" and "the city of error, of evil, and disorder and confusion." Commenting on this dichotomy, Gilson writes: "Midway between these two cities, of which one is the negation of the other, there is situated a neutral zone where the men of our day hope to construct a third city, which would be temporal like the earthly city, yet just in a temporal way, that is striving toward temporal justice obtainable by appropriate means. Such an idea seems never to have occurred to St. Augustine, at least, he never spoke of it."[274]

To what degree does Shari'a "speak of it?" Much of the history of the West is largely the working out of this middle idea. Augustine deals mystically with the competing heavenly and worldly loves of man, while the *dar al-Islam/dar al-harb* dichotomy refers to worldly domains where members of the Islamic ummah regard themselves safe (or not) in the practice of their particular but religious way of life. The third way—"composite" zone which is neither the Islamic State nor an allegedly hostile dar al-harb (House of War)—is the compact modern world.[275] The needed grammar between Islam and the West is the universal natural law and the real "common good," eventually more than practical endeavors toward practical ends.

Required is for the followers of Islam to bracket from cultural accretions those traces of natural law found in parts of the fitra, the *Qur'an* and hadith; and required of the West is the courage to regain what it has lost of the natural law. The *Qur'an* does not fully oppose such an opening to reason. Allah has sent down "scriptures *and the scales of justice*, so that men might conduct themselves with justice" (Q 57:25, italics added). The term "sent down" (*anzala*) means that there is "created in him (man) the capacity of understanding and using" what has been given."[276] The *capacity* is *created in him*? Freed of the constraints of the archaic world, this same capacity, written directly on the human heart, was the opening for Christian society. After two millennia and above any practical outcomes to practical endeavors, when asked whether Christianity could ever really regain its "organic power in human society it once possessed" the Father of Vatican II, Cardinal John Henry Newman, responded: "I am not a politician; I am proposing no measures, but exposing a fallacy and resisting a pretense."[277]

In the history of Islam, the foundational principle of Catholic social doctrine—personal dignity—is evident in an almost random way that has altered world history. Mohammed is credibly portrayed as a quiet and peaceable man by nature and a lover of family and children, and as emotionally vulnerable due to the very early deaths of his parents and to his likely epilepsy. He later becomes passionately religious as a self-proclaimed prophet open finally to defensive and then aggressive forms of jihad. How much of this tipping point and contradiction can be traced finally to deep humiliations—to violations of his personal dignity? Preaching at the Ka'ba he was routinely scorned by his fellow tribesmen. And when driven from Mecca, and before settling in Medina among protective followers, he first was rejected and even stoned by the villagers of Taif. Historian John Glubb speculates on the historical significance of the Meccan rejection. He writes: "It is quite possible that this campaign of defamation did the Apostle more good than harm . . . the hostile remarks which the Qurayish leaders took such trouble to disseminate among the pilgrims may perhaps have served to enhance Mohammed's importance and to carry his name to distant parts of Arabia."[278] And far beyond Arabia and even into the Third Millennium.

NOTES

1. Marcello Pera contrasts these features while making the case that the West is better on these points, but he also rejects the view that conflict with Islam is unavoidably necessary ("Relativism, Christianity, and the West" in Ratzinger and Pera, *Without Roots* [New York: Basic Books, 2006], 10).

2. Peter Lawler, "The Logos in Western Thought," *Modern Age* (Bryn Mawr, Penn.: Intercollegiate Studies Institute, Spring 2009), 45.

3. Jacques Maritain, *The Range of Reason* (New York: Charles Scribner's Sons, 1952), pp. 26–27, cited by Patrick McKinley Brennan, in John Witt, Jr. and Frank Alexander (eds.), *The Teachings of Modern Roman Catholicism on Law, Politics, and Human Nature* (New York: Columbia University Press, 2007), 120.

4. Ibid., 235.

5. Alfred Guillaume, *Islam* (New York: Penguin Books, 1956), 135.

6. Original source identified in Hugo Rahner, *Church and State in Early Christianity* (San Francisco: Ignatius, 1992), 144.

7. Walter Ullmann, *Medieval Papalism: The Political Theories of the Medieval Canonists* (London: Metheun and Co. Ltd., 1949), passim., 159, 195.

8. The sometimes maligned celibacy of Catholic priests is partly attached to this house cleaning action. This "evangelical council," when reinforced by poverty and obedience, removes any chance of a hereditary or dynastic legacy to be passed along under lay control of the office of bishop. Government influence over the selection of bishops remained a concern until the Second Vatican Council (1963–5) and finally was banned in the 1983 Code of Canon Law.

9. Some historians note that in the actual wording of *Unam Sanctam* Boniface VIII addressed differently and at two levels (doctrine, and separate opinion) whether the supremacy of the spiritual over the temporal might (or might not) also involve a direct political authority of popes over kings.

10. Dante (Donald Nicholl, trans.), *Monarchy, and Three Political Letters* (New York: Noonday Press, 1954), 61–94 (Bk. 3). Dante does admit to a degree of subordination "since in a certain fashion our temporal happiness is subordinate to our eternal happiness" (94).

11. Heinrich Rommen, *A Study in Legal and Social History and Philosophy* (Indianapolis: Liberty Fund, 1998), 5.

12. Erik von Kuehnelt-Leddihn, "Reflections on the Revolution," *National Review* (July 14, 1989), 38–40. His recurring thesis is that monarchies have sometimes served the public good better than democracies, by protecting the public from ethnic warfare and from "experts." A modern case in point would be Congressional abdication of life-and-death powers to an expert Independent Payment Advisory Board established in 2010 under health care reform (the Patient Protection and Affordability Act). Cost-cutting decisions can be overridden by Congress only in the single month of January 2012, by a three-fifths vote which would not to take effect until 2020.

13. Farooq Hassan, *The Concept of State and Law in Islam* (Washington D.C.: University Press of America, 1981), 29.

14. Also from the Old Testament, "I will place my law within them, and write it upon their hearts; I will be their God, and they shall be my people" (Jer 31:33). "For such He has written Faith In their hearts, and strengthened Them with a spirit From Himself" (Q 58:22).

15. Eric von Kuehnelt-Leddhin, *Liberty or Equality* (Caldwell, Idaho: Caxton Press, 1952), 83. Likewise and coming out of Nazi Germany, the scientist credited with discovering quantum physics (Max Planck) asserted his life long belief in God when he could find no other way to challenge the assumptions of Totalitarianism.

16. "Sartor Resartus" (Ch. III) in M.H. Abrams et al (eds.), *The Norton Anthology of English Literature* (New York: W.W. Norton and Co., 1962), 1798.

17. *Centesimus Annus* (The One Hundred Years), 1991, n. 38. This encyclical marked the collapse of the Soviet Empire, one hundred years after the first formal encyclical on the condition of the working class (Pope Leo XIII, *Rerum Novarum* [New Things], 1891).

18. Hassan, 109–11. The term "abstract justice" is possibly parallel to "natural law" in Western jurisprudence. Misunderstandings between Muslims and Christians can be surprisingly basic. Hassan contrasts active Islam with Christianity: "(Thus) unlike the Christian belief of some kind of 'automatic' salvation for those who believe in Jesus, Islam stresses action as the basis of salvation and the life hereafter" (83). Hassan might be reacting to some Christians who hold that being "baptized in the spirit" and the so-called "fundamental option" confer an exemption of day-to-day actions from specific moral scrutiny.

19. Edith Stein, (translated by Marianne Sawicki), *An Investigation Concerning the State* (Washington D.C.: Institute of Carmelite Studies Publications, 2006 [1925]), 83.

20. Unlike an individual, "the man of engagement, as a mature person, confronts life integrally; he assimilates it to himself, reflects upon it, moulds it, chooses it and synthesizes its apparent disparate and unconnected events into a shining harmony of a crusade for a communion of loving collaboration here enroute to a communion of

loving happiness hereafter" (Vincent Miceli, *Ascent to Being: Marcel's Philosophy of Communion* [New York: Desclee Co., 1965], 117).

21. Romans begins "There is no authority except from God, and those which exist are established by God" (Rom 13:1).

22. Second Vatican Council, *Gaudium et Spes* (The Church in the Modern World), n. 22.

23. Owen Chadwick, *Catholicism and History: The Opening of the Vatican Archives* (New York: Cambridge University Press, 1978), 46–71.

24. John Paul II, *Christifidelis Laici* (Vocation of the Laity), n. 29. The Second Vatican Council gives further weight to this understanding: "Lay people ought to take on themselves, as their distinctive task this renewal of the temporal order . . . As citizens among citizens they must bring to their cooperation with others their own special competence, and act on their own responsibility" (*Apostolicam actuositatem*, [Decree on the Laity], n. 7). See also the *Lumen Gentium* (Constitution of the Church in the Modern World), n. 33.

25. Second Vatican Council, *Gaudium et Spes* (The Church in the Modern World), n. 54, and John Paul II, *Centesimus Annus* (One Hundred Years), n. 53.

26. Hassan, 98.

27. The quote appears in the *Qur'an* fifty times. The meaning of fitrah (not fitnah) is beautifully explained by Aliaa and Aisha Rafea, "An Essential Language" in Camille Adams Helminski (ed.), *Women of Sufism: A Hidden Treasure* (Boston: Shambhala, 2003), 196–214.

28. W.H. McNeill, *The Rise of the West,* (New York, University of Chicago Press, 1963) 642.

29. *Gaudium et Spes,* n. 36.

30. Heinrich A. Rommen, LL.D., *The State in Catholic Thought: A Treatise in Political Philosophy* (St. Louis, Mo.: Herder Book Co., 1945), 220–1 (italics added).

31. Hassan, 40.

32. Dawson, *The Making of Europe* (New York: Meridian Books, 1964), 191.

33. Scripturally, on the separation of powers see Lk 20:25 and 22:38, Jn 18:36, Mt 16:19, I Peter 2:17, Acts 5:29, and 1 Cor 2:6. In the United States the hardened and ideological phrase "wall of separation between church and state" begins to appear in two Supreme Court decisions *(Everson v Board of Education* (1947), *and McCollum v Board of Education* (1948). This catch phrase "a wall of separation" is not from the Constitution, but rather is taken from a private letter written to a group of Baptists in Connecticut by Thomas Jefferson in 1802. The First Amendment simply prohibits Congress from *establishing* a religion (taken literally, the prohibition does not apply to states). In *Everson* Justice Hugo Black applied the Constitutional amendment for the first time to legislative actions taken at the state level, i.e., the Court approved local reimbursement to parents for public transportation to and from Catholic schools (as equivalent to the use of school buses to public schools).

34. Under England's King Henry VIII only one bishop resisted subordination of the Church to the secular power. The later and more radical French Revolution beguiled only seven of 160 bishops. Half of impoverished French priests succumbed.

Some thirty to forty thousand priests and nuns were then exiled and between two and five thousand priests executed.

35. Joseph McSorley, *An Outline of History of the Church by Centuries* (St. Louis, Missouri: Herder Book Co. 1945), 632.

36. Following the Council of Vienna (1815), concordats signed between the Church and the restored hereditary monarchies does not imply a Church preference for the monarchic form of government over other forms serving the common good. When Napoleon re-entered the European stage, the Pope refused to excommunicate him, as requested by the Bourbons. Tsar Alexander's request for a blessing on his Holy Alliance of restored monarchs was also dismissed (E.E.Y Hayes, *The Catholic Church in the Modern World* [Garden City, New York: Image, 1960], 75–76).

37. "*Letter* of the Holy Father Pope Benedict XVI to the Bishops, Priests, Consecrated Persons and Lay Faithful of the Catholic Church in the People's Republic of China," May 27, 2007.

38. In particular, the Council reasserted the ecclesial jurisdiction of the Pope over every bishop in Christendom, stripped from Pope Pius VII when Napoleon imposed the Concordat of 1801 and the attached Gallican "Organic Articles" dating back to 1682 (William Barry, *The Papacy and Modern Times* [New York: Henry Holt and Col, 1911], 204–5).

39. First Vatican Council, *Dei Filius*, n. 3003.

40. Correspondence quoted in Bernard Lewis, *The Muslim Discovery of Europe* (New York: W.W. Norton, 1982), 177.

41. Leopold Ranke, *History of the Popes,* Vol. II (London: George Bell and Sons, 1870), 467.

42. Owen Chadwick, op. cit., 44–45.

43. Beyond the focus of the Council's precise and narrow definition of papal infallibility were the earlier approaches to temporal power made by Gregory VII, Innocent III and Boniface VIII. With the definition in 1870, the Austro-Hungarian Emperor Frans Josef cancelled the 1855 Concordat with the Church, claiming that this definition changed the nature of the signing party. In previous years the Empire had instituted civil marriages, state control of schools and equivalency among different Christian creeds (Edward Crankshaw, *The Fall of the House of Habsburg* [New York: Viking Press, 1963], 244).

44. The Bull (official decree) *Cum ex Apostolatus officio* (1558), cited in "Janus," *The Pope and the Council* (London: Roberts Brothers, 1870), 311.

45. One detailed account available in English is Dom Cuthbert Butler, *The Vatican Council 1869–70* (London: Collins and Harvill Press, 1962 [1930]). A less sympathetic and less detailed account at the time of the Council is Lord Acton 1834–1902), *Essays on Freedom and Power* (New York: Meridian Books, 1960), 275–327.

The precise definition on infallibility reads as follows: "The Roman Pontiff when he speaks *ex cathedra*, that is, when exercising the office of pastor and teacher of all Christians, he defines with his supreme apostolic authority a doctrine concerning faith or morals to be held by the universal Church, through the divine assistance promised to him in St. Peter, is possessed of that infallibility with which the divine Redeemer willed his Church to be endowed in defining doctrine concerning faith and morals:

and therefore such definitions of the Roman Pontiff are irreformable of themselves (and not from the consent of the Church)" (Butler, 385). This teaching is reaffirmed by the Second Vatican Council in *Lumen Gentium* (Light of the World), n. 25. The notorious failure of Pope Honorius in 634 A.D. to respond clearly to Patriarch Sergius of Constantinople on the issue of Monothelitism—whether Christ had both a human and divine will—was an informal negligence rather than a formal pronouncement.

46. John Henry Cardinal Newman, *Apologia Pro Vita Sua* (Garden City, New York: Image, 1962), 329.

47. Kathleen G. Cushing, *Papacy and Law in the Gregorian Revolution* (Oxford: Clarendon Press, 1998).

48. Al-Munqidh translated by R.J. McCarthy, *Al-Ghazali's Path to Sufism: His Deliverance from Error* (Louisville: Fons Vitae, 1999 [1131]), 44.

49. Newman converted when he saw the parallel between his Anglican home and the doctrinal movements of the first centuries that departed from, rather than maintained, the original teachings of the Church.

50. Owen Chadwick, op. cit., 92.

51. Newman offers us a resilient and non-Darwinian perspective on human understanding: "There is no corruption if it retains one and the same type, the same principles, the same organization; if its beginnings anticipate its subsequent phases, and its later phenomena protect and subserve its earlier, if it has a power of assimilation and revival, and a vigorous action from first to last . . ." (*Essay*, London and New York: Longmans, Green, 1885, Ch. V, cited by Vincent Ferrer Blehl [ed.], *The Essential Newman* [New York: Mentor-Omega, 1963], 136–7).

52. Philip Boyce (ed.), *Mary: the Virgin Mary in the Life and Writings of John Henry Newman* (Grand Rapids: William Eerdmans Publishing Co., 2001), 337.

53. The expression "servant of the servants of God" is scripture-based (Mk 10: 44–45), and used early by Pope Gregory the Great and coined by St. Augustine in reference to his mother.

54. In (experimentally verified) physics the sequence of simplifying assumptions combined with more intricate equations has taken us from Newton's mechanics of separate bodies, to the duality of subatomic particles and charges, to field theory and the interchangeability of matter and energy, to the continuity of space and time, and to special relativity theory as a subset of general relativity, and then to the probabilistic physics of quantum mechanics. (Albert Einstein and Leopold Infeld, *The Evolution of Physics* [New York: Simon and Schuster, 1938]). Recent theory and research continues this trajectory. Each earlier stage of understanding fits within the broader stage, but not the other way around. Even for the structure of science, one might say there is a hierarchy of truths.

55. The divinely revealed teachings are the articles of the Creed, the implicit and now explicit Christological and Marian dogmas, the institution of the sacraments by Christ, the efficacy of grace, the substantive presence of Christ in the Eucharist, the foundation of the Church by Christ and the primacy of the pontiff, and his role in the Church's gift of infallibility as precisely defined, the reality of redemption from original sin, the immortality of the soul, the inerrancy of Scripture with regard to the message of salvation, and the immorality of killing innocent life. Examples of moral

doctrines—the natural law—include the illicitness of euthanasia and prostitution. (*Ad Tuendum Fidem* [to Protect the Faith], Congregation for the Doctrine of the Faith, 1998, nn. 10–12).

56. See Lk 10:16, Mt 18:17–18, Jn 20:23, and Acts 15, 16:4. The beginnings of the Church structure are indicated in 1 Cor 16:16, 12:28, Heb 13:17, and Acts 20:28. Foundational actions are traced to Peter in Acts 2:14–18, 4:8, and 15:8, as well as Paul in Acts 13, and 16:6, 20. The primacy of Peter as the witnessing and concrete man of faith, and not simply the faith found incidentally in Peter, is also recorded in Acts 1:13–26, 12:17 and 15:6–12.

57. Daniel Madigan, *The Qur'an's Self-Image: Writing and Authority in Islam's Scriptures* (Princeton, N.J.: Princeton University Press, 2001).

58. Giorgio de Santillana, *The Crime of Galileo*, (Chicago: University of Chicago Press, 1955), 98. Augustine remarked: "Whatsoever in holy writ cannot be properly said to be concerned either with morality or with the faith must be allegorical" (Farrar, *History of Scriptural Interpretation* [1886], cited in Basil Willey, *The Seventeenth Century Background* (Garden City: Doubleday, 1953 [1935]), 68.

59. Santillana shows that the instruction to not teach appears to have been secretly added to the case file some time after the first Tribunal action of 1616 and before the trial in 1633 (Giorgio de Santillana, *The Crime of Galileo* [Chicago: University of Chicago Press, 1955], passim).

60. Galileo (1563–1641) remarked "Scripture cannot err, but its interpreters can." Bellarmine, his primary interlocutor, erred in many ways including his superficial familiarity with the earlier Copernicus based only on the Introduction of his unchallenged writing (1543). Santillana (ibid., 101) writes that the Introduction describes the heliocentric view as "purely a mathematical supposition . . . with no bearing on the reality of the heavens." The Introduction to Copernicus was written by "Osiander, a Lutheran pastor who was trying in this way to make it acceptable to fundamentalist prejudice." Prior to Copernicus, DaVinci (d. 1519) wrote in his journal "The sun does not set" (cited in E.H. Gombrich, *The Story of Art* [Englewood Cliffs, N.J.,: Prentice-Hall, 1983] 222). Before the Galileo incident, Johann Kepler was excommunicated from the Lutheran church (1613) for holding the moon was a solid body rather than a "lesser light to rule the night."

Bellarmine did look through the telescope, while today court orders restrict the access to the sonograms that unveil an unborn living universe within. Bellarmine wrote: "I say that if it were really demonstrated that the sun is at the center of the world and the Earth is in the third heaven, and that it is not the sun which revolves round the Earth, but the Earth round the sun, then it would be necessary to proceed with great circumspection in the explanation of Scriptural texts which seem contrary to this assertion and to say that we do not understand them, rather than to say that what is demonstrated is false" (cited by Cardinal Poupard, "Galileo: Report on Papal Commission Findings," *Origins* [22:22], Washington, D.C.: Catholic News Service, 1992).

61. Friedrich Heer, *The Intellectual History of Europe* (New York: World Publishing Co., 1953), 308.

62. Al-Munqidh min al-Dalal, op. cit., 33

63. The nineteenth Cardinal John Henry Newman demonstrates that the Galileo affair is only one of several instances of Church actions that do not discredit "infallibility" as actually defined. "What have excommunication and interdict to do with infallibility? Was St. Peter infallible on that occasion at Antioch when St. Paul withstood him? Was St. Victor infallible when he separated from his communion the Asiatic Churches? Or Liberius when in like manner he excommunicated Athanasius? And, to come to later times, was Gregory XIII, when he had a medal struck in honour of the Bartholomew massacre? Or Paul IV in his conduct towards Elizabeth? Or Sextus V when he blessed the Armada? Or Urban VIII when he persecuted Galileo? No Catholic ever pretends that these Popes were infallible in these acts" (from a Letter to the Duke of Norfolk [1876], in Vincent Blehl (ed.), *The Essential Newman* [New York: Mentor Omega, 1963]. 269).

64. Theologians and philosophers use the term *ex nihilo* (out of nothing). *Ex nihilo* is not to be confused with "space" or even "energy" as apart from matter, since it is matter itself (or better, mass-energy) that generates space (or better, physical inertial coordinate systems). It is the *being* (of "things") in all of its dimensions that stands apart from the metaphysical "nothing" designated by the term *ex nihilo*.

65. See the International Theological Commission, "Communion and Stewardship" (July 23, 2004). Also, Charles Darwin's son, Francis, edited Darwin's letters in which we find this: "Now I have never systematically thought much on religion in relation to science, or on morals in relation to society; and without steadily keeping in mind on such subjects for a long period, I am really incapable of writing anything worth sending..." (*The Life and Letters of Charles Darwin* [D. Appleton-Century Co., n.d.], 275–6). Darwin's later attitudes apparently solidified shortly after the sudden death of his ten-year old daughter Anne.

66. Preface to a 1986 Symposium, cited at length in Christopher Cardinal Schonborn, *Creation and Evolution* (San Francisco: Ignatius, 2008), 9.

67. During the period, prior to pressuring the pope to sign a Concordat (a signature almost immediately rescinded), Napoleon confided his religious beliefs to Thibaudeau, counselor of state: "They will say that I am a papist—I am no such thing. I was a Mahomedan in Egypt—I will be a Catholic here, for the good of the people. I do not believe in forms of religion, but in the existence of God" (Walter Scott, *Life of Napoleon: Emperor of the French*, Vol II [Exeter: J & B Williams, 1832], 400).

68. Literally "beyond the mountains" referring to the supremacy of Rome over nation-based churches (e.g., French Gallicanism). The New Ultramontanes sought to extend this internal Church structure into extreme interpretations to cover political and social questions, i.e., they asserted an imagined "omnipotence of the Pope, as the source of all authority, spiritual and temporal" (Veuillot), and condemned modern constitutional forms of government. (Dom Cuthbert Butler, *The Vatican Council 1869–1870*, 61–2.)

69. Striking are the parallel to the ummah, the ulema, and the state as an executor of divine law. Luther's bid for secular protection from the emerging nation-state is likely connected to his support for the bigamy of Philip of Hesse. Under the secular Holy Roman Empire the penalty for bigamy and its sympathizers was beheading

(Stanley Jaki, *Praying the Psalms*, Grand Rapids, Michigan: William B. Eerdmans, 2001, 132.

70. Eric von Kuehnelt-Leddihn, *Liberty or Equality*, 221.

71. One English bishop who attended all but four of the eighty-eight sessions made this comparison: "I have known the House of Commons since my boyhood, and I have witnessed more disorder and heard and seen more violence in that assembly— aye by one hundredfold—than I have ever heard or seen in the Council." Among other citations are those of American bishops of the Opposition who reported "a liberty of speech in the Council which is not exceeded in Congress" (John Francis Maguire, op. cit., 543–554). Impressed by earlier biases, the modern historian Paul Johnson asserts that the council action constituted "popular despotism" and the "extinction of the liberal Catholics" (A *History of Christianity* [New York: Atheneum, 1979], 394–5).

72. Consistent with the First Vatican Council's *Pastor Aeternus* (Eternal Pastor) Pope Leo XIII's encyclical *Satis cognitum* and the later 1917 Code of Canon Law (canons 329, 197) provided that the pope's universal jurisdiction does not impair the true episcopal jurisdiction of bishops in their respective dioceses.

73. Among other changes, a revised concordat in 1984 removed Roman Catholicism as the state religion and Rome's status as a "sacred city."

74. "Vatican I, after defining the primacy and infallibility of the Roman Pontiff, had intended to consider the Episcopal office, but the labors of the Council were interrupted by political upheavals. Thus Vatican II on this point resumes where Vatican I left off . . ." (Second Vatican Council, *Lumen Gentium* [Constitution on the Church], fn. 65).

75. The advantage of having lost territorial power is noted by John Allen, Notre Dame University, in verbal remarks on Inside the Vatican (EWTN telecast, February 2009), and sets the Church very much apart institutionally from the other world religion of Islam with its fused Islamic state.

76. Leopold Ranke, *History of the Popes*, Vol. I (London: George Bell and Sons, 1878), 266.

77. Raymond Jaems Sontag, *European Diplomtic History, 1871–1932* (New York: D. Appleton-Century Co., 1933, 241).

78. *Des Le Debut* (To the Belligerent Peoples), August 1, 1917, in Anne Fremantle (ed.), *The Social Teachings of the Church* (New York: Mentor Omega, 1963), 75–79. Summarizing, the propositions were the need to assert moral force over material force, simultaneous disarmament, arbitration in place of conscription, free movement of people and commerce especially at sea, disarmament, restitution of territories seized during the War, and harmony among national aspirations and with the common good. The relationship between these proposals and Wilson's is noted in research by Professor James Felak, University of Washington, "The Vatican in the Twentieth Century: The Pope's Confront a Turbulent World" (College of Arts and Sciences and Alumni Association History annual Costigan Lecture Series, 2009).

79. Energetic debate and dissent over the meaning of the Second Vatican Council hinges on the alleged difference between the "spirit of Vatican II" and the actual documents. To address this point, an extraordinary synod of bishops was convened in 1985. One of several suggestions to advance and "objective" reception of the Council simply called for a reading of the documents: ". . . a new diffusion of the documents

themselves . . ." (*The Extraordinary Synod: 1985* [Boston: Daughters of St. Paul, 1985], 42).

80. Cited in Thomas P. Neill, *Religion and Culture* (Milwaukee: The Bruce Publishing Co., 1951), 68. On the heels of the Second World War, Pope Pius XII remarked to the College of Cardinals "The Church cannot confine itself inert in the secrets of its temples; in this wise it deserts the mission Divine Providence confided to it of forming the complete man" (Ibid., 69, from *Catholic Mind*, April 1946, 201).

81. Joseph Ratzinger, On the Way to Jesus Christ, *On the Way to Jesus Christ* (San Francisco: Ignatius, 2005), 76–8.

82. In a critique of "Pope John II on Islam," Irfan A. Omar (ed.), Mahmoud Ayoub, A *Muslim View of Christianity* (Maryknoll, New York: Orbis Books, 2007), 241.

83. Second Vatican Council, *Dei Verbum*, (The Word of God), n. 4. On the other hand, from the later Muslim perspective: "Moreover, saying categorically that Mohammed is the last Prophet, the door to future claims and calls was thus closed for good. This is the final message of Islam" (Hassan, 233).

84. Ibid. (italics added). The reference to both words *and* deeds protects scriptural theology, and the revealed nature of the human person, from the erosion of an overzealous historical-critical approach to biblical testimony.

85. Ayoub in Omar (ed.), 135.

86. The remaining two constitutions are on (*Sacrosanctum Concilium*, (Sacred Liturgy) and *Lumen Gentium* (The Church).

87. Second Vatican Council, *Gaudium et Spes* (The Church in the Modern World), n. 2, italics added. The "When one member of the body suffers, we all suffer" (1 Cor 12:26). Pope Benedict XVI finds the document problematic for a second reason as well, which he balances in his encyclical *Deus Caritas Est (*God is Love, 2006). Tracy Roland explains that *Gaurdium et Spes* expounds a spirituality of intellect, conscience, and freedom, but fails to include the central concepts of the person and of love (*Ratzinger's Faith: The Theology of Pope Benedict XVI* [Oxford University Press, 2009]).

88. Second Vatican Council, *Gaudium et Spes*, n. 22. While Vatican II draws from John Courtney Murray in its doctrine on religious liberty (from state pressure), it seems here to go beyond a possible shortcoming in Murray's thesis. Murray is critiqued for trusting in "articles of peace" disconnected from "articles of faith," that is, for believing that a public forum consistently protective of the public good can be value neutral at its base, or whether it must tend first toward holiness. See David L. Schindler, *Heart of the World, Center of the Church* (Grand Rapids, Michigan: William Eerdmans Publishing Co., 1996), 53–65, and "Interview: The Culture of Love," *Catholic World Report* (October 1994), 42–49. In the early nineteenth century Alexis de Tocqueville also foresaw deterioration of a culture that admitted to both obedience and individualistic liberty: "...our posterity will tend more and more to a division into two parts, *some relinguishing Christianity entirely* and others returning to the Church of Rome" (*Democracy in America*, vol. II, Ch. 6, italics added).

89. Ibid., n. 76.

90. Cited by Benedict in "St. Basil: A Voice for Today," Weekly General Audience for August 1, 2007, in the *National Catholic Register*, August 12, 2007.

91. Second Vatican Council, *Gaudium et Spes* (The Church in the Modern World), n. 24.

92. Ibid., "And God created man to his own image: to the image of God he created him: male and female he created them" (Gen 1:27). Man occupies a unique place in creation (Gen 2:20, Ps 8:6–7, Wisdom 9:2–3).

93. *The Glory of the Lord: A Theological Aesthetics*, Vol. II (San Francisco: Ignatius, 1998), 15. The seven-volume series is divided internally by the year 1300 between Clerical Styles (Vol. II) and Lay Styles (Vol. III). Succeeding the synthesis developed by Aquinas, the lay styles begin with Dante and include Erasmus and Luther, Pascal and Leibniz, Peguy and Bernanos, Hopkins and Newman, and others.

94. St. Francis de Sales, *Introduction to the Devout Life* (Garden City, New York: Image Books, 1950), 39.

95. Second Vatican Council, *Lumen Gentium* (Dogmatic Constitution of the Church), n. 16. At a very different point in history, Saint Polycarp, writing within living memory of the Apostles and centuries before the advent of Islam, said this: "For anyone who does not confess that Jesus has come in the flesh is the antichrist. And anyone who refuses to admit the testimony of the cross is of the devil. Whoever perverts the Lord's words to suit his own desires and denies that there is a resurrection or a judgment is the firstborn of Satan" (From a letter to the Philippians, in *The Liturgy of the Hours*, Vol. IV [New York: Catholic Book Publishing, 1975], 323).

Islam accepts resurrection and judgment. The key terms cited from *Lumen Gentium* are "profess to hold" and "adore." *Dominus Iesus* (The Lord Jesus [Congregation for the Doctrine of the Faith, 2000]) announces the "doctrine of faith... willed by the One and Triune God" which *"must be believed"* (italics in original) . . . (has) at the source and center . . . the mystery of the incarnation" (n. 11). A distinction is made between the gift of *theological faith* as acceptance of revealed truth, and the *belief* found in other religions which are to be respected (nn. 7, 21).

96. Second Vatican Council, *Nostra Aetate* (Declaration on the Relationship of the Church to Non-Christian Religions), n. 1. Even authentic ecumenism among Christian religions requires respectful attention to differences: "Nothing is so foreign to the spirit of ecumenism as a false conciliatory approach which harms the purity of Catholic doctrine and obscures its assured genuine meaning" (*Decree on Ecumenism*, n. 11).

97. Ibid., n. 2.

98. Ibid., n. 3.

99. Second Vatican Council, *Declaration on Religious Freedom*, n. 6, fn. 19.

100. John Paul II, *Centesimus Annus* (One Hundred Years), May 1, 1991, n. 44.

101. Second Vatican Council, *Declaration on Religious Freedom*, n. 6.

102. *Centesimus Annus* (One Hundred Years), n. 46, italics added.

103. Ibid., n. 14.

104. Farooq Hassan, *The Concept of State and Law in Islam*, 87.

105. David Schindler is critical of Murray's analysis. He argues that the "neutral" public square evades a positive understanding of the human person and of freedom involving a truth content. Therefore, it inevitably drifts toward the fig leaf of proceduralism and finally coercion. See *Heart of the World, Center of the Church* (Grand Rapids, Michigan: William B. Eerdmans, 1996), passim, and 177–84.

106. Examples of confessional states are Ireland which is Catholic but also admits other religions, Calvin's Geneva, sectarian domains based on the 1555 Council of Augsburg, and today the nation-state subdivisions of dar al-Islam.

107. See the comment and footnote on John Courtney Murray, S.J., in Chapter Two. In the context of Islam, rather than totalitarian Western states, is it conceivable that a neutral (non-Christian) definition of Natural Law might serve less as a path to tolerance than as a half-way house to the more assertive Shari'a Law?

108. Angela Carmella, "Commentary on John Courtney Murray," in John Witte Jr. and Frank S. Alexander (eds.), *The Teachings of Modern Roman Catholicism* (Washington, D.C.: Catholic University Press, 2007), 207.

109. "It was, in a sense, the self-fulfilling prophecy: knowing that the Catholic Church would vigorously oppose abortion we laced the campaign with generous dollops of anti-Catholicism, and once the monster was lured out of the cave in response to the abortion challenge and the nakedly biased line we could make the Catholic Church the point man on the opposition" (Bernard Nathanson, M.D., *The Abortion Papers: Inside the Abortion Mentality* [New York: Frederick Fell Publishers, 1983], 196).

110. Carol Everett television interview on "Highlights," May 8, 2009.

111. The Universal Islamic Declaration of Human Rights (September 19, 1981) has "Islam" as the first word in its Foreword, and contains one sentence (Section XIII) on religious freedom: "Every person has the right to *freedom of worship* in accordance with his religious beliefs" (italics added).

112. For readability, the more recent versions of the Vatican II documents omit the sometimes essential footnotes on this point and others, as found in the unofficial Abbott version (Abbott, Walter (editor), *The Documents of Vatican II* [New York: Guild Press, 1966]). Several clarifying footnotes were included as a condition for Council adoption of the documents (Wiltgen, Ralph, *The Rhine Flows Into the Tiber: A History of Vatican II* [Rockford, Illinois: Tan Publishers, 1966]).

113. See especially the *Catechism of the Catholic Church,* (1994); as well as the concurrent encyclical *Veritatis Splendor* (The Splendor of the Truth), John Paul II, St. Paul: Pauline Books and Media, 1999.

114. Aleksandr Solzhenitsyn, "We have ceased to see the Purpose," Liechtenstein, Sept. 14, 1993, in Edward Ericson and Daniel Mahoney (eds.), *The Solzhenitsyn Reader* (Wilmington, DE.: Intercollegiate Studies Institute, 2008), 591–601.

115. Second Vatican Council, *Gaudium et Spes* (The Church in the Modern World),n. 16, italics added.

116. Interview with *Samedi-Soir,* Nov. 8, 1947, cited in Hans Urs von Balthasar, *Bernanos: An Ecclesial Existence* (San Francisco: Ignatius, 1996), 457.

117. Second Vatican Council, *Lumen Gentium* (Dogmatic Constitution on the Church), "Prefatory Note," n. 2. The text refers to the bishops in relation to their pope, but considering the "universal call to holiness," and the shared sacramental life, is in service to and embraces all of the laity. The self understanding of the Church is that Church of Christ "subsists" in the Catholic Church, that it began with the coming of the Holy Spirit at Pentecost and the commissioning of the apostles by Christ, as narrated in Scripture (e.g., *Lumen Gentium*, n. 8).

118. Ibid., n. 22.

119. This scriptural foundation of primacy achieved explicit importance in the middle of the third century under Pope Steven and later under Pope Damasus in 382 A.D. (Henry Chadwick, *The Early Church* (New York: Penguin, 1970), 237–8.

120. Joseph Cardinal Ratzinger (Pope Benedict XVI), *God's Word: Scripture, Tradition and Office* (San Francisco: Ignatius Press, 2008), 15–22.

121. John Paul II, *Apostolos Suos*, ("On the Theological and Juridical Nature of Episcopal Conferences)," Apostolic Letter, May 21, 1998, n. 24, referencing the Extraordinary Synod of Bishops (convened on the twentieth anniversary year of the Second Vatican Council), 1985. Beyond a few narrowly defined exceptions "the competence of individual diocesan Bishops remains intact; and neither the Conference nor its president may act in the name of all the Bishops unless each and every Bishop has given his own apostolically grounded consent" (*Code of Canon Law,* Canon 455:4, cited in *Apostolos Suos*. The "exceptions" noted in the text are either unanimity, or a two thirds vote combined with confirming action by the whole Church, that is, the Vatican.

122. Yves Congar, *Traditions and Tradition* (Irving, Texas: Basilica Books, 1997).

123. For individuals, the English Calvinist Reverend Hawker (1753–1827) says this as well as any: "Moreover, has thou ever looked with an eye of faith and love to Jesus? If so, it must have been wrought by this eye of Christ upon thee, my soul: for, mark it, we never look to him with an eye of faith, until Jesus hath first looked on us with an eye of love. If we love him, it is because he first loved us. (Robert Hawker, *The Poor Man's Morning and Evening Portions* [Grand Rapids, Mich.: Reformation Heritage Books 1995 and 1831], 697). The Catholic faith stresses the communal aspect of personal union with Christ as complementing the more individual one-on-one and *sola Scriptura* approach of Protestant assemblies.

124. T.S. Eliot, *The Idea of a Christian Society* (New York: Harcourt, Brace and Co., 1940), 14.

125. Peter Lawler, "The Human Dignity Conspiracy," *The Intercollegiate Review,* Wilmington, DE: Intercollegiate Studies Institute, Spring 2009, 40–50. Lawler was a member of former President Bush's disbanded Council on Bioethics. Critics of the replacement Commission on Bioethics under a new president identify a shift of focus from the morality of proposed actions toward a narrower, utilitarian and procedural agenda, i.e., the development of "recommendations through practical and policy related analyses" (wording of a White House statement included in Eric Cohen and Yuval Levin, "Nothing to See Here," *First Things* [New York: Institute on Religion and Public Life, June/July 2010], 29–31).

126. Pierre-Jean De Smet, *Origin, Progress, and Prospects of the Catholic Mission to the Rocky Mountains* (Fairfield, Washington: Ye Galleon Press, 1967) [reprint from a possibly unique original in the Oregon Province Archives dated 1843, 12 pages]). Reminiscent of St. Francis on the banks of the Nile, In 1868 De Smet ignored threats of death and entered Sitting Bull's camp unarmed, in this case to arrange a truce. Violation of this treaty led to Custer's defeat at the Battle of the Little Big Horn in 1876.

127. Jim Wallis, "No More 'Lesser of Two Evils' Politics," *USA Today*, Oct. 8, 1996; author of *Who Speaks for God?*

128. That we constitute ourselves through action, and in relationship, is central to Christianity and is a theme developed theologically in Ratzinger (Pope Benedict XVI), *In the Beginning*, Grand Rapids, Michigan: William Eerdmans, 1995, passim and 69, 73; and philosophically in Karol Wojtyla (John Paul II), *The Acting Person*, The Yearbook of Phenomenological Research, Vol. X (D. Reidel Publishing Co., Boston, 1979), passim.

129. Thomas Molnar, *Christian Humanism: A Critique of the Secular City and It's Ideology* (Chicago: Franciscan Herald Press, 1978), 117.

130. John Paul II, *Veritatis Splendor* (The Splendor of the Truth), 1993, n. 52 (paraphrased).

131. Ibid., n. 76.

132. John Paul II, *Christefidelis Liaci* (Faithful Christian Laity) n. 37; See Mk 8:36.

133. Pope Benedict XVI, *Jesus of Nazareth* (New York: Doubleday, 2007), 118.

134. Second Vatican Council, *Gaudium et Spes*, n. 31. The 1983 *Code of Canon Law* reflects this constraint against unwarranted pronouncements on merely contingent or political matters: "To the Church belongs the right always and everywhere to announce moral principles, including those pertaining to the social order, and to make judgments on any human *affairs to the extent that they are required by the fundamental rights of the human person or the salvation of souls*" (Canon 747/2, italics added).

135. Ibid., n. 36 (italics added).

136. Farooq Hassan, *The Concept of State and Law in Islam*, 109–11, 126.

137. Ibid., 111, italics added.

138. The principles are not new, and in pragmatic form are found in the earliest days of the Church. See Igino Giordani, *The Social Message of the Early Church Fathers* (Boston: St. Paul Editions, 1977).

139. The relevant numbered sections in the *Catechism of the Catholic Church* (CCC) are: the Dignity of the Human Person: nn. 1700–1702, and 1929; a Call to Family, Community and Participation in three sections: Family: nn. 2204–2213, Community: nn. 1877–1912, and Participation: nn.1913–1917; personal Rights in several sections: n. 1930, Rights: n. 2237, Right to Life: n. 2270, Right to Immigrate: n. 2241, Right to Freedom: n. 1738, Right to Work: nn. 2429–30, 2433; personal Responsibilities of citizens: nn. 2238–2240; Concern for the Poor and Vulnerable: nn. 2444, and 2447–49; The Dignity and Rights of Workers: nn. 2427–2428, 2211, 2436, and 2429–35; Solidarity: nn.1939–1942; Care for God's Creation: nn. 2415–2418, and 339–373.

140. Biblical references to human dignity include: Gen 1:22–27 (image of God), Gen 2:17 (conscience and tree of life), Deut 30:19 (choose life), Psalms 8:5–7 (man "little less than a god"), Rom 3:8 (not licit to do evil that good might come of it), Lk 20:25 (render unto Caesar and render unto God).

141. The *Muslim Universal Declaration of Human Rights* (Sept. 19, 1981) reads in part "Human rights in Islam are firmly rooted in the belief that God, and God alone,

is the Law Giver and the Source of all human rights . . . (from the Foreword, www. alhewar.com/ISLAMDECL. html).

142. Edith Stein (Waltraut Stein, trans.), *On the Problem of Empathy* (Washington, D.C.: ICS Publications, 1989), 110.

143. Second Vatican Council, *Gaudium et Spes* (The Church in the Modern World), n. 27.

144. Max Eastman, *Reflections on the Failure of Socialism,* New York: Devin-Adair, 1955, in William F. Buckley (ed.), *American Conservative Thought in the Twentieth Century* (New York: The Bobbs-Merrill Co., 1970), 203. In his "Defense of Poetry" the earlier poet Shelley (1792–1822) stresses "the creative faculty to imagine that which we know."

145. Litigation in 2008 upholding a South Dakota law establishes that "abortion will terminate the life of a whole, separate, unique, living human being" and that this is a statement of fact rather than a "statement of ideology" (Eighth Circuit Court of Appeals; 530 F.3d 724).

146. In cloning, the nucleus of any cell of the body other than a sperm or egg cell is inserted into an egg (ovum) cell from which the egg cell's nucleus has been removed. With electrical stimulation the egg reacts as if it had been fertilized by a sperm cell, producing a one-cell zygote which divides and develops. For the first eight weeks it is called an *embryo*, and is genetically identical to the donor of the somatic cell.

147. Preference for speculative embryonic stem cell research reflects that fact that the results can be patented for lucrative marketing, while adult stem cells lines cannot. The parallel with corporate monopolies on agribusiness seed strains and crop yields is difficult to overlook.

148. Euthanasia is now well established in the Netherlands and Belgium and on the horizon in France, the United Kingdom and New Zealand. Regarding deliberate suicide, the *Qur'an* reads "Do not kill yourselves. God is merciful to you, but he that does that through wickedness and injustice shall be burned in fire. That is easy enough for God" (Q 4:28).

149. Second Vatican Council, *Gaudium et Spes*, n. 27. Through the *Catechism* the magisterium (nn. 2033–5) identifies intrinsically evil acts, including: intentional killing of the innocent (n. 2273*),* infanticide (n. 2268), abortion (n. 2273), euthanasia (n. 2277); (and sexual immorality: nn. 2352, 2353, 2356, 2357, 2370, 2380, 2381). The "fundamental option" is inseparable from actions (VS, n. 67). And*:* "Indeed, the failure to protect and defend life in its most vulnerable stages renders suspect any claims to the 'rightness' of positions in other matters affecting the poorest and least powerful of the human community" (United States Catholic Conference of Bishops [USCCB], *Living the Gospel of Life*, 1998, n. 23). In a memorandum to Cardinal McCarrick (made public July 2004), Cardinal Joseph Ratzinger clarified persistent misunderstandings in the United States on the just war and on capital punishment: "While the Church exhorts civil authorities to seek peace, not war, and to exercise discretion and mercy in imposing punishment on criminals, it may still be permissible to take up arms to repel an aggressor or to have recourse to capital punishment" (n. 3). A diversity of opinion is legitimate on these points, "but not however with regard to abortion and euthanasia."

150. Ibid., n. 73. "The common good does not consist in the simple sum of the particular goods of each subject of a social entity. Belonging to everyone and to each person, it is and remains 'common,' because it is indivisible and because only together is it possible to attain it, increase it and safeguard its effectiveness, with regard also to the future" (*Compendium of the Social Doctrine of the Church*, 2004, 164).

151. John Paul II, *Christifideles Liaci*, n. 4.

152. United States Conference of Catholic Bishops (USCCB), *Living the Gospel of Life*, 1998, n. 23, italics added. The clarity of this affirmation should arouse sympathy for Muslim thinkers like Hassan who see in the West a "dichotomy" between righteousness and politics.

153. Biblical references to Family, Community and Participation include: Acts 2:42–7, 4:32–5, 6:1–7 (deacons serve), John 2: 1–12 (marriage feast at Cana), Gen 17:7–8 and Exodus 6:6–8 (covenant), Psalms 72:1–30 (just and peaceful realm), Mark 1:14–15 (reign of God social image), Mt 19:3–6, Jn 2:1–11 (marriage), Lk 22:14–20 and Cor 11:23–6 and Hebrews 8:7–12 (Christ's new covenant).

154. John Paul II, *Centesimus Annus* (One Hundred Years), n. 39. CA updated the entire social doctrine and was delivered on the one hundredth anniversary of the first major formal document (*Rerum Novarum*, or New Things) and the occasion of the collapse of the Soviet Empire in 1991. A related resource is *Guidelines for Teaching the Church's Social Doctrine in Forming Priests*, Congregation for Catholic Education, *in The Pope Speaks* (Huntington, Indiana: Our Sunday Visitor, 34:4, 1989), 293–333.

155. Gabriel Marcel, *The Mystery of Being*, Vol. 1 (Chicago: Gateway, 1950), 241.

156. Scriptural entries can be found in both the Old and New Testament (Rom 1:18–32; see also in the Bible 1 Tim 1:10, 1 Cor 6:9, Gen 19:1–11 and Lev 18:22 and 20:13) and in the *Qur'an* (Q 4:16, 7:80, 11:77–83, 26:166, 27:54–58, 29:28). With regard to Islam, Enrique Rueda speculates that if American Christian churches were to cast their lot with the homosexual movement . . . a fair number of individuals would seek refuge in other religious creeds . . . in agreement with the natural law" (*The Homosexual Network* [Old Greenwich, Connecticut: 1982], 263–4).

157. In reaffirming relevant Church teaching on sexual ethics and the critical distinction between sexual orientation and actions, the Church actually reaffirms a respect for all persons: "It is deplorable that homosexual persons have been and are the object of violent malice in speech or in action. Such treatment deserves condemnation from the Church's pastors wherever it occurs...The intrinsic dignity of each person must always be respected in word, in action and in law" (Congregation for the Doctrine of the Faith, "Letter to the Bishops of the Catholic Church on the Pastoral Care of Homosexual Persons (1986)," (San Francisco: Ignatius Press, 1987), n. 10.

158. Aleksandr I. Solzhenitsyn, (Thomas Whitney, trans.), *The Nobel Lecture on Literature* (New York: Harper and Row, 1972), 38.

159. Up to a million a year are lured or stolen into cross boundary prostitution where they are typically drugged and herded into as many as ten or twenty violations a day. Labor and sex slavery within national boundaries involves millions more each year.

160. De Lacy O'Leary, *Arabia Before Muhammad* [New York: E.P. Dutton and Co., 1927]), 202. The author cites Q 6:141, 152; 16:60–1; and 17:31–33; see also

Q 81:3). In two extended accounts, Mohammed is reduced to tears when hearing of such live burials (Jean Sasson, *Princess Sultana's Daughters* [New York: Doubleday, 1994], 90–96). Mohammed's response to the guilty father is recorded: "Sons and daughters are both gifts of God, the Prophet reminded him. Both are equally gifts, and so they should always be treated equally."

161. John Paul II, "Letter to Families," Feb. 2, 1994, in *The Pope Speaks*, 39:4, Huntington, Ind.: Our Sunday Visitor, 1994.

162. In a 2004 interview (www.IslamOnline.net) Hassan commented that had it not been for Islamic countries work in 2003 and 2004, the Sexual Orientation Resolution—declaring sodomy and homosexuality as a human right and presented by Brazil and Canada—would have been approved by the United Nations. United Families International, a prominent member of the very broad World Family Alliance, actively promotes a monogamous understanding of the family. In late 2008 France proposed to the United Nations a resolution supporting non-discrimination for homosexual activity. As in national settings, the predictable follow up adjustment internationally could be direct challenges to the traditional nuclear family.

163. Vatican statement carried by the *Associated Press*, November 7, 2007. The Vatican maintains diplomatic relations with 176 states and institutions, many in the Islamic world, but Wahhabism in Saudi Arabia rejects diplomatic relations with a Christian entity.

164. See www.asianews.it/ (March 19, 2009).

165. The apparent reluctance of European states to enforce laws against polygamy, as the United States under different circumstances was able to do with Mormonism (a condition for statehood), is a concern raised by the journalist Oriana Fallaci who faults her homeland of Italy for not enforcing (at the time of her writing) Article 556 of the Criminal Code (*The Rage and the Pride* [New York: Rizolli, 2001], 58).

166. Biblical references to solidarity include: Lk 10:25–37; and Rom 10:12, Gal 3:28 (no distinctions), Jn 4:4–42, Mt 15–21–8 (Samaritan woman at the well), Lk 10:25–37 (Good Samaritan*)*, Acts 2:1–12 (Spirit and languages), and Mt 5:9 (peacemakers).

In *Mater et Magistra* (Mother and Teacher, 1961), Pope John XXIII addresses "development of the social phenomenon" and "multiplication of social relationships"—solidarity *with* subsidiarity. These principles are often mistranslated as "socialization" (*socialisatio*, a term he did not use). Thomas Molnar understands this abbreviated translation as having been useful to those wanting to portray the Church as leaning toward socialism (*The Counter-Revolution* [New York: Funk and Wagnalls, 1969], 202, fn. 14). In 1995, the Second Vatican Council used the term *socialisatio* combined with Pope John's more nuanced and clarifying definitions (Second Vatican Council, *Gaudium et Spes* [The Church in the Modern World], n. 25).

167. Hassan, p. 83.

168. John Paul II, *Centesimus Annus*, n. 55; originally in *Rerum Novarum* (New Things), n. 143.

169. Aleksandr Solzhenitsyn proposes that courageous human beings need not be complicit in evil, and that "writers and artists have a greater opportunity: to conquer the lie!" He alerts his reader to our complicity when "Everything distant from us, ev-

erything that does not threaten to roll across the threshold of our home this very day, is seen by us with all its moans, groans, stifled screams, destroyed lives—even when millions of victims are involved—as being by and large endurable and existing within tolerable dimensions" (*The Nobel Lecture on Literature*, 37, 15).

170. Mary Ann Glendon, "Looking for 'Persons' in the Law," *First Things* (New York: Institute on Religion and Public Life, December 2006).

171. The preeminent theological schools of Augustine and Aquinas hold opposed views on the nature of the state. Augustine held that the state is an arm of the Church and a consequence of original sin. The principle of community is not intellect, but will: "A state is an assemblage of reasonable being bound together by a *common agreement concerning the objects of their love.*" (Norman Baynes, *The Political Ideas of St Augustine's De Civitate Dei* [The Historical Association, 1968]). With Aristotle, Aquinas held that man is a political animal, and that his collaborative efforts are integrated through the state as part of the natural law.

172. William Simon, "The Bishops' Folly" (*National Review*, April 5, 1985). See also the final and now somewhat dated *Economic Justice for All: Pastoral Letter on Catholic Social Teaching and the United States* (Washington, D.C.: United States Catholic Conference, 1986). While conditions have changed since publication, the underlying social principles endure, and are explored in Chapter 4, pages 248–262.

173. Pope Pius XI, *Quadragesimo anno* (On Reconstructing the Social Order), 1931, n. 80.

174. The European Union is marked by an apparent de facto transfer of public policy issues from sovereign states to activism by non-governmental organizations (NGOs), particularly in with respect to national traditions of marriage, family, and human life. Maciej Golubiewski documents that the presumed protection of member states by the "subsidiarity" principle endorsed by the European Union is "ill-defined and practically ineffectual on social policy issues." The author also observes that pre-emptive influence of unaccountable NGOs extends beyond the European Union to other international organizations such as the United Nations. See *Europe's Social Agenda: Why is the European Union Regulating Morality?* (New York: Catholic Family and Human Rights Institute, 866 United Nations Plaza, Suite 495, New York, NY 10017, 2008).

175. Bernard Lewis, *What Went Wrong?* (New York: Harper Perennial, 2003), 111.

176. Alexis de Tocqueville, *Democracy in America*, Vol. II (New York: Vintage, 1945), 321–333.

177. Vincent Ferrer Blehl (ed.), *The Essential Newman* (New York: Mentor Omega, 1963), 264: "Conscience has rights because it has duties . . . ."

178. Phenomenology is the philosophical focus of Karol Wojtyla (John Paul II), *The Acting Person,* The Yearbook of Phenomenological Research, Vol. X (D. Reidel Publishing Co., Boston, 1979). Jean Jacques Rousseau, author of *The General Will* and an icon of modernity, preached the rights of abstract man while he sent his own illegitimate children to orphanages.

179. John Paul II, *Centesimus Annus* (One Hundred Years), n.17.

180. Biblical references to Rights and Responsibilities include: Isa 10:1–2 (Israel's unfaithfulness), Deut 5:17, 30:19 (the Fifth Commandment), Sirach 34:22 (rights of workers), and Psalms146:5–8 (freedom from oppression).

181. Biblical references to the poor and vulnerable include: Dt 24:14, 17–8 ("You too were once slaves…"), Mt 25: 31–46 (treatment of the poor), Lk 4:16–20 (glad tidings for the poor), Mt 25:31–46 (judgment of nations), James 2:1–5, 9 (dishonor not the poor), Lk 14:12–14 (reach out to the poor), Exodus 22:20–22, Lev 19:33–34, and Dt 24:17–18 (aliens, widow, orphans).

182. John Paul II, *Centesimus Annus* (One Hundred Years), n. 38.

183. Paul Sigmund notices this change in wording from *the Instruction on Christian Freedom and Liberation* (1986), in his a commentary on Gustavo Gutierrez, in John Witte Jr. and Frank Alexander (eds.), *The Teaching of Modern Roman Catholicism* (New York: Columbia University Press, 2007), 296. The issue is impartial justice, not politics: "Show neither partiality to the weak nor deference to the mighty, but judge your fellow men justly" (Lev 19:15).

184. Gleaned from Benedict XVI, World Summit on Food Security, *L'Osservatore Romano* (Vatican City: Wednesday, Nov. 18, 2009), 3.

185. John Paul II, op. cit., n. 44.

186. The West faults the Church in history for equating financial risk sharing in modern economies with usury. And yet, today new forms of usury are institutionalized in some practices of the private United States Federal Reserve Banking System. This occurs when interest is paid to private banks for either printing money to support federal debts, or for charging a percentage on loans greater than foregone investment opportunities. The economic crisis of 2008 exposes usury in a more novel form—trafficking in insecure financial instruments by bundled them with creditworthy investments (derivatives), and then trading the new packages with still high credit ratings while undermining confidence in national economies and currencies.

187. Hassan, 182. Regarding private property, Mohammed is quoted by Hassan to have said in his last sermon (*hadith*), "Verily your blood, your wealth and your property are sacred and inviolable."

188. John Paul II, op. cit., n. 32.

189. Ibid., n. 57; see *Catechism of the Catholic Church,* n. 1807. St. Leo the Great remarks that, "…when he says: Blessed are the poor in spirit, he shows that the kingdom of heaven is to be given to those who are distinguished by their humility of soul rather than their lack of worldly goods."

190. Biblical references to the Rights of Workers include: Mt 20:1–16 (agreed upon wage), Mk 2:27 (Sabbath for the people), Mk 6:3 (Jesus was a carpenter), Mt 20:1–16 (wages used in parable), Lk 10:7, Mt 10:9–10, and Tim 5:17–8 (the laborer is worth his pay).

191. John Paul II, *Laborem Exercens* (Human Work), n. 13, 14.

192. Observations made by Resat Kasaba, professor of international studies, "Turkey: Between Secularism and Modernity," part of the series *Hot Spots in Our World 2008*, Jackson School of International Studies, University of Washington, March 19, 2008. Calvinism fostered worldly success partly by tilting the Christian notion of "calling" toward private and measurable activity in the world.

193. Some historians trace the real beginnings of Western economic and political liberties to the earlier self-governing guilds and especially the international traders of Christian and late Medieval Europe, and only later to the nation-state markets and

resources of England and France and the Protestant Reformation (Amintore Fanfani, *Catholicism, Protestantism and Capitalism* [New York: Sheed and Ward, 1939]).

194. Biblical references to Care for Creation include: Gn 1:1–2:3 (the goodness of creation), Gn 2:15 (we are stewards), Mt 7:25–34, Lk 12:22–34 (birds of the air and wild flowers), and Ps 104:1–35 (a hymn of creation).

195. The distinction between *ownership* and *use* of property appears in *Rerum Novarum*, 1891, nn. 22, 23. One school of thought, termed "distributism" champions wide distribution of ownership of family-sized plots of land, as contrasted with collective anonymity. The modern and non-agrarian equivalent in industrial society might be some form of employee stock ownership/control and direct profit sharing.

196. The draft Copenhagen Treaty, September 15, 2009, Annex 1, paragraphs 36 and 38.

197. John Paul II, *Centesimus Annus* (One Hundred Years), n. 49.

198. Case law in the United States moves toward conferring rights on animals and plants, while at the same time declines to recognize the right to life of unborn children. At least one prominent academic publishing house, approached unsuccessfully by this author, has begun a series addressing the "subjective experience and the moral status of animals as well as of the nature and place of human beings."

199. John Paul II, op. cit., n. 54.

200. Advice to a Military Commander Boniface," Letter 199, in Henry Paolucci (ed.), *The Political Writings of St. Augustine* (New York: Henry Regnery Co., 1962), 285.

201. The "tragedy of the commons" is both historical and a metaphor (presented by Garrett Hardin in the 1970s). In early England as a fixed amount of common land was more and more exploited by the addition of private flocks, this resource eventually exceeded its carrying capacity and collapsed to the detriment of all. Each user reasoned that the commons would be degraded by others anyway, so each acted for short term profit. The *enclosures* movement divided the commons such that each user bore a private interest in stewarding resources under his ownership. The correct and effective mix of private and collective responsibility for the common good is a philosophical and policy issue for many ecological dilemmas.

202. One unified collection of commentaries is Michael A. Barkey (ed.), *Environmental Stewardship in the Judeo-Christian Tradition: Jewish, Catholic, and Protestant Wisdom on the Environment* (Grand Rapids, Mich.: Acton Institute for the Study of Religion and Liberty, 2000). John Paul II and Ecumenical Patriarch Bartholomew issued a "Joint Declaration on Articulating a Code of Environmental Ethics" stressing six goals: mindfulness of future generations, the priority of Natural Law and the non-utilitarian use of science and technology, stewardship and solidarity beyond exaggerated ownership, a variety of roles and responsibilities, and the need for trust beyond legitimate controversy (*Origins*, Washington, D.C.: CNS Documentary Service, June 20, 2002).

203. On a global scale, the current situation is a total population growth less than was feared in the 1970s, but with actual decline in some regions such as Europe, offset by greater increases in other regions such as China, India, Latin America and parts of Africa.

204. John Paul II, *Centesimus Annus* (One Hundred Years), n. 58.

205. Ibid., n. 38.

206. Pope Paul VI, *Humanae Vitae* (Human Life, 1968) affirms that the spousal unity and openness to procreation cannot be morally disconnected, either from the other, as through directly anti-conceptive practices or artificial insemination. The position is as a counterattack to the *Kinsey Report* mentality as it is a corrective to the earlier (Anglican) Lambeth Conference decision to endorse the direct separation of human intercourse from even the possibility of procreation. Wrote Paul VI, far in advance of the culture wars of the new century: ". . . It is also to be feared that the man, growing used to the employment of anti-conceptive practices, may finally lose respect for the woman and, no longer caring for her physical and psychological equilibrium, may come to the point of considering her as a mere instrument of selfish enjoyment, and no longer as his respected and beloved companion" (n. 17).

207. Points reiterated by John Paul II, "Address of the Holy Father to the Participants of the Seventh Plenary Session" of the, *Proceedings' on Globalization: Ethical and Institutional Concerns* (Vatican City: Pontifical Academy of Social Sciences, April 25–8, 2001).

208. Pope John XXIII, *Mater et Magistra*, (Mother and Teacher), 1961, n. 191.

209. Zbigniew Brzezinski, *Second Chance: Three Presidents and the Crisis of American Superpower* (New York: Basic Books, 2007), 204. The author is now with the Center for Strategic and International Studies and a professor at John Hopkins University.

210. Ibid.

211. Pope Benedict XVI, *Deus et Caritas* (God is Love, 2006), n. 31.

212. Henry Kissinger, "The Philosophical Problem," in Henry Schwarz (ed.), *Problems in European Civilization: Metternich, the Coachman of Europe* (Boston: D.C. Heath and Co., 1962), 103–4; originally "The Conservative Dilemma: Reflections on the Political Thought of Metternich," *The American Political Science Review*, December, 1954. Modern social science and Scripture sometimes converge: "Foundations once destroyed, what can the upright do?" (Ps 11:3) Kissinger's insight is cross cultural and parallels advice given by Alcuin to Charlemagne in 778 A.D.: "And those people should not be listened to who keep saying the voice of the people is the voice of God, since the riotousness of the crowd is always very close to madness" (cited by Ibn Warroq (pseudonym) interview by Carol Iannone, in *Academic Questions*, 24:1 [New York: National Association of Scholars, Spring 2011], 22).

213. George Weigel, *The Final Revolution* (New York: Oxford University Press, 1992). passim. Some pious historians note additionally Marian apparitions at points in history, in modern times associated with the refusal of the military to turn their guns on their citizens (as in the Philippines in the mid 1980s).

214. Ibid, 35.

215. Over one million Afghanis and countless Russian/Ukranian soldiers were killed in the Afghan War. Of Islamic jihad in Afghanistan, an Italian journalist reports "I got crucified (by the Politically Correct) as a racist . . . when I printed out what they used to do to Soviet prisoners. I mean when they cut off their arms and legs . . . They didn't even like the fact that I cried on the armless and legless Ukrainian recruits

who, having been abandoned by those barbarians and recovered by their comrades lay in field hospitals . . . ." (Ariana Fallaci, *The Rage and the Pride* [New York: Rizzoli, 2001], 86). In completely separate accounts, Western historians record similar behavior against the Vendee resistance during the French Revolution (e.g., unpublished manuscript of Austrian writer Erik von Kuehnelt-Leddihn, "Two Hundred Years since the French Revolution," Seattle, Washington, October 20, 1989). The French historian Baudricourt (1853) records how sometimes during pacification actions in Algeria the colonial French soldiers retrieved from Muslim women their silver ear-rings, leg-rings and arm-rings: "To get them off our soldiers used to cut off their limbs and leave them alive in a mutilated condition" (cited in Karen Armstrong, *Muhammad* [New York: Harper Collier, 1993], 40).

216. Bernard Lewis, Address at the Second Annual Dinner for Western Civilization of the Intercollegiate Studies Institute, Wilmington D.C., Delaware, May 2, 2007. Lewis is widely published and held the Cleveland E. Dodge Chair of Near Eastern Studies at Princeton University, and was a long-term member of the Institute for Advanced Study. Extending the above quote, we should not that also "not implausible" is the weaponry supplied by the United States, and the technology of the broadcasting system and especially the Internet which poked electronic holes in Soviet disinformation, and which is now a nemesis to similar controls in China and in parts of the Muslim world.

217. Imam Riza, cited by Imam Khomeini, in *Islam and Revolution: Writings and Declarations* (London: KPI, 1981), 51. Riza was the eighth of the twelve Imams (765–817 A.D.).

218. Luigi Giussani, *Why the Church?* (Ithaca: McGill-Queen's University Press, 2001), 162.

219. Hassan, 206 (writing in 1981). Medieval Christian writers addressed the same question with different conclusions. The Crusades were first justified as attempts to reclaim formerly Roman lands.

220. Yahaya Michot separates a key historic figure from violent ideology attributed to him today by radical jihadists (*Muslims Under Non-Muslim Rule: Ibn Taymiyya* [New York: Interface Publications, 2006). Seven centuries ago Ibn Tayamiyya issued a fatwa for the Muslims in Mardin, a city in southeastern Anatolia that had been overtaking by Mongols and their institutions of unbelief. Did the inner jihad of Muslims require them to flee the changed external setting? Today "the exact terms may vary from place to place but the same bifurcation—of Islamic as against non-Islamic—resonates across all the debates (ed. from Palestine to Indonesia) and fires Muslim political controversy"(xii). Michot defends the view that the icon of jihadists (Ibn Tayamiyya) and the Prophet were not men of violence and, further, that they do not require "new crusades to save 'civilization' from a so-called 'Islamic threat'" (author' preface, page x). He demonstrates that it is an abuse for radical Islam to legitimize its own "Mongolization" of Islam with the name of Ibn Tayamiyya. Michot translates and includes four of his short texts.

221. Bernard Lewis, *The Muslim Discovery of Europe,* op. cit., 66–7.

222. Malcolm Barber, *The Two Cities: Medieval Europe 1050–1320* (New York: Routledge, 1992), 508.

223. Walter Ullmann, 131–2.

224. Barber, op. cit.

225. See also Deut 18:12 on human immolations, fortune-tellers, soothsayers, charmers, diviners and the like—"because of such abominations the Lord, your God, is driving these nations out of your way."

226. Frederich Heer, *The Medieval World* (New York: Mentor Books, 1962), 140. During the Fourth Crusade, the murder of Alexius IV, heir to Constantinople and supported by the Crusaders, is said by the commentator Villehardouin to have triggered the conquest of Constantinople: "Thus did the war begin." The clergy proclaimed: "Wherefore we tell you, that this war is lawful and just, and that if you have a right purpose to conquer this land, to put it under obedience to Rome, you will have pardon as the pope has granted it, all those who die confessed" (in Lewis Spitz and Richard Lyman (eds.), *Major Crises in Western Civilization,* Vol. 1 [New York: Harcourt, Brace and World, 1965], 131).

227. Adda Bozeman, *The Future of Law in a Multicultural World,* (Princteton, NJ: Princeton University Press, 1971, 82–3..

228. Hassan, 202–4.

229. The relative simplicity of Islam, which offers few criteria for discernment, finds a parallel in those ethicists who promote a simplistic "fundamental option"—a personal conversion after which the immorality of specific and subsequent actions is trumped by the subjectivity of faith and of being saved once and for all.

230. Citation from G. von Rad (*Der heilige Krieg im alten Israel,* Second Edition, [1952], in Von Balthasar, *The Glory of the Lord: A Theological Aesthetics, Vol. VI– Theology of the Old Covenant* (San Francisco: Ignatius, 1991), 253–4, n. 10.

231. See Michael Stoff et al, *The Manhattan Project: A Documentary Introduction to the Atomic Age* (New York: McGraw-Hill, 1991), 181; drawing from Akira Iriye, *Power and Culture: The Japanese-American War, 1941–1945* (Cambridge: Harvard, 1962). The ambiguity of the Japanese response is no greater than the ambiguity of the ultimatum presented by the West, which in the Potsdam Declaration spoke of unconditional surrender, but in another critical and official communication (Captain Zacharias, United States Navy) offered as a definition the less objectionable Atlantic Charter (see Gar Alperovitz, *The Decision to Use the Atomic Bomb* [London: Harper Collins, 1995], 394–404).

232. Hassan, 97 (italics added).

233. Mualanna Muhammad Ali, *Muhammad the Prophet* (Lahore, Pakistan: Ripon Printing Press, 1984 [1924]), 252.

234. Ayoub in Omar (ed.), 208.

235. Benazir Bhutto cites Khadduri in *Reconciliation: Islam, Democracy, and the West* (New York: Harper, 2008), 24–5.

236. "If we abrogate a verse or cause it to be forgotten, we will replace it with a better one or one similar. Did you not know that God has power over all things?" (Q 2:106). Remotely similar to Islamic sequential messaging in the *Qur'an* is the Western evolution of just war theory among theologians (not in Scripture). Some commentators note that with Augustine a just war involved pursuit of sinners responsible for warfare, while under Aquinas the focus is not on punishment but on restoring the disrupted condition of justice.

237. Americans might recall George III who said "I desire what is good; therefore, every one who does not agree with me is a traitor" (George Seldes, *The Great Quotations* [New York: Pocket Books, 1970], 913).

238. John Paul II, *Centesimus Annus* (One Hundred Years), n. 23.

239. Hassan, 205. In the extended text Hassan cites these related ayats are Q 2:190, 192, 256; 4:75; 8:39; 10:100; 22:39, 40.

240. Hassan, 202. Grotius refers to Classical thinkers and Jewish and Christian writers. He appeals to the Natural Law: "This principle (defense) is founded on reason and equity, so evident, that even in the brute creation, who have no idea of right, we make a distinction between attack and defense" (*The Rights of War and Peace* [Washington, D.C.: M. Walter Dunn, 1901], Chapter 2, citation p. 35).

241. Igino Giordani, *The Social Message of the Early Fathers* (Boston: St. Paul Editions, 1977), 178.

242. *Catechism of the Catholic Church*, n. 2309.

243. Abdullah Yusuf Ali, *The Holy Qur'an: Text, Translation and Commentary* (Lahore: SH. Muhammad Ashraf, 1983 [1938]), 75, n. 204.

244. John Paul II, *Memory and Identity* (New York: Rizzoli, 2005), 141. In their exercise of responsibility, the "Polish authorities" are distinct from the Church. The question now is asked whether Churchill acted imprudently to encourage the Poles with a promise of support he could not honor, and then unavoidably to declare war on Germany. With benefit of hindsight, Patrick Buchanan develops this thesis (*The Unnecessary War*, New York: Random House, 2008).

245. The compelling case can be made that any immorality came at the end of active hostilities in the West's surrender of the Polish people to the Soviet orbit, under the Yalta Agreements.

246. Monitored by the Polish Government in London, the Uprising (August 1944) assumed that the German army was in retreat. It depended upon Russian support and Western supplies, but the Soviet Government condemned the action and after two months Warsaw was leveled.

247. Several national Episcopal conferences produced non-doctrinal pastoral letters on nuclear weapons. Major differences were on the nature of the problem itself, the risk of collateral damage or the "slippery slope" (American), the strategic imbalance of armaments on the eastern front (German), or the intrinsic threat of Marxist ideology (French). See *The Challenge to Peace* ("Pastoral Letter" of the National Conference of Catholic Bishops, 1983), and James Schall, S.J., *Out of Justice, Peace* (Joint Pastoral Letter of the West German Bishops) and *Winning the Peace* (Joint Pastoral Letter of the French Bishops) [San Francisco: Ignatius Press, 1984].

248. Interviews and declassified documents reveal what was actually known at the time of the bombing decision. These are examined in Gar Alperovitz, *The Decision to Use the Atomic Bomb* (London: Harper Collins, 1995). Major themes include the questionable need or actual casualty estimates for a land invasion as the only alternative strategy, the potential role of Russia in the Far East as a deciding factor in Japanese resistance and in post-war Europe, the weight to be given to early peace feelers coming from Japan, the diverse positions of military leaders in the United States on impending use of the bomb, institutional complexities in Japan and the West together with important instances of miscommunication as on the terms of peace (e.g., unconditional

surrender and the future role of the emperor of Japan), and shortly after the war the findings of the *U.S. Strategic Bombing Survey* (1946).

249. George Weigel and Rowan Williams, "War and Statecraft: An Exchange," *First Things* (New York: Institute for Religion and Public Life, March 2004), 19.

250. The Soviet leadership signed the nuclear weapons treaty in 1987. The American bishops' draft peace pastoral of 1983, revised only two weeks before the decisive Senate vote, was altered to call for a (prudential) "curb" on nuclear weapons production rather than a probably more ideological "halt" in such production. See Paul Kengor, "The Judge," *Catholic World Report* (San Francisco: Ignatius Press, December 7, 2007), 42–46. Earlier drafts misconstrued the defensive nature of American nuclear strategy and failed to recognize complex initiatives toward arms reduction.

251. The inseparability of prudence and simplicity is explained by Fr. Gabriel of St. Mary Magdalen *Divine Intimacy* (Rockford, Ill.: Tan Books, 1996), 826.

252. St. Gregory, Moral Reflections on Job, in *Liturgy of the Hours*, Vol. 3, 261.

253. *Catechism of the Catholic Church*, n. 2309. In their detailed appeal for the President of the United States to continue to "pursue actively alternatives to war" (with Iraq), the nation's bishops also included this: "There are no easy answers. People of good will may apply ethical principles and come to different prudential judgments, depending upon their assessment of the facts at hand and other issues" (United States Catholic Conference of Bishops' Administrative Committee, "Letter to President Bush on the Iraq Situation," *Origins,* 32:16 (Washington, D.C.: Catholic News Service Documentary Service, September 26, 2002).

254. *The Challenge to Peace*, op. cit. (iii, iv, v) and *Gaudium et Spes* (Pastoral Constitution on the Church in the Modern World, nn. 78–82). In 1982 Pope John Paul II sent a compatible address to the Second Special Session of the United Nations dedicated to disarmament (*Negotiation: The Only Realistic Solution to the Continuing Threat of War* [Boston: St. Paul Editions, 1982]): "In current conditions 'deterrence' based on balance, certainly not as an end in itself but as a step on the way toward a progressive disarmament, may still be judged morally acceptable" (p. 10).

255. Williams and Weigel, op. cit.

256. Weigel and Williams, 16, 19. Apostates from Islam, most of whom seek safety through writer anonymity, confirm that the vast majority of Muslims are peaceful and moderate. Terrorism and violence are practiced by only the closest and most literal followers of Islam using or manipulating isolated parts of the *Qur'an* (Ibn Warraq, *Leaving Islam: Apostates Speak Out* [Amherst, New York: Prometheus Books, 2003]. Included in this volume is a chapter comprised of quotations from the *Qur'an* and numerous commentators in the hadith: "Islam on Trial: The Textual Evidence," 391–429).

257. Bernard Lewis and Buntzie Ellis Churchill, *Islam: The Religion and the People* (Wharton School Publishing, 2008), 53.

258. Barry Cooper, "Jihadists' and the War on Terrorism," *The Intercollegiate Review*, Spring 2007. In 2007 on the eve of her return from exile to Pakistan former Prime Minister Benazir Bhutto was asked about the personal risk of suicide attacks or roadside bombings. Her response was that "Islam forbids suicide bombings and attacks on her. 'Muslims know if they attack a woman, they will burn in hell" (Mat-

thew Pennington, "Ex Premier will return Thursday," Associated Press, October 17, 2007). The following day roadside bombs detonated near the motorcade in a massive crowd of over one million, killing at least one hundred thirty-six and injuring twice this number. Bhutto herself was assassinated two months later. Her suspected assassin (Baitullah Mehsud) was killed in a missile attack in August 2009. Published shortly after her death, Bhutto's book (*Reconciliation*) proposes democratization and economic interdependence as the *realpolitik* alternative to Samuel Huntington's "clash of civilizations" (a termed coined by Bernard Lewis in "The Roots of Muslim Rage" [Atlantic Monthly, September 1990]).

259. Late Medieval "flagellants" publicly scourged themselves to inspire penitence. The similarity with jihad terrorists lies in their resurgence under times of affliction which were viewed as divine punishment, such as famines, continuous warfare and especially the Black Death (1346–50 A.D.). A dissimilarity with fractious Islam was the authority of the Church and specifically the pope to declare such movements heretical (1349 A.D.) and inconsistent with the Christian faith.

260. Pope Benedict XVI, *Values in a Time of Upheaval* (New York: Crossroad, 2006), 81; citation in Benedict is from Albert Gorres.

261. Ps 19:12–13: "Though your servant is careful of them, very diligent in keeping them, Yet, who can detect failings. Cleanse me of my unknown faults." On the deadening of conscience, a compatible verse from the *Qur'an* reads: "And who doth more wrong than one who is reminded of the Signs of the Lord, but turns away from them, forgetting the (deeds) which his hands have sent forth? Verily, we have set veils over their hearts lest they should understand this, and over their ears, deafness, if thou callest them to guidance, even then will they never accept guidance" (Q 18:57).

262. Pope Benedict XVI, op cit., 81, 83.

263. I am indebted to Kirk Kanzelberger for the extended quote from which this phrase is drawn, and for alerting me to the concept of "forgetfulness" as part of a broad psychology of sin (doctrinal dissertation, *The Mystical Daydream*, Fordham University, New York: May 2011; citation is from Hannah Arendt, Eichman in Jerusalem: A Report on the Banality of Evil [New York: Penguin, 1964], 3–5).

264. After the earlier attacks in Nairobi and Dar el Salaam in which the victims were mostly non-Americans, Bin Laden is quoted as saying: "When it becomes apparent that it would be impossible to repel these Americans without assaulting them, even if this involved the killing of Muslims, this is permissible under Islam." In 1998 he announced, "We do not differentiate between those dressed in military uniforms and civilians; they are all targets of this fatwa." Bin Laden is quoted again, "If the present injustice continues…it will move the battle to American soil." See National Commission on Terrorist Attacks Upon the United States, *The 9/11 Commission Report* (New York: W.W. Norton and Co., 2004), 48, 69, 70.

265. Ibid.

266. The report was later revealed to be based on non-scientific research based on a very *non-random* survey including willing prison inmates with a disproportionate share of abnormal personalities (Judith Reisman and Edward Eichel, *Kinsey, Sex and Fraud: The Indoctrination of People* [Huntington House Publishers, 1990]). The Kinsey findings are based on 18,000 "sex histories" all of whom were self-selected

volunteers, a quarter to half of whom were prison inmates and 1,400 of whom were sex offenders, and apparently even included direct experimentation by a group of nine sex offenders on children aged two months to fifteen years. Prostitutes and cohabiting females were classified as married, leading to the claim that a quarter of married women committed adultery. Janice Shaw adds further that Kinsey "was promiscuously bisexual, sado-mashochistic, and a decadent voyeur who enjoyed filming his wife having sex with his staff" (see Janice Shaw Crouse, "Kinsey's Kids," at www. nationalreview.com/comment/crouse200311140923.asp.

267. Half of all abortion clients in the United States regard abortion as a backup to failed contraception. Eighty percent of this figure is unmarried. Many public schools double as contraceptive dispensaries and abortion referral services. The short jump from abortion to euthanasia and other perversions is obvious. Such consequences were explicitly warned against in *Humanae Vitae* (Human Life), the neglected analysis and teaching of Pope Paul VI in 1968: e.g., "one must necessarily recognize insurmountable limits to the possibility of man's domination over his own body and its functions; limits which no man, whether a private individual or one invested with authority, may licitly surpass" (n. 17).

268. Donald and Idella Gallagher (eds.), *A Maritain Reader* (Garden City, New York: Image Books, 1966), 302–3.

269. Pope Benedict XVI, *Caritas in Veritate* (Charity in Truth), June 29, 2009. We are obliged "to broaden our concept of poverty and underdevelopment to include questions connected with the acceptance of life, especially in cases where it is impeded in a variety of ways" (n. 28).

270. Ibid., n.41 (italics added). In this one sentence one possibly detects oblique reference to states lacking written constitutions (English Common Law, Israel and Saudi Arabia) and possibly to the United Nations; the problematic and unitary Islamic State in general; the religious institution of the Vatican City State which has only 110 acres of "territory;" the possible mediator role for religious leaders in our postmodern world of asymmetric power structures such as states of declining credibility; the obsolescence of John Courtney Murray's thesis that a popularly based Natural Law culture can be counted on to shine through morally neutral constitutions (see Chapter 1).

271. Wael B. Hallaq, *An Introduction to Islamic Law* (New York: Cambridge University Press, 2009), 141.

272. Ibid.

273. Edwin Bliss, *Turkey and the Armenian Atrocities* (New York: M.J. Coghlan, 1896), Ch. XIII (225–37).

274. Foreword by Etienne Gilson, St. Augustine, *The City of God* (Garden City, N.Y., 1958), 32.

275. Jihad is not the most legitimate Islamic response to the "composite" zone, to be drawn from the Prophet and from the pivotal fourteenth century Ibn Tayamiyya. This is the contribution made by Yahya Michot in his *Muslims Under Non-Muslim Rule: Ibn Tayamiyya* (London: Interface Publications, 2006). According to Thomas Aquinas, Christians who find themselves in a composite political setting, under the rule of infidels, are bound to obedience unless the natural law is contradicted, because

"power was instituted by *ius gentium*, a human law, and the distinction between believers and infidels exists by virtue of divine law, which does not destroy human law" (*Summa*, II-II, Q. 12, A. 2., citation in Dina Bigongiari (ed.), *The Political Ideas of St. Thomas Aquinas* [Hew York: Haafner Publishing, 1953), xxxvi). In the case of Islam, for a Christian to render obedience would seem to carry the implication that Shari'a is a natural religion and a "human law," not divine.

276. Citations are from Abdullah Yusuf Ali, 1505, fnn. 5313, 5314.

277. John Henry Newman (Vincent Ferrer Blehl, ed.) "Faith, Reason and Philosophy," in *The Essential Newman* (New York: Mentor-Omega, 1963), 297.

278. John Bagot Glubb, The Life and Times of Muhammad (London: Hodder and Stoughton, 1970), 109.

Chapter Five

Modernity:
Monologues and Conversations

Islam and the West have disputed the map of Europe and beyond for thirteen centuries. And today Islam and the West each face an internal crisis. And partly within the West and teaching "in season and out of season," the Church will always be in some state of crisis of its own in the world. In the late nineteenth and twentieth century Vatican councils the Church engaged the dark side and the light side of modernity, both outwardly and inwardly (Chapter 4). Chapter 5 now addresses the crises of the Mosque in the modern world and the dark side of Modernity, and then expands Mohammed's discovery that "paradise lies at the feet of mothers," and reflects on the Muslim interest in the Two Great Commandments as a theme for future conversation.

The Muslim scholar Farooq Hassan concludes his *Concept of State and Law in Islam* with this concise interreligious assessment: "The controversy between Christianity and Islam can now be reduced to three main issues: the doctrine of the Divinity of Christ, the problem of the Crucifixion, and the question of the Gospels."[1] Hassan repeats clearly the Muslim view that his three theological issues pose the question of anthropomorphism and represent a "difference though important" that still is "slight." Alleged Christian anthropomorphism is attributed to corrupted biblical texts that substitute for teachings said to be restored in the later Islamic texts. He proposes a possible "true understanding between Christianity and Islam" with these points in common: that the religion of Islam and the Judeo-Christian faith both believe in a Supreme Being; that both believe in the spirit and the moral life; that both believe in the immortality of the soul; and that both offer guiding principles that are similar. Hassan points to similarities between the Shari'a and the synoptic Gospels (from which it borrows) and to similarities with the philosophical schools on such themes as the classical proofs of God's existence.[2]

Hassan proposes cooperation which "does not mean any concession or attempt for compromise in the two religions." He suggests that to avoid fault finding Muslim missionaries should not attack the doctrine of the Trinity, should study the Sermon on the Mount, and (going beyond the synoptic Gospels) the Samaritan woman in St. John as well as the lessons on faith, hope and charity as these appear in Corinthians.[3] He proposes that Christians should remain silent on polygamy and the Holy War (Hassan wrote two decades before the heightened conflict inflicted in 2001), and should stress the genuine moral and social teachings of the *Qur'an* (Q 23).[4]

On the moral and social teachings, the point of contention from the Christian (and Western) perspective is the Muslim presumption that restoration of original morality in seventh century Arabia does not mean that the larger world likewise labored in such "days of ignorance." This said, a promising opening for scriptural dialogue between the Christians and the followers of Islam is the few Qur'anic verses—partly identified for us by Hassan—that imply what pre-Islamic non-Muslims have long understood as a universal natural law (e.g., Q 16:36 and 30:30, but also Q 9:71, all Chapter 2) accessible to human reason. Chapter 4 stresses as a core principle the transcendent and received dignity of each and every concrete human person, without exception, and the second principle of the common good as an inseparable dimension of *this universal* principle. Both of these imprinted principles, and the implied freedom of man's very nature differ from the more abstract and ethnocentric starting point of Shari'a.

Trusting *encounter* can be deepened by also remembering and by understanding such differences and even depends upon this degree of transparency. There is respectful disagreement on Hassan's stated presupposition: "Islam recognizes all religions in their true form to be Islam."[5] With this pre-emption toward Islam as a starting point—the notion that natural law is not only in but of the *Qur'an*—does the Western understanding of interpersonal dialogue on basics with the followers of Islam any longer have a solid footing to begin?

THE THIRD ENCOUNTER

The initial meeting between the eventual followers of Islam and Christianity was probably during the early life of Mohammed himself (Chapter 2) and contributed to the formation of Islam as a religion. Compiled after his death, the *Qur'an* shows that Mohammed was influenced in part by the divisiveness and the content of Christian theologies scattered across the Byzantine Empire and overheard at first on the trade routes to Mecca, and probably from a Nestorian monk (Bahira). The three later and major encounters between the world of Islam and Europe are the Islamic invasion in the West checked at the Battle of Tours (732 A.D), then the even larger incursion in the East finally repulsed at Vienna (1683), and now the post-Cold War resurgence of Islam as experienced from the late twentieth century to the present. Dawson characterizes the first encounter in the West at Tours as "the last act of the thousand years of interaction between East and West, the complete victory of the oriental spirit . . . Mohammed was the answer of the East to the challenge of Alexander"[6] (Alexander the Great, 356–323 B.C.). From the recent Islamic point of view, these three events alternate with other encounters. These include the crusades, the Muslim victory at Constantinople in 1453, and later colonial expansion by the Western political powers.

The West now fears another deep confrontation and colonization of post-Christian territory by an expansive and assimilating Islam, a possibility certain to extend over centuries rather than decades. This event is the third historic encounter, and at the same time is a second Arian crisis as occurred three centuries before the birth of Mohammed. Probably quoting the late journalist Ariana Fallaci, Bernard Lewis suggests that the third encounter involves the likely choice whether the Europe of the future we will be a "Europeanized Islam or an Islamicized Europe."[7] Fallaci quoted earlier Bassam Tibi, a "moderate" Muslim in Germany: "The problem is not to establish whether in 2100 the greatest majority of the totality of Europeans will be Muslim: one way or another they will. The problem is whether (the) Islam destined to dominate Europe will be a Euro-Islam or the Islam of Shari'a." Fallaci did not believe in dialogue with Islam. She added that dialogue with Islam is "a monologue, a soliloquy nourished by our naïveté or unconfessed despair." She continued, "I strongly dissent from Pope Ratzinger (Benedict XVI) who insists on that monologue with dismaying hope."[8] Demographically at least, rapid trends are not as apparent from early statistics as recently believed. Globally, Muslims are 23.4 percent of the world population (and six percent of Europe), a ratio that is expected to rise to 26.4 percent in 2030 (eight percent of Europe compared to Christians who are currently estimated at 30 to 33 percent).[9] These figures reflect a net increase worldwide of 700 million Muslims.

If Islam becomes the dominant regional or even global religion or culture compared to a post-Christian West, will it be as a product of foreign design or simply as a demographic and cultural trend enabled by Western indifference? In either case, eclectic Islam may further absorb and digest into itself its version the Judeo-Christian message as well as the classical heritage to which the West less vaguely still attaches itself. In academics, Muslim scholars today study the classical *trivium* (grammar, rhetoric, logic) and especially Aristotle, while Western university curricula downplay both philosophy and rhetorical persuasion more in favor of career preparation, the cash flow approach to political discourse, and technical research and languages of data transfer. Christendom once awakened to find itself Arian. Is this to be repeated by a digital culture confronted with an analogue and religious Islamic culture?

Even the fundamental vocabulary of the "nation-state"—a dominant artifact of identity politics—is in jeopardy. Might this jeopardy extend to the secular state in general, which again is more of a Western artifact than a necessary and lasting outcome of history always open ended. The Islamic scholar Mahmoud Ayoub concludes that Muslims and Christians must work harder to understand each other on each others' terms, but then like Hassan ends his essay with what could be read as hinting toward an absorbent Muslim victory over the Christian faith: "although Christians and Muslims have followed different roads toward the goal of human fulfillment in God, the goal is one and the roads meet at many points."[10]

Ayoub identifies the final rub point with Christianity as specifically between Catholicism and Islam, but he is too quick to interpret this difference as a lack of sincerity on the part of the late Pope John Paul II. Ayoub and Muslims in general are sensitive to the late pope's clarity that "interreligious dialogue is part of the Church's evangelizing mission."[11] Each half of the dialogue appears to the other as claiming for itself the imagined middle ground. Ayoub does this by assuming that faith is finally a matter of religious expression, that "the *ultimate goal* of dialogue (is) to achieve a fellowship of faith, a sort of 'religious consensus' that would see in the diversity of expressions of this common faith a divine blessing."[12] To the Catholic, at least, the *ultimate question*—the more final rub point—is whether faith really is reducible to a matter of popular "expression," ultimately, or whether it is fidelity to the One who expresses and even reveals and discloses himself in self-donation. Islam offers the *Qu'ran* and human submission to the One, under Shari'a law, as a "way of life." Christianity witnesses to Christ as both the heart of man and the incarnate image of the Father and accepts His "new life" (Rom 8:1–13). Ayoub suggests that "fellowship will not be achieved between institutions (but is) the quest of sincere seekers of the truth, pious men and women of whom Christ said, 'You shall know the truth and the truth shall set you free' (Jn 8:32)." With the experience of often less than successful large-scale *ecumenical* efforts among Christian churches and ecclesial communities, all under the initiative of the Second Vatican Council, John Paul II and now Pope Benedict XVI also seek personal encounter as the most promising ecumenical path among Christians. Personal witness is also the best interreligious approach to the *followers* of Islam.

Judaism, the third of the monotheistic world religions, in important ways is both like and unlike either the later Islam or Christianity. Judaism is nonabsorbing and non-proselytizing. In this sense it remains a closed religion, and in this sociological sense also resembles the insular aspect of the much larger Muslim community or ummah.[13] This similarity is not surprising since Islam draws heavily from the Jewish Pentateuch. While Islam is expansive, it also retains Old Testament insularity for its members. Islam generally cuts a deep trench between those who accept the five pillars of Islam (dar al-Islam) and those who do not (dar al-harb). In contrast with both Judaism and Islam, the Christian self-understanding is that of a startling encounter. Unlike their "elder brothers" the Jews, Christians view Christ as the definitive fulfillment prefigured in the Hebrew prophecies of Judaism and as exclusive of no one.[14]

As its starting point, Islam views the members of all three monotheistic religions similarly as "people of the book." This premise involves only a partial understanding of Catholicism which is grounded not in a book, but in the reality, words and deeds of the Risen One as narrated in the book. By virtue of being sent by Christ himself, the Church fully existed by oral proclamation of the Word even before any books of the New Testament were written. The significance of Elijah in the Old Testament is that he did not recognize the Lord until, rather than seeing Him in an earthquake or a windstorm or a fire, he listened to "a tiny whispering sound" (1 Ki 19:11).[15] When the imprisoned John the Baptist, the final prophet, sends his followers to ask whether Christ is "he who is to come," Christ's response is not to read and debate with the Scribes, but to hear and see: "Go and tell John what you hear and see: the blind receive their sight and the lame walk, lepers are cleansed and the deaf hear, and the dead are raised up . . ." (Mat 11:2–5).

How members of the three monotheistic religions are to share this compact planet in the future is not predictable and entails a mix of possible outcomes. Hypothetically the range of Christian cultures and niches could vary from some new version of small Papal States (like the Vatican city-state) within a non-religious or even an expanded Muslim matrix, all the way to Benedict's globally scattered "creative minorities"—St. Augustine's "pilgrims in a foreign land"—who are called first to live the sacramental life and bloom wherever they are planted. Just as alliances with monarchies are a passing phase for the Church in history, so too is the fading confidence that people of faith are safe within an initially neutral institutional setting where public (government) education is constrained from passing on values that are reinforced by religion. The creative minorities are to leaven a wide range of uncomprehending and often hostile social and political settings, probably within a pattern of blurred nation-states and some zones of Islamic culture cleansed of the Christian presence. Defining his creative minorities, Benedict foresees a Church: "Less identified with the great societies, more a minority Church; she will live in small, vital circles of really convinced believers who live the faith . . . the salt of the earth. In this upheaval, constancy—keeping what is essential to man from being destroyed—is once again more important, and the powers of preservation that can sustain him in his humanity are even more necessary."[16]

Generally the West still offers resilient political, economic, cultural and social institutions unmatched in history, always less than perfect but also with no claims to be so. The external forces affecting nation-states include the religious and the cultural, and are not limited to the emerging layer of international political organizations such as the United Nations or the European Union or the multinational corporation. As a state and by default, the ummah could become kind of revamped *Pax Rome* or *Pax Britannica*, but now a "congregational monotheism" inserted from outside and from before the dominant Western narrative. As a post-Christian religious symbiosis this outcome would be self-inflicted if only to fill a spiritual void too hollow for even a materialistic consumer culture to fill indefinitely. Islam would reclaim its former cosmopolitan role.

Western societies, possessed by an opposite myth of technical perfectibility, would remain anesthetized, and the historic Catholic core would become a non-territorial dhimmi. It would be anchored geographically and ecclesiastically in Rome, but would be equally marginalized in the remaining strongholds of both secular humanism and the Islamic domain. In earlier times dhimmis were allowed to persist while simply paying annual tribute, as an alternative to less lucrative conversion to Islam.[17] Holding only enough real estate to contain some art work and a few filing cabinets—the one hundred ten acres of Vatican City—the papacy might be strangely useful and accepted as a mediator among residual nation-states and between these secular states especially in the Third World southern hemisphere and the strategically entrenched Islamic State. Such an almost pristine and global shepherding role would be reminiscent of what monarchies were in their better days as mediators among *multi*-national populations and between these and the ever present elites.

Religious freedom, rooted in the received dignity of the human person, could have to wait for times more enlightened than can be supplied by modernity's multicultural pragmatism—the religion of irreligion. But even within a mix of Shari'a and transplanted Western institutional shells, the natural law and the Church in its new setting would still proclaim and serve the permanence of the one-at-a-time concrete human person and the common good. Anchored in the absoluteness of the Incarnation, the Church would consistently propose "in season and out of season"—to every culture, politics, social or economic setting—its social principles, including the institutional and personal right to "immunity from coercion" in religion.

Hassan suggests that the path for dialogue today is that of *personal* spirituality. This path is distinct from any more abstract and organizational dialogue and institution building. At this personal level and within Islam, some aspects of moderate Sufism might match up well with the interior—not merely "subjective"—path of Augustinian theology with the purgative and illuminative and unitive steps toward God.[18] The eleventh century al-Ghazali characterizes Sufi thought in words that sound much like nineteenth century Cardinal John Henry Newman. Al-Ghazali writes "The aim of their (Sufi) knowledge is to *lop off the obstacles present in the soul* . . . in order to attain thereby a heart empty of all save God and adorned with the constant remembrance of God" (italics added).[19] Huston Smith likens the Sufi orders (*tariqahs*) to the contemplative orders of Catholicism. He proposes that Mohammed's journey to heaven was an ecstatic experience of the kind sought by all Sufis.[20] Ayoub reports that in North Africa the Catholic missionary Charles de Foucauld was actually regarded as both a Sufi saint and a saintly Christian.[21] And in her study of Pakistani Sufism, Katherine Ewing finds that Sufi literature is filled with accounts of Christian-like purifying conversion and repentance.[22] Catherine Helminski collects Sufi writings and finds a path to Mary, the mother of Christ: "Mary, the mother of Jesus, is very much revered in Sufism and Islam as an example of one who continually took refuge within the womb of her being."[23] (Because of the divinity of Christ, Catholic theology finds Mary to be more than an example, but the singular *Theotokos*, the Mother of God.)

A joint search for further similarities and differences between Christian and Muslim mystical or contemplative theology could be fruitful. Mainstream Islam guards against the notion that Sufis directly experience Allah. Christianity is the same: "No one has seen God . . . The only-begotten Son . . . has revealed Him" (Jn 1:18). Christian contemplation also restrains any dilution of the many into the one, and even an oversimplified definition of the oneness of God: "We should not identify God in Himself with his divine attributes, such as His goodness, bountifulness, justice, holiness, wisdom . . . (etc.). He . . . is known only to Himself, one God in three hypostases, unoriginate, unending, beyond goodness, above all praise. All that is said of God in divine Scripture is said with this sense of our inadequacy . . . He is incomprehensible to every being endowed with intellect and reason."[24]

A primary difference between Sufism and Christianity is that the former finds the self in the enlightening presence of a distant divinity, while the latter is Trinitarian and recognizes a Father who gives access through his Son. The Son, never apart from the Father, crosses the distance toward us so that in a real sense we might be one with Him. With Islam the Lord is above us, but with Christ the Lord is above us, with us, and within us. For Christians it is through the workings of the Holy Spirit that the Incarnation endures even our suffering to the dregs (I Cor 13:7), as he also shares with us our ecstasy and joys. This is the glory of God inseparable from a mysterious and divine humility in which we are to share. We are invited by Him not only to submission, but to "follow me" (Lk 9:23).

For Catholics, this is the meaning of the extraordinary moment of concentrated presence of all things in Christ who is truly in the Mass. Christian mystics speak of extraordinary favors that sometimes come in the form of substantial locutions, meaning words "that bring to pass in the soul what they signify[25]. . . And this is the power of His word in the Gospel, wherewith He healed the sick, raised the dead, etc., by no more than a word."[26] To accept this enduring power of the spoken word at different points in history might help us to appreciate, if not accept, a Catholic teaching rooted and reflected in Scripture. In the consecration of the Mass it is Christ who acts directly, but he also acts through the priest ordained for this purpose and who fully acts in his own capacity as another Christ (*alter Christus*). From the Last Supper the Catholic fully accepts the words of consecration today, believing that we are truly given the full unity of His body and blood, soul and divinity, in the Eucharist: "This is *my* body . . . This is *my* blood, the blood of the covenant to be poured out on behalf of many" (Mk 14:22–23, italics added, see also Mt 26:26–29, Lk 22:16–20, and 1 Cor 26:23–26).[27]

Unlike food and drink that is taken into the body and converted into the one partaking, the Eucharist promises to transforms the communicant into life of the One partaken: "You will not change me into you as happens with bodily food; rather, you will be changed into me."[28] It is the grace of divine life that is offered and partaken; we are to understand "spiritual realities in spiritual terms" (1 Cor 2:13). "Father, I desire that as you and I are one, so they may be one with us" (Jn 17:21). This reality of His embracing presence as the path to the Father is professed moments later at the elevation of the now consecrated host: "Through Him, and with Him and in Him, is to Thee, God the Father Almighty, in the unity of the Holy Spirit, all honor and glory, forever and ever." The Word of God has entered into his own creation as the Incarnation: "His is a single, uninterrupted utterance, because it is continuous and unending"[29] from before the foundation of the world.

Unlike Islamic submission to a less accessible God, encounter with the Real Presence also unveils the distinct *real*-ness of ourselves. It is in Christ as uncreated love that we come to know our created selves to be most real as persons, rather than as subjects or modernity's floating bundles of instincts—the modern pantheist deconstruction.[30] It is almost as if all of creation is a moment of ecstatic love, where Christ—the alpha and the omega (Rev 22:13)—is a kind of singularity initiating and fulfilling everything that is toward wholeness. With the Real Presence there is the interior reality of Cardinal Newman's motto of *cor ad cor loquitor* ("heart speaking to heart"). When still an Anglican he already proposed an intellectual basis for belief in the Real Presence unencumbered by distance. In a lyrical way he happened upon a finding of modern physics when he denied "the existence of space except as a subjective idea of our minds."[31] In the reality of the real heart, every act of charity and every fleeting prayer offered in time is already factored into the original music of creation from before time began. Thus, it is in time that a real person, Abraham, becomes the "father of faith." And at the moment that this faith is fulfilled, Mary who is found to be "full of grace" (Lk 1:28) likewise becomes the "mother of God." In his mystical body which is the Church, he is perpetually renewed and extended in an unbloody way in the celebration of the Mass, for "nothing is impossible with God" (Lk 1:37).

Oriental mysticism is less perceptive of the concretely real; the "most distinctive feature of Oriental as possibly a fragment of European mysticism is its profound consciousness of an omnipresent, all pervading unity. Every vestige of individuality is swallowed up."[32] Christians can move part way in this direction. Under Dionysius the Areopagite, Western mysticism became less equivalent to the word "sacramental" and "took on a more personal and intimate meaning: It expresses the soul's journey toward God."[33] But in its extreme form, Sufism itself becomes, in Western terms, pantheistic.[34] A counterpart in Catholic theology is probably some of the work of the widely influential Tielhard de Chardin whose poetics were easily mistaken for theology. The pantheistic tendency might be expected to arise within in Islam in the absence of the particularity of the Incarnation—Christ as a mediator who is always still one with the Father. It is through a very small aperture—a manger and as man like us in all things but sin—that the Truth comes to us, and yet He fills and transcends the entire universe.

The precise discussion point with mainstream Islam would be Muslim toleration of Sufism at least as a personal path toward *ideas* about God, even if not as a path approaching actual union with God. At its final and highest level, contemplation in the West is not an idea or even a spiritual achievement, but a direct and undeserved *gift* from God. In the West Eckhardt and Aquinas both affirm that God is a different order of being from ourselves, and that He is ever above the intellect and can never be comprehended (and Islam would agree), although He is *seen* by the blessed.[35] The Second Vatican Council teaches that the Church as a whole is both an institution *and* a charismatic mystery. The institutional Church is both hierarchical *and* charismatic (Eph 4:11–12; I Cor 12:4; Gal 5:22). In his favorable study of the Catholic mystics, Thomas Dubay faults Western thought for its excesses toward too much differentiation and compartmentalization:

> The separation of moral theology from doctrinal, and both of them from mystical, indicates that something is fundamentally awry. It is true, of course, that one cannot be a specialist in everything, but the fact remains that few theolo-

gians make any real effort to consider and introduce mystical reality into their discussion of human acts . . . of the basic principles of morality . . . of achieving heroic holiness . . . of the correlation of all these to infused contemplation and the transforming union.[36]

The study of comparative mysticism, as well as comparative theology, might trigger an excellent response to the underlying and divergent predispositions of Muslim and Christian theologies regarding unity and distinctions, such as between faith and reason, and how the new life is also a way of life.

The Muslim apologist Ayoub finds that the Sufis do not completely reject the redemptive suffering of Christ. Sufis hold, however, that the significance of Christ's death is not in how or when this took place, but "rather in its meaning to a humanity bound to this material plane of existence by lust, greed, and anxiety . . . (and as *only* an) *example* as a specially favored human being who has risen beyond the world of material existence to the divine presence."[37] In the end, Christ is reduced to one example of (Gnostic-like) enlightenment, and is no longer the Redeemer. Ayoub adds that from the Muslim perspective, the Gnostic gospel of *Barnabas* has "provided the answer to many Christological questions for modern commentators . . . (he speculates that it is) probably a late work, written under Islamic influence and agreeing with Islam on many crucial points."[38]

The non-canonical (that is, not inspired) *Barnabas* reinforces the Muslim "substitutionist" theory. This is the theory, shared by some Western rationalists, that it was not Christ who died on the cross, but a secretly placed volunteer and stand in.[39] Among other Gnostic heresies within Christian history, Docetism held instead that Christ was not really a man and in this way that He was preserved from death, and therefore that Christ did not suffer crucifixion and death on the cross. Of "substitution," for the Christian it is Christ who substitutes for us. Christ stands in our place as if to receive the justice of an angry God, but then as von Balthasar shows, He even chooses to become our self-banishment from Himself as the infinite love of the Father. This is the singular mystery of the cross. "God made Christ Who knew no sin *to be sin* on our behalf, that we might become the righteousness of God in Him" (2 Cor 5:21). Through the cross Christ empowers us into the new life. Christ inhabits and then, to an infinite degree, becomes and transforms our desolation into Himself.

An interreligious comparison between mystics simply has not been developed to the same degree as between Muslim and Christian theologians and philosophers. The Medieval era Muslim and Christian systematizers, for example, Averroes and St. Thomas Aquinas, were intent on a broad synthesis of faith with the path of reason, as influenced by the rediscovered natural philosophy of Aristotle.[40] The earlier St. Augustine offers a different and less comfortable examination capable of speaking to very unstable times like his and ours: "So it falls out that in this world, in evil days like these, the Church walks onward like a wayfarer stricken by the world's hostility, but comforted by the mercy of God . . . It was never any different . . . So shall it be until this world is no more."[41]

Recent *ecumenical* dialogue between the Church and other Christian churches and ecclesial communities is valuable practice for a different kind of Catholic-Muslim *interreligious* engagement. The Second Vatican Council may have prepared for a candid, clarifying, and graced interreligious encounter *among persons* of very different religions even more than it did for more ecumenical dialogue among Christian institutions. Successful approaches and the errors of ambiguity are both instructive. Muslims hold that human fulfillment is found not in access to the Father through his self-disclosure in the incarnate Christ, but rather in a guidance and recurring spiritual presence in all of history. Christians agree only to a point. The Church calls upon a distinct and universal natural law in the hearts of all mankind, combined with the advancing works of the Holy Spirit, who spoke through the prophets of the Old Testament and now indwells his Church. Still, in some real and always unconfined sense, the Spirit also moves as the wind where it will (Jn 3:14).

MIRROR TWINS: THE CRISES OF ISLAM AND MODERNITY

The "crisis of Islam" comes at two levels that are inseparably linked. The first tier is the apostasy that it is feared comes with clearly distinguishing a profane realm from the sacred. But Ataturk's pragmatic formula for Turkey yielded a cultural change that nevertheless has also kept Islam fully intact as a way of life. The Caliphate is replaced by a secular constitution, but the minarets remain as daily prayer is called, in Turkish rather than Arabic. The often pragmatic ways of Islam show a latent ability to harbor such apparent contradictions. The second tier of the crisis is the need to find, possibly reflected in fragments of the Shari'a, a way to more fully value the free and responsible human person as such. Hassan looks for scant evidence of natural law in the *Qur'an* as a kind of bridge, and suggests restoration of the traditional Itjihad consensus approach under careful "rules of derivation" (Chapter 3). Others have abstracted principles from the *Qur'an,* but these remain grounded in the book rather than more directly the concrete man himself.

The resulting and immediate political crisis of Islam is generally summarized in these points. There is a measure of self hatred for the past, as in the rejection of the "days of ignorance" in Arabia (and in dar al-harb) preceding the coming of Mohammed. With Islam today anger is aimed largely at those who are currently in power in the Middle East and those who keep them there. The goal of radicals is to destabilize these often autocratic regimes. The popular goal is to follow less violent means, even at the risk of violent suppression. The "Arab Spring" in Egypt, Libya, Syria and Yemen may be the turning of the corner, but with no assurance that these societies can come together toward a stable future. Muslims also feel a fury over the imported and often corrupting popular culture from the West. In the West as well as the Middle East there is now an advance guard of radical Wahabbi Islamic schools, probably seventy percent financed by windfall oil money mined from the deserts of Saudi Arabia.

Institutionally the Islamic State is a combination of the felt worldwide um-mah with a patchwork of administrative units engrafted from the nation-state system in the West. In the long view of religion, neither the Islamic State nor the constitutional nation-state is the end of history. The crisis of Islam chal-lenges its followers to either transform or possibly encapsulate Shari'a Law somewhat as is done in Turkey. Were natural law still consistently accepted by the constitutional states of the West, accountability to universal morality (roughly equated/replaced by Muslims with Islam) might better support polit-ical growth in the Islamic world and reduced tensions with the West. The path for Islam as a world religion with possible openings to natural law as such could then be encouraged with greater conviction. The openings within Islam are tenuous at best, inseparable from the polyglot *Qur'an* as the presumptive singular reference and source of universal human values.

The institutions of Islam display a few rough parallels with the early Protestant Christianity, as compared to the more sacramental Church. The sixteenth century Calvin proclaimed the Supreme Godhead in a new doctrine of predestination (exaggerated from the relatively wide-ranging writings of the fourth century St. Augustine[42]). Martin Luther proposed the opposite core doctrine of salvation through subjective faith alone. The mind of Calvin aligns with the Islamic sense of an unknowable and arbitrary God and the predestined members of dar al-Islam. The mysticism of Luther aligns with the soaring and very personal spirituality of Sufi mysticism. Calvin builds a theocracy in Geneva while Luther births the secular-religious and lay-dominated state, a snub to both the ordained priesthood and the emperor. The historian Philip Hughes develops a connection between the Luther's notion of an arbitrary and supreme God and his ideas about human law. In place of the Church, for Luther it is the Western secular state that acts as "God's agent" and stands "alone as an authority representing the social order." The Church is superfluous as a separate public institution.[43] In comparison, in Islam there is no laity because there is no formal clerical status, so the Mosque-state becomes the only public institution. In the twenty-first century the lay-dominated state moves ever more toward positivist law, while the Islamic State remains bounded by all-inclusive and divinely revealed Shari'a. In a sermon, St. Augustine said of clerics and the laity: "Because we are placed in charge, we are ranked among you as shepherds, if we are good: but because we are Christians, we too are members of the flock with you." The Second Vatican Council concurs with its accent on "the universal call to holiness."

Following the Second Vatican Council the Church proposes and articulated and fully human approach, not a path, into and for the modern world (Chapter 4). These principles hold that there are some things absolutely prohibited by common morality, but it also affirms *a legitimate domain* for prudential decision making by free and responsible people dealing together with their more worldly needs and relations. Under the pressure of the Reformation, the first successful Catholic reform of possible interest to the Islamic world took shape at the Council of Trent (1545–63). During the Council the Church clarified what was permanent and charted a course in a turbulent world. In 1557, desperate for help against Spanish expansionism, Pope Paul IV even appealed to the Turkish sovereign to abstain from his attacks on Hungary and instead to support the papal war in Sicily. (Before the Council, in 1500, the German emperor had been skimming two-thirds of "indulgence" revenues—the flashpoint for the Luther's Reformation—for use in fighting the Turks in the east.[44])

The three major points of polarization at Trent were relations between the Church and civil government and other external threats, but also within the Church itself, the tension between papal decrees and scripture, and between papal primacy and ecumenical or proposed national Church councils. The local priest was too often "little more than a hired functionary" trafficking in "spiritual commodities (and) stereotyped exhortations."[45] In the same way, papal primacy had become "inseparably identified with its caricature in the form of an absolute monarchy" and the priesthood and Eucharistic Sacrifice too often had "assumed only the shape to which they had been perverted and degraded, of domination over the laity, and a systematic traffic in masses . . ."[46] Where Luther sought a Church restored to its primitive simplicity, Mohammed jumped over the earlier Arabian "days of ignorance" to replace paganism with the original faith of Abraham from prior to most Jewish history and the Christ event. Comparing the modern world with Islam, the secular West offers three elements. First is the "rule of law," meaning positive law presumably based in some reliable way on the universal natural law. Secular positive law is distinct from the separate canon law internal to the Church. The second element is the establishment in a different cultural setting of pluralistic political structures within each of the numerous secular and sovereign states. And third is a market economy which Muslims would hope does not violate their own doctrinal sense of economic equality and welfare.

Corresponding to these three positive institutions of modernity we find quite different features in the Islamic State. First, Shari'a is the universal "law," but serves in place of the rule of law as understood in the West. Second, while there are political parties in parliamentary Islamic states, they often remain communally based and even feudal, and typically blur across the relatively arbitrary and recent nation-state boundaries into adjoining and even distant states. And third, in practice many of the Islamic economies are severely split-level, especially in the oil-rich Middle East. Such a political economy makes it difficult to generate and enfranchise a politically responsible middle class of citizens. But from the Muslim perspective exaggerated Western individualism is seen as eroding the broader pre-modern culture of domestic economies and extended family networks that previously supported women.[47]

From these and other differences between the West and Islam, the very prominent Western authority on Islam, Bernard Lewis, identifies a broad lack of personal freedom as the major obstacle to moving from the Islamic State toward some form of democracy as his presumed end point: "To a Western observer, schooled in the theory and practice of Western freedom, it is precisely the lack of freedom—freedom of the mind from constraint and indoctrination, to question and inquire and speak; freedom of the economy from corrupt and pervasive mismanagement, freedom of women from male oppression; freedom of citizens from tyranny—that underlies so many of the troubles of the Muslim world. But the road to democracy, as the Western experience amply demonstrates, is long and hard, full of pitfalls and obstacles."[48]

During one of the countless "pitfalls," the writer Charles Peguy, a convert to the God who would be called and known as Father, was killed by a single shot through the head in the Battle of the Marne (1914). But the young Peguy already had lived long enough to pen his poem *God Speaks*." He finds that "all prostrations . . . all the submission . . . in the world . . . (fall short of) . . . the soaring up point of one single invocation, from a love that is free."[49] In the Christian heart this freedom expands into the irreversible and new dimension of the "new life" and the "good news" of the Gospel which is Jesus Christ. We share the freedom of actually *belonging* to the One who in absolute freedom first *chose to belong to all and each of us*, even to the point of carrying our self-inflicted cross as His own.

At the more confined political level and in Lewis's mind there are only two alternative choices for the followers of Islam in the future, and both find broad support in the Middle East. One is the path of a more isolated Islam in search of an imagined past and the return to ancient glories. And the other is the secular and anomalous path of Turkey.[50] Lacking the centuries that allowed institutional evolution in the West, the Islamic State is challenged to find its path into responsible freedom, even as the West must rediscover its heritage of universal natural law over the welfare state and inevitable identity politics.[51] Within Islam, disciplined scriptural reinterpretation through Itjihad consensus is still accepted by only the Shi'ite minority sect. As Hassan proposes, an internally consistent evolution of Islam in the twenty-first century could depend upon inter-sectarian agreement to restore the potential consensus of Itjihad to the interpretation of the *Qur'an* and hadith.[52]

How might the cryptic openings toward man as the bearer of universal natural law be fostered? Openings are found in the *Qu'ran* (for example, Q16:36, 30:30, 9:71), and the meaning of fitrah (see Chapter 3).[53] Or will believing Muslim's have to mirror either Kierkegaard's Western "leap of faith" with an equivalent and Islamic "leap of pragmatism," with ever more incoherent adjustments? The path of extreme pragmatism claimed by the radical fringe and their slogans is too apparent to Western critics—suicide bombings, hostages beheaded and mutilated, a fourteen year old Christian boy crucified in the back streets of Baghdad, and in the war zone the use of fellow Muslims as human shields.

In the early and less disrupted 1990s an aging European intellectual and aristocrat appeared as a conspicuous guest at a large meeting of Islamic scholars in Muscat, Oman. Without advance notice it was asked of the Austrian Erik von Kuehnelt-Leddhin what he actually thought was the source of the crisis of Islam. During its ancient glory the Islamic world had been so superior to the West in so many ways—in philosophy as evidenced by the transmittal through Moorish Spain of Aristotle to twelfth-century Paris, and in medicine, astronomy, and mathematics. Why, he was asked, had the Muslim world been so eclipsed in recent centuries? Erik could have pointed to the heaviness of Islam itself and what Bernard Lewis identifies as its "arrogance" toward intercultural learning,[54] or to social and economic and political reasons such as the loss of plunder income, and to the aversion for discoverable laws of nature and science, or simply to the competing rise of the West and the naval and military inferiority of the Ottoman Empire.[55] He could have confirmed Bernard Lewis' summary view that the lack of basic personal freedoms explains all.

At possible personal risk and almost as a summary of a most complex subject, this guest ventured one distilled sentence for the passing of the golden age of Islam: "*It is because you do not respect your women.*"[56] Starting at the smallest scale it is not enough to observe the Qur'anic injunction to treat multiple wives equally with each other. The standard of Christian equality is to treat one's spouse as both different from oneself and equal with oneself.[57] But the invited visitor meant even more than this. Family members and fully human societies and cultures all incarnate a respect and reciprocity and even self-donation for what is "other." At all levels we either grow in relationship with the distinctly other, as between spouses or between cultures, or we decline and fail to generate a future beyond ourselves. Looking at a West that is not corruption-free, Shi'ites regard "liberated" women in the West as "manipulated by society to become sex objects, consumers of cosmetics and other products of the Western economy. They see this degradation as leading to "promiscuity, adultery, divorce and the break-down of the family unit in the West."[58]

At about the same time as the Muscat visitor made this remark a princess from the extended royal family of Saudi Arabia published through an English writer[59] her insider accounts of the place of women in much of the Islamic world: "I told my family that in my opinion, the traditions remaining from that era[60] and not the *Koran* were what kept us women in bondage. Few people know the facts that the Koran does not call for veiling, nor the restrictions women endure in the Muslim world. It is the traditions passed down that so hinder us from moving forward."[61] Based on these remarks might even Mohammed say that the too traditionalist elements of Islam are not Islamic enough?[62] The parallel critique heard of (doctrinaire) evolutionists is that even Charles Darwin might not find a place at the table with modern Darwin-ists.

To the early Western mind, Islam seems unable to recognize the stature of man as a reasoning being who is additionally touched by grace. Islam collapses natural law into a divine law which Muslims understand to be the Shari'a. By comparison, one thousand years later and as part of the rationalist Enlightenment, modernity denies the possible and unique mystery and historical fact of Christ as the gratuitous incarnation of the divine within human experience.

As in the crisis of Islam, the crisis of the West comes at two levels. The first tier is to rescue pragmatic reason, now nearly amputated from faith, from closing in even further on itself. Reason becomes a cocoon of disbelief and self-adulation masquerading as open mindedness. This open mindedness reduces faith to the level of subjective opinion and narrative, and then like Islamic politics preoccupies itself with self-identity. The universal natural law does not exist; it is no longer constitutive of the human person. As with the philosophical discontinuity of early Islam, irreconcilable theological and philosophical positions are to be unexamined and treated as equally "true." The public forum backs itself into Shari'a-like consensus orthodoxy of political correctness, and as a first principle among some academics prohibits the questioning of the underlying moral assumptions.[63]

Within the philosophical confusion of the West, the second tier of crisis involves a plausible liason between Western value indifference and Islamic ideology. Invertebrate multiculturalism in the West, either ideological or a collage of self-interests, may find itself a good fit with an Islam that historically has patronized and colonized other unsuspecting religions and cultures—all as lesser versions of itself. Multicultural leveling actually diminishes the human person and now the overdrawn secularist project offers no resilient guarantee of personal freedom and responsibility. Despite the different trappings, is there a pending cultural convergence of expediency between the pragmatic ideology of Islamic leaders and the ideological pragmatism of the West? Arbitrary fatwas dispensed under Shari'a occasionally find their counterpart in the West under court-imposed legislation from the bench.

St. Augustine warns that freedom "cannot be reduced to a sense of choice: it is (instead) freedom to act fully . . ." and to resist what he termed *fantastica fornicatio*—"the prostitution of the mind to its own fancies." Hospitals were originally founded as a vocational service in a Christendom that predated the very existence of the modern state. Hospitals will be forced to close if they refuse to bend to state mandates for euthanasia and abortion.[64] If not actual closure, then we can look forward to an open and resilient counterculture of civil disobedience. Are we in the West now served by the academic equivalent to Stalin's "useful idiots," those Western investors who serviced the Soviet machine for profit and career? Some Western academics of interreligious studies openly lament the fact that unilateral Qur'anic monotheism (Q 30:62–5) has been too long delayed.

For their part, Muslims entertain an opposite suspicion toward the West. For example, of the Muslim-Catholic dialogue initiated by the Second Vatican Council, they ask: "Is this openness true dialogue, or could it be simply condescending tolerance aimed at facilitating evangelization?"[65] In response, a better understanding of *what is meant* theologically by the triune oneness of God—and therefore what this might mean of our relationship to God—can be elementary education rather than affirmation toward conversion. When rudimentary misunderstanding of doctrine and theological terms blocks dialogue, victimization may be in the enforced retention of misinformation.[66]

In his appeal for respectful dialogue, Ayoub turns to the *Qur'an* and proposes four universal rules to qualify the truth claims of any religion. First, the truth claim must be "enshrined in a divinely revealed scripture . . . (second) it must acknowledge and proclaim God's absolute Oneness . . . (third) it must enjoin dynamic faith in God and the last day . . . and (fourth) it should foster righteous living."[67] Ayoub asserts "that the *Qur'an* came not to establish an Islamic empire but a *community of faiths* that would include Muslims, Jews, Christians, Sabaeans, and any other faith community that claims to live by the four principles outlined above."[68] In formulating a possible response, the disjunction to be soberly understood by Christians and the West is that the second ultimatum, the absolute Oneness of a monolithic God, appears to be a pre-emptive rejection of the defining Christian truth claim, namely the gifted, intimate and historical presence—and therefore triune nature of this same (?) one God. Islamic oneness summarily rejects as idolatrous the Jesus Christ who for Christians is the divinity and irreducible basis for personal freedom and responsibility. He is "the truth that will set us free" (Jn 8:32). Islam proposes a universal community of faith, while Christians are suppressed in their desire for "reciprocity" and personal freedom of religion as part of the universal natural law.

The defense of natural law—and resistance to the assimilation of Christianity into the presumptive faith community of Islam—even includes insights from an avowed *atheist*, the late Ariana Fallaci. Fallaci chastises the Catholic Church for winking at the "ideological robberies" of Islam throughout history, the unchallenged Muslim presumption that "Christianity is an abortion of Islam," and for not raising clearly the banner of Western self defense.[69] Fallaci's critique came before Pope Benedict XVI's very clear *Regensburg Lecture* in 2006 (Chapter 1). Fallaci calls herself a "Christian atheist" because for all of its mythology, in her judgment, "Christianity truly is an irresistible provocation, a sensational bet that Man makes himself . . ." We have a catastrophe, she says, "Because before invading our territory and destroying our culture, before canceling our identity, Islam aims to extinguish that irresistible provocation."[70]

As an atheist, Fallaci opines that man created God, not the other way around, and that man does this out of despair . . . *but,* (she continues) that Christ even as only a man demands liberty and freedom. Phoenix-like, He is ever rising up to renew these claims and in this way to "seduce" even her (Fallaci) into belief. As a "Christian atheist . . . (she finds that) Life always resurrects, Life is eternal . . . That most seduces me. Because in it I see the rejection of Death, the refusal of Death, the apotheosis of Life which can be evil: yes. Which is also evil, which eats itself. But its alternative is Nothingness. And let's face it: such is the principle which leads and feeds our civilization."[71] Of Europe's reported flacid convictions, its self-hatred and sickness and "moral and intellectual cancer," Fallaci observes, "If a Pope and an atheist say the same thing, in that thing there must be something tremendously true."[72]

Given this core sameness with the late Pope John Paul II, a remaining difference between Fallaci and the papacy is that she believes radically that man makes himself.[73] Where Christianity rejects this view as a half truth, Islam possibly rejects it as totally false. And the current Pope Benedict hands on the living fact of Christ who in His disclosure of God as Father, also more fully reveals man to himself.[74] The fact of Christ reveals each of us as a transcendent person, so much more than a self-made construct. Ultimately, it is God who creates and reveals man as a recipient of divine hope and victory over any impending and worldly despair. To meet the current crisis of the West the Church proposes a commitment to the coherence of faithful reasoning and reasoning faith, in the person of Christ. It is in Christ that the Spirit is given to us. In the unity of a triune God these are never separate.

All are called to be vigilant against both rationalism and intuitionism (1 Jn 4:1), exercising a kind of reason that also knows that His ways are not our ways. The full meaning of Pope John Paul II's effort in 1990 toward theological integrity in Catholic universities is basically about the integrity of the human person (*1990 Norms for Catholic Universities*).[75] Warning is given against both nihilism and multicultural relativism, as much as theological errors porous to a relativism ("dictatorship of relativism" is the later Pope Benedict's term) sometimes found within the affected theology departments.[76] The norms include this intellectual and cultural perspective: "Among the criteria that characterize the values of a culture are, above all, the full meaning of the human person and his or her liberty, dignity, sense of responsibility and openness to the transcendent." At issue is not only fidelity to the faith, but also to reason above all brands of factionalism or self promotion. Western cultural rationalism can distance itself from God in two steps. The first is to separate religious and civic society, and the second is the disordered assertion of self through positivistic abuse of civil law. Islamic cultural rationalism can distance a transcendent God from itself who then logically engulfs everything else including latent civic institutions into the Islamic State. In both cases, modern and archaic, the relational and living God no longer informs human self understanding. The two cultural patterns disable dialogue in their disregard for an underlying and universal natural law as a common grammar.

A pragmatic common ground between Christians, the West, and the followers of Islam brackets to the side areas not held in common. A deep esteem for the human person still requires a later opening toward deferred core areas of disagreement. This option is lost to the West if the "full meaning of the human person" is forgotten. Theological common ground need not concede a symmetrical relationship between the scriptures as a condition for interreligious work. Because Muslim belief is that the *Qur'an* is a direct copy of the same book in heaven, this "word made book" displaces a clear understanding of natural law as a distinct element of divine law—"The word made flesh" as witnessed in the New Testament writings. Where the distinguishing Western and Christian mind seeks to work toward a common ground within agreed brackets, Islam understands itself as being the always inclusive brackets.

Discourse remains theological and theological discourse remains within the context of the *Qur'an*. As violent jihad with the West possibly subsides, cultural osmosis continues in proposals for dual legal systems in Western states. Muslim building complexes in Western cities are combined with community centers to be managed by subordinate interreligious boards. Do such complexes replicate and in this way expand the domain of the unitary Islamic State? Under Islam all religions are assured a cooperative role in the shadow of the mosque, while under the Western tradition we find a separate realm of community development (the secular state) within which has been found personal freedom of religion.

In the formative years of Islam, the original definition of jihad mutated from the central notion of personal inner struggle. In similar fashion today in the West the most basic human relationship of the "family," and even the meaning of "rights," similarly reverts from clear definition. Qur'anic acceptance of parts of the Arabian "days of ignorance" alongside monotheism finds its parallel in modern linguistic accommodation of word meanings to a surrounding subculture. Distinct meanings are reduced to the status of special cases. Marriage of a man and woman is an anomaly within a broadly redefined and even undefined "marriage," and natural law—the source of family rights—is bracketed aside. The distinction between marriage parity and parody of marriage is anathematized by the guardians of secular culture. If the term jihad can embrace contradictory meanings, and "civil rights" can impose equivalence between the civil rights of Blacks and promotion of ersatz morality, then it seems only a small step for Western multiculturalism to be pragmatically absorbed into a much broader Islamic multiculturalism. Is the so-called "clash of civilizations" any more likely than a polyglot accommodation and across the board dismissal of the natural law foundation for civic institutions? The common ground becomes the agreement to live with contradictions superimposed by protections against all manner of "hate crimes." Western civic rationalism removes God from the public square, while the Islamic State removes the public square from man. The substitution of slogans or single words for concepts, followed by the redefinition of the words, is both the archaic and the modern technique of deconstruction. When asked what would be his first action to save his country, a Chinese emperor answered "I will restore the meaning of words."

In the domain of (Sunni) Islam the watchdog of the unitary state becomes the imam, while in the West the modern variant under the division of powers is either presidential Executive Orders, an arithmetic and funded majority interest, or legislation from the bench. From opposite directions it is only a small step for the logic of Islamic theocratic rationalism and Western pragmatism to converge or overlap. In his search for truth, Al-Ghazali proposed overlapping "hoof prints" between natural and divine law (Chapter 3), and in our lesser search for common ground we might settle for overlapping hoof prints between Islamic and Western pragmatism under a more or less incoherent government-supervised harmony. The mixing zone could easily feature an untouched Qur'anic option for polygamy under divine law alongside same-sex marriage as an overreaction to discrimination and cross dressed as a limited appeal for equality in hospital visitation rights and government benefits. In the West the overlapping hoofprints of Shari'a and of secularism would sequester Christianity as a private indulgence from the public forum. In 2011 the federal Department of Health and Human Services (United States) issued regulations under the Affordable Care Act requiring religious institutions to perform such objectionable functions as abortions and sterilizations, unless the majority of their staffs *and* the majority of those benefiting from their services embrace the institutions' religious and moral convictions. Catholic hospitals, service agencies and schools, for example, are permitted to exist as such only if they discriminate against and exclude the non-Catholic general population. Under this post-modern pretense, Islamic encapsulation is retrieved from the fallen Ottoman Empire—the Church in the West is a modern day dhimmi. Religions in general are to become self-enclosed dhimmis within the secularist state. Under the doctrine of "equality" and aggressive neutrality toward natural law modernity reveals itself as a kind of madness and demonstrates at the same moment "a logical completeness and a spiritual contraction."[77] The chase after equality of outcomes replaces equality of persons. Equality comes to mean sameness.

The legitimate search for common ground between the West and Islam might be in shared efforts to relieve real social and economic injustices (Chapter 4). The risk of cooption comes when the West neglects the natural law or when the Church declines to proclaim the gospel however discretely "in season and out of season." Intellectual integrity at least calls for clarity between the natural law which is universal and accessible by human reason, and any claimed proprietary divine law imbedded in the Islamic self-identity and the Islamic State. Integrity also calls for clarity between human reason and any leveling equality that would transform churches into modern day dhimmis within a secularist regime where freedom of conscience and of religion are paved over. Making no distinction between itself and what is humanly universal, Islam conflates natural law with itself. Islam is at once both a religion and a universal guidance standing apart from religion: "(God) has sent forth His apostle with guidance and the True Faith that he may exalt it *above all religion*, though the idolaters abhor it" (Q 9:33, italics added). Radically secular humanism denies the existence of natural law altogether. In doing so it discards this possible grammar for discourse with Muslims of good will.

Islam for its part absorbs at least parts of the universal natural law into Shari'a in a way that disclaims the common (non-Shari'a) origin. Discourse within the grammar of natural law is blocked in both directions, by either willful denial or oblivious relabeling.

To rescue his nation the Chinese emperor would "restore the meaning of words." Jihad is such a word of indefinite definition.The tipping point in the history of Islam toward ambivalence on the meaning of jihad was the moment of Mohammed's exodus to Medina in 622 A.D. (Chapter 2). Military jihad began then and was vastly expanded by his successors. For the United States a similar tipping point toward blurring of meanings on crucial issues came many centuries later in a landmark legal decision. In 1973 Supreme Court Justice Blackman ruled in *Roe v. Wade* that the unborn human right to live is trumped by the "penumbra" of the asserted "right to privacy" of others. Because the United States Constitution does not explicitly mention the natural law, by judicial fiat (or fatwah . . .) an inventive penumbra law precludes its reality. At the national level the redefinition of abortion as "reproductive health services" and now the push to redefine the very meaning of "family" are logical consequences. Similarly, at the international level proposed United Nations resolutions could prohibit as "hate crimes" public critique of Islam or of homosexuality with perceived violations subject to secular courts.[78]

Of such modern day conceptual graffiti, Benjamin Constant, a French painter rather than a politician or philosopher, saw the big picture: "In certain epochs one must run the whole cycle of madness in order to return to reason." The combined weight of Western intuitionism and positivism converges with T.E. Lawrence's assessment of early Arab cultural presuppositions (Chapter 2): "Sometimes inconsistencies seemed to possess them at once in joint sway; but they never compromised: they pursued the logic of several incompatible opinions to absurd ends, without perceiving the incongruity."[79] Modernity and ancient Arabia are not that far apart. The spread of incompatible opinions without perceiving the incongruity, that is, without the compass of natural law, imposes itself on the West and the multicultural modern world.

At the international level today, the Muslim migration into Europe—problematic but potentially rejuvenating to an agnostic culture—is largely a flight from economic disadvantages in the Middle East. Spotty research[80] of the immigrant population in Europe suggests that rather than shedding their Muslim religion, young Muslims in Europe are actually more religious than their parents. As a practical matter, it also appears that within the European setting the Muslims are organizing congregationally at the local level and are only then possibly federating into larger coalitions. Surprisingly, it also appears that these groups are somewhat autonomous from the Islam of their homelands. It might be that this pattern is totally consistent with and verifies

Islam's self-image as a "congregational theocracy"—that in the global um-mah as a whole the local Muslim associations have always been divided along cultural, doctrinal and ethnic lines. Muslims in the European Union are not interested in assimilating to the same degree as they are in the different United States setting[81] (with the exception of foreign-trained al-Qaeda terrorists). Yet they are also unable at least temporarily to coalesce sufficiently within any of the European Union countries to achieve recognized corporate status. If they achieve such status similar to the Christian denominations, they will then regard themselves as qualified to seek state educational subsidies like those long provided for particular historical reasons (compensation for property confiscation) to Catholic and Protestant religious communities. A comparative survey of Muslims populations in the United States concludes that Muslims in France, Spain and Britain are nearly twice as likely to regard suicide bombing as sometimes justified (fifteen percent rather than seven percent). Nearly two-thirds of American adult Muslims were born abroad and, while conservative socially, they lean heavily toward the Democratic Party by six to one. African American Muslims are apparently more radical than the new immigrants.[82]

Similar to the victimhood psychology of many Muslims is personal vulner-ability within Western modernity. This is our restless anxiety and weariness in the face of seemingly endless existential doubt.[83] Both self-hatreds, Islamic resentment and Western amnesia, evidence an alienation more spiritual than political. Of the two self-hatreds, no brand of pragmatism is sufficient as a cure whether Islamic or Western: "Can the blind man act as a guide to a blind man? Will they not both fall into a ditch" (Lk 6:39). As in pre-Christian paganism and oracles, post-Christian paganism renders uncomfortable forces tolerable by political double-speak. Media elites assert abstract human rights to justify concrete acts of destruction. A false "victimization" mentality is sensitively crafted by the abortion industry for the staffs of neighborhood aborturaries.[84] The attacks of a very few led credibility to this exploited cari-cature. When the *un*-recognition of the unborn human being was fatwah-ed in 1973 by the United States Supreme Court, the court offered two-faced ambivalence: "We need not resolve the difficult question when life begins when those trained in the respective disciplines of medicine, philosophy, and theology, are unable to arrive at any consensus. The judiciary at this point in the development of man's knowledge, is not in a position to speculate as to the answer" (*Roe v. Wade*). And following the court, all are coerced, instead, to speculate confidently on the unknowability of reality and, like the pa-gans of Jericho (Josh. 6:21) or the mobs at the Coliseum, to also *act* on this speculation. With mandatory federal taxes all are complicit in the sacrifice our own children to this deconstruction of the obvious that a second human life is involved. But unlike the gladiators, the unborn are always smaller and unarmed. To borrow a phrase from Hobbes' Leviathan, for those rhetorically and really cast outside of the social compact and its penumbra, life is "nasty, solitary, poor, brutish and short."

In the modern day intellectual and moral vacuum, the fiction of privatized and totally incompatible truth claims was fully enfranchised in another ruling in 1992 (*Casey v. Planned Parenthood*): "at the heart of liberty (as protected by the due process clause of the Constitution), is the right to define one's own concept of existence, of meaning and of the mystery of human life."[85] Is the truth of "other selves" at risk of being defined by a pre-Copernican modernity with myself at the center? Defenders of the unborn find themselves in the position of Galileo. It is permitted to see through the ultrasound the reality that every abortion involves two human beings rather than one, so long as this finding remains politically "hypothetical" (and they) "must neither hold, defend, nor teach that opinion in any way whatsoever."[86]

For its part, members of the Church demonstrate all to often that all other earthy institutions even when combined still do not have a monopoly on human fallibility and corruption. In 1992 Pope John Paul II publicly petitioned forgiveness for transgressions of the Gospel message by members of the Church in prior centuries. The record is inescapable and yet there does remain a distinction (as in all institutions) between the divinely instituted Church and its members. By his gesture he also Christians especially to broadly examine our current "responsibilities . . . regarding atheism, religious indifference, secularism, ethical relativism, the violations of the right to life, disregard for the poor in many countries."[87] Forgiveness, said St. Paul, "prevents Satan— whose guile we know too well—from outwitting us" (2 Cor 2:11). More than a sentiment, forgiveness is a decision to not allow the past to infiltrate the present moment or to become the future. Forgiveness is a radiant act of self respect, and of sovereignty over the situation, in place of resentment and dominance toward the other. Pope John Paul II's gesture is a reminder that apology rising from an interior life is the most communal act of all, often because we are often more like others in their faults than are they.

A survivor of Communist imprisonment in 1918, Pitirim Sorokin (for thirty years chair of the Harvard Department of Sociology) challenged our despondency and one-sided accusations (the most extreme form of which today is radical Islamic jihad). He proposed that personal and cultural disruption do *not always* produce polarization and then aggression. He documented scientifically a range of predictably Freudian responses to evil, but then found a contradiction to Freudianism and many Western schools of thought. He discovered "creative altruism" as a researchable and yet unpredictable path of reintegration. He also found that creative altruism is usually preceded by a period of self-isolation and usually forced introspection. Together with the varied list of Lao-tzu, Buddha,

Confucius, Moses and Christ and many others, Sorokin includes Mohammed as an altruistic founder of religion. These figures followed the creative path, at least initially, rather than the more predictable path of self-righteous victim-hood and aggression.[88] It is such persons and groups that John Paul II hoped to engage in 2000, and that Pope Benedict has in mind when he encourages "creative minorities" to live radiantly faithful lives together in whatever setting they find themselves, to bloom where they are planted.

The highly respected Jewish scholar Bernard Lewis compares institutional Islam today with institutional Christianity in the past. He writes, "If the rulers of the Islamic Republic but knew it, what they are doing is Christianizing Islam in an institutional sense, though not of course in a religious sense. They have already endowed Iran with the functional equivalents of a pontificate, a college of cardinals, a bench of bishops, and, especially, an inquisition, all previously alien to Islam. They may in time provoke a Reformation."[89] Rather than the Reformation, the two recent Vatican Councils better serve as a pos-sible inspiration and in some limited sense a model for Islamic re-evaluation, internal renewal and then more promising external engagement at all levels.

Lewis' careful qualification "not of course in a religious sense," points the reader to other differences deeper than the similarities he lists. Lewis asserts similarities between Islam and Christianity as offshoots of Jewish monotheism and benefactors of Greek thought,[90] but the greater comparisons are between Judaism and Islam. Christianity differs from both in that it is not centered on a book per se, but ultimately on the incarnation of God in history. The ecclesial structure of the Church does not entail a class of ulema-like interpreters and executors of divine law positioned *between* submissive man and the diety. In the Catholic self-understanding, the Church is a communion. The call to holiness is universal with only a distinction in roles.[91] Those who are called as *presbyters* are missionary as are the leaders of Islam, but they receive their mandate of service from Christ—the living God—who *sends* them out into the world, and the laity has a special call of their own for work in the world. In St. Augustine's term, given new currency by John Paul II, the apostles and their successor bishops are the "servants of the servants of God." In a Letter to the Ephesians St. Ignatius of Antioch finds in the Church a sacramental unity: "for you are as united with him (the bishop) as the Church is to Jesus Christ, and Jesus Christ to the Father, so that all things are in *harmony through unity*" (italics added).[92] The teaching role of the Church's magisterium (Chapter 4), visible in both Vatican councils, is both traditional and farsighted. Given precision partly by the Reformation, a clear under-standing of the magisterium protects against the politics of parliamentary approaches toward divine revelation as might attach to the new engagement with the religion of Islam.

Lewis' reference to the Inquisition recalls a dark blot of mingled church-state history in the West, but not so dark as the nearly post-Christian age of conflicting secular ideologies and two world wars. Not two or three thousand victims falsely executed over two or three centuries as under the Spanish Inquisition but, multiplied by modern technology, hundreds of millions killed within decades (and four or five thousand aborted each *day* in the United States alone). Secular political abuses of mass democracies in the twentieth century are sometimes traced back to bad theology. And radical theological individualism is in a sense a mutation from the Reformation doctrine of *sola Scriptura*[93] and easily lends itself to mass political manipulation and then to mass militarization further instructed by mass communication.

At the doctrinal level, Islam's response to modernity can be one of multi-cultural posturing. The congruence of Muslim theology and Western indifference will find little opposition in Western centers of learning. Theologically, if an indifferent West accommodates Shari'a into the elastic tent of multiculturalism, then early fourth century history may repeat itself. The fractious and distracted Christian world awoke to find itself under the spell of Arius who also sought to take Christ down by only a single peg. In the famous words of St. Jerome "The whole world groaned and marveled at finding itself Arian." The simple outcome of the past fourteen centuries will be to transplant a Nestorian offshoot of Arianism into the twenty-first century. Nestorianism makes Mary the mother of only Jesus, and not of Christ. Islam likewise celebrates Christ as holy, but only as one prophet among many. Modern day secularism accepts Christ as a subjective fixation of the unenlightened. The twenty-first century would be recorded as the period when a remarkably resilient Islam expanded for a third time into what is fast becoming a value-neutral and ripe European peninsula.

Like his secularists counterparts in the West, the Muslim thinker Ayoub dismisses a key point made by John Paul II. Ayoub labels as merely personal conviction the pope's clarity on the difference between Islam and the faith of Judaism and Christianity. Ayoub writes, "His Holiness repudiated the principle of religious pluralism, which is crucial to any religious dialogue."[94] At one level all surely agree with Ayoub, but what is meant precisely by pluralism? In the civic realm pluralism is to be much preferred over secularism, but in the self-understanding of many Muslim commentators pluralism easily becomes another term for the universal religion of Islam. Jan Assman, an Egyptologist, offers a focused religious message what is termed the "Mosaic distinction: . . . . a distinction between *true and false* in the realm of religion. Hitherto, religion had been based upon the distinction between pure and impure, or between sacred and profane, and had no place at all for the idea of 'false gods'. . . . whom one should not worship."[95] The polytheism of interchangeable gods was replaced by the concept of idolatry as the most serious of all sins. At this level of monotheism, Islam and Christianity and Judaism find themselves standing close together within a shared silence. Each rejects the polytheism of the past as well, as the modern day idolatry that each conscience is autonomously its own god. In all cases we imagine false realities and then assert the self as a neutral platform for making a selection. Christianity shares with Islam a devotion to the one God. Going beyond Assman, the foundational difference between the two on the nature of this one God is whether He is unknowable, or whether He is self-disclosing and self-donating, that is, Trinitarian.

The Western premise of separated religious and political realms and then of political concord at the *international* level is incomprehensible to Islamic monotheism and the Islamic monologue. At the theological level, Benedict writes: "Equality, which is a presupposition of interreligious dialogue, refers to the *equal personal dignity of the parties* in dialogue, not to doctrinal content, nor even less to the position of Jesus Christ—who is God himself made man—in relation to the founders of the other religions."[96] Political institutions shift with the theological grounding. Modernity in its septic form reduces all faith to a subjective opinion to be removed from the public square,[97] while Islam expands its system of belief to where nothing remains but a single sphere that is both theological and public. The individual is subordinate to the ummah and the Islamic State, as in the pre-Christian West when the human person was defined by and subordinate to the *polis*.

The Crisis of the West is that it no longer clearly grounds the rights of the transcendent human person in the universal natural law. As a consequence, the West proposes a new *polis* of multicultural indifference as a path into a future of convergent and symbiotic politics. The possible fit between a spirituality caged from the public forum and the expansiveness of an absorbent Islam as a way of life is either ignored or denied. Syncretic modernity elides and excels in nuance. Islam proposes condominium monotheism, a sort of *theological contract*, in the same way that the rationalist and post-modern West peddles the myth of a *social contract* centered on a false dilemma between either cyclopean individualism or cyclopean collectivism.

In any case, where in all of this is the core truth of the human person? What is the fate of the one-at-a-time *transcendent human person* in the "larger" history of political accommodation? In some of the particulars of today, Islam would accept all monotheisms as equivalence and tolerated lesser versions of itself, perhaps as members of multi-religious boards governing this or that network of cultural centers, each attached to a mosque. Assimilation at the cultural level sidesteps both theology and politics. In the religious skepticism of his own day, the monk Jean-Pierre de Caussade (1675–1751), proponent of the "sacrament of the present moment," still wondered at Islam: "Why (he asked) does God allow Turks and heretics to flourish?" And he answers himself, "They proclaim his infinite perfection."[98] This was partly a judgment against the growing disbelief he saw even then in his Western culture. But unlike the "Turks and heretics," believing Christians retain a nuptial—mutually enlarging—relationship between the gift of faith in "his infinite perfection" and the gift of reason ever ready to challenge our imperfection. The rationalist crises of the West and of Islam are mirror opposites, and point up the dual challenge facing the Church as it engages the modern world in this millennium.

The challenge involves two different concepts central to our analysis thus far—submission and reciprocity—and takes the following shape. First, the Church is challenged to resists any Islamic-like *submission* to an increasingly aggressive Western state that is operating under the slogan of separation of Church and State co-opted by and validated a society of political correctness. In Canada special commissions and court rulings are poised to punish as religious hate crimes the teaching of the universal natural law and its included exercise of free speech. And second, in the Muslim world and the possibly future Europe the Church must find at least a formula for coexistence between itself and the believing world of Islam. In both cases the formula may be some form of "reciprocity" that adequately recognizes the right of the Church simply to be what it is in a unitary Mosque-state setting. The past model from Western experience would be the many concordats signed with the secular nation-states including pre-Second World War Germany and Italy. Four consistent Church requirements in the West have been the freedom to celebrate the sacraments, to hold property, to foster monastic orders (the primacy of contemplation over action), and Catholic education.[99]

In addition to co-existence and reciprocity, the other major contact point between the Church and Islam deals with natural law. At the interreligious level the opening topic might be a parallel reading of fitrah and verses from the *Qur'an* that tilt toward universal natural law (e.g., Q 16:36, 30:30), together with the Second Vatican Council's *Declaration on Religious Freedom.* In this set of texts might be found a shared appreciation of natural law as it attaches to human persons, and the fact that the right to religious freedom is founded not in political bartering, nor in revelation alone (the *Qur'an*), nor "in the subjective disposition of the person, but *in his very nature*" (italics added).[100] In the *Qur'an* we find that Mohammed denounced and prohibited the burial alive of female offspring (Q 16:58, 59; 81:8). Of such actions "The Prophet burst into tears of pity."[101] This response came from the unwritten book of the heart, from "his very nature" before his followers assembled a *Qur'an.*

In a different setting and on a larger scale, the very numbers of early Christians were swelled by outcasts saved by the charitable relief activities of the Church, and "There is some reason likewise to believe, that great numbers of infants, who, according to the inhuman practice of the times, had been exposed by their parents, were frequently rescued from death, baptized, educated, and maintained by the piety of Christians, and at the expense of the public treasury."[102] Again, this response came from the book of the heart where the natural law is written from the beginning. Of the righteous Gentiles, Paul said that lacking the written book they already "show the work of the Law written in their hearts" (Rom 2:14–15). Christians should do at least the same.

In words that apply to Unitarianism in all of its historic forms, C.S. Lewis writes of a non-Christian or Deist god: "We could talk religiously about the Absolute: but there was no danger of Its doing anything about us. It was 'there'; safely and immovably 'there.' It would never come 'here,' never (to be blunt) make a nuisance of Itself."[103] In Christ his eternal Son made Man, the living and Absolute Father makes a loving nuisance of himself. Following the Church Fathers, "the New Testament is to be found latent in the Old, and the Old is made manifest in the New." In this expectation, and looking vaguely to this future, Abraham "believed against (all) hope" (Rom 4:18).[104]

Baited by religious fanatics acting in the name of religion, the secularist asks: "If religious fanaticism is one of the sources on which terrorism draws— and it is—*can it be correct to call religion a healing and saving force? Is it not rather an archaic and dangerous force* that constructs false universalisms, thereby leading to intolerance and terror? Must not religion be placed under the guardianship of reason and be strictly circumscribed?"[105] Guardianship by whom? Executors for Allah under Shari'a . . . elitist judicial activists and special interests in the West . . . or (as speculated above) a global patchwork? In a lecture delivered the year before he made this remark, the then Cardinal Ratzinger first identified the "tyranny of relativism" as the deepest threat to man. The tyranny of relativism is the deception that man is self-authorized and enslaved to do whatever he *can* rather than what he *ought*. Of Islamic radicalism—not Islam or religion as such—this spokesman for most of Christianity concluded that "In the end, terrorism is also based on this modality of man's self-authorization, and not on the teachings of the *Koran*."[106]

FAITH, REASON AND SCIENCE

Self-authorization disconnected from any larger and reasoned reality can occur in any culture. In recent history, the West has been a testing ground for any number of "isms" in place of non-ideological openness or even curiosity. Unrestrained nationalism is the most obvious political example of reducing complexity to manageable proportions. The most extreme case of total control other than suicide terrorism is pornography and human trafficking. But pornography is only a subset of a much more prevalent and socially acceptable personal willingness to be used—as one market segment or another. The nature of Consumerism is often the opposite of what it appears to be. The reduction of man as a means rather than an end, combined with the digital revolution of instantaneous access to electronic impressions, undermines consciousness. Digital addiction numbs the will and erases any worldview beyond one's opposable thumb. Overindulgence in digital and virtual reality is found to produce corresponding physical changes to the brain itself. A possible hypothesis that the brain alteration and addiction are *determined* by genetic influence rather than culture and behavior would be clearly misguided. In his *Democracy in America*, nearly two centuries ago, Alexis de Tocqueville warned that by an exaggerated principle of equality "a kind of virtuous materialism may ultimately be established in the world, which would not corrupt, but enervate, the soul and noiselessly unbend its springs of action."

The Book of Genesis demythologizes nature and dispatches the pagan idols of the Semitic world. Christianity then witnesses that the "I AM" (Ex 3:14) disclosed to Moses at Mount Sinai is present personally in the world of human experience. With faith rescued from the pagan imagination, the door is also opened wide to scientific investigation of the natural world. And yet, modern day secularism asserts a contradiction between faith and reason, even while Islamic thinkers struggle to reconsider the possible compatibility.[107] Where pagan myths once addressed stable constellations with narratives, the language of mathematics presumes to unilaterally explain the cosmos and even the "universe" as clustered aggregates of galactic dust. With its physical secrets unraveled the meaning of the universe becomes opaque once more in a modern dark age.

Looking instead to the divine even at the expense of nature, early Islam eventually worked to understand allegorically in its many descriptions of a God who stands above his creation. Al-Ghazali (1058–1111), the greatest theologian of Islam, wrote against any such opening toward natural philosophy in a work entitled the *Destruction of Philosophy*. And then in the back-and-forth sequence came the *Destruction of the Destruction* by Ibn Rushd (also known as Averroes), who was a direct influence on the Christian thought of the thirteenth century St. Thomas Aquinas at the University of Paris. Ibn Rushd's work was followed by the *Destruction of the Destruction of the Destruction* by Hodia Zada (d. 1487), who at the command of Mohammed II again wrote against philosophical inquiry, following the successful siege of Constantinople in 1453.[108] With this historic victory over Christianity, Islam had no need for philosophy. Muslim ideology was fully vindicated by the direct action of Allah in history, as had been centuries earlier in the sweeping military successes of the seventh and eighth century.

Oscillation between faith and reason in either the West of the world of Islam contrasts with the coherence of faith with reason developed by Aquinas. He proposed an elevation of each inquiry in the presence of the other, rather than a confused middle case capable of blurring both faith and reason. Despite their differing views, both Al-Ghazali and Aquinas are traced to the earlier Philopenus who distinguished between God's eternal will and the (non)eternity of creation, the object of his will.[109] Aquinas understood that God created without at the same time changing and violating His own unity and oneness. Part of traditional Islam (especially Sufi) leaves no space for the separate autonomy of natural science or the physical laws of nature. Rather, all-that-is is a result of "occasionalism" or direct divine action from moment to moment.

In the West the successful opening of theology toward reason and science (and vice versa) came partly as spin-off from the concept of *analogy*. In theology the concept of analogy means that while God is ever above our reaching minds, He is still knowable in some real sense. By natural theology we can know *that* God is, but not *what* He is. The writer Dumas reflects that: "Not even genius avails to explain what God is; but the kindness of men is a proof that He is." He is recognizable as reasonable and good, but always immeasurably more so than are we. Even from the early fourth century we have this from a bishop Gregory: "'By a certain ana-logy, one arrives at a knowledge of being.' Knowledge . . . therefore, holds the middle ground between knowing and ignorance. It is useful only to those who do not misuse it. To misuse it would be to misuse the divine mystery itself. Human knowledge is therefore true only to the degree that it *renounces by a perpetual effort its own nature, which is to 'seize' its prey*" (italics added).[110] At this early date it is already knowledge, not revelation, that holds the middle ground.

Albert Einstein neatly compressed the above points with this, "The eternally incomprehensible about the world, is its comprehensibility."[111] In his words he had not "fallen into the hands of the priests," but he did sense the significance of the underlying assumption of science, that there is a discoverable order at least at the physical level. He and others detect in the "universe" an order that pre-exists our own mental constructs, and without which even our rational efforts to understand this universe would have no meaning. This meaning, he said, "we are decidedly not entitled to expect *a priori*."[112] That this order is predictable, Einstein said, is a "miracle"[113] (his quotes). In a note written a year before his death, Einstein reportedly dismissed religions as "childish superstitions," but then a few days before his death he confided again to his fellow scientist Francesco Seferi, "He who does not admit the unfathomable mystery cannot even be a scientist."[114]

Christian thinkers hold that the universe exists totally by the freedom of divine action and, at the same time, sustains itself by laws discernible by human reason.[115] Experimental science receives a big boost when Newton's law of inertia replaces the Aristotelian and Islamic notion that it is only through constant intervention that anything in motion remains in motion.[116] These two aspects—the *why* and *how* of the physical universe—touch each other but are not mutually exclusive. The simultaneity of theological, philosophical and scientific inquiry need not be reduced to dichotomy as under Islamic belief or Western scientific atheism. To Islam science is threatening as field of independent inquiry into the causality and objective predictabilities of nature. Pure science is dismissed because the implied regularity and order of the universe—its autonomy—infringes on the absolute autonomy and willfulness of a God who remains forever unknowable. Even two of the most influential early Muslim thinkers believed either that the universe emanated from God—a form of pantheism accepted by Avicenna and pre-Christian Greeks—or that God acted directly from instant to instant (al-Ghazali).[117] All the universe and each instance of the regularities of nature are seen as separately permitted events.

Apologists for the existence and importance of early Muslim science during the Golden Age of Islam (eighth to especially the sixteenth century) point to figures in many fields. Ibn al-Haytham (Athazen, 965–1039) was an early pioneer in optics and the experimental scientific method.[118] He possibly influenced Roger Bacon and Johann Kepler in the West. Abu Rayhan al-Biruni (973–1048) introduced an experimental approach to mineralogy, mechanics and astronomy.[119] But even some Muslim scientists today adhere to a moment-to-moment universe, and are still quoted as saying, "that when you bring hydrogen and oxygen together *then by the will of Allah* water was created."[120] A fanciful parallel in lyrical Western thought comes from C.S. Lewis who even as he endorsed scientific abstraction also celebrated other ways of seeing reality. Lewis wondered, "Is oxygen-and-hydrogen the divine idea of water? . . . There is no water in oxygen and no water in hydrogen; it comes bubbling fresh from the imagination of the living God."[121] In a mystical tone, the nineteenth century Cardinal Newman saw angels active in the physical world: "Every breath of air and ray of light and heat, every beautiful prospect, is, as it were, the skirts of their garments, the waving of the robes of those whose faces see God."[122]

In 1991 a Pakistani physicist estimated that Muslims account for only one percent of the world's scientists but almost a fifth of the total population.

He found that Israel has twice as many scientists as all the Muslim countries combined.[123] A Muslim astrophysicist in Paris faults the Muslim fundamentalists for rejecting science simply because it is Western. Others simply hope to "Islamicize" science—much as the Chinese scholars in the early nineteenth century dealt with the West through structured essays based on ancient Confucian scriptures (the "six-legged essay"). A Muslim chemist in Canada summarizes a concern that applies equally to Muslims and the West: "Modern science doesn't claim to address the purpose of life; that is outside the domain. In the Islamic world, purpose is integral, part of that life."[124]

Cross-cultural tensions posed by science are best illustrated by advances in astrophysics. Using the decimal number system (delivered to the West from India by the Muslims) Western science now collapses all the manifestations of nature's laws into a unique moment or "singularity." The singularity is located at the front edge of a "space-time asymmetry" which is the explosive appearance of the physical universe as we know it—the strongly evidenced Big Bang.[125] The possibility that there is *congruence* (not con-fusion) between a scientifically understandable moment and a possibly "creative" and persisting moment at the "hands" of an absolutely simple, transcendent and creating God raises the enthusiasm of many Western thinkers while it offends many others.[126]

Islamic ideology rejects the legitimate autonomy of science because it undermines the supreme autonomy of Allah. Fourteenth century Christendom produced a parallel school of philosophy. William of Occam's "Nominalism" held that universal concepts are linguistic fictions (or mere names: hence nominalism) attached to absolutely individual things. According to nominalism God is reachable by faith alone and not at all by the fiction of human "reason." It is on the priority of the earlier *realism* over nominalism that the earlier theologian Thomas Aquinas better understood the tie between existence as an event and of God as *relational.* Realism acknowledges the reality of relationships and the contingency of the physical universe with its cause and effect sequences. God is the "cause of causes." Philosophical realism is indifferent to whether the physical universe is eternal as with Aristotle, or not, as with modern physics.[127]

For Christians the creation of the universe in time is partly a matter of faith—and is not disproved by science. The physical universe is contingent and not a closed system; it has a "beginning" in time and at all stages can be distinguished from the "nothing" which it is not.[128] Where the ancients rested the universe on the back of a turtle in space, pre-Copernicans modeled the universe as a series of concentric spheres, each explained by the next larger, and all supported by the farthest sphere—the "empyrean"—consisting of fire and light. Modern day pre-Copernicans would seem to include those who dismiss metaphysical questions by marrying authentic science with an inde-terminate series of Hindu reincarnations. They propose an endless cycle of Big Bangs all trailing off into each other.

The Hebrew people received the revelation that God is above the cosmos and any assembly of human idols however elaborate. Under the Elohist tra-dition of the northern kingdom He is totally "other" *and* yet following the Jawhist tradition of the southern kingdom He is also very near to man. The divine is both God and Lord, and man is both spiritual and physical. In Chris-tianity the self-revelation of the divine is uniquely particularized in the event of Christ—such that the cosmos is no longer divine, and scientific investiga-tion of physical causes and effects no longer risks sacrilege. If things of faith and science are not mutually exclusive, then science does not trump faith. The imperial term the "survival of the fittest"—this exact term is the writer Her-bert Spencer's not the scientist Charles Darwin's—does not explain enough the absolute existence and beauty of a single snowflake, or the Milky Way, or the amoeba or any other elegant part of every food chain.

Why does there exist more than nothing? Does Darwin's "natural selec-tion" of internal variability combined with surrounding circumstances fully explain the self-conscious mind that beholds all *what is* and wonders deeply even as it measures and calculates? Physics and microbiology cannot nullify a stringed symphony by Mozart or any trivial act of kindness done by an obscure martyr in Auschwitz or the Gulag. It does not explain why Stalin who did slave labor in Siberia for four years (1913–1917) built an entire Gulag society for others around this model. It cannot explain the first smile of a newborn toward the sheltering smile of its mother.[129] Nor can science heal the broken heart of a mother who has lost a child, perhaps a unique Son of God suspended between heaven and earth on intersecting planks atop a barren boulder in Palestine. Where Darwin was scandalized into atheism by cannibalism within the insect kingdom, the Christian finds that "There is no creature so little and so vile, that it shows not forth the goodness of God."[130] Above the insects, a quantitative physical universe does not explain why one might willingly die for another: "No one has greater love than this, to lay down one's life for one's friends. You are my friends . . ." (Jn 15:13–14).

Darwin explains that he prefers for brevity the more personified term of "natural selection (as) an intelligent power—in the same way as astronomers speak of the attraction of gravity as ruling the movements of the planets, or as agriculturists speak of man making domestic races by his power of selection." Likewise, he uses the personified word Nature, but means "only the aggregate action and product of many natural laws—and by laws only the ascertained sequence of events."[131] The conviction that any such sequence of events has an origin, not simply an unexplained and chronological start point, is beyond the purview of science. The higher explanation or "cause of causes" is the added point examined by metaphysicians and theologians or by any thinking person. Christian metaphysics holds that the essence of God *is* simplicity; that *being* is his very essence, and that this act of existing is shared through the sovereign action of a divine freedom. The manifestation of man to himself— the whole man—is not by natural selection, but by supernatural election of the "chosen people" of the Old Testament, and beyond.

The Muslim Farooq Hassan explains that under Islamic thought, too, the beauty of God is totally simple and creates from nothing: "God brought the Universe into existence from non-existence," and He maintains the universe by "providing facilities of progress and evolutionary development . . . (an) attribute of God (that is) called *'Rubuiyat'*"[132] As in Western thought, existence is an event more than it is a process. With Islam, Judaism and Christianity continue to uphold the view that in some embracing sense, in addition to creating, the transcendent God also holds all created things in existence.[133] Looking to one's personal future, the Muslim is admonished to always (fatalistically) add "in sha'a' Llah" (if Allah wills). This phrase, resistant to scientific analysis, is actually reminiscent of an obscure and "fatalistic (?)" line in the Epistle of James: "You have no idea what your life will be like tomorrow . . . (you should say) 'If the Lord wills it, we shall live to do this or that'" (James 4:14–15).

The Muslim historian Ibn Khaldoun (1332–1406) centuries ago resolved specialized scientific questions simply by putting them on hold indefinitely. As a "thoroughgoing pragmatist," he wrote "We must refrain from studying these things since such restraint falls under the duty of the Muslim not to do what does not concern him. The problems of physics are of no importance for us in our religious affairs or our livelihoods. Therefore, we must leave them alone."[134] With an attitude shared even by many later secular humanists, early biblical and Christian writers at first said much the same: "Creation is made subject to futility . . . by him who subjected it, but it is not without hope" (Rom 8:20). In the fourth century, still centuries before Ibn Khaldoun, St. Ambrose remarked "To discuss the nature and the position of the earth does not help us in the hope of life to come."[135]

More experienced and confident, the Second Vatican Council (1963–65) is adamant about the autonomy of science and, equally, the validity of faith and the intrinsic compatibility between science and faith: "We cannot but deplore certain habits of mind, sometimes found among Christians, which do not sufficiently attend to the rightful independence of science. The arguments and controversies which they spark lead many minds to conclude that faith and science are mutually opposed."[136] Those of faith do not propose that Genesis is a book on cosmology, and those of science know that they do not *create ex nihilo* what they observe. The complete universe of existence and truth is rich and large enough for scientists who want to know the *ultimate answers* to questions—what and how (?), and for philosophers, theologians and all men and women who want to live the answers to *ultimate questions*, such as birth, death, evil and suffering . . . and the why of it all. Does the reach of the Hubble telescope silence man's ultimate questions about what he sees outside and within himself, or in the larger silence that our instruments reveal is there a higher God who still speaks to us of Himself? Not reducible to mathematics alone, the silence of outer space remains a metaphor for the silence mystery of inner space within the human soul which has its own dimensions.

The early Greek philosophers Democritus and Leucippus precede by over two millennia scientists of our day who would reduce the universe and each of us to a cloud of elemental particles. For the Greeks the explanatory building block was assumed to be internally simple, whether the atom or, as later for Darwin, the living cell.[137] A century and a half after Darwin, the mathematics of infinitely smaller "strings" now might account for not only the smallest parts of the physical universe that are familiar to us, for example, rocks, stars, books, ourselves, but also the broader cosmos. The curvature of the almost infinitely small strings (the same relative size as a gopher compared to our entire galaxy) and of immense cosmic space, both, might be cut from the same cloth. String theory may explain that the physical universe as we know it is a byproduct not of symmetry, but of non-symmetry. For each ten billion particles of matter and antimatter that annihilated each other at the singularity in front of the cosmos, a solitary extra particle of matter at a time—termed the Higgs boson—might have been instantaneously formed. From the miniscule residue of this imbalance every atom and galaxy in the universe was formed.[138] A delightful coincidence links the advanced science of bosons with a poetic intuition of the third century St. Athanasius: "He who is the good Word of the good Father produced order in all creation, joining opposites together, and forming from them one harmonious sound."[139] The physics of the Higgs boson could explain how miniscule particles have physical mass, while the theologian seeks understanding why the universe as a whole is "a whole" and why it has existence at all. Modern science shows us the very same primordial questions, only through a new picture frame that is both smaller and larger than the view given to earlier classical thinkers.

Physicists and theologians begin as back-to-back neighbors and possibly friends; they ask different but congruent questions. Stephen Hawking, the eminent mathematician and physicist, opens his very readable *Brief History of Time* with "Where did the universe come from . . . did the universe have a beginning, and if so, what happened before then?"[140] St. Augustine in the fourth century looked at the same stars with not so different words: "My mind is on fire to understand this most intricate riddle . . . In what space, then, do we measure passing time?.. . . there can be no time without creation."[141] Seeking continuity with our engaging universe always as *a given*, the Darwinian proposes a seamless garment of totally random and gradual natural selection.[142] Nobel laureate Steven Weinberg remarks: "The reductionist worldview is chilling and impersonal. It has to be accepted as it is, not because we like it, but because that is the way the world works."[143]

Theologian Luigi Giussani offers a broader and deeper view. Our vocation is "to the mystery of Being, to the Measure that made us, that far surpasses us in every direction and that we cannot measure—it is to This that an educator's love must entrust the ever-widening space of unpredictable pathways which are opened up by the new man in his dialogue with the universe."[144] Standing back from cosmology, even the string theorist Brian Greene suspects that scientific explanation may have its asymptotic outer limits: "Maybe we will have to accept that certain features of the universe are the way they are because of happenstance, accident, *or divine choice*" (italics added).[145] In work similar to Greene's, Robert Oerter remarks, "There is a possibility, then that the origin of the universe could be explained as a transition from a state with no spacetime to a state with a spacetime like ours: a real creation *ex nihilo*."[146] Oerter concludes his work with this quotation of a colleague: "(I think) that as we learn many additional facts, we will also come to comprehend more clearly how much we don't know—and, let us hope, learn an appropriate *humility*."[147] Science becomes a prayer. The Christian dispensation is that Christ is the infinite humility of an infinite and personal God.

Because of his determinism, Einstein was slow to concede the probablism of quantum mechanics. To his assertion that "God does not play dice with the universe," we might respond the God may "play universe" with whatever dice he chooses. The Christian humbly believes that "By faith we understand that the universe was ordered by the word of God, so that what is visible came into being through the invisible" (Heb 11:3). Isaac Asimov, the science fiction writer, understood best the wisdom of fractals as microcosms of the real: "I believe that scientific knowledge has fractal properties; that no matter how much we learn, whatever is left, however small it may seem, is just as infinitely complex as the whole was to start with. That, I think, is the secret of the Universe."[148] That the human genome is found to be so nearly identical to that of some primates, but not quite, is cause for greater wonder, not less.

Whether galactic cosmos or infinitely small strings, we are reminded even through science of the biblical truth that "His greatness cannot be measured" (Ps 145:3). The difference between a universe formed from chaos and one drawn from nothing—*ex nihilo*—is the difference between mathematics written on paper and the total contingency of both. The original and final meaning of the universe is exhausted in God, but God remains inexhaustibly more and Other. As in the ancient Hebrew scriptures, God is both Yahweh and Elohim, and for the Christian the incarnate Lord is "sustained by his own creation which he himself sustains in being"[149] This intimate circularity cannot be comprehended by science alone, and is at best heavily veiled in the poetics of the *Qur'an*.

The Christian turns toward the cosmos as it is known within the words of Christ, "My kingdom does not belong to this world" (Jn 18:36). Pope Benedict XVI simply finds that "Christianity's claim to be true cannot correspond to the standard of certainty posed by modern science, because the form of verification here is of a quite different kind from the realm of testing by experiment—pledging one's life for this—is of a quite different kind. The saints, who have undergone the experiment, can stand as guarantors of its truth, but the possibility of disregarding this strong evidence remains."[150] As religions of both reason and revelation, Judaism and Christianity know a God who first simply is.[151] And Islam, for its part as historic restorer in Arabia of monotheistic belief, draws heavily from the revelation testified in Jewish and Christian scriptures. More than linear, the Christian narrative is also analogous to a fractal universe where the one and the many point to each other: "For if, by the transgression of the one, death came to reign through that one, how much more will those who receive the abundance of grace and of the gift of justification come to reign in life through the one Jesus Christ" (Rom 5:17).

Yet, as Pascal's "thinking reed" man is to remain humble, formed as he is "out of the clay of the ground" (Gen 2:7), biblically much lower even than the proto-species asserted in 1859 by Charles Darwin. Science itself adds a new twist, or "bottleneck" to the scientific doctrine of proto-species. This is physical evolution as it is narrowly channeled by outside pruning, according to one possible line of reasoning. Genome research (1995) suggests that "Homo sapiens "came into existence and replaced a more primitive ancestor, often called 'archaic Homo sapiens', which appeared perhaps half a million years ago as the descendent of Homo erectus."[152] This picture reinforces the genetic DNA-based finding nearly ten years earlier that "strengthened the claim that all humans alive today are descended from a single African woman" who lived perhaps 140,000 years ago[153] (DNA: deoxyribonucleic acid: the complex key to heredity and physical life). If this DNA finding is accurate, then at the human scale Darwin's natural selection for the natural side of man is a fold within a larger picture.

This larger picture, not inconsistent with science, supports a focused genetic family of human beings each capable of being uniquely touched from without by a new humanity as "persons." This new humanity of the person is different in kind as well a degree, as all other lineages drop from sight. Genetic evidence, not conclusive, suggests that "Neanderthals, anatomically modern humans and an older species called Homo erectus, apparently co-existed until about thirty thousand years ago in parts of Europe and Asia."[154] The short-lived theory of polygenesis, multiple human origins, favored even by some avant-garde theologians in the mid twentieth century, is specifically rejected by a consensus of qualified scientists using a breadth of recent evidence. The DNA and ethnic research points to racial categories as "a social, cultural and political concept based largely on superficial appearances," and not fundamental genetic variations.[155] Natural pruning or in some sense purposive weaving toward an abruptly narrow platform or bottleneck of anatomical hominids would not be incompatible with a general scientific hypothesis of evolution that includes external and so-called "mechanisms" of natural selection.[156] Is it possible that natural selection occurs in a larger context, and that "Biological life is one example of a universal tendency of nature, all of which—animate and inanimate—is a great process of unfolding wholeness (?)."[157] Anthropologists hold that "at every other phase of evolutionary history there have always been multiple species at any one time," both for humans and for other species.[158] Some scientists push the emergence of modern man back many more tens of thousands of years than previously thought. But recent site excavations in South Africa reveal new evidence of technological and possible symbolic behavior. These "sites . . . belie the claim that modern cognition evolved late in our lineage and suggest instead that our species had this faculty at its inception."[159]

Pruning of adjacent species does not conflict with either adaptation or the added and gifted and formative entry from above of each human soul. Each body and soul person is created "for its own sake,"[160] in the image and likeness of God (Gen 1:27–29) and in this sense a complete species unto himself. Physical science is complemented by the proposition that each person "carries within him the seed of eternity, which cannot be reduced to matter alone . . . ."[161] The precise moment of emergence as an integral human person is termed the "ontological leap (into) the uniquely human factors of consciousness, intentionality, freedom, and creativity."[162] In the Psalms we read "What is man that you should be mindful of him . . . You have made him little less than the angels, and crowned him with glory and honor" (Ps 8:5–6). More than simply another step in mechanistic or even evolutionary complexity, the ontological leap evidences a spiritual simplicity that cannot be reduced to mere complexity.

The "person" is always a whole capable of freedom toward the truth of one another. Biblically, the sequential covenant—or the inborn and revealed promise of God—expands from the inner truth of the human person alone, to

marriage as a fecund oneness of the flesh, to the family, to the tribe, and finally to a chosen people, and in Christ to the ultimate calling of all to share in
the inner life of God. Freedom is the ability to be and act together as pilgrims
and strangers in a strange land, and to choose our humanity and self-donation
over our instincts and circumstances, however complex.[163] The "human individual cannot be subordinated as a pure means or a pure instrument, either
to the species or to society."[164] The historian Jacob Burckhardt, inventor of
the idea of "the Renaissance," still rejects modern self-flattery, "If, even in
bygone times, men gave their lives for each other, we have not progressed
since." The leap—the integral person in the world but not of the world—is a
permanent incongruity freely affirmed into existence by a Giver who imprints
himself into his work ("the image and likeness of God").

The theologian, thinking thoughts even about how we "think," would
hazard the claim that the moment of the unique "person"—and of his eternal
destiny—occurs anew in each of its billions of *non-replicable* instances. The
unique creation "of each human soul . . . addresses the ontological discontinuity between matter and spirit (and) establishes the basis for a divine intimacy
which embraces every single human person . . . ."[165] While cosmologists and
fundamentalists argue the meaning of "six days" the author of Genesis sees
through the eyes, and not merely with the eyes. He knows that compared to
one human soul all the millions of galaxies in the cosmos are a most extraordinary prelude, clippings scattered across the editing room floor. Edith Stein,
one of six million souls incinerated into eternity at Auschwitz, shows us the
reality of each human person: "The most exact statement of all that Frederick
the Great did from the day of his birth up to his last breath does not give us a
glimmer of the spirit which, transforming, reached into the history of Europe.
Yet the *understanding glance* may seize upon this in a chance remark in a
short letter."[166] Stein discovers that recognition of the given-ness of the other
and of the self as an "I" is an act "completely attributable to spirit . . . without
parallel in physical nature."[167] Rather than a random data point in the speech-
less depths of space, each person is more of a divine holiday that the Lord is
willing to celebrate for all eternity if man is also willing.

In Judea a man died and then was raised divinely from the dead. Faith in
the One in this historical event is not unreasonable. This faith is not simply
another non-historical mystery religion from the East. Recalling St. Paul's
preaching to the Gentiles and Greeks, and the difference between Christianity
and the merely symbolic world religions of the day, Benedict writes: "If one
investigates this concept more closely, however, one encounters something
unexpected that—as far as I can tell—is glossed over in almost all the pertinent
studies. The Church Fathers found the seeds of the Word, *not in the religions
of the world, but rather in philosophy,* that is, in the process of critical reason

directed against the (pagan) religions, in the history of progressive reason, and not in the history of religion."[168]

Einstein and Benedict XVI sit at the same table, even if not sharing the same plate. "The question is whether reality originated on the basis of chance and necessity . . . and, thus, from what is irrational; that is, whether reason, being a chance by-product of irrationality, is ultimately just as meaningless or whether . . . at the beginning of all things stands the creative power of reason."[169] Half century ago, Einstein made this remark: "What is the meaning of human life, or for that matter, of the life of any creature? To know an answer to this question means to be religious. You ask: Does it make any sense, then, to pose this question? I answer: The man who regards his own life and that of his fellow creatures as meaningless is not merely unhappy but hardly fit to live."[170]

To loosen our spatial way of thinking—the presupposition that faith and reason cannot simultaneously occupy our attention—the primitive zero-sum imagery must be replaced with a better image, the spiraling double helix of the genetic DNA molecule. The imaginary dichotomy between faith and reason might be better imagined as analogous to the double helix marriage of two mutually spiraling coils in each DNA molecule. Like faith and reason (and even like the paired social principles of solidarity and subsidiarity, Chapter 4), the paired coils wind together in seemingly *opposite* directions. They are spaced by a series of molecular ladder-like rungs simultaneously holding them together *and yet* also holding them distinctly apart. Neither spiral is diminished by the other, but rather each exists and is transformed with the other into a larger entity. Cosmologists of a materialist bent confidently announce an expanding universe of spiraling disorganization (entropy), even as they overlook the growing organization at the other "smaller" end of the spectrum. Jumping to theological inquiry, a more intriguing image today than St. Patrick's shamrock for the Trinity is the DNA image, but this analogy also falls short. Beyond analogy and beyond our imagination, there in the Trinitarian One God in three Persons, and the three Persons in the Oneness of God. Finally, we are invited not to spatially imagine, but to listen. "Eye has not seen, ear has not heard, nor has it entered into the heart of man what things God has prepared for those who love him" (1 Cor 2:9).

Jean Abele, a contributor to a series that includes his *Christianity and Science*, explores the fit between the irreducible mystery of the human person and the incontestable productivity of the scientific method. He makes this comparison: "It is clear that this (scientific) method rests on *a choice*, namely, that of the relations that can recur in identical conditions. It therefore leaves quite to one side the universe of persons, since the latter is in fact formed on what is not repeatable, *for each person brings to the sum total of other per-*

sons his own originality and his own irreplaceable contribution . . . (Further) Religion is in fact essentially a relationship of the person of man and the person of God."[171]

The scientific method discovers explanatory relationships in what can be replicated in nature, while the nature of the divinity—a jealous God—and of spiritual truth and the person of man is to be defined as indefinable non-replication. The lay philosopher Josef Pieper contrasts the ultimate theories of physics with a meaning that is always more than physical in its essence. Without discounting the best kept secrets of nature or the brilliant inquiries of science, he suggests this about the spirit: "More critical is the living realization of that unlimited and all-encompassing openness to everything that is, something that is not so much an attitude or a virtue of the spirit as it is its very essence—in short, its nature."[172]

PARADISE LIES AT THE FEET OF MOTHERS

The nature of maternity, like that of the spirit, is an "openness to everything that is." During the relatively benign 1950s, Bishop Fulton J. Sheen suspected that the religious opening between Islam and the West eventually would be not only Christ, but also his mother Mary. This reference is not to past battles and prayerful appeals to Mary on the eve of the Battle of Lepanto in 1571 or later the second Battle of Vienna in 1683. Sheen refers instead to Mary's maternal receptivity that brought Christ into the world. Through Mary the eternal God exceeds even the divine willfulness so revered in Islam, by making the *Logos* or Word which is himself fully present to man in the world. In Mary's "fiat" ("May it be done to me according to your word;" Lk 1:38) the Christian and especially the Catholic finds the freedom of God mirrored in Mary's unobstructed freedom to fully respond within his infinite freedom. Also affirmed is enduring fidelity, as in the enduring Old Testament covenant unbroken by the infidelities of Israel, and in the fidelity of the Church modeled after her, e.g., Newman's insight into continuity of doctrine (Chapter 4), and even the nature of marriage as a fidelity actually made fecund because of human differences within human equality.

Mohammed saw in a lyrical and domestic way a cosmic truth echoed in human maternity. Twelve centuries before Western materialism required dogmatic response regarding human stature and then Mary's unique role as the mother of Christ, Mohammed displayed exclusive devotion to at least his first wife, Khadijha, and great respect and affection for his own daughter Fatima. He often would say, "Respect your children" and "paradise lies at the feet of mothers."[173] And thinking still of his own mother, rather than the Mother of God, St. Augustine already overflowed: "The tears of a single woman are worth more to me than all the emotions of the Roman people."[174] Mary is a pathway because as the perfect human and because she points us to the One who is infinitely beyond us and, because of her, no longer foreign. In Trinitarian Christianity we discover with Mary that "The meaning of life is found, not by moving outside of the moment, but by 'burning into' the moment" (T. S. Elliot). Through Mary the eternal moment becomes burned into time.

Human presence to this Presence comes even before any fully authentic human creativity in the world. Theologian David S. Schindler develops the case that human *creativity*—as in an ostensibly neutral public square displaying its wares of tolerance, pluralism and civility—is a poor and inadequate substitute for what comes prior, namely a prior *receptivity* to God.[175] This reawakening toward the mystically concrete can free women especially from the limits of post-Christian and imitative self-definition, and from the inherited patterns of domination embedded at least as much in Islamic culture. In Mary we see that the key to the kingdom is not management and control—by either the Islamic ulema, or by Western elites in the mold of Descartes and Bacon. Descartes applied the revolutionary premise that the human mind evaluates reality as an outside observer ("I think, therefore I am," *Discourse on Method*, 1637[176]); Bacon then peeked systematically at the secrets of external nature with a kind of unilateral disrespect in order to extract her services. Mary is not a reincarnated pagan goddess, nor is she the third part of a misconstrued Trinity as thought by some Islamic commentators. Despite devotional excesses, she is not an object of Catholic worship. Within the Church, the Marian doctrines protect and point to the core reality that the orientation of "man" (male and female) is not that of a unilateral outsider, and to teachings on the Incarnation and human free will, and to the meaning of divine passion or love at the heart of all creation[177]

Mary is not believed to be semi-divine as were the offspring of pagan gods and their human consorts. Marian theology teaches that she is simply one of us, but completely unruffled by our inner contradictions. Without alloy she is totally matured and fulfilled by remaining receptive to an infused and guiding grace from one Other than herself. Sharing our fundamentally good human nature, and yet without any flaw original to ourselves (rather than inflicted by God), it is in her lack of self-authorization and her creaturely "fiat" that Mary examples complete self-donation. At the wedding feast in Cana Mary addressed the wine stewards in the same fully collected manner: "Do whatever He tells you" (Jn 2:5). Only Mary could respond "fiat" the instant that she understood the facts of her earlier and unique encounter with the Holy Spirit. It was only for greater understanding that she asked "How can this be, since I have no relations with a man" (Luke 1:34)? She is told "nothing will be impossible with God" (Lk 1:37). In Mary we do not find another nature. We find our own human nature as it was meant to be, but always one of us Mary remains forever less than the God we call Father.

What do we find inserted in the *Qur'an* on the uncreated sacrificial love of God as it is mirrored in the creature Mary? The *Qur'an* disclaims a God of such total self-donation as an illusion: "And because of their saying: We slew the Messiah, Jesus son of Mary, God's messenger—they slew him not nor crucified him, but it appeared so unto them; and lo! Those who disagree concerning it are in doubt thereof; they have no knowledge thereof save pursuit of a conjecture; they slew him not for certain" (Q 4:157). "Those who disagree" refers to a theologically divided Byzantine Empire. In place of a self-donating (Trinitarian) God, Islam inserts a human substitution. It was not Christ who died for us, but another who stepped in and was killed in his place. This invention is guarded against by an undiminished Mary. It is guarded against by St. Cyril of Alexandria 370–444 A.D.), bishop, who exposed the subtle error of Nestorius that eventually found its way into the unsuspecting ear of Mohammed. Still, in the collected verses of the *Qur'an* we also find profoundly respectful verses on Mary and her Immaculate Conception, the Annunciation, the Visitation, and the Nativity (Q 19).

Surely with these lines from the *Qur'an* in mind Sheen offers this opinion: "I believe that the Blessed Virgin chose to be known as 'Our Lady of Fatima' as a pledge and a sign of hope to the Moslem people and as an assurance that they, who show her so much respect, will one day accept her Divine Son, too."[178] The first modern Marian dogma (the Immaculate Conception) was made explicit in 1858 partly as a protection of the human person against the West's ideological illusions of naturalism, materialism, and rationalism. Might the Spirit also have been working with an eye to the future? Might it be that in the global context today of the Marian dogmas, as sealing the full meaning of the natural law, also provide a path for the followers of Islam, whose respect for Mary is poetically intact, toward their own particular future of reform and hope?

A recent mystic, a physician and stigmatist, is Adrienne von Speyr (d. 1968) who for several decades had as her spiritual advisor the theologian Hans Urs von Balthasar. He records one of her visions that took place not in a cave, but in the town of Estavayer at Neunburg Lake. In short, never having read the Apocalypse, on an August evening, Adrienne reports to him an ongoing vision. He reads to her Revelation 11:19 to 12:3. In return, from her vision she dictates chapters twelve to twenty, followed by chapters one through eleven. Von Balthasar rejects the possible notion that such private experiences—and there are others in history—are merely subjective imagination.[179] For our purposes, the symbolism of Mary in the cited scriptures might suggest that the "clash of civilizations" between the West and Islam is at its core not a clash but an historic incompleteness still waiting to be filled.

Mohammed's mystical experiences beginning in 410 A.D. and Islam's later deification of the *Qur'an* are not on the same plane as Mary's experience when she became—not the recipient of a book—but the mother of the incarnate Christ, "the Word made flesh." (Jn 1:14). Mary, a Jewish teenager, was the first to truly believe from the heart which itself is a mystery. She believed first at the Annunciation and later at the catastrophe of the crucifixion and then at the resurrection. Even more than Abraham, our earthly father in faith shared with Judaism and Islam, Mary is the first to have hoped totally beyond all human optimism. Rather than a pious excess as Protestants fear, we find through Mary—"blessed among women"—a singular demonstration of the transparency of God. The birth of Christ—fully God and fully Man, not half one and half the other—through Mary removes every hint of Manichaean dualism. Even to the American naturalist poet William Wordsworth the Annunciation was "our tainted nature's solitary boast."

Catholic devotion reports from her apparition at Lourdes in 1858, that Mary is not the product—as if derivatively—of an immaculate conception.[180] She herself *is* this complete receptivity to the *Logos*: "I *am* the Immaculate Conception," just as all human beings are sometimes defined less perfectly as "the capacity for God." As this receptivity increases, the calculus of not being God also accelerates. Only God said to Moses "I am who AM" (Ex 3:14); and Jesus repeated, "Amen, amen, I say to you, before Abraham came to be, I AM" (Jn 8:53–58). Mary is the supreme power of God's grace acting within nature and yet fully above nature. Through Mary the Word becomes flesh. The unique place of Mary in the memory of God, if we can speak this way, is due to the total depth of her reception which in turn is due to her being conceived without barriers (immaculately). While Christ is eternally with the Father, Jesus also is in a sense the *everlasting memory* of Mary's reception. Of human memory as a possible analogy, Edith Stein (victim of Auschwitz) writes: "How long something is retained in memory depends—not exclusively, but to a large degree—on how deeply it has originally penetrated. And the depth of the original penetration depends in turn on the depth of the original reception"[181]

The testimony of Christian scripture is that Mary knew how to wait. She who was unencumbered, "pondered these things in her heart" (Lk 2:19, 51). From Blaise Pascal we learn that "The whole calamity of man comes from one single thing, that he cannot keep quiet in a room." In our Father's house there are many mansions, and likewise in the house of the world there are many quiet rooms or paths. Sometimes the path is a synthesis as with St. Thomas Aquinas who juggled faith and reason and stressed the hierarchic path up through the world. And sometimes the path is one of profound reform and conversion of heart as with St. Augustine and with John Calvin.[182] During times of personal or cultural disruption, it is through Mary that the Spirit is manifested in our midst. Mary is *Theotokos*, "God-bearer," the Mother of God, as affirmed by the Council of Ephesus in 431 A.D. (and Cyril of Alexandria, above). Mary as "God-bearer" is what was denied by the Nestorians who had such an influence on Mohammed.

In modern times in the Islamic world a princess shielded with her own body another young woman who was about to be stoned for an infraction of the Shari'a Law. The penalty was withheld and not inflicted. The closing remark of this courageous princess is this: "We will create a circle of support (for each other)."[183] This maternal circle of support is Marian, an expression of openness toward God and one another—that is, toward the natural law. At the Annunciation and with her "fiat," Mary created with her own body a circle of support for Christ. This Mary perfectly mirrors the later transparency of Christ who said at Gethsemane, "yet not my will but yours be done" (Lk 22:42). Enfleshed through Mary it was Christ who first challenged the law of stoning that persists even into modern times: "Let the man among you who has no sin be the first to cast a stone at her" (Jn 8:7). With a deepening perception of Mary, who again is revered in the *Qur'an*, the hearts of a growing number of Muslim women might transform the meaning of the "followers" of Islam. More than a submission to God, Mary's receptivity is a *response* to a gift and to a Giver, a *surrender* of trust and mutual respect given and received, unalloyed and unexcelled.[184] In Mary's "fiat" and in her treasuring in her heart, we see that the human mind fully healed is most at home in the heart: "It is all too understandable that the old definition of prayer as the 'rising of the mind to God' should have come to be mistranslated as the 'raising of the mind to God,' and that the old liturgical exclamation, 'Up hearts!' should have become 'Lift up your hearts.' *It barely even occurs to us that the upward movement is natural to hearts*" (italics added).[185]

Marshall McLuhan, who coined the term "global village," reminds us that Mary the Mother of God is in fact the Mother of Learning. This title refers less to the esoteric advances in one academic field or another than to the cure for rationalism and overspecialization, as are all mothers in any household. To McLuhan Mary is the queen of a "joyful discovery." Of (Marian) joy, we have this from St. Athanasius: "True joy, genuine festival, means the casting out of wickedness. To achieve this one must live a life of perfect goodness and, in the serenity of the fear of God, practice contemplation in one's heart."[186] From the Acts of the Apostles and Paul's first entry into Macedonia, we should be struck by "the fact that Christianity began in Europe through a housewife's response to God's calling" (see Acts 13:5–15).[187]

With more than political insight, Archbishop Sheen mirrored Belloc's 1938 assessment (Chapter 2) on the dormant threat of a militant Islam. Over fifty years ago Sheen also predicted our modern day:

> At the present time, the hatred of the Moslem countries against the West is becoming a hatred against Christianity itself. Although the statesmen have not yet taken it into account, there is still grave danger that the temporal power of Islam may return and, with it, the menace that it may shake off a West that has ceased to be Christian and affirm itself as a great anti-Christian world power.[188]

Thus, Islam rises to fill an even deeper spiritual vacuum than the political gap left by the end of the Cold War. But long before our era, during the crusades, both Muslims and Christians together made pilgrimages to an image of the Virgin at a monastery in Damascus.[189] This common devotion was more than an anomaly. In the 1950s, Sheen refers to enthusiastic modern day receptions by Moslems of the pilgrim statue of Our Lady of Fatima, in Africa and India and especially in Mozambique. In Mozambique onsite conversions were reported.

Sheen suggests that lines in the *Qur'an* referring to the birth of Mary from a sterile mother indicate a careful Muslim reading of the apocryphal gospel of the birth of Mary: "O Lord, I vow and I consecrate to you what is already within me. Accept it from me" (Q 3:35). The apocryphal gospel reads: "And I consecrate her with all of her posterity under thy protection, O Lord, against Satan."[190] The *subha*, a string of thirty-three beads joined in a circle, is used by Muslims to recite the ninety-nine names for God.[191] Most of these names come directly from the *Qur'an* (over a dozen from Q 59:22–24, for example, Most Merciful, Most Compassionate). Is the seemingly missing one hundredth bead an opening for something much more than dialogue?

Is the silent space the unspoken name, unspoken because unspeakable? Is the missing bead analogous to the temple to the "unknown god" that arrested St. Paul at the Areopagus in Athens when he preached Christ to the Greeks (Acts 17:23)? One of the hidden meanings of Genesis might be that man names the finite things of this world (Gen 2:19) precisely to show that God is infinitely beyond such human naming. Called by the Unnamed One, Moses asks at the burning bush for a name and is told "I AM who am" (Ex 3:14). Devout Jews leave this name of God (YHWH) unspoken, substituting the term Lord. Is the missing bead of Islam the *Word* spoken not by us but by the Father: "And the Word was made flesh" (Jn 1:14)? Something so small as a missing bead best summarizes the similarity and eternal difference between Islam and Christianity. The single bead of the Unknowable, the "pearl of great price," has made Himself known to us. Is there another hidden meaning of the Gospel parable of the sheep? The Father transcends the

ninety-nine names or perfections later seen in Him by man, but He has come
to show us that, as the very creating Soul of our seeking souls, He is the still
missing one hundredth lamb who first seeks and finds us (Lk 15:4–7). Rather
than deferring to any number of cultic or modern echoes, that is, rather than
multiplying the names and voices of God up to ninety-nine, St. Augustine
discovers through, with and in the Word a threesome oneness, and "how there
is a trinity in the very simplicity of God."[192]

The nineteenth century John Henry Cardinal Newman responded to the
Utilitarians or moral relativists of his day with the Marian and heartfelt insight that faith turns finally on concrete things, not ideas. Newman writes of
the heart: "The heart is commonly reached, not through reason, but through
the imagination, by means of direct impressions, by the testimony of facts
and events, by history, by description."[193] If the Marian possibility is the
subordination of action to contemplation and concrete receptivity, then
Mary is a solution for brittle aridity of both Islamic and Western rationalism. Hugo Rahner finds in a very early fifth century liturgy of Milan, still
two centuries before Mohammed, a text speaking of Mary as "mother of all
the living, blessed woman with a multitude of children. Every day she bears
children to God by the Holy Ghost."[194] In the last century the (conservative)
Joseph de Maistre also penned this: "It is love which sings, and that is why
we chant our symbols, for faith is only belief through love."[195] Today real
"progress" is to be measured by whether singing can still be heard on the
face of the earth.

In the final decades of the crusades (the 1230s) the Carmelite monks,
who were devoted to Mary as Patroness, left the Holy Land for the relative
security of Europe.[196] The return of Mary to the Holy Land today would
mark the long awaited and frequently announced ending of the crusades. A
deepened understanding of Mary would be a kind of singing, a cure for those
rationalistic "heresies" in both the East and West. Such heresies all deny the
complementary relationship between the persons of the Trinity, between man
and woman as a unified "person," between matter and spirit, and between
faith and reason within our common human journey through this world into
the next. The unitive line of thought is stressed by Pope Benedict when he
quotes little noticed and opposing verses from the popular Gnostic gospels of
the *Egyptians* and *Thomas*. The first (*non*-canonical) line has Christ saying
"I have come to destroy the works of the feminine," and the second: "When
you make the two one . . . and the upper as the lower, and when you make the
masculine and the feminine one only, so that the masculine is not masculine
and the feminine not feminine . . . you will enter the kingdom."[197] The standard interpretation of the almost androgynous second saying is that it simply
rejects the body and instead follows the esoteric belief that only the spirit is

important. By being for the higher truth or "fiat," Mary is the first witness against this Gnostic belief in all of its forms, ancient and modern.

In his major work on devotion to Mary as the mother of the complete Christ, John Paul II writes: "May she do so (intercede) until *all the peoples of the human family,* whether they are honored with the name of Christian or whether they still do not know their Savior, are happily gathered together in peace and harmony into the one people of God, for the glory of the Most Holy and Undivided Trinity" (italics added).[198] The appeal to Mary is a song and a holiday. For believers and for unbelievers there is the fresh Marian path of . . . beauty: "Being overcome by the beauty of Christ is a more real, more profound knowledge than mere rational deduction . . . (to despise) the impact proclaimed by the heart's encounter with beauty, or to reject it as a true form of knowledge, would impoverish us and dry up both faith and theology. We must rediscover this form of knowledge—it is an urgent demand of the present hour."[199]

This "form of knowledge" (beauty) finds expression in architectural forms of the past. Christian and especially Catholic reality proclaims a synthesis of the supernatural and the natural, of faith and reason. Each in its own culture Christianity and Islam share a common appreciation for beauty. In the West, the Baroque world and its architecture reminds us that God speaks through the heart and emotions even more than the mind. And yet they work together. The composition of complex curvatures is analogous with The Calculus and possibly calculated only with this mathematical tool. The whole expands into the illusionism of heavenly ceilings and the harmonies of polyphonic musical scales. All of this speaks of a God who is clarified by, but always transcends the theological precisions of post-Reformation Europe. Before the colonial era, Muslims and Hindus in rural India often alternated their use of the same temple spaces. And, the Taj Mahal (1630–1653) is a timeless contribution from Islam. This message is Shah Jahan's enduring devotion for his favorite and entombed wife. This composition of stone and lattice vibrates within the oneness of Allah. The pure beauty of the mausoleum reappears in the still silence of a reflecting pool reaching from the horizon, much as man best finds himself in silent reflection. In fourteenth century Moorish Spain the Alhambra floats in the larger harmonies of fountain waters and garden courtyards.

Culturally in both East and West the beauty of the divine—this special form of knowledge—overflows our poor efforts to separate, define, and contain. Western Gothic cathedrals reach beyond themselves in a way only made possible by pointed arches tracing back to Islamic designs imported from Sicily by returning crusaders. Sheets of translucent stained glass, like messages from heaven, fill the voids. Beauty is a conversation worth having. Islamic art floats across a blended message of oneness. Christian art is open to multiplicity and variety, but in the oneness of a God who is also self-revealed. This difference in spiritual metabolism is most evident in Averroes' classic work. Hourani writes: "Ibn Rushd (Averroes) is a master of intellectual alchemy, that typically Islamic art of blending ideas from different sources into a harmonious whole; and there is no doubt that in *Fasl* (*The Harmony of Religion and Philosophy*) the whole is something new and original."[200] The Christian, with Marian access to the particularity of the Redemption, is drawn instead to the light that comes from one Source who is ecstatic-boundless love, and (Jn 1:9) who enlightens everyone and came into the world.

THE COMMANDMENT OF LOVE:
A MUSLIM REQUEST

Late 2007 marked a new phase of the official dialogue by the Catholic-Muslim Forum. The forum settled on three initial themes for future dialogue. These are the nature of the human person, the relationship between religion and the body politic, and specifically proposed by Islamic respondents: the meaning of the Two Great Commandments—love of God and of neighbor. An immediate response from 138 Muslim leaders is entitled "A Common Word as Between You and Us" (see www.acommonword.com) the Two Great Commandments in some form find a place in the scriptures of all three monotheistic religions, although in the *Qur'an* the accent is mostly on the wisdom of almsgiving.[201] Based on our inquiry (this book) it appears that a sustained dialogue could expand into more than one level of discourse. The Muslim request reveals a difference in presuppositions as well as possible content. A recurring theme throughout this inquiry is the contribution of necessary distinctions compared to the Muslim taste for more poetic and cultural presuppositions. Behind the most welcome letter is the working premise that the path of encounter is inter-scriptural, while the symmetry between Islam and Christianity is not between the scriptures, but between the divinized *Qur'an* and the person of the incarnate Christ (Chapter 3).

In his homily in Notre Dame Cathedral in Paris (September 2008), Pope Benedict XVI did remark that the Commandments are "the sum total of all of Sacred Scripture" (the Bible). Still, the Two Great Commandments cannot be cast as a cross-scriptural "golden rule" or only a basis for possibly shared actions of goodwill in the world. The two commandments are really one commandment. The first—"to love the Lord your God with all your heart . . ." (Lk 10:27)—expands into and anticipates the second—"and your neighbor as yourself"—much as the Old Testament prophecies anticipate and are fulfilled in the historical "words and deeds . . . signs and wonders . . . of Christ witnessed in the New, especially his death, resurrection, and sending of the Holy Spirit" (Second Vatican Council, *Divine Revelation*, n. 4). Drawn from the Old Testament, the Commandments are completed in the Christ of the Beatitudes who invites us into the blessedness and greater charity of the new life in him (Lk 2:20–25).

Addressed to the Christian world (and to Jews), the title of the response from the Muslim scholars is a phrase bracketed from a longer verse in the *Qur'an*: "O People of the Scripture! Come to a common word as between us and you: that we *worship* none but God and that we shall *ascribe* no partner unto Him, that we *erect not*, from among ourselves, lords and patrons other than Allah." (Q 3:64). Aside from its *sola Scriptura* approach, the "Common Word" interprets the complete set of propositions as meaning that none have "to prostrate before kings and the like." This meaning could conceivably interact differently in differing cultural and institutional settings of today— in either the context of the fused Mosque-state, or the context of the West where Church and state are distinct. Regarding the historical meaning of the combined propositions (Q 3:64)—Abdullah Yusuf Ali explained in his annotations to the *Qur'an* (1934): "Apart from doctrinal lapses from the unity of the One True God, there is the question of a consecrated priesthood . . . as if a mere human being—Cohen, or Pope, or Priest, or Brahman—could claim superiority . . . or could stand between man and God in some special sense."[202] The Catholic institution of the priesthood is not that priests stand between man and God, but that they simply have a distinct role (apostle: to be sent) to advance "the common call to holiness," coming from the hands of Christ through the apostolic succession. The "Common Word" verse recalls a more unifying meaning from another to the effect that human conflicts are vain and inconclusive, and that God is the final judge: "Our Lord will gather us together and will in the end decide the matter *between us (and you)* in truth and justice: and He is the One to decide, the One who knows all" (Q 34:26, italics added). But here, again, is the point of final revelation, whether in Jesus Christ the One God makes himself present even today and not always later "in the end."

The Church is the original dialogue partner to the exchange initiated at Regensburg in 2006. Each priest, with all of his personal shortcomings, serves as "another Christ" (*alter Christi*)—by imaging the humility of God as a "servant of the servants of God." Additional differences with Islam on the more cultural level might also assure that "Common Word" enables a balanced and sustained dialogue between the parties. The very nature of interpersonal dialogue is approached differently in the West and in the world of Islam. Following an earlier response by thirty-eight Muslim leaders, the Vatican suggested a possible benefit of a unified and smaller number of face-to-face spokesmen, with an early goal (reciprocity) on which to build. The "Common Word" increases the number to 138 (with hundreds more signing later) and is broadly addressed to not only to the Vatican parties but to all Christians (and Jews) in the West. The Church is predisposed toward internal structure as a basis for interreligious discourse, while Muslim participants apparently respond with their internal version of ecumenism, the consensus building approach of Ijma (Chapter 3). A promising encounter for the long term begins with divergent and culturally well established understandings about method. The Muslim response may suggest lack of recognition that Christianity is differentiated into sects as is Islam. The pope does not speak for the Protestant world nor for the Orthodox Churches. In effect the response tends to dismiss the Vatican as the initiating party by possibly foreclosing a more focused dialogue between the Church and willing members of the Muslim world.

The "Common Word" turns toward the Two Great Commandments. An important element of the Christian dispensation is not that man's love for God is to be replicated in our love for one another. Rather "Love consists in this: not that we have loved God *but that he has loved us* and has sent his Son as an offering for our sins" (1 Jn 4:10, italics added). Each surah or chapter of the *Qur'an* begins with the poetic phrase "In the name of Allah, the compassionate and the merciful," but Pope John Paul II proposes that "This God *is, above all, Love.* God not only has compassion and mercy, but he is love—the Triune God is such a complete unity in One that he is what he does. God is a Father who 'gave his only Son, so that everyone who believes in him might not perish but might have eternal life' (cf. Jn 3:16)."[203] St. Augustine concludes that rather than coming from us, charitable love is a divine gift: "Love does indeed renew the man who hears, or rather obeys its command; but only that love which *Jesus distinguished from a natural love by the qualification: As I have loved you.*"[204]

One promising contact point between witnesses to Christ and the follower of Islam might be between the respective mystical traditions. The Western mystical tradition holds that God cannot be known to the intellect, He "can be known directly to the soul in his essence through love."[205] The opening to be shared with the followers of Islam is the harmony of faith and love even more than the coherence of faith and reason. This opening also involves the irreducible difference between the incarnate Christ as the love of God made flesh, and the premise of Islam to let God remain God and man to remain man. What is man that he is to remain man? Broadened by a charity of grace, the dialogue between Christianity and Islam pauses at the nature of the original innocence, and the original sin that passes through the hearts of us all—and at the mystery and reality of a Redeemer. Evil is not only a bad choice or forgetfulness. "Without love and charity," writes Maritain, "Man

turns the best in him into an evil that is yet greater."[206] Evil is a presumed
veto, a profound reversal and direct perversion of the truth, and yet Christ
loved us to the end even while we remained in this condition. The God who
gives us the Commandment(s) of love *is* the same love who frees us. This is
illumined by the coming of Christ and recalled from the Pentateuch by John
the Evangelist: "Beloved, I am writing no new commandment to you but an
old commandment that you had from the beginning" (1 Jn 2:7). The mystery
of human existence as an event is that God does indeed love with infinite particularity each of us, without exception. To enter into this new life is our calling.[207] More than a moral sentiment, this "love" is the Word made flesh, and
a revelation of God that elevates us even beyond our imagining. It is a matter
of faith, and this is faith in a savior rather than a value, even a value held in
common. God's law of love, from the beginning and ever new, shatters every
construction thrown up by man: "I give you a new commandment: Love one
another. *As I have loved you*, so you also should love one another" (Jn 13:34,
italics added; see also and St. Paul in Rom 13:8–10). "Do to others whatever
you would have them do to you. This is the law and the prophets" (Mt 7:12).

The law of love is directed at God but at the same time is an intensification
and elevation of the universal natural law already found from the beginning
within each of us. For the followers of Islam, is their interest in the Commandments as a law of love prodded by the *Qur'an*, or does this stirring
actually come more from the law written from the beginning in the hearts of
all, including the Muslim interlocutors? For the Christian this inborn natural
law turns firstly and directly to the free and responsible exercise of the moral
virtues—prudence, temperance, courage and especially justice—rather than
to a book.

In contrast with the chasm between dar ar-Islam and dar al-harb based on
the *Qur'an* is the Christian continuity between the natural law and the higher
reality of grace and charity as the perfection of human nature: "He who does
not love his brother, whom he sees, cannot love God, whom he does not see"
(1 Jn 4:20). Under the Commandment(s): "Whoever says he is in the light,
but hates his brother, is still in the darkness" (1 Jn 2:10). Daniel Madigan,
a participant in the current dialogue with Islam, stresses an assurance given
for Christians in the "Common Word" that Muslims "are not against them
and that Islam is not against them" (Q 60:8). He highlights this clause as "an
important focus for our continuing dialogue with the group of 138 and other
Muslims."[208] This continuing dialogue—which is interreligious and intercultural—could benefit from ecumenical experiences within the Christian world
following the Second Vatican Council. Some of these ecumenical discussions
have focused on the fit between divine grace and human works—a formulation potentially representing two autonomies and therefore incompatible

with Islamic thought. The best example is the recent Catholic/Lutheran *Joint Declaration on the Doctrine of Justification* (1999).[209]

This sequence of encounters, first ecumenical within the Christian world, and now interreligious with the followers of Islam, may be providential in origin. Muslims insist on the oneness of God and yet express an interest in the Two Great Commandments as an assumed common foundation for the monotheistic religions. Early Protestant theology once held that these were really two different commandments. The consistent Catholic view is that these are two aspects of a single divine invitation revealed in Christ.[210] Early Protestant theology also held that fallen man was fatally marked and incapable of transformation into the new life. For them the first commandment reflected God's infinite love for us, while the second actually spoke of a lesser and only human love. Luther sometimes spoke of the sacrament of marriage as "that worldly institution," and yet it was at the wedding feast of Cana where Christ first revealed Himself such that "his disciples began to believe in him" (Jn 2:11).[211]

Under the unified Catholic view the single commandment of love even now calls the integral human person to full communion with one another. The accent is on the oneness of the commandment, rendering it more like sacramental marriage where the two become one flesh (Gen 2:24). Love of "neighbor" in time is even now our abandonment into the love of God in eternity. As a single commandment, the Two Great Commandments call us to love with our *whole* heart, the whole soul and mind and strength (Mk 12:30–31). Such love is inseparable from love of neighbor. The letter "A Common Word" renders love of neighbor as the test whether one also has faith. It reads, "None of you has faith until you love for your neighbor what you love for yourself" (no citation).[212] With Islam's profound attraction to unity of belief and the oneness of God, Muslims might be attracted by the Catholic parsing of the Christian commandment(s) on divine grace and human works in the world. With Luther we have the singular idea of grace over works, while with Mohammed the singular idea is the oneness of God. St. Teresa of Calcutta tells us more simply that "our work is to encourage Christians and non-Christians to do works of love. And every work of love, done with a full heart, always brings people closer to God."[213] John writes in his fourth Gospel: "*everyone who loves is begotten by God and knows God*" (1 Jn 4:7).

The Calvinist Protestant Ethic stresses works in this world and is credited with fostering the "spirit of capitalism."[214] This ethic is one inspiration behind Sufi Islamic-Calvinism (the Anatolian Tigers) in central Turkey (Chapter 4). Under Islam as a whole, meritorious works is traditionally defined by the five pillars—prayer, alms, fasting, pilgrimage and loyalty to the Prophet. Protestants and Muslims give primacy to their respective scriptures and reject some

aspects of the Church's living "tradition" as too associated with fatal corruptions and apostasy, and both depart from the Church's self-understanding
regarding scripture. The Church holds that scripture is part of the Tradition,
the corporate indwelling of the Holy Spirit partly as expressed in the writings
of the Church Fathers.

Charity, contained in the Commandments and the Beatitudes, is one of
three theological virtues. For purposes of clarity, the Catholic and Protestant
understandings of this and other theological virtues have their own points of
emphasis. Charity is inseparable from the faith and hope. The Church traditionally has defined faith as involving explicit assent of both intellect and will
to the content of shared propositions connecting us to Christ. This assent then
gives birth to a more convinced hope and, yes, love.[215] The Reformers stress
faith as a *way of life* that already includes hope and love (the other two theological virtues), while the Church thinks more in terms of charity, faith and
hope as distinct theological virtues that come together. Under Islam, whose
self-understanding is also a "way of life," the decisive act of membership is
one of will alone. To become a Muslim one simply submits once and for all
to the five pillars of Islam and by this act becomes a member of the global
ummah. In their intellectual predispositions Protestantism and Islam, both, tilt
toward possible distinctions within a prior unity, while the Catholic apologetic accepts distinctions first as the basis for a greater unity. The Catholic
tradition goes on to distinguish two kinds of faith. In addition to an intellectual assent to truths is faith as a totally gratuitous gift from God. As the first
step in faith, the Second Vatican Council speaks of the "obedience of faith"
(*ob-audire*, to listen deeply) as not simply as assent to propositions, or even
common ground, but as an engagement and act of loyalty to the self-revealing
Other involving both the will and the intellect.[216]

Pope Benedict's critique of polarized trends of fundamentalism and
rationalism within Western biblical scholarship might apply as well to the
mirror-image crisis of the Islamic State. On fundamentalism and rationalism within Christianity he writes: "On one side we have the retreat from
the truth of reason into a realm of mere piety, mere faith, mere revelation;
a retreat . . . from truth to beautiful custom, from nature to politics. On the
other side, we have an approach I will call for short 'interpreted Christianity': the stumbling blocks in Christianity are removed by the interpretive
method . . . rendering it unobjectionable . . . (Christianity's) actual contents
written off as dispensable phraseology . . ."[217] Islam carries both dimensions—piety and interpretation—to much greater lengths. Islam offers belief in the jealous oneness of Allah, and then combines this with a strongly
felt and abstract amalgam called the *ummah* which is guided and monitored
by executors of Shari'a.

Apart from "A Common Word" members of the forum crafted a concise statement on common goals and differences.[218] Leading points of concurrence were these: "faith and reason are both gifts of God to mankind . . . (and) do not contradict each other, but faith might in some cases be above reason, but never against it . . . (and that faith and reason) are intrinsically non-violent."[219] (Historically, the tenth century Mu'tazilites were suppressed partly for suggesting that good and evil were freestanding categories possibly apart from Allah.) Both sides of the forum intend to continue to work together in the interests of "genuine religiosity, in particular spirituality, to encourage respect for symbols considered to be sacred and to promote moral values" . . . (and it is agreed that) they "should go beyond tolerance, accepting differences, while remaining aware of commonalities and thanking God for them."[220] In 2007 the Muslim scholars proposed that the dual commandment of love is a "common word" linking the religion of Islam and the faith of Christians. Pope Benedict affirmed in place of any possibly implied scriptural equivalency, that the commandment itself is received more personally as "the heart of Islam and Christianity alike."[221]

The Commandments are not extraneous to man, but from the beginning are written in his heart. The Christian distinction, obscure in Islam, identifies natural law as prior to any of the scriptures. Islam claims for the *Qur'an* the "guidance" given from the beginning, and seems to unilaterally encapsulate it in the *Qur'an* (Chapter 3). Love does not erase the place of justice under the universal natural law, and it may be that the natural law as described here is the common ground that is actually intended in "A Common Word between Us." This distinction has the potential of rendering less necessary the politics of mutually respected religious symbols. Beyond the natural law, for the Christian the transfigured morality of the commandments is grounded not in a pluralist model of unity, but in a personal encounter with Christ who is not a mere symbol. Christ is the divinity in person, fully God and fully man (I Jn 2:3–6, and 3:23–24). The Christian puts his faith in the person of Christ, and only by Him do we really know about the Father and the full meaning of the Two Great Commandments of love. The Trinitarian mystery remains and deepens and cannot be jointly edited away even by a consensus process. To say that "God is love" (1 Jn 4:16) is not to say the reverse that love (alone) is God. We are to live the truth, but we are to be found "living the truth in love" (Eph 4:15). This question of truth is the question posed by the historical Pilate to the historical Christ, "What is truth" (Jn 18:38)?

The similarity and the difference between the submission of Islam and the divine self-surrender in Christ is hinted in the letters of the eighteenth century Jesuit, Jean-Pierre do Caussade: "The state of self-abandonment is a blending of faith, hope and love in one single act which unites us to God and all his activities."[222] God shows himself directly as the incarnation, and through *the words and deeds* of the Second Person of the Trinity made flesh. Christ measures us not by the Law as such (the Commandments), but by the new life of freedom which He is: "I no longer speak to you as slaves, for a slave does not know what his master is about. Instead, I call you friends, since I have made known to you all that I heard from my Father" (Jn 15:15). Even beyond the law: "Be perfect as your Father in heaven is perfect" (Matt 5:48).[223]

Unlike traditional religions, Christian and Muslim and others, the disbelief of modernity—the third entry in our subtitle and triangular inquiry—is marked by an inability to simply reverence singular events, particularly the Christ event. Standing apart from any religion or even insights from the liberal arts, modernity also stalls in its prior loss of poetic imagination. The poetic imagination fosters the respect and, yes, love that is to be given to the reality of individual "things." Modernity too often would have us believe that it is only our concepts and goals that are real. Operatives of power "make a habit of abstract thinking" and in this way stifle within themselves "the faculty to imagine that which they know."[224] To the promoters of utopia the screams of the real victims are not real because not imagined. The victims themselves are out of sight and out of mind. Idolatry of "the economy," or of reform or a promised utopia, frees the imagination from the reality of the Gulag or of Auschwitz. And today, the "silent scream" of the countless aborted unborn goes unnoticed.

Beyond a certain point, the disruption between faith and these darker forms of modernity is finally rationalized in *a prior choice* between two kinds of imagination. These are the analog appreciation of concrete reality, and a more removed and disassembled digital assembled from the binary electronic pathways behind modern computer software programs. Descartes spoke of God as "the ghost in the machine"! The fully human start point toward reality is less "religious" than it is a restored analog universe of real things that are irreducible to a digital and statistical cosmos. The immediate theological and human question today is not whether God exists, but whether man exists. Pope Benedict asserts that ultimately, "Christian faith is not based on poetry and politics, the two great sources of religion; it is based on knowledge."[225] But poetic imagination does prepare the ground for more ultimate knowledge of the real. Absent the poetic imagination as a window to the beautiful and a seedbed for conceptual and verifiable truth, it is no longer possible to discern those beautiful ideas, few in number, which are actually true.[226] A century ago Lenin remarked on purely political power: "It is the hour in which it is no longer possible to listen to music, because music arouses the desire to caress children's heads, while the moment has come to cut them off."[227] Faith is more than belief, and belief is more than imagination, and imagination is more than fiction. Divine grace is more than nature, and both exist. In his *Confessions,* St. Augustine laments his stealing of pears from a neighbor's tree. It is only because of his refined moral *imagination* that he understands the magnitude of his infidelity. His remorse is not that he took the pears—he needed no pears (analogue) and probably did not even count them (digital). His remorse and contrition is that he freely delighted in the act of taking (analog). By his free will, an image of the freedom of God, he violated reality and betrayed his neighbor, but also himself because he first violated the Spirit who dwells within. Without the movements of the poetic imagination, the marriage of faith and reason is simply cut off, guillotined, aborted, no longer possible, crucified. C.S. Lewis captures this truth: "I do not think the resemblance between the Christian and the merely imaginative experience is accidental. I think that all things, in their way, reflect heavenly truth, the imagination not least. 'Reflect' is the important word. This lower life of the imagination is not a beginning of, nor a step toward, the higher life of the spirit, merely an image . . . But (for me) it still had, at however many removes, the shape of the reality it reflected."[228]

In the reflected reality the devout Muslim prays a submissive prayer in supplication (Du'aa) five times daily, while the converted Christian lives within and possibly contemplates the five penetrating wounds of the self-donated, crucified, and Risen One. Witnesses to Christ proclaim neither a practice nor even a doctrine so much as an active *encounter*. When asked how we should pray, the encountered and Incarnate One our Lord gave us his Prayer. Not necessarily five times a day, the prayer to the Father with whom he is One is not five times, but rather five-fold. As adoptive sons and daughter's of a God who is Father, the prayer given to us is a trusting prayer first of *petition* that His kingdom might come even now into this moment, and then it is a prayer of *praise* and of *providence*. And finally ours is a prayer for *pardon* and total healing, and for *protection* as pilgrims in a strange land.

For the secularist everything may have its worth, but nothing is sacred. "(F)or the Jews there is no distinction between holy and profane times; every action is rendered sacred by the benediction which accompanies it . . ."[229] For the followers of Islam Allah is above, but an amalgam natural religion and ummah are below with a division from dar al-harb. And the moment before the Church of the Incarnate One opens itself to the Gentiles, Peter is admonished by the voice of God: "What God has made clean, you are not to call profane" (Acts 10:15). The present moment of the third millennium beckons. Its Design might yet weave together all that is best—the Christ of the witnesses, the piety in Islam, and that part of the West that brought reason to the Areopagus. In the ninth century the rationalist Mutazilites were suppressed for seeking a God of law rather than a God of (arbitrary) will. The

Christian law of love surpasses both will and law, and in this way opens for the human person a harmony of will, intellect and memory—the focus of our concluding chapter.

NOTES

1. Farooq Hassan, *The Concept of Church and State in Islam* (Washington, D.C.: University Press of America, 1981), 243.

2. Ibid.

3. A bridge between the three theological virtues and righteousness, a value shared by Christians and Muslims, is supplied in a second century letter to the Philippians by St. Polycarp. He writes of Christian faith: "This faith is the mother of us all, followed by hope, preceded by love—love of God, of Christ, of neighbor. Whoever lives within this framework has fulfilled the commandment of righteousness. For anyone who has love is far from sin" (*Liturgy of the Hours*, Vol. IV [New York: Catholic Book Publishing Co., 1975], 319).

4. Ibid. 242.

5. Ibid, 232.

6. Christopher Dawson, *The Making of Modern Europe* (New York: Meridian, 1956), 127. Based on original sources Lynn White places less weight than Dawson or originally Gibbon on the Battle of Tours. Martel consolidated his holdings prior to this battle engaging an Islamic presence already weakened by internal dissensions among the Moors (*Medieval Technology and Social Change* [New York: Oxford University Press, 1962], 11–14).

7. Bernard Lewis, op. cit. A somewhat analogous parallel in Western history can be detected from an editorial footnote to an earlier writing by Joseph de Maistre, *On God and Society,* op. cit. Napoleon signed the Concordat with Rome in 1801, but then "promulgated unilaterally an organic law which provided for the teaching of the Gallican Articles in all seminaries" (p. 26; King Louis XIV earlier had discontinued this dynastic requirement). Among the four Gallican Articles is one that would subordinate the universal church in France to the French nation. Lewis alerts the West to the prospect of liberty and freedom of religion subordinated to the absorbent or universalist pretensions of Shari'a.

8. Ariana Fallaci, *The Force of Reason* (New York: Rizzoli, 2004), 300. Martin Walker questions the conventional wisdom of underlying global demographic forecasts (such as expressed by Fallaci), in "the World's New Numbers," *The Wilson Quarterly* (Washington, D.C.: Woodrow Wilson International Center, Spring 2009). He cites declining Muslim birth rates worldwide and some recent national increases by Europeans.

9. Pew Research Forum on Religion and Public Life, *The Future of the Global Muslim Population—Projections for 2010 and 2030,* January 27, 2011; also reported in the *New York Times*, January 27, 2011.

10. Mahmoud Ayoub in Irfan A. Omar, (ed.), *A Muslim View of Christianity: Essays on Dialogue by Mahmoud Ayoub* (New York: Orbis Books, Maryknoll, 2007), 229.

11. John Paul II, *Redemptoris Missio* (Mission of the Redeemer), 1991, n. 55, cited by Ayoub in Omar (ed.), 243.

12. Ayoub in Omar (ed.) 240 (italics added).

13. In this vein, Frederich Heer compares the Muslim separation from infidels (Dar-al-harb) to the Byzantine concept of *eremos*, or desert, and the Carolingian liturgical *gentes* (*The Intellectual History of Europe* [New York: World Publishing Co., 1953], 96).

14. The New Testament includes over three hundred fifty quotations from the Old Testament. Fully one third of these are taken from the psalms.

15. A listening culture is an *encounter* culture. Other biblical references to listening include: Eze 37:4, Isa 59:1, Dt 6:4 and 31:13, Mk 12:29 and 16:15, and Heb 3:7.

16. Joseph Cardinal Ratzinger (Pope Benedict XVI), *Salt of the Earth* (San Francisco: Ignatius Press, 1997), 222.

17. The injunction to suppress non-Muslim groups (dhimmis) is found in the *Qur'an*: "Fight against such as those . . . (who) do not embrace the true Faith, until they pay tribute out of hand and are utterly subdued" (Q 9:29).

18. A theme proposed by Reynold A. Nicholson, *The Mystics of Islam* (New York: Penguin, 1989 [1914]), passim.

19. Al-Munqidh min al-Dalal, translated by R.J. Mc Carthy, *Al-Ghazali's Path to Sufism: His Deliverance from Error* (Louisville: Fons Vitae, 1999), 51.

20. Huston Smith, *Islam: An Introduction* (San Francisco: Harper, 2001), 77, 80.

21. Ayoub in Omar (ed.), 235.

22. Kathernine Pratt Ewing, *Arguing Sainthood: Modernity, Psychology and Islam* (Durham: Kuke University Press, 1997), 157.

23. Camille Adams Helminski, *Women of Sufism: A Hidden Treasure* (Boston; Shambhala, 2003), xxv.

24. G.E.H. Palmer, Philip Sherrard, Kallistos Ware, *The Philokalia* (compiled by St. Nikodimos of the Holy Mountain and St. Makariou of Corinth), Vol. 3 (Boston: Faber and Faber, 1995), 143.

25. P. Marie-Eugene, OCD, 250.

26. Ibid., from St. John of the Cross, *Ascent of Mt. Carmel*, xxxi, 2205–6.

27. The dogmatic definition of "transubstantiation" (the Real Presence of Christ under the accidents of bread and wine) from the Council of Trent uses the epistemological term *species*, not *substance*, and in this way remains apart from Aristotelian physics with its specific limitations or any other physics. Involved is the relationship between the soul of the knower and the thing known which makes an object out of what is otherwise simply a physical thing. "The role of the human soul in relation to its objects is much more analogous to the Sleeping Beauty waiting for Prince Charming to come and awaken her than it is to the role of Don Juan always pursuing new victims!" See L.M. Regis, *Empistemology* (New York: Macmillan Co., 1959), 252.

28. St. Augustine, *Confessions*, Bk. 7, Ch. 10, n. 16.

29. Sermon by St. Bernard, *Liturgy of the Hours*, Vol. IV, 231.

30. Examples: Freud reduced the personality to a disordered sexual instinct. His one-time colleague C.J. Jung defined the individual as more of a response to the external world around him, and Adler focused on the internal and intellectual instinct toward pride.

31. Letter to Faussett (1838), cited in Vincent Ferrer Blehl, *The Essential Newman* (New York: Mentor-Omega, 1963), 54.

32. Ibid., 88.

33. Pope Benedict XVI, "Dionysius the Areopagite: On Mediation and Dialogue," Weekly General Audience of May 14, 2008.

34. Ibid., 27.

35. Brant Pelphrey, *The Theology and Mysticism of Julian of Norwich* (Salzburg: University of Salzburg, 1982), 65, citing the *Summa*, I, Q. 12 where Aquinas defers to St. Augustine.

36. Thomas Dubay, S.M., *Fire Within: St. Teresa of Avila, St. John of the Cross, and the Gospel–on Prayer* (San Francisco: Ignatius, 1989), 310.

37. Ayoub in Omar (ed.), 170, italics added.

38. Ibid., 173.

39. Ibid., 160.

40. The Christian side of the discussion would begin with Henri de Lubac's *Augustinianism and Modern Theology* (New York: Crossroad Publishing Co., 2000). De Lubac restores the Augustinian position of nature reaching toward and being fulfilled by grace from *beyond itself*. He even refers to falsified Augustinianism (an exaggerated dichotomy between alleged active intellect and a creaturely passive intellect), a misunderstanding of Augustine termed by scholars as "Avicennian Augustinianism" (276–7; Avicenna: the prominent Muslim philosopher). De Lubac's clarification of Augustine's vision of the fit between the natural and the spiritual is a corrective to both disconnected naturalism and spiritualism, and has influenced the unified appreciation of the person as explored by the Second Vatican Council (1963–5).

41. St. Augustine, *The City of God*, Book xviii, Ch. 51.

42. "This doctrine (predestination) . . . I began to understand more clearly in that examination of the question which I wrote . . . then I recognized that the very beginning itself of faith was God's gift, and I asserted that doctrine" (citation in Hugh Pope, *Saint Augustine of Hippo: Essays* [Garden City, NY: Image, 1961], 377, n. 62).

43. Philip Hughes, *A History of the Church*, Vol. III (New York: Sheed and Ward, 1947), 519–522.

44. Leopold Ranke, *History of the Popes*, Vol. I, (London: George Bell and Sons, 1878), 30, 223.

45. John Dolan, *History of the Reformation* (New York: Mentor-Omega, 1967), passim. and 242, 256. Not at Trent, but at the Second Vatican Council (1963–5) the collegial and evangelizing role of all bishops and their priests, still in union with Rome, would be clearly developed.

46. "Janus," *The Pope and the Council* (Boston: Roberts Brothers, 1870), 301.

47. Wael B. Hallaq, *An Introduction to Islamic Law* (New York: Cambridge, 2009), 121–4.

48. Bernard Lewis, *What Went Wrong?* (New York: Harper Perennial, 2003), 159.

49. Charles Peguy, (Julian Green, trans.), *God Speaks* (New York: Pantheon Books, 1950), 29.

50. The possibility of additional paths of Islamic evolution is researched early on by the anthropologist Clifford Geertz. In an exploratory monograph Geertz contrasts doctrinaire Islam in the historically tribal Morocco to a more flexible pattern found in peasant dominated Indonesia (*Islam Observed: Religious Development in Morocco and Indonesia* [Chicago: University of Chicago Press, 1968]).

51. The Church, which in some regions seeks to reaffirm a "Catholic identity," must not subordinate its unambiguous witness to any lesser role within the prevailing culture of identity politics. The Christian worldview reinforces a distinct understanding accessible to sound reason—of the universal natural law. In contrast with purely secular rules of the game, or proceduralism, the Church maintains that human rights are "incomprehensible without the *presupposition* that man *qua* man . . . is the subject of rights and that his being bears within itself values and norms that must be discovered—but not invented" (See Jurgan Habermas and Joseph Ratzinger, *The Dialectics of Secularization* [San Francisco: Ignatius Press, 2006], 71).

52. Limited use of *Itjihad* is non binding on future generations and continues among the Shi'ites. The outside observer is moved to wonder whether it was under (non-binding) Itjihad consensus in ninth century Baghdad that the *Qur'an* was elevated above interpretation to a sharing in the very essence of God. If so, then does the possibility exist under a more original Ijtihad that the Qur'anic core of Shari'a is reformable in later generations in a way acceptable to the followers of Islam?

53. "God's creation cannot be changed" (Q 30:30); "Allah be worshipped and evil be shunned" (Q 16:36); "(true believers) . . . enjoin what is just and forbid what is evil" (Q 9:71).

54. Bernard Lewis, "The Roots of Muslim Rage," *Atlantic Monthly* (September 1990).

55. Part of the Kemalist vision was that the Sultans sowed the seeds of their own defeat when they crossed the Bosporus into Europe from Asia. Had Constantinople not become an albatross around its neck, the Empire might have thrived a bit longer in Anatolia, Mesopotamia and the Levant. The Kemalist theory is recalled by Alan Palmer, *The Decline and Fall of the Ottoman Empire* (Barnes and Noble, 1992), 267.

56. Personal conversation (Seattle, Washington, 1998) with Erik von Kuehnelt-Leddihn, author, educator, linguist, novelist, and well-traveled speaker, who died in 1999 at the age of 90. Bernard Lewis writes that Christian deference toward women always startled Muslim visitors. He quotes a visitor to Vienna (Evliya Celebi): "Women have the chief say, and they are honored and respected for the sake of Mary" (Bernard Lewis, *The Muslim Discovery of Europe* [New York: W.W. Norton, 1982], 287–8).

57. Depending upon the very elastic translation of *daraba*, especially when rendered in English, the *Qur'an* (Q 4:34) can mean to Muslim extremists an injunction to sometimes "beat" one's wife. And if beating was ever intended, other writings restrict the instrument to a twig or toothbrush. An opposite saying in the hadith is "Do not beat your wife like you would beat your camel, for you will be flogging her early in the day and taking her to bed at night" (Neil Mac Farquhar, *New York Times*, March 25, 2007).

58. Moojan Momen, *An Introduction to Shi'I Islam* (New Haven: Yale University Press, 1985), 245.

59. Jean Sassoon, *Princess* (Atlanta, Georgia: Windsor-Brooke Books, 2004 [1992]), *Princess Sultana's Daughters* (New York: Doubleday, 1994), and *Princess Sultana's Circle* (Woodstock, New York: Windsor-Brooke Books, 2000). Terrors in Iraq are collected *Mayada: Daughter of Iraq* (New York: New American Press, 2003).

60. The "days of ignorance" in Arabia refers to the time prior to the coming of Mohammed.

61. Ibid., *Princess Sultana's Circle*, 96. In his prison era research, Jawaharlal Nehru attributed the seclusion of Muslim women—not original to Islam—to the influence of the two older neighboring empires, Eastern Roman and Persian (*Glimpses of World History* [New York: John Day Company, 1942], 148 (italics added). Guillaume points out that the *Qur'an*, (Q 24:2) specifies a hundred stripes, *not* stoning for adultery (Guillaume, 191).

62. Muslim scholars incorrectly fault the Christian scriptures for not having been written until over a century after the time of Christ. By both tradition and archeology the charge of historical fabrication is known to be false. The final version of the *Qur'an* was compiled and edited in two decades, but assembly of the variously transmitted hadith extended over a period of two centuries.

63. The primary exponent of this thesis is John Rawls, *Political Liberalism* (New York: Columbia University Press, 1993). At his Notre Dame University commencement address (May 17, 2009), the President asserted that opposed national positions on abortion are "irreconcilable," and alluded instead to a "sensible conscience clause" in forthcoming national health legislation. Ritual sacrifice in Aztec Mexico is a comparable case, also irreconcilable with even a minimal standard of Natural Law and decency. In Mexico the practice affected a lesser number than those aborted in the United States alone, only one hundred thousand per year as compared to over one million. Regarding allegedly "irreconcilable" positions, Pope John Paul II observed that "To believe it possible to know a universally valid truth is in no way to encourage intolerance; on the contrary, it is the essential condition for sincere and authentic dialogue between persons" (*Fides et Ratio*, 1998, n. 92).

64. In the United States a team of Catholic laymen in high government offices is now in place to impose such policies. In a monarchic context, in 1789 the lower clergy (not the lay public), as the majority of the Third Estate (208 of 296 votes), joined the smaller First and Second Estates to compel the monarchy to recognize a single combined Assembly. The Assembly first subjected the Church to populist supervision, confiscations and institutional and doctrinal deconstruction, and then ushered in the total Revolution (E.E.Y. Hales, *The Catholic Church in the Modern World* [Garden City, New York: Image, 1960], 34–50).

65. Ayoub in Omar (ed.), 240.

66. The epic *Song of Roland* (composed between 1066 and 1090 A.D.), was used as a propaganda piece for the First Crusade. In it the Saracens in Spain were portrayed as worshiping three gods: e.g., "And right earnestly did the emir call upon his gods, on Apollo and Tervagant and Mohammed..." (Jessie Crosland (tr.), *Song*

of Roland, [London: Chatto and Windus Publishers, 1907], 163–4). This early and inexact perception of Islam is not held or even heard of in the Christian West today. Contrasting with the later Crusades, the Frankish Roland allied himself with the Umayyad Muslims in Spain against Abdur Rahman, the only surviving member of the liquidated Abassid dynasty (Richard Winston, *Charlemagne* [New York: Vintage, 1954], 134–7).

67. Ayoub in Omar (ed.), 2.

68. Ibid., 3, italics added.

69. Ariani Fallaci, *The Force of Reason* (New York: Rizzoli, 2004), 194–6. While Fallaci mostly faults the Left for forming a natural alliance against the West after the collapse of Communism (210), she also cites a pattern of specific failings by Church officials in the selling of convents and churches, in support in Paris for the Islamic Cultural Institute, in remaining silent when crucifixes are removed from hospitals, in assisting in the locating of a mosque in Lyon, and for saying nothing about polygamy, wife-repudiation, and about slavery which still exists in Sudan, Mauritania, and other parts of Muslim Africa.

70. Ibid., 188–9.

71. Ibid., 185–9. Scripture warns us repeatedly against the worship of false gods, but only once ventures into the total negation of faith, the wasteland of atheism: "The fool says in his heart, 'There is no God'" (Ps 14:1).

72. Ibid., 288.

73. Fallaci, 191.

74. Second Vatican Council, *Gaudium et Spes*, (The Church in the Modern World), n. 22.

75. The poorly received 1990 "Norms for Catholic Universities," *Ex corde Ecclesiae* (From the Heart of the Church*)*, addressed the meaning of scientific and technical research, social life and culture. The Introduction to the document reads, "On an even more profound level, what is at stake *is the very meaning of the human person*" (italics in the original). The norms are partly a response to the 1967 Land O' Lakes Statement signed by educators from ten Catholic colleges and universities purporting to retain their identity as Catholic while also claiming "a true autonomy and academic freedom in the face of authority of whatever kind, lay or clerical, external to the academic community itself." What in the sixties postured as freedom from undue submission sounds today more like careerism in cap and gown. Where the Minnesota lakes are many they are also shallow. Obedience to the social principles—sometimes termed the "negation of ideology"—contrasts with submission and can be sufficiently open to "listen deeply" (*ob-audire*).

76. During his visit to the United States in 2008, in his "Address to Catholic Educators," Pope Benedict (John Paul II's successor) made no direct reference to the Norms, but broadly proposed a renewed educational philosophy, e.g., ". . . the Church never tires of upholding the essential moral categories of right and wrong, without which hope could only wither, giving way to cold pragmatic calculations of utility which render the person little more than a pawn on some ideological chess-board."

77. G.K. Chesterton's famous analysis of madness begins to apply. He writes that "The madman's explanation of a thing is always complete, and often in a purely rational

sense satisfactory . . . his mind moves in a perfect but narrow circle. A small circle is quite as infinite as a large circle, but, though it is quite as infinite, it is not so large . . . the strongest and most unmistakable *mark* of madness is this combination between a logical completeness and a spiritual contraction. The lunatic's theory explains a large number of things, but it does not explain them in a large way" (*Orthodoxy* [Garden City, NY: Image, 1959], 19–20).

78. The forms that persecution might take under a new law of the land are legion. In Massachusetts, as state that recognizes same sex "marriages," one of the oldest adoption agencies in the country was forced out of existence in 2008 because it refused to place orphans in the hands of adoptive homosexual pairs. Historically, the most abrupt early change in Islam was advanced by deliberate language manipulation. Replacement of the Ummayids by the Abbasids in 750 A.D. was facilitated by how the followers of Abbas labeled themselves to confuse the followers of Ali, direct heir, cousin and son-in-law of Mohammed (husband of Fatima). Ali was the son of one of three brothers, Abu Talib, uncle and protector of Muhammed; Abbas and Abdullah, Muhammed's father, were the other two brothers. The Abbasids assembled clan military support by presenting themselves as descendents of the grarndfather Hashim (Reynold A. Nicholson, *A Literary History of the Arabs* [New York: Charles Scribner's Sons, 1907], 250–253). In the politics of today, Islamic "democracy" can have a quite different meaning that what is understood in the West.

79. T.E. Lawrence, *Seven Pillars of Wisdom* (New York: Anchor Books, 1991), 38–43.

80. This paragraph summarized from an address by Professor Steven Pfaff, University of Washington Lecture Series (November 18, 2007). Joseph Weiler, a Jewish scholar, attributes European "Christophobia" to the resentment that the aging elite formed in the revolt of 1968 have toward their children who are "turning to Jesus Christ and Christianity to fill the void in their lives" (Weiler's litany of factors is summarized by George Weigel (*The Cube and the Cathedral* [New York: Basic Books, 2005], 72–77).

81. Immigrants to America distinguished themselves by their tendency to form associations of all kinds, but these were inspired by interests rather than by any overriding religion. The stabilizing backdrop to the American project, however, remains a widely and possibly deeply shared religious commitment distinct from the realm of politics. Alexis De Tocqueville attends to this contrast: "Mohammed professed to derive from Heaven, and has inserted in the Koran, not only religious doctrines, but political maxims, civil and criminal laws, and theories of science. The Gospel, on the contrary, speaks only of the general relations of men to God and to each other....the former of these religions will never long predominate in a cultivated and democratic age, while the latter is destined to retain its sway at these as at all other periods." (*Democracy in America*, Vol. 2, Ch. 5 [New York: Vintage, 1945], 24.)

De Tocqueville warns of an excessively unifying tendency for citizens of democracy toward pantheism (might we say multiculturalism?): "It naturally attracts and fixes their imagination; it fosters the pride while it soothes the indolence of their minds . . . Against it all who abide in their attachment to the true greatness of man should combine and struggle." (Ibid., Ch. 7, 33).

82. Immigrant Muslims are three percent favorable toward al-Qaeda, compared to nine percent of African American Muslims, while 36 percent are unfavorable compared to 63 percent for immigrants (Alan Cooperman, "America's Mainstreamed Muslims," *Washington Post*, May 23, 2007; telephone survey advised by Muslims Amaney Jamal and Farid Senzai of 1,050 adults with a margin of sampling error of five percentage points). These results were generally confirmed in a followup Pew Research Center survey ("Muslim Americans: No Signs of Growth in Alienation or Support for Extremism," August 30, 2011 [http://people-press.org).

83. Jacques Servais writes that in modernity "Man loses the trust that he had spontaneously placed up to that point in the mystery of his destiny, and he perceives in an intensified way the danger and at the same time the necessity of his condition . . . .restlessness, and even more, angst, come to represent more and more the fundamental attitude and the means of knowing reality . . . The first impulse that guides reason here is no longer the spontaneous belief in the goodness of being as a gift, but the existential doubt of an unhappy consciousness that, faced with the world that constantly jars or deceives him, feels inescapably imprisoned in what Hegel calls the 'bad infinity'" ("Restlessness and Anxiety: Toward a Christian Discernment," *Communio* (34:2), Washington, D.C.: Communio Incorporated, Summer 2007, 260).

84. "When you're working there, they try to make you feel like you're under attack by these pro-life groups" (Abby Johnson, a convert and former director of Planned Parenthood in Bryan, Texas, cited in "Nation," *National Catholic Register* [North Haven, Conn.: Circle Media, Nov. 22, 2009]. 4.

85. The implied arrogance is more reactionary than liberating, exceeding even that of Louis XIV who declared "L'estate, c'est moi" (I am the state), and possibly Pope Pius IX who in defending clumsily the Church at one point during the First Vatican Council, remarked "I am tradition."

86. Gieorgio de Santillana, Transcript of April 12, 1633, *The Crime of Galileo* (Chicago: University of Chicago Press, 1955), 238–242. The comparison is inexact. The controversy today is between science and political correctness. In the case of Galileo the controversy was less between theology and science than it was between *two different kinds of reasoning*: Aristotelianism as opposed to Copernicanism, or "*a priori* reasoning against observation and experiment; the syllogism against the telescope" (John Zahm, *Evolution and Dogma* [Hicksville, New York: Regina Press, 1975 (1896)], 395).

87. John Paul II, "Day of Pardon" (n. 4), included by the International Theological Commission, *Memory and Reconciliation: The Church and the Faults of the Past* (Boston: Pauline Books and Media, 2000).

88. Pitirim A. Sorokin, *The Ways and Power of Love* (Chicago: Henry Regnery, 1967 [1954]), 211–254. In his preface, Sorokin cites A. H. Maslow on the shunning of "love energy" by the empirical sciences especially at his time of writing: "Particularly strange is the silence of the psychologists. Sometimes this is merely sad or irritating, as in the case of the textbooks of psychology and sociology, practically none of which treat the subject . . . More often the situation becomes completely ludicrous. (As a rule) the world 'love' is not even indexed (in psychological and sociological works)" (vi).

89. Bernard Lewis, *What Went Wrong?* (New York: Harper Perennial, 2002), 109. Historically, McNeill proposes that after 1453 the already structured Christian clergy ossified to become "a mirror image of the ulema itself, bearing authority over Christians comparable to that which the legal experts of Islam exercised over Moslems" and, conversely, that the ulema were influenced toward a more hierarchical structure and more direct involvement in affairs of state (*The Rise of the West*, 552).

90. Bernard Lewis (ed. and trans.), *Islam: from the Prophet Muhammad to the Capture of Constantinople,* II: Religion and Society (New York: Oxford University Press, 1987), Introduction.

91. Second Vatican Council, *Lumen Gentium* (Dogmatic Constitution on the Church), nn. 39–42. The elevation of the laity primarily means that "the call to the perfection of charity…a life of prayer and, as much as possible, of contemplative recollection . . . (is not) the exclusive concern of monks" (Jacques Maritain, *The Peasant of the Garonne* [New York: Holt, Rinehart and Winston, 1968], 49).

92. St. Ignatius, Letter to the Ephesians, *Liturgy of the Hours,* Vol. III, 80–81.

93. Erik von Kuehnelt-Leddhin, *Liberty or Equality?* (Caldwell, Idaho: Caxton Press, 1952). Erik includes maps of voting patterns in Catholic and Lutheran Germany for the pivotal elections of 1932.

94. Ayoub, 241–3.

95. Pope Benedict XVI, *Truth and Tolerance: Christian Belief and World Religions* (San Francisco: Ignatius, 2004). This work published in 2004 was not available in time for Ayoub's writing originally published in 1999, 211–12.

96. Congregation for the Doctrine of the Faith, *Dominus Iesus* (The Lord Jesus), 2000, n. 22, italics added.

97. Pope Benedict XVI makes this observation: "Freedom for universality and so for the legitimate secularity of the state has been transformed into an absolute secularism, for which forgetfulness of God and exclusive concern with success seem to have become guiding principles . . ." (*Jesus of Nazareth* [New York: Doubleday, 2007],119).

98. John Beevers (trans.), *Abandonment to Divine Providence* (New York: Image Books, 1975), 43.

99. Roland Bainton, *The Age of the Reformation* (Princeton, N.J.: D. Van Nostrand Co., 1956), 85–6.

100. *Declaration on Religious Freedom*, n. 2.

101. Mualana Muhammad Ali, *Muhammad the Prophet* (Lahore, Pakistan: Ripon Press, 1984 [1924]), 23–4.

102. Edward Gibbon, *Christians and the Fall of Rome* (New York: Penguin Books, 2004), 65; extract from *The Decline and Fall of the Roman Empire,* Vol. I, first published 1776.

103. C.S. Lewis, *Surprised by Joy* (New York: Harvest Books, 1955), 210.

104. From the *Navarre Bible*, Introduction to Hebrews (Dublin: Four Courts Press, 1991), 44 and fn. 9.

105. Pope Benedict XVI, *Values in a Time of Upheaval* (New York: Crossroad Publishing, 2006), 36.

106. Joseph Cardinal Ratzinger (Pope Benedict XVI), on Europe's Crisis of Culture," at the convent of Saint Scholastica in Subiaco, Italy, the day before Pope John Paul II www.catholiceducation.org/article/politics.

107. Sayyid Muhammad Rashid Rida (d. 1935), referenced by Ayoub in Omar, Irfan A. (ed.), *A Muslim View of Christianity: Essays on Dialogue by Mahmoud Ayoub* (New York: Orbis Books, Maryknoll, 2007), 118–220.

108. W.H. McNeill, the *Rise of the West* (New York: Mentor, 1963), 555.

109. Guillaume, citing Van den Bergh, 139.

110. See Hans Urs von Balthasar, *Presence and Thought: An Essay on the Religious Philosophy of Gregory of Nyssa* (San Francisco: Ignatius Press, 1995, 93). Gregory was a fourth century bishop and theologian whose writings were in part a response to Arianism, the taproot of Nestorian Christian errors later conveyed by the monk Bahira to Mohammed in the seventh century.

111. Quoted in Etienne Gilson, *The Elements of Christian Philosophy* (New York: Mentor Omega, 1960), 356. See Albert Einstein, "Physics and Reality" (1936*), Out of My Later Years* (New York: Philosophical Library, 1950), 61. Einstein also remarked "science without religion is lame, religion without science is blind."

112. Ibid.

113. Einstein knew that once the physical universe was understood to be a totality of interacting entities, natural theology was no longer inherently discredited. Einstein warned that some would attempt to conflate physics with metaphysics. In a letter to his friend Solovine, written four years before his own death, He explained "It cannot be helped . . .The strange thing is that we have to be satisfied with recognizing the 'miracle' without having any legitimate way of getting any further. I have to add the last point explicitly, in case you think that I am so weakened by age that I have fallen into the hands of the priests" (Letter of March 30, 1952, cited in Stanley L. Jaki, *The Absolute Beneath the Relative, and Other Essays* [Lanham, MD: Intercollegiate Studies Institute, 1988], 1–18).

114. Don Luigi Giussani, *The Religious Sense* (San Francisco: Ignatius Press, 1970), 68.

115. See Heb 1:3, and see Jn 1:10 on the creation of the world through Christ who sustains it in being, all in a single act of creation from outside of time.

116. Even before Newton, in the fourteenth century, Oresme and Buridan formulated the idea of inertial motion and impetus (momentum). This discovery is documented by Pierre Duhem in a ten-volume set (1904 and 1916) as discussed by Stanley Jaki, *Uneasy Genius: The Life and Work of Pierre Duhem* (Boston: Martinus Nijhoff, 1984).

117. "The Physics of Impetus and the Impetus of the Koran," *Modern Age* (Bryn Mawr, Penn.: Intercollegiate Studies Institute, Spring 1985), 153–160.

118. The scientific method seeks verifiable answers to questions using five steps that can be *replicated*: information gathering, formation of a hypothesis, experimentation, analysis, and interpretation.

119. http://en.wikipedia.org/Abu Rayhan al-Biruni (updated July 31, 2011).

120. Dennis Overbye, "How Islam Won, and Lost, the Lead in Science," *New York Times*, Oct. 30, 2001, Section D5.

121. Cited by Evan Gibson, in Andrew Tadie and Michael Macdonald (eds.), *Permanent Things* (Grand Rapids, Michigan: William B. Eerdmans Publishing Co., 1995), 243.

122. Sermon of 1831, cited in Vincent Ferrer Blehl (ed.), *The Essential Newman* (New York: Mentor Omega, 1963), 39.

123. Overbye, op. cit. The author's finding for Israel came before the distorting exodus in the 1990s of Russian professionals into Israel.

124. Ibid.

125. "The fact is that the world was made simultaneously with time . . . As for the 'days', it is difficult, perhaps impossible to think—let alone explain in words—what they mean" (St. Augustine, *The City of God*, Part 3, Book 6 (c. 213–226 A.D.).

126. The Big Bang theory explains the workings of a natural process, but does not explain its existence (not the spiritual side of the whole man). The theory begins after one billionth of a second with the four forces of the universe (gravity, electromagnetic forces and small and large nuclear forces*)* *already existing* as an intensely compact and single super force much smaller than a single atom. Disintegration yields simple atoms after three minutes, atomic radiation after 380,000 years, and matter and gravity combining into star formations and our universe, after nine billion years. The Pre-scientific fiction that maggots arise *spontaneously* from rotten meat finds a place in the non-metaphysical thinkers of the new cosmology: "Spontaneous creation is the reason there is something rather than nothing" (Stephen Hawking, *The Grand Design* (New York: Bantam Books, 2010), 180.

127. Etienne Gilson, *The Elements of Christian Philosophy* (New York: Mentor Omega, 1960), 214. Aquinas was of the opinion that but for revelation (Jn 1:1–3) there is no necessary reason to believe that the physical universe is finite in time rather than not. On this point he argued with fellow theologians.

128. The Gospel of John (1:1–3), and reflected in the Fourth Lateran Council, 1215.

129. The correct disposition toward creation is that of a child when he first experiences a "Thou: in its mother's smile through which it learns that it is contained, affirmed and loved in a relationship which is incomprehensively encompassing, already actual, sheltering and nourishing. . . The communication of Being lies . . . simply enclosed in the child's wonder at reality with the first opening of its eyes: in the fact that it is *permitted* to be in the midst of what exists." The moment of this recognition is the foundation for all of Hans Urs von Balthasar's wide-ranging theology (*The Glory of the Lord: A Theological Aesthetics*, Vol. V, [San Francisco: Ignatius Press, 1991], 613–56, citations 616, 633).

130. *The Imitation of Christ*, (attributed to Thomas A. Kempis), Book II, Ch. 4

131. Charles Darwin, *The Variation of Animals and Plants under Domestication*, Vol. I (New York: Appleton and Co., 1883), 6–7.

132. Hassan, 227.

133. On this point the Muslim philosopher Averroes, who defended a permanent universe, departed from the earlier Avicenna, who defended an eternally created universe (Gilson, 215).

134. Stanley Jaki, "The Physics of Impetus and the Impetus of the Koran," 153–160.

135. Cited in Stephen F. Mason, *A History of Science* (New York: Collier-Macmillan, 1970), 67.

136. Second Vatican Council, *Gaudium et Spes (*The Church in the Modern World), n. 36.

137. Darwin refers to "cells or organic units, or simply units" and an "inherent power which the cells possess, and not (to) any external agency." In proposing Pangenesis, Darwin hypothesizes additional "granules" or "gemmules" which aggregate to enable, for example, the regeneration of lost limbs in some life forms (*The Variation of Animals and Plants under Domestication*, Vol. II, 366–78. That the cell and fictional gemmules are not building blocks is later demonstrated in the discovered microscopic assemblies involving a foundational alphabet of twenty amino acids, and thirty thousand different derived proteins produced by DNA molecules (deoxyribonucleic acid) when these are each transcribed according to varied assembly instructions involving three billion characters contained in the RNA (ribonucleic acid). Scientific research is asking whether microscopic biotic (rather than pre-biotic) processes actually began not with elaborate DNA but with simpler RNA molecules.

138. Brian Greene, 362. Some string theorists even question the so-called Big Bang by proposing a pre-big bang scenario. For them, the equations of string theory suggest that "before" time "the universe started out as cold and essentially *infinite* in spatial extent."

139. From "Discourse Against the Pagans," *Liturgy of the Hours*, Vol. III, 68 (italics added).

140. Stephen Hawking, *A Brief History of Time* (New York: Bantam Books, 1988), 1.

141. St. Augustine, *Confessions*, Book 11, Chapters 21, 22, 30.

142. Darwinism itself mutated when in 1901 Hugo de Vries, a Dutch botanist, inserted Mutation Theory, based on the earlier work on genetics (1866) by Gregor Mendel, an Augustinian monk.

143. Cited in Greene, 17.

144. Don Luigi Giussani, *Why the Church?* (Ithaca: McGill-Queen's University Press, 2001), 155.

145. Green, 385.

146. Robert Oerter, *The Theory of Almost Everything* (New York: Pi Press, 2006), 271. In his work as head of the Human Genome Project, Francis Collins moved from atheism to faith, a path narrated in *The Language of God: A Scientist Presents Evidence for Belief* (New York: Free Press, 2006). As head of the National Institute of Health, Collins as a man of faith has disappointed critics on one of the moral issues of our time, that of embryonic (fetal) versus adult stem cell research and treatments.

147. Ibid., 278, citing Frank Wilczek from a CERN talk (European Organization for Nuclear Research), October 11, 2000. CERN is the world's largest particle accelerator facility, in Geneva, Switzerland.

148. Attributed to Isaac Asimov in book reviews by Stratford Caldicott (ed.), *Second Spring*, XIII, (Merimack, N.N.: Thomas More College of Liberal Arts, 2011), 77.

149. St. Irenaeus, treatise Against Heresies, *Liturgy of the Hours*, Vol. I, 244.

150. Joseph Cardinal Ratzinger (Pope Benedict XVI), *Truth and Tolerance: Christian Belief and World Religions*, 226.

151. Pope Pius XI (1922–39) addresses modern efforts to reduce God to the level of nature. "Whoever identifies, by pantheistic confusion, God and the universe, by either lowering God to the dimensions of the world, or raising the world to the dimensions of God, is not a believer in God" (*Mit Brennender Sorge*, [With Deep Anxiety:

On the Present Position of the Catholic Church in the German Empire], March 14, 1937), in Anne Fremantle (ed.), *The Papal Encyclicals* (New York: Mentor-Omega, 1963), 214–220.

152. Boyce Rensberger, "Research Points to Descent from Shared Ancestor," Washington Post, May 26, 1995, summarizing Dorit, Gilbert and Hiroshi, in the journal *Science* (same date).

153. Thomas Maugh II, "Out of Africa: New Evidence One Woman is 'Mother of us All'," *Los Angeles Times*, October 5, 1989, summarizing molecular biologist Allan Wilson, University of California, at an international genetics conference.

154. Robert lee Hotz, "Neanderthals not Linked to Humans, says Study," (*Los Angeles Times*, July 11, 1997), summarizing a six year effort by German and United States researchers led by genetics expert Svante Paabo, University of Munich, to successfully extract DNA from a one hundred thousand year old Neanderthal bone (published in the journal *Cell*, July 11, 1997). Fleeting but possible inbreeding between Homo sapiens and Neanderthals leaves untouched the doctrine that the personal human soul comes directly from God.

155. Robert Boyd, "Scientists reject the Traditional Notion of Races," (*Knight-Ridder Newspapers*, Oct. 9, 1996). Cited sources are biologist Jonathon Marks (Yale University), ethnicist Michael Omi (University of California), geneticists Luigi Cavalli-Sforza (Stanford) and Kenneth Kidd (Yale), anthropologist Solomon Katz (University of Pennsylvania), and anthropologist Loring Brace (University of Michigan) who in 1996 was writing a book contending that intelligence is the only human trait that does not vary across populations (that IQ variances are due to social influences).

156. The scientific method is not questioned in the above discussion, only its occasionally artless application and interpretation. An analogous case is our scientific understanding of the Shroud of Turin, reputed by many as the burial cloth of Christ. In 1978 carbon 14 dating of a small segment established a discrediting fourteenth century date. In 2005, Ray Rogers, a member of the investigating team, demonstrated that the tested cloth samples came from an anomalous and interweaved patch. The carbon date is the average of older and original flax (linen)—possibly two thousand years old—and later interwoven strands of cotton from the sixteenth century.

157. A theme developed by Stratford Caldicott in "The Awakening of Space: An Introduction to Christopher Alexander," *Second Spring*, XIII (Merimack, N.H.: Thomas More College of the Liberal Arts, 2011), 36–45.

158. Todd Disotell, New York University Center for the Study of Human Origins, cited in "New Human Ancestor Found," *Los Angeles Times*, March 25, 2010. Historically, St. Augustine considered the evidence—the molar tooth of a mammoth that he had seen at Utica—and concluded that there had once been a race of giants. Anticipating modern science, he writes: "The real proof, as I have said, is to be found in the frequent discoveries of ancient bones of immense size, and this proof will hold good in centuries far in the future, since such bones do not easily decay" (*City of God*, Bk. XV, ch. 9).

159. Curtis Marean, "When the Sea Saved Humanity," *Atlantic Monthly* (August 2010), 55–61. Marean is a professor at the School of Human Evolution and Social Change at Arizona State University and a member of the Institute of Human Origins.

Independent research by archeologist Christopher Henshilwood, east of Cape Town, South Africa, has also uncovered "paint kits" dating back one hundred thousand years. This find "implies that people at the time had complex cognition . . . (and that they could) . . . multitask and think in abstract terms . . . they probably understood basic chemistry" (Brian Vastag, *Washington Times*, October 14, 2011).

160. Second Vatican Council, *Gaudium et Spes* (The Church in the Modern World), n. 24.

161. Ibid., n. 18. Thomas Henry Huxley, a disciple of Darwin, "asserted that human progress does not consist in imitating the cosmic process, still less in running away from it, but in combating it" (Lecture entitled "Evolution and Ethics," 1893, cited in Stephen F. Mason, A History of the Sciences [New York: Collier Books, 1962], 423).

162. International Theological Commission, op. cit., nn. 25, 64, 70. The term "ontological leap" appears earlier in John Paul II, "Message on Evolution to the Pontifical Academy of Sciences," (October 23, 1996) where he explicitly agrees that "the theory of evolutions is more than a hypothesis" (n. 4). He proposes that the ontological leap—"a moment of transition to the spiritual" and a discontinuity—is not incompatible to the "physical continuity which seems to be the main thread of research into evolution in the field of physics and chemistry" (n. 6). Of the scientific method, he writes: "The moment of transition to the spiritual cannot be the object of this kind of observation, which nevertheless can discover at the experimental level a series of very valuable signs indicating what is specific to the human being. But the experience of metaphysical knowledge, of self-awareness and self-reflection, of moral conscience, freedom, or again of aesthetic and religious experience, fall within the competence of philosophical analysis and reflection, while theology brings out its ultimate meaning according to the Creator's plans"(n. 6).

163. "Mental activity, consciousness, thought, is a special property of matter, but not a special kind of matter" (*Fundamentals of Marxism-Leninism* [Moscow: Foreign Languages Publishing House, 1961], 36).

164. John Paul II, op. cit., n. 5.

165. International Theological Commission, op. cit., nn. 25, 64, 65, 70.

166. Edith Stein (Waltraut Stein, trans.), *On the Problem of Empathy* (Washington D.C.: ICS Publications, 1989), 113, italics added.

167. Ibid., 96.

168. Joseph Ratzinger (Pope Benedict XVI), *On the Way to Jesus Christ* (San Francisco: Ignatius, 2005), 72, italics added.

169. Joseph Cardinal Ratzinger (Pope Benedict XVI), *Truth and Tolerance*, 181.

170. *New York Times Magazine*, April 24, 1955, cited in George Seldes, *The Great Quotations* (New York: Pocket Books, 1970), 610.

171. Jean Abele, S.J., *Christianity and Science*, Vol. 14 of the Twentieth Century Encyclopedia of Catholicism (New York: Hawthorne Books, 1961), 120 (italics added).

172. Joseph Pieper, *For the Love of Wisdom* (San Francisco: Ignatius, 2006), 156, italics added.

173. Muhammad Ali, 284.

174. St. Augustine, *The City of God*, Book III, Ch. 14.

175. David L. Schindler, *Heart of the World, Center of the Church: Communio Ecclesiology, Liberalism, and Liberation* (Grand Rapids, MI: William B. Eerdmans Pub. Co., 1997). 231, and passim.

176. St. Augustine in the fifth century said much the same without rupturing the human mind from God as a premise: "For if I am deceived, I am. For he who does not exist cannot be deceived. And if I am deceived, by this same token I am" (*City of God*, Book 11, Chapter 26).

177. See the Second Vatican Council, *Lumen Gentium* (Dogmatic Constitution on the Church), nn. 52–68. A tension within modern Catholic theology is whether *being* or action is primary, that is, whether the Marian "fiat"—that of a human nature that is also called—is the first assumption, or whether the starting point is first in the *doing* as is the accent allegedly placed by neo-conservatives on human creativity in exercising such virtues as civility, tolerance and pluralism. (Schindler, op. cit.., 103–4, and the entire text).

178. Muhammad Ali, op. cit., 184.

179. Hans Urs von Balthasar, *First Glance at Adrienne von Speyr* (San Francisco: Ignatius, 1981 [1968]), 90–94.

180. The view that Thomas Aquinas, speaking as a theologian, denied this later declaration of doctrine is questioned by John Eudes. Eudes appeals in part to early editions of Aquinas' *Summa*, in Vienna, Paris and other archives. (*The Admirable Infancy of the Most Holy Virgin Mother of God*, Vol. I [Waterford: James O'Neill, 1841], 56–60).

181. Edith Stein (Kurt Reinhardt, trans.), "The Interiority of the Soul" (Ch. 7), *Finite and Eternal Being*, (Washington, D.C.: ICS Publications, 2002), 437.

182. This typology is drawn from Thomas P. Neill (ed.), *The Building of the Human City* (Garden City: Doubleday Christendom Books, 1960), 81(fn. 28). As a theologian, Benedict XVI is known as an Augustinian more than a Thomist.

183. Jean Sassoon, *Princess Sultana's Circle* (Woodstock, New York: Windsor-Brooke Books, 2000), 247.

184. In the Western experience, Aristotle's *Active Reason* contrasts with the submission of the Stoics (Victor Watts in Boethius' *Consolation of Philosophy* [New York: Penguin, 1999 (1969)], 128, fn. 7). The seemingly slight difference between the *submission* of Islam and full and active surrender of Christianity (e.g., the "fiat" of Mary—"Be it done to me according to thy word") is the difference between the *Qur'an* and the incarnate Christ, the annual hejira and the Eucharistic presence, the hadith and the Two Great Commandments, the ummah and the entire Communion of Saints.

185. Fr. Simon Tugwell, O.P., *The Beatitudes: Soundings in Christian Traditions* (Springfield, Il.: Templegate Publishers, 1980), cited in *Magnificat* (Yonkers, New York: Magnificat, Feb. 2010), 389.

186. St. Athanasius, Easter Letter, in *Liturgy of the Hours*, Vol. II, 341.

187. This passage refers to Lydia. Commentary is provided in the *Navarre Bible*: Acts of the Apostles (Dublin, Ireland: Four Courts Press, 1992), 173.

188. Fulton J. Sheen in Jacques Jomier, *The Bible and the Qur'an* (San Francisco: Igantius Press, 1964), Appendix, 124.

189. Heer, *The Medieval World*, 145.

190. Bishop Sheen in Jomier, 123.

191. John Borelli, "Who is God for a Hindu, Buddhist or Muslim," *Origins* (22:44), (Washington, D.C.: Catholic News Service, April 15, 1993). The earlier pagan belief was that knowledge of the name of the deities conferred to the holder a power over them. This belief is traced to the earlier Chaldeans, and only then to the Egyptians, Assyrians, and later cabalist Jews, and Arabs (Francois Lenormant, *Chaldean Magic: Its Origin and Development* [London: Samuel Bagster and Sons, 1877], 42–4).

192. Title to Book XV, Chapter 6 in his *On the Trinity*.

193. From *An Essay in Aid of a Grammar of Assent* (London and New York: Longmans, Green, 1903 [IV:3]), cited in Vincent Ferrer Blehl, *The Essential Newman* (New York: Mentor-Omega, 1963), 297.

194. Hugo Rahner, S.J., *Our Lady and the Church* (Chicago: Henry Regnery Co., 1965), 46.

195. Joseph de Maistre, *On God and Society* (Chicago: Henry Regnery Co, 1959), fn. 13, 21.

196. Joseph Chalmers, Prior General, *Mary the Contemplative* (Roma: Edzioni Carmelitane, 2001), 7–8. Appendix One is the "Letter of His Holiness Pope John Paul II for the Carmelite Marian Year" in which he writes that the faithful should ". . . radiate in the world the presence of this Woman of silence and of prayer, who is invoked as the Mother of mercy, the Mother of hope and of grace" (85–8).

197. Hans Urs von Balthasar and Joseph Cardinal Ratzinger, *Mary: The Church at its Source* (San Francisco: Ignatius, 2005) 41.

198. John Paul II, *Redemptoris Mater* (Mother of the Redeemer), 1987, n.50, from the *Lumen Gentium* (Dogmatic Constitution on the Church), n. 69.

199. Joseph Cardinal Ratzinger (Pope Benedict XVI), *On the Way to Jesus Christ* (San Francisco: Ignatius Press, 2004), 36. In 1985 Ratzinger remarked: "A theologian who does not love art, poetry, music and nature can be dangerous. Blindness and deafness toward the beautiful are not incidental: they necessarily are reflected in his theology" (*The Ratzinger Report* [San Francisco: Ignatius, 1985], 130).

200. George Hourani (trans. and Introduction), *Averroes: On the Harmony of Religion and Philosophy, 1179–1180 A.D.* (London: Messrs, Luzac and Co., 1967 [1961], Introduction (39).

201. The verse most like Christian charity explicitly centered on God (if not on his love first for us) is probably this: "But it is righteousness—to believe in Allah . . . to spend of your substance, out of love for Him, for you kin, for orphans, for the needy, for the wayfarer, for those who ask, and for the ransom of slaves, to be steadfast in prayer, and practice regular charity . . ." (Q 2:177).

202. Ali, Abdullah Yusuf, *The Holy Qur'an: Text, Translation and Commentary*, Lahore, Pakistan: S.H. Muhammad Ashraf, 1983 (1938), Q 3:64, note 402. The commentator's reference to the "unity of the one true God" contests the core difference

between Islam and Christianity, the Trinitarian Oneness, with a pagan preconception: "How can he have a son when he hath no consort?" (Q 6:101).

203. John Paul II, *Crossing the Threshold of Hope* (New York: Alfred Knopf, 1994), 184.

204. St. Augustine, a treatise on John, in *Liturgy of the Hours*, Vol. II, 788.

205. Brant Pelphrey, *The Theology and Mysticism of Julian of Norwich* (Salzburg: The University of Salzburg, 1982), 64–5, italics added. The author contrasts *The Cloud of Unknowing* with Orthodox mystical celebration of the difference between the cloud of glory ever surrounding God (*shekinah* in the Old Testament) and His actual *essence* or being.

206. *Confession of Faith* (New York: Editions de la Maison Francais, 1941), re-printed in Joseph Evans and Leo Ward (eds.), *The Social and Political Philosophy of Jacques Maritain* (Garden City, New York: Image, 1965), 330.

207. In an oblique but clear comment, Pope Benedict XVI says that "There are certain religious cultures in the world today that do not oblige men and women to live in communion, but rather cut them off from one another in a search for individual well-being, limited to the gratification of psychological desires" (*Caritas in Veritae* [Charity and Truth: On Integral Human Development], June 29, 2009, n. 55).

208. Daniel Madigan, citation from "A Common Word," Section III, repeated in "Some Initial Reflections," www.acommonword.com.

209. *Declaration with Annex*, The Lutheran World Federation and the Roman Catholic Church, English Language Edition (Grand Rapids, Michigan: Wm. B. Eerd-mans Pub. Co., 2000). In point of fact, the *Declaration* tracks very closely with the Tridentine lessons the sixteenth century St. Francis de Sales on the relation between free will and grace, that good works are gifts of grace and that eternal life is a grace and a reward. Of works, he that "...the Catholic Church teaches at the same time, that these good Works are the Gifts of God, that we do nothing of ourselves, but can do all in him who strengthens us, and that our whole Confidence ought to center in Jesus Christ" (in Mons. Marsollier, *The Life of St. Francis de Sales* (London: Thomas Meighon, 1737), Vol. 1, 170–171.

210. "Therefore we love God and our neighbor from one and the same love; but we love God for the sake of God, and ourselves and our neighbors for the sake of God" (St. Augustine, *On the Trinity*, Book X, Ch. 8).

211. In his commentary on the Wedding Feast at Cana, Luther sermonized that "It is honorable to the matrimonial state, that Christ himself goes to the marriage with his mother and his disciples, and in addition becomes the chief cup-bearer to the bride. Since Christ honors and encourages marriage, it follows that every one should regard it favorably and commendable, and let the heart be cheerful, because it is certain that God loves this state, and we should cheerfully endure what ever may be hard to bear therein" (E. Mueller, trans. by P. Anstadt, *Luther's Explanatory Notes on the Gospels* (York, Penn.: P. Anstadt and Sons, 1899), 281.

212. If not from the *Qur'an* or the hadith, this statement might illustrate the self-authorizing quality (and opportunism) of the *Qur'an* to move with Allah's gift of "writing" and "rewriting" the book through continuous revelation, in response to ever new circumstances. On the theory of continuous revelation under Islam see Daniel

Madigan, *The Qur'an's Self-Image: Writing and Authority in Islam's Scriptures* (Princeton, N. J.: Princeton, 2001). A less sympathetic interpretation, recalling the profusion of prophets claimed throughout early Arabian history (remarks from T.E. Lawrence, Chapter 2), would stress the similarity between exclusive confidence in ongoing inspiration (and fatwas) and the Western excess termed "fideism," defined as (over)reliance on faith rather than reason.

213. Eileen Egan, *Such a Vision of the Street: Mother Teresa—The Spirit and the Work* (Garden City, New York: Doubleday, 1985), 357.

214. Max Weber, *The Protestant Ethic and the Spirit of Capitalism* (1904–5). For an assessment see Robert W. Green (ed.), *Protestantism and Capitalism: The Weber Thesis and Its Critics* (Boston: D.C. Heath and Co., 1959).

215. For the Catholic, "Faith is the theological virtue by which we believe in God and believe all that he has said and revealed to us, and that the Holy Church proposes for our belief, *because he is truth itself . . .*" (*Catechism of the Catholic Church*, n. 1814, italics added).

216. "'The obedience of faith' (Rom 16:26; cf. 1:5; 2 Cor. 10:5–6) must be given to God who reveals, an obedience by which man entrusts his whole self freely to God, offering 'the full submission of intellect and will to God who reveals,' and freely assenting to the truth revealed by Him" (*Dei Verbum* [Divine Revelation], n. 5).

217. Josef Cardinal Ratzinger (Pope Benedict XVI*), Introduction to Christianity* (San Francisco: Ignatius, 2004 [1968]), 142.

218. "Joint Declaration of the Pontifical Council for Interreligious Dialogue (Vatican) and the Center for Interreligious Dialogue of the Islamic Culture and Relations Organization" (April 28–30).

219. See www/vatican.va/roman_curia/pontifical_councils/interelg/documents/. St. Paul invites us "to know the love of Christ that surpasses knowledge..." (Eph 3:19).

220. Ibid.

221. Catholic-Muslim Forum, reported in *Catholic Northwest Progress*, (Seattle: Archdiocese of Seattle, November 13, 2008).

222. Jean-Pierre de Caussade, *Abandonment to Divine Providence* (New York: Image, 1975), 14.

223. Aquinas comments: "It is therefore evident that the model for human virtue pre-exists in God, and the reasons for all things pre-exist in him . . . It belongs to man to draw as close to the divine as he can, as even the Philosopher (Aristotle) says and as is recommended to us in Sacred Scripture in various ways:" (citation of Matt 5:48). From the *Summa theologicae*, in Jean-Pierre Torrell, *Saint Thomas Aquinas,* Vol. II (Washington, D.C., Catholic University of America, 2007), 114.

224. Max Eastman, *Reflections on the Failure of Socialism* (New York: Devin-Adair, 1955), in William F. Buckley (ed.), *American Conservative Thought in the Twentieth Century* (New York: The Bobbs-Merrill Co., 1970), 203.

225. Joseph Cardinal Ratzinger (Pope Benedict XVI), *Truth and Tolerance*, 170.

226. In his critique of political power Bertrand de Jouvenel gives us almost Islamic imagery: "we human beings are not...equal to the task of evolving a bubbling stream of ever new verities. Ideas are, truly, like infrequent oases in the barren wastes of human

thought; once discovered, they are for ever precious, even though they are left to be silted up by the sands of stupidity and ignorance" (*On Power: Its Nature and the History of its Growth* [Boston: Beacon Press, 1962], 314).

227. Cited in Luigi Giussani, *The Religious Sense* (San Francisco: Ignatius Press, 1990), 124. In the judicial logic of today, with the application of science accountable to only its own method, the heads of half-born children are punctured with scissors in the process of late term abortions.

228. C.S.Lewis, *Surprised by Joy*, 167.

229. Gabriele Amorth, *The Gospel of Mary—A Month with the Mother of God,* (Staten Island: Alba House, 2000), cited in *Magnificat* (New York: Magnificat, Dec. 2008, 141).

Chapter Six

Present to the Presence

In Istanbul in late 2006, Pope Benedict XVI stood alongside others in Santa Sofia. This is the Church of the Holy Wisdom, later converted to a Mosque under Islamic rule, and now a public museum. Elevating this secular space, he offered a personal prayer in silence. Is it in such a shared silence, deeper even than any forum of mere civility, that whole persons might fully find each other and a God who is both above and within? And might such a discovery of deepened respect render to one another an inner and sacred space that is also free to act in the public forum?

Dialogue that is faithful is not a facile merger between a "community of religions" under Islamic initiative as a theological contract with the Western "social contract" of Locke or Rousseau. It is difficult to comprehend two such worldviews in a resolved symbiosis of civility, the theological and the secular. The community of religions asserts that as human expressions all religions are imperfect versions of Islam as the original religion, while the social contract of a too-secularized natural law presumes that religion is as marginalized in other societies as it is today in the West. Pragmatism is called upon to bridge the gap when the pre-requisite mutual respect of a deeper and universal natural law, a law accessible to all, would better serve all. The natural law is in eclipse in the West, and in the world of Islam is encumbered by the historical and cultural accretions, particularly the unitary Islamic State and the historical insularity of dar al-Islam relative to infidels.

Secularism today sees little distinction between matter and spirit, with spirit being part of the history of matter and fully explained by science. This modern discovery is actually ancient and pantheistic Monism is new garb. Islam holds the opposite view that all things remain within the oneness of God, including the Islamic State. But, outside of these bookends is the thinking of St. Augustine who defends and examines human consciousness in its own right. Given as a concrete *start point*—both revealed and knowable by use of reason—is the dignity of concrete (and transcendent) human persons, all persons without exception. Of the human person and human consciousness, St. Augustine reminds us that beyond the *intellect* and its tension between faith and reason there are two additional dimensions of consciousness to which we might appeal as openings for broadened dialogue. These faculties are the *memory* as the place within ourselves where we find reasoning, and then *free will*.[1] Augustine is often falsely credited with a misleading parallelism between intellect, memory and will, and the triune nature of God. Groeschel explains that these faculties are not equal nor even distinct, stressing that they are "different functions of the same psyche."[2] Where the crisis of Islam is merely extended by asserting itself as a common ground, the crisis of modernity is the tri-furcation of the integrated human psyche. Intellect becomes rationalism devoid of faith, and the will becomes the politics of interests and power, and memory becomes identity politics.

The three faculties of intellect, will and memory offer ground for future dialogue with Islam, and within the Church, the West, and Islam. Based on passages cited from the *Qur'an,* the Muslim "Common Word Between Us" (2007) includes the remark that "souls are depicted in the Holy *Qur'an* as having three main faculties: the mind or the intelligence . . . the will . . . and sentiment which is made for loving the good and the beautiful. Put in another way, we could say that man's soul knows through *understanding* the truth, through *willing* the good, and through virtuous emotions and *feeling* love for God" (italics in the original). While there is significant overlap between Augustine and this recent Muslim statement on the faculties of intellect and will, the initial divergence is between memory and the different and more open ended Muslim listing of love as a sentiment and a feeling love for God. In Christian theology charity is a theological virtue that may or may not include the feelings of natural religion.

MORE THAN FAITH AND REASON

The enduring genius of Augustine was to discover lurking within the fractured intellect another injury of the soul running at least as deep as the split between faith and reason. From his own memory and experience Augustine points to a "sickness of the mind" itself, in the unresolved tension between *two wills*, one toward the truth and the other still bound by habit.[3] For him, the thrust of history is less the question "what do we know" than it is "what do we want." In his *City of God,* Augustine views all of history as the byproduct of the divided heart, the difference between belonging truly and our too often wayward longings. This potential division between communion and experience applies equally at the personal level.

Human nature and its natural law, deeper than the heart's divisions, are discovered directly in the human mind and heart as well as in the Christian scripture (Rom 2: 15–16). In Islam, any such scriptural openings toward natural law are highly tenuous at best, but Hassan and other Muslim scholars point to verses in the *Qur'an* that can be read as validating or at least pointing to or seizing the natural law (Chapter 3). An offsetting verse reasserts divine arbitrariness toward each of us in particular: "We created them, and endowed their limbs and joints with strength; but if We please, We can replace them by other men" (Q 76:22)—almost as if drawing from a harem of options. Such an arbitrary worldview toward the personhood of man matches poorly with the Christian understanding of the fatherhood of God. In this apparently indifferent Muslim theology of people as finally equal and interchangeable parts—as in the modern view of man as equal and not at the same time different—each human person as a unique bearer of the natural law becomes less than a special event deserving respect and freedom.

The Second Vatican Council finds that each person is in fact a unique event. Man (male and female) "is the only creature on earth which God has willed for itself," and the nature of man is to find himself only by making a "sincere gift of himself."[4] A Carmelite contemplative connects the theological virtues to Augustine's three natural faculties (intellect, memory and will) of the gifted human person: "Starting with the principle that the theological virtues are engrafted in the natural faculties—faith in the intellect; charity in the will, hope in the imagination and the memory—St. John of the Cross teaches us to discipline the natural faculties by exercising the theological virtues that correspond to them."[5] This is the discipline of the new life that perfects nature from within, instead of being added to it, and that help define morally grounded social principles for personal encounter and engagement in the world (Chapter 4).

We are moved beyond—in the sense of further into—the Old Testament and the "discipline" of the law borrowed into the *Qur'an* (Q:2:46). Influenced by the Medieval drama contained of his Spanish landscape, Miguel Unamuno did not reason his path into faith. Instead he backed into the new life first of *hope* by outgrowing a gnawing skepticism nearing despair. His hope is not for a past golden age or a possible future utopia, because it is a theological hope that is not of this world. His are not the words of a cloistered Medieval theologian scholasticism. As a possible intercultural pathway, Unamuno's thought can speak to Muslims who still feel the rumbling echoes of seven hundred years from the intercultural Moorish landscape: "To believe in God is to long for His existence and, further, it is to act as if He existed; it is to live by this longing and to make it the inner spring of our action. *This longing or hunger for divinity begets hope, hope begets faith, and faith and hope beget charity. Of this divine longing is born our sense of beauty, of finality, of goodness"* (italics added).[6] Rather than possibly a disguised prod for Christians to live up to Gospel values, the request to discuss the Two Great Commandments might be a path toward hope for the Islamic world as well as the West, and faith joined to expectation.

St. Augustine was the first to wonder deeply about charity as the fit between grace and free will. Just as some Lutheran ecumenists again point to Augustine as a promising contact point for Catholic-Lutheran dialogue,[7] Augustine's attention to intellect, memory and will—more than just faith and reason— might also serve as an interreligious bridge between Christians and the followers of Islam. Augustine is not part of interreligious thought with Islam as he is ecumenically with the Lutheran tradition, but by birth he is North African rather than European. He defended the local Punic language against charges from the Latin world that this tongue was barbaric. Before the time of St. Augustine the demoralized local populations under Roman rule found some relief in Christianity much as the Arabians tribes later found in Islam relief from Byzantine rule.

The mentor of Thomas Aquinas, St. Albert (1206–1280), saw in Augustine's thought a latent link between the human and the more than human: "The image of God which is imprinted upon the soul is found in the three powers of the reason, memory, and will. But (he adds) since these do not perfectly bear the divine likeness, they have not the same resemblance to God as in the first days of man's creation."[8] St. Paul reminds us of the reason for our faith, "if the dead are not raised, then Christ was not raised; and if Christ was not raised, your faith is worthless" (1 Cor 15:16–17). But St. Peter then goes on to counsel us on the tie between our hope and our faith "without seeing you now believe in him, and rejoice with inexpressible joy touched with glory because you are achieving faith's goal, your salvation" (1 Pe 1:8–9). And even he, at the very beginning of the Christian mission, ties reason to hope: "Should anyone ask you for the reason for this hope of yours, be ever ready to reply . . ." (1 Pe 3:15). The late Luigi Giussani encourages us that "if faith is to recognize a Presence that is certain, if faith is to recognize a Presence with certainty, hope is to recognize a certainty for the future that is born in this Presence."[9]

Toning down the place of grace gratuitously given, Islam as a more natural religion holds back with submission. Islam insists that the disobedience of man was healed not by redemption, but by guidance on the straight path of Islam, or knowledge, given from very near the beginning (St. Albert's "first days of creation"). The Christian revelation opens us to a higher key, holding that *because* of the radical denial contained in radical evil, healing can come only through the Incarnation of the divine into the human. Redemption requires a response given less as a horizontal dialectic between forgetting and submissive remembering, but vertically between the depth of our being and the forgetful wisdom of God. It is in this realm of gifted freedom that the Christian finds himself created in His image.

INTELLECT AND FAITH

The *Qur'an* asserts that in the Bible Christians have edited into idolatry the more original religion of Islam. Christian apologists proclaim the one God, and in addition the revelation of his interior life in the incarnate Christ. The Islamic focus on the total transcendence of God is already very much part of the earlier Christian vision. This powerful intuition also dominates the theology of twentieth century Karl Barth, the "leap of faith" of the earlier Soren Kierkegaard, and even the touchstone theology of Martin Luther (1483–1546) with his aversion for the rationalism and corruption of Renaissance Europe south of the Alps.[10] But under Islamic belief attention to the oneness of God is so focused and even fixated that it excludes even the possibility of the incarnation of the Word. The Muslims turn to Arabic words assembled into the *Qur'an,* while the Christian finds new life in the words and deeds of "the Word made flesh" (1 Jn 1:14). The Christian intellect is neither subservient nor autonomous, nor cerebral alone: "We fail to realize that he who seeks to see Christ should look not outside himself, but within himself, emulating Christ's life in the world, and becoming sinless in body and mind, as Christ was. His intellect should apprehend everything through Christ."[11]

How are we to understand the easy path of ambiguity with Islam served up by a Dutch bishop? This bishop predicts that within a century or two, Dutch Catholics will address their prayers not to a Father but to "Allah." In a country that is now home to one million Muslims, he simply finds that "God doesn't really care how we address him."[12] Is he quoted out of context? The term Allah already was used by Arab Jews and by Christians even before the coming of Islam.[13] In Aramaic the term is "Elaha," and in Hebrew "Elohim." But even if the term "Allah" is more original to Judaism and Christianity that it is to later Islam, what does this statement on its face really mean *today*? Pragmatism is not sufficient to smooth over the non-symmetrical differences between Islam and Christianity. While an understanding of the Trinity does not compromise the oneness of God treasured by Muslims, the Islamic understanding of oneness deletes any understanding of the Trinity and of the Christ event in human history. For resident Christians the ideology of the Islamic State renders this difference more than academic.

In Malaysia a dispute arose in 2009 over the Christian use of the term "Allah." One allegation is that broad usage would be confusing to Muslims. In a global setting is it not likely that the greater confusion will be for poorly formed Christians battered by multicultural ideology? Monsignor Lorenzo Albacete, National Spiritual Advisory for the Communion and Liberation Movement, gives us this: "It is not enough to say that Jesus is the name we give to the Truth. Jesus is the man who is the incarnation of the Truth."[14] If God calls each of us by name, must we not return this degree of recognition? More than a name, given to us through this name is the Word which is Jesus Christ. Does Trinitarian revelation matter to the God who so reveals his interior life by sharing himself with us even to the point of embracing our humanity from Golgotha?

In his analysis of St. Augustine's understanding of the Triune presence, one historian sees a lesson capable of being lost even by some bishops as in Arian times: "For, in the Trinity, he (Augustine) discovered a principle capable of saving the reason as well as the will, and thus redeeming the human personality as a whole. It saved reason because, while denying its pretensions to omniscience and infallibility, it nevertheless affirmed the existence of an order of truth and value which, *being in the world as well as beyond it*, was within the power of many to apprehend. And, in saving the reason, at the same time it saved the will, by imparting to it that element of rationality without which it must degenerate into mere subjective willfulness."[15]

What we call God matters not only because it does affect the content of faith, but also and inseparably it affects the reason and the will. Reason involves a complex of intelligence, decision and experience of the entire person past and future, especially as we deal with the data in history narrating the words and deeds of the Christ of the Trinity. Reason is "man's defense against obscurantism and fanaticism, and the empirical base by which men intend to name the hidden and (strictly) inconceivable God."[16] Benedict reminds us that faith "is not a mere construct of human thought," but rather a gift given in proportion to our readiness to receive it, and that "because the goal is the correct apprehension of God's Word, however, and distinguishing it from mere human words, we cannot leave God out of account here."[17] Might it actually matter to the crucified Lord what *we* call Him or, possibly, to whom we are calling?

Not hearing clearly of the Incarnation and dismissing the biblical witness, Islam restores a more distancing and even pre-Christian premise that "that God alone is God." The revealed inner life of God is collapsed into a monolith a bit like the symbolic black stone housed from ancient times in the Ka'ba of Mecca. But from St. Paul, we discover that already within each of us is no longer a heart of stone but the universal natural law (Rom 2:14–15), and that we are temples of the Holy Spirit (1 Cor 3:16). God alone is God, but He also dwells within as the divine gift of self who walked with us on the Road to Emmaus (Lk 24:13–35). The Trinitarian God is the Lord above, with, within us. Given our monotheism, in both Christianity and Islam (and Judaism), is there not also an expansive difference between the transcendent "Allah" (God is one) and the God who enters our history as "Emmanuel" (God is with us)?

Christians and Muslims differ on the historical record. The Muslim scholar Ayoub questions the biblical accounts on several points. He even tenders the notion that the *Qur'an* and Muslim traditionalists were not even aware or influenced by theological doctrines of the Church Fathers and Church councils. Yet he also suggests that at the time of his visions, Mohammed's wife of twenty-five years, Khadijha, might have been Christian. Based on Muslim commentators, Ayoub proposes that the unique place given to St. Paul in Christian history is overstated. He claims St. Paul was not an apostle in his own right, but instead was first held for a year in a sanctuary and schooled in the Gospel before preaching, and before departing for Jerusalem.[18] This is a reference to his later one-year stay in Antioch (Acts 11:26), a church founded by Peter and the city where the followers of Christ were first called "Christians."

Medieval western commentators discounted Mohammed's visions in the same way. They held that the Jewish and Christian elements of Mohammed's revelations at Mt. Hira (610–612) were actually the benefit of earthly tutoring that he allegedly received in secret from itinerate Jews and Christians. The Muslim view of St. Paul could be a rebuttal nearly a millennium out of date and attached to Western prejudices now long forgotten. Preceding the oral teachings and liturgical experiences shared with him at Antioch, St. Paul recounts his powerfully compact revelation of the resurrected Christ and his mystical body the Church, on the Road to Damascus (Acts 9:3–19; 22:6–16; 26:12–18).

Paul eventually becomes the apostle to the Gentiles. Private visions continued and he was "snatched up to Paradise" (2 Cor 12:2–4). Paul himself reports that "without seeking human advisers," he initially did stay "some days with the disciples in Damascus," but then preached independently another three years in Arabia and Damascus before spending a short fifteen days with Peter in Jerusalem (Acts 9:26–30, and Gal 1:11–24). "I did not meet any other apostles (reports Paul) except James . . ." (Gal 1:19) and John (Gal 2:9). Fourteen years after his first visit to Jerusalem, Paul returned to again verified with the other apostles his teachings now to the Gentiles (Gal 2:1–2, 7–10).

During his brief visit in Jerusalem Paul eventually confirmed his message with the already established "tradition." This tradition is the teaching of the

crucifixion and resurrection, and regarding the Eucharist with its place as the
"center of the Church's life" (2 Cor 5:21, 8:9; 1 Cor 15:3–4; 1 Cor 11:23–25,
12:27).[19] In his letter to the Galatians, Paul is most clear about both the tradition of the historical Jesus and about his own distinct calling: "Now I want
you to know, brothers, that the gospel preached by me is not of human origin.
For I did not receive it from a human being, nor was I taught it, but it came
through a revelation of Jesus Christ" (Gal 1:11–12).

Ayoub appears to hold that even St. Paul taught that Jesus was God *rather
than* man. This is the Monophysitism notion, part of that complex of Christian heresies addressed in the first series of seven Church councils, specifically the Council of Chalcedon in 451. More than a century before the coming
of Mohammed, Monophysitism had already made its way into Arabia under
the protection of the Byzantine Empress Theodora (d. 548). Ayoub goes on
to recount a view found among only a few Islamic scholars that St. Paul said,
"I saw Jesus in a dream, and he was pleased with me, I shall therefore sacrifice myself for his pleasure" and then slew himself on the altar. This very
minority commentary is also used to "explain(s) the origin of the three major
Eastern Christian sects: the Jacobites, Nestorians, and Melkites." These sects
are inventively traced back to three emissaries whom Paul is said to have
dispatched in his name. But Western history records the much later origins
of the named sects.[20] And we know from his letters in the Bible, that St. Paul
had more than a dream: "A light from the sky suddenly flashed about him
. . . "Saul, Saul, why to you persecute me? . . . I am Jesus, the one you are
persecuting" (Acts 9:4). It is the very self of Christ who is persecuted *in His
witnesses* as the Mystical Body extending even to the present, his persecuted
Church. One reason why Muslim commentators would propose that St. Paul
killed himself might be the earlier and offensive and discredited Western
speculation that Mohammed committed suicide.

The Christian reader wonders why the Apostle Paul must be singled out by
Islam and discredited? Is it so that a later Arabian messenger for monotheism
and a new or restored way of life can escape possible redundancy with the
earlier Apostle to the Gentiles and to Arabia? As the final Prophet, Mohammed is repeatedly identified in the *Qur'an* as the (final) Apostle (2:104, 4:46,
48:12, 13, 27, 28). Is Paul disliked because he raises a doubt about angelic
visions, warning that Satan can "masquerade an angel of light" in order to
deceive (2 Cor 11:14), and because he calls upon the intellect to distinguish
between gifts of the Spirit and demonic fantasies? Or is it because St. Paul
taught that while the core of the old Law is fulfilled in Christ, the Law is at the
same time replaced by Christ and his sending of the Holy Spirit into history
and His people? "*In the past* God spoke to our fathers through the prophets
in various ways and manners, *but now in our times*, the last days, he has spo-

ken to us in his Son" (Heb 1:3, italics added). As part of Islam's ambiguous respect and deconstruction of Christian narrative, Christ's references to the coming of the eternal Comforter are also recast in the *Qur'an*. The Holy Spirit who, according to the gospels, "will guide you in all truth" (Jn 16:12–13, 17) is in the *Qur'an*, "intended to betoken the Promised one . . . the Holy Prophet Mohammed," after whom there would be no future prophet (Q 33:40).[21]

Is St. Paul discredited because he says of the Gentiles: "They show the work of the Law written in their hearts," (Rom 2:14–15)? In this way he locates natural law—part of divine law—as something already universally inborn rather than as accessible only through a final messenger in the *Qur'an*. Having preceded Mohammed by six centuries in pagan Arabia and elsewhere, St. Paul already confronts the polytheism of the classical and pagan worlds: "Men of Athens, I note that in every respect you are scrupulously religious. As I walked around looking at your shrines, I even discovered an altar inscribed, "To a God Unknown. Now, what you are thus worshiping in ignorance" I intend to make known to you . . . In him we live and move and have our being (Acts 17:22–23, 28). And then in his writings, "It pleased God to make absolute fullness reside in him . . . making peace through the blood of his cross" (Col 1:19–20).

Muslim attention to Paul is probably because the "new life" of love that he proclaims not only restores, but illumines the preparatory law of Moses: "It is no longer I who live, but Christ who lives in me" (Gal 2:20). Of the commandments, Paul proclaims: "'You shall not commit adultery; you shall not kill; you shall not steal; you shall not covet,' and whatever other commandment there may be, are summed up in this saying, (namely) 'You shall love your neighbor as yourself.' Love does no evil to the neighbor; hence love is the fulfillment of the law" (Rom 13:9–10). More than a messenger of guidance restored, Paul is an apostle of redemption and beatitude as well. In this light, Islam is sometimes seen as a natural religion because transgressions of the law come mingled alongside prayer and devotion. The early Arabian cult of multiple wives and concubines is permitted to blur the more transforming message of salvation and resurrection. St. Paul, on the other hand, forces a clear choice between the old life and redemption (e.g., Rom 8:5–13, 1 Cor 6:9–11, 18–20). He insists that "There is neither Jew nor Greek, there is neither slave nor free person, there is not male and female, for you are all one in Christ Jesus" (Gal 3:38). St. Paul would allow no more space for Mohammed's alloy of "fragrance (perfume), women and prayer"[22] than for the pre-Christian or post-Christian paganism of "wine, women and song"(e.g., 1 Cor 6:9–11) and such Western episodes as America's ante-bellum trio of aristocracy, slave sex and King Cotton. St. Paul confronts the dark side of modernity in any age—the posturing to validate both halves of our double lives, whether in the ancient world, the seventh century, or the twenty-first.

The more accommodating *Qur'an* is made equivalent to the clearly new life in Christ—the transforming fulfillment of the law. Islam substitutes Mohammed for the Apostles and all of those disciples who received the Holy Spirit from Christ at Pentecost. Unlike Mohammed who assembles the collective ummah around his unique visit to heaven, the Holy Spirit at Pentecost descends sacramentally from the oneness of the Trinity to all those witnesses to Christ who are the Church. This "universal call to holiness"—this spiritual democracy—is grounded in the natural law and authentic humility, and supplies a theological basis for political democracy in the world. The common good can be well served directly by those who carry within themselves the freedom and the responsibility to respect others as they do themselves.

For Mohammed the followers of Abraham are the descendents of Ishmael, while Paul preaches Christ even to the Gentiles. St. Paul held that it is no longer ethnic descent, but rather "it is those who have faith who are children of Abraham" (Gal 3:7). Like the later Mohammed, St. Paul notices the transgressions of Israel as with the golden calf at the foot of Mount Sinai. But rather than re-establishing the lost covenant with Abraham, St. Paul interprets the Law as a phase within an unbroken covenant: "the gifts and the call of God are irrevocable" (Rom 11–29). In Christ and his Church the promise to Abraham is fulfilled: "This is what I mean: the law, which came four hundred and thirty years afterward, does not annul a covenant previously ratified by God, so as to make the promise void" (Gal 3:17). Paul asks, "Why the law?" The answer: "It was added because of the transgressions till the offspring (meaning Christ) should come to whom the promise had been made (meaning Abraham) . . ." (Gal 3:19).

Historians find a similarity between Paul and Mohammed at least as messengers, even a redundancy, but the difference is still much greater. Like Mohammed, Paul was in Arabia, but rather than living any law, Christ *is* the law of the new life living in Paul (Gal 2:20). Of himself, the Arab Muslim finds that he is living in God, although a non-Trinitarian Allah. He "Could not look for God within him; he was too sure that he was within God. He could not conceive anything which was or was not God, Who alone was great . . ."[23] Where Mohammed upholds the Law and affirms that "there is no God but Allah, and Mohammed is his prophet," Paul said instead: "there is one God, the Father, from whom all things are and for whom we exist, and one Lord, Jesus Christ, through whom all things are and through whom we exist" (I Cor 8:6). Under Islam we live in God, and following St. Paul we both live in God and He lives in us.

In his Letter to the Galatians St. Paul finally contrasts slavery under the Law with this new freedom of Christ. Through allegory he identifies Hagar and Ishmael with slavery under the Law (Gal 4:21). These figures are known by

Mohammed as the ancestors of his tribes and are selected as the touchstone of Islam. Paul quotes the Torah, and then gives an update, "'Drive out the slave woman and her son! For the son of the slave woman shall not share the inheritance with the son' of the freeborn' . . . Therefore, brothers, we are children not of the slave woman but of the freeborn woman" (Gal 4:30b, 31c). An ironic parallel within Islam is that Mohammed's only possible surviving son, the son of the Coptic slave girl Mariya, was driven out of Arabia by Mohammed's surviving favorite wife A'isha.[24] Hagar and Ishmael suffered an identical fate respectively at the hands of Abraham and at the demand of Sarah. Ishmael later returned to join Isaac in burying their father Abraham (Gen 25:9).

Paul preaches a law of freedom unscripted by legalistic Phariseeism: "Through Christ we have full confidence in God, who has made us suitable ministers of his new covenant, *not of a written code* but in the Spirit" (2 Cor 3:4, italics added). The direct contact point with Islam is that the *promise* made to Abraham is to be found fulfilled in the Word made flesh, not simply restored in the *Qur'an*, the claimed Word made book. The *Qur'an* divides both the Torah and Christ from Abraham our father in faith: "Say: People of the Book, let us come to an agreement: that we will worship none but God . . . why do you argue about Abraham when both the Torah and the Gospel were not revealed till after him. Have you no sense?" (Q 3:62–5) Ayoub reminds us that Christ is very highly esteemed in Islam: "The assertion that early Christians were actually Muslims reflects, first, the high place that Christ occupies in Muslim faith and piety and, second, the persistent belief that Christianity is essentially a true religion."[25] Christianity is viewed as a distorted member of the Muslim family and only in this sense "essentially a true religion."

Muslim scholars often apply their own reasoning about the Bible not to terms used in this scripture, but instead to only roughly equivalent Arabic terms found in the *Qur'an,* a book written six centuries later. In his consistently very informative and candid articles, Ayoub cites other Muslim commentators (e.g., Rashid Rida, d. 1935) on the meaning of such Qur'anic terms *ibn* and *walad–Ibn* which means "son" and *walad* which means "offspring." This oblique approach of parsing Arabic words introduces a recurring layer of confusion for Muslims on the essentials of Western thought and of Christianity regarding the Trinity and the divinity of Christ.[26] The Western distinction between words and concepts renders it a fallacy to substitute words for concepts and then to appeal to the often ambiguous meaning of such words. In the realm of religious creed, conceptual propositions such as the Trinity are equally removed from such substitutions of concepts with vocabulary even in the same language.

But Muslim commentators also draw from nominally "Christian thinkers who have rationally rejected the Trinity."[27] This reference applies to the many creedal propositions being tested against the Christian tradition in the eastern Mediterranean in the time of Mohammed, but more likely to eighteenth century Deists and to Unitarians in the nineteenth century. The Deists, analogous to Mohammed, saw themselves not as transforming Christianity, but as restoring an original Christianity with Christ as a philosopher, "before its corruption by St Paul, the Fathers and the Councils."[28] Despite the irreducible difference between Trinitarian Christianity and all forms of Deism, a promising path of personal engagement between Christianity and Islam today might be to draw upon individual mystics from each tradition (see Chapter 5). On this path we can be encouraged by an account of a recent mystic in post-Confucian culture. The collapse of Confucianism in China was replaced only superficially by Marxism-Leninism-Mao Zedong, and spiritually today China is in "something of a free-for-all."[29] In this Chinese case the harmony between personal paths was so compelling that a reading of the autobiographical *Story of a Soul* by Therese of Lisieux (1873–1897) converted a prominent Chinese mystic to Christianity.[30] Lindblom recounts how the Chinese convert John C. Wu (1899–1986), an influential modern thinker and writer, found Christianity to be the transforming fulfillment of all that is best in the ancient religions of the East.[31]

Might it be that Therese, patron saint of missions, offers a hint for some inquiring twenty-first century followers of Islam? Might Therese be a path that strengthens and then releases rather than undermines traditional belief in Islamic submission? Like Islam, the message of Therese is a radically simple one. The small but telling difference with St. Therese is the difference between submission to the *Qur'an* and the Mary-like encounter and surrender to the person of Christ. With Mary, surrender is less a matter of submitting than of a loving "obedience." Therese defines her "Little Way" toward a self-donating and infinitely inviting God in these words: "It is the way of spiritual childhood, the way of trust and absolute surrender."[32] A historical comparison between Theresian spirituality and the mystical spirituality of selected Muslims might begin by noticing the influence on Therese of the Jesuit Jean-Pierre de Caussade.[33] Caussade's core message is the reality of the "sacrament of the present moment" as a rich path to God through ordinary things. The followers of Islam claim to reverence all of existence in somewhat the same way, as a succession of divine interventions not fully explicable by any laws of nature.

On the matter of faith and intellect, we have not yet heard from our rationalist brethren and their belief in dis-belief, the *de facto* "religion" of modernity in its atheist or agnostic variations. What do the believers in suspended belief—or possibly the ascedia of willing disbelief—think about any fit between the human intellect and faith? The pre-rational religious mind is often faulted for muddling man and God in the person of Christ, or muddling the Mosque and state under Islam, or muddling faith and reason in a confused and archaic bundle. Confidence is better deserved by the irreversible breakthrough the scientific method. Truth is quantifiable and resides in demonstrable results capable of being repeated under controlled conditions. Learning of this type is cumulative, progressive, and advanced by an interplay between verifiable knowledge and imagination. Within the modern sciences, Isaac Newton was correct in 1676 when he announced, "If I have seen further it is by standing on the shoulders of giants."[34]

The religious believer simply suspects that this understanding on one plane does not disprove truths found by thinking on more than one plane. By itself the scientific method yields a low ceiling universe. The finite is measured against the infinite, but the infinite is not necessarily material. Like Newton the Christian also rests on the shoulders of others—the books of the Old Testament and then the person of Christ (Lk 15:1–7, Jn 10:3–18). Were the wise men of the east necessarily mistaken to look "further," in an ever new way? They found God in a manger . . . surprisingly very nearby *beneath* his stars and constellations.

Even today, Aquinas would have us see our intellects as involving not only evidence, but always internal *judgments* about bundles of evidence. Eras of theology, metaphysics, and then physics do not necessarily cancel each other in history one after the other, the regnant ideology first advanced by the French mathematician and philosopher August Comte (1798–1857). Measurement is not the only self-evident first principle nor is it the whole of reason, and reason is not the sum total of the intellect. For Aquinas, neither inductive nor deductive ways of reasoning are directly data driven, but are judgmental acts of composition and division. As a building block, a brick is not completely a brick until it is part of a larger and higher form like the Christian cathedrals of Europe or the Moorish Alhambra. Verbal language provides us with signs of objective things like atoms and mathematics, but also with the meaning of things, that is, with our *relationship* to the reality of these "things." Language clarifies ideas; ideas are not limited to clarifying language. Even science defers in a way to the realm of meaning when it discovers in the cosmos "black holes," events that at the level of science are neither black nor holes. Part of the Galileo incident was the insistence of theologians who—in the same way—insisted that the sun "rose" in the east. Four centuries before Galileo, and lacking a telescope and the beginnings of new science, Aquinas already wrote that a totally new theory of "heavenly movements," consistent with additional evidence, was possible.[35] As both a theologian and a philosopher, Aquinas knew the difference between contingent things that *have* existence and a God who in his simplicity *is* his own act of existence. The nature of God is to ever transcend His own transcendence.

Even within the sciences, Newton's mechanical laws of inertia retain a place within the broader "field theory" of modern physics. Field theory sets aside an assumed qualitative difference between particles and charges, and between matter and energy, and discovers that these phenomena are interchangeable according to new mathematical laws. Field theory, or the special theory of relativity, provides new laws in instances where the old laws of mechanics no longer apply, as when a moving particle approaches the constant speed of light. The old theory fits within the new, *but* the new is not reducible to the old. "What distinguishes science is that it is a systematic attempt to establish closed systems one after another. But all fundamental scientific discovery opens the system again . . . The act of imagination is the opening of the system so that it shows new connections."[36]

The growth of thought within science is not zero-sum, nor is science in a zero-sum relationship with other kinds of inquiry. While field theory explains much more than Newtonian mechanics, mechanics remains valid as a subset suitable for our normal experience. In an analogous way, metaphysics holds that this entire evolution of physics remains focused on physical phenomena. This plane is not in a zero-sum relation with other planes of inquiry. Phenomena do not explain a single act of human kindness or even the smallest deception, or anything "spiritual," except through a tyranny of rationalism. Aristotle's *Metaphysics,* still current and now better known to Muslims than to Western physical scientists, observes our thoughts about thought itself. This pre-Christian tract offers three principles rooted in humility before the existence of that which is: "the Divine Intellect is a measure, not a thing measured; Natural things are both measure and a thing measured; (and) The human intellect is a thing measured, not a measure" or the source of truth.[37] Measuring his own finiteness, man can conclude that he is not the measure of all things.

This pluriform line of reasoning defends the proposition truth is not simply a good fit between reality and any thoughts or ideas we might wish to impose. Rather, for Aquinas truth is the *relation* between the mind and that which is. The medieval Islamic scholar, Averroes, said much the same thing: "that the existence of being is a cause and reason for our knowledge, while the eternal Knowledge is a cause and reason for beings."[38] The alternative start point for Cartesian thought, the shaper of much modern philosophy, is a departure from this tolerance of reality as well as of Trinitarian Christianity. Cartesianism assumes that with respect to reality and God, man is on the outside looking in. Luigi Giussani quotes the fifth century St. Augustine: "I inquire in order to know something, not to think it."[39]

In our day the perennial and more agnostic option—merely "to think it"—*attaches itself* to the legitimate scientific method, somewhat as Islam attaches the state and the public forum to itself. Explanatory equations are thought to be the existential reality. Some agnostics, not their science which as a method is indifferent, doubt the *existence* of "things" as such and then doubt the existence of a living God. The atheist believes that the existence of even an orderly cosmos is exhaustively understood to be the result of cooling gasses. Nothing exists except aggregates of smaller nothings. This is paralysis before the real. Of our "modern" predicament, the early Hugh of St. Victor (1096–1141) wrote: "A certain man retorted to a philosopher, saying, 'Do you not see that men are laughing at you?' To which the philosopher replied, 'They laugh at me, and the asses bray at them.'"[40]

Inspecting the flat universe of the agnostic, the Christian, Muslim and Jew still remembers that there is a "deep calling upon deep" (Ps 42:8), and that the fullness of what is—the "I AM" (Exodus 3:14)—has revealed himself. The Christian, however unworthy, becomes a transparency and a "temple of God"—(1 Cor 3:9, 16; Eph 2:19–22).[41] The difference between Christian membership in the Church and Muslim membership in the ummah is basic. Membership in the ummah is ancestral and a matter of will alone, not will with reason. The validity of the decision within the Muslim community "is independent of the precise knowledge of the ways and beliefs of the Muslim community that motivates and accompanies it . . . (further) the apostate is condemned not on the ground of doctrinal error but, to put it in modern terms, because of 'high treason' to the umma."[42] Islam submits to a God beyond reason by submitting to the way of life of a folk culture. The contact point between the followers of Islam and Christians is also the point of greatest difference. St. Paul reaches to a reasonable wisdom beyond reason: "I will destroy the wisdom of the wise, and thwart the cleverness of the clever . . . has not God turned the wisdom of this world into folly . . . we preach Christ crucified—a stumbling block to Jews, and an absurdity to Gentiles . . . For God's folly is wiser than men, and his weakness more powerful than men" (1 Cor 1:19–25).

WILL AND POLITICS

Christian faith is compatible with reason and intellect, but finally as a free act also enlists our memory and our will. The "will" translates from the Hebrew and Latin as "yearning," or Augustine's "restlessness," rather than implying simply control or willfulness. In the West, St. Augustine's early tilt toward divine foreknowledge, a diminishment of human will, becomes the prominent foundation one thousand years later for John Calvin's sacrifice of human will altogether to his doctrine of predestination which is also found in Islam. Luther moves in the opposite direction to discover arbitrary and gifted buoyancy in the grace of God. One way of understanding Islam as a natural religion is to see it as laminating together the familiar opposites of fatal predestination and of unmerited grace. Under Islam one either submits or one does not. By Western standards, contradictions are embraced and culturally suppressed in the Muslim "way of life." One decides even as he is predestined. Even irrevocable membership in the ummah is based totally on an act of the will, either individually or by the group or one's ancestors. To leave Islam is not a change of citizenship as in the Western secular order, but possibly an act of treason.

Left to its own devices, Western rationalism tends also to dissolve reason and natural law into something less. Rommen finds that the British philosopher John Locke (1632–1704) errs by elevating human will over reason as a "moral reflex" to the order of creation. In his view Locke substitutes a "conception of natural law as a rather nominalistic symbol for a catalogue or bundle of individual rights that stem from individual self interest."[43] Such an uprooted and ethnocentric, even self-centered, definition of natural law serves poorly as a possible bridge toward other cultures and the followers of Islam. In an address the year before his 2006 *Regensburg Lecture* Pope Benedict identified the anti-religious righteousness of radical secularists: "The true contrariety which characterizes the world of today is not that among diverse religious cultures, but that between the radical emancipation of man from God, from the roots of life, on the one hand, and the great religious cultures on the other."[44] We are dealing here with rebellious willfulness in the face of God, not merely academic disagreements or even passionate ones over the relative legitimacy of faith and reason. Academic discourse and convincing appeals to reason are not enough to close this chasm once opened by the will, nor is diplomatic statecraft. Better information and better management are not sufficient to solve global problems that at their root are spiritual, theological, and moral.

Alexis De Tocqueville made this telling remark about the simplifying power of the will in league with slogans, "A false notion which is clear and precise will always have more power in the world than a true principle which is obscure and involved."[45] The principles of universal natural law will always face an upstream battle against the "terrible simplifiers," both Western and Islamic. By his addresses and trips, Pope Benedict XVI is looking centuries back and ahead. In his directness the pope stretches the finely crafted political language of nation-states and the more typical Vatican diplomacy of statecraft. As a moral teacher in a time of cultural decline, he is possibly less concerned with "strict diplomatic rules" than was the mid-twentieth century Pope Pius XII in his general warnings against German Fascism.[46] What diplomacy among states possibly could have effectively met the rise of categorically primitive barbarism in Germany, only thinly disguised in the trappings of the modern nation-state?[47] In today's different political circumstances, even more than Pius XII, Benedict speaks not only as a statesman but consistently and apart as a religious and cultural voice in the wilderness. A potential mediator, he and his predecessor Pope John II are riding and influencing the larger wave lengths of human history. In a break from the relatively recent mold the pope's appointment to the Vatican secretary of state position came from the teaching side of the Church rather than the diplomatic corps.

Not implausible for the future is a growing obsolescence of both the Western church-state distinction *and* the nation-state model to which it is attached. Benedict directs his critique not to Islam, but to the West:

> I am urging people to realize that a war has indeed been declared on the West. I am *not* pushing for a rejection of dialogue, which we need more than ever with those Islamic countries that wish to live in peaceful coexistence with the West, to our mutual benefit. *I am asking for something more fundamental: I am asking for people to realize that dialogue will be a waste of time if one of the two partners to the dialogue states beforehand that one idea is as good as the other* (italics added).[48]

Of the depth of American consumerism, a former American poet laureate imagines this remark to the Christ who expelled demons into swine (Mt 8:28). Of being separated from his demons, the modern day figure says to Christ, "If you cannot cure us without destroying our swine, we had rather you shoved off."[49] The dialogue becomes even more problematic if the second party (Islam) is unilaterally convinced that dialogue with others and its own monologue are synonymous, that all religions are but imperfect copies of universal Islam.[50] At a Vatican synod in late 1999 the study topic was how to improve rapport between Christians and Muslims. An attending churchman recalls this Muslim remark: "By means of your democracy we will invade you, by means of our religion we shall dominate you."[51]

The Church exists to give us not political solutions, but access to the final things. The Church simply "demands the space to be what it is."[52] It claims its place as an ecclesial body, whose members are not atomized individuals holding subjective opinions, but "the salt . . . (and the) light of the world" (Mt 5:13, 14). The Church is a barrier against totalitarianism. This Church space protects us as transcendent beings from either being reduced to political digits as in the pagan polis or Roman Empire, or in the flatland of radical secularism, or in any subsidiary status assigned under a restless Shari'a Law—or any chaotic combination of these. There is little difference between being suffocated by dhimmi status or by a patronizing "tolerance" (or worse) under an equally expansive and unilateral secular humanism. The Church is a "witness" to the world for the intrinsic dignity of each person, and for each human life above any calculus of political correctness or societal benefits and costs.[53]

Isaiah reminds us "my thoughts are not your thoughts, nor are your ways my ways, says the Lord" (Isa 55:8), and St. Paul proclaims "Christ crucified, a stumbling block to Jews and foolishness to the Gentiles . . . For the foolishness of God is wiser than human wisdom, and the weakness of God is stronger than human strength" (1 Cor 1:23–25). In the Christian self-understanding, the Church was ignited at Pentecost and ever since has gathered at the perpetual Last Supper. While the Church finds permanent unity through the papacy, it is more essentially a non-political Eucharistic family.[54] At the last supper Christ instituted the Eucharist when He said "do this in remembrance of me" (Mt 26:26–30; Mk 14:22–25, Lk 22:14–20, I Cor 22:23–27). Eucharistic solidarity is the heart of the "creative minorities" who by a personal decision cohere in Christ and are enabled to leaven from within whatever world is given to us, however atomized and chaotic. In an increasingly globalized and non-territorial world, the Catholic Church will be identified institutionally by the Vatican papal state together with each diocese headed by its bishop—but spiritually it will be identified by the lives and sometimes radiant influence of its many and very diverse members. Rather than a path for shrinkage and a remnant mentality, the path of creative minorities is much more one of hospitality toward one another and toward more distant others. "This is how all will know that you are my disciples, if you have love for one another" (Jn 13:35).

In advance of a new global landscape which includes a resurgent Islam, the Church's 2007 restoration of the *transnational* and uniform Mass form installed at the Council of Trent (Tridentine) may be both a prudent and a providential action. Rather than a separate rite within the Roman Catholic tradition, this liturgy is simply the "extraordinary form" of the now familiar and locally acculturated *Novus Ordo* (New Order) Mass dating from the most recent council. In this single rite of both forms, as from the beginning (Acts 2:42), the Church clearly affirms for its members its continuity within the Eucharistic unity of *communio*[55] as a new way of being and acting. Communio is the new life in the living present, each member always with the Church as a whole and all with God.[56] Where traditionalism is the dead faith of the living, vibrant tradition remains the living faith of the dead. The ever new life of grace and inner conversion and encounter is an enduring corrective to the post-modern identity politics in all of its forms, not simply another form. For Christians the coming of the Holy Spirit is a mysterious gift of the One from above, not a political construction from below that is totally contained within history. Given the added mystery of the human person, He comes mysteriously as a divine fire: "Then there appeared to them tongues as of fire, which parted and came to rest on each one of them" (Acts 2:3).

The Christian worldview is not eclipsed by any anachronistic duality to simply "let God be God" and man to be man (an Islamic tenet). He ever transcends us and ever is with us and we can be in Him; but we still are not He. In his "Prayer Before Mass" Pope John Paul II hints that the details of our lives with God enable more of a fabric than a duality: at the Mass the worshippers are invited to weave the threads of their prayers, works and sufferings, joys and very self to the (corresponding) body, blood, soul and divinity of Christ. The final prophet, John the Baptist, proclaimed: "He must increase; and I must decrease" (Jn 3:30). Even for those who are not members, the Church holds that "The Holy Spirit offers to all the possibility of being united with this paschal mystery in a way known only to God."[57] Under the Catholic sacramental vision of creation, even marriage is transformed into a sacrament whereby the marriage partners are capable of conferring marriage as a sacrament upon one another. For all Christians, history is less a political ascension through time than it is a moving connection point located always between time and eternity. Specifically for Catholics, the Mass, as a continuity and tradition, serves partly as a permanent reminder celebrated in the Counter Reformation "Baroque spirit (which) lives in and for the triumphant moment of creative ecstasy."[58] History kneels before the Psalms: "One day within your courts is better than a thousand elsewhere" (Ps 84:11). We are freed to be totally His *because* the Second Person of the Trintarian One has first humbled and totally donated himself into our uncomprehending hands. This degree of His belonging to us is the meaning of the sacrifice and communal banquet of each Mass. It is St. John's meaning when he proclaims "God *is* love" (1 Jn 4:8) and "whoever confesses the Son has the Father as well" (1 Jn 2:23).

Attentiveness to the eternal moment will always stand in contrast with an alternative spirit of the times, especially the already fading spirit of regimented bourgeoisie capitalism or socialism. The latter "has the mechanical rhythm of a clock, the Baroque the musical rhythm of a fugue or a sonata."[59] Under the baroque spirit, the dome and the sonata are by-products of the creative moment, much as the sum of existence is the by-product of divine creativity. Yet north of the Alps the Protestant mystique is also found, as in Rembrandt's domestic and rustic scenes. Instead of trying to *imagine* the glory, Protestant Christianity very simply *listens* to the word under a *sola Scriptura* theology. And today, five centuries after Trent, the Mass of the Second Vatican Council more fully incorporates the Word of the Lord before the Eucharist. The scripture is a dimension of the liturgy Tradition, and remains protected from either literal fundamentalism or historical-critical deconstruction.

The sociologist of European history, Christopher Dawson, suggests that had not sixteenth and seventeenth century Spain and the Protestant world—the two worlds of the Baroque and the Reformation—worn themselves to a standstill in their opposed efforts to assimilate France, "Europe might have fallen apart into two closed worlds, as alien and opposed to one another as Christendom and Islam . . ."[60] In modern times the theology of the Incarnation permanently resists assimilation into either an offshoot post-Protestant and secularist culture or the peripheral and now expanding Muslim presence. While Islam is in some ways a religion of ecstatic belief, even at the expense of reason, the contrast between Eucharistic unity from above and Islamic amalgamation into a cosmopolitan ummah is elementary. Where the principle of unity for the ummah is abstract and non-historical, Eucharistic *communion* is both concrete and mystical. It is incarnational and inspired through, with, and in the self-disclosing Other.

Eucharistic worship within the Catholic Church deals less with the "inaccessible transcendence" than with "divine condescension," the purifying fact of Christ as Redeemer.[61] The Eucharist "is at one and the same time a Sacrifice-Sacrament, a Communion-Sacrament, and a Presence-Sacrament."[62] In the Eucharist—more a verb than a noun—is found the self-emptying Son who remains both with us yet never apart from the Father and the Holy Spirit. The Eucharist "is the only true revolution in the world: faith as knowledge, and charity—looking Christ in the face—as morality."[63] His invitation is for each of us to be incorporated into both his death and resurrection, that is his Mystical Body in history. That is, we discover that we are part of the universal "communion of saints" which embraces all members in all generations, each personality so fully intact as to be transformed, not simply mingled as an element alongside the divine. Said St. Paul: "I consider the sufferings of the present to be as nothing compared with the glory *to be revealed in us*" (Rom 8:18, italics added).

Needed today at the personal level is the re-*cognition* of body and soul not in duality, but in the original unity of the human person. Contradictions to be pruned away in the post-Christian West include a culture based too much on common appetites and on the distractions of consumerism. From the Christian perspective the West too often humiliates both the masculine and maternity, too often genuflects before pornography at the cash register, and the androgynous tendencies of a "culture of death"—including highly sanitized rite of child-sacrifice under the slogan "freedom of choice." Contradictions of Islamic culture, carried forward *in the foundational texts themselves* from the "days of ignorance" are polygamy even tendencies toward self-vindication through conquest and plunder in either its aggressive or subtle forms, a patchwork culture of criminality, and openings toward a new subculture, with no parallels in history, of suicide bombing as a path toward personal salvation. In both the West and the world of Islam, the perennial crisis at its most basic level, is a very traditional one of "having it both ways," or serving two masters. In the mid-nineteenth century the European and Jewish-born convert to

Islam, author Muhammad Asad, found in Islam especially "the satisfaction of spiritual yearnings without the necessity to renounce the satisfaction of those of this world. Islam, for him, is the religion of the body and spirit in one."[64]

Sectarian Christian communities are based on the functional principle of local preaching and *sola Scriptura* theology,[65] the Tradition of the Church offers the sacramental Real Presence—both a symbol and that which it symbolizes—through the concurrent action by the validly ordained priest (sent in apostolic succession by Christ) and the indwelling Holy Spirit (e.g., Mk 14:22).[66] Also concurrent with this prayer is another offering: our works, sufferings, joys and selves, together with His real body, blood, soul and divinity.[67] The Real Presence, the eternal Delight of the Father, is the whole meaning of resurrection *and* redemption, and gives a special possibility at least of holiness in His image.

The Mass liturgy will continue to clearly sustain transnational Catholic solidarity among bishops, their extended priesthood, and equally the laity even as they leaven the world with the good news of universal human dignity. The transnational Church, both an institution and a mystical union, is neither national nor international, nor is it a construction of human inventiveness or the applied social sciences.[68] The Church universal thrived in each of the local catacombs, and in its self understanding even today "the one, holy, catholic and apostolic Church of Christ is truly present and active in each particular church."[69] One benefit of modern technology becomes clear. Any local suppression and martyrdom of the human person or of the Church itself in a post-modern world, as we see already in India, the Sudan and Nigeria, is instantaneously visible globally—and even in this sense is suffered by all. But it was by such witnessing by a persecuted minority of ten percent that the entire Roman Empire was overcome and converted.[70]

Bernard Lewis defines the pedigree for the current conflict between (Western) secularism and (Islamic) nationalism: "The revolutionaries in France had summarized their ideology in a formula of classical terseness—liberty, equality, fraternity. Some time was to pass before they, and ultimately their disciples elsewhere, came to realize that the first two were mutually exclusive and the third meaningless. Of far greater effect, in the impact of Western ideas on Islam, were two related notions—neither of them originating with the French Revolution, but both of them classically formulated and actively disseminated by its leaders; namely, secularism and nationalism. The one sought to displace religion as the ultimate basis of identity, loyalty, and authority in society; the other provided an alternative."[71] The false god of nationalism is bankrupt and nearly dead, and radical secularism is an episode already on the life support of fading political largesse. Liberty and equality are always at risk of being mutually exclusive. Fraternity dissolves in the heat of the day, although in the Muslim world the ummah continues unscathed as an abstract fraternity.

Pope Benedict addresses the issue of displaced religion, and the "pathologies of religion" and willfulness:

> A partisan image of God, which identifies the absoluteness of God with one's own community or its interests, thereby elevating something empirical and relative to a state of absoluteness, dissolves law and morality . . . We see this in the terrorists' ideology of martyrdom, which of course in individual cases may also be the expression of despair at the lawlessness of the world. Sects in the Western world also provide examples of irrationality and a perversion of religion that show how dangerous religion becomes when it loses its orientation.[72]

A leading example of sectarian terrorism in the West is certainly the assassination of Mountbatten (1900–1979), great grandson of Queen Victoria, by the Irish Republican Army who planted a bomb on his fishing boat. Mountbatten was the lead negotiator for the separate independence of Hindu India and Muslim Pakistan in 1947. Whether Islam is a "partisan image of God" is the ambiguity addressed in several parts of this book. The proposal is that Islam might be more a confusion between natural law and some form of private intuition and sectarian natural religion. This deficiency in making distinctions, and the universality of natural law, would explain why Muslims sincerely regard their religion (of natural law) as universal and inclusive of all other religions.

St. Augustine put his finger on the deeper problem, shared equally in the West and under Islam. The "sickness of the mind" is the coexistence within the person of "two wills, since one of them is not complete, and what is lacking in the other of them is present in the other." The soul, writes Augustine, has a single nature and is not God, and "is rent asunder by grievous hurt as long as it prefers the first because of its truth but does not put away the other because of habit."[73] To let man be man—an Islamic premise—finally is to not let a saving God be God.

In this fallen world, the West and Muslims can always fine social justice opportunities to work on together. But Christian charity finally transcends even public and private programs of social justice: "There will never be a situation where the charity of each individual Christian is unnecessary, because in addition to justice man needs, and will always need, love." As a member of the Church and like the incarnate Lord—"I must be personally present in my gift."[74] It is this personal presence that transforms a mere cup of water given in His name into a foretaste of heaven—a fractal of the divine Presence.

MEMORY AND IMAGES

A third dimension of the human consciousness is our memory. Memory is more than electronic imprints on brain tissue. It is the needed environment for the intellect to operate and calls us to further growth: "We stand in front of our past, which closes and opens at the same time . . . The past is the time of birth, not of death."[75] The Christian knows from the Jews, his "elder brothers," that even a chosen people is not fully defined by what they have done, or what has been done to them. And for the followers of Islam, the healing of history is not found in the restoration of a golden age. But like the Christian, the Muslim remembers first his God. For the Muslim the practice of *dhikr* is this remembrance. From the *Qur'an*, "Please God and call your Lord to mind when you forget" (Q 18:24) and "remember God often" (Q 33:41).

How then to replace all the bad memories of history? It is only because of memory, often manipulated, that events of the day can trigger flashbacks every bit as real as the triggering event itself: Auschwitz, martyrs, Galileo, Constantinople in 1453 or even 1204 and Jerusalem encircled and then sacked and retaken. Before any of these events, in the early fifth century St. Augustine pondered the meaning history and of memory. The certitudes of the seemingly eternal Roman Empire and its projection of an ordered cosmos were falling to the barbarians at the gates. In his *City of God* he defended the Christians against the comforting Roman memory of more secure times under the pagan gods. Loyalty to a jealous God over pagan hearth decorations was not the cause of the current catastrophe. And two centuries later Mohammed installed in Arabia the memory of Abraham and monotheism against the tribal memory banks and warfare under the multiple idols of Mecca. Of the right to even defend a patch of ground, a prominent theme in the Old Testament, Augustine would have proposed that: "Our only real excuse for what we do is that there has been an infinite series of plunders, of iniquities behind ours."[76] Muslims seek to reclaim Andalusia and southeastern Europe, while Christians recall that nearly all Muslim territory was once Christian—Spain, Turkey, the Holy Land and all of North Africa.

Pope John Paul II's year 2000 gesture to heal memories of the past millennium was his "Homily of the Holy Father: 'Day of Pardon.'" On behalf of the Church with its turbulent history, this pope asked forgiveness for those members of the Church who have failed to match the message that the Church transmits. He asked for forgiveness for "the infidelities to the Gospel committed by some of our brethren." The text is published together with an explanatory tract authored by the International Theological Commission. The Commission addresses interreligious responses to this unilateral act of self-accusation: "What must be avoided is that these acts (recognition of past wrongs) be mistaken as confirmation of possible prejudices against Christians. It would also be desirable if these acts of repentance would stimulate the members of other religions to acknowledge the faults of their own past. Just as the history of humanity is full of violence, genocide, violations of human rights and the rights of peoples, exploitation of the weak and glorification of the powerful, so too the history of the various religions is marked by intolerance, superstition, complicity with unjust powers, and the denial of the dignity and freedom of conscience. Christians have been no exception and are aware that all are sinners before God!"[77]

In his apology John Paul II calls attention to 'the violence some have used in the service of the truth (and) toward the followers of other religions."[78] Even more than a sin against others, such violence is a sin against the Holy Spirit who too often is enlisted as an ally on the geographic game board. The division between eastern and western Christianity, much older than the Reformation, broods over the modern world from a wound dating back a nearly a millennium (Constantinople, 1204) and more. How hard it is to reweave the tapestry of history and encounter once it is severed. The first history of the Crusades appeared only in 1899, and now the Middle East remembers and recoils from their particular inflamed memories.

Today, with the benefit of historical distance, believing Muslims and the Christians might at least begin together in their understanding that belief and culture—more than the economies and power of nation-states or empires—are what moves men, women, and history. This deepening is an inkling of the natural law being resurrected into the modern world. The dark side of all "modernity" is the avoidance of our moral dilemmas through the artful habit on simply not remembering, of a prior forgetfulness of reality (Chapter 4). Of our deepest memory of God within, the early Muslim Al-Ghazali and the Christian St. Augustine both wrote a personal confession of their inner journey. Augustine begins and ends his entire treatise with an insight: "our heart is restless until it rests in you."[79] Augustine and Al-Ghazali, together, might very likely afford us a shared path of deepening memory and fruitful encounter among individual Christians and individual followers of Islam.

The Christian memory is that the Christ of the Trinitarian Unity is not to be falsely grouped together with Islam's unhappy memories of idolatrous Mecca. The living memory of the Church recalls its origin and its future: "The Christian dispensation, as the new and definitive covenant, will never pass away, and we now await no further public revelation before the glorious manifestation of our Lord Jesus Christ (cf. Tim. 6:14 and Tit. 2:13)."[80] In the self understanding of the Church, "What else is Tradition but the task assumed by the Church of transmitting (in Latin, *tradere*) the mystery of

Christ and the entirety of his teaching preserved in memory?"[81] The living Christ is the remembered promise made to Abraham. In the Church are his spiritual descendents (Gen 15:5). As a guest of Zacchaeus, Christ announced: "Today salvation has come to this house, for *this* is what it means to be a son of Abraham" (Lk 19:9, italics added).

The Christian memory is both similar to and different from the memory that is Islam. There is no longer a closed clan of the Law, or no absolute polis and no closed ummah, and there are no tribally defined sectarian divides or outsider infidels. The difference is in the glance and petition of the good thief encountered by Christ at Golgotha. In this fleeting moment of encounter he asks: "*remember* me . . . ," and the immediate response from the Pierced One is "today you will be with me in Paradise" (Lk 23:42–3). History is long, but eternity takes but a moment. By comparison radical jihad—a fringe group in the world of Islam—is partly a frantic attempt to recapture the quite different memory of a golden age of past Muslim glory. Judaism, for its part, claims rightly its memory of a Covenant with a God who never abandons them.[82] The memory of Judaism is of eternal Israel, that the Covenant with the tribes of Judah endures: "If they violate my statutes and keep not my commandments . . . I will never violate my covenant, not go back on the word I have spoken" (Ps 89:32,35).

The "deadening of conscience" (Chapter 4) in East and West is a loss of memory, the memory or "echo" of a God who calls each of us. "For man has in his heart a law inscribed by God . . . His conscience is man's most secret core and his sanctuary. There he is alone with God whose voice *echoes* in his depths."[83] This echo is memory of the deepest kind. In the temple Christ read aloud the remembered passage from Isaiah prefiguring his own coming. He announced with authority that, "Today this Scripture passage is fulfilled in your hearing" (Lk 4:21). The life of Christians is also memory extended forward by the indwelling of the Holy Spirit: "The Advocate, the holy Spirit that the Father will send in my name—he will teach you everything and remind you of all that I told you" (Jn 14:26). The memory of events past, sheltered by the Presence, brings us into the future: "By his coming, which never ceases, the Holy Spirit causes the world to enter into the 'last days,' the time of the Church, the Kingdom already inherited though not yet consummated."[84] The memory of Christians in these last days and within the Spirit is toward "a future full of hope" (Jer 29:11).

The distinctly Christian view or memory is captured by a student of history: "Among the historical religions Christianity is the mark along with Judaism and Islam, of seeing existence in terms of encounters between a personal God and human beings, and these encounters 'take the form of historical acts and events in this world.' Christianity, however, by its attitude to suffering and in its central belief, Christ's incarnation and crucifixion, can claim to be 'the historical religion *par excellence* . . .'"[85] John Paul II writes of the Crucifixion: "The event at Calvary is a historical fact. Nevertheless, it is not limited in time and space. It goes back into the past, to the beginning, and opens toward the future until the end of history. It encompasses all places and times and all of mankind."[86]

Together with Christianity, Judaism and Islam are prophetic religions, each tracing historically to Abraham. It is first in Abraham that the grip of past memory and ancestral totems is transcended. Abraham breaks loose into a totally new openness toward a singular and true God that he cannot see. It is this novelty of completely turning around that sets all of history on a new course and makes Abraham our common "father in faith." Israel learns over time that to be possessed by the one true God it is necessary to not be possessed by or alloyed with the world. Christianity accepts the progressive unfolding of revelation in history up to the incomprehensible self-disclosure of an infinitely personal God in the fullness of time.[87] By comparison, Islam breaks from the lineage of Judeo-Christian revelation and history with a memory of ascent from Ishmael rather than Isaac.

With St. Thomas Aquinas the Christian is more than St. Augustine's sojourner with a memory. For Aquinas, "Man was a wayfarer by *nature* as well as by *history*, and history was no more than his nature enacting itself in time. Man's history was the story of his being, and his being could be seen both revealing and fulfilling itself in history."[88] The implanted inner law, the memory and echo of the divine law, is dynamic rather than passive, and incarnate rather than an idea. The interior law or universal natural law points through and beyond this world to the Son as our True Self, the one in history who *already* is both "the Way (and) the Truth and the Life" (Jn 14:6).

What of man who by his nature is a pilgrim with memory? What are our different cultural predispositions of memory and of human "time" and do these shape, or how are these shaped by, our theologies? The theologian Hans Urs von Balthasar provides a possible opening at least for Christian meditation: "To believe, to hope, to love means, in fact, to imitate the faithful obedience, the self-denying patience of Jesus, by which he *brings the eternal into time*."[89] He elaborates, "God is not only transcendent to the world as one who is 'other' (for then he would be subject to limits), but is *also totally immanent to the world precisely because of his total transcendence*" (both italics added).[90] Von Balthasar discovers that in the Incarnation the eternal enters into time, and that in the Resurrection time enters into eternity. The incarnation at a moment in time, "in the fullness of time" (Gal 4:4), is as much about the present as it is about the past or even the future. Commenting on the thought of Simon Weil, Finch offers a view similar to von Balthasar: "If we study the Gospels we will find that it is life in the present—not in the timeless present of past and future, but in the (timeful) present of the Now—that is the essence of Christianity. The secret of the teaching of Christ is *that all true life is life in the present*, as distinct from the past and future. This is where reality is. If there is no experience of the present as the *Now*, then there is no real *life* at all" (italics added).[91]

The Pauline letters include this: "Oh, that *today* you would hear his voice . . ." (Heb 3:7, italics added). Do we find in different cultural perspectives on time and memory, as well as the stature of human reason, an opening for a possibly wonderful inter-*cultural* conversation? The secular historian of Islam William Cantwell Smith, highly regarded by Muslim scholars, says this about how time is understood differently in different cultures: "In the Old Testament attitude, history itself is continuingly revelatory. History is to revelation as subject to predicate, rather than vice versa. Classical Hebrew thought learned from history, and—so the modern interpretation runs—put what it learned into scripture. Islamic thought learned from scripture, and put what it learned into history."[92] Islam does not accept God's total and incarnate presence in history (as Christ), yet the *Qur'an* contains brief wording similar to Revelation and finds Allah to be very close as well as distantly above us: "He is the First and the Last, the Evident and the Immanent: And He has full knowledge of all things" (Q57:3).

Refining Smith's cross cultural profile is Israel's appreciation of time as *abruptly* revelatory as continuously so. The history of Israel is one of continuous invasions and disruptions, such that God is often seen through the cracks so to speak, and is feared. In the history of Israel God writes straight with crooked lines. The Christian profile differs. Christ comes as an enduring surprise compared to what is expected, and yet as one whose kingdom is not of this world. Preaching to the Jews and echoing the great prophets, the apostles held that the eternal design (Acts 2:23, 3:18) was now fulfilled in time, and that Israel should "listen to his voice, today."[93] Paralleling Smith (above): Christianity waits with the Old Testament and then learns from a God who puts himself into history. Unlike the Western utopian visions, the future is "today" for those who are open to receive and give radical forgiveness. But then again, centuries after Christ and at the sack of Rome, and foreseeing the collapse of the Empire and the cosmic empyrean itself, St. Augustine reminds his flock that as Christians they are citizens of an unearthly city, the *City of God.* Augustine's hierarchical image of time is retained but moderated in the Medieval era with the rise of economic activity and quantification of time. Translucent rose windows of stained glass are eventually replaced with mechanical clocks. But in general the Jewish and Christian perception of events is linear. This perception is also fractal in that all of human history is created by time-bound events, with each and every part touched by great tragedy and greater grace.[94] By a kind of field theory (as in modern physics) human events occur in linear history, but comprehensible history is generated by the inscrutable events it contains. And, Christ is the insertion of the eternal divine into the sum of all moments, the fullness of time. His followers (the Church) are called to continuous personal conversion today and in this way to be the leaven of all future history.

The monotheistic religions see history as less of a system, as distinctly human, and as open to divine prophecies to be fulfilled. History is ultimately urged forward and upward by our own freedom, in the same way that any other chaotic work of art is a byproduct of something more than itself. For the Christian, Christ takes all of human history into himself in a hymn of praise and thanksgiving to the Father. Even at the Last Supper, on the eve of His passion, he first gives thanks to the Father (Mk 14:23). Of this radiance, St. Paul writes: "While God has overlooked the times of human ignorance, now he commands all people everywhere to repent, because he has fixed a day on which he will have the world judged in righteousness by a man whom he has appointed, and *of this he has given assurance to all by raising him from the dead*" (Acts 17:30–31, italics added).

Islam is more suspended in time, looking back to the ancient world and its more recent golden age. There is a mythical resurrection but not divine redemption both in and above time. Christ speaks of this middling approach to Reality: "And no one puts a patch of raw cloth on an old garment, for the patch tears away from the garment, and a worse rent is made. Nor do people pour new wine into old wine-skins, else the skins burst, the wine is spilt, and the skins are ruined. But they put new wine into fresh skins, and both are saved" (Mt 9:16–17). Nineteenth century critics of Islam (particularly regarding the Turks as perceived in that era) detected two opposite poles in Islam related to time.

(The) very absoluteness of Islam makes (the Muslim) overbearing and insolent to all who are not of his faith. Its exaltation of the sensual paradise frees him from all restraint in the gratification of his passions . . . (when provoked) he becomes immediately the most dangerous revolutionist known to history; this in aggression. But in another sense the same religion develops within him an indolence . . . in the enjoyment (of sensual pleasures) he is *careless of the future and the past*, and lives only in the present" (italics added). Of those times, a Turkish pasha refused Europeans a concession to mine coal from his land: "If God Almighty had intended that coal to be used, He would put it near the surface where it could have been got at, not away below, where you have to dig for it. It is blasphemy to change His plans.[95]

For the Muslim world today, the overlooked and greatest interreligious memory from before the time of Mohammed might actually be the discounted

St. Paul. St. Paul preached first in Arabia and then in Damascus (the first Christian city later to be conquered by Islam). But with St. Paul we learn that eternity enters time not through submission or conquest, but in the Christ event that in this final age inspires praise and gratitude. Of past abuses we are now free, and free to remember how to forget. "Memory of evil is an injustice . . . a sentinel who protects sins, . . . alienation of life, a nail that pierces the soul, wickedness that never sleeps, . . a daily death."[96]

In the poised moment between the Resurrection and the Ascension, Christ restrains Mary Magdalene's hand. He releases her from the still desperate grip of her own past. She still remembers how she first sat at the feet of Christ, and why. He draws her instead into the eternal present and the presence of the eternal: "Stop holding on to me, for I have not yet ascended to the Father" (Jn 20:17). Islam also lives in the present and Judaism speaks of Eternal Israel. Christ at Pentecost sends the eternal fire of the Holy Spirit who is simultaneously his very self in the presence of the Father. Within this living "memory" of Him, we are to finally "have life and have it more abundantly" (Jn 10:10). Even death in all of its forms including the physical "is swallowed up in victory" (1 Cor 15:54). St. Paul proclaims, "Nature for grace, grace for glory—these are the supreme synthesis . . . 'All are yours, you are Christ's and Christ is God's'" (1 Cor 3:23).[97]

In twelfth century Europe the crusader Louis IX adhered to the "Truce of God," the interval when combatants in Europe interrupted their particular bad memories and together dropped their feuding. A faint memory of the Truce of God still emerged centuries later from the trenches of the First World War. Within earshot of each other, combatants of opposing German and the French lines sang Christmas carols together. Similar moments of peace interrupted the Crusade battlefields in the Holy Land. The two sides took time to exchange gifts or else match their skills in tournaments rather than in combat. How are we to discover and then enlarge such interlude moments in the drumbeat of history? Josef Pieper explains: (good memory means) "nothing less than 'true-to-being' memory, meaning that objective grasp of reality is the basis of good action, and that the truth of real things is grasped only by true-to-being memory.[98]

He warns that the greatest danger to such memory is that, "the truth of real things will be falsified by the assent or negation of the will. There is no more insidious way for error to establish itself than by this falsification of the memory through slight retouches, displacements, discolorations, omissions, shifts of accent . . . The honesty of the memory can be ensured only by a rectitude of the whole human being which purifies the most hidden roots of volition" (will).[99] In late 2006 in Istanbul Pope Benedict prayed for a moment in the shared silence of Santa Sophia. When might such a shared inner silence and listening become the larger half of a global dialogue where three continents— Europe, Asia and Africa—all touch in the same Holy Land?

AN *UNCOMMON* WORD

Intellect, memory and will come as parts of the one human psyche in the mystery of the person. History is their domain. The West stresses the intellect as a path to clarity regarding the Real and the Word of God; Islam stresses more the will as a path given through the words of Allah, the word made book. Historically these two impulses, more than instincts, played out very differently on the peninsulas of European Christendom and in Arabia. In the first century, in the Christian's still oral preaching to the pagans, "such as those in Asia Minor or in Philippi or Corinth or Rome, it was not enough to speak about the Risen Christ, for the hearers would automatically have thought that Christianity was just another mystery religion about a demi-god. The Greek speaking world was full of mythological cults of this type, and St. Paul found that he was misunderstood in precisely this way at Athens (Ac 17:18). The only safeguard against such misunderstanding lay in emphasizing, to pagans, the concrete details of his life" (e,g., Acts 10:37–47, St. Peter's address to the centurion).[100] The catechetical framework of all four gospels became the sequential preparation, ministry, journey to Jerusalem, and the passion, death and resurrection in Jerusalem of the absolutely unique Christ now made present in history.[101]

In another case, the crucial importance of a few words and their meaning is supplied by the "*filioque*," wording inserted by the Church in the Creed (partly at the prodding of the emperor Charlemagne) to better express in human language and in the West the equality of "persons" in the Triune oneness of God. Were the Spirit to be given pre-eminence through the tool of human language—a tool both essential and inadequate—then the incarnate Christ would become less than unique, only one of many possible and lesser manifestations. The Christian world formally split (1054 A.D.) largely over linguistic subtleties raised by the filioque, fully five centuries before the more reported Reformation in the West. In seventh century Arabia, Mohammed was so scandalized—or opportunistic toward—this kind of apparent hairsplitting in the seventh century Byzantine world that he dismissed Trinitarian Christianity along with the pagan idolatry of his environs, and much of Judaism as well.

The intellect, will and memory are distinct but inseparable. The intellect is given that we might discern at least what is meant by doing good while also avoiding evil. This is the universal natural law unfolded in the West and at least obliquely folded into a few verses on the *Qur'an* (e.g., Q 9:71). Memory extends beyond past events in the world to the inner core of man—our shared original sin and our more original innocence. And the human will is a wellspring of freedom toward the truth, rather than a liberty from constraint.

In the fourteenth Century Church, St. Catherine of Siena, a lay woman and secular Third Order Carmelite, weaves our three human and personal themes of intellect, memory and will into a single prayer to the Father who is One. She elevates each of us toward a God who works within: "O Father, grant that I may unite my *memory* to you by always remembering that You are the beginning from which all things proceed. O Son, unite my *intellect* to Yours and grant that I may perfectly judge all things according to the order established by Your wisdom. O Holy Spirit, grant that I may unite my *will* to You by loving perfectly that mercy and love which are the reason for my creation and for every grace given to me, without any merit on my part."[102]

In our century and two days before his *Regensburg Lecture* in 2006, the fears of the post-Christian world were on his mind of Pope Benedict XVI as he spoke in Munich of Europe: "They do not see the real threat to their identity in the Christian faith, but in the contempt for God and the cynicism that considers mockery of the sacred to be an exercise of freedom and that holds up utility as the supreme moral criterion for the future of scientific research."[103] To re-ignite Christian faith, in his *Jesus of Nazareth* the pope frames an unsolicited dialogue with the writings of Rabbi Jacob Neusner. He pinpoints Neusner's objection to Christ, that "Perfection, the state of being holy as God is holy (cf. Lev 19:2, 11:44), as demanded by the Torah, now consists in following Jesus."[104] In a later piece that might resonate with some followers of Islam, Neusner underscores why he remains *not* a Christian: "Where Jesus diverges from the revelation of God to Moses at Mount Sinai that is the Torah, he is wrong, and Moses is right . . . But if Christians take seriously the claim that the criterion of Matthew is valid—not to destroy but to fulfill—then I do think Christians may well have to reconsider the Torah ('Judaism' in secular language): Sinai calls, the Torah tells us how God wants us to be."[105] To Christian ears, Neusner has the same response as did the Pharisees when Christ healed the man blind from birth on the Sabbath: "We are disciples of Moses," they said, "We know that God spoke to Moses, but we have no idea where this man comes from" (Jn 9:28–29).

No innovator can add or detract from the original testimony Scripture. On this charge, Peter remarks: "Know this first of all, that there is no prophecy of scripture that is a matter of personal interpretation, for no prophecy ever came through human will; but rather human beings moved by the holy Spirit spoke under the influence of God" (2 Pe 1:20–21). It was not innovation that was in Christ but rather the Spirit, the author of prophecy. And with the Father, Christ and the Spirit are one. Is all of this simply a circular argument? The first followers of Christ are alarmed by the Resurrection and at His departure by Christ's sending of the Spirit at Pentecost. They find that this "divergence" from Mosaic prophecy is the fullness of Mosaic expectation in the fullness of

time—the divine fulfillment. The Holy Spirit speaks through the prophets of
the Torah and then, sent by the resurrected Christ, this same Holy Spirit who
for Moses anointed the seventy elders (Num 11:25) now witnesses to the Son
to perpetually remind us of all that He did and said (Jn 14:26).

The *Qur'an*, which borrows from the Pentateuch, crudely echoes the Torah
as the eternal Law, overlaid as it is by additional Arab poetics and cultural
remnants. Just as Neusner finds fault with a prophet Christ for departing
from the Torah, Mohammed faults the earlier Jews for breaking the covenant
made with Abraham. Compared to the Torah which tells us "what to be,"
the *Qur'an* also tells us what to do. Compared with both, God first shows us
himself in Christ who then shows us *who we are* and then what we are to be
and do and expect: "I am the way, and the truth, and the life; no one comes
to the Father but through me" (Jn 14:5). The absolutely unique truth claim of
the witnesses to Christ, unlike followers of any other religion, is not only that
God manifests himself in many ways, but that in our history God goes further
to actually reveal his very self—and to reveal us to ourselves—by becoming
man: "The Word was made flesh" (Jn 1:14).

As a witness to this alarming and astonishing event, and dramatically recruited
on the Road to Damascus (modern day Syria), St. Paul writes in Galatia of his
encounter with the very person of the post-Resurrection Christ (Gal 1:11–12,
15–17). In Corinth he explains his astonishment: "Having therefore such hope
(the fullness of glory), we show great boldness. We do not act as Moses did, who
used to put a veil over his face that the Israelites might not observe the glory of
his countenance, which was to pass away. But their minds were darkened; for
to this day, when the Old Testament is read to them, the self-same veil remains,
not being lifted to disclose the Christ in whom it is made void . . . but when they
turn in repentance to God, the veil shall be taken away (2 Cor 3:12–14). (And,
Paul continues) Now the Lord is spirit; and where the Spirit of the Lord is, there
is freedom. But we all, with faces unveiled, reflecting as in a mirror the glory
of the Lord, are being transformed into his very image from glory to glory, as
through the Spirit of the Lord (2 Cor 3:15–18)."[106]

Where the Lord is, there is the "spirit of freedom," always larger than the
external and often random turning points of history and shattering every order
constructed by man. On the Road to Emmaus it was finally the resurrected
Christ who personally explained the connection between the Old Testament
and Himself (Lk 24:13–35): "Beginning, then, with Moses and all the prophets, he interpreted for them every passage of Scripture which referred to him
. . ." And their eyes were opened "happily to the sight of their own glorified
humanity."[107] To his disciples, in the villages of Caesarea Philippi, Christ
himself posed this question regarding his divinity: "Who do men say that I
am," and then, *"who do you say that I am?" (Mk 8:27–30).*[108]

Sufi al-Ghazali lingers with the prophets: "Listen to the utterances of the prophets: for they have indeed experienced and seen what is true in all that revelation has brought us. Follow in their path, and you will perceive some of that by direct vision."[109] To wary Muslim eyes, the Christian is guilty of blasphemy because the Oneness claimed by Christ violates the oneness of God. But to the Christian the Prophet Mohammed, possibly a true mystic given an intuition into the oneness of God, was not called to confuse the depth of this Truth as shown atop Golgotha with the stone carvings of pagan Mecca. For the Christian, Mary is infused by the Holy Spirit and, through the triune nature of the one God, the always human Mary is made the mother of the whole Christ. In Mary we are stunned by the full meaning of Mohammed's words when he said "paradise lies at the feet of mothers." To the "good thief" Christ said: "This day you will be with me in Paradise" (Lk 23:43). Revealed through the mystery of maternity, the Prophet Isaiah discovered the permanence of God's promise to Zion: "Can a mother forget her infant, be without tenderness for the child of her womb? Even should she forget, I will never forget you" (Isaiah 49:15).

Augustine discovers "Our heart is restless until it rests in You."[110] Is it possible that by claiming the human heart the Risen One adds to human stature and freedom without diminishing the divine autonomy and power? The prayer of the Church is "May our faith prove we are not slaves, but sons, not so much subjected to your law as *sharing in your power*" (italics added).[111] None of us sees God, but Saint Gregory of Nyssa explains that the verse: "Blessed are the pure of heart, for they shall see God" (Mt 5:8) combines with "the Kingdom of God is within you" (Lk:20–1) to mean that the pure of heart is blessed even now to "see the image of the divine nature in the beauty of his own soul."[112] The Christian hears: "If anyone love Me . . . My Father will love him, and *We will come to him, and will make Our abode with him*" (Jn 14:23). Such indwelling by the Spirit—and what this means about the nature of man (male and female)—is the irreducible gap between the faithful surrender of Christians and devout submission by the followers of Islam. At a very general level, Pope John Paul II remarked "when a culture becomes inward looking, and tries to perpetuate obsolete ways of living by rejecting any exchange or debate with regard to the truth about man, then it becomes sterile and is heading for decadence."[113] The almost predictable response of Islamic commentators would be that the notion of "exchange or debate" is a defective premise since whatever is of value is already contained within Islam as the original and all-inclusive revelation, including distinctly non-religious discussion of human nature (the natural law) based on reason alone.

Muslims are scandalized by crucified love and explain that a transcendent God simply cannot be victimized. They hold that "(their) denial of the killing of Jesus is a denial of the power of human beings to vanquish and destroy the divine Word, which is forever victorious."[114] The Muslim view is the mirror opposite of the atheist journalist, Ariana Fallaci, when she explains that she is a "Christian atheist" *because* Christ even "as a man only can be never vanquished."[115] To the Christian, Christ reveals such a God who cannot be victimized, but who can choose to fully know and live our self-inflicted victimhood. Because of this boundless degree of freedom, He also can be found in such little things as a simple act of graced kindness, or the womb of an obscure Jewish maiden. Divinity is found in a manger beneath the stars rather than as recluse in a heaven hidden beyond the stars—equally untouchable and untouching.

The journalist Fallaci (d. 2004) rages over the Church and the assistance it gives to the building mosques, especially when combined with the simultaneous removal of crucifixes from hospital walls. This rage from an atheist! Only a few years past, Polish students—mere students!—demanded the restoration of classroom crucifixes, during those final years before the Berlin Wall fell into the streets of Berlin in 1989 causing a rumble that shattered the entire Soviet Union in 1991. But not to be outdone by the historic collapse of the Communist State as a history shaping myth, in 2009 the European Court on Human Rights tried removing cultural/religious crucifixes from classroom walls. In the fifth century as now, St. Ambrose dealt with simply a plea from polytheism, for the cause of civility, to open his cathedral niches to the placement of gods of the state. In his time Valentinian was tempted by the useful urgency to see if "a common basis between Christianity and a monotheistic Paganism could be found in the Unknowability of God."[116]

Two centuries later, Mohammed sought out potential Christian and Jewish allies to help him impose the oneness of the unknowable God on an idolatrous Mecca. And today, secular multiculturalists and allied Muslim scholars from within their own self-understanding again propose ever "modern" multiculturalism as ancient tradition in new clothes. As in the worlds of Mohammed and Ambrose, the Muslim scholar Ayoub asks why not put all three monotheistic Scriptures under one cover? He writes: "The *Qur'an* presents the three people of the Book(s) a challenge and a promise. The challenge is for all to live by the moral and spiritual dictates of the Torah, the Gospel, and the *Qur'an*" (see Q 5:66) . . . Can Jews, Christians, and Muslims hear the voice of God speaking to each in their own language through all three scriptures? This (he says) is the challenge for the twenty-first century."[117] Yet, is the challenge to find a common binder for our similarities, or is it more about an equality that respects and even thrives on differences?

Different people of faith are called equally to be witnesses and protectors of the beautiful because beauty, too, is a path to the one, the true and the good.

The Muslim tradition clearly reveres the power of God *and* his beauty: "He is Allah, the Creator, the Maker, the Fashioner. His are the most beautiful names. Whatever is in the heavens and the earth declares His glory; and he is Mighty and Wise" (Q 59:24). In the Judeo-Christian tradition the beauty is found especially in the Psalms and in the unguarded words and deeds of Christ narrated in the Gospels, not least of which is His resurrection. It is through transcendental beauty, which "can never be separated from the covenant," and as "a datum of faith," that Israel looks past its own transgressions (Ps 105 and 106) to "offer up to God in praise the splendour which God granted to the world and man."[118] Apart from the needed harmony between faith and reason, might the Christian apologetic offer a direct appreciation for the beautiful as a contact point with the followers of Islam?

In the history of science, two biographers notice that Charles Darwin may have converted from science to scientist-agnostic for a reason of a lost beauty totally outside of his science.[119] Moore and Desmond suggest that Darwin's final tipping point coincides less with the sorting and ranking of flora and fauna on the Galapagos Islands than with the tragic death of his daughter, Annie, in 1851 at the age of ten.[120] In another case, the more contemporary communist-atheist Whittaker Chambers writes that his personal tipping point away from communism and toward Christian beauty and truth was little more than an accidental glance. In a beam of hallway light noticed the exquisite form of something so seemingly trivial as his sleeping daughter's ear. More than a function, he saw a lovely design. Like the later Darwin, the American writer Mark Twain was a consistent determinist, but he was still drawn to the possibility of grace by the anomaly in history of Joan of Arc. Her name is the title of his lesser known but personally favorite work[121] which was likely inspired by the radiance of his treasured daughter Susy (who at the age of twenty-four tragically died of spinal meningitis in 1896). In the Christian tradition the theologian von Balthasar challenges us to lift out heads and to be "responsible guardians of the glory of creation." All of his many volumes pivot off the beauty of a child's first smile as he is cradled in his mother's arms and for the first time notices and responds her. Through her smile he becomes conscious of relationship and of self. In this first moment of love, something is revealed—the spontaneous love for the mother, and the fact that Being is good, true, and cause for joy, that is, beautiful.[122]

The coherence between things of faith and things of reason, both with the truth of hope and charity, lies partly in this gifted ability to see beauty in and through the world. We are to see reality as a splendor, to see *through* the eyes and not simply with the eyes. We are to see with the thirsty eyes of the heart, rather than with only the physical eyes as receptors of light, whether corpuscles or waves.[123] For the Christian, the "Son is the reflection of the Father's *glory*, the exact representation of the Father's being . . ." (Heb 1:1–2:4, italics added). The apologetics of Genesis and Christianity begins abruptly with a creation outside of the doings of man and apart from the pagan gods of the Semitic world. It begins with the gifted majesty of a jealous Lover God and with an almost inexplicable separation and our need for gifted redemption. Without diminishing these doctrines regarding our original innocence (and a sin original to ourselves rather than to God), the medieval theologian Duns Scotus proposed a refreshing solution. He proposed that the ambient glory of the infinite God would have freely donated himself fully into His creation, which is inherently good, as the Incarnation *even apart from the Fall*. God is not so distant from the fabric of His creation that He would enter only as a concession to human frailty and for "damage control." In other words, "the concept of 'redemption' does not necessarily imply liberation from sin . . . the Fall was not the determining cause of the Incarnation . . . A preservative redemption. i.e., one that prevents a person from falling into sin, is just as much a redemption as a liberating redemption, i.e., one that frees a person from a sin already incurred." Mary, "the Mother of God" to Catholics and revered by Muslims, is the unique example of one who like us is redeemed by her Son, but in the former sense of preventive redemption.[124] Duns Scotus held that the beauty of the Incarnation is "not subordinated to the Fall." Christ is the "firstborn of all creation" and not an "afterthought." The splendor of creation is such that the Incarnation could have been given with or without the Fall which comes more as a later and added (speaking ontologically, not chronologically) need for liberating redemption.[125]

Christian and Western critics of Islam seek a common grammar, possibly the universal natural law, while Muslims propose as an opening a "common word" from the respective scriptures, and this is thought to be the Two Great Commandments. This gesture of friendship is welcome, but even the referenced Commandments of love are not the foundation of Christian faith (Chapter 5). Instead, the *foundation* is the Incarnation and resurrection, God in the person of Christ fully God and fully man, who in revealing the Father's love also *reveals man to himself*. This asymmetry between the divinized *Qur'an* and the Bible testimony is discussed in Chapter 3. The natural law—the numinous light of God within his own creation—is illumined by his actual presence. No one of us is an accident or interchangeable. This is self-revealed love "in person," more than scriptural or even "the word made book." Under the interchangeable word made book(s) Christians see the Word-made-flesh rendered Father-less and disunited from the cross, and then returned into the hands of the Church to be held more in common.

Building on Scotus, what else might we find as a first step in dialogue between those who restore the faith of Abraham and those who proclaim the fulfillment of this faith in the savior Jesus Christ? Borrowing from von Balthasar we find an inadvertent clue: "While Abraham's obedience is a purely abstract function of the covenant of grace, untouched by the sinful condition of humanity, the covenant which God will enter upon through Moses is deeply coloured by the concrete state of sin."[126] When Islam connects to Abraham through Ishmael, rather than through the Judeo-Christian line extending from Isaac through Moses, it disconnects from the unfolding understanding of man at his deeper level of original innocence marred (but not erased as in Protestant theology) by original sin. The contact point for dialogue is here in the nature of man himself, as might be inferred from Scotus. He proposes a God who would have become incarnate with or without original sin, that is, consistent with the Christian faith but also resonant with the more primitive and limited presuppositions of Islam inattentive to original sin.

While this Scotist theological opinion is not mainstream Christian tradition, neither is it heretical.[127] Scotus accords with those likeminded Christian theologians who find that the "unsalvation" of Man before Christ is illumined less by the Fall than by the gratuitous coming of the eternal Christ into time. The Fall and redemption are not really understood until the coming of Christ: "The Pauline expression of original sin is elaborated from the understanding of Christ's redemptive work and grace, such that Adam's sin and its consequences are grasped in the gift of the saving benefits Christ brings *and not vice-versa.*"[128]

Might the followers of Islam consider the beauty of an Incarnation— tragically not part of human history—such as Scotus presents, above their own dichotomy between God of infinite insight and foresight and Man? In Christ, God is both transcendent and present: Emmanuel (God with Us). And equally, might Scotus help Western thinkers to read with greater curiosity the recent "Common Word Between Us and You" (2007)? The Muslim writers say that "souls are depicted in the Holy *Qur'an* as having three main faculties: the mind or the intelligence . . . the will . . . and *sentiment which is made for loving the good and the beautiful*" (italics added). The incongruity with Augustinian thought is the substitution of sentiment for memory, and the departure from Christian theology is the dilution of graced charity into a more natural sentiment. But Mohammed's perception into the *beauty* of the One God—the least theological of the four or five transcendentals—is like all other private revelations.

The love of beauty does not stand alone, but might serve as a portal to the other transcendentals—to love, the one, the true and the good—and hints however obscurely at the incarnate Christ who is and yet transcends them all. Beauty loses its luster if it, too, is idolized beyond what is discovered by other means and transcendentals, the one, the true and the good. More in harmony with Catholic theology than classical Protestant, the Muslim love for beauty holds that man is "unalterably good, so they are entitled to self-respect and a healthy self-image."[129] Complementing the broad Catholic doctrine of original sin as not corrupting man to the core is the Muslim concept of fitra (our inborn tendency toward good actions). In the *Qur'an* the nature of sin as the depths of betrayal is often understated as more of an individual "forgetfulness" (*ghaflah*), but for all Christians it derives universally from a primordial rupture. Original sin ruptures the still intact beauty of original innocence (or fitra?) because it destroys the beauty of our relationship to a Creator who is both justice and love.[130]

This perplexing question of the additional gift of beauty and grace has tested Western theologians ever since St. Augustine picked it up with rigor in the late fourth century. A useful insight pioneered by Henri de Lubac shortly before the Second Vatican Council holds that man in his natural state—unlike the rest of nature—seeks an end that *by himself he is unable to attain*.[131] The Redeemer of Christianity hears and then fulfills the nostalgic, poetic and beautiful, but incomplete refrain retained all throughout the *Qur'an*. The refrain appears at the beginning of all but one of the one hundred fourteen chapters (surahs): "In the name of God, the Compassionate, the Merciful."[132] In the end the Christian knows that the encountered Word is One. The Lord *does* what He *is* and *is* what He *does*: "The Lord *is* compassion and love" (Ps 111:4). So much so that the beauty of Christ, in whom we see the Father in the unity of the Holy Spirit, is that he freely enters into our alienation *and* suffering as his very own.[133]

Within this contact point of the Incarnation as beauty and mercy, we have more than intellectual knowledge of our origin: "The effect of grace, as the upsurging of the eternal love within him, is to bring a man's faculties back again into their original course, and so to disengage them completely and *set them free*. Therefore grace *is more than compassionate mercy* . . . (but) a vital force, which awakens and summons the powers of man's soul, understanding, will and feeling . . ." (italics added).[134] Remarkably, the reference is to understanding, will *and feeling* . . . Again, for the Christian such sentiments and yearning are rewarded in the encounter with Christ as closing *from above* the distance between the ever distant God (Allah) and any prayers we might offer, including the communal prayers of solicitation (*Du'aa*) raised five times each day by the followers of Islam. The Christian proclamation, prefigured in the Old Testament and echoing in every line of the New Testament, is in the unsurpassable beauty that "The Word became flesh" (Jn 1:14). In the infinite simplicity of God there is no division, not even between the One who acts and the action taken. At the raising of Lazarus Christ did not say "I bring the value of resurrection;" He said "I *am* the resurrection and the life" (Jn 11:25).

Bernard of Clairvaux, preacher of the Second Crusade, preserves the uncompromised transcendence, including the beauty, which is so important to both Christians and Muslims and to Jews. The beauty of God is total but unsullied: "God cannot suffer, but he can *suffer with*."[135] "Incapable of suffering as God, he did not refuse to be a man, capable of suffering."[136] In the Son, God chooses to become the abyss of our self-betrayal and even deeper abandonment from Himself. In this inexhaustible mystery is also the coincidence between Christian faith and the Muslim belief, so protective of beauty, that man cannot victimize God. The heart of Christianity is that God is victim only in the sense that it is by his eternally free choice. He is the beauty of infinite self-donation. Christian recognition of this mystery within the superabundance of God identifies Christianity as *the only religion that profoundly heals human suffering*.

Whittaker Chambers finds that "Nothing is more characteristic of this age than its obsession with an avoidance of suffering. Nothing dooms it more certainly to that condition which is not childlike but an infantilism which is an incapacity for growth that implies an end. The mind which has rejected the soul, and marched alone, has brought the age to the brink of disaster."[137] But St. Paul's discovery is that "the sufferings of this present time are as nothing compared with the glory to be revealed for us" (Rm 8:18). Of the "Compassionate, the Merciful" God (*Qur'an*, and the earlier James 5:11 and originally Exodus 34:6), the very definition of "*com*-passion" is to "suffer with." In the beauty of "suffering with," the God who is love becomes our suffering as a unified "person." Not the idolatry of multiple gods, but the beautiful unity of two complete natures, one fully divine and the other fully human.

And as God partakes in our humanity without diminishing himself, we are also to be personally incorporated into Him: "Even now I find my joy in the suffering I endure for you. In my own flesh, I fill up what is lacking in the sufferings of Christ . . ." (Col 1:24). Within the grace of God, man is called and invited to participate in his own salvation and the suffering self-donation of Christ.[138] For the Christian, the Trinity is the living God who is both infinitely transcendent and who as the Ultimate Craftsman of beauty puts Himself into the work of his hands.

In the classical world, Archimedes of Syracuse (d. 212 B.C.), whose works were translated into Arabic by Thebit ben Corat (836–901), literally put himself in his own tiny and relatively mundane work. The riddle was to know genuine gold from a deceptive alloy. And then, "Eureka, I have found it!" Having entered a tub of water he suddenly understood. He understood from the inside the exact equivalence of physical displacement by any shape however irregular within a surrounding environment. From the simple facts about volume displacement and known metallic weights compared to the weight and volume of displaced water, he was able to solve the riddle for his ruler Hiero II. In the king's crown the royal artisans had not substituted tin for gold. Happily so since Archimedes' own head was possibly at stake—as is our soul with our larger riddle of choosing against alloy in serving our Master.

Ayoub cites the Muslim theologian-philosopher Fakhr al-Din al-Razi. Al-Razi arrives unsuspecting at a tipping point very similar to the "eureka" of Archimedes. The Muslim philosopher writes: "It therefore follows that everything other than God is created in time, and hence preceded by nonbeing. This also means that all things came into being through God's creative act and His power of bringing things from nonbeing to being. From this it follows that everything other than God is His slave and possession. *It is therefore impossible that anything other than He is His offspring*" (italics added).[139] He is His offspring! John's Gospel testifies to this *mirabile* (wonderful to relate): "In the beginning was the Word, and the Word was with God, and the Word was God" (Jn 1:1).

Eureka! To pause at this insight—"It is therefore impossible that anything other than He is His offspring"—is to encounter the triune unity of God who is the Lord of History. Beneath the intellect there is first the memory and the choice to be of good will.[140] Prior to the decision is the willingness to not lapse into a pre-emptive forgetfulness that renders all things mundane, ordinary, and even outside of conscience. The Western error of distancing is that of Descartes who set the trajectory of Western coldness by presuming too much to approach the entire cosmos as an outside observer. It is the forgetfulness of the civic public square devoid of all values except the possible technique of civility, which the Muslim observed finds too wanting (Hassan, Chapter 2). And it is the forgetfulness of Islam which elides the depth of sin (original sin) and the heights of a Redeemer on a hilltop. With an optimism that today might look naïve, Jean Guitton, a lay observer of the Second Vatican Council, in the concluding year quoted the Muslim el Akkad (1956): "It all comes down to knowing whether one should hold strictly to the fundamental religious values which were those of Abraham and Moses, on pain of falling into blasphemy—as the Muslims believe; or whether God has called men to approach him more closely, revealing to them little by little their fundamental condition as sinful men, and the forgiveness that transforms them and prepares them for the beatific vision—as Christian dogma teaches."[141]

With beauty as one measure, the choice is between the *beauty of Arabic words made book or the totally unique and unfathomable beauty of "the Word made flesh."* The choice is between an Islamic State frozen in time and with executors of the divine will, or a Redeemer who is the divine Way, and Truth and the Life. The Word is not simply another being or "existent," but "the very appearance of Being itself" (Von Balthasar). Such is the meaning, the beauty, precisely set forth at the Council of Nicaea (325 A.D.). In the early fifth century ,nearly a century after the Council of Constantinople dogmatized the Triune oneness of God, St. Augustine readily conceded the inadequacy of the term *persona* for each distinct member of the Trinity, but asserted that we use this term only because in human thought and language there is none better.[142] St. Bernard places time in the context of eternity: "God has spoken once. Once, indeed, because for ever. His is a single, uninterrupted utterance, because it is continuous and unending."[143] According to Madigan, Islam sees the uncreated *Qur'an* as a "metaphor" for a continuous revelation of divine writing and rewriting: "communication must remain above the limits that human expression or physical display would place on it."[144] But where Islam sees itself as the ongoing receptor of God's revelation, St. Teresa of Jesus finds that Mary's incomparable and complete humility "drew Him down from heaven into the Virgin's womb."[145]

To discover the reality of Christ as the uninterrupted utterance of the Word is to discover the truth about the whole man. Converted, man by his interior nature is destined for God. The continuing utterance, as a reminder, is the Holy Spirit sent by Christ to work in his Church, his historical and mystical body, as word and sacrament. Converted, the blind man in the Scripture gains his sight, not because his eyes are healed. Rather, he is healed and gains his eyes because of his faith in the Word. "One thing I do know is that I was blind and now I see" (Jn 9:25). Reason fully works in coherence with faith in the One, rather than in presumed (and distrusting) isolation.

The crisis of Islam at its source, like the crisis of the West, is not political, social or even (multi)cultural as modernity would have it. At its root, the crisis is a crisis of its vision of the human person and spirit. Is it possible for each of the followers of Islam to suspect that at the heart of the *Qur'an*, however much eclipsed, that the guidance given to Adam was given at the very beginning *as his own nature*, rather than extrinsically and even a moment later. We are to remember the universal natural law whose imperfect expression may be a cultural artifact, but which is first of all a fact. It is a fact whose existence *ex nihilo* is steadfast and of divine origin. In the long run, "*The natural law always buries its undertakers.*"[146] At the turn of the twentieth century, the priest Lacordaire did much to reintroduce to secularist France the meaning of faith to a nation dominated by a new rationalist ideology. His insight applies as much to the amalgam of Islam as it does to the "multicultural" relativism that has hijacked legitimate modernity: "the principle of success of Jesus Christ . . . *was not a principle of fusion, but a principle of contradiction . . .* if you would understand how difficult is the triumph of Jesus Christ, I propose to you, not the conversion of the world, but of one (any) single man."[147] Proposing the new life of inner conversion in and from the world, the Church also seeks to unfold for the world an "integral human development" by which is meant both the "advancement of all men and of the whole man."[148]

Rabbi Neusner arrives at and also stops the same Eureka tipping point as Al-Razi (above). He writes: "I now realize, only God can demand of me what Jesus is asking."[149] The Jewish Neusner and the Muslim Al-Razi, like the Christian convert, discover this universal threshold of Encounter. The modern secularist, too, must wonder at Neusner's insight, the real question whether the Christ of history is who he says he is, or whether he is simply another of the countless pre-modern myths. Does God make so much of a nuisance as the Son of God that in Him we become adoptive sons and daughters (Gal 4:4–7)? In the West C.S. Lewis discovers this tipping point late in his own conversion from atheism to Theism, and then to Christ: "Early in 1926 the hardest boiled of all the atheists I ever knew sat in my room on the other side of the fire and remarked that the evidence for the historicity of the Gospels was really surprisingly good. "All that stuff . . . about the Dying God . . . It almost looks as if it had really happened once. To understand the shattering impact of it, you would need to know the man . . . If he, the cynic of cynics, the toughest of the toughs, were not—as I would still have put it—'safe,' where could I turn?"[150]

The road before us becomes a crossroad, and in this imperfect world the crossroad becomes a cross. St. Paul identifies this cross as a "stumbling block to Jews and foolishness to Gentiles . . . the foolishness of God is wiser than human wisdom, and the weakness of God is stronger than human strength" (1 Cor 1:23, 25). And for Islam, Christ is both a stumbling block and foolishness. Having seen the oneness and mercy of God, Mohammed remained wrapped in Arabian communalism (much as the chosen people of Judaism celebrate the eternal Israel). For the Christian, prophecy alerts us to the eternal presence of God, and apocalyptic vision that points to the end times. It is the thought of this new life of communio through the cross that causes even St. Peter to falter. Peter is sure that the Lord will be quite—reasonable, "God forbid, Lord! No such thing shall ever happen to you" (Mt 16:22). By this false optimism, not Christian hope, graced beatitude would be submerged forever into the routines of the world—an alloy. Never would anything ever be new under the sun. This is the most subtle idol of all, the divine made routine. Was Peter's first "denial" more of a predisposing bewilderment: "I do not *know* Him" (Lk 22:37)? To our desire for a manageable god, Christ responds, "Get behind me, Satan! You are an obstacle to me. You are thinking not as God does, but as human beings do" (Mt 16:23).

The totally unique truth claim of Christianity is not a claim *made by* Christians, but is a claim that is *made upon* us: "Blessed are those who have not seen and have believed" (Jn 20:29). A penitent Peter later said "Lord, to whom shall we go? You have the words of eternal life. We have come to believe, we are convinced that you are God's holy one" (Jn 6:68–69). To the believing Jew and Muslim as well as the Christian, the entire world is no longer mundane, but consecrated. Von Balthasar rejects all historical constructs and even dogmas in favor of an "ultimate reality" that is both infinitely transcendent and infinitely personal: "It is only the mystery of the Trinity that makes it possible to conceive of such an act of transcending without loss: the Word of God (the Father) is so personal that it itself is a person; but as God it is so essentially one with the Father, and as man so transparent to the Father in obedience, that it becomes the visible presence of God; acting and speaking in the world"[151] . . . Trinitarian Christianity presents itself, not as dogma, but as the rejection of dogma, not as the assertion but rather the denial of anthropomorphism and myth, and it calls for a final and conclusive expulsion of these elements from the description of ultimate reality as the preliminary to a starkly realistic account of nature and of man."[152]

In God's self revelation in Christ, the full stature of man is equally revealed. St. Irenaeus startles us, "God is man's glory. Man is the vessel which receives God's action and all his wisdom and power . . . It will be a glory which will grow ever brighter until it takes on the likeness of the one who died for him."[153] We are to become like Him when we see Him face to face (Rev 22:4). Leibniz, a mathematician rather than any kind of theologian, pauses at the perennial and religious question, "Why should there be something rather than nothing?"[154] And Balthasar, the theologian of beauty, gives answer again:

> The responses of the Old Testament and *a fortiori* of Islam (which remains essentially in the enclosure of the religion of Israel) are incapable of giving a satisfactory answer to the question of why Yahweh, why Allah, created a world of which he did not have need in order to be God. *Only the fact is affirmed in the two religions, not the why.* The Christian response is contained in these two fundamental dogmas: that of the Trinity and that of the Incarnation.[155]

The Christian will continue to propose, not impose, a thought expressed well by the English writer, G.K. Chesterton. Chesterton says of the apostles and the unbroken line of disciples, their successor bishops: "Those runners gather impetus as they run. Ages afterwards they still speak as if something had just happened . . . .We might sometimes fancy that *the Church grows younger as the world grows old.*"[156] The followers of Islamic restoration are drawn yearly to their center at the Black Stone of the Ka'ba in Mecca, and the voices of modernity count the stars in the Spiral Nebula and then discount any higher Wisdom. The Christian encounters an ever new event, and his vision is lifted upward from the rock of Golgotha to a cross, and inward to the all-embracing intersection of the entire universe with its Creator whose name is love (Jn 1:14). With St. Paul the Church now gives witness in the global Areopagus, in New York, in Rome and in Istanbul. Christian hope is proclaimed in all arenas. Evidence of such hope comes even from a mouthpiece of the Soviet purges of the 1930s. In his unpredictable defense of Pasternak a communist man of letters roused himself from his hardness: "If the whole world were to be covered with asphalt, one day a crack would appear in the asphalt, and in that crack grass would grow."[157] Fifty years later, after his conversion from a prominent Socialist upbringing, the British commentator Malcolm Muggeridge remarked that Christian faith in the face of relentless Soviet oppression and brainwashing was "the most extraordinary single fact of the twentieth century."[158]

From its own crisis, the Church emerges from its siege mentality of the Reformation with the two recent and inseparable Vatican councils. In two thousand years the Second Vatican Council is the first to use the term "evangelization." It is the first to address its teachings outward to all those of good will. As a gift rather than a possession, the gospel or "good news" of Christ is to be shared and can be kept only by being given away. The axis to all the carefully whittled wording of the Second Vatican Council is this message to modern man: "*By the revelation of the mystery of the Father and His love, (Christ also) fully reveals man to man himself . . . .*"[159] Where the secular realm divides the external world from the world of religion, it too readily dismisses even the reality of the human person as a subjective opinion and therefore objectively irrelevant. Fidelity and grace are replaced with management of a more random paradigm of man and the universe. But such a *cosmos* of a hundred trillion thermonuclear reactions does not hold a candle to a *universe* or a "world" illumined by Christ who is One with the Father, and through whom all things are. A humble and prayerful soul might light such a candle in the back of an obscure wayside chapel, as an ever new witness in every age to a higher truth than self-sufficient modernity.

The gift from Christ into his "new life" of the Beatitudes exceeds even the Two Great Commandments proposed as the foundation and common word among monotheistic religions. "He was known *before* the foundation of the world but revealed in the *final time* . . ." (1 Pe 1:20)." Matthew testifies, "This messianic people . . . though it does not in fact embrace all mankind, and may more than once look like a small flock, is yet the enduring source of unity, hope and salvation for the whole human race. It is established by Christ as a communion of life, of love and of truth . . . and is sent out into the whole world as the light of the world and the salt of the earth" (Mt 5:13–16).[160] More than a "common word" between us, Christ is the singular and uncommon Word made flesh.

Muslims of good will are a reminder to western modernity that cultural forgetfulness does not negate the reality of God and the God of reality. As from the biblical Wisdom texts, "(The Lord) is found by those who test him not, and he manifests himself to those *who do not disbelieve* him" (Wis 1:2, italics added). Like the witnesses to Christ,the followers of Islam also remember God: "Please God and call your Lord to mind when you forget" (Q 18:24), and "remember God often" (Q 33:41). The stark and yet serene canvas of the Bedouin mind on which the *Qur'an* and its "guidance" are painted was best captured by T.E. Lawrence: "(He) could not look for God within him; he was too sure that he was within God. He could not conceive anything which was or was not God . . . ."[161]

The Christian memory and some of the West recalls that the natural law is the universal guidance discoverable within man himself, and then that it is within the memory of the Triune God that we now await "the glory to be revealed in us" (Rom 8:18). The Christian recalls the admonition of Peter for readiness to give a reason for one's new life of faith: "Always be ready to give an explanation to anyone who asks you for a reason for your hope . . ." (1 Pe 3:15). The secularist of good will holds, instead, that man is the measure of all things, and places his remembrance of the future and his optimism (different than the new life of faith, hope and charity) exclusively in the exercise of human reason.

At the intersection of the mosque, the manger and modernity we sometimes find the gesture of friendship—the path of St. Francis and it also the reciprocity given to him by the Sultan al-Kamil in a handshake and a certificate of free passage. Compared to a fully human universe of received guidance and the friendship of true face-to-face encounter, is secular civility sufficient to create and sustain itself? How might we find ourselves beyond the confines of secularism or jihad, or the outside the bubble of pluralist indifference and ijma? Can a society worthy of human flourishing evolve or be constructed spontaneously from nothing (ex nihilo)? "Everyone who listens to these words of mine but does not act on them will be like a fool who built his house on sand" (Mt 7"26). Less than ten years before Mohammed (d. 632) and his followers began their conquest of the Arabian peninsula, the Irish St. Columban (d. 615) had already completed his missionary work on the northerly peninsula which is Europe. His Gospel message and method were kindled at first in the solid monasteries he founded. This was before the Trinitarian revelation was domesticated into language-based sects and nation-states based on language, gunpowder and the printing press, or set aside in Arabic writings and a more multi-national Islamic State.

Even today St. Columban preaches alongside St. John who said in his first letter: "When anyone acknowledges that Jesus is the Son of God, God dwells in him and he in God" (1 Jn 15). St. Columban adds:"It is no God dwelling far off from us that we seek, whom if we merit it we have within us. For he resides in us like soul in body, if only we are sound members of him, if we are not dead in sins, if we are uninfected by the taint of a corrupt will; then truly does he reside in us who said, 'And I will reside in them and walk in their midst.'"[162] On whether we live in God as Islam affirms, or whether God also lives in us as the Christians affirm, St. John proclaims: "We have seen and testify that the Father sent his Son as savior of the world. Whoever acknowledges that Jesus is the Son of God, God remains in him and he in God" (1 Jn 4:14–15).

NOTES

1. St. Augustine, *Confessions*, Bk. 13, Ch. 11, n. 12.

2. Groeschel explains that the image of the One and Trinitarian God—the Son imaging the Father and the mutual love of both in the Spirit—is in "the mind's operations of its own self-directed love toward self . . . when it remembers itself, understands itself, or wills or loves itself" (Benedict Groeschel, Augustine: *Major Writings* (New York: Crossroad Publications, 1999), 113. Groeschel traces the misapplication of intellect, memory and will (to the Trinity) to the medieval theologian Peter Lombard (in Edmund Hill, *The Works of St. Augustine* (The Trinity) [Brooklyn: New City Press, 1991]), 25.

3. St. Augustine, *Confessions*, Bk. 8, Ch. 9; Bk. 10, Ch. 22 and 24.

4. Second Vatican Council, *Gaudium et Spes* (The Church in the Modern World), n. 24.

5. P. Marie-Eugene, OCD, *I Want to See God: A Practical Synthesis of Carmelite Spirituality* (Chicago: Fides, 1953), 438.

6. Miguel de Unamuno, *Tragic Sense of Life* (New York: Dover Publications, Inc., 1954), 185.

7. David Yeago, Lutheran Theological Southern Seminary, Charleston, South Carolina, Panel comments at "Future Lutheran and Roman Catholic Ecumenism," Seattle, Washington, January 19, 2008. Luther, in his letter "To the Councilmen of All Cities in Germany," held that the direct study of Hebrew and Greek gave him "the gospel just as pure and undefiled as the apostles had it, that it has been wholly restored to its original purity, far beyond what it was in the days of St. Jerome and St. Augustine" (in Richard M. Gamble (ed.), *The Great Tradition* [Wilmington, Delaware: Intercollegiate Studies Institute, 2007], 371–381).

8. Quoted in *Magnificat*, Yonkers, New York: IX:9, Nov. 2007, 199.

9. Luigi Giussani, *Is it Possible to Live this Way?*, Vol. 2: Hope (Ithaca: McGill-Queen's University Press, 2008), 8.

10. The tenor of the age is characterized by Church critics: "Every one who came from Rome brought back word that in the metropolis of Christendom, and in the bosom of the great mother and mistress of all Churches, the clergy, with scarcely an

exception, kept concubines" ("Janus," *The Pope and the Council* [Boston: Roberts Brothers, 1870], 281).

11. St. Peter of Damaskos, in G.E.H. Palmer, Philip Sherrard and Kallistos Ware, *The Philokalia*, Vol. 3, (Boston, Faber and Faber, 1995 [1984]), 235. The kingdom is found inside the human heart (Lk 17:21, 13:19, Mt 13:33 and 45), 25.

12. Bishop Martinus Muskens reported in *Catholic World Report* (CWR), (San Francisco: Ignatius Press, October 2007), 13. In a separate and opposite case and in the face of government opposition, the archbishop of Kuala Lumpur (Malaysia) in 2009 continues to use "Allah" as an accepted translation of "God" (CWR, March 2009).

13. Mahmoud Ayoub in Irfan A. Omar (ed.), *A Muslim View of Christianity* (Maryknoll, New York: Orbis, 2007), 243.

14. *Magnificat*, Yonkers, New York: Magnificat, December 2007, 9:11, 88.

15. Charles Norris Cochrane, *Christianity and Classical Culture: A Study of Thought and Action from Augustus to Augustine* (New York: Oxford University Press, 1974), 384.

16. Michael Novak, *Belief and Unbelief* (New York: Mentor Omega, 1967), 177, fn. 9.

17. Pope Benedict XVI, *Pilgrim Fellowship of Faith* (San Francisco: Ignatius, 2005), 257.

18. In the separate context of the *Dead Sea Scrolls*, the independent scholar Robert Eisenman maintained a popularized view widely rejected by scholars. He held that the Qumran community were Zealots rather than Essenes, that James was among them, and that St. Paul resided at Qumran for full three years as an archrival who also turned Jesus into a God (Hershel Shanks (ed.), *Understanding the Dead Sea Scrolls* [New York: Random House, 1992], 285, and James C. Vanderkam, Chapter 14, 182–202).

19. Pope Benedict XVI, "St. Paul and the Twelve," "St. Paul and the Historical Jesus," (Weekly General Audiences Sept. 24 and Oct. 8, 2008), in *National Catholic Register*, October 5 and 19, 2008.

20. The three major Catholic Rites (not lesser or heretical sects) in the East are also apostolic in origin. St. Peter ruled in Antioch prior to Rome, and Alexandria began under St. Mark. Jerusalem was an early center for pilgrims and monastics. Paul predates by centuries the three named sects: The Jacobites were founded by Jacobus Baradai, sixth century Bishop of Edessa, the Nestorians by Nestorius (patriarch of Constantinople in 428 A.D.), and the Melkites trace to the Emperor supporters of the Council of Chalcedon (451 A.D.).

21. Maulana Muhammad Ali, *Muhammad the Prophet* (Lahore, Pakistan: Ripon, 1984 [1924]), 44–5.

22. Mohammed's preferences are attributed by Ghazali, Ibn Sa'd and others. The Western parallel is attributed to Luther: "Who does not love wine, women and song remains a fool his whole life," or more likely to Johann Heinrich Voss (1751–1826) (*Bartlett's Familiar Quotations*).

23. Ibid.

24. Humphrey Prideaux, *Life of Mahomet* (London: Curll, Hooke, Fleetstreet, Mears and Clay without Temple-Bar, 1718[1696]), 86.

25. Ayoub in Omar (ed.). 123.

26. Referring to us, rather than Christ, St. Paul remarks "Even as some of your poets have said, 'For we too are his offspring'" (Acts 17:28). He is quoting Aratus of Soli, a third-century B.C. poet from Cilicia (Donald Senior and John Collins (eds.), *The Catholic Study Bible* [New York: Oxford University Press, 2005], 1474 fn.).

27. Ibid.

28. Eric Voegelin, *From Enlightenment to Revolution* (Durham, North Carolina, 1975), 80. Where Church councils seek to clarify with consistency the precise meaning of the fact and concept that "Jesus Christ is Lord," Islam seems to defer to the Arabic language and vocabulary as the source of possibly new meanings. Coming from Allah, new expressions of meaning may or may not abrogate past meanings. Old and new meanings comprise a continuous revelation coming from the "self-awareness" of the *Qur'an*. See Madigan, below. In the Western tradition where reason is differentiated from faith, it is a fallacy to substitute words for concepts, particularly with the final goal of redefining the words.

29. John Lindblom, "John C.H. Wu and the Evangelization of China," *Logos*, 8:2 (St. Paul, Minn.: University of St. Thomas, Spring 2005), 134, citing Perry Link, *Evening Chats in Beijing: Probing China's Predicament* (New York: Norton)l 1992), 116–17.

30. In Europe, the Jewish born author Edith Stein converted from atheism upon reading in a single evening a classic writing by the sixteenth century mystic Teresa of Avila.

31. Lindblom, op. cit., Unrelated to John Wu, Harry Wu is a campaigner for human rights in China. The organization *laogai* (reform through labor) documents the existence of at least 909 labor camps in China, with between forty and fifty million forced inmates since 1949. Wu calls attention to the Western failure to track the origin of billions of dollars of routine trade products accepted from China (See laogai.org).

32. *The Story of a Soul: The Autobiography of St. Therese of Lisieux* (New York: Doubleday Image Book, 1957), 159.

33. Jean-Pierre de Caussade (translated and introduced by John Beevers), *Abandonment to Divine Providence: Classic Wisdom from the Past on Living Fully in the Present* (New York: Doubleday, 1975), 9–21 (Introduction).

34. Cited in Robert Oerter, *The Theory of Almost Everything* (New York: Pi Press, 2006), 276. Another source reports that at his death Newton said, "I don't know what I may seem to the world. But as to myself I seem to have been only like a boy playing on the seashore and diverting myself now and then finding a smoother pebble or a prettier shell than the ordinary, whilst the great ocean of truth lay all undiscovered before me."

35. Aquinas commented: "Reasoning is employed (in another way), not as furnishing sufficient proof of a principle but as showing how the remaining effects are in harmony with an already posited principle; as in astronomy the theory of eccentrics and epicycles is considered as established because thereby the sensible appearances of the heavenly movements can be explained; *not however as if this proof were sufficient, since some other theory might explain them*" (*Summa Theologica*, cited in L.M. Regis, *Epistemology*, 455, italics added).

36. Jacob Brownowski, *The Origins of Knowledge and Imagination* (New Haven: Yale University Press, 1978), 108–9.

37. Cited in Fulton J. Sheen, *God and Intelligence in Modern Philosophy* (Garden City, New York: Image, 1958), 244.

38. Averroes (George Hourani, trans.), *On the Harmony of Religion and Philosophy*, 1179–1180 (London: Mssrs. Luzac and Co., 1967 [1961]), UNESCO Collection of Great Works: Arabic Series, Appendix, 74.

39. Don Luigi Giussani, *The Religious Sense* (San Francisco: Ignatius Press, 1990), 8.

40. From the "Didascalion," in Richard Gamble (ed.), *The Great Tradition* (Wilmington, Delaware: Intercollegiate Studies Institute, 2007), 255–66.

41. "The philosopher says that composition and division exist in the intellect and not in things." (Aquinas on Aristotle, cited in L.M. Regis, *Epistemology* [New York: MacMillan, 1959], 346.)

42. Farooq Hassan, *The Concept of State and Law in Islam* (Washington, D.C.: University Press of American, 1981), 87. The situation compares to Sixteenth Century Europe. "Luther's Christian State, Henry of England's Royal Supremacy, Calvin's 'Institutes,' the 'Spiritual Exercises' of St. Ignatius, the Augsburg Confession, the decrees of Trent, the Thirty-Nine Articles, the Westminster Catechisms, are all framed on the principle of submission to the powers that be . . . Heresy was treason, and treason was heresy" (William Berry, *The Papacy and Modern Times: A Political Sketch, 1303–1870* [New York: Henry Holt and Co., 1911], 121.

43. Cited by Russell Hittinger in Heinrich Rommen, *The Natural Law* (Indianapolis: Liberty Fund, 1998), xxviii.

44. Cited by Mustafa Akyol, *First Things*, March 2007, 15. Akyol is a devout and thoughtful Muslim as well as a liberal Turkish journalist and author of *Islam Without Extremes: A Muslim Case for Liberty* (New York: W.W. Norton, 2011). From the cross-cultural perspective, Akyol celebrates the potential modern role of Mu'tazilite thought (rejected in the ninth century), while understating the distinctly western and even Catholic tradition of coherence between faith and reason (e.g., Thomas Aquinas in the thirteenth century). He advocates a pluralist world in which Islam and its sects participate alongside rather than above other faiths. But, how Islam as a religion repudiates its additional claim that it stands "above all religions" (Q 9:33) remains elusive. The natural law tradition is the missing key offered from the West, with its focus directly on the nature of the human person, and is central to the social doctrine of the Church (Chapter 4).

45. Alexis de Tocqueville, *Democracy in America*, Vol. 1 (New York: Vintage Books, 1961), 172. The conversion is obstructed more by the will than by the intellect, a theme we have visited, is developed by Thomas Dubay, *Authenticity: A Biblical Theology of Discernment* (San Francisco: Ignatius, 1997 [1977]), 186–199.

46. See Jose Sanchez, *Pius XII and the Holocaust* (Washington, DC: Catholic University Press, 2002), 112. Pope Pius XII rose to the papacy through a distinguished career in the Vatican state department.

47. "The Nazis were not that horde of dumb and brutal creatures who came from the darkness of history in some unexplainable fashion, but (a group) that constitute

instead an example of the consequences of a massive collapse of Christian ethics . . . to comprehend this fact we have to recognize also the value of Christian morality and not disqualify it, as an old 'Liberalism' has done and modern progressives still do, by considering it as a collection of absurd 'taboos'" (Ambrose Eszer, "Edition Stein, Jewish Catholic Martyr," in *Carmelite Studies*, IV, Washington, D.C.: International Carmelite Studies Publications, 1987, 318–19).

48. Pope Benedict XVI, *Without Roots: The West, Relativism, Christianity, Islam* (New York: Basic Books, 2006), 45.

49. Richard Wilbur, *New and Collected Poems* (New York: First Harvest Edition, Harcourt, Inc., 1989), 43.

50. Maimonides, the great Medieval Jewish philosopher, held the same attitude toward both Christianity and Islam. David Novak writes: "Like philosophy, Christianity and Islam are true when they are variations of themes most completely presented in Judaism; and they are in error when they contradict Judaism" ("The Mind of Maimonides, in Richard John Neuhaus (ed.) *The Second One Thousand Years* [Grand Rapids, MI: William B. Eerdmans, 2001], 15–27).

51. His Eminence monsignor Guiseppe Bernardini, archbishop of the Turkish Diocese of Smyrns, in Oriana Fallaci, *The Rage and the Pride* (New York: Rizzoli, 2001), 98.

52. George Weigel, "What the Church Asks of the World," an address delivered at Seattle Pacific University, Feb. 27, 2007. This insight probably draws from Pope Benedict XVI who sees that separation of church and state can be conceived positively, "since it is meant to allow religion to be itself, a religion that respects and protects its own living space distinctly from the state and its ordinances" (*Without Roots*, op. cit, 111).

53. A reverse calculus comes into play when the Vatican refrains from evangelizing in Muslim countries for fear of endangering their minority Catholics.

54. Muslims note that among Christian institutions, the Catholic Church provides a unity remotely like that of the transnational ummah of Islam. Hassan attributes this unity to the papacy: "the Roman Catholic Church, particularly because of the institution of the papacy, which provides a focal point for all Catholics, loosely resembles in practice, though not in doctrine, the 'unity' of Islamic communities . . ." (*The Concept of State and Law in Islam* [Washington, D.C.: University Press of America, 1981], 88.

55. The use of Latin in the liturgy is less a rejection of the vernacular than the valuing of a "dead language" whose living meanings remain stable through time.

56. Don Luigi Giussani, *Why the Church?* (San Francisco: Ignatius Press, 2001), 95.

57. Second Vatican Council, *Gaudium et Spes* (The Church in the Modern World), n. 22.

58. Christopher Dawson, *The Dynamics of World History* (New York: Mentor Omega, 1956), 206, italics added.

59. Ibid.

60. Ibid.

61. James Keating, "A Share of God's Life: Mystical/Liturgical Foundations for a Catholic Morality," *Logos*, 8:2 (Spring 2005), 65–88. Quoted terms in Keating are from John Paul II (68–69).

62. John Paul II, *Redemptor Hominis* (Redeemer of Man), (Washington, D.C.: United States Catholic Conference, 1979), 83. See also *Mystici Corporus* (Mystical Body of Christ), Pius XII, June 29, 1943.

63. Giussani, *Is it Possible to Live this Way?* Vol. 2: Hope, op. cit., 118.

64. The words of Norman Daniel, commenting on Asad's *The Road to Mecca* (1954), in *Islam and the West* (Oxford, Oneworld, 1960), 315.

65. According to Emilien Lamirande, Luther reduces communion (*Gemeinschaft*) to community (*Gemeinde*), "making this article of the Creed simply a definition of the Church in the Protestant sense" (*The Communion of Saints* [New York: Hawthorn Books, 1963], 20; vol. 26 of the *Twentieth Century Encyclopedia of Catholicism*, ed. Henri Daniel-Rops [New York: Hawthorn Books, 1962].

66. Invocation of the Spirit is recorded no later than fourth century Egypt, where it is untouched by Arian or Nicene influences. "Here the prayer is, first, that the divine Word may come upon the elements 'that the bread may become the body of the Word' and 'that the cup may become the blood of the Truth,' and, secondly, that all the communicants may receive the medicine of life to their benefit and not to their condemnation" (Henry Chadwick, *The Early Church* [New York: Penguin, 1990], 265).

67. In his "Prayer before Mass," Pope John Paul II expressed an offering of "our prayers, works, suffering, joys and even ourselves to the Eternal Father with this sacrifice of the Body, Blood, Soul and Divinity of His dearly beloved Son . . ." (published posthumously in the *National Catholic Register*, May 19–22, 2006; See also the *Catechism of the Catholic Church*, Second Edition [Rome: Libreria Editrice Vaticania, 1997], n. 1374.

68. The sacramental and the functional notions of church institutions are developed in Josef Cardinal Ratzinger (Pope Benedict XVI), *Principles of Catholic Theology* (San Francisco: Ignatius, 1987), 242–263.

69. Second Vatican Council, *Christus Dominus* (Decree on the Bishops' Pastoral Office in the Church), n. 11, 1965.

70. McNeill identifies cases in history of religious conversions coming in response to the extension of new civilizations. Alternative and sometimes minor religions become rallying points for encysted survival. The Khazars in the Volga region became Jews, the Uighurs (early Turks) became Manichaeans. "The religion of Mohommad (he notes) represents a similar, though far more significant and original adaptation of civilized religion to local needs" (W.H. McNeill, *The Rise of the West: A History of the Human Community* [New York: Mentor, 1963], 461).

71. Bernard Lewis, "The State and Society under Islam," *Wilson Quarterly* (Washington, D.C.: Woodrow Wilson International Center, Autumn 1989), 47. The American Benjamin Franklin suggested the slogan to French leaders: "Liberté, Egalité, Fraternité" (George Seldes, *The Great Quotations* [New York: Pocket Book, 1960], 872), which in their hands became a new holy trinity to replace the discarded Trinity of Father, Son and Holy Ghost (Freidrich Heer, *The Intellectual History of Europe* [New York: World Publishing Co., 1953], 405).

72. Pope Benedict XVI, *Values in a Time of Upheaval* (San Francisco: Ignatius Press, 2005), 109.

73. St. Augustine, *Confessions*, Book 8, Ch. 9, n. 21 and Ch. 10, n. 22, 24.

74. Pope Benedict XVI, *Deus Caritas est* (God is Love), 2007, nn. 28, 29 31a and b, 34. The clear donation of self together with the gift is one difference between Christian charity and the zakat tax collected from Muslims and distributed to the needy by the state. In the latter case, again, the mosque-state serves multiple roles.

75. Jerzy Peterkiewicz (trans.), Karol Wojtyla, "A Conversation with Man Begins: The Meaning of Things," *The Place Within: The Poetry of Pope John Paul II* (New York: Random House, 1982), 124.

76. Henry Paolucci (ed.), *The Political Ideas of St. Augustine* (New York: Gateway Editions of Henry Regnery Co., 1962), Appendix by Dino Bigongiari, 353.

77. International Theological Commission, *Memory and Reconciliation: The Church and the Faults of the Past* (Boston: Pauline Books and Media, 2000), n. 6.3.

78. Ibid., Appendix, "Homily of the Holy Father 'Day of Pardon' (March 12, 2000), n. 4.

79. St. Augustine, *Confessions*, Book 1, Chapter 1, and Book 13, Chapter 38. While there is no compulsion, under the persuasive knowledge of Islam (Q2:256), Augustine earlier held that, on the one hand, while we are *drawn* to believe (perhaps violating free will), on the other: "It is not enough that you are moved by the will, for you are drawn *also by desire.*" Belief is a matter of love, not knowledge alone, and it is in this crucial and Christian sense that there is then no compulsion of the will. (From a treatise on John, extract in *Liturgy of the Hours*, Vol. IV, New York: Catholic Book Publishing, 1976, 391.)

80. Second Vatican Council, *Dei Verbum* (Dogmatic Constitution on Divine Revelation), n. 4.

81. John Paul II, *Memory and Identity* (New York: Rizzoli, 2005), 149. John Paul II continues: "It is a task in which the Church is constantly sustained by the Holy Spirit. During his farewell discourse, Christ speaks to the Apostles of the Holy Spirit: 'He will teach you everything and remind you of all that I have said to you' (Jn 14:26)."

82. Is Islam half of Judaism, in that it knows the Elohist tradition of a distant God, but randomly does not recall any convincing telling of the Jahwist tradition of a close (not simply anthropomorphic) God? Did the Elohist tradition of the Northern Kingdom find its way into early Arabia separate from its joining with the Jahwist tradition in the finally written Old Testament?

83. Second Vatican Council, *Gaudium et Spe* (The Church in the Modern World), n, 16.

84. *Catechism of the Catholic Church*, op. cit., n. 732.

85. Quotes are from Toynbee in M.C. D'Arcy, *The Meaning and Matter of History: A Christian View* (New York: Meridian Books, 1959), 115. Von Balthasar differentiates the spectrum of solutions offered by founders of religion to the basic tension between the existence of God and the existence of the world, or the One and the Many: "Possible solutions are: (a) to remain midway between the One and the Many (the way of Mohammed); (b) to abolish the Many for the sake of the One (the way of all forms of non-Christian mysticism, including Sufism); (c) to incorporate the One into the Many (the way of polytheism and pantheism)." See Hans Urs von

Balthasar, *The Glory of the Lord: A Theological Aesthetics, Vol. I— Seeing the Form* (San Francisco: Ignatius Press, 1998), 506.

86. John Paul II, *Crossing the Threshold of Hope* (New York: Alfred Knopf, 1994), 68. In contrast, while human suffering looms large in the metaphysics of Buddhism, the solution is to annihilate human existence by breaking the cycle of repetitive human reincarnation.

87. Of a personal God who might act in history (or even reveal Himself) Einstein remarks that "The main source of the present-day conflicts between the sphere of religion and of science lies in the concept of a personal God . . . In their struggle for the ethical good, teachers of religion must have the stature to give up on the doctrine of a personal God..." ("Science of Religion" [1939], in *Out of My Later Years* [New York: Philosophical Library, 1950], 27–8.

88. Anton Pegis, *At the Origins of the Thomistic Notion of Man*, The St. Augustine Lecture Series under the auspices of Villanova University (New York: The Macmillan Co., 1963), 58–9. "The human soul . . . is in an entirely unique way an intelligence that can *be* itself only by *enacting* within itself a personal history . . . ." (52). Augustine's anthropology is compatible, as in his controversy with Pelagius and has defense of human freedom as both an endowment and as something to be achieved in cooperation with grace through a lifetime of healing (Peter Brown, *Augustine of Hippo* [Berkeley: University of California Press, 1969], 372–3).

89. Hans Urs von Balthasar, *A Theology of History,* San Francisco: Ignatius, 1994 [1963], 47–50. Benedict XVI writes that the "God of the philosophers, whose pure eternity and unchangeability had excluded any relation with the changeable and transitory, now appeared to the eye of faith as the God of men, who is not only thought of all thoughts, the eternal mathematics of the universe, gut also agape, the power of creative love" (*Introduction to Christianity* [San Francisco: Ignatius, 2004 (19680], 143).

90. Hans Urs von Balthasar, *The Glory of the Lord: A Theological Aesthetics, VI: Theology—The Old Testament* (San Francisco: Ignatius, 1991), 351.

91. Henry Leroy Finch, *Simon Weil and the Intellect of Grace* (Ithaca: McGill-Queen's University Press, 2001), 130.

92. William Cantwell Smith, *Islam in Modern History* (Princeton: New York: Mentor, 1957), 34 (italics added). Regarding the Islamic community in history, Hassan explains that while cohesion in the West is based less on symbols and more on a shared heritage of action within history, Islamic membership in the ummah is radically different. It is based on a simple and *"common act of will"* that identifies (them as) Muslims" (*The Concept of State and Law in Islam*, op. cit., 89, italics added).

93. Xavier Leon-Dufour (translated and edited by John McHugh), *The Gospels and the Jesus of History* (Garden City, New York: Image Books, 1970), 199.

94. For the secularist, the analogy would be modern understandings of space-time, wherein "space" is not a container for stars and galaxies, but is formed by the physical objects themselves, taking on curvatures proportionate to their size and density.

95. Edwin Bliss, *Turkey and the Armenian Atrocities* (New York: M.J. Coghlan, 1896), 82–3.

96. Francis of Paola, cited by Joseph Cardinal Ratzinger *in Principles of Catholic Theology: Building Stones for a Fundamental Theology*, op. cit., 212.

97. Bishop Fulton J. Sheen, *God and Intelligence in Modern Philosophy* (New York: Image, 1958), 243.

98. Josef Pieper, *Prudence* (New York: Pantheon Books, 1959), 32.

99. Ibid., 32–3.

100. Xavier Leon-Dufour, 203.

101. Ibid.

102. Fr. Gabriel of St. Mary Magdalen, *Divine Intimacy* (Rockford, Ill.: Tan Books and Publishing, 1996), 665 (italics added).

103. *Catholic World Report*, Nov.2006, 20.

104. Pope Benedict XVI, *Jesus of Nazareth* (New York: Doubleday, 2007), 105.

105. Jacob Neusner, *A Rabbi Talks with Jesus* (Montreal: Mc-Gill-Queen's University Press 2000); and "Renewing Religious Disputation in the Quest of Theological Truth: In Dialogue with Benedict XVI's Jesus of Nazareth," *Communio International Catholic Review*, Washington, DC: Communio, Inc., Summer 2007, 328–334.

106. Culturally, face veils are not unique to Muslim societies. In Medieval Europe ladies of high birth often wore veils in public and most used a head cloth, and ideally women in Elizabethan England remained within their homes except on special occasions (Gideon Sjoberg, *The Preindustrial City* [New York: The Free Press, 1960], 167–8, with citations.

107. Sermon by St. Leo the Great, *Liturgy of the Hours*, op. cit.,Vol. II, 898–9.

108. Christ fulfills revelation ". . . through his words and deeds, His signs and wonders, but especially through His death and glorious resurrection from the dead and final sending of the Spirit of truth"(Second Vatican Council, *Dei Verbum* [Divine Revelation], n. 4).

109. Al-Munqidh min al-Dalal, translated by R.J. McCarthy, *Al-Ghazali's Path to Sufism: His Deliverance from Error*, Louisville: Fons Vitae, 1999 (1131 A.D.), 77.

110. St. Augustine, *Confessions*, Bk. 1, Ch. 1. And the final "But you, the Good, needful of no good, are forever at rest, for your rest is yourself" Bk. 13, Ch. 38.

111. *Liturgy of the Hours*, op. cit., 1112.

112. Ibid., 412–14.

113. *Centesimus Annus* (One Hundred Years), 1991, n. 50.

114. Ayoub in Omar (ed.), 176.

115. Ariana Fallaci, *The Force of Reason* (New York: Rizzoli, 2004), 188–9.

116. Brown, op. cit., 32. In the broader picture still, there came the confrontation between Ambrose and his communicant, the emperor Theodosius, who had order the retaliatory slaughter of seven thousand assembled citizens in Thessalonica. For the independent and internal order of the Church, Ambrose extracted public repentance from the emperor before he could return to the communion rail.

117. Ayoub in Omar (ed.), 209. Responding, we might note that multiculturalism in the West is vulnerable to this notion that all revelations are narratives only, and that they are equal, and equally subordinate to the distant God of the *Qur'an* (regarded as the essence of God), as newly revealed through the messenger-prophet.

118. Hans Urs von Balthasar, op. cit., (drawing from G. von Rad), Vol. VI: *Theology of the Old Covenant* (San Francisco: Ignatius, 1991), 208–210.

119. Of evolution, the Chinese philosopher Tson Tse anticipates Darwin's particular version of evolution by 2700 years: "All organizations are originated from a single species. This single species had undergone many gradual and continuous changes, and then gave rise to all organisms of different forms. Such organisms were not differentiated immediately, but, on the contrary, they acquired their differences through gradual change, generation after generation" (cited by Jawaharlal Nehru, *Glimpses of World History*, New York: John Day Co., 1942, 525–6).

120. The reference to Darwin's daughter traces to James Moore and Adrian Desmond (*Darwin*, London, 1991), referenced in John Brooke, "The Distinctive Agnosticism of Charles Darwin," in Stratford Caldecott (ed.), *Second Spring*, Vol. 8 (2007), 53. Darwin's early "unwillingness to express myself on religious subjects" is evident in his letters which are selectively quoted in Bakewell Morrison, *The Catholic Church and the Modern Mind* (New York: Bruce Publishing Co., 1933), 169–177, citing Francis Darwin (ed.), *The Life and Letters of Charles Darwin*, Vol. 1 (D. Appleton-Century Co., n.d.). Darwin (b. 1809) also once commented that he abandoned Christianity when he was forty, a date which nearly corresponds with the death of his Annie (1851).

121. Mark Twain (foreword by Andrew Tadie), *Joan of Arc* (San Francisco: Ignatius, 1989 [1896, serialized in Harper's in 1895]).

122. Hans Urs von Balthasar, op cit., Vol. IV, *The Realm of Metaphysics in Antiquity*, San Francisco: Ignatius, 1989, p. 26; and *My Work in Retrospect* (San Francisco: Ignatius, 1993), 114.

123. The Catholic convert Malcolm Muggeridge attributes this familiar distinction (of seeing through and with) to the mystical artist William Blake (*The End of Christendom* [Grand Rapids: William B. Eerdmans, 1980], 62). See also "A Vision of the Last Judgment" from Blake's Notebook: "I question not my Corporeal or Vegetative Eye any more than I would Question a Window concerning a Sight. *I look thro it & not with it.*"

124. Citation of William Marshner in Juniper B. Carol, OFM, STD, *Why Jesus Christ: Thomistic, Scotist, and Conciliatory Perspectives*, dedicated to His Eminence James Cardinal Biffi, (Manassas, Virginia: Trinity Communications, 1986), 134, 474. Carol summarizes his meticulous research: "The *ultimate* reason why God decreed the Incarnation is His intrinsic goodness. This applies to creation in general. The *proximate* reason for the Incarnation is twofold." The author goes on to articulate that the *primary* reason is "the supreme love and worship which only Christ can render to the Father" (in the context of this book, surpassing our "submission"). And the *secondary* reasons (plural) include the "deification" of rational creatures through Christ's meritorious causality" (476).

125. Ibid., 472–4.

126. Hans Urs Von Balthasar, *The Glory of the Lord, A Theological Aesthetics*, Vol. VI, *Theology of the Old Covenant* (San Francisco: Ignatius, 1991), 226.

127. In the Church, theological opinion is distinct from formal teaching, unlike the collective consensus views found under Islam and that often conflict. Church theology is ultimately accountable to the discernment of the Holy Spirit acting through a single teaching authority (the magisterium) as noted in Chapter 4.

128. Robert Egan, S.J., *New Direction in the Doctrine of Original Sin* (doctrinal dissertation, Fordham University, 1973), 230. The author also carefully explores varied understandings of "original sin," e.g., the emphasis in eastern writers (influential in Byzantine Christianity most accessible to Arabia) on shared punishment or weakness rather than on shared guilt.

129. Huston Smith, *Islam: A Concise Introduction* (San Francisco: Harper, 2001), 39. The Catholic dogma is that Man is only damaged by original sin (inclined to evil, but not inherently evil); the Lutheran premise is that Man is both essentially good and essentially evil. Calvinism originally involved predestination. Under the Catholic dogma man is weakened and in need of divine assistance, but essentially good and sacramentally gifted to enter the additional New Life of grace available through the ministries of a Church ignited at Pentecost.

130. The unique instance of Mary's Immaculate Conception shows that our universal human nature is graced, and not that this nature is replaced with a different nature in the special case of Mary. That the Immaculate Conception is a fruit of grace and not a change of human nature is a point made by Newman (Philip Boyce (ed.), *Mary: The Virgin Mary in the Life and Writings of John Henry Newman* (Grand Rapids, Michigan: W.B. Eerdmans, 2001), 335. Respect in the Church for Mary does not deify a human being—a Protestant misunderstanding. Nor does it render Mary a consort with God and in this way the third part of the trinity, Father, Son and Mary—a Muslim misunderstanding.

131. Henri de Lubac, *Augustinianism and Modern Theology* (New York: Crossroad Publishing Co., 2000 [1946]).

132. This wording, which might trace to Exodus (Ex 34:6), also coincides with James several centuries prior to Mohammed (62 A.D.): "You have heard of the steadfastness of Job, and have seen what the Lord, who is *compassionate and merciful*, did in the end" (James 5:11).

133. Aquinas gives us this theological reflection: "Just as, properly speaking, it is not 'compassion' but 'suffering' that describes our condition when we ourselves experience some cruel treatment, so also, if there are some persons so united to us as to be, in a way, something of ourselves, such as children or parents, we do not have compassion at the distress but rather we suffer as in our own wounds" (*Summa Theologiae*, II-II, 30.1. ad2).

134. Karl Adam, *The Spirit of Catholicism*, Dom Justin McCann (trans.) (New York: Crossroad Publishing Co., 1997.

135. Cited by Benedict XVI in *Spe Salvi* (In Hope), Encyclical Letter, Nov. 30, 2007, n. 39.

136. Letter from St Leo the Great, *Liturgy of the Hours*, Vol. II (New York: Catholic Books Publishing, 1975), 1745–6.

137. Whittaker Chambers, "The Direct Glance," in William F. Buckley, Jr. (ed.), *American Conservative Thought in the Twentieth Century* (New York: The Bobbs-Merrill Co., 1970), 508.

138. In expounding this theme of "co-redemption," Jacques Maritain (*The Peasant of the Garonne* [New York: Holt, Rinehart and Winston, 1968] 248–253) quotes extensively from his wife, Raissa, and from Fr. Marie-Joseph Nicolas ("La Co-

redemption" [*Revue Thomiste*, 1947, I]) who writes: "The difficulty does not lie in explaining this simple truth; it lies rather in explaining how Protestantism came to reject it" (221). Lutherans would demand an explanation how the Church could tolerate its members treating grace as a commodity (sale of indulgences).

139. Ayoub in Omar (ed.), 127.

140. Raniero Cantalamessa, *Jesus Christ: The Holy One of God* (Collegeville Minn.: Liturgical Press, 1990), 148.

141. Jean Guitton, *The Great Heresies and Church Councils* (New York: Harper and Row, 1965), 117.

142. Thomas Dubay attributes the lack of faith among Westerners to both a lack of knowledge *and* to bad will—the habituated inability to give assent. Biblical citations include 1 Cor 15:33–4 and 2 Cor 4:4; Jn 3:20, 8:43–44, 8:47 and 15:24; Mk 1:15; Lk 10:9–15 and 16:31. See Dubay, *Authenticity* (San Francisco: Ignatius, 1997), 186–198.

143. St. Bernard, Sermon, *Liturgy of the Hours,* Vol. IV, op. cit.,, 231.

144. Daniel Madigan, *The Qur'an's Self-Image: Writings and Authority in Islam's Scripture* (Princeton, N.J.: Princeton University Press, 2001), 186, and passim. Where Muslim theology allows new revelations from above to abrogate past writings, the coherence of faith and reason in the Catholic tradition allows theology to deepen the definitive "deposit of faith" rooted in the Incarnation, but not to replace it (see in Chapter 4 Cardinal Newman and the *Development of Christian Doctrine*).

145. Quote (not the linkage to Islam) is from *The Way of Perfection* (16), cited Gabriel of St. Mary Magdalen, O.C.D., *Divine Intimacy: Meditations on the Interior Life* (Rockford, Ill.: Tan Books, 1996), in 528.

146. Etienne Gilson, *The Unity of Philosophical Experience* (New York: C. Scribner's Sons, 1965), 306.

147. Pere Lacordaire, *Jesus Christ, God, God and Man* (Manchester: James Robinson, 1907), 147–8.

148. Pope Benedict XVI, *Caritas in Veritate* (Charity in the Truth), 2009, n. 18. The term "integral humanism" is from Jacques Maritain, "Christian Humanism," *The Range of Reason* (New York: Charles Scribner' Sons, 1949), republished in *A Maritain Reader* (Garden City, New York: Image, 1966), 226. Integral humanism "would consider man in all his natural grandeur and weakness, in the entirety of his wounded being inhabited by God, in the full reality of nature, sin, and sanctity."

149. Pope Benedict XVI, *Jesus of Nazareth* (New York: Doubleday, 2007), 115; citing Jacob Neusner, *A Rabbi Talks with Jesus* (Montreal: McGill-Queen's University Press, 2000), 68.

150. C.S. Lewis, *Surprised by Joy* (New York: Harcourt Inc., 1955), 223–4.

151. Hans Urs von Balthasar, *The Glory of the Lord: A Theological Aesthetics*, Vol. VII: *Theology: The New Covenant* (San Francisco: Ignatius Press, 1989), 274.

152. Charles Norris Cochrane, op. cit., 432, italics added.

153. From "Against Heresies," *The Liturgy of the Hours*, Vol. 1 (New York: Catholic Book Publishing Co., 1975), 337.

154. Demonstrated in this arresting question a congruence between metaphysics and mathematics. Etienne Gilson traces the expression not to works of Thomas Aqui-

nas, but to Leibniz, the discoverer of The Calculus. As a mathematician, Leibniz fully appreciates inductive reason based on particulars, but unlike later Darwinists, he sees equally the validity of the metaphysical question of existence versus non-existence, in its particulars and cosmologically. See Etienne Gilson, *The Elements of Christian Philosophy* (New York: Mentor Omega, 1963), 180.

155. Hans Urs von Balthasar, *My Work in Retrospect* (San Francisco: Ignatius Press, 1993), 118, italics added. Yet, the Spirit moves where it will.

156. G.K. Chesterton, *The Everlasting Man* (Garden City, New York: Image, 1955 [1925]), 268, italics added.

157. Cited in Whittaker Chambers, *Cold Friday* (New York: Random House, 1964), 324.

158. Malcolm Muggeridge, *The End of Christendom* (Grand Rapids: William B. Eerdmans Publishing Co., 1980), 38. As a Soviet exile in the West, in 1973 Solzhenitsyn resigned as Rector of the University of Edinburgh rather than approve a student demand to distribute "pot and pills" (drugs and contraceptives).

159. Second Vatican Council, *Gaudium et Spes* (The Church in the Modern World), n. 22.

160. Second Vatican Council, *Lumen Gentium* (Light of the World), n. 9.

161. T.E. Lawrence, *Seven Pillars of Wisdom* (New York: Anchor Books, 1991), 39.

162. From *Sermons of Columbanus*, Sermon 1, Corpus of Electronic Texts Edition compiled by Beatrix Farber, University College: Cork, Ireland, 2004 (www.ucc. ie/celt/published). A saying from Christ: "Again, I say to you, if two of you agree on earth about anything for which they are to pray, it shall be granted to them by my heavenly Father. For where two or three are gathered together in my name, there am I in the midst of them" (Mt 18:18–19).

Bibliography

Abbott, Walter (editor), *The Documents of Vatican II,* New York: Guild Press, 1966.

Ali, Abdullah Yusuf, *The Holy Qur'an: Text, Translation and Commentary*, Lahore, Pakistan: S.H. Muhammad Ashraf, 1983 (1938).

Augustine (Introduction by Etienne Gilson), *The City of God,* Garden City, New York: Image Books, 1958.

Armstrong, Karen, *Muhammad: A Biography of the Prophet*, San Francisco: Harper Collins, 1993.

Assfy, Zaid H., *Islam and Christianity,* York, England: William Sessions, Ltd., 1977.

Augustine (Foreword by Etienne Gilson), *The City of God,* Garden City, N.Y.: Image, 1958.

Averroes (George Hourani, trans.), *On the Harmony of Religion and Philosophy, 1179–1180*, London: Mssrs. Luzac and Co., 1967 (1961), UNESCO Collection of Great Works: Arabic Series.

Bainton, Roland, *The Age of the Reformation*, Princeton, N.J., D. Van Nostrand Co., Inc., 1956.

———. *Early Christianity*, Malabar, FL: Krieger Publishing, 1960.

———. *The Medieval Church*, Malabar, FL: Kreiger Publishing, 1962.

Barber, Malcolm, *The Two Cities: Medieval Europe 1050–1320,* New York: Routledge, 1992.

Bauckham, Richard, *Jesus and the Eyewitnesses: The Gospels as Eyewitness Testimony*, Grand Rapids, MI: William Eerdmans Publishing, 2006.

Baynes, Norman, *The Political Ideas of St. Augustine*, New York: The Historical Association, 1968.

Belloc, Hilaire, *The Great Heresies*, Rockford, Ill.: Tan Books, 1991 (1938).

Bennett, Isaiah, *Inside Mormonism: What Mormons Really Believe*, San Diego: Catholic Answers, 1999.

Bhutto, Benazir, *Reconciliation: Islam, Democracy, and the West*, New York: Harper, 2008.

Bigongiari, Dino (ed.), *The Political Ideas of St. Thomas Aquinas*, New York: Hafner Publishing Co., 1953.

Bonner, Michael, *Jihad in Islamic History*, Princeton University Press, 2006.

Bostom, Andrew G. (ed.), *The Legacy of Jihad: Islamic Holy War and the Fate of Non-Muslims*, Amherst, New York: Prometheus, 2005.

Bosworth, Donzel, Heinrichs, Pellat, editors, *Encyclopedia of Islam*, Volume VII, New York: E.J. Brill, 1993.

Bozeman, Adda, *The Future of Law in a Multicultural World*, Princeton University Press, 1971.

Brockopp, Jonathon (ed.), *The Cambridge Companion to Muhammad*, New York: Cambridge, 2010.

Brodie, Fawn M, *No Man Knows My History*, New York: Alfred Knopf, 1995 (1945).

Brzezinski, Zbigniew, *Second Chance*, New York: Basic Books, 2007.

Butler, Dom Cuthbert, *The Vatican Council 1869–1870*, London: Collins and Harvill Press, 1962 (1930).

Campbell, R.J., *The Story of Christmas*, New York: The Macmillan Co. (1941).

Carol, J.B., OFM, *Why Jesus Christ?: Thomistic, Scotistic, and Conciliatory Perspectives*, Manassas, Virginia: Trinity Publications, 1986.

Carroll, Warren, *The Building of Christendom*, Vol. II, Christendom College Press, 1987.

Chadwick, Owen, *Catholicism and History*, New York: Cambridge University Press, 1978.

Charles, Rodger, SJ, *An Introduction to Catholic Social Teaching*, San Francisco: Ignatius Press, 1999.

Congar, Yves, *Tradition and Traditions, Irving*, Texas: Basilica Press, 1997.

Cooper, Barry, "'Jihadists' and the War on Terror," *The Intercollegiate Review*, Wilmington, DE: Spring 2007.

Daniel, Norman, *Islam and the West: The Making of an Image*, Oxford: Oneworld, 1993 (1960).

Daniel-Rops, Henri, *History of the Church of Christ*, Garden City, New York: Image, 1961–7.

Daughters of St. Paul, *Extraordinary Synod—1985*, Message to the People of God, Boston: 1985.

Dawood, N.J. (trans.), *The Koran*, London: Penguin Books, 2003.

Dawson, Christopher, *The Making of Europe*, New York: Meridian Books, 1956.

———. *The Dynamics of World History*, New York: Mentor Omega, 1956.

Denny, Frederick Matheson, *An Introduction to Islam*, New York: Macmillan, 1994.

Egan, Robert, S.J., *New Direction in the Doctrine of Original Sin* (doctoral dissertation), Fordham University, 1973.

Einstein, Albert and Leopold Infeld, *The Evolution of Physics: The Growth of Ideas from Early Concepts to Relativity and Quanta*, New York: Simon and Schuster, 1938.

Esposito, John, *The Islamic Threat: Myth or Reality*, New York: Oxford University Press, 1999 (1992).

———. *Islam: The Straight Path*, New York: Oxford University Press, 1998.

———. *Unholy War: Terror in the Name of Islam*, New York: Oxford University Press, 2002.

Fallaci, Oriana, *The Force of Reason*, New York: Rizzoli, 2006 (2004).

Fairbank, John, Edwin Reischaeur and Albert Craig, *East Asia—The Modern Transformation*, Boston: Houghton Mifflin Co., 1965.

Freemantle, Anne, *The Social Teachings of the Church*, New York: Mentor Omega, 1963.

Gibb, H.A.R., *Mohammedanism: A Historical Survey*, New York: Oxford University Press, 1962.

Gibb, H.A.R., and J.H. Kramers, *Shorter Encyclopedia of Islam*, Ithaca: Cornell University Press, 1953.

Gibbon, Edward, *Christians and the Fall of Rome*, New York: Penguin Books, 2004; extract from *The Decline and Fall of the Roman Empire*, Vol. I, first published 1776.

Gilson, Etienne (ed.), *The Church Speaks to the Modern World: The Social Teachings of Leo XIII*, Garden City, New York: Image Books, 1954.

Giussani, Luigi, *Why the Church?*, Ithaca: McGill-Queen's University Press, 2001.

———. *The Religious Sense*, San Francisco: Ignatius Press, 1990.

Glubb, John Bagot, *The Life and Times of Muhammad*, London: Hodder and Stoughton, 1970.

Grotius, Hugo, *The Rights of War and Peace: Including the Law of Nature and of Nations*, London: Walter Dunne, 1901.

von Grunebaum, G.E., *Islam: Essays in the Nature and Growth of a Cultural Tradition*, London: Routledge and Kegan Paul Ltd., 1955.

Guillaume, Alfred, *The Life of Muhammad: A Translation of Ibn Ishaq's Sirat Rasul Allah*, Oxford: Oxford University Press, 1967 (1955).

———. *Islam*, New York: Penguin Books, 1956.

Habermas, Jurgen and Joseph Cardinal Ratzinger (Brian McNeil, trans.), *Dialectics of Secularization: On Reason and Religion*, San Francisco: Ignatius, 2006.

Hallaq, Wael B., *An Introduction to Islamic Law*, New York: Cambridge University Press, 2009.

Hassan, Farooq, *The Concept of the State and Law in Islam*, Washington, D.C.: University Press of America, 1981.

Hayes, E.E.Y., *The Catholic Church in the Modern World*, Garden City, New York: Image, 1960.

Heer, Friedrich, *The Intellectual History of Europe*, New York: The World Publishing Co., 1953.

———. *The Medieval World*, New York: Mentor, 1963.

Helminski, Camille Adams (ed.), *Women of Sufism: A Hidden Treasure*, Boston: Shamphala, 2003.

Hindley, Geoffrey, *The Crusades: Islam and Christianity in the Struggle for World Supremacy*, New York: Carroll and Graf Publishers, 2003.

Hourani, Albert, *A History of the Arab Peoples*, Cambridge, Mass.: Harvard University Press, 1991.

Hughes, Philip, The Church in Crisis: *A History of the General Councils, 325–1870*, New York: Hanover House, 1960.

Jaki, Stanley, "The Physics of Impetus and the Impetus of the Koran," *Modern Age*, Intercollegiate Studies Institute, Spring 1985.

Janus (anonymous, translated from the German), *The Pope and the Council*, Boston: Roberts Brothers, 1870.

John Paul II, *Original Unity of Man and Woman: Catechesis on the Book of Genesis*, Boston: Daughters of St. Paul, 1981; included in *The Theology of the Body*, Boston: Pauline Books and Media, 1997.

———. *Centesimus Annus* (One Hundred Years), 1991.

Jenkins, Philip, *The Hidden Gospels*, New York: Oxford University Press, 2001.

———. *The Next Christendom: The Coming of Global Christianity*, New York: Oxford University Press, 2002.

———. *God's Continent:Christianity, Islam, and Europe's Religious Crisis*, New York: Oxford University Press, 2007.

Joinville, Jean de and Geoffroy de Villehardouin (Margaret Shaw, trans.), *Chronicles of the Crusades*, New York: Penguin, 1963.

Jomier, Jacques, *The Bible and the Qur'an*, San Francisco: Ignatius Press, 2002.

Karim, Maulana Fazlul, *Al-Hadith: An English Translation and Commentary of Mishkat-ul-Masabih* (4 volumes), New Delhi: Islamic Book Service, 1988.

Khomeini, Imam, Translated and annotated by Hamid Algar, *Islam and Revolution: Writings and Declarations*, London: KMI, 1981.

Kuenhelt-Leddihn, Erik von, *Leftism: From de Sade and Marx to Hitler and Marcuse*, New Rochelle, New York: Arlington House, 1974.

Laffin, John, *The Dagger of Islam*, Boston: Bantam Books, 1981.

Lapidus, Ira M., A History of Islamic Societies, New York: Cambridge University Press, 1988.

Lawler, Peter, "The Human Dignity Conspiracy," *The Intercollegiate Review*, Wilmington, DE: The Intercollegiate Studies Institute, Spring 2009.

Levy, Reuben, *The Social Structure of Islam*, New York: Cambridge University Press, 1957.

Lewis, Bernard, *The Emergence of Modern Turkey*, London: Oxford University Press, 1961.

———. "State and Society under Islam," *Wilson Quarterly*, Washington, D.C.: Woodrow Wilson International Center, Autumn 1989.

———. *The Crisis of Islam*, New York: Random House, 2004.

———, ed. and trans., *Islam: from the Prophet Muhammad to the Capture of Constantinople*, Vol. II: Religion and Society, New York: Oxford University Press, 1987.

———. *What Went Wrong: The Clash between Islam and Modernity in the Middle East,* New York: Harper Perennial, 2003.

Lippman, Thomas, Understanding Islam: *An Introduction to the Muslim World* (revised), New York: Mentor, 1990.

Madigan, Daniel, *The Qur'an's Self-Image: Writing and Authority in Islam's Scriptures*, Princeton, N.J.: Princeton University Press, 2001.

Maddy-Weitzman, Bruce, ed., *Middle East Contemporary Survey—2000*, Vol. XXIV, Tel Aviv University, Moshe Dayan Center for Middle Eastern and African Studies, the Shiloah Institute, 2002.

Margoliouth, D.S., *The Early Development of Mohammedanism* (The Hibbert Letures of 1913), New York: Charles Scribner's Sons, 1914.

Maritain, Jacques, *Man and the State*, Chicago: Phoenix Press, 1951.

Michot, Yahya, *Muslims Under Non-Muslim Rule: Taymiyya, Ibn.,* Oxford: Interface Publications, 2006.

Molnar, Thomas, *Christian Humanism: A Critique of the Secular City and It's Ideology*, Chicago: Franciscan Herald Press, 1978.

McGonigle, Thomas, and James Quigley, *A History of the Christian Tradition: From the Reformation to the Present,* New York: Paulist Press, 1996.

Momen, Moohan, *An Introduction to Shi'i Islam: The History and Doctrines of Twelver Shi'ism,* New Haven: Yale University Press, 1985.

Muhammad Ali, Maulana, *Muhammad the Prophet*, Lahore, Pakistan: Ripon Press, 1984 (1924).

Al-Munqidh min al-Dalai, translated by R.J. McCarthy, *Al-Ghazali's Path to Sufism: His Deliverance from Error*, Louisville: Fons Vitae, 1999 (1131 A.D.).

Murray, John Courtney, S.J., *Government Repression of Heresy*, Proceedings of the Catholic Theological Society, no date (c. 1950).

Nagel, William, (ed.), *Morality and Modern Warfare: The State of the Question*, Baltimore: Helicon Press, 1960.

National Conference of Catholic Bishops, *The Challenge of Peace*, Washington, D.C.: United States Catholic Conference, 1983.

Norwich, John, *A Short History of Byzantium*, New York: Vintage, 1997.

Nicholson, Reynold A., *A Literary History of the Arabs*, New York: Charles Scribner's Sons, 1907.

———. *The Mystics of Islam*, New York: Penguin, 1989 (1914).

O'Leary, de Lacy, *Arabia Before Muhammad*, New York: E.P. Dutton and Co., 1927.

Omar, Irfan A. (ed.), *A Muslim View of Christianity: Essays on Dialogue by Mahmoud Ayoub*, New York: Orbis Books, Maryknoll, 2007.

Palmer, Alan, *The Decline and Fall of the Ottoman Empire*, New York: Barnes and Noble, 1992.

Paolucci, Henry (ed., interpretive essay by Dino Bigongiari), *The Political Writings of St. Augustine*, Chicago: Gateway Edition, 1962.

Pauley, Bruce, *The Habsburg Legacy*, Kreiger Publishers, 1972.

Peterson, Daniel C., *Mohammed: Prophet of God* (Grand Rapids, Michigan: William B. Eerdmans Publishing Co, 2001).

Pontifical Academy of Social Sciences, *Globalization: Ethical and Institutional Concerns*, Proceedings of the Seventh Plenary Session of the Academy, Vatican City, April 2001.

Pontifical Council for Justice and Peace, *Compendium of the Social Doctrine of the Church*, 2004.

Prideaux, Humphrey, *The Life of Mahomet*, London: Curll/Hooke/Fleetstreet/Mears/Clay, 1718 (1695).

Rahner, Hugo, *Church and State in Early Christianity*, San Francisco: Ignatius, 1992.

Ramadan, Tariq, *In the Footsteps of the Prophet: Lessons from the Life of Muhammad*, New York: Oxford University Press, 2007.

Ranke, Leopold (E. Foster, trans.), *History of the Popes and Especially of their Conflicts with Protestantism in the Sixteenth and Seventeenth Centuries*, London: George Bell and Sons, 1878.

Ratzinger, Joseph Cardinal (Pope Benedict XVI), *Turning Point for Europe*, San Francisco: Ignatius, 1991.

———. *Truth and Tolerance*, San Francisco: Ignatius, 2003.

———. *On the Way to Jesus Christ* (translated by Michael J. Miller), (San Francisco: Ignatius, 2005).

———. *Without Roots*, Basic Books, 2006.

———. *Values in a Time of Upheaval*, New York: Crossroad Books, 2006.

———. "Faith, Reason and the University: Memories and Reflections," University of Regensburg Lecture, in *Catholic World Report*, October 2006.

———. *Jesus of Nazareth*, New York: Doubleday, 2007.

———. *God's Word*, San Francisco: Ignatius Press, 2008.

Regis, L.M., *Epistemology*, New York: The Macmillan Co., 1959.

Robson, James, *Christ in Islam* (Wisdom of the East Series), London: John Murray, 1929.

Rommen, Heinrich, *The State in Catholic Thought: A Treatise on Political Philosophy*, St. Louis: Herder Book Co., 1945.

———. *A Study in Legal and Social History and Philosophy*, Indianapolis: Liberty Fund, 1998.

———. Royal Aal al-Bayt Institute for Islamic Thought, "A Common Word Between Us and You," 2007 (www.acommonword.com).

Russell, Jeffrey Burton, *A History of Heaven*, Princeton, New Jersey: Princeton University Press, 1997.

Sasson, Jean, *Princess*, Atlanta, Georgia: Windsor-Brooke Books, 2004 (1992).

———. *Princess Sultana's Daughters,* New York: Doubleday, 1994.

———. *Princess Sultana's Circle*, Woodstock, New York: Windsor-Brooke Books, 2000.

———. *Mayada: Daughter of Iraq*, New York: New American Library, 2003.

Schall, James V., S.J., (ed.) Pastoral Letters: Joint Pastoral Letter of the West German Bishops, *Out of Justice, Peace*; and Joint Pastoral Letter of the French Bishops, *Winning the Peace*, San Francisco: Ignatius, 1984.

———. *The Regensburg Lecture*, South Bend, Indiana: St. Augustine's Press, 2007.

Schindler, David L., *Heart of the World, Center of the Church*, Grand Rapids, MI: William B. Eerdmans, 1997.

Schonborn, Cardinal Christopher (foreword), *Creation and Evolution*, San Franciso: Ignatius, 2008.

Sherwin-White, A.N., *Roman Society and Roman Law in the New Testament*, Oxford: Clarendon Press, 1963.

Shih, Vincent Y.C., *The Taiping Ideology: Its Sources, Interpretations, and Influences*, Seattle: University of Washington Press, 1967.

Sjoberg, Gideon, *The Preindustrial City*, New York: The Free Press, 1960.

Smith, Wilfred Cantwell, *Islam in the Modern World*, New York: Mentor, 1957.

Smith, William Robertson, *Lectures on the Religion of the Semites*, London: A. and C. Black, Ltd., 1927 (1889).

Sontag, Raymond James, *European Diplomatic History 1871–1932*, New York: D. Appleton-Century Co., 1933.

Spitz, Lewis and Richard Lyman (eds.), *Major Crises in Western Civilization*, Vol. I, New York: Harcourt, Brace and World, Inc., 1965.

Stein, Edith (Waltraus Stein, trans.), *On the Problem of Empathy*, Washington D.C.: ICS Publications, 1989.

Tellenback, Gerd, *Church, State and Christian Society at the Time of the Investiture Contest*, New York, Harper Torchbook, 1959.

Torrell, Hean-Pierre, *Saint Thomas Aquinas*, Volumes 1 and 2, Washington, D.C.: Catholic University of America, 2007.

Ullmann, Walter, *Medieval Papalism: The Political Theories of the Medieval Canonists*, London: Methuen and Co. Ltd., 1949.

Urs von Balthasar, Hans, *The Glory of the Lord: A Theological Aesthetic* (seven volumes), San Francisco: Ignatius Press, 1989–1998.

Walsh, Michael, *An Illustrated History of the Popes*, New York: St. Martin's Press, 1980.

Warraq, Ibn, *Leaving Islam Behind: Apostates Speak Out*, Amherst: New York: Prometheus Books, 2003.

Weigel, George, *The Cube and the Cathedral: Europe, America, and Politics Without God*, New York: Basic Books, 2005.

———. *Faith, Reason, and the War Against Jihadism*, New York: Doubleday, 2007.

Wiltgen, Ralph, *The Rhine Flows Into the Tiber: A History of Vatican II*, Rockford, Illinois: Tan Publishers, 1966.

Index